REBUILDING ST. PAUL'S OUTSIDE THE WALLS

ARCHITECTURE AND THE CATHOLIC REVIVAL IN THE NINETEENTH CENTURY

RICHARD WITTMAN
University of California, Santa Barbara

Shaftesbury Road, Cambridge CB2 8EA, United Kingdom

One Liberty Plaza, 20th Floor, New York, NY 10006, USA

477 Williamstown Road, Port Melbourne, VIC 3207, Australia

314–321, 3rd Floor, Plot 3, Splendor Forum, Jasola District Centre, New Delhi – 110025, India

103 Penang Road, #05–06/07, Visioncrest Commercial, Singapore 238467

Cambridge University Press is part of Cambridge University Press & Assessment, a department of the University of Cambridge.

We share the University's mission to contribute to society through the pursuit of education, learning and research at the highest international levels of excellence.

www.cambridge.org
Information on this title: www.cambridge.org/9781009414524

DOI: 10.1017/9781009414548

© Richard Wittman 2024

This publication is in copyright. Subject to statutory exception and to the provisions of relevant collective licensing agreements, no reproduction of any part may take place without the written permission of Cambridge University Press & Assessment.

First published 2024

Printed in the United Kingdom by CPI Group Ltd, Croydon CR0 4YY

A catalogue record for this publication is available from the British Library

Library of Congress Cataloging-in-Publication Data
NAMES: Wittman, Richard, 1967- author.
TITLE: Rebuilding St. Paul's Outside the Walls : architecture and the Catholic revival in the nineteenth century / Richard Wittman, University of California, Santa Barbara.
OTHER TITLES: Rebuilding Saint Paul's Outside the Walls
DESCRIPTION: Cambridge, United Kingdom ; New York, NY, USA : Cambridge University Press, [2023] | Includes bibliographical references.
IDENTIFIERS: LCCN 2023025415 (print) | LCCN 2023025416 (ebook) | ISBN 9781009414524 (hardback) | ISBN 9781009414555 (paperback) | ISBN 9781009414548 (epub)
SUBJECTS: LCSH: San Paolo fuori le mura (Church : Rome, Italy)–History. | Architecture and religion–History–19th century | Church renewal–Catholic Church–History–19th century. | Historic buildings–Italy–Rome–Conservation and restoration–History–19th century.
CLASSIFICATION: LCC NA5620.S8 W57 2023 (print) | LCC NA5620.S8 (ebook) | DDC 726.6/40945632–dc23/eng/20230724
LC record available at https://lccn.loc.gov/2023025415
LC ebook record available at https://lccn.loc.gov/2023025416

ISBN 978-1-009-41452-4 Hardback

Cambridge University Press & Assessment has no responsibility for the persistence or accuracy of URLs for external or third-party internet websites referred to in this publication and does not guarantee that any content on such websites is, or will remain, accurate or appropriate.

CONTENTS

List of Plates	*page* vii
List of Figures	ix
Acknowledgments	xv
List of Abbreviations	xix

INTRODUCTION	1

PART I FIRE IN THE TEMPLE

1	DISENCHANTING HISTORIES	13
2	"A PORTENT, BEYOND STATUES SWEATING BLOOD IN THE FORUM . . ."	41
3	FUTURE VISIONS	65
4	BROADENING THE DEBATE	84
5	REFRAMING THE DEBATE	100
6	CATHOLIC ROMANTICISM	125

PART II RESURRECTING SAN PAOLO

7	MATTERS OF MONEY	139
8	RESISTING RESURRECTION	157
9	THE END OF A GENERATION	186

PART III REIMAGINED SACRED HISTORIES

10	LUIGI POLETTI AND THE CHALLENGE OF REBUILDING SAN PAOLO	207

vi CONTENTS

11 PAUL AND PETER — 246

12 MATERIAL HISTORIES — 264

13 PRELUDE TO A REVOLUTION — 295

14 EIGHTEEN FORTY-EIGHT — 321

PART IV FROM PAUL TO MARY

15 PIUS IX AND ROMANTIC AESTHETICS — 333

16 TWO DAYS IN DECEMBER — 349

CONCLUSION — 365

Bibliography — 387

Index — 413

Color plates can be found between pages 204 and 205.

PLATES

1 Luigi Rossini, *View of the Ruin of the Basilica of San Paolo*, 1824.

2 Carlo Marchionni, New Vatican Sacristy, Vatican City, 1776–1784.

3 Commissioner of Antiquities Carlo Fea showing Pope Pius VII the new archaeological discoveries at Ostia, from the cycle of frescos depicting episodes from the life of Pius VII Chiaramonti by Domenico De Angelis and Domenico Del Frate, c. 1818, in the Clementine Gallery in the Vatican Library.

4 Giovanni Paolo Panini, *Interior of San Paolo fuori le mura*, oil on canvas, c. 1750.

5 Milvian Bridge, Rome, as reconstructed by Giuseppe Valadier, 1805–1806.

6 Elevation of the basilica of San Paolo fuori le mura, showing its prefire state (left) and Angelo Uggeri's vision for its repair and reconstruction (right) (from Uggeri [1823]).

7 Unidentified plan project for San Paolo, possibly Gianbattista Martinetti's project of April 1824.

8 Giuseppe Valadier (assisted by Gaspare Salvi), longitudinal section, revised project for San Paolo, June 1824.

9 Jean-Victor-Louis Faure, *San Paolo fuori le mura after the Fire of July 1823*, 1823.

10 Pasquale Belli, proposed longitudinal section for the reconstruction of the basilica of San Paolo, 16 November 1830.

11 View of the north porch of the rebuilt basilica of San Paolo.

12 The apse at San Paolo as reconstructed between 1833 and 1840.

13 Inner side of the Arch of Placidia facing the apse.

14 West face of the superstructure of Arnolfo di Cambio's ciborium over the confessio at San Paolo, as restored 1836–1840.

15 View from the nave of San Paolo looking east.

16 The pontifical throne designed by Luigi Poletti, in the apse of San Paolo fuori le mura.

17 The St. Benedict chapel at San Paolo fuori le mura, designed by Luigi Poletti.

viii LIST OF PLATES

18 A variant of Poletti's second façade option for the basilica of San Paolo, roughly corresponding to Gregory XVI's order in 1844 to reconstruct the original façade and portico. Gregory had ordered the quadriporticus eliminated from the project, and Poletti's memorandum described the project as not having one, but the variant shown in this drawing has one.

19 George Wigley, Sant'Alfonso de' Liguori, Rome, 1855–1859.

20 Area beneath the choir at San Lorenzo fuori le mura at the floor level of the fourth-century basilica, created by Virginio Vespignani following excavations in the 1850s.

FIGURES

1 The basilica and monastery of San Paolo fuori le mura (detail) (Giovanni Maggi, *Le dieci basiliche del giubileo*, Rome, c. 1620).   *page 2*

2 Francesco Demesmey, third-prize project for the 1758 Concorso Clementino second-class competition in architecture.   3

3 Interior of San Giovanni in Laterano, Rome, as restored by Francesco Borromini in the 1640s.   15

4 Interior of Santa Maria Maggiore, Rome, as restored by Ferdinando Fuga in the 1740s.   16

5 Felice Giani, patriotic altar erected in St. Peter's Square for the Festival of the Federation, 1798.   19

6 Jacques-Louis David, *Portrait of Pius VII*, 1805.   20

7 Amphitheatrum Flavium, from the cycle of frescos depicting episodes from the life of Pius VII Chiaramonti by Domenico De Angelis and Domenico Del Frate, c. 1818, in the Clementine Gallery in the Vatican Library.   21

8 Arch of Constantine, Rome, showing the enclosure erected by Pope Pius VII in 1805 (from Giovanni Battista Cipriani, *Vedute principali e piu interessanti di Roma* [Rome, 1799 {sic; 1806}]).   22

9 Excavations at the Colosseum (from Angelo Uggieri, *Journées pittoresques de Roma* [Rome, n.d. {c. 1808}]).   25

10 Longitudinal section of the basilica of San Paolo fuori le mura, drawn by Andrea Alippi and engraved by Pietro Ruga (from Nicolai [1815]).   30

11 Interior of the basilica of San Paolo (from Gutensohn and Knapp [1822–1826]).   32

12 Milvian Bridge, Rome, before its reconstruction by Giuseppe Valadier (from Angelo Uggieri, *Journées pittoresques de Roma*. Rome, n.d. [c. 1800–1802]).   35

13 Giuseppe Valadier, project for the Milvian Bridge and environs, 1805.   36

14 Façade of San Paolo fuori le mura (from Giuseppe Agostino Pietro Vasi, *Raccolta delle più belle vedute antiche, e moderne di Roma*, v. 1, Rome, 1786).   42

15 Andrea Alippi, section toward the east through the nave and aisles of the basilica of San Paolo; engraved by Pietro Ruga (from Nicolai [1815]).   45

16 Frontispiece illustration from Uggeri (1823).   46

17	Ascanio Savorgnan di Brazzà, *Fire at San Paolo*, 1824, depicting the arrival of the fire brigade.	47
18	Luigi Rossini, *View of the Ruin of the Basilica of San Paolo*, 1824.	48
19	Thomas Lawrence, *Portrait of Pius VII*, 1819.	51
20	Luigi Rossini, *View of the Ruin of the Basilica of San Paolo*, 1824.	52
21	Cyprien Gaulon, *Portrait of Leo XII*, c. 1826.	56
22	Antoine Joseph Wiertz, *Portrait of Angelo Uggeri*, 1835.	66
23	Plan of the basilica of San Paolo fuori le mura, indicating which columns had been damaged or destroyed in the fire of July 1823 (from Uggeri [1823]).	67
24	Jean-Baptiste-Cicéron Le Sueur, *San Paolo fuori le mura after the Fire of July 1823*, 1823.	68
25	Jean-Baptiste Joseph Wicar, *Portrait of Giuseppe Valadier*, 1827.	72
26	Giuseppe Valadier, plan, first project for San Paolo, December 1823.	76
27	Giuseppe Valadier (assisted by Gaspare Salvi), plan, revised project for San Paolo, June 1824.	85
28	Giuseppe Valadier (assisted by Gaspare Salvi), lateral exterior elevation, revised project for San Paolo, June 1824.	86
29	Giuseppe Valadier (assisted by Gaspare Salvi), west elevation (left; section through courtyard) and east exterior elevation (right), revised project for San Paolo, June 1824.	87
30	Detail of Plate 8 showing the church interior.	88
31	Gaetano Gnassi, longitudinal section, winning project for a new basilica of San Paolo fuori le mura, Concorso Clementino 1824, first-class competition in architecture.	90
32	Gaetano Gnassi, plan, winning project for a new basilica of San Paolo fuori le mura, Concorso Clementino 1824, first-class competition in architecture.	91
33	Francesco Santini, project for a new basilica of San Paolo fuori le mura, May 1824.	92
34	Giovanni Molli, preparatory drawing for Molli's lost project for a new basilica of San Paolo for the 1824 Concorso Clementino.	95
35	Giovanni Molli, architectural plan labeled "S. Paolo in Roma= Ar^to Gio Molli, ideō," identified here as a preparatory drawing for Molli's lost project for a new basilica of San Paolo for the 1824 Concorso Clementino.	96
36	*Portrait of Carlo Fea*, after a drawing by Jean-Baptiste Wicar, 1813 (from Carlo Fea, *Varietà di notizie economiche fisiche antiquarie*, Rome: Bourlié, 1820).	101
37	"Nota delle Oblazioni volontarie fatte per la riedificazione della Basilica di S. Paolo," unpaginated supplement to *DdR*, 21 December 1825.	144
38	Map showing the geographical distribution of all donors listed in the *Prima nota* covering the period from 25 January 1825 to 21 December 1825.	149
39	Map showing the geographical distribution of all donors listed in the *Seconda nota* covering the period from 1 January 1826 to 31 March 1826.	150

LIST OF FIGURES

40	Map showing the geographical distribution of all donors listed in the third through the final *Eleventh nota*, covering the period from 1 April 1826 to 30 June 1833.	151
41	Antonio Aquaroni, *View of the Ruins of San Paolo fuori le mura*, 1823.	160
42	Illustration by Angelo Uggeri from his article arguing for the reinforcement of the Arch of Galla Placidia at San Paolo ("Dell'arco trionfale detto di Placidia. Prima conferenza," *Memorie romane di antichità e belle arti* 4 (1827), pp. 113–124).	161
43	Angelo Uggeri, "Chronological Table of the Ostian Basilica," from his report to Treasurer General Mario Mattei, June 1827.	167
44	Angelo Uggeri, "Plan of the Basilica of San Paolo," June 1827.	168
45	Severian spolia capital from the original nave arcade of the basilica displayed in the Passeggiata Archaeologica at the basilica of San Paolo.	170
46	Angelo Uggeri, engraving showing his counterproject for the nave arcade capitals (published in Uggeri [1828]).	171
47	Gaspare Fossati, sketch depicting the raising of one of the columns of the triumphal arch at San Paolo, 6 August 1829.	176
48	Pasquale Belli, proposed plan for the reconstruction of the basilica of San Paolo, 16 November 1830.	178
49	Comparison approximately to scale of the elevation of the old basilica as depicted in Nicolai's monograph (left) with Belli's proposed nave elevation of 16 November 1830 (right).	179
50	Pasquale Belli, proposed section through the transept looking west (top) and nave looking west (bottom) for the reconstruction of the basilica of San Paolo, 16 November 1830.	181
51	Paul Delaroche, *Portrait of Pope Gregory XVI*, 1844.	187
52	Pasquale Belli (and Luigi Poletti?), demonstration of how the nave floor at San Paolo was to be raised, 22 January 1833.	195
53	Plate VIII *bis* from Uggeri (1833).	197
54	Plate VIII *ter* from Uggeri (1833).	198
55	Plate XXXIV from Uggeri (1833).	199
56	Plate XXXVIII from Uggeri (1833).	200
57	Raffaele Fidanza, *Portrait of Luigi Poletti*, 1838.	208
58	Louis-Hippolyte Lebas, Notre-Dame-de-Lorette, Paris, 1823–1836.	213
59	Poletti's plan for the rearrangement of the apse at San Paolo, March 1834.	215
60	The 1:50 wooden model for the reconstruction of San Paolo created on Poletti's orders in 1834.	219
61	Detail of Poletti's wooden model of San Paolo showing the join where the nave (left) and the west façade (right) meet. This join indicates where the pronaos façade originally built onto the model was removed sometime after 1852 and replaced with the current one, following the decision to build the façade in the Paleochristian style.	221
62	Older photographs of Poletti's wooden model before it was placed in its plexiglass case.	222
63	Luigi Poletti, initial project for a ciborio over Paul's tomb to replace Arnolfo di Cambio's ciborium.	224
64	Title page from Poletti (1838a).	229

LIST OF FIGURES

65 Giulio Romano, Mantova Cathedral, nave, 1545–1546. 233

66 Friedrich Ziebland, St. Bonifaz, Munich, 1836–1847. 234

67 Reused column from the north aisle of San Paolo fuori le mura, reemployed by Poletti among the other old aisle columns supporting the north porch of the rebuilt basilica. 239

68 Elevation of the apse of San Paolo fuori le mura in its ruined state, by Angelo Uggeri, 1833. 247

69 Virginio Vespignani's sketches from 18 January 1838, when the confessio at San Paolo was excavated. This sketch depicts the slab bearing the inscription "PAULO APOSTOLO MART." 250

70 Detail of the apse mosaic at San Paolo. 256

71 Engraving showing the Early Christian inscriptions discovered on the underside of one of the keystones of Arnolfo di Cambio's ciborium at San Paolo fuori le mura when it was restored in 1836–1840. 258

72 Detail of Gregory XVI's tomb in St. Peter's basilica. 261

73 The Veii Columns along the south wall of the St. Benedict chapel. 272

74 The interior of Pope Gregory XVI's new Etruscan museum (from L'Album, 24 March 1838). 273

75 Piazza Colonna, Rome, showing the Column of Marcus Aurelius (second century; with a statue of St. Paul at its summit, added by Pope Sixtus V in 1589) and the Palazzo della Posta e Gran Guardia (known today as the Palazzo Wedekind) by Pietro Camporese the Younger with input from Giuseppe Valadier, 1830–1837. 275

76 Detail of the Palazzo della Posta e Gran Guardia. 276

77 Detail of one of Luigi Poletti's first designs for the apse and eastern chapels of the basilica of San Paolo fuori le mura. 277

78 The entry of Pope Gregory XVI's new Egyptian museum (from L'Album, 16 February 1839). 281

79 The Pontifical Expedition to Egypt loading the alabaster columns donated by Mehmet Ali aboard their ships for the return to Rome (from L'Album, 21 August 1841). 283

80 The first of Ravioli's dispatches from the Pontifical Expedition to Egypt, showing its arrival at the First Cataract of the Nile facing Philae (from L'Album, 13 March 1841). 285

81 The rebuilt transept of the basilica of San Paolo fuori le mura in 1840 (from L'Album, 11 July 1840). 286

82 Pope Gregory XVI consecrating the papal altar at the basilica of San Paolo fuori le mura (from Collezione di costumi sacri Romani, 1841–1843). 288

83 Gregory XVI reads his allocution during the ceremonies for the consecration of the transept at San Paolo fuori le mura in October 1840 (from Moreschi [1840]). 290

84 José Galofre y Coma, Portrait of Pope Pius IX, 1847. 305

85 Luigi Poletti's project to reinstate his ciborium proposal by erecting it over that of Arnolfo di Cambio, June 1846. 310

86 Façade of St. Peter's basilica. The statues of Peter and Paul stand on plinths to the far left and right (partially obscured by video screens). 311

LIST OF FIGURES

87 Elevation drawing of Poletti's pronaos façade option for the west front
    of the basilica of San Paolo fuori le mura, with the quadriporticus
    extending to either side. Signed by Poletti and dated November 1845. 312

88 Undated sketch by Poletti showing the north flank of his vision
    for the reconstructed San Paolo fuori le mura. 313

89 Engraving by Andrea Alippi showing the façade and portico of San
    Paolo fuori le mura before the fire of 1823 (from Nicolai [1815]). 314

90 Poletti's third façade option for the basilica of San Paolo,
    representing a rationalized Paleochristian-style façade and
    quadriporticus. 315

91 Luigi Poletti's design for a *girandola* structure representing the new
    façade of the basilica of San Paolo fuori le mura, created for the
    public celebrations of the festival of Peter and Paul, 29 June 1854. 346

92 The consecration ceremony at the basilica of San Paolo fuori
    le mura on 10 December 1854 (from *L'Album*, 16 December 1854). 355

93 Giuseppe De Fabris's project for a monument in Rome dedicated
    to the Immaculate Conception of Mary, December 1854 (from
    Orioli [1855]). 360

94 Luigi Poletti, Colonna dell'Immacolata, Rome, 1855–1857. 361

95 Poletti's 1846 project for a Pauline column to be erected outside
    the north porch of San Paolo fuori le mura. 362

96 Santa Maria sopra Minerva, Rome, fourteenth century; restored
    between 1848 and 1855 by the Dominican fathers of the adjacent
    monastery following designs by Fra'Girolamo Bianchedi. 366

97 Virginio Vespignani, Santa Maria della Misericordia, Verano
    Cemetery, Rome, 1855–1859. 367

98 *The excavations under the southeast side of the Palatine Hill* (from
    Cacchiatelli and Cleter [1865]). 368

99 Annibale Angelini, *Il Ponte del Soldino*, 1869. 369

100 Electric-telegraph wires extending out of Rome to the southeast
    (from Cacchiatelli and Cleter [1865]). 370

101 The Ponte Senatorio, a new iron suspension bridge over the Tiber
    built atop the second-century BCE remains of the Pons Aemilius
    (from Cacchiatelli and Cleter [1865]). 371

102 The basilica of San Lorenzo fuori le mura, mainly from the sixth and
    thirteenth centuries; restored by Virginio Vespignani, 1855–1864.
    As the photograph was taken before the bombing of 1943, it shows
    the now-lost fresco paintings along the nave walls. 372

103 *Excavations beneath the church of San Clemente*, Rome (from
    Cacchiatelli and Cleter [1865]). 374

104 *The basilica of Santo Stefano in the via Latina* on the southern
    edge of Rome, excavated starting in 1859 (from Cacchiatelli and
    Cleter [1865]). 375

105 *The basilica of S. Alesandro on the via Nomentana*, discovered
    in 1854, surmounted by the half-built church begun by the architect
    Luigi Boldrini in 1857 but abandoned in the early 1860s (from
    Cacchiatelli and Cleter [1865]). 376

ACKNOWLEDGMENTS

It is daunting to enumerate the debts of gratitude accumulated over more than a decade of research. I shall try, but I ask forgiveness in advance for any omissions.

I begin by acknowledging a profound debt to two pioneering scholars of nineteenth-century San Paolo, Elisabetta Pallottino and Michael Groblewski, both names that proliferate in my footnotes. This study is in continuous dialogue with their works, and I hope that it measures up to the high standards they set.

An essential thank you goes to the staffs at the numerous libraries and archives where my research was conducted. At the Archivio di Stato in Rome, I thank the whole staff but especially Monica Calzolari and more recently Claudia Ambrosio, who both not only spared no trouble in making the archive of the Special Commission available to me during the long years when it was being reorganized but also cheerfully and generously shared their expertise with me in countless other ways. At San Paolo fuori le mura itself, I would like formally to thank the Abbot, his Most Reverend Excellency Dom Donato Ogliari, as well as the director of the Historical Archive, Father Pierfrancesco De Feo, and the several very helpful archivists with whom I worked directly over the years there. At the Archive of the Academy of St. Luke in Rome, I especially thank Elisa Camboni for her kind assistance. At the Library of the American Academy in Rome, my thanks go to the late Christine Huemer and the whole of her excellent staff. At the Biblioteca Nazionale Vittorio Emanuele in Rome, I thank Laura Biancini in particular for her help; at the Biblioteca di Storia Moderna e Contemporanea in Rome, Aida Marazzi and her colleagues were always of great help to me; and at many other Roman libraries and archives, countless staff members went out of their way to help me over the years – at the Archivio Storico Capitolino, the Biblioteca del Senato, the Biblioteca di Archaeologia e Storia dell'Arte, the Bibliotheca Hertziana, the Biblioteca Casanatense, the Biblioteca Alessandrina, the Bibliothèque de l'Ecole Française, the Library of the British School in Rome, and the Fondazione Besso. I extend grateful thanks also for the cheerful professionalism of the helpful librarians and archivists at the Archivio Apostolico Vaticano, the Biblioteca Apostolica Vaticana, and the Archivio della Reverenda Fabbrica di

San Pietro, all in Vatican City. Further afield, very special thanks are due to Maria Elisa della Casa at the Biblioteca Civica d'Arte Luigi Poletti in Modena, who could not have been more welcoming and helpful when I was working at the Archivio Luigi Poletti there; and to the director of the Fondazione Achille Marazza in Borgomanero, Giovanni Cerutti, and to archivist Barbara Gattone, whose great hospitality and helpfulness were an invaluable help to my research on the Molli family archive there. Thanks are also due to the staff at the Archive de l'Institut and the Bibliothèque de l'Institut national d'histoire de l'art in Paris, the Getty Research Institute in Los Angeles, the Library at Villa I Tatti outside Florence, and the AHO Library in Oslo. The Carnegie Library in Suva, Fiji, offered a peaceful if incongruous workplace when my wife's work brought us for a season to the South Pacific. And finally I thank the staff at Davidson Library at the University of California at Santa Barbara, especially the tireless Interlibrary Loan Department.

I have had the great good fortune to receive copious support for my research on San Paolo. Early starts on this project were funded by a Barbieri Grant in Italian History (2002) from Trinity College in Hartford; an NEH Summer Research Grant (2003); and a National Endowment for the Humanities (NEH) Fellowship (2005–2006). The second and decisive stage of research was inaugurated with a Millicent Mercer Johnsen Post-Doctoral Rome Prize in Modern Italian Studies at the American Academy in Rome (2009–2010); two Academic Senate Research Grants from UCSB (2011 and 2016); invited research residencies at the Institut National d'Histoire de l'Art in Paris (2016) and the Oslo School of Architecture and Design (2016); and finally by a six-month Wallace Fellowship at Villa I Tatti/the Harvard University Center for Italian Renaissance Studies in Florence. I am deeply grateful to all these institutions for their generosity. I am also deeply grateful to Villa I Tatti, and to its director, Professor Alina Payne, for the Lila Wallace/Reader's Digest Publication Grant that helps support the production costs of this book. I extend warmest thanks also to my academic home, the Department of the History of Art and Architecture at the University of California at Santa Barbara, where a wonderful group of colleagues and students (and a succession of sympathetic department chairs) helped, supported, and stimulated me in innumerable ways during the long gestation of this book.

Myriad individuals have helped me on this project in ways big and small. I offer a very special thank you to a quartet of Roman colleagues who at the start of this project were intimidating names whose work I admired, but who by the end have become friends, as all of them in their different ways welcomed me to their city with exceptional generosity and warmth: Susanna Pasquali, Elisabetta Pallottino, Marina Docci, and especially Giovanna Capitelli, who in addition to countless other kindnesses undertook an invaluable critical reading of the completed manuscript. I also wish to thank, in no

ACKNOWLEDGMENTS xvii

particular order, the many other friends and colleagues who helped me write this book: Maarten Delbeke, Yuri Strozzieri, Jasper Van Parys, Christopher Wood (for a very thought-provoking exchange on nineteenth-century historicism), Robert Coates-Stevens, Catherine Brice, Peter Fane-Saunders, the late Terry Kirk, Heather Hyde Minor, Fabio Barry (for Roman site visits, scholarly consultations and debates, and general hilarity over the years), Nicola Camerlenghi, Jean-Philippe Garric, Claudio Fogu, Jon Snyder, Tommaso Caliò, Barry Bergdoll, Robin Middleton, Mia Fuller (in conversation with whom I first conceived this project), Adrián Almoguera, Ilaria Fiumi Sermattei, Francesco Ceccarelli, Mari Hvattum, Lucia Allais (for indispensable editorial suggestions on the *Grey Room* article from which my conclusion derives), Anne Hultzsch, Christopher Korten, James Harrell (for answering within an hour my out-of-the-blue email query about Egyptian alabaster), Laura DiZerega, Laura Wittman, and finally my old friend Joseph Imorde.

My parents, Sarah and Richard Wittman, have always supported me in everything, and this book has been no exception. I can never thank them enough for all their love and encouragement, and for concealing what must have been their puzzlement that I could be working for so long on one book. I offer the dearest thanks of all to my wife Claudia Martínez Mansell and our daughter Estrella Wittman Martínez, two lights that entered my life in Rome during the course of this project. I dedicate this book to them, with all my love.

ABBREVIATIONS

Archives and Libraries

AASL:	Archivio dell'Accademia di San Luca, Rome
AAV:	Archivio Apostolico Vaticano, Vatican City
ANF:	Archives Nationals, Paris
ASC:	Archivio Storico Capitolino, Rome
ASP:	Archivio dell'Abbazia di San Paolo fuori le mura, Rome
ASR:	Archivio di Stato, Rome
CSRBSP:	Archivio della Commissione (or Congregazione) Speciale per la riedificazione della Basilica di San Paolo
BAV:	Biblioteca Apostolica Vaticana, Vatican City
BCALP:	Biblioteca Civica d'Arte Luigi Poletti: Archivio Luigi Poletti, Modena
BEM:	Biblioteca Estense, Modena
BiASA:	Biblioteca di Archaeologia e Storia dell'Arte, Rome
BNR:	Biblioteca Nazionale Centrale Vittorio Emanuele II, Rome
BSMC:	Biblioteca di Storia Moderna e Contemporanea, Rome
FM:	Fondazione Achille Marazza, Borgomanero
PCAS:	Pontificia Commissione di Archaeologia Sacra, Vatican City

Manuscripts

Cronaca I, II, III:	Chronacle of the Monastery of San Paolo fuori le mura. Three volumes: *Cronaca I*: up to 1823; *Cronaca II*: 1823–1850; *Cronaca III*: 1850–1859 (ASP: 16/c)
SPF:	Raffaello Liberati, "Storia dei principali fatti accaduti nel Monastero di S. Paolo fuori Roma e contrade ivi dintorno dal 1 gennaio 1849 a tutto luglio del medesimo anno," 1866 (ASP: 16/c)

Publications

CAPDR:	*Collezione degli articoli pubblicati nel Diario di Roma e nelle Notizie del giorno relativi alla nuova fabbrica della Basilica di S. Paolo*, ed. Luigi Moreschi, Rome: Tipografia della R.C.A., 1845.

DESE:	Moroni, Gaetano, *Dizionario di erudizione storico-ecclesiastica*, 103v., Venice: Tipografia Emiliana, 1840–1861.
TEPD:	*Tutte le encicliche e i principali documenti pontifici emanati dal 1740*, ed. Ugo Bellocchi, 12v., Vatican City: Libreria editrice vaticana, 1993-.

Periodicals

BMMGP:	*Bollettino dei monumenti musei e gallerie pontificie*
CHR:	*Catholic Historical Review*
DdR:	*Il diario di Roma*
DPARA:	*Dissertazioni della Pontificia accademia romana di archeologia*
GASLA:	*Giornale arcadico di scienze, lettere, ed arti*
GdR:	*Gazzetta di Roma*
JSAH:	*Journal of the Society of Architectural Historians*
MRABA:	*Memorie romane di antichità e di belle arti*
RSdA:	*Ricerche di storia dell'arte*

Other Abbreviations

tiG:	transcribed in Groblewski (2001)
tiSAD:	transcribed in Strozzieri (2021) in the *Appendice Documentaria*

INTRODUCTION

> You know, I suppose, that the ancient and respectable tumble-down Basilica of San Paolo *fuori delle mure* is burnt down at Rome ...
>
> William Gell to Dr. Frederic Forster Quin
> Naples, Tuesday, [22] July 1823[1]

Paul of Tarsus – St. Paul the Apostle, the Apostle to the Gentiles, God's Chosen Vessel – was martyred in Rome sometime between 65 and 67 CE. He was laid to rest along the via Ostiense, south of Rome, in a sepulchral area owned by a Christian woman named Lucina, where his tomb soon attracted great veneration. Not long after Emperor Constantine accepted Christianity in 313, a modest basilica was erected to shelter the tomb, sponsored, probably, by Constantine himself. Within a few decades, local devotion had outgrown this first basilica, so in 384 (or 386) the co-emperors Theodosius I, Valentinian II, and Arcadius launched the construction of a far bigger one. This prodigious new monument was consecrated under Honorius early in the fifth century and came to be known as San Paolo fuori le mura for its location beyond the old Aurelian city walls. It was to endure for more than fourteen centuries as one of the most important churches in Christendom and, with St. Peter's, one of Rome's two most important pilgrimage centers[2] (**Figure 1**).

In July 1823, this sprawling, precious monument to Catholic antiquity was destroyed in what was most likely an accidental fire caused by workmen restoring

1. The basilica and monastery of San Paolo fuori le mura (detail) (Giovanni Maggi, *Le Dieci Basiliche del Giubileo*, Rome, c. 1620).
Source: Wikimedia Commons; Collection Skokloster Castle; photo Jens Mohr.

the basilica's roof[3] (**Plate 1**). If this had occurred just a few decades earlier, the response would probably have been swift and uncontroversial: the ruins would have been cleared away and a new basilica in the contemporary classical style erected in their place. As recently as 1758, the students participating in the annual Concorso Clementino at the Academy of St. Luke had greedily imagined doing just that (**Figure 2**), and it is what some contemporaries expected would happen now. But the idea proved to be anything but uncontroversial this time around. Instead, a contentious debate was unleashed that was to dominate the Roman cultural scene for two years. This pitted those in favor of a new modern classical church against opponents who demanded a historically unprecedented solution: that of reconstructing the original fourth-century Early Christian basilica in its pristine totality, in what came to be known as the *in pristinum* option.

The resolution of the debate in 1825 by Pope Leo XII in favor of the *in pristinum* option set in motion the largest and most expensive construction project in Rome since the rebuilding of St. Peter's.[4] Unprecedented though it was to undertake an archaeologically precise reconstruction of a destroyed building, Leo's decision sprang from ostensibly conservative longings. But it also reflected the climate of anxious, searching introspection that had begun to

2. Francesco Demesmey, third-prize project for the 1758 Concorso Clementino second-class competition in architecture, in which competitors were asked to design a new basilica of San Paolo "in modern form."
Source: © Accademia Nazionale di San Luca, Roma.

settle over the Eternal City following decades of trauma, and this already by 1823 had created conditions ripe for new ideas and departures. The traumas dated back at least to the time of the French Revolution, in the aftermath of which Rome endured two desecrating French occupations, the death of a pope in a French prison, another pope bullied into a series of enfeebling international agreements, the removal of much of the pontifical archives and art collections, and the demolition or degradation of numerous historic churches. After the fall of Napoleon in 1814, Church leaders confronted an unrecognizable social, political, religious, and economic landscape: Catholic observance was in decline across Europe; political liberalism was ascendant; rights and privileges the Church had long enjoyed abroad were truncated or gone; Catholic missionary activity beyond Europe was in precipitous decline; and the normative discourses of modern science, historiography, and philosophy were speaking a different language entirely to the old Catholic conception of the world. Church leaders began to dream of launching a campaign of principled response abroad and institutional rejuvenation within. Yet the old European system of national Catholic Churches had collapsed in the face of post-Revolutionary nationalisms and concordats, leaving an ill-prepared Roman Curia increasingly on its own to figure out how to support the fortunes of the Church Universal. On top of everything else, the pontifical territories were collapsing financially: by the 1820s, as the economies of other European states were starting to liberalize and expand, the Papal States remained a stagnant feudal economy supporting a sprawling domestic welfare state.[5]

The fire at San Paolo arrived like an exclamation point at the end of this *Via Crucis*. A sour atmosphere of alienation and fear – but also defiance – had settled over official Rome by 1823, as clerical leaders began to reckon seriously with the grave and possibly existential challenges their Church still faced. In retrospect, the fire at San Paolo could scarcely have avoided being perceived as a supercharged metaphor: as a sign of divine fury or a harbinger of still greater catastrophes to come. This precisely was what made reconstruction seem such a pressing necessity. With such high stakes, it is little wonder that an intense debate erupted over exactly what kind of church should be built. Modern? Smaller? An economical repair? Exactly the same as before? For it was never a debate solely or even principally about architecture.

This book is accordingly also not just about architecture. Rather it reevaluates architectural culture in Rome during these decades in relation to the Catholic Church's long, metamorphic response to the losses and humiliations inflicted by the French Revolution, Napoleon, and the subsequent triumph of the liberal order in Western Europe. In pursuit of these larger questions, the reconstruction of San Paolo from 1825 to 1854 will occupy most of our attention, forming a bridge between two distinct periods: that of initial trauma over the half-century before the fire of 1823, then the decades of papal restoration, and, later, Catholic revival that followed the Roman insurrection of 1849.

The opening chapter details how longstanding attitudes about architecture and architectural heritage in Rome had begun to mutate in the decades prior to 1823, and especially during the Revolutionary and Napoleonic periods. These mutations are linked here to the pressure of contemporary tribulations and are presented as evidence of unacknowledged shifts in how clerical leaders perceived both the Church's history and its relationship to the world. The middle chapters of the book then focus on San Paolo: on how the debates precipitated by the fire grew out of the dismal memory of recent events, and how the discourses that then animated the reconstruction responded to a spectrum of evolving and sometimes competing desires: to reconnect with threatened histories, to insist upon the Church's distance from the secular world, to manifest the Church's resilience, to found a popular Catholic revival, or to place Roman Catholic architecture on a new modern footing. The chapters on the post-1850 period, finally, argue that although the rebuilt San Paolo was widely seen by contemporaries (and subsequently by architectural historians) as a failure, the reconstruction effort in a broader sense proved to be an essential trial-and-error laboratory in which Church leaders learned many of the lessons that later made possible the international revival of Catholic fortunes that occurred after 1850.

This is, in other words, a book concerned not only with architectural matters per se, but also with the prominent public role architectural matters played in the Church's efforts to navigate, control, and project its own nineteenth-century modernity. And by insisting on framing this process as the history of a modernity, the book also aims to raise questions about an outdated historiographical consensus concerning where and when the European modern can and cannot be found. In formulating these questions, I have drawn inspiration from the exhortation to students of global modernities to "provincialize Europe" and to envisage "multiple modernities" in order to attempt something similar *within* the European geographical space.[6] Early nineteenth-century Rome is usually depicted as a reactionary backwater, and it figures in European histories of the period (especially architectural histories) principally as a backdrop to the Romantic reveries of more sophisticated northern visitors.[7] Many participants in the artistic and cultural debates at issue in this book took stridently antimodern positions, and even the rebuilding of San Paolo itself was framed as an act of antimodern defiance. But it certainly does not follow that this history is therefore somehow irrelevant or antithetical to the story of nineteenth-century European modernities, for antimodern discourses are necessarily modern themselves. This book therefore rejects hierarchical conceptions of European modernity as a unitary emancipatory phenomenon that emerged first in Paris, London, or Berlin and only later and in weaker, derivative form in places like Rome. It argues instead that the new economic, political, cultural, philosophical, religious, geographical, and scientific forces that shaped European modernities in particular ways in Paris, London, or Berlin were *necessarily* shaping a modernity in Rome too, but one in which a different history and different relative conditions caused those forces to be experienced, contested, absorbed, and transformed in very different ways.

The goal of this reframing is not to promote Rome to the company of Paris and London at an imagined high table of European modernity, but to lay out the complexities and ambiguities of the Roman experience, in all their peculiarity, as a paradigmatic modern story of response and initiative. In so doing, this book gestures toward the less homogenizing understanding available when we provincialize Paris and London, as it were, by adopting a less hierarchical framework for analyzing the intersecting structural and epistemological changes that we refer to with the term "modern."

This argument is developed here through a variety of intertwined thematics. At the level of architectural history, this book reveals that early nineteenth-century Roman architects and their clerical patrons did not simply cling to outdated ideas, as the historiographical caricatures have it, but rather were deeply engaged with the same doubts and dilemmas that preoccupied contemporaries such as Karl Friedrich Schinkel and Henri Labrouste elsewhere in

Europe. These concerned the relationship of the past to the present, the nature of history, the subjectivity of aesthetic experience, and whether traditions inherited from the past retained validity in an unprecedented new context. They approached these questions, however, from a very different perspective than their contemporaries in Paris or London, one informed by Rome's exceptional ancient and recent history. Thus whereas northern architects were able to repudiate Vitruvian idealism by looking to the local and the indigenous – to the Gothic, for instance, or to eclectic syntheses – Roman architects faced the difficulty that the classical tradition actually *was* their old indigenous way of building. Their challenge was thus not to switch styles but to learn to think about an old style in new ways: more historically, more relativistically. This is partly why, to eyes habituated to Berlin or Paris, Roman work of this period can seem the product of a mulish and provincial classicism, even though in reality it often sprang from the same aspirations to be self-consciously modern and national. At the same time, however, the complexities of the Roman situation were rendered even denser by religious considerations: by the enduring local sense of Rome's suprahistorical status in Christianity, or by the long Catholic tradition of seeing universalist classicism in the arts as an emblem of God's providential plan for his Church in the Eternal City. They were also inflected by the peculiarly expansive nationalisms that became available in Rome after 1800, which concluded from history that the Italic race(s) were the divinely chosen civilizers of humanity. Being Roman, in other words, dictated that universalist claims were never quite off the table, which naturally weighed on the theoretical reflections and design decisions of Roman architects in unique ways. And yet this was in no respect a provincial enterprise. The architect who commanded the reconstruction of San Paolo from 1833 to 1869, Luigi Poletti, was not only a voracious scholar of ancient Italic architectures, but also possessed one of the biggest personal libraries of recent architectural theory in Europe, with numerous works in French, Latin, and Italian, all of which he read fluently, as well as in German and English, of which he may have had some knowledge. A basic concern in this book, then, is to disclose an intellectual richness in Roman architectural debates and designs that most of the recent scholarship on European nineteenth-century architecture has assumed to be absent.

Another key theme here concerns the radical break within Catholic tradition represented by the unacknowledged historicism that began to orient thinking about the past in Rome during these decades. The normative historiography of historicism has long assumed it to be northern in origin, culturally Protestant, and opposed in its essence to the providentialist temporality of Catholic tradition; and Catholic apologists have largely agreed. This book instead reveals how a modern historicist consciousness of time as linear and inert – as unsusceptible to supernatural anachronic instabilities – began during this period to orient not just architectural reflection, but also the Holy See's superintendence of historical narratives and their physical traces in Rome, and even of Church history itself. As a result, ancient remains progressively lost their old capacity to bend or reactivate time and instead began to present their distinction as fragile and decaying witnesses to the depth of an ever-receding past. Historicist assumptions were fundamental to Pope Leo XII's resolution to rebuild San Paolo in its original fourth-century form, while after 1850 they also came to orient Pius IX's sprawling campaign to deploy Christian antiquities in Rome for didactic and propagandistic ends. This major epistemological shift – hiding in plain sight in architectural culture – hints at the depth of change that was quietly occurring within a Church famously unwilling to acknowledge its own doctrinal development, and points to the high stakes inherent in reengineering venerable Catholic traditions for new missions in a changed world.

The notion of the rebuilt San Paolo as a metaphor was eventually to prove more apt than anyone could have anticipated, for in pursuing the immense task of reconstruction, Church leaders found themselves engaging with many of the same challenges and opportunities they faced, and would continue to face, in their larger project of rebuilding the vitality, prestige, and self-confidence of the Catholic Church as a whole after the setbacks that opened the century. The funding of the reconstruction offers perhaps the most pertinent example. Prior to Leo XII's bold decision to rebuild a replica San Paolo at full scale, many had advocated cheaper and simpler solutions in the knowledge that the impoverished pontifical treasury would collapse under the strain of anything more ambitious. Leo's choice was predicated instead on the gamble that sufficient resources could be raised through an international fundraising drive, which he hoped might eventually snowball into an international Catholic revival under the sign of St. Paul. The fundraising campaign for the reconstruction of St. Peter's Basilica during the Renaissance had depended on the sale of indulgences and on top-down forms of coercion, neither of which were available to the Church anymore. Fundraising drives for San Paolo instead had to be conceived as bottom-up, identitarian appeals in which ordinary Catholics would be persuaded to contribute freely. The result was the first genuinely global fundraising campaigns in world history, extending already in the 1820s and 1830s beyond Europe to North and South America, India, the Philippines, and China. In aiming to persuade the faithful to contribute to the reconstruction of San Paolo, the clerical organizers of the fundraising campaign quickly perceived the difficulty of engaging potential donors in what was after all a faraway building that most would never see in person. This difficulty was overcome by means of publicity, which made of the reconstruction the most publicized architectural project in history up until that time, written about in newspapers from *The Courier* of Hobart, Tasmania, to the *Bengal Catholic Herald* of Calcutta. This occurred through the concerted efforts of a few key individuals in Rome who dedicated themselves to informationalizing this irreducible sacred space to give it the mobility required to reach a dispersed international public. This was yet another unprecedented enterprise – unprecedented anywhere, not just in supposedly backward Catholic Rome.

These drives did not end up sparking Leo's international Catholic revival, but they did teach the Catholic leadership essential lessons about how the channels of power binding the faithful to the institutional Church might be reimagined in an emergent modern world. The real fruit of this experiment then came with the great Catholic revival that *did* unfold in Europe after 1850: a popular movement predicated on greater official openness toward popular religiosity (Marian devotion, the Immaculate Conception, mass pilgrimages to places like Lourdes and La Salette), expanded reliance on popular donations (for instance, the Obolo, known as Peter's Pence, a popular fund inaugurated by international Catholic donors that supported the Holy See financially during the years of Italian reunification) and increased Church backing of Catholic newspapers and associations, societies, and eventually political parties. No longer was it the old ruling classes but rather a broadly popular Catholic movement that increasingly sustained the Church's cultural and political influence.[8] That new calculus had been first glimpsed in the international fundraising drives for the reconstruction of San Paolo decades earlier, which proved an essential laboratory for the international revival of Catholic fortunes that occurred after 1850.

The publicity surrounding the reconstruction of San Paolo regularly highlighted architectural and historical themes, as well as the successes of the fundraising drive. But its central theme was the person whose sacred body gave the whole enterprise its raison d'être: St. Paul. The most remarkable survival of the fire that devoured San Paolo in 1823 was the tall Gothic ciborium that marked the location of Paul's grave. It was a survival no one needed to be told was a miracle containing a precious message from God: that the fire and reconstruction should occasion a collective Catholic rededication to Paul's legacy. Who, after all, might the Church more profitably look to than the Doctor to the Gentiles in confronting a world of religious indifferentism and dangerous new doctrines? Paul was the Church's great peripatetic evangelizer among the pagans; he was the primary author of its stern and Christ-centered theology. A quarter century of justifying the reconstruction of San Paolo in such terms was to prove instructive to Church leaders; instructive, however, chiefly about the *limits* of Pauline rhetoric in kindling excitement beyond the confines of the clerical and educated elites. The underwhelming results of this Pauline experiment likewise form part of the prehistory of the post-1850 Catholic revival, for they contributed to the Holy See's revolutionary decision after 1850 to relax its official distrust of popular religiosity and to tap instead into its adamantine power.

Thus it was that in a season of enormous uncertainty for Church leaders, when the disorienting new realities of the post-Napoleonic world were only just being recognized in their full dimensions, the San Paolo reconstruction provided an arena for experimenting with a whole range of new strategies for thinking about architecture, for publicly mobilizing history and the legacies of Rome, and above all for reengaging with the faithful. The reconstruction of the church, in short, served as a practice run for the reconstruction of the Church.

The consecration of San Paolo occurred in 1854, when the essential architectural envelope was completed but many decorative and peripheral features still remained to be executed. This was celebrated in a suitably pompous ceremony, attended by hundreds of high-ranking clerics from around the Catholic world. None, however, had actually come to Rome for that purpose; they had all come instead to be present at Pope Pius IX's proclamation of the dogma of the Immaculate Conception of Mary two days prior. One event barely registered on the world's consciousness, while the other was important news everywhere. By the time both ceremonies were over, the Catholic Church had consummated a profound shift from one set of strategies for institutional renewal to another: from an austere vision hatched in the wake of Revolution and Napoleon, and which the reconstruction of Paul's basilica had been intended to actuate, to new strategies forged amid the disappointments and lessons of those years, and predicated instead on popular religiosity, Marian devotion, and reconfigured pastoral, social, and cultural ideals. This is the story that this book aims to tell, with a special emphasis on the role played by the reconstruction of Paul's basilica in revealing to Church leaders both the limits and the possibilities of a modernity that they anathemized, but also slowly learned to exploit as they rebuilt a Church that might yet thrive in the future.

NOTES

1   Madden (1855), v. 3, p. 392.
2   Docci (2006); Camerlenghi (2018).
3   On the parallels with the 2019 fire at Notre Dame in Paris, see Wittman (2019) and (2020a).
4   The main studies of the reconstruction are Del Signore (1988); Pallottino (1995), (1997), (2003), and (2012); Groblewski (2001).
5   Crocella (1982), pp. 21–28; Felisini (1990).
6   Yack (1997); Chakrabarty (2000); Eisenstadt (2000); Cazzato (2017a) and (2017b).
7   For example, the recent 693-page volume *Nineteenth-Century Architecture* (Bressani and Contandriopoulos, 2017), volume 3 in a multivolume *Companions to the History of Architecture* series published by Wiley, devotes all of two paragraphs to nineteenth-century Italy.
8   Mazzonis (1980); Crocella (1982), pp. 95–153.

PART I

FIRE IN THE TEMPLE

ONE

DISENCHANTING HISTORIES

THE REVIVAL OF CLASSICAL ARCHITECTURAL FORMS DURING THE Italian Renaissance proved an astonishingly durable development, setting a course that was to be followed for 300 years and more. The forms and theory of the classical tradition were of course constantly evolving over these centuries, and the tradition itself was subject to doubts and criticism (particularly toward the end; Carlo Lodoli in Venice or Francesco Milizia in Rome spring to mind). But because classical architecture was so unambiguously indigenous to Italy, and because growing awareness of the variety of architectural history had still not yet overcome the ideal of stylistic normativity, the impact of criticism on patronage and practice was limited. Nowhere was this truer than in Rome itself, where classicism was woven into the everyday fiber of an elite local identity that for both historical and religious reasons held deeply internalized universalist pretensions. The classical artistic tradition in Rome hinged on the Church's understanding of the Roman Empire as the providential prototype and forerunner for the Christian Empire of the Church – a conceit that itself reflected belief in the divinely mediated quality of sacred history, and in the anachronic propinquity of the ancient past to the present.[1] Between the Renaissance and the end of the eighteenth century, this view of history gradually lost its credibility and ossified into a kind of rhetorical formality. By 1800, as the suspicion continued to grow that the relationships between historical periods were defined more by difference than by continuity, most Roman artists reacted like their contemporaries elsewhere in Europe: by doubling down on an increasingly essentialist theory of the superiority of classical aesthetics.[2] But at the same time – and again as in ostensibly secular Europe – the "memory crisis" of these decades also sparked a searching reassessment of the architectural past, of which architectural modes from the past were worthy of study, preservation, or revival in the present, and why, and with what meaning.[3] No historic architectural mode enjoyed a more dramatic reversal of fortune during these years than that of the Early Christians. This chapter explores this evolution in its relation to contemporary historical events.

The Roman Church witnessed regular episodes of Paleochristianism before 1800, mostly when external challenges or reforming impulses stoked a longing for the purity of sainted early days. The reforming zeal born of the sixteenth-century combat with Protestantism, for instance, led to new Catholic scholarship on Early Christianity and its monuments, along with a few fascinating church restorations aimed at reinstantiating something of the Paleochristian spirit – even if this was also the century when demolition began on the most important Paleochristian church of all, old St. Peter's.[4] Early Christian stones were treated with greater reverence in the seventeenth century, as when the canons of St. Peter's petitioned Paul V to preserve the last remains of Peter's half-demolished old basilica, or when Innocent X commissioned Francesco Borromini to refurbish the dilapidated Lateran basilica with explicit instructions to preserve as much of the old building as possible.[5] But Borromini still obliged by concealing the reinforced Early Christian walls beneath a modern skin (**Figure 3**). The new reverence, in short, did not correlate to a new taste for Early Christian aesthetics. Even in the two fiercely erudite Paleochristian-revival church restorations commissioned by Cardinal Cesare Baronio around 1600, the purity of the Christian past was evoked less with an historicizing aesthetic than by reconstructing "the ancient content, vocabulary, and syntax" of Early Christian usages.[6]

Early Christian mania again surged in the eighteenth century, at which point it began to receive a rather different artistic expression. Pope Clement XI (1700–1721) took a special interest in the Early Christians and oversaw an extensive series of church restorations.[7] In the second quarter of the century, the steady accumulation of revisionary church histories by Protestants inspired a group of Roman clerical reformers centered on the historians Giovanni Bottari and Prospero Lambertini to advocate a more critical Catholic historiography, one more deeply rooted in the scientific evaluation of source materials, and that aspired to new discoveries and verifiability rather than just the validation of existing beliefs.[8] This intellectually exacting movement was elitist, anti-Jesuit, and openly hostile to popular religiosity, and it coincided

3. Interior of San Giovanni in Laterano Rome, as restored by Francesco Borromini in the 1640s. *Source*: Author.

with an intensified rationalization of dogma and bureaucratization of the clergy. When Lambertini was then elected Pope Benedict XIV in 1740, he directed major institutional energies toward a renewal of historical scholarship, founding no fewer than three academies devoted to historical research, endowing new academic chairs at the Collegio Romano in church history and liturgical history, and patronizing the work of Bottari, a pioneering specialist in the material culture of early Christianity.[9] This reform manifested itself also in a doctrinaire tendency in architecture that was hostile to the Baroque mode inherited from Francesco Borromini and his contemporaries, and aimed instead to inject the new criticality into thinking about architecture and its past. Its signature achievement was Ferdinando Fuga's major restoration of the Early Christian basilica of Santa Maria Maggiore in Rome (**Figure 4**), which exhibited an unprecedented historical rigor and concern for the building's original form and can, in certain respects, even be regarded as proto-historicist.[10] In all, then, most of the ancient churches in Rome were targeted for renovation of one sort or another over the first half of the century, including St. John Lateran, San Clemente, SS. Apostoli, Santa Croce in

4. Interior of Santa Maria Maggiore, Rome, as restored by Ferdinando Fuga in the 1740s. *Source*: Author.

Gerusalemme, Santa Prassede, Santa Maria in Trastevere, San Crisogono, and San Paolo fuori le mura (where the ancient mosaics were systematically restored and a new narthex renewed what was believed to be its Early Christian predecessor).[11]

Bottari's reforms fell from favor with the election in 1758 of Pope Clement XIII, who perceived them as a secularizing threat.[12] What took their place was a reactionary return to the idea of a providential relationship between the Church and ancient Rome; that is, to exactly the kind of historical claim the reformers had criticized as privileging holy mysteries over verifiable chronological developments. A changed policy toward pagan antiquities was one result. In an effort to refortify the Church's providential association with classical antiquity, Pope Clement XIV (1769–1774) decreed new art export prohibitions and new excavations aimed at unearthing fresh antiquities, and accelerated acquisitions in the antiquities market; he also built a large new Museo Pio-Clementino behind the Vatican palace to contain it all. Yet in spite of the determinedly conservative tenor of these efforts, the status of classical works in Clement's new museum was different than it might have been a century earlier. The works were now presented as primarily artistic in nature, their political significance limited to the suggestion of a Roman timelessness, and the idea that Rome formed civilization's bulwark against unwelcome modern upheavals. In the encomical literature celebrating Clement's policies, Time was always held up as the enemy, while the embattled papal hero was lauded for protecting the city from change.[13] That was the horizon of Clement's efforts, which avoided instrumentalizing antiquities to proclaim a parallel with the Empire of the Caesars, as Renaissance popes had done. As the century progressed, Roman guidebooks likewise progressively abandoned their organization around sacred itineraries and started to present the city instead as a storehouse of aesthetic treasures for secular tourists.[14]

Clement's treasurer, Gianangelo Braschi, had been instrumental in shaping this policy of reaction, and when Clement died it was Braschi who was elected his successor. As Pope Pius VI (1775–1799), he holds the distinction of being the first pontiff to explicitly identify the Enlightenment as an enemy of the Church, and he launched a Counter-Reformation-style "reconquest" to combat it.[15] Pius's Jubilee of 1775 was the first to be explicitly framed as a response to secular currents.[16] The politically active antiquity of the Renaissance popes was also rehabilitated: Pius's classically hyperbolic *possesso* ceremony of 1775, for instance, was larded with references to the Age of Augustus that aimed to shore up the old parallel between pope and Caesar.[17] The Church also continued its dogged efforts to reassert its custodianship of ancient artworks.[18] The signature architectural project of the Braschi pontificate was a new Vatican sacristy, the exterior of which alluded to Rome's Baroque heritage (**Plate 2**). Its construction had also necessitated the demolition of Santa Maria della Febbre, an important Early Christian structure that represented the final surviving vestige of old St. Peter's. This old-fashioned sense of the substitutability of new monuments for old was starkly at odds with the historical solicitude Fuga had shown just a few decades earlier at Santa Maria Maggiore. By insisting that the Church alone was the legitimate heir of the Roman Empire, Pius VI aimed to assert Rome's vitality and privilege, and to face down Voltaire as the Church had once faced down Luther. With Time anathemized as emblematic of change, the custodianship of ancient art became an emblem of political immunity and an unquestioned Roman stasis.[19] These historical attitudes were presented under the sign of continuity with tradition, but in reality they constituted willful gestures of reaction and resistance, and therefore their original significance was distorted. In this case, the obdurate revival of old anachronic temporal perspectives paradoxically carried within itself something of the historicist urge to affect the future with willful course corrections on the historical journey that produced the present.

Braschi was prescient in identifying Time as his enemy, for the challenges faced by the Church soon metastasized with the coming of the French Revolution. Revolutionary culture drew greedily on Athens and Rome, reviving but also reimagining antiquity in a secular key. Everybody from the revolutionaries to their enemies posited the Revolution as an epochal break with history, and this tended to advance both the modern sense of the past as receding, decaying, and eventually as alien, as well as the corollary understanding of time as inexorably linear. These ruptures arrived spectacularly in the Eternal City itself in February 1798, when Napoleon sent General Louis Alexandre Berthier to depose Pius VI and found a new Repubblica Romana. There were to be two French occupations between 1798 and 1814, unequal in length and of very different characters, and each followed by a papal restoration. By the time of the definitive restoration in 1814, perspectives on the Church's relationship to the monuments of antiquity and to those of its own history had been violently recalibrated – to the point that it had become conceivable for the first time in centuries that the convictions binding the old idea of a universal classicism to its pedestal might really come into question in Rome.

The Repubblica Romana of 1798, mocked locally as the *repubblica per ridere* ("The Risible Republic"), explicitly set out to recreate its ancient namesake, though in the event it only lasted nineteen months. This was still long enough for Pius VI to die in a French prison and for Catholic Rome to endure harrowing transformations. The Republic set up a new secular administrative order that systematically revoked Rome's historic exceptionalism. It instituted house numbers where before there had been only descriptive means of indicating location; street lighting was installed where the Church had simply discouraged people from being out at night; civil equality was conferred on the city's Jewish community and their bursting ghetto was opened up.[20] Tremendous damage was inflicted on the ecclesiastical patrimony of the city, with churches closed, vandalized, looted, turned to other uses, or sold at auction.[21] The Republic in general pursued a thoroughgoing ideological redefinition of the spaces and places of the city, using archaeological pageants and festivals at key classical sites to present the baffled Roman citizenry with a decidedly non-Catholic image of the classical past and, by extension, the whole Roman landscape.[22] Classical monuments long ago appropriated for the Church were brazenly reappropriated. A Liberty Tree was erected at the city's historic foundation place on the Capitoline Hill; a statue of Liberty appeared atop the Column of Marcus Aurelius, where it held the Sistine statue of St. Paul on a leash; civic meetings were convened in the Forum as they had been in ancient times.[23] The Rome of antiquity was enveloped in a bracing sense of *Jetztzeit*. For the Festival of the Federation in 1798, a giant altar complex with austere Doric columns was erected on St. Peter's Square (**Figure 5**). Famous classical statues like the Capitoline Wolf and the Palazzo Spada Pompey were lugged onstage as props for performances of Voltaire's *Le mort de César*.[24] Hordes of classical artworks were removed to Paris, in an epic act of plunder that was piously presented as "repatriation."[25]

5. Felice Giani, patriotic altar erected in St. Peter's Square for the Festival of the Federation, 1798.
Source: © Roma – Sovrintendenza Capitolina, Museo di Roma.

This spectacle ended with a first papal restoration following the Battle of Marengo, when then-First Consul Bonaparte granted the newly elected Pius VII (1800–1823) the privilege of returning to Rome (**Figure 6**). Pius returned fully aware that he ruled now at Napoleon's pleasure, and immediately, in 1801, he was compelled to sign a Concordat that for the first time ever subordinated the Catholic Church in France to the secular state. At home, meanwhile, he faced tremendous challenges. A visitor in 1802 estimated that the population had been reduced from 180,000 or even 200,000 on the eve of the occupation to just 90,000 after.[26] Despairing at the condition of his desecrated and plundered capital, Pius resumed his government under the sign of "restoration," restarting archaeological work and restocking the pontifical art collections in a restorative effort that clearly figured his hopes of a more general political and religious restoration.[27] Classical sites were scrubbed of their brief association with revolution, and a landmark chirograph was promulgated in 1802 that amplified Clement XIV's earlier strictures against the export of classical artworks. To administer these policies, Pius VII appointed the great sculptor Antonio Canova as his inspector general of fine arts and the razor-sharp jurist-antiquarian Carlo Fea as his commissioner of antiquities.[28]

6. Jacques-Louis David, *Portrait of Pius VII*, 1805.
Source: © RMN-Grand Palais / Art Resource, New York.

Archaeological excavations were initiated at Ostia and in the Forum, the Museo Pio-Clementino was expanded, and the Vatican's decimated collection of ancient art was again restocked[29] (**Plate 3**). What might be regarded as the first modern restorations of entire buildings were also undertaken, as the Arch of Septimius Severus (1803) and the Arch of Constantine (1805) were both dug out and isolated, and the Colosseum (1805–1807) was cleared, isolated, and buttressed with the great spur that secures its half-ruined outer wall on the east (**Figure 7**). Efforts were made to remove the baker's shop and fish markets that

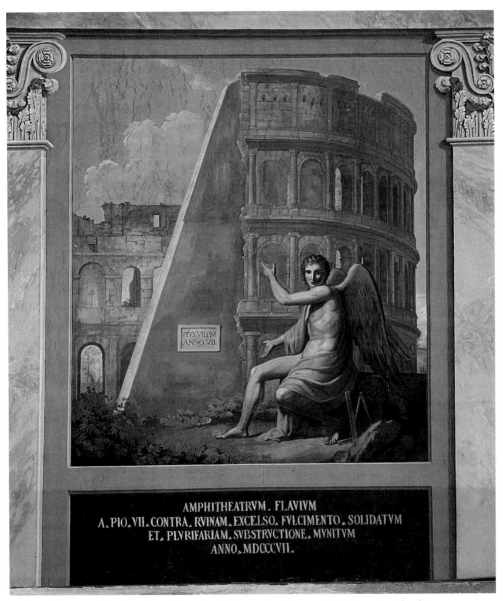

7. Amphitheatrum Flavium, from the cycle of frescos depicting episodes from the life of Pius VII Chiaramonti by Domenico De Angelis and Domenico Del Frate, c. 1818, in the Clementine Gallery in the Vatican Library.
Source: Author.

occupied the porch and flanks of the Pantheon (1804–1806).[30] These works were all publicized in Rome's small coterie of fine arts journals.[31]

Pius VII's aim was to draw a distinction between two visions of antiquity: that of the Republic and that of the Church. After seeing apostles of revolution on alarmingly familiar terms with ancient monuments, the restored pontiff seemed determined now to defamiliarize those monuments. Where revolutionary performers had acted scenes alongside the Capitoline wolf, walls were

8. Arch of Constantine, Rome, showing the enclosure erected by Pope Pius VII in 1805 (from Giovanni Battista Cipriani, *Vedute principali e piu interessanti di Roma* [Rome, 1799 {sic; 1806}]). *Source*: Getty Research Institute, Los Angeles (92-B28075).

now constructed to mark antiquities off from the quotidian life of the city, while later accretions and "undignified" contemporary users (like the fishmonger at the Pantheon) were scrubbed away[32] (**Figure 8**). These efforts to evoke the anodyne space of a museum in the midst of the city presented historic monuments not as flaming torches of liberty to be passed from one era to another, but as delicate architectural mummies that whispered reassuringly of timelessness and shelter from change.

The relinquishment of pagan antiquity as a vital emblem of divine providence opened up a gap in the Church's economy of representation, one soon filled by new perspectives on the city's patrimony of ecclesiastical architecture. Pius VII's 1802 Chirograph had also forbidden church repairs and reconstructions whose historical accuracy was not first approved by Canova and Fea, despite the backlog of urgent work required following the depredations of the Republic.[33] This marked a major change and indicates how deeply perspectives on history were shifting. Repairs and restorations of old churches had traditionally been a matter for the clergy to decide, on the argument that churches were living religious spaces whose historical value inhered in their site, history, and name and therefore were not diminished by repairs that substituted new elements for old.[34] The 1802 Chirograph instead implied a materialist vision of the church building as decomposed into a hierarchy of emblematic historic components, the loss or deterioration of any one of which would diminish the historical value of the whole. The life of the past in the present, in other words, was no longer to be taken for granted; ever withdrawing on time's inexorable tide, only laborious, erudite protection could maintain the past's availability for the present and future.[35] The overall budget devoted to work on damaged churches remained less than that allocated to antique pagan sites, but Pius's Chirograph nonetheless marked an unprecedented redirection of intellectual resources toward Rome's ecclesiastical patrimony.[36]

It can hardly surprise that the shock of seeing so many churches damaged or destroyed by anti-Catholic occupiers had awakened a sharper awareness of these structures as part of a suddenly threatened Roman Catholic identity; this was simply the Roman version of that great experience of loss and rupture that across revolutionary Europe nurtured a growing sense of historic artifacts as irreplaceable witnesses to a vanishing past.[37] The idea that the buildings of a nation or city formed a collective patrimony that might inspire an identitarian sense of pride within the wider population had developed during the eighteenth century in France, amid anxieties about national decline and the emergence of nationalist patriotism.[38] Roman clerical leaders confronting not dissimilar anxieties began gravitating after 1800 to related ideas, and would seek increasingly to use the restoration of ecclesiastical edifices as means of fortifying the loyalty and resolve of the Roman faithful. During the nine years of Pius VII's first restoration, official periodicals carried no less than sixty-five articles celebrating the repairs being done at some forty-eight different churches.[39] If the challenges of revolutionary ideology had unlocked a war for the hearts and minds of the faithful, most Roman Catholics in the Eternal City preferred the sight of a damaged house of God made good again to the unearthed ruins of yet another pagan temple. This seems to have been especially true in the popular classes, who, according to the contemporary poet Giuseppe Giacchino Belli, regarded the excavation of pagan antiquities as a foreign foible tantamount to grave robbing.[40]

Pius VII's efforts to restore Rome's luster succeeded, and Napoleon – Emperor of the French since 1804 and King of Italy since 1805 – was soon tempted to help himself. But the French army that reentered Rome on 2 February 1808 was very different from that of a decade earlier: it was a disciplined imperial force tasked with transforming Rome into a modern regional capital within an expanding French Empire. The newly appointed Prefect of Rome, Count Camille de Tournon, began at once reeling the Eternal City back into secular, bureaucratic time.[41] Sweeping juridical and legislative reform brought the law into line with the rest of the Empire, Rome's Jews were reemancipated, and the creation of the vast Campo Verano cemetery halted the tradition of burial of the dead within the city walls.[42] The city was also aggressively declericalized, with cardinals expelled, clerics dispersed, the papal court abolished, the Vatican archives removed to Paris, and the religious congregations disbanded. Priests who resisted were disappeared into exile.

At the level of architecture and planning, a decree of July 1811 created a powerful and well-funded organism called the Commission des Embellissements, which launched a major campaign of renovation on the monuments and infrastructure of what was now called the Département de Rome.[43] The most important involved demolitions below the Pincian Hill in preparation for a magnificent new Piazza del Popolo with adjacent public park.[44] And of course the French again took steps to appropriate Rome's classical heritage. The ecclesiastical apparati installed in a number of ancient monuments were purged, and excavations in the urban center quickened, with the Roman Forum dug down to the antique ground level along with the area around Trajan's column. Among the many monuments exposed to clearer view (often through demolitions of churches and conventual buildings) were the Colosseum (**Figure 9**), the Temple of Fortuna Virilis, the Temple of Vesta, the Arch of Janus, the Temple of Peace [Basilica of Maxentius], and the Horti Caesaris in Trastevere. Like the papal work of the previous decade, these efforts tended to isolate monuments in highly formalized spaces separated from everyday life. But their significance was different now; they spoke instead of the French occupier's power to superintend a history with whose magnificence he hoped to associate himself. The parallel was more a question now of branding than of providence. And finally, as mature imperialists the French also did not neglect to assist Pius VII's program of repairing churches damaged under the Republic, often working alongside their Roman counterparts. At the end of 1811, the French created the Commissione delle Chiese to systematize the maintenance of churches and assigned a special budget to repair and restore the sprawling Vatican complex as well as the derelict roof at San Paolo fuori le mura. More than 1,000 men were employed on these tasks; Stendhal crowed that the French administration was accomplishing more in a few years than the popes had in ten pontificates.[45]

But the French were compelled to withdraw from Rome in February 1814, and by late May Pius VII had returned.[46] Reactionaries in the Curia initially pursued a "hard" restoration that would annul everything French and turn the

9. Excavations at the Colosseum (from Angelo Uggieri, *Journées pittoresques de Roma* [Rome, n.d. {c. 1808}]).
Source: gallica.bnf.fr / BnF.

clock back to the way things had been before; even the feudal system was reintroduced after a discreet interval. But soon enough it became apparent that clerical leaders could not simply refuse all engagement with the emerging new norms of European government, culture, and society. Within a year, a more accommodationist approach prevailed under the steady leadership of Pius's worldly secretary of state, Cardinal Ercole Consalvi.[47] With respect to architecture and antiquities, recent legislation was consolidated in the famous Pacca Edict of 1820, while a few of the classical monuments that the French had emptied of religious trappings were reconverted to religious use, most famously the Colosseum.[48] But if Pius's administration more generally returned to the pre-1809 policy of museumizing the city's antique architecture while repairing churches damaged during the Republic (of which very many still remained), the relationship between the city's antique and ecclesiastical patrimonies nonetheless continued to evolve. Excavations of antique monuments were increasingly farmed out via Consalvi's shrewd practice of inviting foreign archaeologists to come do the work at their own expense.[49] Historic ecclesiastical architecture, on the other hand, continued to be a focus of attention, with the official press carrying sixty-six celebratory notices between 1814 and 1823 relating to repairs and restorations at forty-four different churches.[50] In reading these notices, it is apparent that the government had come to regard this body of monuments as a repository of Christian identity and thus as one of the city's most important possessions. The world of architectural history scholarship, to which we turn next, further bears this out. For although the momentum of centuries dictated that scholarship on antique monuments still dominated in the academies and learned journals, the most original developments in Roman scholarship after 1814 were to come in scholarship on Early Christian architecture.

To manage the countless Roman churches still in need of repair in 1814, Pius's government developed an official system of prioritization.[51] This turned on historical criteria and only secondarily on aesthetic criteria, with the result that architects were soon being set to work on buildings that, for all their historical importance, they regarded as artistically decadent – Early Christian churches, for example. But the emerging historicism that had shaped recent monuments legislation dictated that these repairs be done with a degree of archaeological precision rather than by simply updating them to the contemporary taste. Indeed, after the violence these buildings had endured at foreign and "modernizing" hands, the idea of substituting forms in the modern taste for the wounded originals had come to seem like an attack on the monument's integrity, one that would obliterate its precious testimony of a departed era with the hostile mark of the present. But there was a problem: functional knowledge of how to work accurately and correctly in the less esteemed historic styles was often lacking. Roman architects had for centuries been educated in the canons of classical correctitude, and the notion of working in a proverbially decadent style like the Early Christian was not dreamed of. One consequence was a burst of new scholarship in Rome on buildings in these unesteemed styles.[52]

The forerunner here was the exiled French aristocrat Jean-Baptiste-Louis-Georges Seroux d'Agincourt, resident in Rome from 1779 until his death in 1814. During those years, Seroux worked out of his house in via Gregoriana with a cadre of assistants to produce the *Histoire de l'Art par les Monumens, depuis sa décadence au IVe siècle jusqu'a son renouvellement au XVe*.[53] This groundbreaking multivolume work was only published between 1810 and 1823, though it was well known to the scholarly community in Rome during the long decades of its gestation. Its achievement was to provide the first systematic history of art and architecture during the long in-between that separated the decline of Rome and the Renaissance: an important age for the history of Christianity, but one whose art and architecture had always been considered unworthy of serious attention. Seroux insisted that his aim was not to redeem this art, but to provide a better understanding of its decadence. Yet his assessments of certain "decadent" monuments were so extremely positive that, later in life, he was to worry, with good reason, that they had encouraged a taste for these works in younger readers.

Consider Seroux's discussion of San Paolo fuori le mura (**Plate 4**). In his introduction to the architecture of the fourth century, Seroux had proclaimed that Greco-Roman classicism was defined by its perfection of the Orders, and that the downfall of classicism lay in subsequent departures from those canons, such as when columns were used to support arches rather than a flat entablature.[54] He indicated San Paolo a page later as an example of this, also criticizing its reuse of elements from antique buildings and the bad taste of its many innovations. But the tone changed dramatically when he then described the interior's overall effect:

> Four rows of columns arranged along the length of the edifice form simple and grand divisions, which produce on the interior effects as admirable as those of the peristyles placed by the ancients on the exteriors of their temples. This beautiful ordonnance possesses a grandeur and magnificence truly worthy of its object. The eye delights in this multitude, in these long lines of columns forming the five naves, and in the most varied and picturesque effects of light and perspective.[55]

His concluding lines made clear that he found the basilica an aesthetic success:

> If today one wishes to enjoy the beautiful effect that this church can still offer the eye, one must halt at the entrance door: there, far from the city, amid the solitude in which this building stands, facing a forest of columns, beneath that rude timberwork that supports the roof, and facing three great arches, the spectator feels himself penetrated with admiration and respect for this venerable basilica, which, while it sins against the rules of antique architecture in many respects, presents an august and sublime image of it nonetheless.[56]

For earlier writers, violations of classical correctitude had translated seamlessly into aesthetic displeasure, but Seroux announces a new generation for whom this was not a reliable equation – a generation that was increasingly to find itself tangled up in denunciations of decadence followed by incongruous admissions of pleasure. It is difficult to exaggerate what a big shift this represented in the Roman context, where scholarship on the early churches of Rome had almost always been interested only in their documentary value.[57] Coming in the wake of the Revolutionary and Napoleonic appropriations of classicism, Seroux's sympathetic response to Early Christian works injected a new sense of aesthetic possibility into the historical research unfolding concurrently in response to the government's efforts to classify and repair damaged churches.

In March 1809, not long after the French occupiers arrived in Rome, an illustrated study of Early Christian churches was published there in French and Italian as part of a sprawling series that was to endure for the next two decades under the title *Journées pittoresques des édifices de Rome ancienne*. The author was the architect and antiquarian Angelo Uggeri, who was later to play a central role in the early stages of the reconstruction of San Paolo. This particular volume was entitled *Edifices de la décadence*, and the influence of Seroux – who Uggeri knew well – was not limited to the title.[58] Uggeri wrote that he was passing "from the beautiful Greco-Roman works" covered in his previous volumes to "those of the period of Decadence," and specifically to "the Churches together with the majestic Constantinan basilicae"; that is, from the "infancy ... adolescence and ... virility" of the classical orders to the "sad old age" in which classicism expired.[59] His goal, he claimed, was not merely to satisfy "a simple historical curiosity" but to discover which of the "ancient maxims" had been the last to disappear, why "foreign and barbarous" practices had been introduced, and how what we now call Romanesque and Gothic architecture eventually arose.[60]

After an unsparing account of architecture's initial descent into decadence, the book presented twenty-six buildings. The first was the Arch of Constantine: "It is the best preserved and the richest of all the triumphal arches, one that presents Architects with a model of the genre, Painters with an agreeable and imposing mass, and Antiquaries with a humiliating proof of the corruption and decadence of art."[61] Not exactly a ringing endorsement, but neither was it confirmation of the gloomy claims of the introduction. Uggeri condemned its builders for scavenging reliefs from earlier monuments, then condemned the elements they actually did execute. But he also thanked Pius VII for clearing the area around it, adding that the arch "is one of the ancient profane monuments that in our own times has been considered the most important to preserve, since it belonged to the great Constantine, that patron of the Christian Religion he solemnly embraced, and which, from that time and under the protection of the Emperor, spread out miraculously across the entire world."[62] Uggeri stops well short here of praising the aesthetic qualities of the arch, but the passage does help us to grasp how his proud identity as a Catholic in Rome, at a time when that identity was under siege from the outside world, had opened him up to feeling stirred by a monument that in a more complacent past had been regarded as simply decadent.

Of the twenty-five other buildings Uggeri discusses, San Paolo fuori le mura receives the longest discussion. The commentary again seems at odds with the book's stated premise:

> ... there is nothing more seductive in architecture (because they are easier to grasp) than peristyles arranged with order and regularity. In addition to announcing a natural and solid architectural construction,

they permit us to enjoy the full extent and capacity of the building, such that the eye, as it penetrates amid the column shafts, is able to take in the furthest extremities of the temple. As a result of that extensive forest of columns, one is marvelously transported and full of admiration wherever one turns, because at each step the perspective of the scene changes and renews itself in a series of grand tableaux that are most agreeable and most interesting. The enjoyment of this view increases still more when the mind considers that these numerous and diverse columns, large and small, and of various materials, are extremely precious on account of the rarity of their marble, the finesse of the work, their massiveness and richness, and their ancient origin.[63]

Uggeri regretted that flat entablatures had not been employed in the nave, as had Seroux and others before him, but then, in an important sign of things to come, he also attempted to exonerate the Early Christians builders from aesthetic responsibility for this error: they had simply lacked access to the large stones necessary to form an entablature and had used arches only as an expedient, most likely with great reluctance. Much later the placement of arches atop columns became a common usage, but this would not have been the intent of the Early Christians.[64]

Uggeri's book reveals a new protectiveness toward the Early Christians and hints at the coming collapse of the traditionally sharp distinction between aesthetic and intrinsic value – of beauty and historical significance – which for centuries had authorized the judgment of Early Christian architecture as decadent and that of the pagan Roman Empire as a timeless ideal. The proverbial aesthetic decadence of Early Christian architecture was now becoming a problem, one that would-be apologists like Uggeri were increasingly to solve in historicist fashion, declaring it a contingent consequence of the social, economic, and political breakdown of the late Roman Empire.

As far back as 1787, the Mantua-based Spanish Jesuit Giovanni (Juan) Andrés had asked why it was that "while we run after not only Greek and Roman antiquities, but even Egyptian and Arab ones, and others even more remote, only Christian ones remain abandoned?" In response, he had sounded a precocious call for a specifically Early Christian archaeology that promised to fortify the faith by confirming sacred history.[65] Andrés's book was subsequently republished in an enlarged edition in Rome in 1808–1817, where a race was under way to produce the first monograph on Rome's greatest Early Christian monument, San Paolo fuori le mura. The race was won in 1815 by Nicola Maria Nicolai, a scholarly monsignor, architect, archaeologist, civil engineer, clerical reformer, and historian who during the Napoleonic occupation had taken on the lonely responsibility of looking after and celebrating the

Divine Office in the deserted basilica.[66] It was during this intimate daily encounter that Nicolai conceived the project of writing a monograph, and the result, *Della Basilica di S. Paolo*, was to vault him to the presidency of the Pontifical Roman Academy of Archaeology.[67]

With Nicolai's book, we no longer have to hunt for the author's guilty pleasure in an Early Christian work, for Nicolai is unabashed. He even expresses astonishment that there had not yet been a full study of the architecture of the basilica – which gives a sense of just how fast attitudes were changing. His book provides an unprecedentedly complete history of the basilica's foundation and early history, followed by a detailed catalog of the many subsequent waves of modification to which it had been subject. It also includes detailed sections and elevations of the old basilica, which following the fire were to stand as its most accurate surviving record (**Figure 10**). After fifteen weighty chapters, Nicolai concluded on a thoroughly historicist note, proclaiming that the great value of San Paolo lay in its status as a palimpsest, as a place where one may study the best and the worst of "the arts in all five of their principal epochs" with one sweeping glance.[68] Nicolai was not prepared to surrender the old historiographical schema of great epochs and decadent ones, but neither did he think it odd to conclude with a plaintive appeal to Pius VII that "this building is deteriorating every day from the injuries of time, to the point that if it is not repaired soon, ruin is inevitable."[69]

Nicolai's book received an important and very positive review from Giovanni Battista Vermiglioli, the conservator of the Antiquities Museum and professor of archaeology and mythology at the University of Perugia.[70] In the opening pages, Vermiglioli tried to set Nicolai's book in a larger historiographical context. He began with a statement that echoed Andrés in

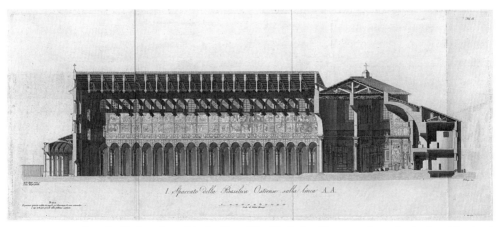

10. Longitudinal section of the basilica of San Paolo fuori le mura, drawn by Andrea Alippi and engraved by Pietro Ruga (from Nicolai [1815]).
Source: Bibliotheca Hertziana – Max Planck Institute for Art History.

asking why there was so much scholarship on pagan antiquity yet so few works like Nicolai's on Christian monuments:

> While such an abundance of study goes into understanding pagan Rome, literary men who profess the Catholic religion ought to devote their efforts equally, with full maturity of thought, and with maximum effort, to understanding Christian Rome, and to investigating it in depth through its numerous celebrated surviving monuments. What enormous fields these would offer for exploration, in which we should find scattered everywhere, no less than in profane antiquities, objects presenting great knowledge and profound doctrine![71]

Such studies would inform us "about the piety of our fathers, about the history of the ancient Christian sites, and about the fine arts, which, from their ruin until their renaissance, over the space of nearly ten centuries, were encountered uniquely in Christian monuments."[72] Vermiglioli evoked the historiography of Early Christian art, from Bosio's *Roma Sottoterranea* of 1630 up through Seroux d'Agincourt, and cited San Paolo as "the most remarkable Christian edifice that remains among the ancient ones surviving in Rome." Without even a hint that he was saying anything controversial, Vermiglioli described San Paolo as remarkable "for its vastness and beauty."[73]

The runner-up to Nicolai in the race to produce a monograph on San Paolo was Giuseppe Giustino di Costanzo, the abbot of the monastery there. Costanzo wrote but never published a now-lost manuscript on San Paolo back in the 1780s, when Seroux's work was still being assembled and circulated in manuscript. This "Memoria della Basilica di San Paolo" was known to scholarly contemporaries, and in 1816, after Costanzo's death, the scholar Francesco Cancellieri began circulating a prospectus for a publication based on it.[74] Cancellieri's 1,353-page manuscript survives and seems to have been mostly completed by 1819, although in the end it too was never published.[75]

Enthusiasm for the architecture of the Early Christian era was, in short, quickening in the opening years of the century.[76] This burgeoning Paleochristianism made its way also to Roman guidebooks and the official press. In 1816, Mariano Vasi devoted several richly complimentary pages of his popular guidebook to the "magnificent and majestic" basilica of San Paolo, and even mentioned the "beautiful cloister" of the thirteenth century, which earlier connoisseurs had regarded as a chaotic embarrassment.[77] In 1820, Carlo Fea's *Nuova descrizione di Roma* noted that the interior of San Paolo "breathes an air of majesty and solid nobility, though the vault be but naked timberwork," adding that the twelfth-century mosaic adorning the Arch of Galla Placidia was "highly esteemed."[78] Repair work that Pius VII ordered at some point after the publication of Nicolai's monograph also received attention in the *Diario di Roma* starting in fall 1818, with at least four accounts of repairs to the roof and doors, as well as of a papal inspection visit in 1821.[79] The new attitudes were discernible in the Roman academies too. On 20 June 1822, Commissioner of Antiquities Carlo Fea read a paper before the Pontifical Academy of Archaeology about the Constantinian basilicae of old St. Peter's, San Paolo fuori le mura, San Lorenzo fuori le mura, and Sant'Agnese fuori le mura.[80] It began with another declaration in favor of Christian archaeology, and noted that Cardinal Pacca, protector of the Academy and Camerlengo of the Holy Roman Church, had on many occasions stated his wish to see more archaeological work on Christian antiquities in Rome. Fea challenged his Roman listeners by noting that foreigners were beating them to it, as evinced by the book of engravings of Paleochristian churches recently published by the German team of Johann Gutensohn and Johann Knapp, *Monumenti della religione cristiana*[81] (**Figure 11**). Gutensohn and Knapp's book was praised in that same year in the Roman *Giornale arcadico* for perpetuating "the historical memory of that era, when architecture maintained itself as best it could amidst the barbarism of the time and the deplorable deeds inflicted by invasions and foreign armies" – an *apologia* for the faults of Early Christian architecture that

11. Interior of the basilica of San Paolo (from Gutensohn and Knapp [1822–1826]).
Source: University Library, University of California, Berkeley.

echoes what Uggeri had said in 1809.[82] The *Giornale arcadico* reviewer described San Paolo in particular as "one of largest and most majestic edifices, and extremely rich on account of the forest of columns in antique marble that support it." He acknowledged the "irregularity of the bases and capitals" and spoke that obligatory word, "decadence," but concluded that "the roof construction with its extremely long trusses is nevertheless a masterpiece on account of its daring and intelligent design" (a verdict that echoed the one reached by the French engineer Jean-Baptiste Rondelet a decade earlier in his *Traité de l'art de bâtir*).[83] Also in 1822, the same Vermiglioli who had reviewed Nicolai's book in 1816 again weighed in on the importance of Christian antiquities, this time in the published version of the influential archaeology course he taught at the University of Perugia.[84] This devoted six chapters to ancient Christian monuments, painting, sculpture, numismatics, and inscriptions, and offered an even more strident argument than six years earlier:

> We who have been born and raised in the sweetness of such an august Religion, must absolutely not leave ourselves open to the reproach that we have destroyed ourselves, rather strangely, with our love of the remains of pagan antiquity, while disparaging the remains of a law and of a religion that, while it blesses us on earth, also assures us of eternal happiness . . .[85]

He added that "if the monuments of Greece and Rome illustrate Homer, Euripides, Virgil, and Ovid, Christian monuments serve no less to illustrate the great book of the old and the new Covenant, as well as the oldest Church Fathers," of whom he reels off a list.[86]

One could furnish plenty of other examples, but the trend is clear enough.[87] Educated Catholics in Rome, in permitting themselves to fall in love with the long-scorned artistic heritage of the Early Christians, gained more intimate access to their own local history, which was of course also the history of Catholic Christendom. At the same time, they were able to escape the shadow of the now painfully outdated rhetoric of Roman classical universality and, armed with a defiant new aesthetic code, assert distinctions between themselves and their enemies. These new ways of thinking about and mobilizing sacred antiquity focused instead on history's objective assurance of the Church's capacity to endure time's depredations: not a providential endurance within a divinely malleable time in which the past is never really past, but a heroic one that perseveres over an immense and inexorably expanding chronological distance. Taken as a whole, the evolution of attitudes and policies in Rome toward historic architectural remains announced a profound shift in understanding the relationship of past and present. Just as the significance of pagan antiquities had been changing, the enthusiasm for Christian archaeology likewise suggests that a disenchanted sense of history was becoming normative even in Rome, despite the claims of both friend and enemy that

Rome stood apart from the advances of modern secularity. Göran Blix has argued that early nineteenth-century archaeology elsewhere offered a kind of secular immortality and a "weak form of compensation" for the lost public certainties of the Christian afterlife, following the liberal reassignment of religion to the private sphere.[88] This is perhaps not quite what was happening in Rome, but something related was occurring: the center of the Catholic world was beginning implicitly to acknowledge a kind of time that no longer accommodated divine mediation but rather was empty, linear, and homogeneous. Contrary to the received historiography, Rome too was participating in the emerging historicist consciousness of nineteenth-century Europe.[89]

The papal territories were already on an eccentric course with respect to the normative European encounter with postrevolutionary modernity. Clerical Rome had been the unwilling subject of a self-proclaimed modernity thrust upon it by foreign military, economic, political, and cultural domination. History, in this context, offered both a familiar reassurance and a comprehensible language of contestation. Catholic intellectuals in this context began losing their old confidence in past–present continuity; they instead increasingly internalized a temporalized view of history that hinged on historical difference, and specifically on a meaningful contrast between a religious, organic, authentic past and a mechanistic, scientistic, impious present. No longer was the past "not really past"; now, its whole virtue lay in its past-ness, in its profound difference to the modern age. This unresolved Catholic historicism lacked the philosophical immanence of some contemporary historicisms, but it was soon to lead conservative Catholic intellectuals into the same kind of historicist redactions more commonly associated with their secular counterparts.

However momentous these new trends were, Roman architects at the start of the century continued to adhere more or less unflinchingly to the canons of contemporary classicism. Yet the slowly mutating historical consciousness we have just surveyed, which formed the cultural context in which new architectural works were publicly interpreted, ensured that formal continuities did not always equate to continuities of meaning and message.

No project demonstrates this more clearly than the reconstruction of the Milvian Bridge in 1805–1806, during Pius VII's first restoration. A milestone along the principal northern approach to Rome on the via Flaminia, about a mile and three quarters north of the Porta del Popolo, the original bridge was already a semi-ruin patched with wooden planks when in 1799 it was damaged in fighting between French and Austrian troops[90] (**Figure 12**). Subsequently repatched with more wooden planks, large portions of the bridge were then swept away by the historic floods of 2 February 1805, leaving it completely

12. Milvian Bridge, Rome, before its reconstruction by Giuseppe Valadier (from Angelo Uggieri, *Journées pittoresques de Roma*. Rome, n.d. [c. 1800–1802]).
Source: gallica.bnf.fr / BnF.

unusable.[91] The timing of this flood was ominous in the true sense of the word, for Pius VII was at the time away on a very unhappy forced visit to Paris for Napoleon's autocoronation as Emperor, and many had already feared this humiliating voyage would end with the pontiff, like his predecessor, in a French jail. Given that Pius's return to Rome required him to traverse the Milvian Bridge, its destruction by natural forces seemed to augur exactly such an outcome.[92] Keen to tamp down anxieties, Secretary of State Consalvi ordered a breakneck reconstruction from his trusted Cameral architect Giuseppe Valadier (about whom we shall have much more to say in the pages ahead). Rather than undertake yet another makeshift repair, Valadier was to rebuild the bridge entirely, transforming the north tower into a monumental triumphal arch and guardhouse and creating an elliptical plaza opposite with double rows of elm trees and a triumphal column (**Figure 13**). Conceived in consultation with Secretary of State Consalvi, this ambitious effort was intended to fix the bridge "once and for all."[93] Work was pursued with all possible dispatch as an entreaty to God that Pius might again be vouchsafed back across the bridge to his Eternal City. In the event, Napoleon did not

13. Giuseppe Valadier, project for the Milvian Bridge and environs, 1805.
Source: © Accademia Nazionale di San Luca, Roma.

kidnap the pope, and when Pius returned to Rome on 26 May 1805, he was met by jubilant crowds at the newly rebuilt bridge, which he officially inaugurated by his passage across it.

These events were fundamentally inflected by the significance of the site itself. In Church tradition, the Milvian Bridge was where God had first announced his divine will that the Roman pontiff, head of the Catholic Church, should also be the temporal ruler over Rome. This had come to pass 1,500 years previously, when the emperor Constantine, marching down the Italian peninsula in the year 313, in the midst of a civil war and in hopes of gaining control of the Western Roman Empire, had had a dramatic vision of the Christian God as he approached the city. The apparition promised Constantine victory if he would inscribe a cross and Christ's monogram on the shields of his soldiers. Constantine did as instructed and was rewarded the next day with victory, in what came to be known as the Battle of the Milvian Bridge. Constantine subsequently adopted Christianity himself and issued the Edict of Milan, decriminalizing the faith across the Empire and paving the way to it eventually becoming the official state religion. In Catholic tradition, these events were offered as irrefutable proof that the pope's temporal power in Rome was a matter of divine will. The Milvian Bridge's reliquary significance, in other words, had never been more topical than in 1805, when the beleaguered Holy See was still recovering from one occupation and feared that another was in the offing. The decision to rebuild it in such monumental fashion was thus not without political significance. The reconstructed bridge was to confront future invaders from the north with a reminder that challenges to the pope's temporal authority violated the manifest will of God.

But while the cosmopolitan Consalvi clearly felt that Valadier's design articulated this defiant message well, more conservative clerical observers did not agree – especially in retrospect, ten or twenty years later. The problem lay in the stylistic idiom that Valadier had employed (**Plate 5**). His reconstructed guardhouse-cum-triumphal arch presents a compound of simple interpenetrating geometrical volumes wrapped in an exaggerated rustication. Stout battered masonry covers its sides and outer face, while a swollen frame of dilating rustication surrounds its north-facing archway, complete with a menacing extralarge dropped keystone. In other words, the design reflects the squat, muscular idiom of international neoclassicism between 1780 and 1810 – an idiom identified most closely with Ledoux's *barrieres* in Paris (more than one modern scholar has termed Valadier's structure Ledolian) but that also characterized many French revolutionary competition projects and festival decors, as well as many secular public monuments and projects elsewhere, such as Friedrich Gilly's Friedrichsdenkmal project for Berlin.[94] It was not very edifying for conservatives in Rome to think that Consalvi hoped to protect the Eternal City with what looked to them like a secondhand French Revolutionary pavilion. Such misgivings were then confirmed when, after the French occupiers returned in 1806, they began eagerly planning embellishments around the bridge, including a public promenade, additional treelined avenues, and a triumphal column – all in celebration of the point at which the "route de la France" arrived at the Eternal City.[95] It certainly did not help that the more conservative Roman clerics already regarded Consalvi and Valadier as compromised by their cooperation with the French.[96]

Extreme discretion remained the watchword in Rome for those who harbored reservations, especially political ones, about the products of official culture. After 1823, however, the situation was to change, and the situation at San Paolo was to be a major catalyst for that change. A sharp and surprisingly public debate was to unfold, shaped more and more by conservative clerics whose views had been formed amid the distress of French domination, who had come to associate all things modern with ideals antithetical to the Church. And among those things, for a time at least, was modern classical architecture. As a result, and for the first time since the Renaissance, clerical intellectuals and Church leaders began to envision building a major new Roman church in a style other than the one providentially bequeathed to them by the Caesars.

NOTES

1   I use the term *anachronic* in the sense defined in Nagel and Wood (2010), pp. 13–14.

2   The figures most commonly associated with that essentialism were the French art theorist Antoine Chrysostome Quatremère de Quincy and the Rome-based German art historian Johann Joachim Winckelmann, although countless others contributed. The classic statement of the changing sense of history around this time occurs in Koselleck (2004), p. 11 ff.

3   On the "memory crisis," see Terdiman (1993). On its cultural and historiographical consequences, see Blix (2009).

4   Zuccari (1981); Vessey (2009); Van Liere et al. (2012). As Cecalupo (2021) points out, the demolition of St. Peter's actually helped kick-start the development of Christian archaeology.

5   Herz (1988), p. 593; Richardson and Story (2013). On other seventeenth-century restorations of Early Christian works, see Mariani (1989); Barry (1999).

6   Herz (1988), quote from p. 612. See also Barry (1999).

7   Johns (1986).

8   Cochrane (1965a) and (1965b); Momigliano (2012). Minor (2010) offers a synthetic overview of this reform movement in relation to architectural thought (p. 25 ff.).

9   Ditchfield (2005), pp. 6–7. The essential product of the new historiography was Orsi (1747–1762). See Minor (2010), pp. 44–58.

10   Minor (2010), pp. 59–90. See also Bellini (1995).

11   Docci (2006), pp. 138–140; Minor (2010), p. 19; Caperna (2014); Camerlenghi (2018), pp. 223–243.

12   Minor (2010), p. 6.

13   Springer (1987), p. 45.

14   Di Nola (1988), (1989), and (1990).

15   Collins (2004), pp. 56–57.

16   Colapietra (2014), pp. 15–16.

17   Collins (2004), pp. 36–37.

18   Pietrangeli (1958); Springer (1987), pp. 43, 54; Collins (2004).

19   Springer (1987), p. 46.

20   Springer (1987), p. 69; Boutry (1997), p. 324.

21   Martone (2007), p. 88.

22   Springer (1987), pp. 65–68; Donato (1994).

23   Sala (1882), v. 1, p. 137; Springer (1987), pp. 66–68.

24   Springer (1987), pp. 65–66.

25   Pommier (1989), pp. 7–67.

26   Eustace (1815), v. 2, p. 2.

27   Springer (1987), p. 75.

28   Springer (1987), p. 75–76; Ridley (1992a), (1996), (2000); Martone (2007), p. 90.

29   Springer (1987), pp. 77–78.

30   Jonsson (1986), pp. 18–38; Ridley (1992a), p. 35ff.

31   Rolfi Ožvald (2012); Wittman (2020b).

32   Uggeri (1817); Ridley (1992a), pp. 35–44.

33   Martone (2007), p. 91.

34   Nagel and Wood (2010) categorize such practices as "substitution" (pp. 29–34).

35   Blix (2009), pp. 1–8.

36   Martone (2007), p. 89; Sette (2007), pp. 190–204.

37   Blix (2009).

38   Wittman (2007), pp. 19–94.

39   Martone (2007), p. 88.

40   Springer (1987), ch. 4.

41   Nardi (1989) and (2005); Boutry (1997), pp. 326–329; Bercé (2001).

42   Boutry (1997), pp. 326–329.

43   Boutry (1997), pp. 328–330; Ridley (2000), pp. 149–150; Nardi (2005), ch. 11.

44   Matthiae (1946); Debenedetti (1987), pp. 540–551.

45   Nardi (2005), ch. 11.

46   For a vivid account, see Andrews (1814).

47   Robinson (1987); Boutry (2002a), pp. 371–377.

48   Curzi (2000); Ridley (2000), pp. 221–240.

49   Robinson (1987), p. 153; Ridley (2000), p. 181.

50   Sette (2007), pp. 190–204, table.

51   Martone (2007), pp. 91–93.

52   Much the same happened a few decades later in France, when following the foundation of the Commission des Monuments Historiques classically trained architects were set to restoring Gothic churches.

53   Seroux d'Agincourt (1823; Italian ed. 1826).

54 Seroux d'Agincourt (1823), v. 1, Architecture, pp. 9–10.

55 Seroux d'Agincourt (1823), v. 1, Architecture, pp. 11.

56 Seroux d'Agincourt (1823), v.1, Architecture, pp. 12. These lines echo Roman theorist Milizia, who in 1781 praised the spatial effects of the nave of San Paolo: "one sees the effects of the grandiose peristyles in S. Paolo fuori le mura, and wishes to have them immediately in the Vatican [i.e., in St. Peter's]" (Milizia [1781], v. 1, p. 347. See also v. 2, pp. 480–481). They also echo Julien-David Le Roy's account of a colonnade being like a forest (itself informed by the reflections of Marc-Antoine Laugier).

57 Cf. Severano (1630); Ciampini (1693); Boldetti (1720); Allegranza (1773).

58 De Boni (1840), p. 1033.

59 Uggeri (1809), dedication and p. 2.

60 Uggeri (1809), pp. 1–2.

61 Uggeri (1809), p. 7.

62 Uggeri (1809), p. 10.

63 Uggeri (1809), pp. 35–36.

64 Uggeri (1809), p. 38.

65 Andrés (1787), pp. 593–594.

66 Pouillard (1817), pp. 154–176, esp. 155; Odescalchi (1835). On Nicolai's collaborations with Consalvi and reputation as a reformer, see Boutry (2002a), pp. 374–379.

67 Nicolai (1815).

68 Nicolai (1815), p. 311.

69 Nicolai (1815), p. 311.

70 Vermiglioli (1816a and 1816b). The only other major review of Nicolai's book appeared after the fire of 1823 (Napione [1824]).

71 Vermiglioli (1816a), p. 22.

72 Vermiglioli (1816a), p. 22.

73 Vermiglioli (1816a), p. 23.

74 Cancellieri (1816). On Cancellieri, see Trollope (1886).

75 Cancellieri, "Storia della Basilica di S. Paolo sulla via Ostiense," 1819 (BAV: Vat.Lat. 9672).

76 In 1823, just weeks after the fire at San Paolo, Cancellieri tried to capitalize by republishing his prospectus for a book based on Castanzo's notes, this time in the *Effemeridi Letterarie di Roma*, only now promising two new chapters, one on the fire and one on the state of the ruin. This was never published either (Cancellieri [1823]).

77 Vasi (1816), v. 2, p. 320.

78 Fea (1820), v. 3, p. 619.

79 *DdR*, 7 October 1818, p. 3; *DdR*, 17 November 1819, p. 1; *DdR*, 2 August 1820, p. 1; *DdR*, 16 October 1821, p. 1. Interest in the restoration spread beyond Rome as well: *L'ami de la Religion et du roi* (Paris), 18 November 1819, pp. 27–28; *Gazzetta di Milano*, 18 August 1820, p. 1185.

80 Fea (1829).

81 Gutensohn and Knapp (1822).

82 *GASLA* 16 (1822): 402–404. German reviewers went further, with one writing that the book simply proved "how much more magnificent the old artistic sensibility is than that of our own time" (*Morgenblatt für gebildete Stände* [Stuttgart and Tübingen], 7 November 1822, pp. 354–355).

83 Rondelet (1812), v. 4, pp. 168–171.

84 Vermiglioli (1822).

85 Vermiglioli (1822), v. 2, p. 350.

86 Vermiglioli (1822), v. 2, pp. 350–351.

87 Cf. Settele (1825). Gutensohn and Knapp planned to enrich their work with a historical text by Professor Antonio Nibby of the University of Rome. Nibby did prepare such a text, and later published it, but it never appeared in any edition of Gutensohn and Knapp's book (Nibby [1825a] and [1825b]).

88 Blix (2009), esp. pp. 1–24.

89 Wittman (2021).

90 Becchetti (1989); Cremona (2008), p. 125 n. 4.

91 *Diario Ordinario*, 18 May 1805, pp. 10–13; Carcani (1858), p. 116; Lagunes (2004), pp. 216–217.

92 Trollope offers a vivid account of the voyage based on the notes of Cancellieri, who accompanied Pius to Paris (Trollope [1886], pp. 289–295).

93 Guattani (1806), p. 6.

94 Meeks, for instance, describes the bridge as Ledolian (Meeks [1966], p. 108).

95 Debenedetti (1987), p. 522.

96 See Chapter 3.

TWO

"A PORTENT, BEYOND STATUES SWEATING BLOOD IN THE FORUM . . ."

THE EARLY NINETEENTH-CENTURY TOURISTS WHO MADE THE mile-and-a-quarter journey from the Porta San Paolo down the deserted via Ostiense to the rustic site of the old basilica of San Paolo fuori le mura were invariably shocked by the church's appalling dilapidation. "Dismal and ruinous" were the words of John Chetwode Eustace, an Anglo-Irish priest who visited in 1802.[1] "Far from splendid" was the verdict of Jane Waldie, a Scotswoman visiting in 1816, who decried its state of "total neglect and abandonment."[2] The Frenchman Jean-Baptiste Reinolds observed simply that "it is falling into ruin."[3] When Napoleon's intrepid cultural attaché Vivant Denon inspected the building in late 1811, he reported that "the entire roof structure threatens to collapse, and if nothing is done, it is to be feared that very soon it *will* collapse."[4] The west façade facing the Tiber had fourteenth-century mosaics above and an exuberant eighteenth-century narthex at ground level; it also listed so far forward that it was slowly detaching itself from the nave.[5] Behind this on the left side rose an infirm eleventh-century campanile, one of the oldest in Rome (**Figure 14**). Three doorways under the narthex led into the nave and aisles, the central one of which held a spectacular pair of eleventh-century Byzantine doors from Constantinople; Louis Simond, a French visitor in 1817, observed that they had been frozen on their hinges for more than a century.[6]

This state of decrepitude was owed to the fact that the basilica and its monastery were deserted, or nearly so, for long stretches every year from May until as late as November, when the thirty-odd monks of the

14. Façade of San Paolo fuori le mura (from Giuseppe Agostino Pietro Vasi, *Raccolta delle più belle vedute antiche, e moderne di Roma*, v. 1, Rome, 1786).
Source: Heidelberg University Library.

Benedictine community relocated to their city house of San Callisto in the Trastevere district of Rome. They went because the basilica's swampy site along the Tiber was plagued by *malaria* – literally "bad air," still believed at that date to cause what is now known to be a mosquito-borne disease. During those months, the monks would trek from San Callisto down to the basilica and back every morning to recite the Holy Office and sing the Mass, but were excused from returning in the afternoon for vespers.[7] The German dramatist August von Kotzebue once witnessed such a celebration, and noted that with the ceremonies confined to one small corner, the rest of the basilica took on "exactly the appearance of a warehouse."[8] Just a few monks stayed behind with the monastery's domestic staff of six to keep watch over the basilica and monastery buildings. The Frenchman Simond was told that "during the bad-air season, only a single monk and his servant remain, *les enfants perdus du monastère*."[9]

Between 1810 and 1814 the abandonment of the site became year-round after the Napoleonic occupiers dissolved the Roman religious communities. Eustace noted during this phase that the church was "abandoned to its own solidity, and left to molder away in damp and neglect."[10] The French took some responsibility for the preservation of the old church, and Denon's report on the crumbling state of the basilica roof (which reflected lobbying by the abbot of the monastery) persuaded Napoleon to fund a season of repairs.[11] But for important stretches of those four years there was just one person who came to the basilica on a regular basis to celebrate the Divine Office and make sure the building had not collapsed in the night: Nicola Maria Nicolai, the scholarly monsignor whose estate neighbored the monastery and who, as we saw, conceived the idea for a monograph on San Paolo while engaged in his melancholy surveillance.[12]

All this neglect left San Paolo the least altered Early Christian church in Rome. The famous Cardinal Archbishop of Westminster Nicholas Wiseman, who arrived in Rome in 1818 as a young seminarian, later recalled that in those days

> little or nothing had been done to modernize [San Paolo] and alter its primitive form and ornaments, excepting the later addition of some modern chapels above the transept; it stood naked and almost rude, but unencumbered with the lumpish and tasteless plaster encasement . . . of a modern Berninesque church, [such as] had disfigured the Lateran cathedral under the pretense of supporting it. It remained genuine.[13]

Joseph Woods, a British architect who visited in 1817, lamented that most Early Christian basilicas had barely "sufficient remains of the old work to trace the plan and distribution of the parts," but that among the "one or two" in Rome where it was still possible to experience the original forms, the most important "in size and in reputation" was San Paolo, where "most of the original construction is not only preserved but still exposed."[14] The nave with its four flanking aisles was so immense – 90 meters in length by nearly 60 meters in width – that in the 1580s Giacomo della Porta and Domenico Fontana had measured out the curve for the cupola of St. Peter's on its pavement; nineteenth-century visitors could still find the grooves in the floor.[15] Thirty meters overhead loomed the great wooden roof trusses spoken of by Denon, famously unconcealed by any kind of vault or ceiling and directly supporting the tile roof. This was carried on very high walls pierced at their summit by round-headed windows (some by then haphazardly bricked up) and decorated with washed-out frescos, probably from the fifth century, depicting the life of Paul and scenes from the Old Testament.[16] Below these, starting in the nave and extending into the transept, was a famous series of frescoed medallions depicting every pope from Peter to the present. These faded portraits were one of the city's most important illustrations of the integrity of the apostolic succession and were regarded as a proof of the *primatus papae*. The nave walls were supported on an arcade of round-headed arches atop forty tall columns, twenty on each side. The twenty-four closest to the entrance – eleven on the left and thirteen on the right – formed a distinct set and were among the church's most famous ornaments: spolia thought to have come from either the Basilica Aemilia or the Mausoleum of Hadrian, they were as prized for their rare *pavonazzetto* marble as for their exquisite workmanship.[17] Northern visitors disappointed in the threadbare basilica always raved at least about these columns. Charlotte Eaton, sister of Jane Waldie and similarly indifferent to the charms of postclassical Rome, recorded her wish to "knock down the horrible old fabric in which they are shrouded, and restore them to light and beauty."[18] Woods described their marble as "white or with a slight tinge of red or buff, and marked with purple veins . . . finely proportioned and perfectly well wrought, with capitals and bases of white marble . . . there can be no doubt that they are the spoils of a building of the best ages of architecture."[19]

For Catholics, these precious columns also held ecclesiological significance. Part of the value of Paul's basilica lay in its connection to the heroic age of Constantine, the emperor whose conversion to Christianity marked the turning point in the providential history of the Roman Church. Roman scholars had reluctantly but correctly concluded after 1800 that San Paolo was not actually the original Constantinian building, as had long been believed, but rather a second and much larger building on the same site; namely, the basilica as enlarged by Theodosius and his successors.[20] As if in compensation for this deflating realization, they theorized that these *pavonazzetto* columns had been carried over from Constantine's first basilica: transferred initially from their pagan site by Constantine for use in basilica number one, and then lovingly extracted by Constantine's successors for reuse in the second, present basilica.[21] This theory had the great advantage of preserving a material link between the existing basilica and the first Christian emperor, and it gained credence from the fact that all the other columns in the nave and aisles were, to nineteenth-century eyes, of execrable quality: "devoid of grace . . . crude . . . the negation of good taste," in the words of Seroux d'Agincourt.[22] It was conjectured that these sorry objects had been manufactured in the time of Theodosius to fill out the vastly enlarged basilica by workmen who Woods observed "could neither make a straight flute, nor an evenly curved surface."[23]

The nave ended to the east in a giant triumphal arch supported on two colossal gray Hymmetic marble Ionic columns, the largest in the building – even, some said, in the whole city (**Figure 15**). This arch was covered with fifth-century mosaics whose inscription indicated the patronage of Galla Placidia, half sister of the Emperor Honorius, who was credited with completing this second basilica. This so-called Arch of Placidia towered over the confessio enclosure that contained Paul's tomb at the center of the basilica, which was marked by a thirteenth-century Gothic ciborium by Arnolfo di Cambio on red porphyry columns. The transept to the east was then raised up by several steps and divided lengthwise by the so-called Dividing Wall, a medieval addition that helped support the long roof trusses above and

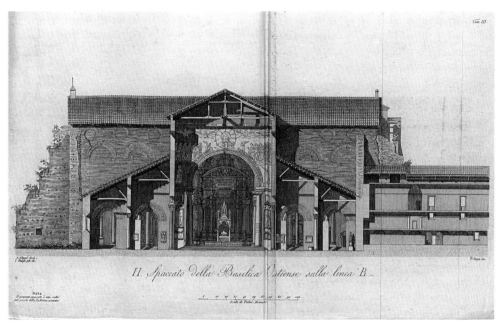

15. Andrea Alippi, section toward the east through the nave and aisles of the basilica of San Paolo; engraved by Pietro Ruga (from Nicolai [1815]).
Source: Bibliotheca Hertziana – Max Planck Institute for Art History.

effectively transformed the wide transept into two narrow transepts.[24] And finally at the center of the east wall opened the great semicircular apse, flanked by the two modern chapels mentioned by Wiseman, one seventeenth- and the other eighteenth-century. The calotte of the apse itself was decorated with a splendid but disintegrating thirteenth-century mosaic that depicted the enthroned Christ surrounded by apostles and evangelists. Beneath this was heaped a preening high altar of the late sixteenth century, whose upper segments rose up and blocked the mosaic's lower registers.

On the hot midsummer evening of 15 July 1823, the sacristan Isidoro Ferri was among the *enfants perdus du monastère* left behind to guard Paul's basilica. With the setting of the sun, Ferri rang out the Ave Maria on the campanile, made his rounds, and, encountering nothing unusual, retired for the night. The monastery's domestic staff likewise noticed nothing odd as they went about their last tasks before bed; nor did a local merchant who passed by the basilica; nor did two other monks who returned to the monastery later that night accompanied by friends.[25] Only around one o'clock in the morning did another local merchant's herdsman, watching over animals in an adjacent field, notice that the roof of the basilica was glowing (**Figure 16**). He ran to the monastery and pounded on the door and yelled up at the windows. The head groundskeeper, Pietro Battisti, awoke and immediately

16. Frontispiece illustration from Uggeri (1823), showing the moment on the night of 15 July 1823 when the fire at San Paolo was discovered.
Source: Collection of the author.

sent his foreman, Nicola Antoniacci, into the dark up the via Ostiense to Rome to raise the alarm and get help. Flames were soon flashing out from the roof. Battisti roused the two monks, and together they plunged into the church and began dragging out anything they could move. Eventually the flames forced them to withdraw, so they mounted the campanile and pounded the bell with a hammer. But there was no one to hear it, since the neighboring farmers also mostly avoided the unhealthy district in summer.

When Antoniacci reached the Porta San Paolo, he told the guards what was happening. They sent a man to fetch the fire brigade from the Sant'Ignazio quarter, another mile and a half away through the crooked city streets. Antoniacci then ran off to wake the building contractor Beretta, who was overseeing Pius VII's campaign of repairs to the basilica's roof. Beretta rounded up as many of his workers as he could find and rushed them down to the basilica.

Members of the Prussian scholarly and diplomatic community later cursed themselves that they were not that night taking the air up on the roof of their palazzo on the Capitoline Hill as they often did, for they would surely have seen the flames in the distance and raised the alarm. Particularly heartbreaking was the discovery the following morning that their housekeeper had actually seen the flames but thought nothing of them.[26]

Only after 3 A.M. did the first six firefighters finally arrive, having learned from the guard as they passed through the Porta San Paolo that the roof of the basilica had already collapsed[27] (**Figure 17**). Upon arriving they encountered a "terrifying Vesuvius."[28] A strong west–east wind had driven the flames through

17. Ascanio Savorgnan di Brazzà, *Fire at San Paolo*, 1824, depicting the arrival of the fire brigade.
Source: © Istituto Nazionale di Archeologia e Storia dell'Arte, Roma.

the roof, bay by bay, toward the apse. Other fire squads soon arrived, accompanied by the City Fire Commissioner, Marchese Origo, while detachments of Pontifical Dragoons along with squads of carabinieri and mounted police raced from the city toward the tragic radiance that now filled the southern sky. Word of the fire somehow only reached the monks at San Callisto around 4:45 A.M., but within an hour they too began arriving on the scene.[29] As sections of the nave roof plummeted to the floor and continued to burn, loud detonations began to ring out: the basilica's famous old columns were exploding from the heat. The only hope now was that at least the apse and the eastern chapels could be saved, along with the adjoining monastery buildings. In this, the firefighters achieved success, with some help from the wind, which calmed as morning dawned. The spread of the inferno was eventually halted though the fire continued to burn at ground level throughout the day, and only on 17 July was the shell-shocked monk who maintained the monastery chronicle able to write: "Finally today the fire is fully extinguished."[30]

18. Luigi Rossini, *View of the Ruin of the Basilica of San Paolo*, 1824.
Source: Architekturmuseum der TUM.

Once the smoke cleared, it was evident that the losses were catastrophic (**Figure 18**). The basilica's shattered ruin presented "a horrible picture, a vast piazza full of broken stones ... Here one saw Corinthian capitals, there attic bases, here giant beams transformed into charcoal, there column fragments and calcined marbles, there iron fittings in enormous confusion, the candelabra of the altars blackened and crushed, and finally pieces of sacred images whose subjects could no longer be discerned."[31] The roof was gone over the nave and fatally damaged over the transept and choir. The nave wall along the north side had collapsed. Sixteen of the forty columns lining the nave had fallen, including exactly half of the twenty-four precious *pavonazzetto* columns associated with the Constantinian basilica.[32] Many of the columns that still stood were calcined and cracked, while the perimeter walls of both nave and transept were unstable. Smoke and heat had devastated their venerable frescos and mosaics. The ground was "covered with large heaps of rubbish, out of which rose the crumbling ruins of the exterior walls, and several most magnificent Corinthian pillars; but these latter were all either broken off, at a greater or less height, or split perpendicularly, from base to capital, by the heat of the fire."[33] Everywhere one looked, one saw "a horrible spectacle. The celebrated and ancient marbles of the superb walls of this edifice were an enormous mass of fragments, and this awakened compassion, and moved one to tears."[34]

When Cardinal Wiseman rejoiced that old San Paolo had "remained genuine," he echoed a long tradition. For centuries, one of the most treasured aspects of old San Paolo had been its capacity to make the heroic Early Christian age seem intimately proximate.[35] Even an atheist like Stendhal sensed that it was "a long way" from the raw simplicity of San Paolo to "the gilded panels of Santa Maria Maggiore and Saint Peter's." For him, the key was the exposed timberwork high above the nave: unselfconscious and sublime, this was the element that "most of all recalled the earliest centuries of the Church and used to give San Paolo its eminently Christian (which is to say, severe and sorrowful) atmosphere." Looking up at those elderly trusses, "not hidden nor disguised by anything," he felt he discerned the past more clearly. "Why not just say it outright? At San Paolo we were truly Christians."[36]

Stendhal's Romantic nostalgia was shared in a very different key by many in clerical Rome. A rumor circulated that Pius VII had awakened repeatedly on the night of 15 July, dimly aware that, somewhere, a grave misfortune was being inflicted on the Roman Church.[37] Visiting not long after, British traveler Moyle Sherer observed that "your valet conducts you to [San Paolo] mourning."[38] For the fire had closed off a portal onto an emphatically vital Church history, one still capable of superseding the limits of earthly temporality and of acting in and on the present. Back in 1800, the scholar and cleric Francesco Cancellieri had described a vision in which he saw all the historic popes from the papal portrait medallions at San Paolo spring to life, descend from the basilica walls, and crowd into the city to be present at the coronation of Pius VII.[39] A fluid historical energy that still offered assurance amid the ruptures and discontinuities of current events seemed to inhere in the very stones of the place. The Romantic Catholic Chateaubriand said that it was while sitting amid the ruins that he realized "the whole history of Western Christianity begins at San Paolo fuori le mura."[40]

Mournful acknowledgments of loss were by then becoming common in Rome. Clerical leaders had spent most of the past twenty-five years unsuccessfully defending the Church against the assaults of *philosophie*, Revolution, and Napoleon; they had witnessed France, the "eldest daughter of the Church," turn savagely against them; seen Church traditions and authority systematically subverted; endured the capture and profanation of their holy city; and felt their habitual sense of continuity with the historical past violently ruptured. The fire that destroyed San Paolo seemed only the latest installment, and a symbolic one at that, emblematic of the Church's contemporary situation. These presentiments were to have a determining impact on the response to the fire.

> Flames were noted last night coming from the roof of the basilica of San Paolo fuori le mura, as a result, it appears, of a tragic accident caused by some tinsmiths who, while working yesterday on the roof of the Basilica, permitted lit coals to fall from a pan ... We will give more exact information on this horrible disaster in the coming days.[41]

The fire at San Paolo was actually not the lead story in the *Diario di Roma* that first baleful morning. What led was instead a report on how Pope Pius VII, approaching his eighty-first birthday, was coping with the broken femur he had suffered in a fall ten days earlier (**Figure 19**). Yet the two events had seemed connected. As recalled years later by Cardinal Wiseman, Pius in his sickbed was already "the object of affectionate solicitude to all Rome" when the city awoke that morning

> to news so melancholy, and so naturally connected with [the pope], that in ancient times it would have been considered a portent, beyond statues sweating blood in the Forum, or victims speaking in the temples. It was rumoured that the great basilica of St. Paul's beyond the walls was burned down, and was already only a heap of smoking ruins.[42]

The "natural" connection lay in the fact that Pius had spent time in his youth at the monastery of San Paolo and "loved the place with the force of an early attachment." (His old cell was a highlight of the tour monks gave to visitors).[43] The legend of this omen only grew with time. Thirteen years later, a respectable Roman journalist would write that the fire had occurred on the very night of Pius's death, just as the Temple of Ephesus had burned the night Alexander the Great had died, and just as when Ariosto died, the theater built for his plays had burned.[44] The dates did not really match quite so neatly, and Pius still had some life left in him that 16 July. But from concern for his fragile health, his attendants kept the tragic news from him.

The daily chronicle of the San Paolo monastery noted that morning that crowds had immediately begun gathering to gape at the smoldering ruin[45] (**Figure 20**). The young Wiseman again:

> [t]he sad news had penetrated into every nook of the city at sunrise. Melancholy indeed was the scene. The tottering external walls were all that was permitted to be seen, even from a respectful distance; for it was impossible to know how long they would stand. A clear space was therefore kept around, in which the skillful and intrepid fire-brigade – an

19. Thomas Lawrence, *Portrait of Pius VII*, 1819.
Source: Royal Collection Trust / © His Majesty King Charles III 2023.

20. Luigi Rossini, *View of the Ruin of the Basilica of San Paolo*, 1824.
Source: Architekturmuseum der TUM.

> admirably organized body – were using all their appliances to prevent the flames breaking out from the smoldering ruins.[46]

Wiseman also evokes the presence there of a man who was to play a leading role in the debates to come:

> There, among others, was the enthusiastic Avvocato Fea [Carlo Fea, Pius VII's Commissioner of Antiquities], almost frantic with grief. He was not merely an antiquarian in sculptures and inscriptions, he was deeply versed in ecclesiastical history, and loved most dearly its monuments. St. Paul's was one of the most venerable, and most precious of these. ... Among the constant and bewildered cries of Fea was: "Save the triumphal arch!"[47]

Over the following days, a series of meetings were held between Cardinal Secretary of State Ercole Consalvi and monastery officials, while the titular architects of the monastery, Pasquale Belli and Andrea Alippi, built wooden supports to shore up the ruin.[48] Despite the guards sent by Consalvi to keep the site closed, thefts were soon detected; the monastery chronicler suspected the workers.[49] On 28 July, an arch on the south side of the nave collapsed, killing two workers and leading to the fall of another *pavonazzetto* column, which brought the total to thirteen.[50]

A French visitor who rode out to the basilica on the morning after the fire was told the same story as appeared in the *Diario di Roma*: the fire had occurred when tinsmiths working on the roof permitted lit coals to fall from a pan.[51] The monastery chronicler recorded a more sinister version: in the course of a violent row, one of the tinsmiths had hurled a pan of hot coals at a group of masons.[52] Some version of this basic tale, hinging on the negligence or misbehavior of the tinsmiths, eventually became the standard explanation for the fire. The Prussian diplomat and scholar, Christian Carl Josias Bunsen, went so far as to tell a friend, incorrectly, that it had been "proven in a court of law" that the fire resulted from a drunken scuffle between the tinsmiths.[53]

What is curious is that, after that first notice in the *Diario di Roma*, the careless or unruly tinsmiths were never again mentioned in any official or semiofficial document. On 26 July, just ten days later, the *Diario di Roma* published a long, detailed, and more or less official account – the "Relazione esatta e veridica delle circostanze che precedettero il fatale incendio della Basilica di S. Paolo fuori le mura" – which reconstructed the fire in forensic detail but gave no information whatsoever on what started it.[54] Subsequent official or semiofficial texts did the same.

The likely reason for this silence comes in a remarkable letter brought to light by Monica Calzolari.[55] Addressed to Consalvi by the Dominican Tommaso Domenico Piazza, an official in the Congregation of the Inquisition, the letter was written during the brief interval between the fire and the publication of the "Relazione."[56] It was not delivered to Consalvi directly but rather sent via the Cardinal Vicar of Rome, Annibale della Genga. Della Genga was associated with the conservative-to-reactionary factions within the Curia who resented what they saw as Consalvi's excessive accommodation with modern doctrines and values.[57] For instance, they felt that Consalvi had failed to contest Rome's demotion from Caput Mundi to Capital of the Arts – to a kind of museum for foreign tourists, where the monuments no longer spoke primarily of the triumph of the Church – and they dreamed of resacralizing Rome, of imposing "a unitary rhetoric and an *obligatory language* on the holy city," in Philippe Boutry's words.[58] During his three years as Cardinal Vicar in Rome, della Genga had imposed austere moral legislation to regulate public behavior and police religious observance. In many respects, then, Consalvi and della Genga had their differences on contemporary religious politics. Piazza's letter was surely provided to della Genga more to win his esteem than in hopes that it would make Consalvi more receptive to its content.[59]

Piazza wrote in the letter that he had been given an advance draft of the "Relazione" and was appalled by it. Only a nonbeliever, he felt, could attribute an event like the fire at San Paolo purely to the negligence of the tinsmiths. What of God's role? Had everyone forgotten the destruction of the First Temple in Jerusalem? Piazza quoted God's warning to Solomon: if you turn from me and do not keep my commandments, then will I cast Israel out of the land I have given them, and this house, which I have hallowed for my name, will I cast out of my sight.[60] True Catholics, Piazza continued, were disposed to fear the anger of the Lord, and seeing the many abominations and blasphemies that had so recently profaned the holy city, he could not fathom why Consalvi would fail to make use of the fire at San Paolo to "build up and confirm the religious sentiments of the Faithful" by portraying it as a "sign from an Omnipotent Hand, angry and threatening Rome." Such would serve as a "refutation of unbelief, a healthy reproach to those who profane our churches." Piazza recommended affirming that, "while the human part in the catastrophe remained uncertain, the part of God was very certain, and had been provoked (as all good people know) by scorn against those who deny and profane the Temples consecrated to God; and that in his Anger God wished to give a threatening sign through the swift and horrible destruction" of one of the "principal basilicas of the Metropole of the Faith."

Della Genga had Piazza's letter copied for his own files, noting on it that the original was submitted to Consalvi the next day. It seems very likely that the reason the "Relazione" did not end up stating a specific cause for the fire when it was published two days later – why the mention of the tinsmiths was deleted – was because of the concerns the Dominican father had voiced. The matter of fundraising for the reconstruction might also have been a factor. Piazza's letter does not mention it specifically, but others later made the point that the faithful would be more likely to donate to a future reconstruction if the fire were presented to them as a message from God rather than as a banal accident. Indeed, just five days after the "Relazione" was published, a notice appeared in the weekly supplement to the *Diario di Roma*, probably by someone in Consalvi's circle, that took up this very point. It highlighted the striking similarities between the San Paolo fire and a fire that had damaged the Lateran basilica during the Middle Ages, which had started "through the negligence of a workman who was repairing the lead sheets of the basilica roof." It also noted that, following the Lateran fire, Pope Clement V had successfully stimulated "the generosity of the Roman people and of all of Christendom" to contribute toward what became a speedy repair.[61] The story aimed to reassure skeptics that donations would still be forthcoming even if the fire were not publicized as an act of divine telegraphy.

So what then was the point of publishing the "Relazione" at all? Mainly to nip rumors in the bud and to insulate the fire brigade as well as the monks of the monastery from criticism. Local antiquarians and foreign visitors had been warning for years about the perils of leaving the basilica abandoned for long stretches every summer. John Eustace, for instance, had noted snidely that the monks left in summer because "of the real or imaginary unwholesomeness of the air," and declaimed that

> the Benedictine monks are, in all countries where the Order exists but particularly in Italy, both rich and public spirited, [so] that it is a subject of surprise, and just reproach, that while so many superb edifices have been erected by them in different towns and countries, one of the most ancient and celebrated temples in the Christian world should even in the capital itself, and under the eye of the pontiff, be allowed to molder away and sink almost unnoticed into ruin.[62]

Certainly the monastery chronicle on the morning after the fire suggests a guilty conscience, for it describes the blaze as having been caused by an absolutely unforeseeable concatenation of misfortunes.[63] There were also plenty of whispers that the fire brigade had not exactly covered itself in glory in taking such a long time to arrive. The diplomat Bunsen told his friend that the fire brigade's ladders were said to have been mysteriously missing when they went to look for them on the morning of the conflagration.[64] A manuscript sonnet preserved in a scrapbook at the National Library in Rome mocks the "gran Pompier" – Marchese Giuseppe Origo, director and commander of the Rome fire brigade – for his hapless firefighting techniques, and the discomfort-averse "fat Fathers" of the monastery who had left the building so vulnerable.[65] When Origo himself lectured in Rome on fire-fighting a few weeks later, an art journal, clearly aware of these whispers, remarked, carefully, that San Paolo had proven how really big fires were beyond human powers to halt.[66] Further evidence that the "Relazione" aimed to deflect rumors and criticism appears in what are almost certainly the drafts of the text, amid the manuscripts of Giuseppe Tambroni, a Roman archaeologist, diplomat, and art critic who may now be identified as its likely author.[67] Tambroni's reworkings prove he was chiefly concerned to stress the vigilance of the monks in watching over the basilica, the heroism they and the fire brigade exhibited once the fire erupted, and the parade of eyewitnesses who noticed nothing suspicious in the hours prior to the blaze.[68]

Tambroni's "Relazione" was reproduced verbatim in the *Gazzetta* of Milan, more or less translated on the front page of the *Constitutionnel* of Paris, summarized on the front page of the *Journal des débats* in Paris, and paraphrased in the *Gazzetta Piemontese* in Turin, the *Gaceta de Madrid*, and the Parisian *Ami de la Religion*.[69] In Rome, however, its reception was complex, because while few people seem to have believed the official line, there was little consensus about what exactly the fire actually *did* signify. Indeed, imaginations ran amok.

21. Cyprien Gaulon, *Portrait of Leo XII*, c. 1826.
Source: Bordeaux, Bibliothèque municipale – Delpit 82/11.

But before turning to that entertaining topic, it is necessary to say a word about a signal event that occurred less than a month after the "Relazione" was published: the death on 20 August of Pope Pius VII, and the surprising election to the papal throne one month later of none other than the conservative Cardinal Vicar of Rome, Annibale della Genga, henceforth to be known as Pope Leo XII (**Figure 21**). For this change in Church leadership was to have a determining effect on all subsequent debate about the situation at San Paolo.

The historian Raffaele Colapietra marks the 1823 conclave as a turning point: a moment when many convictions the Church had cleaved to in negotiating the traumas of the past half-century finally gave way to new approaches.[70] The College of Cardinals was divided into two broad factions: a smaller moderate one and a larger *zelante* one, within each of which there were subfactions.[71] The moderates were mostly content with the internal administration of the Papal States under Pius VII and Consalvi, but felt that their external policy of ostensible neutrality had been misguided. The moderates hoped instead for a pope who would strengthen the so-called Throne and Altar alliances that bound the Church to the Catholic sovereigns of Europe – in Austria especially – in exchange for a certain subservience. The *zelanti*, instead, wished to move the Church in the opposite direction, as they mostly understood that their old world was not coming back: rather than adapt to the structural reconfigurations of the post-1815 European restoration, which they perceived as instrumentalizing the Church, they wanted to declare even greater independence and to centralize ecclesiastical authority in Rome (an ideal known as ultramontanism, which had a long future ahead of it).[72] They also wanted the Church to use that independence to foment a great renewal of Catholic religious life, at once public and internal, institutional and popular. Many *zelanti* had noticed and were attracted to the Catholic religious revivals of the first decades of the century in Germany and France, which were associated with early Catholic Romantics such as Chateaubriand, Lamennais, and various likeminded German authors.[73] This fledgling Catholic revival, which in Germany led to several high-profile conversions from Protestantism, hinged on a reenergized, personally affective religiosity that stood in stark contrast to the official religiosity of guilt and obligation inherited from the Counter-Reformation. Many in Rome hoped that these new energies might awaken the Catholic masses and make protagonists of them in a direct confrontation with the ascendant values of secular liberalism.

The conclave of 1823 was a typically complex and intrigue-filled event, but the eventual election of Leo XII was regarded as a triumph for the *zelanti*. Leo was very much of the group that perceived in contemporary Catholic Romanticism, and in the work of Lamennais particularly, a formidable new resource for the Church in reimagining its place in a changed European society.[74] Leo took his regnal name from Pope Leo I, also known as St. Leo the Great (440–461), in homage to St. Leo's tireless combat against heresies that had threatened the unity of the early Church, his efforts to protect Rome from barbarian invaders (most famously in 452, when he personally talked Attila the Hun into a withdrawal), and his advocacy for the absolute power of the pope within the Church. All three accomplishments had analogs in Leo XII's vision of the challenges he faced in reforming the modern Church.

In his first encyclical, *Ubi Primum* (5 May 1824), Leo thundered against the erroneous doctrines of the modern world, which beneath a "meek appearance of piety and liberality" concealed a sinister "indifferentism" that claimed, "God has given free leave to every person to embrace or adopt, without any risk of his salvation, whatever sect is most pleasing to him, according to his own private judgment or opinion."[75] This stress on worldly "indifferentism" drew straight from the recent publications of Lamennais, who argued that indifference posed a greater threat to the modern Church than the outright denial that had so perturbed clerical leaders during the eighteenth century.[76] Leo also condemned both the practice of distributing vernacular translations of the Bible to ordinary people and the modern doctrines of ecumenicalism and toleration, insisting instead that the Catholic Church offered the only path to salvation:

> We are taught, and with a divine faith believe in, *one Lord, one faith, one baptism, and that no other name under heaven is given to men besides the name of Jesus Christ of Nazareth, in which we can be saved*; on which account also we profess that *out of the Church there is no salvation*.[77]

Leo's angry vision of a Church at war with a wayward contemporary world would have been foreign to Pope Pius VII or Consalvi, but it was to be shared by all his nineteenth-century successors.

Nineteen days after *Ubi Primum*, Leo issued a second encyclical – *Quod Hoc Ineunte* – which proclaimed that 1825 would be a Jubilee year, the first since 1775. This Jubilee was in many respects the defining act of Leo's pontificate.[78] When his treasurer told him the budget would not support it, and when his new secretary of state warned that political conspirators would use the occasion to smuggle their operatives into Rome, Leo brushed them off.[79] Instead he read a Latin allocution in the College of Cardinals, printed the next day in Italian on the front page of the *Diario di Roma*, informing the assembled clerics that the eyes of pilgrims from across Catholic Christendom would soon be upon them, and that he expected them to present a luminous example of "worthy, pure, and holy" life.[80] Leo's hope for the Jubilee was to capitalize on the recent upsurge in Catholic devotions across Europe; it made a declaration to European Catholics, over the heads of their national governments, that Rome embraced the new trends in Catholic religiosity and wished to see them grow into in a triumphant Catholic renewal for modern times.[81]

In preparation, Leo ordered a complete series of extraordinary apostolic visits to the churches of Rome to verify that they measured up to his stringent standards of visible sanctity and orderliness.[82] As Wiseman relates, a Swiss guardsman was stationed in every church to prevent "artistic or curious perambulations at improper times, and assist in repressing any unbecoming conduct."[83] Leo ordered the removal from St. Peter's of a large illuminated cross that hung suspended from the dome, on account of the joyful crowds of tourists it attracted to what he insisted should be a place solely of piety and worship.[84] A battery of new moral legislation aimed to stamp out putatively immoral behaviors that clerics complacently attributed to the recent French occupations: prostitution, card games, obscenity, street violence, immodest dress, improper language, the letting of rooms for immoral purposes, private meetings of large groups, and, of course, unauthorized "sects." Leo also suspended the popular Carnival and made it illegal to consume wine on the premises of *osterie*, which effectively eliminated one of the major forms of nonecclesiastical sociability available to the city's inhabitants.[85] During the Jubilee itself, he made it his practice to walk shoeless in religious processions and multiplied his visits to hospitals and prisons, where he would partake of humble meals with residents and wash their feet.[86] He further signaled his piety by transferring his residence from the opulent Quirinal Palace to the more visible Vatican Palace next to St. Peter's, despite – or rather because of – its reputation for being uncomfortable and unhealthy.[87]

This atmosphere of febrile otherworldliness proved to be rich soil for conspiracy theories about the fire at San Paolo. Wiseman recalled that "every sort of rumour was started and believed. [The fire] was confidently reported to be the work of incendiaries, and part of an atrocious plan to destroy the sacred monuments of Rome."[88] The young Luigi Poletti wrote to his brother in the provinces that "such a loss is felt so strongly here that everyone behaves as though he has lost something personal, and you see melancholy sages in the streets, while idiots deduce from it sad consequences, prophesying misfortunes and calamity."[89] A minor cleric wrote to Cardinal Secretary of State della Somaglia to say that the imprisonment of Pius VII and the fire at San Paolo were proof that terrible trials were coming, and suggested that the Christian people would soon end up in slavery like the ancient Hebrews.[90] Such anxieties were not limited to clerics. Stendhal observed that there was "something mysterious connected with the fire at San Paolo" even in the minds of *le peuple*, representatives of which had informed him that the fire occurred because the basilica's famous sequence of papal portrait medallions was out of space: "there is no more room to mount a portrait of Pius VII's successor. From this there is talk that the Holy See is to be eliminated."[91]

From the contemporary diary of Gregorio Speroni, a priest and functionary at the Papal Curia, we get a fuller sense of this atmosphere.[92] Speroni records that a certain tinsmith named Giacomo, son of Eugenio, had been arrested shortly after the fire at San Paolo and charged with being the guilty party who had been so careless with his coals. This Giacomo was held in prison, but for "only fifty-seven hours," after which he was quietly released and told to get out of town. Obediently he went off to a friend's house in nearby Albano but remained there for only a few days before returning to Rome, where he had been living unmolested ever since. According to Speroni, the common view was that Giacomo was innocent: "the Public is not persuaded" any longer by the story of the negligent tinsmiths, and was increasingly fixated on the improbable speed with which the roof had been consumed by the flames – especially after the news reached Rome that an almost identical fire had destroyed the church of Espiritu Santo in Madrid just days later, moments after the end of a mass attended by a large crowd of dignitaries.[93] Many people, Speroni wrote, had drawn from this the logical conclusion that both fires were the work of a diabolical sect of arsonists.[94]

Similar claims emerge in an extensively annotated copy of the printed "Relazione," preserved at the National Library in Rome.[95] The annotation begins with an asterisk at the point in the text where the discovery of the fire is recounted. The nameless annotator asks how, in the two-and-a-quarter hours between the discovery and the arrival of the fire brigade, the fire could have grown from a few flames to devouring the entire roof structure; how in three hours one spark could have consumed "an immense Temple built so solidly that it had resisted the wounds of time for several centuries!" The wood of the beams could never have burned that quickly, while the beams themselves were too far apart for the flame to have leaped between them. The more plausible explanation was "currently being talked about publicly in Rome," namely, that there had been three "oltramontani" – northern Europeans, with the implication of their being Protestants – who, after the departure of the workers on the afternoon of the 15 July, had received permission from the custodian to go up on the workers' scaffolds to sketch and take measurements of the basilica. After the fire, the monks who had climbed the campanile to sound the alarm claimed that they had "clearly seen" that the fire had four points of origin, not one. Given this, continued the annotator, it was clear that it had been the "oltramontani" who set the fire, not the tinsmiths, and this was why Giacomo, son of Eugenio, had been released by the police. The proof that the government knew full well what had really happened was that new citywide regulations had subsequently been announced that forbade custodians at major monuments to open closed areas to visitors without the written permission of the secretary of state.

Such speculations bundle together many of the anxieties that preoccupied contemporary Roman clerics: fear of violent enemies scheming to destroy all that was dear to Catholics, or suspicions that the government was concealing the magnitude of the threat facing the Church. Even the fact that the arsonists should appear in the guise of foreign antiquarians – an infidel population that preferred to sketch and measure basilicas rather than worship in them – reflected pious resentments. Anti-Semitism also circulated in the San Paolo rumor mill. An anonymous contemporary manuscript at the National Library claims that "the arrival in Rome of the extremely rich Jewish banker Rothschild, contemporaneously with the fire, led some to suspect that it had been accomplished on his orders."[96] It should be noted that Leo XII himself was noxiously anti-Semitic, and would certainly have been sympathetic to such claims. As Cardinal Vicar, his zeal after the French occupation in enforcing the return of the city's Jews to the ghetto had been so fervent that the ghetto eventually had to be enlarged.[97] He also reestablished the old tradition of the *predica coatta*, whereby the Jews were forced to hear a hectoring sermon every Saturday from an official "Preacher to the Jews," an office Leo filled with the clerical author of a tract entitled *Ebraismo senza replica* [*Judaism without Rejoinder*].[98] As pope, in 1827, he was to resurrect Pius VI's draconian "Edict Concerning the Jews," among other measures that effectively criminalized Jewishness across the Papal States.[99] Such measures had a long history in Roman Catholic tradition, but they enjoyed a new respectability in the atmosphere announced by *Ubi Primum*, as more than one foreign visitor attests.[100] The British traveler Moyle Sherer visited the ruins of San Paolo a year or two after the blaze and wrote that "you see people from the city muttering regrets and suspicions [about the fire]; and divided in the latter between the Jew accursed by them and the English heretic, of whom some of them think no better."[101] Bunsen likewise asserted that the Romans he knew mostly claimed ("or at least do not wish to admit the unlikelihood of the claim") that the fire at San Paolo had been set by "the Jews (alias Englishmen, alias Jews dressed as Englishmen, i.e. Jews or heretics)."[102]

As the shock of the blaze wore off, the most extreme voices faded out and cooler heads pushed on deciphering the divine message encoded in the fire. At the end of 1823, Giuseppe Marocchi, a reliable supporter of authority, published his *Dettaglio del terribile incendio accaduto il di 15 luglio 1823 della famosa basilica di S. Paolo di Rome*, a clear-eyed account that on its final page compared the blaze to the destruction of the Temple of Jerusalem.[103] The comparison had been made previously by hotheads like Piazza, but Marocchi offered it in measured tones as a tragic local event of cosmic significance holding implications for the life of God's people. He even pointed out that the Jewish festival commemorating the destruction of the Temple fell that year on 15 July – a coincidence that left little doubt that God had intended the fire to be a watershed in the life of Roman Catholics.[104]

That Roman Catholic writers in Rome were prepared to identify the present situation of the Church with the persecutions endured in ancient times by God's chosen people shows how much things had changed over the past quarter century with respect to the Church's sense of its position in the world. The festival that Marocchi was referencing – the festival of Tisha b'Av – is the great day of lamentation in the Jewish calendar: a time to mourn as well as to renew the determination to survive. Moving past the bluster of some of the first reactions we have just surveyed, a similar path of mourning and renewal now opened before Catholics in Rome as they began the contentious process of reflecting on this latest catastrophe to befall them – on its self-evident connections to the figure of Constantine, to the Early Christians, and above all to St. Paul – and started debating the response God was so clearly trying to call forth from His Church.

NOTES

1   Eustace (1815), v. 2, p. 120.
2   Waldie (1820), v. 2, pp. 348–349.
3   Reinolds (1816), p. 121.
4   Vivant Denon, "L'Eglise de Saint-Paul-hors-des-murs, à Rome," 31 January 1812 (ANF: AF IV 1050 doss. 8, n. 20).
5   Nicolai (1815), p. 311.
6   Simond (1828), p. 323.
7   Plessis (1903), p. 259.
8   Von Kotzebue (1806), v. 3, p. 399.
9   Simond (1828), p. 323.
10 Eustace (1815), v. 4, p. 459.
11 Vermiglioli (1825), v. 4, pp. 177–178; Denon (31 January 1812), as in Chapter 2 n. 4.
12 Pouillard (1817), p. 155.
13 Wiseman (1858), p. 200.
14 Woods (1828), v. 1, p. 383.
15 Fontana (1694), p. 329; Filippi et al. (2006).
16 By the early nineteenth century, these frescos were nearly obliterated. See Eustace (1815), v. 2, p. 122, and Woods (1828), v. 1, p. 386. Julian Gardner argues that the nave frescos were not fifth century but "substantially late-mediaeval" (Gardner [1999], p. 251).
17 On these columns, see Docci (2006), pp. 59–63.
18 Eaton (1820), v. 2, p. 271.
19 Woods (1828), p. 385.
20 Nicolai (1815), p. 310.
21 Nicolai (1815), p. 302; Seroux d'Agincourt (1823), v. 1, Architecture, p. 13.
22 Seroux d'Agincourt (1823), v. 1, Architecture, p. 13.
23 Woods (1828), p. 385.
24 Camerlenghi (2013).
25 This account is mostly based on [Tambroni] (1823) and Marocchi (1823).
26 Bunsen and Nippold (1868), pp. 206–207.
27 Giuseppe Tambroni, untitled documents, July 1823 (BAV: Ferrajoli 517, f. 245).
28 Marocchi (1823), p. 6.
29 *Cronaca* I, 16 July 1823.
30 *Cronaca* I, 17 July 1823.
31 Marocchi (1823), pp. 7–8.
32 And a thirteenth fell a few days later (*Cronaca* II, 28 July 1823).

33 Beste (1826), v. 1, pp. 55–56.

34 Marocchi (1823), pp. 15–16. See also *Journal des débats politiques et littéraires* (Paris), 31 July 1823, p. 1; *The Times* (London), 5 August 1823, p. 2b.

35 A seventeenth-century account, for instance, noted that the "old walls" of San Paolo evoked rich ideas in those who knew Early Christian history (Connors and Rice [1991], p. 62).

36 Stendhal (1829), v. 2, pp. 180–185.

37 Stendhal (1829), v. 2, p. 182. Stendhal claimed to have visited San Paolo the morning after the fire, but in fact arrived in Rome only in December (Hjort [1970], pp. 157–158).

38 Sherer (1825), p. 352.

39 Cancellieri (1802), pp. v–vi.

40 Chateaubriand (1850 [written 1829]), v. 9, p. 107.

41 *DdR*, 16 July 1823, p. 1.

42 Wiseman (1858), p. 198.

43 Plessis (1903), p. 259.

44 Sacchi (1836), pp. 316–317.

45 *Cronaca* I, 16 July 1823.

46 Wiseman (1858), pp. 199–200.

47 Wiseman (1858), p. 200.

48 *Cronaca* II, 18–19 July 1823.

49 *Cronaca* II, 20 and 25 July 1823.

50 *Cronaca* II, 28 July 1823. See the plan in Uggeri (1823).

51 *Journal des débats politiques et littéraires* (Paris), 31 July 1823, p. 1; *DdR*, 16 July 1823, p. 1.

52 *Cronaca* I, 16 July 1823.

53 Bunsen and Nippold (1868), p. 207.

54 [Tambroni] (July 1823).

55 Calzolari (2012).

56 "Copia di una Lettera Scritta dal P[adre] M[aestr]o Piazza . . ." (AAV: Segreteria di Stato, Spogli dei Cardinali, Della Somaglia Giulio, b.2B, f.E), cited in Calzolari (2012), pp. 90–91.

57 Colapietra (1963), esp. pp. 137–144; Regoli (2016).

58 Boutry (1997), p. 343, emphasis in the original text.

59 Alan J. Reinerman calls della Genga a "bitter enemy" of Consalvi, while Wiseman highlights the popular perception of their emnity only then to deny it. (Reinerman [1978], p. 41; Wiseman [1858], pp. 231–234). Colapietra instead stresses the commonalities between the two (Colapietra [1963], p. 140).

60 1 Kings 9:7 (King James Version).

61 *DdR: NdG*, 31 July 1823, p. 1.

62 Eustace (1815), v. 2, pp. 120–122. Ironically, Eustace himself was to die of malaria a few years later in Naples.

63 *Cronaca* I, 16 July 1823.

64 Bunsen and Nippold (1868), p. 207.

65 Sebastianelli (2004), p. 547.

66 *MRABA* 1:1 (1824): 145–148.

67 Tambroni (July 1823), as in Chapter 2 n. 27. Tambroni at this date was a protector of the young Luigi Poletti, who a decade later was to assume the directorship of the reconstruction of San Paolo (Strozzieri [2021], p. 40).

68 Tambroni (July 1823), as in Chapter 2 n. 27.and f.245r. Wiseman, too, in the passage cited earlier, still in the 1850s made a point of stressing the "admirable organization" of the brigade.

69 *Gazzetta di Milano*, 4 August 1823, p. 1305, and 5 August 1823, pp. 1308–1309; *Le Constitutionnel* (Paris), 10 August 1823, pp. 1–2; *Journal des débats politiques et littéraires* (Paris), 10 August 1823, p. 1; *Gazzetta Piemontese* (Turin), 26 July 1823, p. 448; *Gaceta de Madrid*, 9 August 1823, p. 208; *L'ami de la Religion* (Paris), 20 August 1823, pp. 39–41.

70   Colapietra (1963), pp. 12–15.

71   For a breakdown of these factions, see Colapietra (1962), pp. 80–83.

72   There was also a reactionary faction among the *zelanti* who wished to turn the clock back to the pre-Revolutionary era, but their influence was limited. See Colapietra (1962) and (2014).

73   Reardon (1985), pp. 117–145.

74   Milbach (2020); Regoli (2020).

75   *TEPD*, v. 3, pp. 9–15; quote p. 12.

76   Colapietra (2014), p. 17.

77   *TEPD*, v. 3, p. 13, emphasis in the original text.

78   On the Jubilee of 1825, see Fiumi Sermattei and Colapietra (2014), especially the essay by Colapietra; see also Burgess (1825) and Geoffroy de Grandmaison (1902).

79   Wiseman (1858), pp. 273–274; Colapietra (2014), p. 25.

80   Boutry (1997), p. 349; *DdR*, 12 June 1824, pp. 1–2.

81   Colapietra (2014), p. 27.

82   Grégoire (1967); Ilari (1967–1969); Boutry (1997), pp. 349–350; Falsetti (2014).

83   Wiseman (1858), p. 257; see also Fraschetti (1906), v. 1, pp. 60–61.

84   Wiseman (1858), pp. 255–257; Boiteux (2020).

85   Wiseman (1858), pp. 258–259; Boutry (1997), pp. 352–358.

86   Boutry (1997), p. 350; Regoli (2020), pp. 25–26.

87   Boutry (1997), p. 350. Pius IX made the same move after the debacle of 1848–1850, for the same reasons.

88   Wiseman (1858), p. 199.

89   Luigi Poletti to Geminiano Poletti, 15 July 1823 (BCALP: LP23a C7).

90   Giovanni Maria Bozzetti to Giulio Maria della Somaglia, 29 June 1825 (AAV: Segreteria di Stato, anno 1825, b. 586 [rubr. 48], #22).

91   Stendhal (1829), v. 2, p. 182.

92   Gregorio Speroni, "La Basilica di San Paolo incendiata," 1823-5 (BAV, Cod.Vat.Lat. 9901, fols. 86–86v; referenced in Camerlenghi [2007], p. 222). On Speroni: Baldassari (1889), v. 2, p. 416.

93   *Gaceta de Madrid*, 22 July 1823, p. 156.

94   Similar rumors spread after the fire at Notre Dame in Paris in 2019. See Wittman (2019) and (2020a).

95   Costantino Maes, "Thesaurus Romanus," c. 1910, v. 68, #11499 (BNR: Sala Romana). The text is discussed in Briganti Colonna (1929) and Sebastianelli (2004).

96   Sebastianelli (2004), p. 546, who provides a transcription.

97   Boutry (1997), pp. 358–362.

98   Boutry (1997), pp. 345–347; Kertzer (2001), pp. 61–64.

99   Sebastianelli (2004), p. 546; Kertzer (2001), pp. 64–70.

100   Boutry (1997), pp. 324–327.

101   Sherer (1825), p. 351.

102   Bunsen and Nippold (1868), p. 207.

103   Marocchi (1823).

104   In fact, Tisha b'Av fell on 17 July in 1823.

THREE

FUTURE VISIONS

Public debate on the reconstruction of San Paolo began just two weeks after the fire, with the publication of *Della basilica di S. Paolo sulla via Ostiense* by Angelo Uggeri, who we encountered previously as the author of the 1809 *Edifices de la décadence*[1] (**Figure 22**). Uggeri's book pleaded for rebuilding San Paolo more or less exactly as it had been before the fire, with a few key adjustments. The suggestion was unprecedented in the history of European architecture. Replacement buildings in the past were certainly known to make reference to their predecessors, or to incorporate fragments of them into their fabric, and repairs or extensions often preserved a certain harmony with the existing building; but a precise reconstitution of an essentially destroyed building was unheard of. The closest precedents were local: Valadier and Stern's reconstruction of the Arch of Titus and Valadier's proposed reconstruction of the Colosseum, both dating to the decade immediately preceding the fire at San Paolo.[2] But these were both antique monuments that had been ruined for centuries, whereas Uggeri's proposal concerned what until very recently had been a living, functioning building, and a Christian one at that. Despite its novelty, however, the idea was swiftly embraced in Rome by clerics, scholars, and especially those who qualified as both. Those who came out in opposition to such a solution were mainly architects, who preferred the more conventional solution of a new and modern San Paolo that would stand as a nineteenth-century pendant to St. Peter's.

22. Antoine Joseph Wiertz, *Portrait of Angelo Uggeri*, 1835.
Source: © Accademia Nazionale di San Luca, Roma.

This chapter delves into the initial iterations and arguments of each position, which were far more characterized by modern historical anxieties than one might suppose from the prevailing caricature of early nineteenth-century Rome as a cultural backwater. The chapter will also highlight the emergence of the symbolic and economic stakes of these two visions for the reconstruction and how they led this first phase of discussion to a surprising – and, again, unprecedented – initial resolution.

The vignette on the title page of Uggeri's *Della basilica* depicted the moment when the fire was discovered (**see Figure 16**). The following page carried a plan of the basilica showing its surviving and destroyed columns as shaded and unshaded circles (**Figure 23**). Both images subtly reinforced Uggeri's

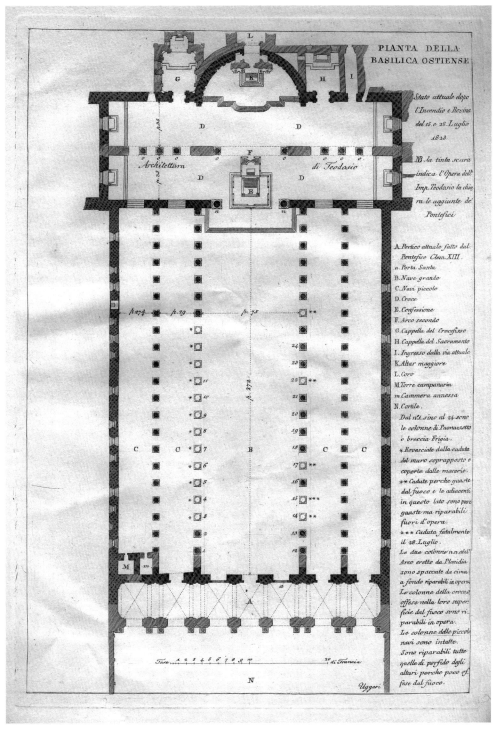

23. Plan of the basilica of San Paolo fuori le mura, indicating which columns had been damaged or destroyed in the fire of July 1823 (from Uggeri [1823]).
Source: Collection of the author.

24. Jean-Baptiste-Cicéron Le Sueur, *San Paolo fuori le mura after the fire of July 1823*, 1823. *Source*: © Beaux-Arts de Paris, Dist. RMN-Grand Palais / Art Resource, New York.

contention that the damage was not that extensive, and certainly not enough to justify clearing away the ruins for a new building. They give the reader a much sunnier impression of the state of the building than, for instance, artists' drawings made shortly after the fire (**Figure 24**).

Uggeri's concern to preserve as much of the old basilica as possible was both historical and aesthetic: "... given the great value we place on the earliest marvels of sacred Christian buildings, who would dare to alter the plan of this building, and withdraw from the eye the enchantment of that simple arrangement of columns?"[3] Preserving the old plan was the "public desire," while a modern reconstruction could only lead to aesthetic loss: "Saint Peter's and the Lateran were destroyed by time and by events; and their architecture converted into gelid masses of bricks." Uggeri already identifies his enemy here as those who would advocate a new and modern basilica – an idea that had not yet been publicly mooted but clearly was already in the air. This was surely part of why he rushed his book into print.

Uggeri instead envisaged a repair in which surviving elements were treated with the same respect as a pagan ruin, with every salvageable element meticulously preserved. He proposed to whittle away the fire-damaged parts of the surviving columns and to patch them with new stones to create composite shafts. Those that were unsalvageable would be substituted with new shafts camouflaged or stuccoed to look like the originals. He also proposed some changes. The palimpsest of old tombs and marble slabs that made up the original floor would be replaced with a modern pavement; a fireproof roof would be concealed above a coffered ceiling; and a flood break would be constructed outside to protect the basilica from the capricious Tiber. The most significant modification, however, came in the reconstituted nave elevation, where Uggeri proposed to replace the arches of the old arcade with a flat entablature, the more correct classical solution. The justification he offered was, again, both aesthetic and historical. The best nave columns, he wrote, were spolia from pagan temples, and by examining their abaci one could see that they had originally supported entablatures, not arches. Expanding on the argument he had made in 1809, he asserted that the Early Christians had introduced arches at San Paolo only out of necessity due to the late antique collapse of the stone quarrying industry. Arches atop columns had been legitimized in the Renaissance, but it would be anachronistic to read that legitimacy back to Early Christian times, and therefore perverse to perpetuate this unwillingly committed violation in the repaired basilica, given that there was no longer any difficulty in quarrying large enough stones to form entablatures. Indeed, one had a responsibility to build an entablature, for it would consummate an Early Christian intention that had been postponed for some fourteen centuries.[4] The most famous plate in Uggeri's book depicted this transformation beneath the dubious epigraph, "IN PRISTINVM"[5] (**Plate 6**).

Uggeri's argument here reflects his lifelong obsession with the relationship of the Early Christian basilicas to the ancient civic basilicas, and of San Paolo specifically to the Basilica Ulpia, the ruins of which had been discovered in the Forum of Trajan in 1812 by French archaeologists.[6] His argument had antecedents in certain late eighteenth-century writings by Francesco Milizia and was gaining popularity among Roman scholars. In 1824, the French *pensionnaire* Lesueur even turned it on its head, producing as his *envoi* from Rome a reconstruction of the Basilica Ulpia based on San Paolo.[7] Uggeri had first floated his own version in 1817, and now he developed it further, noting that the major difference between the two buildings was that the Basilica Ulpia had had flat entablatures.[8] So in one sense Uggeri makes an historicist argument, in that he is concerned to legitimize Early Christian architecture as a logical development on its own terms, and as a function of the interplay of inherited norms and new needs. In this regard, the argument mirrors the historicism that was helping to revalorize local architectural traditions across Europe during these years. But Uggeri also seeks to ennoble Early Christian architecture by stressing its formal continuity with the ideals of pagan architecture, at least on the level of intention. Ostensibly this reflects stylistic idealism; but it also implies a historicist sense that styles correlate with particular historical moments. And so Uggeri ends up in the very peculiar position of using one historicist argument, about the contingent lack of large stones to make entablatures, to explain an anomaly in another more hybrid argument, which concerns the betrayal at San Paolo of the classicizing aesthetic intentions proper to the Early Christian historical moment.

It was an argument, in other words, that wove together historicist and essentialist threads in a manner we shall encounter more than once from other protagonists in the chapters to come. The key to this very Roman, but also very modern, ambiguity lies in recognizing that the ancient pagan classical tradition could be seen in many different lights in Rome, even in the mind of a single individual. In much recent theory, it offered a universal ideal; but for those becoming critical of the classical tradition, Roman classicism presented the hegemonic ideal against which the local Early Christian idiom had been so unfairly measured, and from which the sympathetic relativism of an Uggeri aimed now liberate it. At the same time, Roman classicism could also appear as the local Roman architecture par excellence: as the indigenous tradition that, irrespective of the universalizing claims later imposed upon it, had the best claim of any to speak with an authentic Roman accent. And note that Uggeri did not see Roman architecture as a subsequent generation of historicists was to do: as an essentially arcuated architecture with Greek orders superficially superimposed on it. He adhered still to the traditional classicist perspective in which the arcuated and the trabeated both had their legitimate place in the Roman tradition, provided they were handled correctly. It might seem contradictory for Uggeri to have been so intent on liberating Early Christian architecture from disapproving classical judgments, only then to make just such a judgment by insisting on an entablature. But the entablature was only partly about classical correctitude. It also reflected his honest desire to preserve from oblivion what he believed were the aesthetic intentions of the Early Christians. Builders in earlier centuries had also regularly transformed or improved upon the buildings they were called upon to repair. However, their confidence in doing so had reflected a belief in historical continuity that, while not denying the alterity of the past, did not make it the essential fact about the past either. It was thereby still able to identify a building's essence with its name, site, relics, and history, regardless of changes in its architectural form.[9] This was not Uggeri's perspective in 1823. Uggeri instead was concerned to preserve an element of knowledge about the Early Christians that he feared would be forever lost and forgotten if the arches were reconstructed.

A thoughtful review of Uggeri's book appeared in October 1823 in *Effemeridi letterarie di Roma*, written by Filippo de Romanis, the journal's editor, who described himself as a friend of Uggeri. De Romanis credited Uggeri with articulating the "general consensus" on San Paolo. He noted that the papal commissioner of antiquities, Carlo Fea, out of his mind with grief, had also been crying out for an *in pristinum* solution, and that the historian Francesco Cancellieri, still working on publishing di Costanzo's unfinished history of San Paolo, had called for one "from his sickbed."[10] But De Romanis was not entirely convinced by Uggeri's sense of what a "repristination" should entail. Could it really be considered a "repristination" when, in substituting entablatures for arches, or a coffered for an open ceiling, it altered essential design features? De Romanis felt that this concept of a corrected reconstruction was a slippery slope. Was putting the basilica back in its pristine form really even Uggeri's goal? Or was it to rebuild the basilica *alla moderna*?[11] Respectfully he declared his opposition to Uggeri's entablatures and ceiling and registered his skepticism that the Early Christians had employed arches only because of technical limitations. Perhaps they simply *liked* arches.[12] This first review of this pioneering publication about the reconstruction of San Paolo thus pinpointed essential questions that ended up characterizing the whole decades-long reconstruction: questions about the relative claims of aesthetic truths versus historical truths, about the claims of the past on the present, and about the responsibilities of the present toward the past.[13]

Sometime in the two weeks following the fire, the powerful Cardinal Camerlengo Bartolomeo Pacca convoked his Consultative Commission on Antiquities and Fine Arts to debate the repair of San Paolo. In mid-August, Giuseppe Valadier, one of the Commission members, submitted a report on the subject to Pacca[14] (**Figure 25**). Valadier, who we encountered previously as the designer of the Milvian Bridge, was by 1823 the most celebrated architect in Rome, at the height of a triumphant career that had begun back in 1775, when at the tender age of thirteen he won first prize in the Concorso Clementino.[15] This success had impressed Pope Pius VI, who later became almost a surrogate parent to Valadier after the young artist's father committed

25. Jean-Baptiste Joseph Wicar, *Portrait of Giuseppe Valadier*, 1827.
Source: © Accademia Nazionale di San Luca, Roma.

suicide in 1785. The following year, Pius appointed Valadier cameral architect. After several decades of archaeological excavations, supervising restorations of classical monuments, and carrying out architectural and town planning projects, Valadier was in 1821 appointed Professor of Practical Architectural at the Academy of St. Luke. One year later, he joined Pacca's Consultative Commission.

The mysterious voice that favored rebuilding San Paolo in a new style and on a new plan – the voice that had prompted Uggeri, De Romanis, Fea, and Cancellieri all to call for an *in pristinum* solution – belonged without question to Valadier, who seems to have felt that the commission to rebuild San Paolo was his almost by right. Uggeri and company knew Valadier as an unreconstructed true believer in the eternal validity of the Vitruvian tradition and were certainly aware that he regarded the Early Christian style of the old basilica as irredeemably decadent. There could be little doubt but that he would favor a new building in a modern classical style. But Valadier was also enough of a courtier to know that he had to move methodically, by first convincing the powers that be that his was the only feasible solution. This was the purpose of his report to Pacca, which methodically set out the crippling, ruinous expense that an *in pristinum* repair or reconstruction would entail to the Holy See – 309,141 scudi to be precise, representing nearly two-and-a-half times a typical annual budget for the government's entire division of Public Instruction and the Fine Arts. This information was humbly offered, he wrote, so that the Holy Father in his great penetration might have all available information in determining the wisest course of action.

But just two days after Valadier sent this report to Pacca, the Holy Father died, ignorant to the last of the catastrophe that had consumed San Paolo.[16] Pius's death was unfortunate for Valadier, as it stripped him of his principal advantage in seeking the commission. The election of Leo XII a month later magnified the setback, for Leo and his allies were unforgiving of Valadier's prior history of collaboration with the French occupation authorities.[17] Under the Repubblica Romana, Valadier had been entrusted with a major role in the selection, packaging, and dispatch of Roman artworks to Paris, while under the Napoleonic occupation he had presented expansive urban and archaeological projects that entailed the demolition of numerous ecclesiastical institutions, including the convents of Santa Maria del Popolo and San Bonaventura, San Sebastiano, the monastery of San Francesca Romana, and all the churches in the Roman and Imperial Fora. Some of these projects had been carried out, including the demolition of the monasteries of Santo Spirito and Santa Eufemia next to Trajan's Column.[18] Valadier also directed the Napoleonic regime's major town–planning initiative, the redesign of the Piazza del Popolo and the creation of a *passeggiata* on the Pincian hill, the latter component of which was completed after 1814 and had entailed the demolition of further ecclesiastical properties, with the permission of Consalvi and Pius.[19] None of this endeared Valadier one bit to the newly ascendant conservatives around Leo XII. In this respect, Valadier's neoclassical Milvian Bridge of 1806 was an emblematic work, for it reflected architectural currents in leading European centers to the north, and in so doing diminished the sense of exceptionalism that for *zelante* observers was supposed to be the monument's — and indeed Rome's — whole point.

Valadier's position did not, however, deteriorate all at once with Pius's death. Leo XII was in famously poor health at the time of his election and reportedly told the conclave that they had "elected a cadaver."[20] There was a general premonition that the pontificate might be brief, and little occurred during its opening months. On 26 October, Leo made an unannounced visit to the ruined San Paolo, where the Prior Curate rather forwardly observed that "there are many projects, but none has yet been approved, it would be good to see something done."[21] But Leo had more pressing matters to attend to, like cleaning house in the Curia. One of the few who managed to hold on was Treasurer General Belisario Cristaldi, who on account of his post was directly concerned with the administration of the San Paolo reconstruction and especially with its costs. Cristaldi also happened to be an old friend and supporter of Valadier. So despite some bad luck, Valadier still had reason to be optimistic.

Two days before Valadier submitted his report on the restoration, the two titular architects of the monastery, Pasquale Belli and Andrea Alippi, submitted their own estimates in favor of a repair rather than a reconstruction.[22] To Alippi belonged the honor of having made the precious plans and elevations published in Nicolai's 1815 monograph on San Paolo, but Belli was the more prominent architect, an almost exact contemporary of Uggeri who was by then nearing the end of a busy if unremarkable career.[23] Though nowhere near the talent Valadier was recognized to be, Belli had also occupied important offices under the Napoleonic regime, was a longstanding and prominent member of the Academy of St. Luke, and had been prized by Consalvi as competent and reliable.[24] Belli's preferred architectural mode was a dry but thoroughly modern classical one, as illustrated by his most famous work, the crypt he collaborated on with the architect Giuseppe Brizi for the basilica at Assisi to house the tomb of St. Francis, after the saint's body was discovered there in 1818.[25] This austerely neoclassical Greek cross structure made no concessions whatsoever to the style of the rest of that famous medieval basilica.[26]

Belli and Alippi had a vested interest in convincing the government to repair rather than rebuild because then the commission would be theirs by virtue of their position at the monastery. And so they estimated that the whole job could be completed for just 235,701 scudi, nearly 25% less than what Valadier estimated a few days later. The shock of Valadier's estimate, however, led them to revise their own just a few weeks later to a more realistic 361,570 scudi.[27] They also enlisted Abbot Zelli of the monastery to lobby the pope on their

FUTURE VISIONS

behalf. Zelli responded with a memo to Leo that evoked San Paolo not only as "one of the most ancient and respectable monuments of our Religion," but as the only Christian monument in Rome that "since its foundation in the distant past has retained its original form."[28] He asserted that it was "unanimously" agreed among the "most renowned artists and the most learned antiquarians" that the rebuilt San Paolo must fully occupy the old basilica's ancient footprint: it was "the desire of the entire citizenry, and the general expectation." Anything else would require new foundations, the cost of which would far exceed simply repairing the existing shell on the old foundations. Zelli also explicitly rejected all solutions that would yield a smaller basilica, whether temporarily or permanently: such plans offended Roman piety by shrinking "the magnificent Theodosian basilica to a little temple." Rejecting Valadier's pessimism, Zelli claimed the damage was mostly limited to the roof and nave columns and checked off a long list of elements that remained "intact" – he kept repeating the word, like an incantation – or needed only minor repair. Zelli's optimism was however belied by the eye-watering estimate from Belli and Alippi that it accompanied.

A few weeks later, Leo XII's health took a turn for the worse. By the first week of December, he had been forced to suspend audiences.[29] On 22 December, Abbot Zelli went to speak with him about the reconstruction and was turned away; on Christmas, Leo received last rites.[30] Cristaldi now wrote to Valadier to suggest that this might be a good time to set down some ideas on paper for his new San Paolo.[31]

Valadier obliged with a five-page memo accompanied by four large drawings illustrating his proposed new design, of which only a copy of the ground plan now survives[32] (**Figure 26**). Here finally was the smaller San Paolo that everyone had been whispering about. Valadier later wrote that every aspect of this project had been determined by economy: by the knowledge that all expenses would have to be borne by the impoverished Papal Treasury.[33] But that is not what he said now, as he praised the design based on its supreme artistic merit. He dismissed the "important men, both learned and unlearned," who, "speaking out of enthusiasm" rather than from knowledge, had been clamoring to rebuild the church at its original size and state. Anyone competent knew that old San Paolo had been poorly constructed, was susceptible to fire, and reflected an era when the arts were "decadent." Its principal virtues had been its antiquity – that patina of centuries that awed any visitor with a sense of history – and the quality of its marbles, and both had been irretrievably destroyed by the fire. A repair could reconstitute only the decadent *forms* of the old building, and only at enormous cost, which Valadier now estimated at 400,000 scudi. Such a fortune, he warned, would be very badly spent. But if the problem were approached more "dispassionately," it would be possible to preserve the memory of the old building with a detailed 1/20–scale wooden

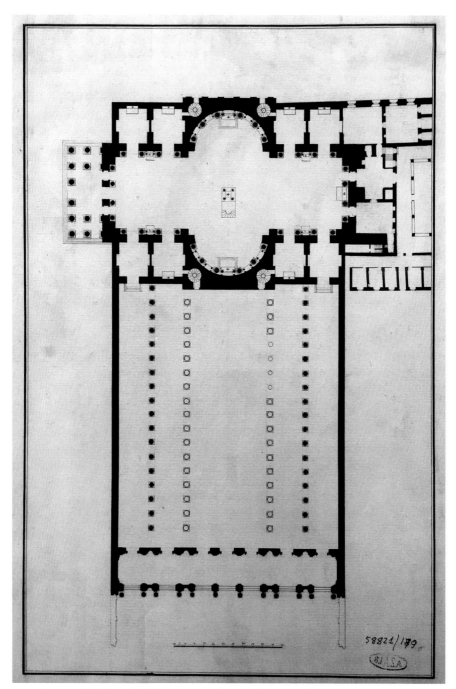

26. Giuseppe Valadier, plan, first project for San Paolo, December 1823.
Source: © Istituto Nazionale di Archeologia e Storia dell'Arte, Rome.

model, and by incorporating into the new church what few precious marbles had survived the fire, and "in particular the beautiful columns," which "might be used, if not in load-bearing capacities, for decoration." This accorded with Roman tradition: most of the rebuilt or refurbished basilicae, from St. Peter's to the Lateran, highlighted memorial elements or materials from the original building. Valadier also proposed to reuse the old foundations to "preserve the memory of the grandeur of the whole and of the parts." But he insisted that above ground the new San Paolo should follow the "true rules of art, and the beautiful examples of the Greeks and Romans, those ancient immortal masters of the Fine Arts."

Where Valadier departed from tradition was in the scale of his new basilica, for he proposed to roof only the area corresponding to the old transept and apse, yielding a smaller basilica reoriented from west–east to north–south. The main façade was now to be on the north face of the former transept, where Valadier envisaged a temple front portico visible head on to those coming down the via Ostiense from Rome. The huge area formerly occupied by the nave would now become an open service courtyard with no public function. Along the walls of this courtyard Valadier proposed to display the papal portrait medallions and other recovered elements, but everything else was to be cleared away, including the old campanile. All salvageable building materials were to be reused. Inside the reoriented church, the apse as well as its mosaics were to be doubled on the west under the arch of Galla Placidia, forming a rounded minitransept.[34] The altar of the confessio marking Paul's burial place would stand at the center, with six smaller chapels ringing the perimeter. Thirty-six columns salvaged or reconstituted from the old basilica were to stand along the interior walls, and the whole was to be lit by three great skylights in the vault. The result, Valadier concluded, would be both cheaper than a full reconstruction and far more in keeping with the rules of good architecture.

What Cristaldi initially thought of the project we do not know, for the archives contain no trace of a response until March 1824. But by then, several new factors had come into play.

Around this time there appeared the first imaginative reflection on how the reconstruction of San Paolo might be funded. The author was Antonio Santelli, a Roman cleric and government functionary who presented his thoughts in a memorandum addressed to the papal government.[35] Santelli was likely inspired by the knowledge – apparently common knowledge in clerical circles – that Valadier was planning to offer, or had already offered, a design for a scaled-back half-basilica. For one who viewed such a prospect as a failure to heed the divine challenge encoded in the fire, it made sense to attack the essential obstacle to a full-scale reconstruction, which was lack of money. Thus Santelli reminded the government that the fire had been an object of tears for "the entire World," and to a degree that would have been impossible in any previous era, this was something more than a Eurocentric exaggeration: for news of the fire had been disseminated in newspapers as far as the northeastern United States mere weeks after the event.[36] Santelli's first suggestion was therefore to appeal for funds to the sovereigns of Europe and the Americas.

Santelli echoed Padre Piazza in suggesting that the generosity of these sovereigns could be encouraged by telling them that the fire had been set deliberately by political sects that threatened them as much as they threatened the Church. But Santelli set his sights also on ordinary Catholics, suggesting that every Catholic bishop in the world be urged to raise funds within his jurisdictions, especially in the wealthier areas. He suggested that a 3 percent tax be levied on all clergy in the Papal States; that all monies destined for other church repairs, maintenance, and construction be temporarily diverted to San Paolo; that ordinary Catholics be given the opportunity to show their devotion by sponsoring a worker for a day, a week, a month, or longer; that a congregation be created to oversee the funds raised and to publish regular tallies; and that major benefactors be rewarded with commemorative medals. As we shall see, nearly all of these measures were eventually instituted.

Santelli unsurprisingly believed that the reconstruction should not only adhere to the original plan and dimensions, but that all mosaics, carvings, and paintings from the old basilica should also be carefully reused in the new building or deposited somewhere for future generations. No corners should be cut in finding the correct materials for a precise reconstruction of what had been lost. He insisted that this had nothing to do with his own personal beliefs or devotion: it simply reflected the reality that people would not visit a transformed modern basilica, would not give money for it, and would not accord it the old building's ancient prestige. The Church could either play it safe and end up spending a still-sizable sum on a building that no one would care about, or it could trust to God that the faithful would respond generously to the challenge of resurrecting the basilica exactly as it had been before the fire.

Leo XII, meanwhile, lying at death's door in late December 1823, summoned the saintly Bishop Strambi of Macerata to his bedside. Strambi arrived on 30 December and reassured Leo that he would soon recover, for he had offered up his own worthless life to God in exchange for the pontiff's. The next day, the accommodating Strambi died, and Leo – "like one from the grave" – miraculously rose up, fully recovered. Or such at least was the story that "all Rome" believed, according to Wiseman.[37] What is certain is that Leo's health did improve markedly in the new year, with the result that he began taking a greater interest in the question of San Paolo.

Over the months following the fire, various architects had submitted projects for the reconstruction. One or two we still possess, while others we know

FUTURE VISIONS 79

of from mentions in contemporary written sources.[38] The architect Carlo Donati even petitioned the government to hold an international architectural competition, noting that such an event might stimulate foreign financial contributions.[39] But even lacking such a competition, projects were accumulating, and so on 24 March 1824 Leo XII's new secretary of state, Giulio Maria della Somaglia, delegated three members from his advisory Arts Council to prepare a report on three proposals in particular: the project Valadier had sent to Cristaldi in December, and two others submitted by his colleague Gaspare Salvi, who taught architectural theory at the Academy of St. Luke.[40]

In evaluating these proposals, the Council made mention of two "aims of the Government," namely, that costs be kept low and that the "image of the old Basilica" be preserved.[41] The first of these went without saying, but the second was new. It may have been related to the discovery just a month earlier that the rains and ice of winter had severely damaged the surviving parts of the old basilica, forcing Belli and Alippi to build several new wooden supports.[42] This deflating discovery made it plain that not everything that remained standing was stable enough to be reincorporated into a repaired church and raised the possibility that the building as a whole might be beyond repair. But in the absence of any new funding resources, a full *in pristinum* reconstruction also seemed highly unlikely. It therefore became a pressing concern for those who, like della Somaglia and Cristaldi, were in positions of responsibility to start thinking about how a tightly budgeted new basilica might retain some kind of palpable relationship with its predecessor.

As for the projects themselves, Salvi had initially sent della Somaglia four proposals at the end of 1823, none of which survive. Della Somaglia had responded by asking him to draw up budgets for two of them: a full-scale Latin Cross option and a smaller option that reoccupied only the transept of the old basilica. Salvi estimated that the full-scale option would cost 343,041 scudi, and the smaller one fully one-third less (228,217 scudi).[43] Della Somaglia therefore excluded the Latin Cross from consideration and provided his Arts Council with only the smaller option to examine, along with another smaller option by Salvi, and finally Valadier's project from December, which of course was also of reduced size. These three conceptually similar projects were identified to the Council only by letter since everyone involved knew one another and della Somaglia wanted the judgments to be as objective as possible.

The Council was composed of Giuseppe Venturoli, director of the Pontifical Engineering School and a leading figure in the Pontifical Corps of Engineers, and his two colleagues Gianbattista Martinetti and Luigi Brandolini, both engineer inspectors.[44] Their brief report, submitted on 19 April, focused initially on just Valadier's project and one of Salvi's two.[45] These they found to be extremely similar in all basic features, though they preferred Valadier's project for certain aspects and Salvi's for others. The last third of their document reviewed Salvi's other proposal: a "grandiose Temple" that they found commendable but were obliged to dismiss out of hand because it failed to restrain costs or to evoke the image of the old basilica. Not that they were looking for direct iconic references: when Salvi had first submitted his reduced-size project to della Somaglia, he had admitted that it did not recall the *form* of the old basilica but compensated by recalling instead its magnificent *character*. It was likely on account of the overwhelming need to restrain costs that della Somaglia and later his council were willing to let such sophistry pass without comment.

The three evaluators concluded nonetheless that a bit more could to be done to highlight the connection between the new and old churches, and so Martinetti, seconded by his two colleagues, drew up a remarkable project of his own that further developed the ideas of Valadier and Salvi.[46] This was submitted separately to Cristaldi (and probably also to della Somaglia) on 16 April, and then echoed in more general terms in the conclusion of the trio's official report three days later.[47]

Martinetti's idea was to erect a church over the transept of the old basilica, as Salvi and Valadier had proposed, but to retain the old east–west orientation and turn the ruins of the old façade and nave walls into a public entrance precinct – *in their ruined state*. Within this desolate precinct, to the east, the new façade of the rebuilt church would rise up like a phoenix:

> ... one could not imagine a more appropriate and decorous entry to the new church than in passing through the ruins of the burned out basilica, which would form a kind of vestibule. Such ruins could not help but stir sentiments of religious veneration, and as precious monuments of Sacred antiquity they would be esteemed just as we see the many remains of Pagan antiquity jealously preserved, and exposed to view whenever they are concealed by other structures.[48]

An unattributed drawing in the Archive of the Monastery of San Paolo may represent Martinetti's project, or at least another very like it (**Plate 7**). Had this extraordinary project been carried out, it would have gone quite some way toward undercutting the common historiographical prejudice that sees Roman architecture of this period as conventional and unengaged with contemporary reassessments of aesthetic experience. It is not just that the project tapped weirdly into the vein of resentment shown by early partisans of sacred archaeology like Andrés or Vermiglioli, who had marveled that their contemporaries valued pagan ruins more than Christian ones. More significant is how vividly it illustrated the resonance that Romantic aesthetics of subjectivity and open-endedness, the concrete and the specific, the violent and the melancholy, could have amid this atmosphere of Catholic defiance and resentment.[49] We shall revisit this theme further ahead.

FUTURE VISIONS

That resonance is again highlighted when we learn that Pope Leo himself announced something quite similar to Martinetti's project just a few weeks later. In May 1824, his second encyclical, *Quod Hoc Ineunte*, proclaimed 1825 a Jubilee year.[50] The pontiff implored the Catholic faithful to make the pilgrimage to Rome so that they could energize their faith by visiting "the basilicas of the blessed Peter and Paul, and also those of St. John Lateran and of St. Mary Major, at least once a day for thirty continuous or interpolated days." The basilica of the blessed Paul was of course a charred ruin at this point, yet this was exactly what Leo had in mind: pilgrims attending masses inside the ruined basilica for the whole Jubilee year. Leo might have been inspired by Martinetti's project, or perhaps it was Martinetti who learned of Leo's intentions and was inspired by them. Either way, the announcement placed the potent image of the ravaged temple front and center. One can well imagine how those venerable broken walls would have been exploited as the image of an embattled Church, wounded but not destroyed by the conflagration of modern godlessness, and yet capable of rising anew through the devotion of the faithful.

A little less than two months after this proclamation, Leo made an apostolic visit to San Paolo to commemorate the first anniversary of the fire, and there he got a first taste of what such open-air masses would actually feel like.[51] As reported in *Diario di Roma*, Leo performed liturgical functions under the blue canopy of a July sky before then visiting the chapel where St. Paul's chains were displayed. Gazing out over the ruins, the pontiff "displayed intense sadness and expressed his determination to get to work as soon as possible on rebuilding this temple, at least its eastern parts where the sepulcher of the Holy Apostle is venerated." That "at least" hardly suggested a ringing endorsement of the half-size projects being proposed by Valadier and Salvi. It must have given Valadier pause also to note that the pontiff was not inclined to experience San Paolo as the disinterested aesthetic beholder imagined by classical theory. Leo seems instead to have responded emotionally to the melancholy narratives the ruin brought forth in his subjective mind.

NOTES

1   Uggeri (1823; 2nd ed. 1825). On this text, see also Groblewski (2001), p. 20 n. 25 and pp. 47–51. The first and second editions both bear the date 30 July 1823, but the second names Leo XII as pope and identifies Uggeri as Secretary to the Special Congregation overseeing the reconstruction, which was only founded in March 1825. On Uggeri, see Moreschi (1837; reprinted with additions in *Cosmorama Pittorico* [Milan] 10:9 [1844]: 66–67); Fabi Montani (1838 and [1837]); Colini (1973); Roberts (2015).

2   Valadier (1833), pp. 15–24; Jonsson (1986), pp. 99–130. Since the time of Quatremère de Quincy, it has been claimed that these reconstructions aimed to distinguish the ancient and modern fabric by the use of different materials. But the travertine of the Arch and the brick of the Colosseum were actually dictated by economy, and were intended to be concealed beneath surface coloring (Fancelli [2008], pp. 270–271).

3 Uggeri (1823), p. 3.
4 Uggeri (1823), pp. 6–8.
5 See the discussion in Groblewski (2001), pp. 42–52.
6 Fea (1813); Ridley (1992a), pp. 154–156, 164.
7 Milizia (1787); Lesueur (1877); Pasquali (1995); Pinon (1995).
8 Uggeri (1817), ch. 15.
9 Nagel and Wood (2010), p. 13; pp. 29–34.
10 De Romanis (1823), p. 35.
11 De Romanis (1823), p. 37.
12 De Romanis (1823), p. 37.
13 Similar concerns were raised by the architect Carlo Donati ("Idea per fare il miglior Progetto di ristauro della Basilica Ostiense," 14 January 1824 [ASR: Camerale III b.1909, #28]).
14 Giuseppe Valadier, "Scandaglio del ristauro della Basilica di S. Paolo," 18 August 1823 (ASR: CSRBSP Segreteria b.276, f.1). See also Groblewski (2001), pp. 29–35.
15 Servi (1840; originally published serially in *Il Tiberino* in 1839); Ciampi (1870); Marconi (1964); Debenedetti (2008), v. 3, pp. 7–30.
16 *DdR*, 20 August 1823, 1.
17 Marconi (1964), pp. 215 ff.
18 Petruccioli and Terranova (1981); Boutry (1997), p. 331.
19 Ciampi (1870), pp. 21, 39–40.
20 Leflon (1951), p. 384.
21 *Cronaca* II, 26 October 1823; *DdR*, 31 October 1823, 1.
22 Andrea Alippi, "Scandaglio per il ristauro della Nave grande della Venble Basilica di S Paolo," 16 August 1823 (ASP: 32/c, b. 1828–1850, f.1); Pasquale Belli and Andrea Alippi, "Scandaglio per il ristauro della Nave traverza della Ven.ble Basilica di S. Paolo," 16 August 1823 (ASR: Camerale III b. 1909, #21). Belli and Alippi had previously submitted estimates for the repair of elements damaged by the fire.
23 Cf. Betti (1833); *DdR*, 2 November 1833, pp. 21–23; Sette (1987); Di Marco (2006).
24 Betti (1833), pp. 359–360, 364–365; Sette (1987), p. 492.
25 The crypt was long attributed to Belli alone, but Mirko Santanicchia ([2017], pp. 320–321) has recently illuminated Brizi's role.
26 Sette (1987), pp. 491–492. Belli and Brizi's work was replaced in the early twentieth century with a neo-Romanesque design.
27 Giovanni Francesco Zelli, "Progetto …onde ripristinare la memoranda Basilica di S. Paolo," 1 December 1823 (ASR: Camerale III b. 1909, #24 and CSRBSP Segreteria b. 282; ASP: 30/c, libro rosso 1; tiG pp. 284–287).
28 Giovanni Francesco Zelli, "Progetto …onde ripristinare la memoranda Basilica di S. Paolo," 1 December 1823 (ASR: Camerale III b. 1909, #24 and CSRBSP Segreteria b. 282; ASP: 30/c, libro rosso 1; tiG pp. 284–287).
29 Wiseman (1858), p. 235.
30 *Cronaca* II, 22 December 1823; Marconi (1964), p. 216.
31 Marconi (1964), p. 216.
32 Giuseppe Valadier, "Progetto per la Basilica di S. Paolo …," 1823 (ASR: Camerale III b.1909, #25). Discussed and mostly reproduced by Marconi (1964), pp. 216–219. See also Pallottino (1995), pp. 38–40; Pallottino (1997), pp. 329–330; Groblewski (2001), pp. 39–42. The drawings are at: BiASA, Sala Lanciani, Roma XI. 100. 179.
33 Giuseppe Valadier to Belisario Cristaldi, 19 November 1825 (ASR: Camerale III b. 1909, #33; Camerale III b. 1910, #143; ASP: 30/c, libro rosso 2).
34 Valadier used this formula elsewhere; see Marconi (1964), pp. 125, 131.
35 Antonio Santelli, "Progetto per procurare i mezzi onde riedificare la famosa Basilica di S. Paolo," 1823 (ASR: CSRBSP Segreteria b.276, f.1; discussed in Groblewski [2001], pp. 38–39 [tiG pp. 287–290]; and Calzolari [2012], pp. 91–93).

36 The news was reported first in northern Italy: *Gazzetta di Milano*, 23 July 1823, p. 1239; *Giornale della Provincia Bresciana* (Brescia), 25 July 1823, p. 268; *Gazzetta Piemontese* (Turin), 26 July 1823, p. 448. It reached French and English newspapers by early August: *The Times* (London), 2 August 1823, p. 2d, and 5 August 1823, p. 2b; *The Gentleman's Magazine* (London), 93:2 (August 1823), p. 172; *The London Literary Gazette*, 9 August 1823, p. 511; *L'ami de la Religion* (Paris), 20 August 1823, pp. 39–41; *The Christian's Pocket Magazine and Anti-Sceptic* (London) 9:3 (September 1823), p. 505. It then reached the United States, in reports mostly but not always drawn from British papers: *Providence Patriot*, 17 September 1823, p. 2; *Baltimore Patriot and Mercantile Advertiser*, 18 September 1823, p. 2; *Village Register and Norfolk County Advertiser*, 19 September 1823, p. 190; *Niles' Weekly Register* (Baltimore), 20 September 1823, p. 43; *Trenton Federalist*, 22 September 1823, p. 2; *New Hampshire Patriot & State Gazette* (Concord), 22 September 1823, p. 2; *Saratoga Sentinel*, 23 September 1823, p. 2; *Watch-Tower* (Cooperstown), 29 September 1823, p. 2; *Portsmouth Journal of Literature and Politics*, 4 October 1823, p. 3; *Trenton Federalist*, 6 October 1823, p. 2; *Providence Gazette*, 15 October 1823, p. 1; *American Mercury* (Hartford), 21 October 1823, p. 2; *Village Register* (Dedham), 24 October 1823, p. 2; *Farmer's Cabinet* (Amherst), 1 November 1823, p. 2; *New Hampshire Sentinel* (Keene), 7 November 1823, p. 2; etc.

37 Wiseman (1858), p. 236.

38 For instance: Francesco Santini, "Progetto di ricostruzione della basilica di San Paolo," 1 May 1824 (private collection; published by Fiumi Sermattei [2013], p. 205). Francesco Paccagnini also submitted a proposal (Belisario Cristaldi to Francesco Paccagnini, 24 September 1824 (ASR: Camerale III b.1909, #35).

39 Donati (14 January 1824), as in Chapter. 3 n.1 3.

40 See also Groblewski (2001), pp. 52–57. On Salvi, see Visconti (1850); Cerutti Fusco (2002), (2007), (2008).

41 Giuseppe Venturoli, Luigi Brandolini, and Giambattista Martinetti to Giulio Maria della Somaglia, 19 April 1824 (ASR: Camerale III b. 1909, #32; also in b. 1910, #122 [incorrectly dated 1825]).

42 Pasquale Belli and Andrea Alippi, "Rapporto," 19 February 1824 (ASR: Camerale III b. 1909, #29).

43 Gaspare Salvi, "Scandagli di due progetti per la riedificazione della Basilica di S. Paolo dell'Architetto Gaspare Salvi," Rome; March [?] 1824 (AAV: Segreteria di Stato; Spogli dei Cardinali; Della Somaglia Giulio, b. 2B, f.E).

44 See Verdi (1997), p. 214.

45 Venturoli et al. (19 April 1824), as in Chapter 3 n. 41. See Pallottino (1995), pp. 38–40; Groblewski (2001), pp. 53–56.

46 On Martinetti: Betti (1830; partly reprinted in *L'architetto girovago* 2 [1842]: 31–34); Ceccarelli (2020).

47 Giambattista Martinetti to Belisario Cristaldi, 16 April 1824 (ASR: Camerale III b. 1909, #31).

48 Venturoli et al. (19 April 1824), as in Chapter 3 n. 41.

49 For an alternative view, see Groblewski (2001), p. 54).

50 *TEPD*, v. 3, pp. 19–25; *DdR*, 24 July 1824, p. 1.

51 *Cronaca* II, 18 July 1824; *DdR*, 24 July 1824, p. 1.

FOUR

BROADENING THE DEBATE

O N 22 JUNE 1824, VALADIER PRESENTED THE ARTS COUNCIL WITH A revised version of his initial project for a new San Paolo.[1] None of the surviving drawings that relate to this project correspond in all details to the description in Valadier's memorandum, nor do they all accord with one another, yet clearly Valadier's revised project had absorbed key features from Martinetti's proposal. It jettisoned the north–south reorientation of his initial project and reinstated the main entrance to the west, eliminating the north-facing façade from the original project (although in some drawings it remains as a secondary entrance) (**Figures 27** and **28**). In all the drawings, the entrance to the basilica precinct is now through the old eighteenth-century narthex to the west, which gives into the open courtyard where the nave had been. The memorandum speaks of a "portico running throughout" the former nave, and most of the surviving drawings illustrate this as a roundheaded arcade supported on columns running on all four sides of the courtyard, in an obvious echo of the old main arcade (**Plate 8**). The surviving plan, however, suggests that the old narthex was to be demolished entirely, save the distinctively rhythmed series of paired and single columns ornamenting its front, which was to remain as a ghostly screen, like the ancient columns before the façade of San Lorenzo in Milan[2] (**Figure 27**). Valadier's memorandum stated that whereas in the original project the salvageable columns of the nave arcade were to be reused in the new church, in this revised project they were to remain standing, isolated, in what would now be an open courtyard. But this

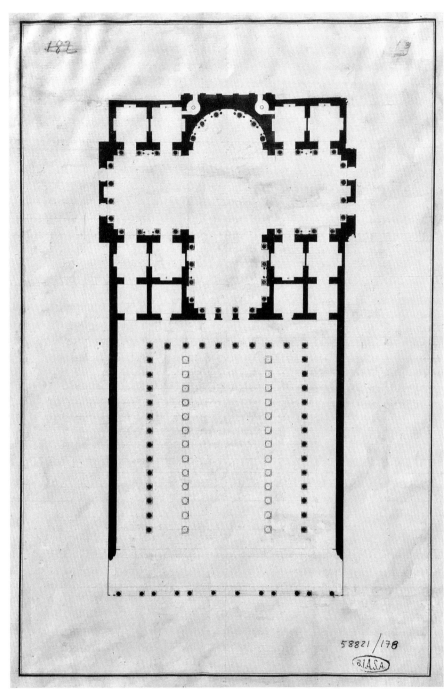

27. Giuseppe Valadier (assisted by Gaspare Salvi), plan, revised project for San Paolo, June 1824.
Source: © Istituto Nazionale di Archeologia e Storia dell'Arte, Rome.

28. Giuseppe Valadier (assisted by Gaspare Salvi), lateral exterior elevation, revised project for San Paolo, June 1824.
Source: © Accademia Nazionale di San Luca, Roma.

puzzling configuration is not illustrated in any of the surviving illustrations.[3] Looming over this courtyard was the high façade of Valadier's new church, with the old Arch of Galla Placidia reconfigured as a giant thermal window (**Figure 29**). The interior then offered a modern classical space: three short arms covered by coffered barrel vaults, the old apse with its mosaic to the east, and a crossing covered by a coffered pendentive dome pierced by a glazed oculus (**Plate 8** and **Figure 30**). The confessio and papal altar were to be shifted several feet to the east so as to stand directly under this oculus. The columns along the interior walls would no longer be salvaged or reconstituted from the old church but were instead to be of new stone.

While it is entertaining to watch a neoclassicist like Valadier trying (with surprising grace) to reconcile himself to Romantic demands, it is easy to discern from his memorandum how he really felt. Virtually every comment underlined how this revised project would reduce the amount of material that could be reused in the new church, and how this would drive up costs and limit its ability to recall the old basilica. He attributed not a single advantage to it, and in places almost actively campaigned against it. He clearly preferred his original idea. But he was also beginning to recognize that it was ineffective to pitch his arguments on the basis of aesthetic purity and classical coherence. It was the economics that mattered.

29. Giuseppe Valadier (assisted by Gaspare Salvi), west elevation (left; section through courtyard) and east exterior elevation (right), revised project for San Paolo, June 1824.
Source: © 2022 Archivio Storico dell'Abbazia di San Paolo f.l.m.

This revised project received no immediate response. On 30 July, Valadier fired off an exasperated letter to Cristaldi dismissing all discussions thus far as too uninformed by the real difficulties the reconstruction entailed, and demanding that a committee of professors of architecture, sculpture, painting, and literature be convened and charged with determining which project was the best.[4]

This did not happen, but Cristaldi may have been stirred to make a new push on Valadier's behalf, for in September a breakthrough occurred. The first hint came on 20 September when Valadier went before a Roman notary to foreswear compensation for any future work he might undertake at San Paolo.[5] He did so almost certainly because he had knowledge of what was to follow four days later: official word that Pope Leo had approved his design for San Paolo, and was appointing him architect director for the project.[6] This victory, however, came with stipulations: Leo decreed that Salvi was to be Valadier's associate on the project, and together they were obliged to accept the modifications requested by the Arts Council by returning the church to its original orientation and retaining the ruined nave as an entrance vestibule. Pope Leo had apparently savored this pungent Romantic concept – one that would have been avant-garde anywhere in Europe at this date – with its juxtaposition of ruins and new construction evoking a poetic narrative of

30. Detail of Plate 8 showing the church interior.
Source: © Accademia Nazionale di San Luca, Roma.

death and resurrection, tragedy and redemption, and a venerable past embracing a resolute present.

Valadier's appointment occurred against a background of controversy connected with that year's relaunch of the Concorso Clementino, the triannual student art competition of the Academy of St. Luke, which had been in suspension since the time of the French occupations.[7] The First Class Architecture competition for the 1824 relaunch had been published at the start of May, right around the time of Leo XII's proclamation of the 1825 Jubilee. It invited student contestants to imagine a "magnificent temple" to replace the gutted San Paolo, in the "same location and position"; one that in restoring in the best proportions the sublime beauty of the internal colonnades, adds to them also the decorousness of external peristyles, and, retaining all the usages to which the old Basilica was destined, forms from them one of the most majestic temples of Christianity, in accordance with the laws of the most severe and elegant architecture.[8]

Six young competitors presented themselves.[9] Pietro Camporese and Quintiliano Raimondi were pedigreed Romans from established architectural families. Three others were provincials: Gaetano Gnassi was from Iesi in the Marche, Francesco Patane was Sicilian, and Giovanni Molli was from Novara in the Kingdom of Sardinia. And finally there was the mysterious Sempliciano Jourdan, about whom nothing is known. The competition brief asked each architect for a large-scale plan, a front and side elevation, and at least one interior section.[10] These were to be submitted anonymously in mid-September, marked with only a motto. The jury would then assign each one a number, and under that number they were to be exhibited publicly on the Capitoline from 19 to 26 September. This turned out to be the very week in which Leo XII awarded Valadier the commission to build the project discussed in the previous section.[11]

The exhibition that week stimulated lively discussions in Rome. The visiting Karl Friedrich Schinkel saw it and wrote in his diary of an evening spent with Baron von Bunsen and guests in the Palazzo Caffarelli debating the projects and brainstorming their own solutions.[12] Pope Leo visited on 27 September, one day after the exhibition had closed to the public, and on 29 September the nine members of the architecture jury met to decide the winner. Four we have already encountered: Valadier, Salvi, Martinetti, and Belli. The other five were Clemente Folchi, Giacomo Palazzi, Pietro Bracci, Giovanni Domenico Navone, and the jury president, Girolamo Scaccia. All nine were members of the architects' class at the Academy. The minutes of their deliberations show that it ended up being a tight contest between two projects, #1 and #4, whose authors can be identified from other documents in the Academy archive.[13]

Project	Architect	YES	NO
#1	Gnassi	5	4
#4	Molli	4	5
#5	Camporese	3	6
#6	Raimondi	3	6
#2	Jourdan	0	9
#3	Patane	0	9

The intention of the winner, Gnassi, to recall the form of the old basilica in his project is immediately apparent[14] (**Figures 31** and **32**). The entire footprint

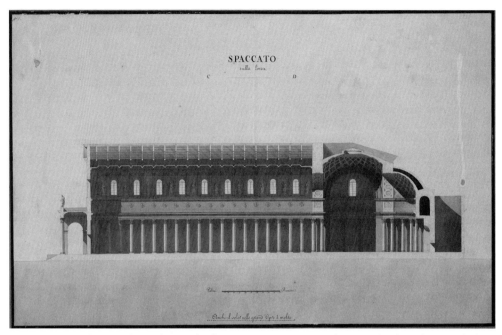

31. Gaetano Gnassi, longitudinal section, winning project for a new basilica of San Paolo fuori le mura, Concorso Clementino 1824, first-class competition in architecture.
Source: © Accademia Nazionale di San Luca, Roma.

of the basilica is reoccupied, an impressive colonnade once again dominates the nave, and the main elevation preserves the old papal portrait medallions and lancet windows of the original building. It is not an *in pristinum* project, as Gnassi also introduces a flat entablature and coffered ceiling along with a west façade with narthex of the kind often added to Early Christian churches during the seventeenth and eighteenth centuries. His crossing and apse are also novel, and more in line with the norms of contemporary neoclassicism. But the Early Christian echoes of the project are unmistakable, and in the minutes of the jury deliberations his is the only project credited with resembling the old basilica.[15] The other entrants' submissions do not survive, but a sense of what they might have looked like is possibly provided by an unofficial Concorso project submitted directly to Leo XII by the architect Francesco Santini of Bologna: this depicts a multidomed basilica in a rich Vitruvian idiom, with echoes of Renaissance classics such as St. Peter's and Sant'Andrea in Mantua (**Figure 33**).

As soon as the tally giving Gnassi his victory was announced, a dispute erupted in the jury room. The four jurors who had voted for Molli's Project #4 – they were Valadier, Salvi, Belli, and Martinetti – insisted that the verdict be annulled and Molli be declared the victor.[16] The president of the jury, Scaccia, declared that there were no grounds for annulment, so the disgruntled four lodged a complaint with the venerable Cardinal Camerlengo Pacca. He too refused to intervene. Nearly a month later, the other competitors

BROADENING THE DEBATE

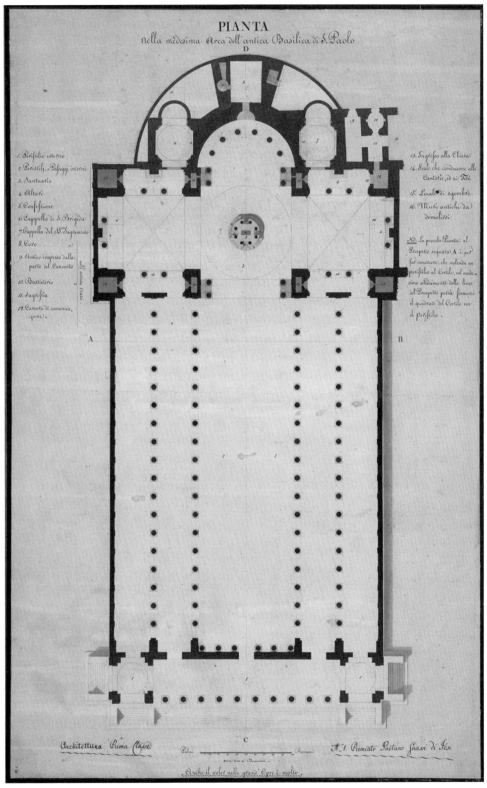

32. Gaetano Gnassi, plan, winning project for a new basilica of San Paolo fuori le mura, Concorso Clementino 1824, first-class competition in architecture.
Source: © Accademia Nazionale di San Luca, Roma.

33. Francesco Santini, project for a new basilica of San Paolo fuori le mura, devised in May 1824 in response to that year's Concorso Clementino but not entered into competition. *Source*: Private collection.

addressed a jointly signed complaint to Leo XII asking that the verdict be overturned, claiming that his project had been plagiarized and that all Rome was abuzz with the scandal.[17] But by then Gnassi had been publicly premiated, and so this too came to nothing.

It is easy to imagine what troubled Valadier, Salvi, Belli, and Martinetti. The Academy was about to publicly bestow a very prestigious award on a project that ran directly counter to the kind of reduced-scale solution that Valadier, with input from Martinetti, Salvi, and Belli's associate Alippi, had just been commissioned by the pope to execute. They probably warned that Gnassi's victory was a provocative contradiction of the Holy Father's recently settled decision on the matter. But in the absence of more information about the other projects, and especially about Molli's Project #4, a fuller understanding of this altercation has remained elusive. A close reading of old sources, however, along with some new archival discoveries, now permit a complete account to be presented. This reveals that the controversy was far more closely tied than previously thought to contemporary debates about the reconstruction of the actual basilica.

It is worth noting that the subject of the architecture competition of the Concorso had been the result of a last-minute change. Back on 2 May, one day *after* the competition briefs were supposed to have been published, the governing council of the Academy of St. Luke met to change the program from "An isolated temple to be used as a large baptistry for a great capital," selected back in March, to a "magnificent basilica" to replace San Paolo. Why would certain parties within the governing council have wanted to change the competition program? At the time, the change was rather unconvincingly justified with reference to the election of a new member to the council, the papal architect Giovanni Domenico Navone (who later became one of the five jurors who voted for Gnassi).[18] But the timing suggests that other factors might have been in play, for the meeting at which the change was voted fell just days after Martinetti had presented his idea for a reduced-scale church with the ruined nave as an entrance court. It is certainly possible that the traction such reduced-scale projects were starting to get prompted the opponents of such a solution to try to use the upcoming Concorso to direct public attention to the matter. If so, their gambit proved extremely effective.

With respect to the five losing projects, there exist two written sources: the minutes of the jury deliberations, and a review of the exhibition published several months after the exhibition closed by the critic Enrico Lovery in the *Memorie romane di antichità e belle arti*.[19] Neither is particularly voluble. The jury minutes consist of bullet-point remarks, whereas Lovery refers briefly to just three projects: those of Raimondi, Camporese, and Molli. His complimentary but rather generic comments reveal little about the actual form of the projects, though he is especially admiring of Molli's project, which "asks to be examined at length," and is "imagined with intelligence equal to the beauty of the style in which it is carried out." But it is what he says next that is most noteworthy: "We say this [about Molli's project] without concealing the burning desire within our soul to see that venerable basilica reborn with its old plan, the majesty of which could perhaps be reduced but never increased." The clear implication is that Molli's project did *not* reproduce that plan; otherwise, the remark makes no sense. Lovery's review was published after Gnassi's controversial victory was a fait accompli, and, as he states more than once, he had no wish to provoke a scandal. All the same, he did not even mention Gnassi's winning project, but instead resumed his praise of Molli's project in the very next line, hymning its "simple and uncommon nobility," its "sweet gradation of scale," and its success at "distilling from [all this] an ensemble of the best proportions."[20]

The big question, of course, given Lovery's remark about the plan, is whether Molli's project was a reduced-scale project of the type Valadier, Salvi, and the others had proposed. The jury minutes note in their second line that Molli's project "exceeds in its length the prescribed limits, having included also a courtyard." This is the only project that the minutes mention as having had a courtyard, and the language would fit a scheme that turned the old nave into a court with an entrance pavilion of some kind. Indeed, the next line of the minutes criticizes what seems to be just such a feature: "one notes the defect of the useless anti-temple, dark, and the [bad] proportions of the overly long middle portion."

Drawings recently discovered in Molli's previously unstudied family archive now offer additional evidence.[21] The finished competition drawings are not among them, but there is a series of mostly plans, some of which are explicitly labeled by Molli as San Paolo projects from 1824, as well as several sketches from the same year that were also clearly executed in the context of the Concorso. A first group is comprised of two large drawings showing a full longitudinal basilica plan, accompanied by a series of detached flaps showing alternatives for different elements[22] (**Figure 34**). There is also a written key for another plan which no longer survives.[23] Given that Lovery's text suggests that Molli's project did not have a longitudinal basilica plan, and given also that none of this group of drawings depicts the courtyard described in the jury minutes, we may safely conclude that this group does not depict Molli's final design.

But the second group of drawings, also labeled in the architect's hand as projects for San Paolo, depict exactly the kind of reduced-scale plan proposed by Valadier et al. The largest is a tracing of Nicolai's plan of the old basilica, upon which Molli has faintly sketched some basic ideas for a reduced church covering just the area of the old transept. The orientation is west–east, and the nave is clearly transformed into a court.[24] Another drawing offers a more developed variant in pen, pencil, and ink[25] (**Figure 35**). This reduced San Paolo is centered on Paul's *confessio*, with the old apse to the east flanked by chapels, two short transept arms to the north and south, and a west arm at the entrance. A temple-front west façade is indicated by four in-antis columns standing forward into the courtyard occupying the former nave. To either side are groups of three smaller columns standing where the aisle arcades formerly began. How exactly Molli had organized the rest of the courtyard to the west, we do not know, for the lower half of the sheet has been torn away, as proven by the cutoff text in the lower-right-hand corner ("S. Pa—," and below that, "Molli Giovanni de—"). Various other sketches in the archive may depict sections of this reduced-plan version of the basilica.[26]

Between Lovery's comments, the description in the jury minutes, and now these plans, it seems all but certain that Molli's controversial Concorso entry was a reduced-scale project reoccupying only the transept of the old basilica with an open courtyard occupying the former nave. This explains the controversy that erupted after Gnassi's victory, which effectively ranged the prestige of the Academy *against* the type of solution that the pope, just five days earlier,

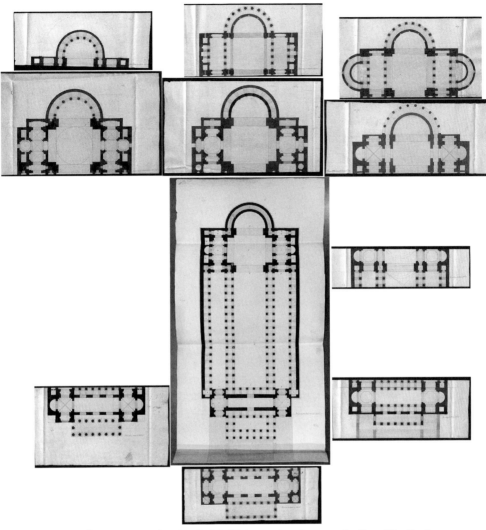

34. Giovanni Molli, preparatory drawing for Molli's lost project for a new basilica of San Paolo for the 1824 Concorso Clementino.
Source: Fondazione Achille Marazza, Fondo Giovanni Molli, GM 66 doc. 18/1-12 – documento riprodotto per gentile concessione della Fondazione A. Marazza di Borgomanero.

had commissioned Valadier to execute, and *in favor of* those who clamored for the sort of full-scale reconstruction the government had ruled out. Given this, it is tempting to speculate that Pacca had refused to intervene because he already sensed or perhaps even knew what future events indeed bore out – namely, that Leo's support for Valadier's project was weak, and that influential voices in the pope's orbit were making progress convincing him that an *in pristinum* solution could work. Valadier might have been aware too, for on the final day of the public exhibition, just 48 hours *after* he had received the commission to rebuild San Paolo, but three days *before* the controversy erupted

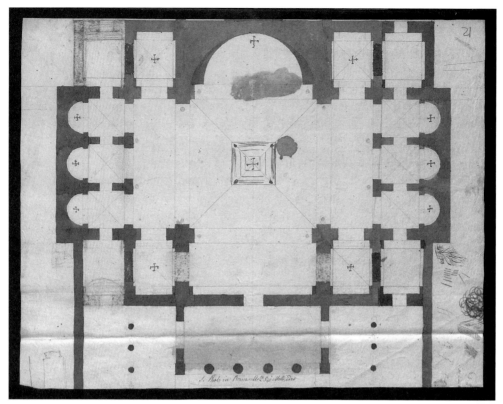

35. Giovanni Molli, architectural plan labeled "S. Paolo in Roma= Ar^{to} Gio Molli, ideō," identified here as a preparatory drawing for Molli's lost project for a new basilica of San Paolo for the 1824 Concorso Clementino.
Source: Fondazione Achille Marazza, Fondo Giovanni Molli, GM 66 doc.21 – documento riprodotto per gentile concessione della Fondazione A. Marazza di Borgomanero.

within the Concorso jury, he had fired off yet another memorandum to Cristaldi insisting that it would be a tragic and ruinously expensive mistake to attempt to rebuild San Paolo as it had been before the fire.[27] It is difficult to see why he would write such a thing just days after receiving the commission to build a reduced basilica, unless it was because he already sensed that the full-scale solution was somehow again in play, perhaps in connection with the responses being elicited by the Concorso exhibition.

And of course on the day after *that*, Pope Leo visited the exhibition. The juror Clemente Folchi later wrote that Leo had paused before the works "one by one," and that he had "spoken about them, and commended them."[28] The *Diario di Roma* reported that Leo "spent a substantial amount of time discussing each of the exhibited projects," while at the prize ceremony in the Senate Palace on the Capitoline a few days later, the jury president, Scaccia, as he awarded Gnassi his prize, reiterated that the pontiff had personally examined and commented on every project.[29] We have no evidence as to what Leo actually thought or said, of course, but perhaps his misgivings about Valadier's reduced church grew into full-blown doubts upon seeing such a design side by side with Gnassi's bigger, bolder solution. It might even have made some difference that Gnassi hailed from Iesi, less than 40 kilometers from Leo's ancestral town of Genga. Certainly some of Leo's closest advisors are on record as having regretted the triviality of the other designs – for instance, his Commissioner of Antiquities, Carlo Fea, who in recalling the exhibition to the pontiff a few months later advised that "the worst outcome would be to adopt one of those childish projects [recently] exhibited on the Capitoline."[30]

What is certain is that the Concorso exhibition reanimated public discussion of the basilica and crystalized for some contemporaries a sense of how much would be lost if a modern and reduced project were executed – just as the Academy's governing council probably hoped when they changed the competition brief back in May.

By this point in our story, the basic positions in the debate have been staked out. One is Valadier's position in favor of a new and modern church. Valadier's project conformed to Roman tradition in every respect aside from its diminutive size, and that was not Valadier's choice but rather reflected the dire realities of the pontifical government's financial situation. In Valadier's view, the project fulfilled the government's needs in the best possible way: it housed Paul's tomb with grandeur and dignity by satisfying the most universal aspirations of the fine arts, it attended thoughtfully to the needs of memory, and it did so economically and realistically.

Then there is the position of Valadier's opponents, who held that the old basilica ought to be rebuilt as close as possible to the way it was *ante incendium*. The only version of this solution that we have seen in any in detail thus far is Uggeri's slightly eccentric one, though we will encounter others in the pages to come. Gnassi's design may be said to have gestured in that direction as well, to a much lesser extent. Based on the survey in Chapter 1, we can agree that *in pristinum* approaches were all but unprecedented. We have also begun to sense what will become clear in the following chapter, which is that this solution was especially favored by conservative revanchists among the clergy and Roman intellectual elite: men who in their different ways had grown impatient with the pragmatism, worldliness, and disenchantment of the Consalvi years and who were energized by Leo XII's ardor for institutional renewal. For men of this stripe, *in pristinum* solutions could represent a rejection of present-day cosmopolitanism; a way of communing with a heroic Early Christian past; a response to a summons from God Almighty; a rejection of deflating claims that the modern Church was in decline; or simply a flat refusal to accept the wound inflicted by the fire.

Somewhere between these two positions stood the Martinetti variant, which Pope Leo, probably at the urging of Cristaldi and della Somaglia, had selected for execution by Valadier. A compromise within a compromise, this approach first of all satisfied the paramount demand for economy. It centered on a new and diminished church that spoke a contemporary architectural language. But with its uncanny juxtapositions of old and new, of ruins and the newly built, it also reached for the kinds of responses that formed the appeal of the *in pristinum* solution: not the satisfactions of disinterested aesthetic contemplation, but rather a subjective contemplation of historical, institutional, and religious narratives that were perceived to inhere in meaningful rather than ostensibly beautiful forms. Indeed, this approach reached further in that direction than the *in pristinum* solution and tried to tell a more complex tale as well.

There are paradoxes aplenty in all this. Not, perhaps, in the fact that conservatives were the cultural innovators here, nor that a pope like Leo XII should have finally chosen an even more innovative solution, for cultural innovation is never the province of any particular ideological tendency. But it is perplexing that the most aesthetically relativistic solutions were embraced by a party that excoriated all forms of relativism; that these defiant essentialists should have so hated Valadier's architectural vision, which was rooted in an essentialist belief in true and false architecture; or, to turn it around, that the most traditional solution should have been regarded by the traditionalists as an innovation. A fuller analysis of these apparent paradoxes may be postponed for now, as the story has plenty of twists and turns still to come. It is enough for now to signal their presence and to suggest that, more than merely a sign of changing aesthetic sensibilities, they point to much deeper changes unfolding in the worldviews of the historical actors concerned.

NOTES

1 Giuseppe Valadier, "Osservazioni sulle varie circostanze che accompagnono l'esecuzione dei due progetti fatti dal sottoscritto per la restaurazione della Basilica di S. Paolo ...," 22 June 1824 (ASR: Camerale III b. 1909, #33; transcribed in Marconi [1964], pp. 222–223). See Pallottino (1995), pp. 38–40; Pallottino (1997), pp. 329–330; Groblewski (2001), pp. 55–56; and Pallottino (2003), pp. 490–401. The drawings, which have been variously linked to this project by the aforelisted authors, are distributed across three Roman archives. Drawings showing the elevations and sections are at the ASL and ASP; some of these are published by Pallottino (2003), p. 491. A copy of the plan is at the BiASA in the Lanciani collection (Roma XI 100 A 178). A modified version of the project was later published by Valadier in the *Giornale di belle arti* (1 [1830]: 13 and Tav. V) and in his *Opere* (Valadier, 1833).
2 The area between the so-called Colonne di San Lorenzo and the basilica was still clogged with houses in 1824, but Valadier would have known the original arrangement.
3 The plan could also be read as indicating an intention to mark the column locations on the pavement.

4   Giuseppe Valadier, "Osservazioni preliminari da farsi per disporre, ed ordinare le preparazioni, e tutt'altro alla riedificazione della Basilica di S. Paolo fuori le mura," 30 July 1824 (ASR: Camerale III b. 1909, #33).

5   Valadier claimed that he did this "on account of my particular devotion to Saint Paul" (Marconi [1964], p. 225).

6   Belisario Cristaldi to Giuseppe Valadier, 24 September 1824 (ASR: Camerale III b. 1909, #33).

7   For more detail, see Wittman (2021); see also Caniglia (2002).

8   Folchi (1824), pp. 3–4.

9   Elenco dei Sig. i Concorrenti al Premio Clementino a di 15 sett. 1824, 15 September 1824 (AASL: v. 74, no. 568). For biographies of the six competitors, see Caniglia (2002), pp. 384–385.

10 Concorso announcement *bando* of 1 May 1824 (AASL: *Miscellanea Concorsi* I, no. 16). Reproduced in Caniglia (2002), p. 375.

11 "Elenco," as in Chapter 4 n. 9.

12 Riemann ed. (1979), p. 212 (diary entry between 5 and 9 October 1824).

13 AASL, v. 74, no. 814; published in Groblewski (2001), pp. 294–297. Caniglia (2002), pp. 387–388 (AASL: *Miscellanea Concorsi* I, no. 18).

14 Little is known about Gnassi. In addition to the details reported by Caniglia (2002), p. 384, an article from 1841 reports that Gnassi bore a striking resemblance to the famous portrait of Vignola in the *Regola delli cinqve ordini*, but despite this good omen went on to a mediocre architectural career cut short by an untimely death (Gasparoni [1841b], pp. 165–166).

15 Gnassi may even have based his project in part on the reconstruction of the Basilica Ulpia produced in 1823 by the French *pensionnaire* Jean-Baptiste Lesueur (Lesueur [1877]).

16 Giuseppe Valadier, Gaspare Salvi, Pasquale Belli, and Giambattista Martinetti, "Giudizio del Concorso Clementino di 1824 " 29 September 1824 (AASL: v. 74, no. 814).

17 The initial complaint does not seem to survive but is referred to in this second complaint (ASR: Camerlengato, P. II, Tit. IV, b. 150, f. 100).

18 Caniglia (2002), pp. 362–363.

19 Lovery (1824). The minutes of the jury deliberation are in the AASL (v. 74, Nr. 814; tiG pp. 295–297).

20 Lovery (1824), p. 36.

21 FM: Archivio Arch. Giovanni Molli (1799–1865).

22 FM: GM 66/18 [1–10, 12].

23 FM: GM 66/18 [11].

24 FM: GM 66/119.

25 FM: GM 66/21.

26 For more detail, see Wittman (2021), pp. 209–228.

27 Giuseppe Valadier, "Osservazioni necessarie e preparatorie per dare le disposizioni necessarie alla Fabbrica della Basilica di S. Paolo," 26 September 1824 (ASR: Camerale III b. 1909, #33).

28 Folchi (1824), pp. 5–6.

29 *DdR*, 2 October 1824, 1.

30 Carlo Fea, "Parere dell'Avvocato Fea Commissario delle Antichità pel restauro della Basilica Ostiense," 8 November 1824 (ASR: Camerale III b. 1909, #36); transcribed in Marconi (1964), p. 227.

FIVE

REFRAMING THE DEBATE

VALADIER RESPONDED TO THE SETBACK OF THE CONCORSO CLEMENTINO by trying to make his directorship seem like a fait accompli. Before a final design had even been approved, he turned San Paolo into a buzzing hive: he submitted cost estimates for materials, reported on the 1/20 model of the old basilica, supervised nave wall demolitions, took delivery of building materials, and organized the prison laborers assigned to the project.[1] By these means, Valadier hoped to take the wind from the sails of his opponents, the most implacable and effective of whom would prove to be Commissioner of Antiquities Carlo Fea[2] (**Figure 36**). Lawyer by training and antiquarian by vocation, Fea was by 1824 the wily veteran of more than two decades of successful legal battles to preserve and protect Rome's historic monuments. He was the principal author of both the 1802 and the 1820 legislation regulating the preservation and export of antiquities and had won innumerable court cases against eminent persons caught seeking to spoliate Rome's cultural heritage. He was also an active scholar who frequently presented learned papers at the Academy of Archaeology.[3] Fea had worked with Valadier in many capacities in the past, but the two men were cut from different cloth. Fea was abrasive, deeply pious, conservative in matters of politics and culture, and gave no quarter in battle; his biographer notes that "the deplorable side of his character consisted in the harshness with which he treated his opponents."[4] Valadier would surely have agreed.

36. *Portrait of Carlo Fea*, after a drawing by Jean-Baptiste Wicar, 1813 (from Carlo Fea, *Varietà di notizie economiche fisiche antiquarie*, Rome: Bourlié, 1820).
Source: http://arachne.uni-koeln.de/item/buchseite/432552.

On 8 November 1824, Fea presented Pope Leo with a one-page "Parere" ("Opinion") on San Paolo that opened with the declaration that "the will of the Romans and the foreign public is that San Paolo should be put back the way it was before; otherwise it would no longer be recognized as the famous

San Paolo."⁵ He continued that rebuildings in the past had always retained the former building's form, including at San Paolo in the fourth century, and had always been enlargements. It would therefore be disgraceful to replace old San Paolo with a reduced-scale church. The precious old columns were a tragic loss, but Fea felt they could easily be substituted with other marbles, possibly even columns composed of drums rather than monoliths if they proved cheaper and easier to transport. What was clear, he wrote, was that the reconstruction would require support from the whole of the Christian world, and this made it essential to attend to the public's will. Punning on the name of the *paolo*, a small-denomination Roman coin, Fea wrote that the faithful "will not donate a *paolo* to transform San Paolo into some different arrangement." Therefore, and "before anything else," it was necessary to engage with public opinion, to shape but also to solicit its will "including by means of the press." It was in this document that he assured the pope that the worst thing would be "to adopt one of the childish projects exhibited [recently] on the Capitoline."

Fea's little memo was the highly concentrated first expression of a new way of approaching the reconstruction that was to gain steady momentum from this point on. At its heart was the idea that the aesthetic objections Valadier had raised, for instance about the irreproducibility of the old basilica's antique patina or its original marbles, were irrelevant. Any columns, so long as they were of respectable quality, would do. What really mattered was the historical and religious narrative. Aspects of the old basilica that were important to Catholics and to the Catholic religion had to be retained, for it would only consummate the destruction wrought by the fire to rebuild with unfamiliar forms and arrangements. Above all, the reconstruction must not become the first in Catholic history in which a major church was reduced in size and altered in form, for this would be to admit that the Church had been alienated from and diminished with respect to its own past.

In turning the emphasis to these broader narratives, Fea initiated a shift in the discussions about San Paolo from a public principally centered in Rome to the infinitely larger one of international Catholicism, whose dispersed members would only learn of the reconstruction by reading or by seeing pictures. The reconstruction was inevitably reframed by this shift, which henceforth was more and more to take on the contours of an international collective Catholic enterprise.

Following the Concorso Clementino controversy, Valadier's opponents sought to convince Pope Leo to change course and commission an *in pristinum* reconstruction. They lobbied the pontiff and his advisors behind the scenes and also organized some minor bureaucratic harassment of Valadier himself. But these familiar techniques were now supplemented by something more unusual in the Roman context: efforts to sway public opinion, as Fea had suggested, and to bring representations of that opinion, framed as the opinion or will of the faithful, to bear on government decision-making.

In principle, popes and their advisors did not consult the views of their subjects. Roman leaders utterly rejected contemporary doctrines of public opinion, believing instead that the public had not the slightest moral claim to influence government. An article on this subject appeared in the *Giornale ecclesiastico di Roma* in the very month when Leo XII rendered his final decision on San Paolo. It declared that so-called "public opinion" was in fact just the opinion of influential intellectuals which was then parroted by the chattering classes:

> ... the government [then] feels itself besieged by an imposing majority ... Even the most enlightened man will have difficulty safe-guarding himself from the influence of such a perceived majority, because the human spirit is formed in such a way that it bends to the weight of the testimonies that surround it. So one takes as the general preference of the people or as the general opinion that which is only "public opinion," which is really just the expression of the manner of thinking of the particular class of persons one is surrounded by. One believes that one is acceding to the desires of the many, but all one is really doing is following the fantasies of the few; one imagines one is pleasing the people with decisions that in reality make them shudder.[6]

Any ruler who bought into such fantasies was the dupe of what Leo and his allies identified as the Protestant principle in the sphere of politics, a principle utterly opposed to unity and order and incompatible with the Church's conception of clerical authority.[7] It is most instructive, then, to see how the will of the faithful Catholic public was evoked in the San Paolo debates and with what intended effect.

Arguments about aesthetic matters are traditionally framed as matters of taste, and in such matters the most powerful resources are expertise and social prestige: that of the artist or connoisseur in the first instance, and that of the noble or ruler who sets the tone in the second. The early advocates of the *in pristinum* solution did not possess much of either, as they were mostly middling intellectual clerics, which is why Valadier repeatedly invoked his own expert-ise in dismissing their claims. To have focused the opposition to Valadier's project on the question of architectural style would thus have been to conduct the battle on his battlefield. By shifting the fight to more favorable ground, reframing it in terms of the preservation of Roman Catholic identity, trad-itions, religious norms, and dignity, the expertise of architects and artists lost relevance. Anyone who cared about the fortunes of the Catholic Church now was entitled to hold an opinion.

The rhetorical figure of the faithful thus took on a new resonance, and this proved effective for two reasons. On the one hand, Leo XII's dreams of a popular devotional revival – one that already in 1825 the Jubilee seemed unlikely to produce – were recharged by claims that the ordinary Catholic faithful instinctively understood the challenge of the fire and therefore favored the more arduous *in pristinum* solution. Such news offered the intoxicating prospect of a unifying, popular, collective endeavor of devotion. The other big advantage of invoking the faithful was economic. By expanding the discussion to the scale of Catholic Christendom, it became possible to contemplate a vast basilica splendid enough to erase the tragedy of 15 July 1823 rather than a half-size compromise destined to perpetuate its memory. For the *in pristinum* campaign ultimately hinged on money: on showing Leo that he was not necessarily locked into what he could find in the Papal Treasury.

When phrases like "common opinion" or "public will" appear in the texts to be discussed in this chapter, they present out-of-place rhetorical figures: they do not mean quite what they would have meant in liberal contexts, but they nonetheless break startlingly with Roman tradition. They show that as relationships of dependency and authority within the Church changed, even a political language associated with the Church's enemies could come to hand in the quest for new tools with which to refashion the old relationship between the Church hierarchy and the faithful.

In January 1825, almost three months after submitting his "Parere," Fea rose among his fellow savants at the Pontifical Academy of Archaeology to speak in support of the *in pristinum* solution. Eyewitnesses reported that his address was "interrupted by frequent pauses and tears" and received "with a great deal of commotion."[8] The text was swiftly printed as a pamphlet with the title *Aneddoti sulla basilica ostiense*.[9] After some historical preliminaries, including a rehearsal of the arguments of Uggeri (who was probably in the audience) concerning the relationship of the basilica to the Basilica Ulpia, Fea settled in to entertain his audience with anecdotes about the fires and earthquakes and subsequent repairs that the basilica had endured during the Middle Ages and after. His point was to show that many "extremely expensive repairs" had been "undertaken even in the times when Rome was depopulated; in times of artistic decadence, and when pecuniary means were slight, and indubitably inferior to our own." Having established this with innumerable examples, he launched into an emotional recollection of the 1823 fire which concluded that the only consolation lay in the "sweet hope of being able to raise up anew this marvel of Rome and of the world, with the appropriate means, with the help of the religious people of our time, as in the days of yore."[10]

He turned next to the question of the form the rebuilt basilica should take. He did not mince words:

> The city is shocked and moved: away with innovations! away with the projects of ambitious academic artists! On all sides one encounters projects to change the Basilica's form with capricious ideas, through which it would lose even its very name, since it would no longer even be a basilica! Prudentius too would cry, *Te Paulus hinc exterminat!* This is not the place, say sensible people, for the sublimnity claimed by the fine arts to shine forth; it is not the place to think of what is fashionable. The fine arts serve Religion, they do not give it orders. When the respectful emperors deemed the Basilica of Constantine unworthy of the apostle of the people, they wanted his church to be larger still, and, following the model of Trajan's basilica [i.e., the Basilica Ulpia], even more magnificent than the one constructed by Constantine for the co-apostle Peter.[11]

For Fea, the fourth-century reconstruction had been the product of a glorious consensus between the Pope, the Senate, and the whole Christian people. It was "a norm of conduct" in religious architecture that when you rebuilt something, you kept its previous form: "Why did Paul V prefer the Latin Cross for the Vatican Basilica, if not from a most respectable desire to preserve the old plan, so as not to profane it in the slightest?" Rebuilt churches were never reduced in size, because the number of the faithful was always growing. What would happen, Fea asked, when immense crowds appeared in Jubilee years only to find that Valadier had reduced the church to its transept? And what would one say "to the holy apostle when he saw his great nave profaned and reduced to a grassy courtyard?" San Paolo was after all "not just any temple, dedicated to the holy apostle with an indifferent memory"; it was a building that lived "in the mind, in the heart, and in the books of Rome, and of all the Christian world, to whom it belongs equally." The stakes could scarcely be higher, for "the temple that the modern idealist innovators want to build is arbitrary, more ambitious than reasoned."[12] One had no choice but to mobilize against them.

Fea acknowledged that various prized features of the old basilica had been lost and could not be brought back, but he insisted, as he had in his "Parere," that this in no way constituted an argument against what he was proposing. The historic columns had been one such feature – although one that, truth be told, only experts had known about – but they did not constitute the entire significance of a building that had been packed with notable ecclesiastical, historical, pictorial, and architectonic elements. The columns, claimed Fea, could be substituted with copies, maybe even in Carrara marble, not expensive monoliths but constructed from drums, which after all had been good enough for many Roman temples. For other materials too – wood, brick, roof tiles – he suggested cheap local sources. Fea reassured his listeners (and readers) that "it would be very easy to restore the sacred Basilica in its ever admirable, universally admired totality, at less expense than the various extravagant new projects" recently proposed.[13]

A last round of pauses and tears likely punctuated the final moments of Fea's discourse, when he brought up the inevitable parallel with St. Peter's. When the Vatican basilica threatened ruin in the sixteenth century, how did Julius II decide to renovate it? In a manner worthy of the Vicar of Jesus Christ and of the emperors who had contributed to the original church. That project unfolded over a century, carefully managed by a succession of popes; a string of rulers and countless private persons contributed to it. The final product surpassed anything accomplished by the Egyptians, the Greeks, or the Roman emperors. It was a church as great as the Catholic Church itself, which it represented. "And us?" Now it was our turn. With so much responsibility to both the living and posterity, how will we respond?[14]

He left the question hanging.

Fea's pamphlet received several very positive public reviews – and one very critical private one.

In Rome, it was discussed at a subsequent séance at the Academy of Archaeology by Stefano Piale, who mostly focused on historical and archaeological matters, but who also ringingly endorsed Fea's vision for an *in pristinum* reconstruction that avoided "the mania for modernizing."[15] The *Aneddoti* was also the subject of the first article on the San Paolo debates to appear outside Italy, in the *Literatur-Blatt* supplement of the important Stuttgart and Tübingen paper *Morgenblatt für gebildete Stände*.[16] Amid long, translated passages from Fea's text, the anonymous reviewer ironically observed that

> several have, in their way, made a pitiful examination and offered something better than what was there before: instead of an unchanging basilica, [they propose] a dainty house of prayer, and instead of an empty main nave, a splendid courtyard, whose rooflessness should stand it in good stead.

In contrast to such "enlightened voices of artistic wisdom and history," Fea's attachment to the history of his fatherland and vision for the reconstruction were warmly saluted.

A longer commentary on Fea's *Aneddoti* appeared in February in the Florentine journal *Antologia*, at that date the most respected cultural journal on the peninsula.[17] It was the first article on the San Paolo debates to be published outside the Papal States, but it was the work of a Roman: the scholar, critic, and journalist Giuseppe Melchiorri.[18] Written in the guise of a letter to a Florentine friend about recent events back in Rome, the article sounded an urgent public alarm on the demolitions Valadier was conducting in the ruined nave of the old basilica.[19] After establishing that the only hope for San Paolo lay in "preserving its old form, and compensating for the loss of the marbles as best as can be," Melchiorri groaned that instead "the temple is being largely demolished, and out of the remains are to be formed a basilica of a new sort that departs from the majestic traditional form of the basilican type." This was why Fea had protested at the Academy, and why "so also did all those who feel even a scintilla of patriotism, and understand what antiquities and the arts are."

Melchiorri's text aimed to draw a broader Italian intellectual elite into the campaign against Valadier. The readership of *Antologia* was not the overwhelmingly clerical one typically found in the Papal States, but rather one that saw itself as patriotic, in a cultural if not a political sense, and to which Fea's portentous religious language might have seemed a bit extravagant.[20] Melchiorri therefore said nothing about St. Paul or the occult meanings of the fire, but instead stressed that a precious Italian *cultural* heritage was being destroyed. Melchiorri misrepresented Fea's text to the point of making it seem as though it were principally art historical in nature, and avoided quoting it by telling his correspondent that he would send him a copy so he could read it for himself.

A one-paragraph review of the *Aneddoti* did appear in *Antologia* three months later, perhaps also by Melchiorri.[21] "Better a ruin that fortifies one's faith in a past greatness, than a restoration that would cancel its image," it began. It would have been easy, it continued, to demonstrate with logic that any new solution for San Paolo would be an insult to the old basilica, that "substitution" is barbarism, and that everything points instead toward "restoration"; but Fea did this using history instead, showing again and again that it had always been restored with scrupulous respect for its original form. Having thus twisted Fea's argument into something essentially historical and drained of its religious essence, the reviewer applauded Fea's persuasive approach to the question.

The most pointed commentary on Fea's *Aneddoti*, however, was unpublished: a commentary by Giuseppe Valadier himself, written at the behest of Abbot Zelli of the monastery, who had sent him a copy and asked him to respond.[22]

Valadier began respectfully enough, by acknowledging his old colleague's "tireless" historical and archaeological scholarship. But before the end of his first page he was already accusing Fea of embellishing history and of cherry picking his sources. Rather than get bogged down on points of historical fact, Valadier aimed to demonstrate that Fea's argument hinged on an intellectual incoherency: namely, a fatal inability to distinguish between *intrinsic* value and *extrinsic* beauty. Valadier illustrated the difference by citing the humble rustic manger at Bethlehem as an example of a site that was intrinsically valuable but not extrinsically beautiful. San Paolo was the same: it had intrinsic value that was religious and historical, but the arts that decorated it reflected the "centuries of maximal decadence in the arts and sciences." In jumbling these two categories together, Fea had been led in Valadier's view to absolve the old building of its defects. Valadier brought up his own work restoring the Arch of Titus and the Colosseum as projects justified not by the intrinsic importance of the monuments but by the extrinsic beauty of their architecture. (If the intent at the Colosseum had been to memorialize the Christian martyrs who died there, he noted, it would have been enough to preserve the perimeter of the arena in which the killings took place.) Valadier insisted repeatedly on the perfect decadence of the architecture of old San Paolo, with its mismatched and misused elements pillaged from Roman temples, its design by "caprice," and its "lack of true artistic principles." In anticipation of the arguments of French Romantic theorists a decade later, Valadier depicted the Early Christians as having completely bungled their historic challenge of inventing the new building type of the Christian church and suggested that they had imitated civic basilicas out of an inability to conceive of anything more original.

Valadier also wrote that Fea, "not content to preach against everyone," also enjoyed "giving opinions that contradicted whatever a knowledgeable person might say about a given subject in art, science, or mechanics," for he believed himself "superior to everyone else in these areas." Fea had clearly gotten under Valadier's skin. But at the same time, Valadier was eager not to be seen as indifferent to matters of historical and religious import. He assured Zelli that he would never have been one to advocate pulling down San Paolo to replace it with something in the modern style. But now that God had done that for us, he felt that as a rule it was always better to build something new. This is what had made Rome the center of the arts in the first place.

Referring wickedly to Fea's recent performance at the Academy of Archaeology, Valadier wrote that "when one reasons about Art . . . one does not want fanaticism, nor that enthusiasm that laughs and cries when it speaks of such things." The fifteen-year-old Raphael might be esteemed, he continued, just as a 120-year-old illiterate peasant might be respected; but in one case it would be on account of merit, and in the other it would be merely on account of the accident of age. The scale model he was building would be more than enough to preserve for posterity the memory of an old basilica that, for him, had been the architectural equivalent of the illiterate old peasant. He then turned, as had Fea, to the obligatory parallel with the reconstruction of St. Peter's: "When the immortal Julius II ordered the famous Bramante to build him a new Saint Peter's, how many madmen cried out against that happy decision? And yet without convoking the Senate and the whole of Christianity, as our author would like the Holy Father to do in such circumstances, he laid down the principles that guided a great and praiseworthy monument, one which is reputable both as a shrine and for its artistic merit." If Leo XII is given by God the health, strength, and wisdom to do likewise, concluded Valadier, he will achieve what Augustus achieved in Rome: he will have found the basilica an ugly pile of bricks and left it a proud temple of marble.

That Valadier would even write such an impassioned response to Fea's arguments reflected his awareness of how precarious his position was. Fea's interventions had succeeded in creating a public impression that the San Paolo debate was not settled, and opportunistic architects were already starting to circulate counterprojects. In February, Pietro Lanciani, a member of Leo XII's Arts Council, proposed an *in pristinum*-type project, insisting that it was the "common desire" to see the basilica rebuilt as it had been.[23] That same month, the Conservatori of Rome addressed a memorandum to the secretary of state calling for an *in pristinum* reconstruction.[24] Still another project was submitted in February to the Camerlengo's office by Antonio Sarti, a young Modenese architect with a bright Roman future ahead of him.[25] His design echoed Valadier's, transforming the surviving eastern parts of the building into a new and smaller church. Sarti claimed he was oriented by economy and a desire "to preserve everything precious that survived the fire, since this is essential for leaving a memory of all that formed the old basilica."[26] Another *in pristinum* proposal from these weeks wondered why large sums were being spent to preserve the old mosaics and papal portrait chronology at the old basilica, given that the new modern design would surely sweep those elements away. It added that, if an entirely new church really was to be the solution, then there ought to be an international competition.[27]

It can seem sometimes like Valadier's impending removal was almost an open secret. Melchiorri had concluded his *Antologia* essay with a cryptic remark: "I would like to be able to tell you in a subsequent letter some less sad news on [San Paolo], and I console myself with the reflection that human counsels can change quickly." When his follow-up letter then appeared in March, dated 28 February, it opened with rejoicing: "no longer will those reprehensible innovations that certain architects [i.e., Valadier] wished to execute take place; instead it is to be returned to that original form that Fea celebrated and the value of whose ancient memories so many know and love."[28] Yet this was simply not true yet at this date; the changes Melchiorri evoked were only to occur officially weeks and months later. A gossipy report from April in the *Morgenblatt für gebildete Stände* likewise announced prematurely that "San Paolo is to be restored as it was, notwithstanding a nonsensical project of Valadier, which, as is his style, was to make a modern building out of it, and had already completely destroyed much of the old."[29] Apparently insiders could see which way the wind was blowing. Had the turning point been the Concorso Clementino? Or had it been something that occurred when Pope Leo visited San Paolo on 7 February, celebrating mass in one of the surviving chapels and touring the ruins?[30] Probably no single event decided the matter. But among many, surely the most important factor, to which we now turn, was the outcome of Leo XII's decision to test the waters for a San Paolo fundraising drive.

The campaign to induce Pope Leo to support the *in pristinum* option was from the start also a campaign to convince him that sufficient funds could be raised from the international faithful to complete such a vast enterprise. Leo XII's encyclical *Ad plurimas easque gravissimas* was the fruit of those efforts: a full-throated and official supplication to the whole Catholic faithful to contribute toward the reconstruction.[31] The encyclical was dated 25 January, when the festival marking Paul's conversion to Christianity was celebrated each year, but that is not when it was actually promulgated. There are no mentions of it in any published or manuscript texts in Rome until early March, when suddenly several articles on it were published, della Somaglia began issuing memoranda relating to it, and the monastery chronicler at San Paolo transcribed it into his register.[32] Only on 21 March did Leo officially constitute the new Special Congregation on San Paolo whose formation the encyclical announced.[33] All of this indicates that the 25 January 1825 date was symbolic, and that the actual date of the encyclical was around 10 March.

As was typical with encyclicals, the letter was addressed to "all the patriarchs, primates, archbishops, and bishops of the entire Catholic world." It put the 1823 fire in a precise context, as the culmination "of the numerous and terrible calamities that afflicted the memorable Pontificate of our glorious predecessor." It added that Pius VII had commanded that "necessary repairs" be undertaken – this was untrue; Pius had never been told of the fire – "but it was apparent that this would require extraordinary means, since the incredible violence of the flames had destroyed almost everything." Upon succeeding Pius, Leo therefore ordered that every resource be directed toward preserving whatever had survived the fire. He recalled his hope at the time of his May 1824 encyclical that Jubilee pilgrims would attend masses in the basilica. But since then, he explained, additional parts of the building had collapsed, leading to the realization that "we could not, without great danger, make the basilica in any way serviceable for the Jubilee."[34] So the idea was abandoned, and it was finally resolved to undertake a rebuilding rather than a repair. But given the paltry government funds available for such work ("which will not surprise anyone after the terrible and numerous calamities that our States have suffered"), Leo rejoiced in his confidence that the faithful would support the reconstruction with their own means.

This was the crux of the endeavor: to take a sounding on what exactly could be expected from a fundraising drive. To this end, Leo laid out the narrative he wanted the clergy to evoke in making their appeals. The challenge posed by the fire was to be framed in terms of the debt that every Catholic must feel toward St. Paul himself. Paul had "traversed so many countries" and endured so many trials and misfortunes on his way to martyrdom, and it was only because of him that "our ancestors were brought out of the darkness and brought into the most admirable light." Given this incalculable debt, what Catholic could be ungrateful enough not to contribute? Leo also alluded to the status of Peter and Paul as co-apostles and protectors of the City of Rome and evoked the parallel between their respective basilicas, which had always benefited from the largesse of both Romans and foreigners. This is how St. Peter's was rebuilt, and why it was to be expected now that the faithful, "both citizens and foreigners," would contribute to San Paolo. Leo was persuaded because this was so manifestly the will of God:

> This thought seems to have come to us from God himself, in that, amidst the horror of the fallen vault of the ruins of the great marble columns reduced to ashes, Paul's sepulcher was preserved in full, just as in ancient times the three youths were saved amidst the fire of Babylon.

> We will build therefore upon the same spot, not far from the place where [Paul] gave his life for Christ; we will build anew a church for Paul, the companion in the merits and the glory of Peter. If it no longer will have those columns and those other ornaments of inestimable value that it once had, the church will be built with the magnificence that the collected offerings will allow.[35]

The encyclical ended with very clear instructions on how Paul was to be used in sermons soliciting donations: the clergy were to speak of Paul's merits, and "to excite the devotion of the faithful towards him ... you will find in his admirable texts the most persuasive arguments to enflame the hearts of those confided to your care with love for Paul, and to incline them to support our efforts."

The challenge of the fundraising drive dovetailed perfectly with Leo's dream of reanimating popular religious zeal within the Church. Little surprise that Leo came to regard as providential God's fiery hint that the Church should make recourse to the Doctor to the Gentiles. The continual comparisons with the reconstruction of Peter's basilica four centuries earlier highlight the topicality of the divine suggestion. In the sixteenth century, it had been the challenge of Protestantism that most threatened the Church, and so God had guided the Church back to Peter, the so-called Rock of Faith who guaranteed that the Papal Succession and thus the institutional authority of the Roman Catholic Church was divinely ordained. In the nineteenth century, however, the issue was the external threat to the Church represented by the world's slide into secularism, indifferentism, and atheism. If Peter the rock had been an image of tradition, place, situatedness, and durability, Paul offered instead an image of conversion, peripatetic mobility, and the dissemination of information across nations. What figure in the Church's pantheon of heroes could possibly have offered a better example of nimble evangelism, saintly perseverance, and dedication to combating false doctrines? As the great letter-writer of the Early Church, he was the obvious guide for a nineteenth-century Catholicism that needed to reengage and reenergize an expanding international community of Catholic believers. Little wonder then that Leo saw the fire as a divine directive to reflect on the legacy of the saint whose basilica it destroyed.

Leo's encyclical followed Fea's recommendation in appropriating the reconstruction from the domain of architecture and reframing it as an affective narrative accessible to a far wider public. If Fea's texts declared a Catholic refusal to accept the fire as an occasion of loss, Leo made an adjustment: he stressed instead the narrative of Paul the holy ancestor to whom every Catholic was indebted, and to whom God was obviously summoning the faithful to rededicate themselves. Leo prudently uttered not a word about architectural form since that would ultimately depend on the success or failure of the fundraising effort he was testing. But if the pope's encyclical may be regarded as a kind of experiment, the very fact that Leo was conducting it amounted to a declaration: that Valadier's approach was now Plan B, to be pursued only if the generosity of the faithful proved unequal to the challenge of the *in pristinum* approach, which was the new Plan A.

Leo's encyclical was accompanied by what in the austere Roman public sphere of 1825 passed for a publicity blitz: three articles in rapid succession, all probably by the same man. The most important appeared in the *Diario di Roma* in March 1825, signed by the Sicilian Theatine Gioacchino Ventura. At this stage in his career – we shall encounter him again in a few chapters, rather transformed – Ventura was a polemicist for Lamennaisian reform and the recently appointed editor of the *Giornale ecclesiastico di Roma*, one of a loose alliance of journals that sprang up during these months around Italy as mouthpieces of a burgeoning Catholic irredentism.[36] Ventura's verdict on the contemporary world at this stage usually fell somewhere between the cata-strophic and the apocalyptic, but here he confined himself to reflecting on how the San Paolo endeavor fit into Leo's thirst for the resacralization of Rome and, by extension, the regeneration of humanity. He opened with a rhetorical fusillade:

> The *immortality* of Rome's duration, whence it emerges ever more magnificent and ever more beautiful from every destruction and ruin, has won it the title of *Eternal City*; and likewise, the *universality* of its influence bestows upon it the name of *Catholic* or *Universal City par excellence*. For this is indeed the city in which no one, least of all a Catholic, is a foreigner; one that is the fatherland of all men, and in which all find shelter, protection, and defense under the peaceful scepter of our common Father; which in this way possesses nothing of its own that, in a certain manner and in a certain way, does not belong to everyone; and whose preservation and maintenance is a matter of universal interest.[37]

Echoing the rhetoric of Leo XII's Jubilee, Ventura here wants nothing to do with Rome as the capital of the fine arts, or as the homeland of classical antiquity. Rome is instead the timeless, perpetual, universal city of God. This blanket of universality was explicitly extended by Ventura to the great Catholic monuments of the city, and none more than the four great basilicas dedicated to Peter, Paul, Mary, and John. Not because of their artistic quality, he observed, but because "the piety of *all men* raised [them] up to honor the memory of the most holy Founders and Fathers of the Religion of *all men*." For this reason alone, they are "*Catholic edifices*."

Ventura then pivoted to Leo's encyclical. Stressing the "miracle" by which Paul's sepulcher survived the blaze, he celebrated Leo's command to the clergy to raise funds by directing the eyes of the faithful to the figure of Paul. If this effort succeeded in erecting a temple worthy of "the greatest of the Christian Apostles," then finally a century that had endured nothing but sacrilege would have hope for the future. The underlying claims were profound: the Catholic edifices of Rome possessed universal significance, and the reconstruction of San Paolo offered hope for the future of humanity. Not a word was said about the form in which the basilica was to be rebuilt, but it would have been obvious to everybody that Ventura's sympathies lay with the *in pristinum* solution.

A second commentary on Leo's encyclical appeared around the same time in Ventura's *Giornale ecclesiastico*, signed "V.T." ("Ventura Teatino").[38] It struck similar notes, declaring that the zeal of every pope to embellish Rome with churches was most strikingly demonstrated by the basilicas of Peter and Paul, two princes of the Church and the holy protectors of Rome. But of course, "the richer, perhaps, and the more precious" of these two basilicas had just been destroyed by fire. Such lavish praise offers startling testimony as to how dramatically the stock of Early Christian architecture had risen vis-à-vis that of the Renaissance in mere months since the fire.[39] But Ventura also warned that when reconstruction began, the Church's enemies would inevitably spew impudent questions about the pope's true intentions, just as they had when St. Peter's was rebuilding during the Renaissance. This warning was accompanied by a footnote that referred to the *Life and Pontificate of Leo X*, first published in 1805 by the English Unitarian William Roscoe and translated into Italian in 1816.[40] According to the note, Roscoe had claimed that "the construction of Saint Peter's was but a miserable pretext by the court in Rome to make money," and that "at the construction site of Saint Peter's the pope had employed only two workmen, one blind and the other crippled."[41] The absurdity of the accusation should not obscure Ventura's intent in repeating it; namely, to underscore how the fire at San Paolo presented a golden opportunity for the faithful to defy the Church's enemies with proofs of their devotion.

A third text, also signed by Ventura and appearing first in a Modenese Catholic journal and then in the *Giornale ecclesiastico* in July 1825, hammered all these themes yet again.[42] Most of this lengthy essay concerned the "current disposition of souls in Europe with respect to religion," and again contrasted with Ventura's usual tone of bitter lamentation: all Ventura could see now when he surveyed the European scene was the coming collapse of the hubristic dreams of Enlightenment and Revolution and the germination of the great religious revival they had inadvertently sewn. San Paolo was not explicitly mentioned, but the giddy sense of possibility the essay projected, coming just as the Roman hierarchy was seeing that an international fundraising call might be met with a positive response, suggests that the San Paolo project was starting to be seen as a potential catalyst for the realization of Leo's dreams of Catholic regeneration. It was surely no coincidence that Ventura ended with this passage from the absolutist tract *Du Pape*, published a few years earlier by the French Catholic ultra Joseph Le Maistre (my italics):

> We are just arriving at the greatest of all religious epochs, *in which each person is expected to bear, to the extent of his capacity, a stone for the august edifice whose plans have been visibly decreed*. The mediocrity of one's talent must not discourage anyone; at least, it has not made me worry. The indigent, who plants only mint, dill, and cumin in his narrow garden may confidently hold the first stalk to the heavens, sure that it will be accepted equally well as [the offering] of the opulent man ...

On 21 March 1825, Pope Leo constituted the Special Congregation for the New Fabric of the Basilica of San Paolo, charged with overseeing and

administering the reconstruction of the basilica.[43] Eventually known more commonly as the Special Commission for the Reedification of the Basilica of San Paolo, this body was presided over by the cardinal secretary of state (della Somaglia at this date) and composed of four additional cardinals and seven additional prelates. Among these were a Belgian, a Frenchman, and a Spaniard, whose appointments confirm Leo's ambition to create an international profile for the reconstruction.[44] The treasurer general was also automatically a member, which for now meant Valadier's old ally Belisario Cristaldi. Among the appointed clerics were two scholars who had written key works of scholarship on the old basilica: Nicola Maria Nicolai and Angelo Uggeri, the latter of whom was named Secretary. Their presence was an unambiguous sign that historical considerations were to be taken seriously in the reconstruction.

Over the following weeks, della Somaglia and the Special Commission planned how best to ensure the success of the fundraising effort. They distributed the encyclical to bishops and abbots throughout Italy, made appeals to wealthy Catholic laymen, and had special deposit forms printed for the bank account that had been created in the Depositeria Camerale.[45] They also began drawing up a list of all the ministries, corps, and institutions in the pontifical government, denoting which official was to organize collections in each one. A few early donations arrived already in March at della Somaglia's office, including contributions from the Bishop of Arezzo (1,500 scudi), the Duke of Bracciano (10,000 scudi), and a certain Signore Vitelli (1,500 scudi).[46]

Several Italian clerics distributed copies of Leo's encyclical while others composed pastoral letters of their own. Bishop Teloni of Macerata and Tolentino published the encyclical within his diocese with a title that claimed to "make it public for the clergy and people of the two dioceses."[47] Archbishop Luigi Lambruschini of Genova circulated a pastoral letter that garnered a reputation in clerical circles: already in August della Somaglia was writing to the Papal Nuncio in Naples to say that he had managed to lay hands on "the last remaining copy" of this letter, "which you have asked me about so many times."[48] Several other such letters survive.[49] One of the richest came from the pen of Cardinal Archbishop Cesare Brancadoro of Fermo, an old pro famed for his eloquent pastoral communications. Brancadoro's letter began with a reflection on the miraculous survival of Paul's tomb as proof of the divine will that Paul's body be preserved in this place and housed in a new temple.[50] It reported Leo's decision to "invoke the charitable competition of spontaneous piety of the Faithful throughout the entire Catholic Orb," then turned to how Catholics must all thank Saint Paul for their acquaintance with Christianity, for his energy in travelling the world, for his "immortal acts," and for his teachings, which Brancadoro recapitulated. He then checked off the level of contribution he expected from each trade and profession, from shopkeepers to farmers, instructing every diocese to set out collection boxes in the most frequented churches with signs on them reading = ALMS FOR THE CONSTRUCTION OF THE BASILICA OF SAINT PAUL =.[51] (Such collections boxes were for a time ubiquitous: an English Catholic visiting the Roman basilicae in mid-May 1825 testified that already "at each of the holy doors is a large box to receive offerings for the re-building of St Paul's church," while an Italian writer in 1831 recalled that they had been placed "in every corner of the land, including the most remote.")[52] Brancadoro concluded with a few paragraphs for his clergy to read from the altar, reminding the faithful of their debt to Paul and urging them to secure his special protection for themselves by outraising every other archdiocese in the Papal States.

Della Somaglia was also in contact with the Papal Nuncios around Europe, who coordinated collection in the territories to which they were assigned.[53] These efforts were closely monitored in Rome for what they forecast about the likely success of the drive beyond Italy. The nuncio in Madrid, Giacomo Giustiniani, wrote that he had received the copies of the encyclical sent in June, that he had reached out to the royal family, was coordinating outreach to the Spanish nobility, and would soon be in contact with the Spanish bishops. Things did not go so smoothly everywhere. The Nuncio in Lisbon, Giacomo Filippo Fransoni, wrote to confirm receipt of thirty copies of the encyclical, but warned that the recent independence of Brazil had had devastating effects there, and that "the critical circumstances of this country do not promise a very happy result" for the drive. (Della Somaglia urged him to approach the task with optimism.) Fransoni confirmed shortly thereafter that things were indeed going badly, with various clerics claiming they were unable to contribute due to the heavy tributes demanded of them by the new liberal government. Still, a few bishops were planning to publish the call for donations in their dioceses. Della Somaglia replied by asking whether Fransoni had yet had a crack at the Portuguese Court, noting that "all the others have promised to contribute, and some have even begun to do so."[54]

Della Somaglia also corresponded with diplomatic representatives of the Protestant majority nations, who became the main conduit for contributions from those countries. The Prussian legation in Rome was led by Bunsen, who on 15 August conveyed to della Somaglia that King Friedrich Wilhelm III had been thrilled to learn of the appeal, and had authorized fundraising "in all the Catholic churches of His monarchy."[55]

The irrepressible Carlo Fea managed in May 1825 to make a spectacular contribution through his personal appeal to King Ludwig I of Bavaria, a staunch Catholic, avid antiquarian, art collector, and architectural patron. Fea was very aware that Ludwig at this date possessed in Rome a cache of antiquities he had acquired for his new Glyptothek in Munich, and that he was awaiting the opportune moment to request an export permit for them from Fea, who was head of the pope's Export Commission. Fea also knew that not too long ago Ludwig had been forced to wait six years for a permit to export the Barberini Faun. Ludwig grasped the situation immediately when he received Fea's invitation to contribute to the reconstruction of San Paolo, replying that a major collection effort would be undertaken in Bavaria at once; he then immediately requested (and received) the export permit for his Roman antiquities.[56] Fea capitalized on this quid pro quo by printing up copies of Ludwig's four-sentence reply on single sheets, which were then wittily folded in the manner of a contemporary letter, complete with Fea's address printed vertically along the left-hand side. These quasi-facsimiles of Ludwig's pledge not only publicized the mounting success of the fundraising effort but also disseminated a standard for cooperation that other European royals and nobles would have felt pressure to compete with.

Meanwhile, Uggeri was trying to organize the inaugural meeting of the Special Commission. When he requested Cristaldi's thoughts about what should be on the agenda, the Treasurer General listed several pressing matters: demolitions of dangerous elements, efforts to record damaged items, scaffolds to be erected, donations to be solicited. It also included the following key points: "Resolve whether the initial design chosen by the Holy Father shall remain. Whether, embracing the idea of reoccupying the whole area, everything must be repristinated as it was, including the defects."[57] Both questions reflected Cristaldi's lingering loyalty to Valadier, one by passive-aggressively recalling that a change of plan effectively meant overruling the pope's original choice, and the other by noting that a rigorous repristination would necessarily involve reconstituting the bad along with the good. Uggeri sensed what Cristaldi was up to and replied tartly that it was not the Commission's place to debate a decision made by the pope: if His Holiness had already chosen a design, "as the query claims," then it was everyone's honor and duty to contribute to its execution. But:

> On the possibility that such is not the resolution taken [by the pope], and that by the institution of this most respectable Congregation His Holiness has left opinions free, and asks that each speak his opinion as to what he thinks most decorous, and most glorious for that Sacred Person, one will not hesitate to declare that the only solution that leads to that end is that of remaking the Basilica in the same manner and form as it was before … and this is the desire of foreigners and of Romans.[58]

Uggeri then addressed Cristaldi's second point:

> It is undoubtedly true that among the many celebrated beauties in the fondly remembered basilica of San Paolo there were also artistic defects, but these were proper to those times in which the Basilica was built, and

therefore they should not be emended ... To correct [such an] original would be tantamount to losing one's reason, like one who wishes to reduce the paintings of Giotto to the manner of Raphael, and who would destroy a painting by him so as to have one by a contemporary artist (even a very prestigious one), rather than restore it in the manner of Giotto.[59]

Taking this passage in isolation, one might conclude that Uggeri had abandoned his impulse to reform the nave arcade with an entablature, and recognized instead that the rationale of the *in pristinum* argument hinged integrally on submission to the forms of the past. This conclusion would however be inaccurate, for around this very time Uggeri brought out a new and essentially unaltered edition of his 1823 book. The only difference was that he now named himself prominently on the title page as Leo XII's Secretary to the Special Commission for the basilica's reconstruction.[60] This edition aimed to increase public pressure on the government not to pursue Valadier's plan, but also indicates that Uggeri's views had not shifted – as subsequent events were soon to confirm. The initial battle lines were thus drawn: on one side was Cristaldi who, seemingly out of loyalty but perhaps also out of economic prudence, still seems to have supported Valadier's position, while Uggeri on the other side was preparing an aggressive push to switch to an *in pristinum* solution.

Uggeri worked up a background paper for the commissioners in advance of their first meeting, rehearsing all the major points in favor of an *in pristinum* reconstruction.[61] It described how much had survived the fire and could be reused. It pointed out the meticulous care lavished on pagan monuments – the examples chosen, significantly, were Valadier's recent restorations of the Colosseum and the Arch of Titus – and implied that to do less for San Paolo would leave the Holy See open to mockery. It argued further that Leo XII's Encyclical clearly stated that the basilica was to be *restored* and made no mention of the *construction* of a church. It asserted that neither religious nor artistic tourists would go to visit Valadier's "brick church." The reason, Uggeri explained, as though the matter were self-evident, was that the arts at present were at a low point: "I do not think," he deadpanned, "that we can presume in our age to triumph over the conceptions of the Buonarrotis, the Palladios, the Vignolas. It is therefore dangerous beyond belief to expose oneself to the choice of a new architecture in the reconstruction of the basilica." The faithful would curtail their contributions. Uggeri returned in conclusion to one of his pet arguments: the flaws of the old basilica were worthy of respect because, after all, they were "born of poverty of means and of the times, and of the architect's ignorance," not of intellectual or aesthetic inadequacy.[62]

Della Somaglia, as president of the Special Commission, read a draft of Uggeri's background paper and forwarded it on to Nicolai, complaining that it was "more an oratorical discourse than a briefing document." He told Nicolai to have Uggeri to boil it down into a list of propositions to be discussed and voted on.⁶³ In particular, he wrote, the Commission should discuss the cost difference between an *in pristinum* reconstruction and "the design presented by Valadier to His Holiness," and to this end della Somaglia had already begun rounding up material for comparison. He asked Belli and Alippi to prepare a new estimate for an *in pristinum* repair/reconstruction, taking into account any additional damage and degradations that had occurred since the time of the fire. This was submitted on 22 April, their estimate increasing about 5 percent to 378,390 scudi. (They apparently thought della Somaglia had requested the estimate because he was considering replacing Valadier, so they optimistically included a fresh copy of Abbot Zelli's letter of support for their project.)⁶⁴ Della Somaglia also inquired via Cristaldi whether Valadier "still" expected to direct the reconstruction. The answer came back affirmative, so Valadier was asked in May to provide an estimate for his project as well.⁶⁵ Valadier replied at once that a full estimate had never been done and therefore he had no such thing on hand; in a message to Uggeri, he protested that it was impossible for him to do an estimate because there were too many unknowns.⁶⁶ Della Somaglia told Cristaldi to extract an estimate from Valadier somehow, and within one month.⁶⁷ In mid-July, della Somaglia's Arts Council declared the Belli-Alippi estimate to be sound.⁶⁸ In that same week an enterprising building supplies contractor named Guglielmo Closse presented an estimate for forty columns in connection with the latest Belli-Alippi proposal, along with his own opinion on the reconstruction (which, unsurprisingly for a building supplies contractor, was that a full-scale *in pristinum* reconstruction was the superior option).⁶⁹ Also in that same busy midsummer week, della Somaglia wrote to Cristaldi to say that he still had not received an estimate from Valadier and urged him to press the architect on this.⁷⁰

Valadier however had become bedridden with a knee injury, and it was only in August that he managed to submit his estimate. By this point, he seems to have realized that the pope was leaning toward an *in pristinum* reconstruction, for he told della Somaglia that he was now working on a project to rebuild San Paolo "at the same size it was before the fire." But he still could not help adding that his project would "correct everything that the miserable artists of the age of Constantine did not know about the beautiful basilicae of antiquity . . ."⁷¹

But by then the wheels of change were already turning. On 21 August, della Somaglia informed the Nuncio in Naples that a major publication was forthcoming any day now that would have a major impact on fundraising.⁷² Three weeks later, Abbot Zelli was confidentially informed in an audience with Pope

Leo that Valadier was to be sacked and replaced by Pasquale Belli.[73] Four days after that audience, on 18 September, Pope Leo sent the final text of his *Chirograph on the reconstruction of the Basilica of San Paolo* to della Somaglia to review. This was the publication della Somaglia had evoked to the Nuncio a month earlier, and it was to represent Leo's final word on the reconstruction. It was published shortly thereafter on the front page of *Diario di Roma* and in a variety of printed forms, and before long was being translated, shipped, and reported on around the world.[74]

The Chirograph opened by attributing the two years of inactivity since the fire at San Paolo to uncertainties over resources:

> However ardent was the desire that we harbored from the first days of Our Pontificate to see the burned basilica of San Paolo re-erected and returned to public worship, it was necessary to delay implementation until Our uncertainty about the means we would have at our disposal for this holy task had been vanquished.

Leo had been encouraged, however, by the many manifestations he had witnessed of devotion and generosity, and this had prompted him to issue his encyclical back in March. The number of donations and pledges recorded since then had surpassed his hopes and led him to "increase the limits of the work, which, had we been limited only to Our own means, we would have been forced to curtail." Leo envisaged that "the inhabitants of every class and condition" would contribute "in proportion to their abilities." Leo himself promised an annual contribution of not less than 50,000 scudi from his own budget.

Leo then made it official: it was to be an *in pristinum* reconstruction. In what was to become a famous and much-discussed passage (to which we shall return), Leo declared:

> We would like in the first place to see fulfilled the wish of the erudite, and of those who commendably yearn for the preservation of antique monuments in the state in which they were created by their founders. Therefore no innovation shall be introduced in the forms and architectonic proportions, nor in the ornaments of the resurgent edifice, unless it be to exclude some small thing that in later times was introduced through the whim of a subsequent era.[75]

Uncertainties were to be referred to the Academy of St. Luke for review, such as the marbles to be used for the new columns, or the form of the new roof.

The Chirograph said nothing about who was to direct the work, but Valadier could read the writing on the wall. On 11 November he wrote a dignified appeal to Cristaldi and Nicolai to remind them that he had been working voluntarily without pay for eighteen months, that the pope had after all originally chosen him for the commission, and that his initial project had been designed when it was thought that the reconstruction was to be funded by the impoverished government. He hoped the Special Commission would remember all this when it met to decide who would be the architect.[76]

That meeting occurred twelve days later.[77] Voting broke down as follows (Uggeri as secretary did not have a vote):

Commission member	Vote
Cardinal President della Somaglia	Belli
Treasurer General Cristaldi	Valadier
Cardinal Galleffi	Belli
Cardinal De Gregorio	Belli
Cardinal Bertazzoli	Belli
Cardinal Riario	Valadier and Belli
Monsignor Nicolai	Valadier
Monsignor d'Argenteau	Belli
Monsignor Sala	Valadier
Monsignor De Marco	Valadier
Monsignor Isoard	Belli

It was surprisingly close: Belli got 6.5 votes, while Valadier got 4.5. Had just one of Belli's supporters voted the other way, the result would have been a tie. Nonetheless, two days later Leo XII reviewed the results and confirmed Pasquale Belli as architect director of the reconstruction of San Paolo. Andrea Alippi and Pietro Bosio were appointed his assistants. Respectful letters were sent to Valadier and Salvi informing them of the decision and letting them know that when in future the Arts Council was consulted on the reconstruction, their opinions would be among those sought.[78] A few days later, Belli's appointment was announced in the *Diario di Roma*.[79]

Belli might seem a puzzling choice, given that he was almost as identified as Valadier had been with Napoleon, Consalvi, and international neoclassicism. But what had doomed Valadier was not just his past associations but also his reputation. Valadier was a man of considerable self-regard, to put it mildly; an accomplished courtier who was comfortable conversing familiarly with popes and who knew his way around the corridors of power. Belli, on the other hand, was described as "sound" in Special Commission documents just prior to his nomination as architect.[80] Far better, it must have seemed, to install a "sound" technician from whom little trouble might be expected than a prima donna like Valadier. It would soon prove a case of "be careful what you wish for."

NOTES

1   ASR: Camerale III b. 1909, #33. See also *Cronaca* II, 16 December 1824 (demolitions) and 22 December 1824 (*forzati*).

2 Ridley (1992a), (1996), and especially (2000).

3 Ridley (1996).

4 Ridley (1992b), p. 146.

5 Fea, "Parere," as in Chapter 4 n. 30.

6 Ventura (1825d), p. 200. Ventura is here the heir to debates in French letters from the previous century and a half.

7 Ventura (1825c), pp. 17–70, esp. pp. 24–26.

8 Melchiorri (1825a); Piale (1833).

9 Fea (1825).

10 Fea (1825), p. 15.

11 Fea (1825), pp. 15–16.

12 Fea (1825), pp. 16–17.

13 Fea (1825), pp. 17–18.

14 Fea (1825), p. 19.

15 Piale (1833).

16 *Literatur-Blatt* (Stuttgart and Tübingen), 24 March 1825, pp. 93–96.

17 Melchiorri (1825a). A second installment appeared a month later (Melchiorri [1825b]).

18 On Melchiorri, see Izzi (2006).

19 The monastery chronacle reported on 16 December 1824 that "work began today on demolishing the walls of the basilica by the garden of the main nave" (*Cronaca* II, 16 December 1824).

20 Carpi (1974); Ferraris (1978).

21 "Sulla raccolta fatta dall'avv. Carlo Fea di aneddoti sopra la Basilica Ostiense di S. Paolo," *Antologia* 18:54 (June 1825): 99.

22 Two versions of Valadier's commentary exist in the monastery archive, both dated 1 March 1825. One is addressed to Zelli and the other to an unnamed correspondant (Giuseppe Valadier, review of Fea's *Anneddoti della Basilica di S. Paolo* [two copies], 1 March 1825 [ASP: 30/c, libro rosso 1]).

23 Pietro Lanciani, "Idea sulla ricostruzione dell'incendiata Basilica di S. Paolo," 24 February 1825 (ASR: CSRBSP Segreteria b. 276, f. 1; ASP: 30/c, libro rosso 1, with the date 24 October 1824).

24 Conservatori di Roma to Giulio Maria della Somaglia, 27 February 1825 (ASR: CSRBSP Segreteria b. 286, f. 2).

25 On Sarti, see Spagnesi (1978), p. 88 ff.

26 Antonio Sarti, "Progetto," 2 February 1825 (ASR: Camerlengato, P. II, Tit. IV, b. 154, f. 185). See Groblewski (2001), pp. 305–307.

27 ASP: 32/c, b. 1828-50, f. 1.

28 Melchiorri (1825b), p. 153.

29 *Morgenblatt für gebildete Stände* (Stuttgart and Tübingen), 16 May 1825, p. 156.

30 *Cronaca* II, 8 February 1825; *DdR*, 12 February 1825, p. 1.

31 *TEPD*, v. 3, pp. 28–30. See discussion in Groblewski (2001), pp. 86–88.

32 *Cronaca* II, March 1825; Ventura (1825a); Giulio Maria della Somaglia to the Special Commission, 16 March 1825 (ASR: CSRBSP Segreteria b. 286, f. 3).

33 Giulio Maria della Somaglia to Belisario Cristaldi, 21 March 1825 (ASR: Camerale III b.1910, #120; Camerlengato, P. II, Tit. IV, b. 155, f. 204). News of the foundation of the Congregazione was reported in *DdR* (26 March 1825, p. 1).

34 This seems to have been recognized in December, when the Jubilee Porta Santa ceremonies were transferred to Santa Maria in Trastevere (*Cronaca* II, 20 December 1824; *DdR*, 24 December 1824, p. 1).

35 *TEPD*, v. 3, p. 30.

36 Ventura (1825a), p.1. This network was comprised by the *Memorie di religione, di morale e di letteratura* (Modena), the *Enciclopedia ecclesiastica e morale* (Naples), the *Giornale ecclesiastico di Roma*, the *Giornale degli apologisti della religione cattolica* (Florence), and the *Amico*

d'Italia (Turin). On Ventura and this essay, see Boutry (2002a), pp. 380–381. The essay was later reprinted at the end of Moreschi (1840b).

37 Ventura (1825a), p. 1. Emphasis in the original text.

38 Ventura (1825b). On this journal, see Pirri (1932a) and (1932b); Majolo Molinari (1963), v. 1, pp. 458–459.

39 See also Napione's 1824 review of Nicoli's 1815 book, which described San Paolo as "stupendo" and discussed its value as though it were self-evident (Napione [1824]).

40 Roscoe (1816, Italian edition; originally printed in 1805). Roscoe was a Liverpool-based Romantic and early collector of late medieval paintings (Andrews [1964], p. 16).

41 Roscoe does not in fact claim this.

42 Ventura (1825e) and (1825c).

43 On the Special Congregation/Commission, see *DESE* v. 15, "Congregazione speciale per la riedificazione della basilica di San Paolo," p. 272; *CAPDR*, pp. 21–22; Groblewski (2001), pp. 88–90; Boutry (2002), II. 25, pp. 203–206.

44 Groblewski (2001), p. 89.

45 "Bilancj del Conto a parte dei depositi voluntarij . . .," March 1825–December 1827 (ASR: CSRBSP Computisteria b.112); "Bilancio del Conto a parte de'Depositi volontarj . . .," 1825 (ASR: Camerale III b. 1910, #121).

46 Della Somaglia to Special Commission and to Cristaldi (16 and 21 March 1825), as in Chapter 5 n. 32, 33.

47 Teloni (1825), cited in Fiume Sermattei (2013), pp. 194–195.

48 Giulio Maria della Somaglia to Giacomo Giustiniani, 21 August 1825 (AAV: Segreteria di Stato, anno 1825, b. 586 [rubr. 48], p. 34). Lambruschini's letter was later published in the *Giornale ecclesiastico*.

49 Cf. Grimaldi (1825), cited in Fiume Sermattei (2013), p. 196; Gandolfi (1825).

50 Brancadoro (1825).

51 Brancadoro (1825), p. 21.

52 Beste (1826), v. 1, p. 151; Costanzi (1831), v. 2 [supplement], pp. 38–39.

53 Giacomo Giustiniani to Giulio Maria della Somaglia, 11 August 1825 (AAV: Segreteria di Stato, anno 1825, b. 586 [rubr. 48], p. 46).

54 Giacomo Filippo Fransoni to Giulio Maria della Somaglia, 9 April 1825; Giulio Maria della Somaglia to Giacomo Filippo Fransoni, 30 May 1825; Giacomo Filippo Fransoni to Giulio Maria della Somaglia, 9 July 1825; Giulio Maria della Somaglia to Giacomo Filippo Fransoni, August 1825 (AAV: Segreteria di Stato, anno 1825, b. 586 [rubr. 48]).

55 Christian Carl Josias Bunsen to Giulio Maria della Somaglia, 15 August 1825 (AAV: Segreteria di Stato, anno 1825, b. 586 [rubr. 48], p. 26).

56 Cf. Wünsche (1980). My thanks to Laura diZerega for bringing this context to my attention.

57 Angelo Uggeri to Belisario Cristaldi, 22 April 1825 (ASR: Camerale III b. 1910, #123); Belisario Cristaldi, "Rapporto di Monsignor Tesoriere," 24 April 1825 (ASR: Camerale III b. 1910, #125).

58 [Angelo Uggeri],"Riflessioni sopra il Rapporto di Monsignor Tesoriere . . .", 24 April 1825 (ASR: Camerale III b. 1910, #125; ASP: 30/c, libro rosso 2).

59 [Angelo Uggeri],"Riflessioni sopra il Rapporto di Monsignor Tesoriere . . .", 24 April 1825 (ASR: Camerale III b. 1910, #125; ASP: 30/c, libro rosso 2).

60 Uggeri (1823; 2nd edition 1825).

61 Angelo Uggeri, "Memoria," 24 April 1825 (ASR: CSRBSP Segreteria b. 286, f. 1; republished as Appendix IV in Moreschi [1840b], p. 195).

62 Angelo Uggeri, "Memoria," 24 April 1825 (ASR: CSRBSP Segreteria b. 286, f. 1; republished as Appendix IV in Moreschi [1840b], p. 195).

63 Giulio Maria della Somaglia to Nicola Maria Nicolai, 20 May 1825 (ASR: Camerale III b. 1910, #128).

124   FIRE IN THE TEMPLE

64 Pasquale Belli and Andrea Alippi, "Scandaglio della spesa che prossimativamente sarebbe per importare l'intero ristauro della Basilica di S. Paolo," 22 April 1825 (ASR: CSRBSP Segreteria b. 276, f. 1; tiG p. 309; Giovanni Francesco Zelli, "L'Abbate di S. Paolo umilia un progetto sopra i ristauri della Basilica . . .," 22 April 1825 (ASP: 32/c, b. 1828–1850, f. 1).

65 The Pro-Memoria of 4 June 1825, cited by Groblewski ([2001], p. 309), indicates that Valadier had been asked before 20 May to supply his estimate within a month (ASR: CSRBSP Segreteria b. 276, f. 3).

66 Giuseppe Valadier to Giulio Maria della Somaglia, 26 May 1825 (ASR: Camerale III b. 1910, b. 5). For the message to Uggeri, see the documents annexed to Uggeri's correspondance with Nicolai, 20 May 1825 (ASR: Camerale III b. 1910, #128).

67 Giulio Maria della Somaglia to Belisario Cristaldi, 10 June 1825 (ASR: Camerale III b. 1909, #33; copy at 1910, #143; ASP: 30/c, libro rosso 2). See also Marconi (1964), p. 230.

68 Giuseppe Venturoli, Giambattista Martinetti, Luigi Brandolini, and Luigi Gozzi to Giulio Maria della Somaglia, 18 June 1825 (ASR: CSRBSP Segreteria b. 276, f. 1; ASP: 30/c, libro rosso 2; tiG pp. 309–310); Pasquale Belli to Angelo Uggeri, "Oggetto: Materiali che hanno servito per determinare lo Scandaglio degli Archit.i Alippi e Belli," 2 July 1825 (ASR: CSRBSP Segreteria b. 276, f. 1; tiG pp. 310–311); Giuseppe Venturoli, Girolamo Scaccia, Luigi Brandolini, and Luigi Gozzi, "Giudizio," 22 July 1825 (ASR: CSRBSP Segreteria b. 276, f. 1; ASP: 30/c, libro rosso 2; tiG p. 315).

69 Guglielmo Closse, "Offerta," 16 July 1825 (ASR: Camerale III b. 1909, #62; Camerlengato, P. II, Tit. IV, b. 155, f. 204; tiG pp. 313–314).

70 Giulio Maria della Somaglia to Belisario Cristaldi, 19 July 1825 (ASR: Camerale III b. 1910, #134).

71 Giuseppe Valadier to Belisario Cristaldi, 2 August 1825 (ASR: Camerale III b. 1910, #136).

72 Della Somaglia to Giustiniani (21 August 1825), as in Chapter 5 n.48.

73 *Cronaca* II, 14 September 1825.

74 Pope Pius VII (1825); *DdR*, 28 September 1825, pp. 1–2.

75 Pope Pius VII (1825), p. 4.

76 Giuseppe Valadier to Belisario Cristaldi, 1825 (ASR: Camerale III b. 1909, #33; b. 1910, #143; ASP: 30/c, libro rosso 2). Giuseppe Valadier to Nicola Maria Nicolai, 1825 (ASR: Camerale III b. 1910, #143).

77 Special Commission, *Dubii e Risoluzioni della Commissione speciale . . .*, 23 November 1825 (ASR: Camerale III b.1910, #143). The annotated copies of both Uggeri (ASR: CSRBSP Segreteria b. 286, f. 2) and della Somaglia (AAV: Segreteria di Stato; Spogli dei Cardinali; Della Somaglia Giulio, b. 2B, f. E) survive. See also the discussion in Groblewski (2001), pp. 98–101.

78 Angelo Uggeri to Giuseppe Valadier, 24 November 1825 (ASR: Camerale III b. 1910, #148); Angelo Uggeri to Gaspare Salvi, 27 November 1825 (ASR: Camerale III b. 1910, #148).

79 *DdR*, 3 December 1825, p. 1.

80 BAV: Cod. Vat.Lat. 13842 (cited in Pallottino [1997], p. 336 n. 21).

SIX

CATHOLIC ROMANTICISM

PREVIOUSLY WE NOTED THE APPARENT PARADOX IN HOW VALADIER'S faith in a universal classical ideal worked against him in the debates of 1823–1825; how at the very moment when the Catholic leadership was defining itself as the final redoubt of resistance to relativism in religion and politics, conservatives were fighting against a proposal advocated by Valadier on the basis of the universal validity of the classical ideal. Not only that, but they branded his traditionalist project an innovation, while advocating in its place a far more innovative – indeed, unprecedented – solution, which they justified not with reference to a timeless ideal but to historical meanings associated with recent local events. Making no claim to universal validity, the *in pristinum* solution proclaimed its meanings by activating subjective associations specific to a particular community of belief.

The *in pristinum* project and its rationale were, to put it differently, Romantic. This claim may seem counterintuitive and warrants a little explanation, since few observers then or now would associate the atmosphere of clerical conservativism that prevailed in early nineteenth-century Rome with Romanticism. The impact of Romanticism on the Catholic Church is most often studied with respect to literature and theology, where the standard story is one of a thwarted revolution. In this account, an array of early nineteenth-century Catholic scholars and theologians around Europe develop new approaches to Catholic religiosity that are identified by contemporaries as Romantic.[1] Countering the dominant rationalist traditions of the

Counter-Reformation, these thinkers envisage a larger place in religious life for the nonrational and subjective aspects of human experience. Enthusiasms for medieval religiosity and mysticism join with intrepid philosophizing to push orthodoxy to its limits and sometimes beyond. While these movements rejuvenate Catholic devotion in certain quarters, the Church hierarchy in Rome comes quickly to mistrust them as incompatible with Catholic traditions of authority.[2] The movement is definitively throttled when Pope Gregory XVI issues not one but two encyclicals, in 1832 and 1834, condemning the Catholic Romanticism associated with the French priest Hugues-Félicité Robert de Lamennais, among others. In the second half of the century, the Church gradually enshrines an orderly neoscholasticist theology as the new orthodoxy, which later hardens into the neo-Thomism that still today represents the main way of Catholic theology. Ergo, the nineteenth-century Roman hierarchy, to the extent that it engaged with Romanticism at all, was against it.[3]

This history, however, omits many of the twists and turns of what was actually a far more complicated relationship. For one thing, Catholic Romanticism was hardly limited to theology. It also informed concerns about the condition of religion and society in Europe, as well as the perception that Catholic Christendom faced an existential crisis in its confrontation with modern secularism.[4] Catholic Romanticism also changed its character significantly between the 1820s and the 1830s, and the Roman hierarchy was not nearly as hostile to its first iterations as it was to those of a decade later.[5] In fact, the writings of Catholic Romantic writers – Lamennais most of all – enjoyed enormous influence in Rome during the first three years of Leo XII's pontificate, which is to say at precisely the moment of the San Paolo debate, on which they unquestionably had a major impact. Leo's pontificate actually began under a banner of religious renewal with a strongly Lamennaisian flavor, with "indifferentism" identified as a key malady afflicting the Church and the promulgation of a vivid "theology of visibility" as the necessary means of regeneration.[6] In distinction to the ultratraditionalist *zelanti* in the Curia, who were steeped in defensiveness and nostalgia, Leo in the first years of his pontificate surrounded himself with an ultramontanist group that saw the new challenges of the era as an opportunity for the Church.[7] This group included figures like Gioacchino Ventura and Giovanni Marchetti, who shared the Lamennasian sense that the humble faithful would soon become the protagonists of a Catholic restoration.[8] It was also from Lamennais that Pope Leo drew his vision for the 1825 Rome Jubilee, in which the Catholic faith was to be vividly externalized in all public places and behaviors, with hopes of inspiring an international revival of Catholic fervor.[9] Several passages of Leo's manifesto *Ubi Primum* drew upon Lamennais's *Essai sur l'indifférence en matière de religion* (1817 ff), and a few months after issuing it Leo even received Lamennais twice in Rome. Leo was known to keep just two portraits in his

CATHOLIC ROMANTICISM

private cabinet, one of the Virgin and one of Lamennais, and there is even reason to believe that in October 1826 Leo appointed Lamennais a cardinal *in pectore*, although the matter is uncertain.[10] This Lamennaisian moment in Rome came to a relatively abrupt end later in 1826, as the failure of the 1825 Jubilee to generate a mass Catholic revival moved Leo XII to a reluctant recognition that Lamennais's project was perhaps not practicable.[11]

Part of the attraction lay in Lamennais's raucous Manichean rhetoric, for instance his claim that Protestantism and atheism were based on the same nefarious principle that rationality should determine belief. Lamennais held that the only true path was rather that of blind and total submission to the unrationalizable authority of Catholic traditions, institutions, and moral precepts. Such antirationalist mystifications were a Romantic Catholic calling card, and they echo resoundingly through *Ubi Primum*. But they were by no means restricted to the utterances of Pope Leo, nor was Lamennais the only figure of influence. The two-year existence of Padre Ventura's *Giornale ecclesiastico di Roma* coincided precisely with the apex of Lamennais's Roman vogue, and its pages bulged with admiring references to Lamennais and the intransigent Louis de Bonald ("a sublime genius" and "the glory of France"), along with citations from works like Joseph Le Maistre's reactionary call to order, *Du Pape* (1819).[12] But above all, Ventura revered Lamennais, whom he met in Naples in 1824 and in a star-struck letter described to a friend as "great and immortal."[13]

So it would certainly be inaccurate to say that Romanticism in a cultural sense was without influence in the Rome of Leo XII. Romanticism is of course a capacious and endlessly contested term, but still a useful one provided it is defined thoughtfully. Rather than narrow it to a literary or artistic or even theological movement, a more suggestive approach, following Michael Löwy and Robert Sayre, is to see in Romanticism the contours of a worldview: one broadly antipathetic toward the new ways of life forged by an ever-advancing capitalism, philosophical Enlightenment, political liberalism, secular progressivism, and the rise of the bourgeoisie.[14] Romanticism in this sense was not a movement; it was too disunified, diffuse, and contradictory for that label. It was rather a polyvalent mode of criticality, protest, and lament that aspired to redeem the disappointments and anxieties born of modern transformations. As such, it accommodated both progressive and reactionary elements and exerted an attraction at all points along the ideological spectrum. Among the innumerable tropes common to it were a keening sense of historical loss; nostalgia for an idealized past; anguish over the disenchantment of the world; dislike of mechanization, abstraction, and rationalization; affinity for the traditional, the local, the concrete, and the particular; abhorrence of rationalism and enlightened universalism; a preference for blind adherence to traditions and authorities, even when – or even because – they were irrational or nonrationizable; adoration of the heroic individual who resists a soulless world; longing for the unity of community and a dream of plenitude to replace modern fragmentation and alienation. Central to all iterations of the Romantic worldview was a fetishization of history, which in turn reflected the conviction that a cold and overweening Enlightenment had unfairly written off the warm past as backward and superstitious. Neither analytical in a materialist sense nor ideologically programmatic, Romanticism in this sense simply bemoaned the discrete ramifications of the modern socioeconomic and epistemic order as they were perceived from any number of specific vantage points. This diffusely reactive quality in Romantic criticism helps explain its contradictory plurality, and the ease with which it was adopted by both the political or religious left and right.

Approaching Romanticism like this helps us to see past the self-interested claims of Church leaders who would present the reactionary discourses of 1820s Rome as expressing a timeless and unchanging Catholicity – an ahistorical analysis that was echoed, in a different key, by the Church's contemporary enemies, for whom the Church was unmodern and stuck in the past. By recognizing that what was being said, thought, and debated in Rome shared a language and habits of critique with other discourses unfolding in very different contexts across Europe, we position ourselves far better to apprehend the Roman debates about San Paolo in the modern context historically proper to them. It helps us, in other words, to see these debates, and the ultimate triumph of the *in pristinum* solution in Leo XII's Chirograph of September 1825, not as the product of an unmodern Church clinging to a repressive and unchanging worldview, but as a quintessentially modern response to modern developments, couched even in a modern language.

Reframed in this way, Pope Leo's Chirograph and the *in pristinum* solution more generally no longer appear so paradoxical but are revealed as the peculiar products of the profound historicist reassessments so familiar from other contemporary contexts. Historicist modes of thought reflect the Romantic mistrust of ahistorical abstractions and absolutes: whereas enlightened rationality sees itself cutting through and unifying lived experience, historicism instead posits history as irreducible and determining, in all its specificity, contingency, and variety.[15] This is worth remembering because most of what has been written about European architectural historicism to date has focused on its links to nationalism and the emergence of bourgeois political elites who, having displaced aristocracies that were legitimized with reference to a divine order, sought a secular legitimacy story of their own. It would be impossible to fit the debates around San Paolo into such a framework if we were to remain satisfied with the long-established narrative of the Church as not only antimodern but unmodern. Our historiographical reframing of the San Paolo debates helps us thereby to see that this narrative requires revision.

Given however that Papal Rome in the 1820s was still a poor feudal economy with a tightly policed public sphere, a theocratic absolute ruler, and only a small and quietist bourgeoisie, one might reasonably be skeptical that the disruptions of modernity were so powerfully palpable there. Certainly they were not experienced in Rome as they were in the future heartlands of industrial capitalism in northern Europe. But the metamorphoses of rich and powerful nations do impact their smaller, weaker neighbors, and it is chiefly in this way that capitalist liberal modernity made its impact in Papal Rome.

Some of this we have already seen. At the geopolitical and economic level, the upheavals of the period 1789–1815 had overthrown the Church's former status and influence in Europe. The post–Congress of Vienna "restoration" ostensibly aimed to stitch the *ancien régime* back together, but in reality a new configuration of political ambition, public power, and economic wealth had taken hold that ruled out a return to the old theocratic ways. A constant refrain in the conservative Romantic literature of 1820s Rome blamed the unbridled egotism and hubris of modern ideologies for destroying the old consensus of submission to the throne of St. Peter, and for replacing it with a chaos of refractory identities and beliefs. To make matters worse, European economies were rapidly liberalizing and expanding after 1815, which magnified the relative poverty of the Holy Father's stagnant feudality.

Modern disruptions also visited Rome with the two French occupations, which each in their different ways attacked the historic exceptionalism of Rome in order to recast the city in a modern image, depersonalizing and bureaucratizing what had traditionally been managed through relations of clientage and fealty, and replacing the poetry of the Eternal City with the prose of the *chef-lieu du département du Tibre*.[16] The French also dismantled the pontifical state's system of charitable almsgiving, on which roughly half the population depended, and liberalized the foodstuffs market, two disastrous "reforms" that only confirmed to clerical apologists that capitalist values and Christianity were antithetical. Why else did mighty England have so many more starving people than the impoverished Papal States?[17] Such attitudes were later to land books like John Stuart Mill's *Principles of Political Economy* on the Index of Prohibited Books and would inform Pius IX's declaration that the Church could never reconcile with the doctrines of "progress, liberalism and modern civilization."[18]

Earlier still, in the eighteenth century, cultural tourists from the north had brought another unwelcome jolt to Rome. These tourists came especially from England, the most developed capitalist economy of the day, where economic growth had put ambitious travel within reach for an unprecedented range of people, most of whom were not Catholic and many of whom harbored anti-Catholic prejudices. This had serious consequences in Rome. Roman guidebooks gradually abandoned their traditional religious presentation of the city, conceived with Catholic pilgrims in mind, and turned to helping cultural tourists educate and entertain themselves.[19] In Roman clerical circles, this was experienced as a brazen appropriation that perverted the city's true vocation of proclaiming the providential triumph of the Catholic Church and the munificence of the popes.[20] The northern tourists to whom these guides catered also increasingly had the means to buy and export artworks, or in some cases even antiquities. The papal government reinforced its legislative controls against such exports, but with limited success, and a number of shrewd dealers – most of them British – grew very rich off a booming trade.[21] The overmatched papal government ultimately had to devote significant resources to safeguarding Rome's patrimony, sometimes even to the point of purchasing at-risk works from collectors and aristocratic families simply to keep them in the city.[22]

By puncturing the status of the Church abroad and by challenging, humiliating, and disenchanting it at home, these repeated blows struck at what had long been seen as immutable realities consecrated by the will of God. And as such they easily called forth Romantic tropes of critique and lament. Löwy and Sayre offer a typology of Romantic worldviews, of which two in particular describe large parts of the conservative spectrum in 1820s Catholic Rome: "restitutionist Romanticism" and "conservative Romanticism."[23] The nostalgia of the former type centered on a distant idealized past, often the Middle Ages, while the nostalgia of the latter looked to the period immediately prior to the French Revolution, to an old regime in which aspects of the modern socioeconomic order were present but not yet perceived as inimical to tradition. Thus Leo XII in his encyclicals blamed modern freedoms for the contemporary contagions of disunity, immorality, instability, and social fragmentation; as a counterpoint, he offered the Lamennasian ideal of the Jubilee pilgrim in Rome who surrenders to blissful immersion in a joyous community of unquestioned faith. The same starkly dualistic tone characterized the works of Padre Ventura, who coached his readers in plangent terms to see the Church as spurned and no doubt unfashionable, yet implacable in its condemnation of newly hegemonic doctrines like the right of individual conscience or tolerance (called *indifference* in his parlance, following Lamennais). Like Leo, Ventura took explicit aim at the eighteenth-century traumas – Rousseau and Voltaire, Enlightenment and Revolution, and finally liberalism – that in his view had erased an earlier idyll of order and stability.[24] Sometimes his nostalgia reached back further still, to the Crusades, when, in his view, the Christian nations had come together in the "marvelous unity of a great family under a single head, which, were it not for Protestantism, would still endure."[25] For Ventura, modern evils were essentially formed upon the individualistic principle inherent in Protestantism, which had bled forth recently from religion to politics.[26] This bitter anathemizing of normative contemporary values was new in the rhetoric of post-Tridentine Catholic apologetics: never before had the Church felt itself so completely betrayed by the world around it.

It would be difficult to imagine an event more apt than the fire at San Paolo to call forth the quintessential Romantic sentiments: the experience of loss; nostalgia for the way things were; desire to overcome a threat to a cherished and idealized historical past; a sense that present misfortunes were the fault of hostile modern ideas brought in from outside; a conviction that "our" tragic loss gives comfort and pleasure to "the world"; and so on. Even before the fire, the pressure of a decade and a half of French domination and occupation had already conjured such sentiments, and as we saw, the result was an unprecedented campaign of scholarly rebuildings aimed at restoring the damaged fabric of Rome's churches *in pristinum*. The fire at San Paolo then concretized these sentiments in a single event. We have seen already what an appetite there was in Rome for the Romantic aesthetics of loss and tragedy, with Leo XII's initial plans to hold Jubilee masses within the charred shell of San Paolo, or in the official approval he subsequently gave to a reconstruction project that foregrounded the ruined nave. This melancholy nostalgia for an idealized past also informed the contemporary swell of affection for the crude grandeur of Early Christian architectural aesthetics, which spoke powerfully to the muscular self-image many Catholics hoped the Church might recover: one that had greedily built its rude churches from the temple carcasses of its former persecutors, with none of the self-effacing admiration of pagan Rome that characterized nineteenth-century attitudes.[27] For Roman clerics reeling from a catastrophic quarter century, that unapologetic confidence formed a telling contrast with the latter-day solicitude toward pagan art. They thrilled to identify with a manifestly Christian architecture that the cultivated tastemakers dismissed as uncouth. Its rawness now looked like an emblem of virile authenticity and substance: a local architecture whose significance extended no further than the Christian, or indeed the Roman Catholic, historical context and that would never offer itself up for use in the design of banal post offices and stock exchanges.

When Fea depicted Valadier's essentialist conception of classical idealism as an "innovation" with respect to Roman Catholic tradition, he was making the classic Romantic move of inventing an ideal past that the present by definition has betrayed. The claim was plausible to contemporaries partly because there was a grain of truth in it: Valadier's approach was traditional in perpetuating the old association between Vitruvian classicism and Rome's providential status, but it was modern in some of the forms it took. The stylistic language of Valadier's designs was in dialogue with architecture in decidedly non-Catholic contexts elsewhere, and we have seen with his Milvian Bridge how this appearance of cosmopolitanism could undermine the sense of Roman primacy that traumatized clerical conservatives demanded. Valadier's position was also modern with respect to the absolutely superior position he assigned the classical ideal vis-à-vis other stylistic modes, which reflected universalizing frameworks developed by Enlightenment theorists. At the end of one of the copies of his commentary on Fea's *Anedotti*, Valadier made a startling slip of the pen when he wrote that if Leo XII executed his project rather than an *in pristinum* one, the pope would be leaving behind as his legacy a "Temple that would honor the arts and the eighteenth century."[28] He meant, of course, the *nineteenth* century, as a contemporary commenter noted in pencil in the margin. One need not be a convinced Freudian to see the error as revealing: as a haunting presentment on Valadier's part that his ideals were being superseded by newer conceptions pegged to different ambitions. His haughty claim that classicism represented an absolute aesthetic truth smacked enough of the values of the Church's enlightened enemies to Fea and his public that they rendered plausible the claim that Valadier's approach constituted an "innovation."

Finally, the very prodigality of the *in pristinum* solution resonated with the defiant antirationalism inherent to Romantic discourses. The reduced-size church Valadier had proposed was, if nothing else, reasonable: the Church was poor, while San Paolo was remote, rarely visited, and half the year abandoned. Its sagging disrepair had occasioned little serious concern in Rome before the fire. Here is what a sensible English visitor – a Catholic, in fact – had to say in 1825:

> A committee is appointed to rebuild this Basilica, I believe on the ancient plan. If so, great sums will be spent to brace up splintered columns, and reconstruct a church, which, were it in the centre of Rome, would still be of an useless, unnecessary size: how much more so, when placed in fields at a distance of two miles from the walls of the town! The Committee would do better, were they to build, out of the ruins of the Basilica, and over the tomb of the Apostle, a handsome chapel, proportioned in size to the number of the religious of the adjoining convent, and of the congregation of the neighbourhood ... I regret having contributed half a paul towards this work, which I have already given you my reason for disapproving of, but which, fortunately, my gift will not very materially advance.[29]

Such reasonable concerns reflected precisely that cold modern spirit of calculation that defiant Romantic clerics reviled. To insist that the only acceptable response to the fire was to embark on a staggeringly expensive reconstruction, for which the Church would have to trust God to inspire massive generosity among the faithful – this proved irresistible, for it repudiated the whole modern regime of ascertaining worth through cold rational abstractions instead of through the unquantifiable warmth of beliefs, faith, obedience, and devotion. A small and economical San Paolo would announce that Rome had internalized its enemies' mode of calculation and accepted their claim that the Church was poor and diminished; it would surrender the Church's self-image of grandeur and magnificence. The *in pristinum* solution, with its imprudent cost and disproportionate scale, presented itself as an act of heedless obedience to the divine command encoded in the fire. As a lavish home for the buried bones of an 1,800-year-old ghost, and a celebration of his decidedly nonmodern philosophy, the very function of the building scorned modern materialist reason. It was meaningfully irresponsible and spoke both to Catholics and the world of a faith that flinched at nothing, of a love unconstrained by reason. As Paul had asked of the Corinthians, "Hath not God made foolish the wisdom of this world?"[30]

The fundraising drive that this reckless devotion required personalized the gesture for Catholics everywhere, inviting them too to relinquish modern acquisitiveness and come together in the plenitude of a unified community of generosity and sacrifice. A spatially exploded and mediatized Jubilee for those unable to make it to the one Leo planned in Rome, the fundraising drive was to be a manifesto of Romantic Catholic revolt against the new gods of the contemporary world and a public demonstration of the Catholic alternative: a generous, selfless, obedient community fearless in its love of God.

The historicism enshrined both in Leo XII's Chirograph and in the *in pristinum* solution also indicates just how alienated Church leaders had come to feel before the values of the modern world. Historicism hinges on the rejection of historical absolutes; it delegitimizes the universalizing narrative of golden ages and ages of decadence and posits rather that the particular historical development of any given community will determine which aspects of history are of special value to it. The new San Paolo announced in Leo's Chirograph depended on precisely such a conception, for it frankly relinquished Valadier's ambition of participating in a universal aesthetic truth and pinned its meaning instead to the narratives of one particular community. Why was this important shift away from the universalizing perspective of especially recent classical theory occurring now, in the 1820s?

Part of the answer lies in the appropriation of classical aesthetics by the Church's enemies during the Enlightenment and French Revolution, as discussed in the first chapter. But part of what had emboldened the forces of Enlightenment and Revolution to reach so confidently for that prize was an assurance that their ideals constituted humanity's new universal touchstone, and part of why the Church ultimately proved ambivalent about the loss of classicism was because its own supposed universality was rapidly ebbing. The notion of a universal Church whose influence would always naturally permeate every aspect of European society could hardly have survived the season of humiliation and tragedy that visited Rome between 1798 and 1814. The language of reactionary Catholic Romanticism in the 1820s was that of a once powerful institution coming to grips with its marginalization. Church leaders were grappling at least subconsciously with the implications of what it meant that the Church had been expelled from so many quarters where it had once been welcome. That made it all but impossible to continue thinking of the Church as coextensive with humanity. The Church was instead a particular community within humanity – one dedicated to a universal truth, to be sure, but that multitudes had turned upon or abandoned. These transformations made some clerical imaginations susceptible to the troubling modern insight that civilizations, as antiquity reminds us, have finite lifespans. And that insight, in turn, was closely related to the willful ambition of historicist architecture to refabricate civilizational continuity.[31] Such admissions were never articulated in so many words, but the surrender of classicism and the enthusiastic embrace of a historicist reconstruction project for San Paolo afford a suggestive glimpse into a never explicitly acknowledged mutation in the Church's own self-image, born of recent crises and traumas.

Bearing this in mind, it becomes easier to situate the historicist ambitions of the San Paolo reconstruction into the European history of architectural historicism. Historicist architectural idioms aimed to tell the stories of particular communities that, for whatever reason, saw universalist styles as generic or lacking meaning, and in response retreated into the Romantic bunker of the specific, the local, and the particular. The very point of the Romantic languages of architectural historicism was that they did not claim to speak equally and, as it were, generically to all communities. (When decades later Viollet-le-Duc was invited to imagine an appropriate modern architecture for Russia, he did not transpose the Gothic idiom he championed in France but rather used his analytical *process* to distill a historical idiom specific to Russia.)[32] The debate on San Paolo helps us to recognize that even at the very moment when the Catholic Church seemed most in thrall to reactionary essentialism, most at odds with the contemporary modern world, it could not escape from the relativizing logic of a newly multipolar sociopolitical world.

*
**

To sum up: Leo XII's decision in 1825 to rebuild San Paolo in its original Paleochristian style constituted an unprecedented break with a long tradition of Roman architectural practice. To describe it as a mere question of changing taste is to beg the question of the significance of this decision. In fact, the decision seems to reflect a shift then playing out within the Church leadership as it surveyed the transformed world of the early nineteenth century and sought to reckon how the Church's place in it had changed. The rejection of Valadier's classicism implicitly acknowledged that the universalist claims associated with the outward signs of Catholic art and culture had lost their credibility; that those classical signs were too often now to be seen celebrating the supposedly universal values of God's rampant enemies. The entwinement of essentialist aesthetics and religion could hold together only as long as Catholic supremacy seemed normative, and as the Church felt assured of its role as the gatekeeper to society's normative deity. By 1825, that world no longer existed. By withdrawing into the isolation of Romantic meaning-making at San Paolo, Church leaders unwittingly internalized the very relativism against which they so violently protested in other areas where specifically religious claims were more obviously at stake. Leo had affirmed a building and an aesthetics that were for "us" and that no longer claimed to be for "all," for he and other Church leaders were readjusting their sense of what place the Church occupied in the world. This is the most important revelation to emerge from the San Paolo debates of 1823–1825.

NOTES

1   Many leading Catholic Romantic intellectuals – Chateaubriand, Lamennais, Le Maistre – were French, but Catholic Romantic theology was centered in Germany, at the universities in Munich and Tübingen. The artistic Romantic Catholicism of Pugin in England and of Montalembert et al. in France was a phenomenon of the 1830s.

2   Bénichou (1977), pp. 217–218.

3   Aubert et al. (1981); O'Meara (1982); Reardon (1985); Gadille and Mayeur (1995), pp. 22–25.

4   See, for example, Ventura's letter to Canosa of 24 September 1824, quoted in Pirri (1932), p. 315.

5   Pirri (1932); Colapietra (1963), esp. pp. 56–71, 220–256, 287–293, 429–448; Boutry (1997), pp. 317–367; Colapietra (2014); Federici (2020), pp. 63–80; Milbach (2020); Regoli (2020).

6   Boutry (1997), p. 349; Milback (2020), pp. 51–60; Regoli (2020), pp. 21–25.

7   Colapietra (1963), pp. 237–256; Milback (2020), pp. 60–61.

8   Colapietra (1963), pp. 238–249; Federici (2020), pp. 68–69.

9   Boutry (1997), p. 349. See also Colapietra (2014), pp. 17 ff.

10 Colapietra (1963), pp. 327–329; Le Guillou (1978), pp. 1–9; Milbach (2020), pp. 53–54.

11 Colapietra (1963), pp. 287–293; Regoli (2020), pp. 27 ff. See also Pirri (1932), pp. 313–314.

12 Ventura (1825d), pp. 197, 231; Pirri (1932), p. 318. On Le Maistre and De Bonald, see Stewart (1920), pp. 370–374.

13 Pirri (1932), pp. 314–318.

14 Löwy and Sayre (2001).

15 Löwy and Sayre (2001), p. 40.

16 Boutry (1997) pp. 326–327.

17 Crocella (1982), p. 23.

18 Mills's *Principles* were placed on the Index on 12 June 1856 (Bujanda and Richter [2002], p. 620); quote from Allocution "Jamdudum cernimus," 18 March 1861 (*TEPD*, v. 4, p. 214).

19 Di Nola (1989).

20 Boutry (1997), p. 336.

21 Coen (2019).

22 Johns (2000), pp. 30–31, 40.
23 Löwy and Sayre (2001), pp. 59–60.
24 Ventura (1825c), pp. 23–31.
25 Ventura (1825d), p.224.
26 Ventura (1825c), p. 24 n. 1.
27 cf. Wiseman (1858), p. 200.
28 Valadier (1 March 1825), as in Chapter 5 n. 22.
29 Beste (1826), v. 1, pp. 57–58.
30 1 Corinthians 1:20.
31 Blix (2009), pp. 4, 96–98.
32 Viollet-le-Duc (1877).

PART II

RESURRECTING SAN PAOLO

SEVEN

MATTERS OF MONEY

Embedded in the debate analyzed in Part I were two distinct conceptions of what exactly one spoke about when one spoke of the basilica of San Paolo. In the perspective associated with Valadier, San Paolo was a material object in real space: an aesthetic and functional structure to be experienced in person. In the perspective associated with the advocates of the *in pristinum* solution, the rebuilt San Paolo offered instead a point of reference for narratives that were to circulate far beyond the building's physical site. These two conceptions thus also implied distinct audiences or publics. In the first, whenever doubts or questions arose in the course of work, the point of reference was to the experience of the spectator at the actual building. In the second, what mattered was instead how the reconstruction enterprise was broadcast to an exponentially larger public, the majority of which would never visit the building but rather know it solely from verbal and graphic representations.

Total victory seemed to have come for the partisans of this latter position when Pope Leo XII issued his Chirograph. But in fact these two perspectives remained in conflict throughout the initial phase of work under the direction of Pasquale Belli (1825–1833). For those involved with the practical task of raising money for the reconstruction, the reconstituted San Paolo was to be the guarantor of a religious narrative about a resurgent Catholic Church, devotion to St. Paul, and the will of God. This was the perspective that texts like Leo XII's Encyclicals and Chirograph promoted, and in the late 1820s it helped create for San Paolo what can justifiably be termed the first ever genuinely global public for a work of architecture. But for the architects and the academic committees that oversaw them, it was the stone-and-mortar reality of the new building that most mattered, with the result that the Chirograph's neat narrative of a precise reconstruction proved deeply problematic. These men were conditioned by a lifetime of designing according to contemporary aesthetic and technical standards, and they found it all but impossible to set those standards aside in order to reproduce what they mostly regarded as the positively inferior standards of an earlier age. The resurgent San Paolo consequently took shape in the late 1820s as an uncertain mosaic of conflicting intentions and perspectives, with publicists and builders alike navigating unavoidable compromises that ultimately rendered many aspects of the rising building unsatisfying, whether as an image of return to the Early Christian era or as a successful contemporary design.

This early struggle to reconcile the two San Paolos – the publicitary and the material – forms the subject of Part II, where it is read as emblematic of the larger challenges the Church faced in navigating between the demands of its traditional beliefs and the new possibilities of an increasingly interconnected, mobile, informationalized Western world. The current chapter will focus on the fundraising drive for the reconstruction: its organization, its publicitary reach, and the demographics and possible rationales of those who contributed to it. The following two chapters will then consider the ferocious debates that erupted between 1825 and 1831 as the various institutions Leo XII had entrusted with responsibility for carrying out the simple mandate of his Chirograph faced the surprisingly contentious task of translating his vision into reality.

The Holy See historically drew its revenues from two main sources: the fees and offerings collected internationally by the Church, and the rents, taxes, and other impositions it collected within the Papal States.[1] Once upon a time, the former had been by far the larger source, but historical events from the Protestant Reformation to the French Revolution had changed that, and by the 1820s the situation was reversed: the latter source was now the larger, despite the poverty and economic stagnation that characterized the pontifical territories and especially the area around Rome.[2] Nearly half the Roman population by this date lived on charity, while those who worked were hardly better off. The Church and local aristocracy owned virtually everything and, whether from complacency or principle, did little to foster economic development. Pius VII and Cardinal Consalvi had just managed to keep the state budget in the black by retaining certain Napoleonic reforms and developing a few new ones of their own, but they had not undertaken any truly

MATTERS OF MONEY

fundamental reforms.[3] In particular, they had not transferred responsibility for economic policy making into the hands of lay experts, which meant that overmatched cardinals and monsignors continued to steer the ship. And once authority passed to the avowedly unworldly Leo XII, the situation became even worse: the days when state budgets finished in the black were soon a distant memory, and would have been even without the staggering expenses entailed by the reconstruction of San Paolo.[4]

The poverty of the pontifical state was an essential factor in the debates on the reconstruction surveyed in Part I: it was why a small-scale reconstruction had been initially favored, and why Leo XII wanted evidence that a fundraising campaign would be effective before he signed off on a full-scale *in pristinum* rebuilding. But what was to be the model for this fundraising campaign? Everyone initially thought of the campaign for the reconstruction of St. Peter's three centuries earlier. But if St. Peter's might still have offered a model for fundraising within the papal territories, it was no longer at all relevant in the world beyond. The Catholic Church in the sixteenth century had been far more influential in European politics and economics than it was in 1825 and had been able to redirect a variety of revenue streams to the rebuilding of Peter's basilica.[5] The Church had also, infamously, made widespread use of the sale of indulgences to fund the rebuilding and had levied special taxes in gold-rich Spain and Portugal.[6] None of these options was available in 1825.

The fundraising drive that summer and autumn therefore unfolded differently. Within the papal territories, a systematic sweep targeted each employee and officeholder of the sprawling pontifical government, down even to the lowliest scribe. Within the international Church as a whole, the upper clergy were mobilized to solicit funds through the lower clergy as well directly from the faithful. Papal nuncios abroad gave personal attention to the courts and nobilities of the Catholic countries to which they were assigned. When della Somaglia sent copies of the Chirograph to the nuncio in Madrid, he expressed the hope that it would reassure anyone there who "might have doubted either the extent of the work to be undertaken, or the part to be paid out of the papal budget."[7] (Efforts to move the actual funds were often complicated by the still improvisational logistics of contemporary international banking. In one instance, the nuncio in Paris, Vincenzo Macchi, reported to della Somaglia that the Bishop of Namur had given him a gift of 3,300 francs for San Paolo, and that in order to effect the transfer of this money to the San Paolo fund, della Somaglia should withdraw an identical sum in Macchi's name from two different Roman institutions, where the nuncio explained he had personal assets.)[8] In the Protestant countries where fundraising was permitted, the state typically interposed itself between Rome and the local clergy who solicited the money. In Prussia, the Protestant king ordered the Catholic archbishops and bishops of his realm to coordinate the drive and to direct its results to the diplomat Bunsen in Rome, who would then transfer them personally to the pope.[9] But little, in general, was expected from such countries: the Netherlands, for instance, received only three copies of the Chirograph, which were given to the Dutch chargé d'affaires in Rome to dispatch to the court in Amsterdam.[10]

Even before September 1825 had ended, della Somaglia was receiving letters of acknowledgment from the diplomatic representatives of European principalities large and small, some of whom accompanied their compliments with personal donations.[11] The most elaborate of these acknowledgments came from Bunsen, who, having received the package of Chirographs for Prussia, raved that it was destined to be "the cornerstone, so to say, of a monument of eternal glory," and that the whole Christian world was sure to feel the same. He also expressed his personal joy "that the generous efforts of His Holiness might succeed in giving us back this noble edifice with its original plan," adding that his king shared these sentiments.[12] News of major contributions was soon arriving daily in della Somaglia's office. In October came word of a massive donation of 4,000 scudi from King Carlo Felice of Sardinia; in November came the results of the first wave of foreign collections in locations from Bavaria to Corfu, as well as a variety of personal donations from the likes of the French minister of foreign affairs (1,000 francs), or from a group at the Viennese court (2,066.03 fiorini d'argento and 182 in zecchini d'oro tedesco).[13] News of one dignitary's gift was circulated to encourage others. The nuncio in Naples wrote in November to della Somaglia to say that when a Neapolitan noble had informed King Francesco I of Naples about the huge donation made by Carlo Felice of Sardinia, Francesco immediately pledged to surpass it by 1,000 scudi. Unfortunately, the noble had misreported the amount donated by Carlo Felice as only 2,000 scudi, so Francesco had only pledged 3,000; but the nuncio reassured della Somaglia that he had corrected Francesco's misapprehension and expected that any day now the king would increase his donation accordingly.[14]

But if the personal touch was essential at the high end of the fundraising drive, it was the printed word that did most of the work in inciting ordinary people to donate. In November, Padre Ventura's *Giornale ecclesiastico* published the pastoral letter written by Archbishop Lambruschini of Genoa, which the papal nuncio in Naples had been badgering della Somaglia for back in August.[15] Joined to a copy of Leo's Encyclical, it followed the pattern of other letters we have seen, identifying Paul as the apostle Christians most regarded as "our Apostle," and speaking of how, in these evil times marked by the loss of faith, God had clearly intended the miraculous survival of Paul's tomb as an incitement to the Church to produce new modern heroes. Lambruschini reminded his readers of the sufferings Paul had endured for their benefit, but also recalled that the old basilica had been especially beloved by Pius VII; those

MATTERS OF MONEY

unmoved by other considerations were urged at least to contribute in memory of the beloved Pius. He warned his Genoese flock in conclusion that Genoa must not allow itself to be outraised by Turin, which he assured his readers was already busy raising funds. The editors of the *Giornale* noted in a brief afterward that the archbishop had recommended the moment when the evangelist was read as the most propitious time to direct the congregation's attention to the collection boxes.

One of the most innovative uses of print in connection with the reconstruction was the decision to publish regular lists of donors and donations in the *Diario di Roma* (one of the many ideas first floated by Antonio Santelli immediately after the fire).[16] Preparations for these lists had been in the works at least since November, when della Somaglia asked his agents for precise tallies of names and figures so that they could be "printed in the *Diario*."[17] The *Prima nota* was published as two separate supplements to the *Diario* in December 1825 and listed all donations received up to that point.[18] The first supplement listed donations received from clerics and high-ranking nobles, starting with Pope Leo's annual bequest of 50,000 scudi and followed by the bequest of the College of Cardinals (2,000 scudi annually)[19] (**Figure 37**). Next came the King of Sardinia (4,000 scudi), then a very large donation from Archbishop Václav Léopold von Chlumčansky of Prague (2,170 scudi), followed by a series of much smaller gifts (200 to 40 scudi) from an assortment of archbishops, nobles, and high-ranking clerics. Then came a series of bishops from across Europe, mostly Italian but also including the aforementioned Bishop of Namur in Belgium, as well as both the Archbishop and Vicar General of Dublin and the controversial Vicar General of the Midlands in England, John Milner. Some had made personal gifts, others were turning over the results of collections made in their dioceses. Then followed the various papal nuncios; an assortment of other clerics, including Abbot Zelli of San Paolo, who passed along a little over 23 scudi that had been donated to him; then some lesser Italian nobles; and finally a few miscellaneous donors, including a German priest who passed along the two and a half scudi he had received for a silver medal he sold to King Ludwig of Bavaria. All of the donors discussed in della Somaglia's correspondence from the previous nine months appear in the list. The total up to this point was 71,479.16 scudi, of which 50,000 came from Leo XII. The second and much longer installment of the *Prima nota* was published a few days later and covered donations mainly from departments and individuals within the government of the Papal States.[20] Many of these pledged a certain sum to be given in installments over the coming several years. Donations ranged from the surprisingly large – 1,500 scudi from a Nettuno landowner – to sums one 100th that size. Funds were received from contractors working on the salt works in Ostia, from a roadways manager in Rome, from Treasurer General Cristaldi (500 scudi) as well as from the staff of Cristaldi's office (1,010 scudi).

37. "Nota delle Oblazioni volontarie fatte per la riedificazione della Basilica di S. Paolo," unpaginated supplement to *DdR*, 21 December 1825.
Source: Author.

The largest gift was the 6,000 scudi collected by the employees of the main government accounting office, the smallest the 3 scudi donated by a cameral minister in Pontecorvo. The sum total for this second part of the *Prima nota* was 142,821.87 scudi, nearly double that of the first part, which meant that, all told, the final haul for pledges in the period prior to 21 December 1825 amounted to a tidy 214,301.03 scudi.

As 1825 turned to 1826, the fundraising effort became more bureaucratized as standardized printed circular letters began flooding out to the administrative subdivisions of the Papal States. Monastic leaders printed appeals to the members of their orders, exhorting them not to let themselves be outraised by other orders.[21] The papal camerlengo Cardinal Galleffi sent out a printed letter to each supervisor in the Reverenda Camera Apostolica instructing them to solicit donations from those working under them, down even to the subaltern level.[22] He explained that the government could contribute only 50,000 scudi per year to the reconstruction, and that since it was a question of no less a figure than St. Paul, everyone was expected to use "the most persuasive methods and employ all possible zeal" in soliciting donations from _____ – and here there was a blank in which to write who exactly the recipient was to target (e.g., "all the employees of your Tribunal"). Other letters were sent by Treasurer General Cristaldi to the departments of the Camera Apostolica scattered across the pontifical territories. The Cameral archive contains the long list of over 100 individuals and offices to which one such letter was sent, from the "General Secretariat of the Treasury," to the "Administration of Streets and Horses," to a series of individuals ("Signore Pellegrino Salvigni, Director of the Papal Mint in Bologna," etc.).[23] The archive also contains responses to these requests, providing detailed lists of which individuals pledged what. For instance, the response sent back to Rome by the vice commissariat for outstanding balances in Ferrara included a spreadsheet listing the eight contributing employees by name and job title (including a porter and the two office scribes) along with their annual and monthly salaries, and finally the amount they each had pledged to the reconstruction (which for the whole vice commissariat added up to just 2.10 scudi).[24]

A bundle of documents in the Archivio Storico Capitolino in Rome permits the reconstruction of the whole sequence of actions that went into the collection efforts of the Camera Capitolina, one of the two civil magistratures that governed Rome at this time, and at the head of which were three Roman aristocrats known as the Conservatori di Roma.[25] The sequence begins in December 1824 with the initial approach from della Somaglia and Uggeri. Writing on behalf of the Special Commission, they requested contributions from the three Conservatori and ask them to circulate the request to the rest of the Camera Capitolina and its employees, adding that they would like a complete list of names so that it might subsequently be "published in the press." The Conservatori then sent out a circular letter to some 74 individuals and offices. In March, they began receiving responses.[26] The Conservatori finally met with Leo XII on 2 September 1826 to present the 15,421.615 scudi worth of pledges they had netted through their efforts. Because some employees had pledged a lump sum while others had promised a monthly or weekly gift for a given period of time, the sum was to be paid in a complex schedule over the coming decade. This was all "benignly approved" by Pope Leo in his audience with the Conservatori. A few days later, della Somaglia wrote to the Conservatori to inform them that he had alerted Treasurer General Cristaldi of the pledge, and before long Cristaldi (and later his successors as treasurer general) was sending over letters of receipt whenever payments were made on the pledges.[27]

The multitude of pledges received for the reconstruction were recorded in various places. On a regional level, there were sheets that listed every individual pledge, no matter how small, from government functionaries in the various Apostolic Delegations of the Papal States (Perugia, Ferrara, Pesaro, etc.).[28] In Rome, these regional lists were then copied into a vast tabbed ledger.[29] The culminating document in the pyramid was an even larger ledger compiled in 1840, which noted not only every pledge since 1825 but also detailed what had actually been paid in respect of each pledge and when.[30] As we will have occasion to discuss later, it turns out that a surprising percentage of what was pledged was never actually paid over, including a significant portion of the pontifical pledge of 50,000 scudi per annum.

At this early stage, however, it was the public promises that mattered most. Not only were long *note* published every several months in the *Diario di Roma*, but the biggest individual pledges were also frequently prepublished as they rolled in.[31] Journalists beyond Rome then often republished these notices, in a publicitary amplification that pontifical government was surely aware of.[32] In March 1826, a noble named Morel de Bauvine offered to make his marble quarries on the Isle of Elba available free of charge for the reconstruction effort; after being reported by the *Diario di Roma* on 4 March, this news was echoed within days in the *Gazzetta Piemontese* [Turin] (16 March), within weeks in the *Oesterreichischer Beobachter* [Vienna] (30 March), the *Gaceta de Madrid* (4 April), and *L'ami de la Religion* [Paris] (5 April), and, within months, in the *United States Catholic Miscellany*, published in Charleston, South Carolina (2 September).[33] Even quicker did the news spread of the gift given by King William I Frederick of the Low Countries, appearing first in the *Diario di Roma* (2 August 1826) and just a month and a half later in the *United States Catholic Miscellany* (23 September).[34] In July 1826, the editors of the *Miscellany* in an aside laid bare this information chain to their South Carolinian readers:

> Our accounts are not later than the last week in May; but the latest publication which has reached us is the *Diario di Roma*, of the 10th of May, No. 37. – His Holiness was in good health, and pretty actively employed in the discharge of his important duties. The last publication of subscriptions for repairing the church of St. Paul was 142,821.87, which added to 71,479.16, previously acknowledged, made a sum total of 214,301 crowns, 3 cents.[35]

The *Diario di Roma* also publicized the results of the national fundraising drives. When King Friedrich Wilhelm III of Prussia paid over the results of his national drive, news of it was soon known as far away as Baltimore, via the "Foreign News" section of *Niles' Weekly Register* (23 September 1826), whose editors included the possibly invented detail that when Pope Leo thanked the Prussian king, he "said that when Protestant churches were to be rebuilt, he hoped that Catholics would prove equally liberal."[36]

Despite initial impressions of frenetic generosity, the number of new pledges dropped off quickly, starting immediately after the *Seconda Nota* of April 1826 (see **Table 1**).

As the table shows, the number of days covered in each *nota* crept upward after the second *nota* was published, presumably in an attempt to mask a decline in giving. In the *Terza nota*, the daily rate of giving declined by 69 percent compared to the period covered by the second. It is also probably no coincidence that the *Quinta nota* covers one more month than the *Quarta nota* had done, since this allowed it to include the massive gift of over 32,000 scudi from the Austrian national fundraising drive and thereby to avoid the appearance of a truly catastrophic drop-off from the previous *nota* (which itself had been swollen by a gift of over 10,000 scudi from the King of France). The remaining *note*, published over the following six years, would continue this trend by each covering a year rather than six months. Despite this, they describe a continually shrinking income stream.

By the time of the *Ottava nota*, the lists of donors were short enough that they no longer appeared as separate supplements but in the columns of the *Diario*. There was a slight uptick in the *Nona nota*, thanks to a few substantial individual bequests, but the *Decima nota* resumed the decline with just eight donors pledging a total of 875.15 scudi, while the *Undecima nota* of 1833 showed only six names pledging just 301.23 scudi – less than the average *daily* receipts from the first two and a half years of the drive. This was to be the final published list. In the end, fully 83 percent of the total pledged during the entire eight-and-a-half-year drive had been pledged already by the end of the second year; as the *Gazzetta Piemontese* reflected philosophically, "sensations, even if they are very powerful at first, inevitably weaken and are sometimes

148 RESURRECTING SAN PAOLO

TABLE 1 *Eleven Funding* Note *Published in the* Diario di Roma

Name	Date published	Period covered	Days covered	Amount (scudi)	Daily Ave. (scudi)	Running Total
Prima nota (1)	21 December 1825	1/25/25–12/21/25	–	71,479.16	–	71,479.16
Prima nota (2)	January 1826	1/25/25–12/21/25	–	142,821.87	–	214,301.03
Prima nota (1+2)	–	1/25/25–12/21/25	330	214,301.03	649.40	214,301.03
Seconda nota[37]	12 April 1826	1/1/26–3/31/26	91	95,995.74	1054.90	310,296.77
Terza nota[38]	2 August 1826	4/1/26–7/25/26	116	38,078.27	328.26	348,375.04
Quarta nota[39]	December 1826	8/1/26–12/31/26	153	53,502.43	349.69	401,877.47
Quinta nota[40]	23 June 1827	1/1/27–6/22/27	174	52,944.79	304.28	454,822.26
Sesta nota[41]	28 June 1828	7/1/27–6/26/28	362	15,110.00	41.74	469,932.26
Settima nota[42]	23 June 1829	7/1/28–6/20/29	356	5,535.14	15.55	475,467.40
Ottava nota[43]	26 June 1830	6/26/29–6/26/30	366	1,744.49	4.77	477,211.89
Nona nota[44]	2 July 1831	6/26/30–7/1/31	369	3,742.06	10.14	480,953.95
Decima nota[45]	30 June 1832	7/1/31–6/30/32	365	875.15	2.40	481,829.10
Undecima nota[46]	10 July 1833	6/30/32–7/10/33	375	301.23	0.88	482,130.33

even forgotten as time passes."[47] The decision to continue the drive for so long was probably as much about publicity as it was about scudi. Publication of the results in the *Diario di Roma* not only helped spread awareness of the drive even overseas, but the practice of giving the geographical location of each donor also enabled contemporaries – as it enables us – to observe how the geographical reach of the fundraising campaign expanded each year even as total receipts were shrinking.[48] The *Prima nota* was predominantly an Italian affair, whereas the *Seconda nota* included more Spanish donors, some donors in Ireland and England, and a smattering of figures from the Netherlands, Bavaria, France, and even as far as Greece (drives on the island of Zante, then a British protectorate, had netted 346 scudi; see **Figures 38** and **39**). By the *Terza nota* in August 1826, the Atlantic Ocean had been crossed, with a substantial donation of 800 scudi from " the Seminary of Montreal in Canada, diocese of Quebec." (More about this in a few paragraphs.) The *Quarta nota*, covering the

MATTERS OF MONEY 149

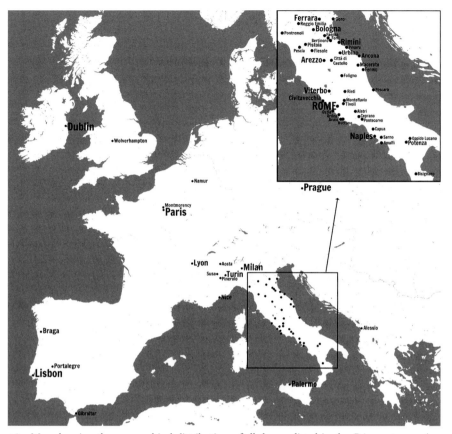

38. Map showing the geographical distribution of all donors listed in the *Prima nota* covering the period from 25 January 1825 to 21 December 1825.
Source: Author.

rest of 1826, opened with pledges from clerics in Italy, Spain, Portugal, and Ireland, as well as from the eastern periphery of Europe (Poznań, Wrocław, Olomouc, Gniezno), but also contained another gift from Canada, this time from the first hospital of the city in Montreal (401 scudi), as well as one from a pair of nobles in Michoacán in central Mexico (100 scudi). In the *Quinta nota* (June 1827), there is a donation from St. Petersburg in Russia, one from "sig. Jucan Jose Ruiz of Guatemala in America" (40 scudi), and one from the bishop of Nueva Caceres in the Philippines (180.98 scudi). The *Sesta nota* reports a gift from the former plenipotentiary minister of the emperor of Brazil to the Holy See (200 scudi) and another from the bishop of Quebec (1,506 scudi), along with continued donations from individuals and groups around Europe (Austria, Hungary, the Netherlands, Portugal, France, and of course Italy). The *Settima nota* included two more donations from the Philippines – the bishops of Nueva Caceres and Nueva Segovia – while the *Ottava nota* relayed news of a series of collections in Ireland and told also of the 5,177.50 scudi that had been collected

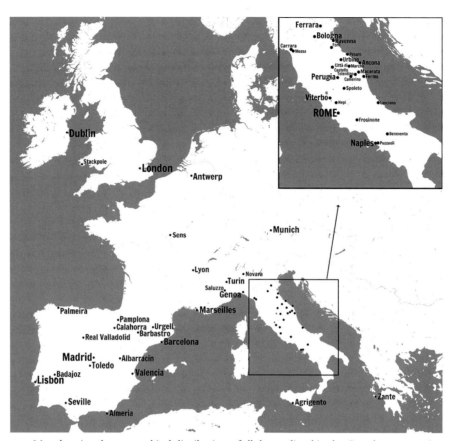

39. Map showing the geographical distribution of all donors listed in the *Seconda nota* covering the period from 1 January 1826 to 31 March 1826.
Source: Author.

by the procurer of the Congregation of Propaganda Fide in the Portuguese colony of Macao in China. Even the anemic *Decima nota* carried news of a certain Signore Bruni's collection of 40 scudi from "various American benefactors"[49] (**Figure 40**). All of these foreign donations are recorded in the aforementioned cumulative ledger of 1840 as having been paid in full.[50]

These published lists thus conjured the image of a vast Catholic world rallying to the cause with energy and generosity. A Roman guidebook of 1830 informed tourists visiting San Paolo that the pope's appeal "to the Catholic world" had led "monarchs, princes, and entire provinces" to respond with eager donations.[51] One Roman writer in 1831 rhapsodized that

> ... not only did bishops rush to inform the members of their dioceses about the new field of merit opened up to them by the fundraising drive for the reconstruction of this church; but from the Isle of Elba came the free offer of marbles and granites of whatever dimension for the new columns that were to support the arches of the nave of this great temple,

MATTERS OF MONEY   151

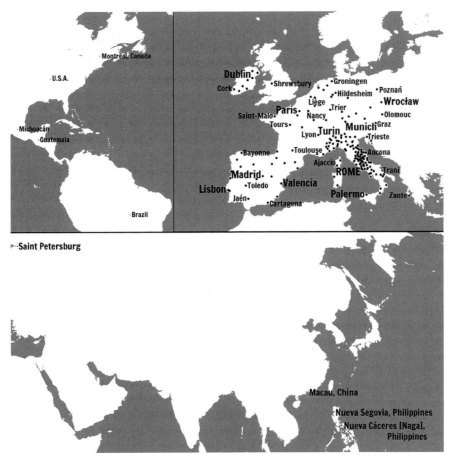

40. Map showing the geographical distribution of all donors listed in the third through the final *Eleventh nota*, covering the period from 1 April 1826 to 30 June 1833. Outside Europe, there are two sites in the Philippines (Nueva Segovia and Nueva Cáceres), one in China (Macao), one in Mexico (Michoacán), and one in Canada (Montreal, from which multiple donations were sent). In addition, one donor is identified simply as "from Guatemala in America," while two people are listed as having turned over donations collected in Brazil and in the United States of America.
Source: Author.

an offer made by the pious Morel de Bauvine, who owned the quarries; from all the civil and military employees of every department throughout the entire Pontifical State substantial sums were contributed; from all the nobility and property owners, from the clerics enjoying benefices, rich quantities of money were lavished for the expenses relating to such a worthy objective; and from the collection boxes placed by the bishops in even the most remote corners of the country came considerable quantities of money; and careful lists of all these offerings and collections were maintained and brought to public attention by means of the press.[52]

Even far beyond Rome, readers had the impression of a worldwide Catholic crusade. The *United States Catholic Miscellany* enthused in 1826 that "HEAVEN is pleased to favour this undertaking" given "the resources, emanating from the subscriptions so abundantly supplied by all classes of people," while the *London Times* noted more dryly that the reconstruction was receiving funds from "the faithful of different parts of the globe."[53] Here was exactly that aroused and revitalized Catholic piety that Leo XII so yearned to place before the eyes of the world.

This appears to have been the first global fundraising drive in history. It also seems to have marked the first time that a building had constituted a genuinely global public for itself; not a passive public that is aware of a given building's existence, but an active public that is motivated to take positive action on the building's behalf. This unprecedented and very modern enterprise hinged on practices of abstraction. The building itself had first been informationalized as narrative, which permitted its liberation from a physical location in Rome and its distribution to a far-flung global public of potential donors. The corollary to this centrifugal action was the centripetal action of the hundreds of donations and pledges, for these too hinged on abstraction: that of labor into money. These monies were then recorded and collated as information by the Roman bureaucracy, with each donor – from the office porter in Ferrara to the colonial officer in Macao – reduced to a name inscribed in a uniform official script into the formularies printed onto the uniform lined pages of a tabbed ledger. For a project that found its most defining impetus in a Romantic revolt against the abstractions of modernity – against the spirit of calculation and the reification of the human; against frictionless impersonal exchange, cosmopolitanism, and faceless bureaucracy – there is irony aplenty in this. If nothing else, these tensions reflect the contradictions inherent in the task that faced Church leaders as they sought to revendicate old truths in a new world.

The concept of space that purportedly lay at the heart of the reconstruction effort was also fundamentally at odds with modern sensibilities. The reconstruction hinged on a fetishization of embodied space: a sacred space sanctified by a venerated sacred body, as well as a basilican structure whose materials were hallowed by history.[54] Yet the fundraising drive we have just surveyed was predicated on exploding the local and the specific, and on reaching beyond proximity – beyond Rome, beyond Italy, and eventually beyond Europe – to convince donors to offer a gift that at this date could sometimes only manage the journey across international borders through an improvisational bartering of different national currencies. We are a long way away here from Romantic dreams of human warmth and enchanted plenitude. The fundraising drive used the most modern and abstracting methods available to

MATTERS OF MONEY 153

constitute an unprecedentedly placeless and anonymous community of discourse, the connective fiber of which was money.

This abstraction can only have become more perceptible the further one was from Rome. Which begs the question: what were donors as far away as Canada or Mexico or the Philippines thinking when they contributed money to repair a church that lay across the oceans in faraway Rome? The archbishop or the colonial administrator in such circumstances may possibly have known Rome at first hand, but most of the people from whom he collected funds did not. How were they persuaded to give money – and to give generously too? Some insight is provided by the remarkable pastoral letter sent on 18 November 1825 by Bishop Joseph-Octave Plessis of Québec to the clergy of his immense rural diocese.[55]

Bishop Plessis's letter was accompanied by a translated copy of Pope Leo's Encyclical *Ad Plurimas* and began by reassuring his priests that he would not require them to speak from their pulpits about the pope's request: he was only supplying the Encyclical for those who wished to do so, or who wished to pursue its exhortations with specific individuals. He observed that it would be impossible to give better reasons for donating to the reconstruction than those given by Leo himself, but he also acknowledged the peculiar situation that his priests were in, far from Europe and speaking to congregations who had no experience of Rome as a real place. "Perhaps it is true," he wrote, "that at our distance from the capital of the Christian world one does not form a proper idea of the importance to be attached to the conservation of these ancient and venerable buildings, the imposing view of which is so apt to awaken faith and excite piety in those who have the good fortune to visit them." He recalled his visit to the old San Paolo in 1820, when he was "overcome with religious respect" and a sense of real connection to Paul's spirit.[56] And yet, he continued, "the perspectives of some people do not extend any further than the objects immediately surrounding them, and such people will object perhaps that our own country presents enough good works still to be done as could easily absorb all our available savings." To such objections, he replied that any diocese might say the same, and exhorted his clergy to believe that one could fulfill the expectations of Québec while also lifting "our gazes a bit higher." There were 150 parishes in the diocese, he wrote, each containing 300 families, more or less, which added up to 45,000 families; if each managed to donate 12 sols or 6 pence, with a bit more from the clergy, from the religious communities, and from the well-to-do, it would be easy to produce "a rather reasonable sum – for a country which has not yet obtained a reputation for opulence." If they failed, they at least would have the satisfaction of having tried. If they succeeded, it would be gratifying to know that the Holy Father had not appealed to them in vain, and that they had given tangible proof of their piety toward the apostle whom God had called to spread Christianity to "the nations from which we originate."

Plessis's metaphor of "lifting up your eyes" from Québec to look toward Rome is telling, as it superimposes the intimate scale of the body on the geographical scale of the fundraising drive. In this, it is emblematic of the quintessentially modern experience of overlapping spatialities on which the fundraising enterprise was built, which connected the intimate to the global in new and uncanny ways.[57]

NOTES

1 For this paragraph: Cameron (1957); Pollard (2005), pp. 23–24.

2 Demarco (1949); Felisini (1990).

3 Crocella (1982), p. 21.

4 Crocella (1982), pp. 22–24.

5 Sabene (2015); Di Sante and Turriziani (2016).

6 Sabene (2015), pp. 51–67, and (2016), pp. 43–62.

7 Giulio Maria della Somaglia to Giacomo Giustiniani, 30 September 1825 (AAV: Segreteria di Stato, anno 1825, b. 586 [rubr. 48], p. 49).

8 Vincenzo Macchi to Giulio Maria della Somaglia, 2 August 1825 (AAV: Segreteria di Stato, anno 1825, b. 586 [rubr. 48], p. 31).

9 Christian Carl Josias Bunsen to Giulio Maria della Somaglia, 24 September 1826 (ASR: CSRBSP Computisteria b. 109, f. 4).

10 AAV: Segreteria di Stato, anno 1825, b. 586 [rubr. 48].

11 Thus for instance the Marchese Crosa, chargé d'affaires for the king of Sardinia in Rome, donated 100 scudi to the reconstruction effort (Marchese Crosa to Giulio Maria della Somaglia, 24 September 1825 [AAV: Segreteria di Stato, anno 1825, b. 586 {rubr. 48}, p. 50]).

12 Christian Carl Josias Bunsen to Giulio Maria della Somaglia, 29 September 1825 (AAV: Segreteria di Stato, anno 1825, b. 586 [rubr. 48], p. 64).

13 Marchese Crosa to Giulio Maria della Somaglia, 22 October 1825; Francesco Serra Cassano to Giulio Maria della Somaglia, 2 November 1825; Marchese Bibas Pieri (ex-Console Pontificio of the Ionian Islands) to Giulio Maria della Somaglia, 20 November 1825; Extraordinary Ambassador of the French King at the Papal Court [illegible name] to Giulio Maria della Somaglia, 21 November 1825; [illegible name; Viennese court] to Giulio Maria della Somaglia, 29 November 1825 (AAV: Segreteria di Stato, anno 1825, b. 586 [rubr. 48], pp. 115, 126, 130, 136, 169).

14 Giacomo Giustiniani to Giulio Maria della Somaglia, 19 November 1825 (AAV: Segreteria di Stato, anno 1825, b. 586 [rubr. 48], p. 133).

15 Lambruschini (1825).

16 See Chapter 3.

17 Giacomo Giustiniani to Giulio Maria della Somaglia, 29 November 1825 (AAV: Segreteria di Stato, anno 1825, b. 586 [rubr. 48], p. 222).

18 These lists can be dated based on the dates of the pledges they report and their position in bound copies of the *Diario di Roma*.

19 "[Prima] Nota delle Oblazioni volontarie fatte per la riedificazione della Basilica di S. Paolo," *DdR*, 21 December 1825, unpaginated supplement.

20 The exact date of publication was sometime between 21 Decemeber 1825 and the first week of January 1826.

21 Don Remigio Crescini to the monks of S. Giovanni Evangelista in Parma, 28 January 1826; Don Vincenzo Bini to the monks of the Benedictine Confederation, 31 January 1826 (ASP: 30/c, libro rosso 2).

22 "Circolare No. 12671," 1826 (ASR: Camerale III b. 1910, #190).

23 "Nota dei Dicasteri ed altri Ministri Cam^li. a cui è stata spedita la Circolare per le offerte per la riedificazione della Basilica di S. Paolo" (ASR: Camerale III b.1910, #162).

24 Vice Commissariato de Residui in Ferrara to Belissario Cristaldi, 6 September 1827 (ASR: CSRBSP Computisteria b. 65, f. 3). Or see also the documents from various military divisions (ASR: CSRBSP Computisteria b. 109, f. 4).

25 "Posizione per la Pia Oblazione per la Riedificazione della Basilica di S. Paolo," starts 23 December 1825 (ASC: Camera Capitolina, Credenzone 18, t. 78, Catena 1601, fol. 1533–1622).

26 "Posizione per la Pia Oblazione per la Riedificazione della Basilica di S. Paolo," starts 23 December 1825 (ASC: Camera Capitolina, Credenzone 18, t. 78, Catena 1601, fol. 1547–1552, 1555, 1563 ff., 1572, 1574–1576.

27 "Posizione per la Pia Oblazione per la Riedificazione della Basilica di S. Paolo," starts 23 December 1825 (ASC: Camera Capitolina, Credenzone 18, t. 78, Catena 1601, fol. 1536–1539, 1553, 1540–1541 ff.

28 Cf. Delegazione Apostolica di Perugia, "Quadro generale dei Publici Funzionarj che percepiscono il soldo dalla Cassa camerale e delle pie offerte da loro presentate per la riedificazione dell'arsa Basilica di S. Paolo...," 31 January 1826 (ASR: CSRBSP Computisteria b. 109, f. 2).

29 "Registro dei versamenti volontarj eseguiti nelle Casse Cam[era]li delle Legazioni, e Delegazioni Pontificie pel ristabilimento della Basilica di S. Paolo," 1826-36 (ASR: CSRBSP Computisteria b.110, f.4). Or see also the "Saldaconti per le volontarie oblazioni esibite tanto dagle Individui addetti alle Sopraintendenze Doganali [etc.] ..." (ASR: CSRBSP Computisteria b.110, f.2). This mountain of unstudied material offers rich insights into the economy and administration of the Papal States during this period.

30 "Registro di tutte le offerte volontarie che si fanno in sussidio delle grandi spese occorrenti per la riedificazione della basilica di S. Paolo ...," 1825–1840 (ASR: CSRBSP Computisteria b. 111).

31 *DdR*, 24 December 1825, p. 1 (the Consistory; 2,000 scudi per year); *DdR*, 7 January 1826, p. 1 (the first regiment of the Pontifical Carabinieri; 1,200 scudi); *DdR*, 14 January 1826, p. 1 (the Papal bodyguard; 3,000 scudi); *DdR*, 4 March 1826, p. 1 (Morel de Bauvine; marble from his quarry); *DdR*, 29 April 1826, p. 1 (another gift from the Pontifical Carabinieri; 962 scudi); *DdR*, 10 May 1826, p. 1 (Collegio de Procuratori; 100 scudi per year for ten years); and on and on.

32 To take a random example, the routine donation of the Guardie Nobili Pontificie was first reported in the *DdR* (14 January 1826) and then a week later in the *Ossevatore del Trasimeno* (Perugia) (21 January 1826, p. 13) and then a week after that in the *Gazzetta Piemontese* of Turin (28 January 1826, p. 68).

33 *DdR*, 4 March 1826, p. 1. See also *DdR*, 15 March 1826, p. 1; *Gazzetta Piemontese* (Turin), 16 March 1826, p. 183 (see also *Gazzetta Piemontese*, 23 March 1826, p. 199); *Oesterreichischer Beobachter* (Vienna), 30 March 1826, pp. 377–378; *Gaceta de Madrid*, 4 April 1826, p. 161; *L'ami de la Religion* (Paris), 5 April 1826, p. 239; *United States Catholic Miscellany* (Charleston), 2 September 1826, p. 54.

34 *DdR*, 2 August 1826, p. 1; *United States Catholic Miscellany* (Charleston), 23 September 1826, p. 79.

35 *United States Catholic Miscellany* (Charleston), 29 July 1826, p. 15.

36 *Niles' Weekly Register* (Baltimore), 23 September 1826, p. 59.

37 *DdR: NdG*, 12 April 1826, p. 1.

38 *DdR: NdG*, 2 August 1826, p. 1. The cumulative subtotal provided at the end of the *Terza nota* confuses the two parts of the *Prima Nota* for separate *note*, and it omits the real *Seconda nota* altogether.

39 *DdR: NdG*, December 1826, p. 1.

40 *DdR: NdG*, 23 June 1827, p. 1.

41 *DdR: NdG*, 28 June 1828, p. 1.

42 *DdR* (supplement), 23 June 1829, pp. 1–2.

43 *DdR*, 26 June 1830, pp. 1–2.

44 *DdR*, 2 July 1831, p. 3.

45 *DdR*, 30 June 1832, p. 2.

46 *DdR*, 10 July 1833, p. 1

47 *Gazzetta Piemontese* (Turin), 25 July 1833, p. 440. The paper covered the fundraising drive extensively: 3 January 1826, p. 3; 22 April 1826, p. 275; 10 August 1826, p. 612; 4 January 1827, p. 9; 9 July 1829, p. 510; 5 July 1830, p. 459. Other northern Italian journals also covered it, for instance, *Messaggiere tirolese* (Trent), 10 July 1827, p. 68.

48 Some of the offices mentioned – the Archbishop of Alexandria, or the Bishop of Castabala – were historic titular sees whose occupants resided in Rome.

49 *DdR*, 30 June 1832, p. 2.

50 "Registro . . ." as in Chapter 7 n. 30.

51 *Roma compiutamente descritta* (1830), p. 258.

52 Costanzi (1831), pp. 38–39.

53 *United States Catholic Miscellany* (Charleston), 9 September 1826, p. 63; *London Times*, 15 October 1825, p. 2.

54 Cf. Low (2003).

55 Têtu and Gagnon (1888), v. 3, pp. 187–197. On Plessis, see Lambert (2003–).

56 Plessis (1903), p. 259.

57 See Wittman (2010), pp. 35–37.

EIGHT

RESISTING RESURRECTION

LEO XII'S CHIROGRAPH APPEARED TO SET A VERY CLEAR COURSE FOR the reconstruction:

> No innovation shall be introduced in the forms and architectonic proportions, nor in the ornaments of the resurgent edifice, unless it be to exclude some small thing that in later times was introduced through the whim of a subsequent era.[1]

And if disagreements arose on some minor point, firm protocols were in place:

> We desire that judgments on such matters be referred uniquely to the Academy of Saint Luke, where it will be decided which type of stone is to be used for the columns and pavement, as well as the solution for roofing the temple.[2]

But as it turned out, Leo was too optimistic by half, for almost immediately the questions and conflicts began to multiply. Were only the destroyed columns to be replaced? Or, in the interest of creating a more uniform building that recalled the "state in which it was first erected by its founders," should they all be replaced? Did the new columns have to follow every detail of the old ones? The old columns and capitals had mostly been *spolia* from different antique sources, and consequently had varied from column to column. Did these variations have to be replicated anew? No one seriously contemplated doing that, but if it was acceptable to change some things, which things was it not acceptable to change? The capitals atop the columns had also been varied; if they were now to be uniform, what model were they to follow? Did the model have to derive from one of the capitals of the ruined basilica? Or could an external model be adopted? The Chirograph also decreed that the building was to be preserved as it had been created by its founders, yet many of its most prized elements dated from well *after* the original construction, like the medieval mosaics that covered the apse and triumphal arch or the Gothic ciborium over Paul's tomb. If these were to be repaired and retained – and no one ever suggested doing otherwise – was it also necessary to retain the less prized elements that had survived the fire, like the medieval campanile, the eighteenth-century narthex, or the medieval wall that divided the transept lengthwise? These could hardly be considered "small things" that had been "introduced through the whim of a subsequent era." But if they were to be demolished, how could they be replaced without erring into "innovation"? Technical matters posed another set of problems. Was it permissible to change the character of the roof to make it fireproof? If so, why not also raise the level of the floor to prevent floods?

In time, all of these questions and more were brought before the Academy of St. Luke and debated by Belli and the membership of the Special Commission. The *in pristinum* solution as formulated in the pure sphere of ideas, in short, fell apart as it was implemented in reality. This chapter and the next will survey these seemingly inexhaustible debates as they played out, first prior to the submission of Belli's master plan for the reconstruction in November 1830 (Chapter 8) and then after his master plan had been received (Chapter 9). Together, they disclose how the ambiguities of the Chirograph were consistently used, not always in the best of faith, as a pretext to justify decisions that were in fact driven by aesthetic preferences or technical concerns.

The key figure in these initial discussions was not the architect Pasquale Belli, as one might expect, but rather the secretary of the Special Commission, Angelo Uggeri. For it was Uggeri who guided the Commission in deciding which decisions to put for adjudication before the Academy of St. Luke; Uggeri who was then also a member of the Architects' Class at the Academy where the adjudicating took place, and was active in lobbying his colleagues there; and then again Uggeri who managed the discussion and even the implementation of the Academy's judgments once they were returned back to the Special Commission. It is not irrelevant in this context that Uggeri was himself something of an architect *manqué* who back in the 1780s had even built a theater in Codogno, near Cremona, before his career developed in other directions.[3] Uggeri definitely saw his early architectural background as lending credibility to his ambition to play a central – perhaps *the* central – role in the reconstruction, and it was no coincidence when, out of the blue and less than one year after his appointment as secretary to the Special Commission, a leading Roman journal published a laudatory essay about his by then more than forty-year-old theater in provincial Codogno.[4] Given Uggeri's ambitions at San Paolo, it made sense for him to ensure that everyone knew he was no mere armchair architect.

As noted, Uggeri had been arguing for years that old San Paolo was inspired by the forms of Trajan's civic Basilica Ulpia, that its virtues were those of Christianity joined to classicism, and that its faults reflected purely contingent limitations. He had also argued after the fire that any repair or reconstruction ought to purify the architecture of the basilica in keeping with the Ulpian model the Early Christians *would have followed* more closely had they not been limited by their circumstances. With his appointment as secretary to the Special Commission, and especially following Belli's appointment as head architect, Uggeri set about trying to impose this vision. The passages of the Chirograph cited at the start of this chapter seem to have convinced him that Leo XII shared his vision.

One of the first surviving parts of the old building to attract attention was the great wall that divided the transept transversally (**Figure 41**). This wall was still of uncertain date in the 1820s, but most scholars, Uggeri among them, discerned correctly that it dated from sometime in the Middle Ages.[5] In January 1826, Uggeri initiated discussions in the Special Commission about demolishing the wall.[6] He claimed that the wall had probably been erected to help support the long span of the roof, and that the Chirograph mandated the demolition of such subsequent additions. Once removed, he added, the transept would recover its original spatial unity. Demolition would also eliminate the expense of restoring the wall and ensure that there would be no unpleasant contrast between its irregular spolia columns and the new columns that would eventually populate the nave. Uggeri perceived from the start that the dividing wall would set a precedent for how the Chirograph was interpreted for the rest of the reconstruction, so he shrewdly framed his proposal in terms of the goal of returning the basilica to its "original Constantinian state."

Uggeri's proposal was forwarded to the Academy of St. Luke, which sent a delegation to inspect the wall and then approved Uggeri's proposal unanimously.[7] A week and a half later, Pope Leo approved the Academy's verdict, and the wall was demolished shortly thereafter.[8] Uggeri had won round one. Yet in so doing he had also demonstrated how easy it was to use the Chirograph to organize a consensus in favor of demolishing unloved remnants

41. Antonio Aquaroni, *View of the Ruins of San Paolo fuori le mura*, 1823. The dividing wall extends from right to left and includes the large arch closer to the viewer.
Source: Thorvaldsens Museum, Copenhagen, D484, photographer Helle Nanny Brendstrup.

of the old basilica. The lesson was not lost on those whose vision of a purified basilica, it soon emerged, went far beyond his own.

Standing several feet in front of the now-doomed dividing wall was the great triumphal arch of Galla Placidia (**Plate 9**). This arch and the wall that contained it were original to the building, while their splendid mosaic decoration dated to about a century later, from the pontificate of Leo XII's namesake St. Leo the Great, who was prominently mentioned in its inscription. The Chirograph implied that elements of such evident importance should be preserved, but the wall had been listing seriously even before the fire and had sustained so much additional damage during the fire that it stood now only with the aid of timber props. The mosaic, meanwhile, despite some consolidation work the previous year, was crumbling, with one contemporary visitor observing that its tesserae lay "scattered over the ruins."[9] Uggeri here submitted a scrupulously preservationist proposal that envisaged repairing and reinforcing the arch while replacing only the two ravaged colossal columns that supported it.[10] The sole change would be of a structural nature: Uggeri's analysis indicated that the inner arch was a reinforcement from the time of Leo I, contemporary with the mosaic that decorated it, and so Uggeri

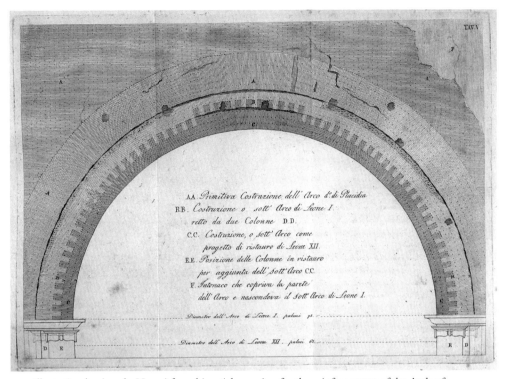

42. Illustration by Angelo Uggeri from his article arguing for the reinforcement of the Arch of Galla Placidia at San Paolo ("Dell'arco trionfale detto di Placidia. Prima conferenza," *Memorie romane di antichità e belle arti* 4 (1827), pp. 113–124).
Source: Getty Research Institute, Los Angeles (85-S95).

proposed to add yet another reinforcing arch within it (**Figure 42**). This necessitated positioning the two new columns closer together, which narrowed the opening. The west face of this new inner arch might, Uggeri suggested, be covered with inscriptions naming Leo XII.

On 26 April 1826, the Academy examined and rejected the proposal.[11] They felt that the wall and arch were far more seriously damaged than the proposal suggested, and that the new inner arch would compromise the overall proportions. They instead recommended demolishing the whole thing and rebuilding it *ex novo*. Pope Leo approved the Academy's recommendation, and in November a contract for the detachment and eventual remounting of the mosaic was signed with Giacomo Raffaelli, a leading authority on mosaics who had been involved in the work since the previous year.[12] The terms of the contract, however, did not reflect a very rigorous ethos of historic preservation, for it stipulated that only the tesserae representing figures, ornaments, and inscriptions need be preserved, while those of the blue background could be discarded and replaced with new ones when the mosaic was remounted.[13] (The English Catholic Beste reported in this same year that "particles of the

Mosaic destroyed by the conflagration are now set in gold and worn as fashionable ornaments by ladies at Rome.")[14]

We do not know if Uggeri had any say in Raffaelli's contract – it was not signed by him – but he disapproved its lack of scientific rigor. Within months, he was complaining to the treasurer general that the work was being rushed and that an accident had recently damaged part of the mosaic, and asking how much more would have to be lost before better conservation practices were instituted.[15] Whatever the peculiarities of Uggeri's understanding of what the Chirograph did or did not protect, he took seriously the need to preserve those elements he felt it *did* cover. Indeed, despite the pope's demolition order, Uggeri continued to press for the retention and repair of the arch and its wall. He presented his case in a lecture at the Roman Academy of Archaeology, then disseminated it in the *Memorie romane di antichità e belle arti*, the same journal that had profiled his theater in Codogno the year before.[16] But all to no avail. This first defeat proved a taste of things to come, as the tide now began to turn against Uggeri's comparatively robust (if also eccentric) preservationist instincts.

The biggest question to be tackled next concerned what were inevitably referred to as *i marmi*: that is, the stone that was to be used for the new columns, bases, and capitals of the nave.[17] Debate on this question had started innocently enough in the days immediately following the fire, when alert building contractors had begun petitioning to supply replacement columns for what they imagined would be just a repair. The first came from the Roman contractor Guglielmo Closse, who with a salesperson's bombast proclaimed in a letter to Treasurer General Cristaldi that he could have San Paolo open for business again "in two years" with "columns even more beautiful than the ones that were destroyed."[18] After some discussion, Closse made a formal offer in July 1825 to supply red granite columns from quarries in Simplon in the north of Italy.[19] In the end, the Special Commission ended up using a different Simplon granite, with Closse as one of the two supplying contractors. But before reaching that decision, the Commission and Academy of St. Luke contrived to pursue a years-long, brain-meltingly repetitious debate in which a parade of different marbles was auditioned, and during which the entire reconstruction effort was more or less paralyzed. This debate can seem pointless (many contemporaries certainly thought so), but it served an essential purpose in hashing out and in a certain manner resolving, for a time anyway, key ambiguities inherent in the Chirograph: ambiguities relating to the overlapping authority of particular individuals and institutions, and to the relative claims of archaeological correctitude and architectural beauty in orienting the reconstruction.

Other speculators followed Closse, each singing the praises of other stones and other quarries. Partisans of Cottanello marble from the mountains north of Rome published a pamphlet recalling how unwarranted prejudice had almost prevented Innocent X from using it in St. Peter's, and warned against the revival of such prejudices now.[20] Carlo Fea weighed in with a *Continuazione* of his *Aneddoti sulla basilica ostiense*, in which he evaluated what he had identified as the nine serious proposals for replacement columns that were circulating.[21] The proposals were:

(1) To make sheathed columns with travertine cores and skins composed of bonded fragments from the original columns.
(2) To gather broken column parts in *granito cenerino* from around the Temple of Peace (Forum of Vespasian) in Rome and to make compound columns from them.
(3) To use Closse's red granite Simplon columns.
(4) To use columns of alabaster from Civitavecchia.
(5) To look for colored marbles in the neighborhoods of Camerino, Spoleto, and Assisi.
(6) To use Cottanello columns from Sabina.
(7) To use a milky *granito cenerino* from the Island of Elba.
(8) To use Carrara marble.
(9) To use a new white granite from a recently rediscovered quarry on the Island of Elba.

Fea proposed three criteria: speed of procurement, structural solidity, and resemblance to the basilica's original columns. Each of the first seven options failed in one respect or another. Option three – Closse's red Simplon granite – was of an unpleasant and inappropriate color, he noted. In response to the recent Cottanello pamphlet, Fea adduced a seventeenth-century document that told of the immense difficulty of getting Cottanello marble from its remote mountainous quarries to St. Peter's. Noting that 215 buffalo had died moving the marble back then, Fea worried that to use the same marble now at San Paolo might result "in the extermination of the entire species."[22] In the end, Fea favored options eight and nine. Both sites already had accessible quarries that produced a stone light in color, and for both the transportation to Rome was over water. To save time and money, Fea felt that the columns could be supplied in two or even three segments: even at San Paolo, not all the old columns had been monoliths. As for Elba (option nine), Fea drew attention to Morel de Bauvine's dramatic offer, which had become public just days before his text was published.[23] This, Fea felt, would be ideal, but it would first require sending experts to make sure the quarries were up to standard.

Morel de Bauvine's offer also sparked the enthusiasm of Secretary of State della Somaglia, who in February ordered Uggeri to send specialists to inspect the quarries and procure samples for the Academy to evaluate.[24] After receiving the samples, the Academy declared that the stone was not suitable for bases and capitals but might be good for column shafts.[25] But the growing international renown of Morel de Bauvine's offer seems to have upped the ante for the other contractors. Closse now shipped a few Simplon granite columns to Rome and exhibited them in the new customs building on Piazza del Popolo.[26] The Cottanello faction, meanwhile, responded to Fea with a witty pamphlet attributed to "a stonecutter" who, in working-class accents, claimed he had no choice but to "drop the chisel from his calloused hands" and refute Fea's various untruths.[27] Fea immediately published a ferocious lawyerly demolition of the *soi-disant* stonecutter's arguments, insisting that archaeologists, not architects, let alone stonecutters, were the people to consult on such matters.[28]

On 4 June 1826, the Academy of St. Luke assembled in its rooms at the Sapienza to make a decision.[29] The options were almost, but not quite, identical to those enumerated by Fea. The academicians defined four criteria for judgment: the columns should be monoliths, they should have a color similar to the old *pavonazzetto* columns, they should be fluted as the old ones had been, and, as requested by the secretary of state, they should be easily and quickly obtained. None of the proposed columns fulfilled all four criteria, but in the end they managed to narrow the choice down to the Elba and Simplon granites.[30] The paler granite from Elba was closer in color to the old nave columns and more susceptible to being fluted, but the academicians were unconvinced that it could be quarried as monoliths. If they were wrong about this, then they recommended using it, but otherwise they advocated monolithic granite columns from Simplon, despite their unattractive color, and despite their unsuitableness for fluting. They recommended Carrara marble for the bases and capitals.[31]

In countenancing the replacement of the original fluted whitish marble columns with unfluted ones in a darker granite, the Academy was essentially disregarding Leo XII's Chirograph. All they could say for themselves was that it was more important to recover the old basilica's sense of "magnificence" than to recreate its specific appearance.[32] Such an interpretation seemed at best Jesuitical, and certainly it was anathema to Uggeri, who as late as 1832, long after the matter had been resolved, was still lamenting that the whitish Elba granite had not been used.[33] But in fact this was to be just the first of many times that the classically minded academicians were to glibly finesse the strictures of the Chirograph when they smelled an opportunity to escape the straightjacket of replicating a building that they all viewed as deeply problematic in its original incarnation.

Uggeri took his time in bringing the Academy's recommendation to the Special Commission, no doubt hoping that a better solution would present itself. Sure enough, a project soon surfaced that called for creating columns out of ancient remnants recently discovered in the Temple of Venus and Rome and in Trajan's Forum. Uggeri sent it to the Academy of St. Luke to review as though their resolution in favor of Simplon granite had never occurred.[34] There it was rejected, but only on grounds of solidity.[35] A variety of other proposals soon appeared, all of which were also considered and rejected.[36]

Even as Uggeri was trying to slow things down, others were complaining about how long everything was taking. On 18 September 1826, Fea directed a tart memorandum at the Special Commission which opened, "It would appear that some kind of evil spirit has materialized to block the reconstruction of the Basilica of San Paolo. Three years have gone by and we are still arguing about what marble to use for the nave columns."[37] Fea's attitude had always been marked by impatience and a concern for public optics, and in this spirit he now withdrew his support for Elba granite and returned to his earlier preference for fluted compound columns of white Carrara marble. Because the Carrara quarries had been operating for centuries, he wrote, columns could be en route very quickly, and there could be no question about their quality being incommensurate with the dignity of the basilica. It was also an intellectually coherent solution that would clearly distinguish new and surviving elements. New elements needed to be of excellent quality, but only had to resemble the old in a general sense since their function was merely to facilitate and not disrupt the viewer's experience of the authentic historic fabric. They should not attempt to deceive the spectator into thinking they were themselves authentic.

Fea's arguments fell on deaf ears. On 5 October, the Academy met again and resolved that the choice was between Morel de Bauvine's Elba granite and a black and white Simplon granite being offered by Closse; on 20 November, they reaffirmed that Carrara marble should be used for the bases and capitals.[38] They also requested Morel and Closse to supply more specimens for examination. Closse promptly obliged, but for unknown reasons Morel de Bauvine missed the deadline. After weeks of waiting, the Special Commission on 22 January 1827 awarded Closse a first commission for two colossal unfluted columns in Simplon granite to support the triumphal arch of Galla Placidia.[39]

Uggeri now sensed that he was losing control over the rebuilding process, so he resolved to draw up a master plan for the entire reconstruction that pulled together all his various ideas on the subject. In May 1827, he sent copies out to his allies Abbot Zelli and Nicolai, as well as to Secretary of State della Somaglia.[40] He explained to Zelli that he was trying to balance the imperatives of the architect charged with systematizing a new building with those of the archaeologist charged with preserving the memory of an old one. As an archaeologist, he considered it essential that the new San Paolo be saturated with tangible relics of the old Constantinian basilica; as an architect, he was concerned to render the new transept and nave internally coherent, but also spatially distinct from one another, so that each could form an autonomous echo of the rectangular concept of the Basilica Ulpia, which for Uggeri remained the essential model. He felt sure that his concern over the basilica *as monument* would not conflict with that "of the operative and executive architects," who were instead concerned with the basilica *as edifice*. Uggeri came closer here than anyone yet had to acknowledging that two different conceptualizations of the basilica underlay the reconstruction enterprise: the basilica as idea, as narrative, as *monument*, and the basilica as *edifice*, as a material construction in stone, wood, and mortar. As both an archaeologist and an architect (even if *manqué*), it is not surprising that he should have been the first to note this dualism.

Uggeri also informed Zelli of his strong preference for Morel de Bauvine's stone from Elba over all other options and stressed that no further decisions should be made until Morel's overdue samples arrived. This finally occurred a few days later. The Academy of St. Luke examined them and then met on 10 June to make its long-awaited final decision on the nave columns. The vote was eighteen in favor of Simplon granite to just three in favor of Elba granite, with poor Uggeri among the three. The Academy's report made no mention of resemblance to the columns of the old basilica and observed only that Simplon granite seemed "more unified and harmonious, and more homogeneous for the interior of an edifice." The quality and uniformity of the stone, in other words, counted for more than its resemblance to the old basilica. Uggeri's signature was absent from the report, in protest.[41] Even so, the recommendation was approved by the Special Commission on 4 July 1827 and sent on for final approval by Leo XII.

At that same meeting, the Special Commission also examined Uggeri's new master plan.[42] Uggeri described his project as strictly obedient to the Chirograph's command to rebuild the basilica in the state "in which it was first erected by its founders," which he took to mean Constantine and those from Valentinian to Galla Placidia who had enlarged it and completed its decoration. His first illustration offered a "Chronological Table of the Ostian Basilica," which set forth his by now familiar fixation on the determining role of the Basilica Ulpia in the design of San Paolo (**Figure 43**). It showed the plan of the Ulpian basilica from the Forma Urbis Romae next to a plan of San Paolo labeled "Constantinian," and then a second plan of San Paolo as it had appeared in 1823. The goal clearly remained to work back toward what he believed were the aesthetic intentions of the original builders.

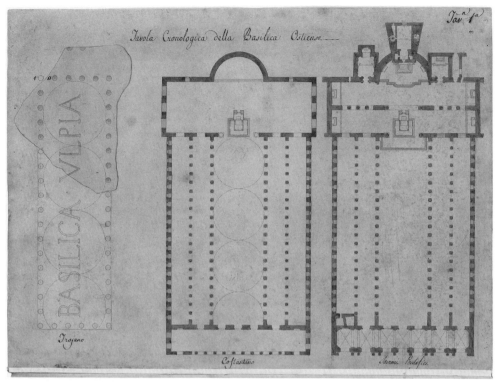

43. Angelo Uggeri, "Chronological Table of the Ostian Basilica," from his report to Treasurer General Mario Mattei, June 1827.
Source: ms. Vat.lat.13444, f.3r, © 2023 Biblioteca Apostolica Vaticana.

Uggeri's second illustration represented the plan of San Paolo as he hoped to reconstruct it (**Figure 44**). One notable feature was the long, narrow, elevated portico he proposed to run from the north end of the transept all the way to the Porta San Paolo. Uggeri claimed that historical documents vouched for the existence of this shelter for pilgrims in the time of the sixth-century pope Symmachus, and that it therefore qualified under the Chirograph to be reconstituted. Another notable component of the project was the arrangement of the columns. The eight *pavonazzetto* columns that had best survived the fire were to be reinstalled as freestanding decorative elements along the transept terminal walls. Sixteen engaged columns fabricated from *pavonazzetto* fragments salvaged from the wreckage along with twelve pilasters fabricated from the hymmetic marble of the colossal columns of the triumphal arch were to be installed in non-load-bearing spots. The most speculative element of the design appeared in Uggeri's third illustration, which gave the elevation of the transept terminal walls: whereas the now-demolished dividing wall had formerly cut the transept terminals into halves, with baroque altars to the left and right, Uggeri now imagined the wall divided into three uneven bays with a single altar in the center.

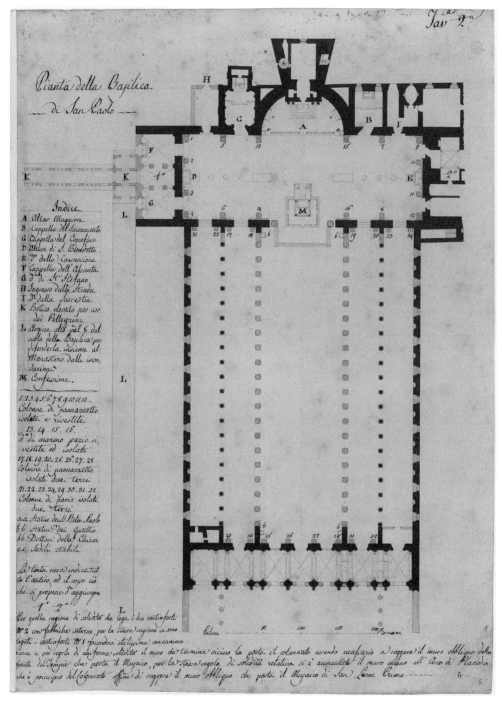

44. Angelo Uggeri, "Plan of the Basilica of San Paolo," from his report to Treasurer General Mario Mattei, June 1827.
Source: ms. Vat.lat.13444, f.4r, © 2023 Biblioteca Apostolica Vaticana.

The Special Commission – which just minutes before had approved the Academy's choice of Simplon granite for the nave columns – politely complimented Uggeri's zeal and voted to forward his proposal to the Academy of St. Luke. But it also rather pointedly observed that the reconstruction did, after all, already have a titular architect whose job it was to direct the work.[43] And so they resolved also to ask Belli what *he* was planning. Belli was not nearly as quick as Uggeri to produce his master plan, and much was to change over the three and a half years that elapsed before he finally managed to do so.

*
**

Uggeri waited a full five months, until the end of 1827, before placing advertisements in the northern Italian press soliciting bids for the forty columns that were to come from the Simplon quarries.[44] He and his allies were active in the interim trying to reopen debate on the columns, especially after the two colossal columns for the triumphal arch arrived in Rome, one in October 1827 and the other at the start of January 1828, and were roundly judged a disappointment.[45] Fea had already criticized their mottled fawn granite as unattractive a year earlier; a young architect in Rome at the time described them as "a Simplon granite of an unbeautiful color."[46] Uggeri insisted that there was still time to find an alternative.

A new crisis arose at the end of 1827 when Belli announced that he was planning to model the capitals for the nave on those of the Pantheon. This seemed incredible to Uggeri, but the Special Commission promptly approved it, provoking him to fire off a furious protest to della Somaglia.[47] The capitals of the nave at the time of the fire were a varied lot, as can be seen still today in the *passeggiata archaeologica* along the south flank of the basilica where many of them are displayed (**Figure 45**). Belli had argued that none of them was in good enough condition to be accurately reconstructed for use as a model, but the idea of substituting ones modeled on those of the Pantheon – traditionally regarded as the ideal type of the Corinthian order – leaves little doubt but that he was motivated by aesthetic rather than archaeological considerations. Uggeri recognized this instantly and thundered to della Somaglia that the whole idea was not just illegal but absurd, given that the Pantheon's columns were decorative rather than load-bearing. He added that the elongated proportions of the Pantheon capitals would necessitate shortening the columns at San Paolo by a whole *palmo* (about 9 inches), because the height of a Corinthian capital was normally equal to one column diameter. This would amount to another violation of the Chirograph and a huge additional expense.

Reminding della Somaglia that the Chirograph required that *all* surviving architectonic elements be preserved and referring to "the shame of the entire Special Commission in having failed to exercise sufficient vigilance," Uggeri raged that at least two of the imperial spolia capitals were in good enough shape to serve

45. Severian spolia capital from the original nave arcade of the basilica displayed in the Passeggiata Archaeologica at the basilica of San Paolo.
Source: Author.

as models for new ones and demanded permission to create a gesso model based on these. He provided an engraving of one capital – the same one his friend Seroux d'Agincourt had illustrated as dating "from the best antique period"[48] (**Figure 46**). Uggeri made it clear that in his view the integrity of the entire reconstruction hung in the balance. Once his gesso model was ready, he wrote, it would be up to della Somaglia and the rest of the Commission to determine whether it really was wise to put "an elegant and delicate capital in place of a severe and masculine one, and thereby destroy from top to bottom the entire merit of the majestic architecture of the nave of the basilica." This opened up a second front in what was turning into an open battle between Uggeri and the architect director.

*
**

46. Angelo Uggeri, engraving showing his counterproject for the nave arcade capitals, in preference to Belli's project for ones modeled on those of the Pantheon (published in Uggeri [1828]).
Source: Archivio di Stato, Roma. Su concessione del Ministero della Cultura; reproduction prohibited.

Belli was informed of Uggeri's objections, and on 14 January wrote to Treasurer General Cristaldi to say that he stood by his decision and would like the matter referred to the Academy of St. Luke, which he clearly now viewed as his ally. (Both Belli and Uggeri were members, but Uggeri only since 1825, and only as a scholar and antiquarian, whereas Belli had been elected in 1810 as an architect and had served there in a variety of offices including bursar and chamberlain.)[49] Della Somaglia granted Belli's wish on 27 January, asking the Academy to answer five questions while keeping in mind the Chirograph's prohibition on innovation:

(1) Is Uggeri's engraving accurate with respect to what survived the fire?
(2) Does the capital Uggeri chose exhibit good proportions, graceful work, and good composition?
(3) If Pantheon-style capitals were to be used instead, would the columns have to be diminished?
(4) How would the price of the stone blocks required for each type of capital differ?
(5) How would the price of execution for each type of capital differ?[50]

Before the Academy met, Uggeri circulated a memorandum insisting that the very questions della Somaglia was asking were illegitimate. The matter was simple: the Chirograph explicitly forbade innovation. Do the capitals of the nave columns count as a "little thing" added by a later era? Clearly not. Yet della Somaglia had even included a question about aesthetic merit, which obviously violated the Chirograph's command to recreate the original forms regardless of merit. (Though Uggeri also hedged his bets, reminding the academicians that the old capitals probably derived from either the Basilica Aemilia or the Mole Adriana, which meant that they were imperial works designed following good Roman norms.) He also reiterated his claim – which underlay the third of della Somaglia's five questions – that Belli would have to change the proportions of the columns if he introduced Pantheon-style capitals.[51]

The academicians went to examine the ruined basilica on 30 January, then retired to rooms at the Sapienza in via Canestrari to reflect. Three hours later, they concluded that Uggeri's engraving conformed to its original, but because the capitals of the basilica as a group had not been uniform, the one Uggeri had illustrated could not be taken as *typical*. As for the aesthetic merits of the capital, they deferred, asking to see a three-dimensional model of a fully restored version. With respect to the proportions of the columns, they indicated that rather than adjust the columns to the capital, it was the capital that would be adjusted to fit the columns, and that the apparent "grace and svelteness of the columns in question would undoubtedly increase" as a result. They side-stepped the question of how this would alter the proportions of the elevation as a whole. On the questions of economy, they concluded that there would be little difference, and that in any case cost was irrelevant. Among the twenty signatories to the statement was Pasquale Belli, who evidently had not thought it necessary to recuse himself.[52]

Della Somaglia instructed Uggeri to prepare the requested gesso model, and by 13 March it was ready.[53] The Academy examined it and quickly addressed a report to della Somaglia denouncing it on purely aesthetic grounds ("The caulicoles are heavy, and too rigid in their upper extremities," etc.). They concluded with an emphatic reaffirmation of their original judgment of 30 January: "preference should be given to the capital from the Pantheon." Belli was again among the signatories.[54]

Uggeri did not bring the Academy's recommendation before the Special Commission but instead continued intriguing behind the scenes. In mid-April della Somaglia requested the advice of the Academy on a new proposal from a Roman contractor named Ferrari who was offering a pale Corsican granite for the nave columns. Della Somaglia also asked the Academy to provide a "decisive resolution" on the capitals that, as he put it, "accorded with the Chirograph."[55] Uggeri interpreted this as a move toward formalizing the Pantheon capitals idea and let loose another blistering protest in response.[56] A switch to Pantheon capitals represented a *clear* violation of the Chirograph, so why even debate it? Why was the Academy even being consulted? The Chirograph obliged the Commission to seek the Academy's expertise only in matters that could not be resolved on the basis of the old basilica. Given that enough of the original capitals survived for use as a model for new ones, the Commission had no choice but to use them, and the Academy had no legitimate claim to comment. Uggeri beseeched della Somaglia to remember that the old columns and capitals had been deliberately selected by the Imperial founders of the basilica. To exclude them would be to erase part of the historical significance that formed the essential rationale for the reconstruction.

Della Somaglia ignored Uggeri, and the Academy reconvened on 20 April. They compared samples of the new Corsican granite with the Simplon granite they had chosen previously and, after some debate, voted sixteen to eleven in favor of the newcomer based on its closer resemblance to the original *pavonazzetto*. Among the sixteen was Belli. Perhaps Uggeri had made some headway in shaming them into taking more seriously their responsibility to evoke the appearance of the old basilica; or perhaps they too had become disillusioned by the muddy-colored granite from Simplon. As for the capitals, they had "already given their opinion twice, in two reports, both times preferring the capital from the Pantheon, and for strong reasons that are clearly explained in those reports."[57] That matter was closed as far as the Academy was concerned.

Uggeri could only postpone a reckoning within the Special Commission for so long, as the Commission's annual congress was scheduled for 10 July. In the run-up to the meeting, lobbying intensified on all sides. An anonymous manuscript circulated that made the bracingly historicist argument that the new capitals should not be modeled on the fine spolia ones reused from imperial buildings, as Uggeri had suggested, but rather on the ones that had been created anew during the Theodosian extension; in other words, the capitals Seroux d'Agincourt had described as "devoid of all grace," and that even the most enthusiastic partisans of Early Christian architecture regarded as incompetent.[58] The rationale for this was that the twenty-four *pavonezzetto* columns with their capitals were only "accidentally" in the basilica and belonged more properly to the time of paganism, whereas the sixteen Theodosian capitals were authentic products of the Early Christian era. The reconstruction ought properly to reflect the "age of Theodosius, not the anachronistic presence in [the basilica] of the Age of Augustus."[59] The author added that using Pantheon capitals would create a truly incoherent hodge-podge and endorsed Carlo Fea's idea of using two-piece columns from Carrara rather than monoliths of granite. The archive is silent as to how the proposal was received by the Special Commission.

In May, Ferrari, the contractor for the new Corsican granite, drew up his bid to supply monolithic columns at 1,450 scudi apiece. In July, Closse and his partners put in a competing bid to supply the same in Simplon granite for 1,200 scudi apiece.[60] In between, della Somaglia resigned as secretary of state, and the presidency of the Special Commission passed to his successor, Tommaso Cardinal Bernetti. Bernetti wasted no time in nominating *yet another* granite for consideration, this one from the island of Giglio off the coast of Tuscany, samples of which he ordered the Academy of St. Luke to evaluate.[61] The Academy duly met in July and agreed that this was the best one yet, far better than the granites of Corsica or Simplon. Belli once again was among the signatories.[62]

The Special Commission then met on 10 July. Despite Uggeri's pleas, they approved the Academy's recommendation to use the capitals from the Pantheon as the model in the nave. That question was now definitively settled. As for the columns, they responded to the Academy's latest recommendation of Bernetti's granite from Giglio by voting to send a team of experts to inspect the quarry.[63] Two weeks later, the delegation returned with several stone samples.[64] Their report observed that there were at least three good quarriable sites on the island but none that produced a granite matching Bernetti's samples.[65]

On 3 August 1828, the Academy convened for the umpteenth time to review the whole question. By now, everyone was aware that debate was dragging on absurdly. Between these debates and the wait for Belli's new master plan, still nowhere in sight, the worksite was dormant. A Frenchman who visited during the summer of 1828 wrote that "there were about fifteen workmen there" – a tiny number for such a vast endeavor.[66] Given this, and given the uncertainties about the new Giglio granite, the Academy now recommended eliminating Giglio from consideration and renarrowing the choice to Simplon and Corsica. After a fresh discussion, the Academy unanimously reaffirmed their vote in favor of the Corsica granite. Belli was again a signatory.[67]

Incredibly, debate went on. In September, the sculptor Ceccarini published a pamphlet defending the Giglio granite.[68] The Special Commission met again and, seemingly out of sheer exhaustion, decided to disregard the recommendations of the Academy. With so much uncertainty surrounding the various island granites (Elba, Corsica, now Giglio), they decided to stick with Simplon granite, which after all was already being used for the two great columns of the triumphal arch.[69] And so in November 1828, three and a half years after Closse's initial offer of Simplon granite, a contract was signed with the contractor Nicola Pirovano, who, in partnership with Closse, agreed to provide within three years, that is, by November 1831, forty monolithic unfluted columns of mottled fawn granite from the quarries at Simplon.[70]

Meanwhile, everyone still awaited Belli's master plan. When Secretary of State Bernetti asked the Academy in January 1829 to weigh in on the interior decoration of the basilica, the Architects' section replied that they were starting to feel uncomfortable offering judgments in the absence of any firm sense of the architect's vision. They urged Bernetti to lean on Belli to submit his master project.[71] The bureaucratic wrangling soon fell silent. Belli toiled away.

Then on 9 February, Leo XII died, and for the next two months Rome was absorbed in the usual dramas and speculations attendant upon a papal conclave.[72] On 31 March, Cardinal Bishop Francesco Saverio Castiglioni was elected Pope Pius VIII. A sickly sixty-seven-year-old whose back and neck were covered with suppurating sores, much of his authority was reputedly wielded by his powerful new secretary of state, Cardinal Giuseppe Albani, who also took over the Special Commission. The main news from the building site in these months concerned the erection of the two colossal columns.[73] The first went up on 2 July 1829, with the *Diario di Roma* reporting that the task took only three hours and that this "greatly honored" Belli and his assistants.[74] (It was one of the only times Belli was ever praised for doing something quickly.) The second column was then erected on 6 August in the presence of a distinguished audience of cardinals, prelates, nobles, and artists – an occasion captured in a sketch by the Swiss architect Gaspare Fossati[75] (**Figure 47**).

In December 1829, Albani told Uggeri that he wanted the Special Commission to make a final decision on the master plan for San Paolo at their

47. Gaspare Fossati, sketch depicting the raising of one of the columns of the triumphal arch at San Paolo, 6 August 1829.
Source: Archivio di Stato del Cantone Ticino (Svizzera), *Fondo famiglia Fossati di Morcote*, N. 597.

very next meeting.[76] Though Belli had had two and a half years to formulate his plan, he was increasingly infirm, and nearly an entire additional year was to elapse before he finally came through on 16 November 1830. Secretary of State Albani sent the project the following day to the Architects Class at the Academy of St. Luke.[77]

Two weeks later, Pius VIII died after a pontificate of just twenty months. From Secretary of State Albani on down, most members of the Curia resigned, as was normal, even if the historical moment then unfolding around them was decidedly not; for Europe was just then being convulsed by a rolling wave of revolutions. The unrest had begun in Paris, where in July 1830 the reactionary Catholic King Charles X had been overthrown by Louis-Philippe d'Orléans. It had spread thence to Brussels, leading in October to the Belgian declaration of independence from Dutch rule. Italian revolutionaries had plotted their own uprisings in hopes of forging a united Italy and even received assurances from Louis-Philippe's new government that France would protect them from retaliation. Clerical Rome watched all this with horror. Yet when the College of Cardinals was convened to elect Pius VIII's successor, it drew to Rome at the worst possible moment the

RESISTING RESURRECTION 177

cardinal-legates who governed many of the most restive northern legations. Suffice it to say, Belli's long-awaited master plan had a lot to compete with.

The project consisted of a memorandum and three images: a plan (**Figure 48**), a longitudinal section (**Plate 10**), and two transverse sections, one from the apse looking west, and one from the nave also looking west.[78] Belli's memorandum began with a withering description of the prefire basilica: most of the nave columns were "bad work" exhibiting a crude lack of entasis and "false proportions"; the arches atop them revealed the "decadence of the arts"; the pavement was a grotesque collection of discarded bricks and marbles; the exposed roof timberwork, for all its charm, had only been visible because a coffered ceiling "whose vestiges are still visible" had been destroyed.[79] Thus he established at the start that he approached his task from the perspective of aesthetics rather than historic preservation.

In the second part, Belli set forth his reconstruction proposal, and here another thing became clear: he had learned his lesson well that the most effective way to justify eliminating features he disapproved of, or recreating lost features he liked, was to invoke the authority of the Chirograph. He opened with an ingratiating mention of that "never sufficiently praised Chirograph" in which Leo XII had mandated that there should be "no innovations." He then advanced a long series of innovations. Flooding, he noted, was a major problem for a church sited on low-lying land adjacent to the Tiber. To remedy this, he proposed to raise the level of the floor by 3 palmi (roughly 27 inches) and to build a tufa breakwater along the building's flanks. As for the interior nave elevation, Belli offered something only loosely related to that of the old basilica. In exchange for retaining the trademark arches atop the nave columns – a transgression he excused by recalling that the Renaissance had sometimes favored similar arrangements – he changed everything else. The busy decorations that originally framed the papal portrait medallions in the arch spandrels were all cleared out, leaving the medallions to float in space. The middle band in the elevation acquired a new blank architrave below the frieze. The upper wall was entirely reconceived as an orderly Corinthian pilaster ordonnance close to that of Fuga's restored Santa Maria Maggiore. Rectangular painted panels filled the lower quarter of the interpilastriations, while up above there were round-headed panels in which clear windows alternated with full-length frescos of saints and apostles. Over all this, Belli proposed to hang a wooden coffered ceiling.

These changes would have transformed the overall proportions. In an absolute sense, Belli's elevation was shorter than that of the old basilica, for while the floor was to be raised, surviving elements to the east and west dictated that the level of the ceiling and roof would remain the same as in the old basilica. The internal proportions changed as well. In the old basilica, the upper wall had been a quarter again as tall as the arcade, whereas Belli had

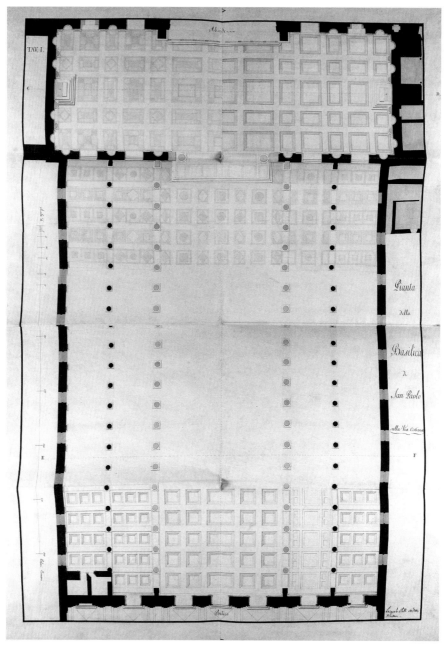

48. Pasquale Belli, proposed plan for the reconstruction of the basilica of San Paolo, 16 November 1830.
Source: Biblioteca Nazionale Centrale "Vittorio Emanuele II" di Roma, Vitt.Em. 638.

evened things out, increasing the proportion of the elevation occupied by the columns and especially the capitals (as Uggeri had predicted with the adoption of the Pantheon capitals) and significantly expanding the portion given over to the middle zone, which was also now higher up the wall (**Figure 49**). As a

49. Comparison approximately to scale of the elevation of the old basilica as depicted in Nicolai's monograph (left) with Belli's proposed nave elevation of 16 November 1830 (right). *Source*: L: Bibliotheca Herziana; R: Biblioteca Nazionale Centrale "Vittorio Emanuele II" di Roma, Vitt.Em. 638.

result, the proportion of the elevation occupied by the upper zone was reduced by roughly 20 percent and now actually occupied less space than the lower arcade. The rhythms were also greatly simplified, with the formerly complex syncopation of the ornament, both vertically and horizontally, reduced to something approaching a linear grid. If Fuga's Santa Maria Maggiore provided the model for the upper wall, Lesueur's restoration drawings of the Basilica Ulpia seem to have supplied the proportions.

In the transept, Belli continued the system of his nave in the upper zones, while in the lower he proposed an austere series of pilasters rising directly to a flat entablature (**Figure 50**). On the transept terminal walls, the middle bays projected slightly to highlight the altar at their center, while pilasters were swopped out for engaged columns. Belli's proposal thus united nave and transept in a manner wholly unlike in the old building, where the two had been entirely different in their decor. This also rejected Uggeri's vision of the new basilica as comprising two fully separate spaces.

On the evenings of 7 and 11 January 1831, amid reports of insurrection in the northern Papal States, and with the papal throne still vacant, the Architecture Section of the academy met, studied Belli's project, and issued a long and positive report. They affirmed that the plan and elevation preserved the original "form, distribution, and proportions," just as the Chirograph commanded. Belli's proposal for the upper walls was "rather well thought out" and in keeping with the character of the building. The academicians also reluctantly agreed to Belli's proposal to erect arches atop the nave columns, even though it was "contrary to good architecture," for "they were thus originally." Perhaps to avoid giving Belli everything he asked for, one minute change was required: the suppression of the half pilaster occupying the angle behind the central projection of the transept terminal wall, which offered a whiff of Baroque tectonic expression. But overall the project was sound, for it preserved "the former temple in its original state, with the most commendable character and decoration of that era."[80]

Belli's colleagues proved equally accommodating of his desire to remedy practical defects. They endorsed his plan to eliminate flooding by raising the floor. They may have been influenced in this by the major flood that had just occurred in Rome, with perfect timing, around Christmas. The Roman press seems not to have reported it, perhaps out of concern for the public mood (Tiber floods had a reputation for correlating with crisis), but other European papers noted it. A breathless account in the *Gaceta de Madrid* reported that "all the streets closest to the river were flooded so suddenly that the inhabitants had to flee instantly; even so, many lost everything including their houses." The countryside around San Paolo was also flooded, and the "works in progress for the reconstruction [of San Paolo] were suspended after the waters destroyed a newly built part of the building and had filled up the nave with water and slime."[81] Belli could hardly have asked for a timelier justification.

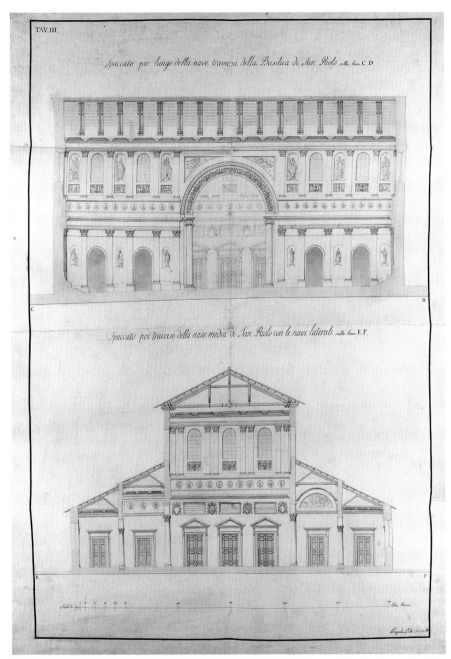

50. Pasquale Belli, proposed section through the transept looking west (top) and nave looking west (bottom) for the reconstruction of the basilica of San Paolo, 16 November 1830.
Source: Biblioteca Nazionale Centrale "Vittorio Emanuele II" di Roma, Vitt.Em. 638.

The flood may even have reminded the academicians that the geological and fluvial life of the land upon which San Paolo stood held magical significance for the Roman *popolani*. The vernacular poet Giuseppe Gioachino Belli (no relation) penned a sonnet in that same year of 1831 entitled "La Fin der

Monno" ("The End of the World"), which evoked how, at the end of time, *er Nocchilia*, a composite of Enoch and Elijah, would emerge from his hole in the ground near San Paolo ("da la bbuscia de San Pavolo") to fight the Antichrist.[82] When the *Neue Augsburger Zeitung* reported on the flood of December 1830, its correspondent added that the common people, who called the river the "Prophet's Stream" ("vates Tiberis"), had interpreted it – as they had the fire at San Paolo eight years earlier – as a divine curse, only this time related to the death of Pius VIII.[83] The wisdom of preserving the basilica from future floods may have been sharpened in the Academy by an awareness of such popular beliefs.

Whatever the case, the vote of the academic architects was but a first step toward the final approval that authorized work to begin. The complex story of what happened next is taken up in the following chapter.

NOTES

1   Leo XII ((1825), p. 4.
2   Leo XII (1825).
3   Fabi Montani (1837), p. 310; Colini (1973), p. 148.
4   Cardinali (1826) (illustrated with plan, section, and elevation).
5   Uggeri followed Fea in dating the wall to the eighth century (Fea [1826a], pp. 5–6; Angelo Uggeri, "Proposizione per ridurre la Basilica Ostiense al primitivo stato Costantiniano" (January 1826) (ASP: 36/c, b. "Basilica S Paolo. Ricostruzione [Diario Romano], Studi importanti"; republished in Uggeri [1826], Sommario 1, Letter A ["Proposizione ..."], pp. 1–3). Seroux d'Agincourt ([1823], v. 2, p. 4) had described it only as posterior to the original construction. Docci dates it to the twelfth century (Docci [2006], p. 72).
6   Uggeri, "Proposizione ...", as in Chapter 8, n. 5. The reply of the Academy of St. Luke is dated 21 January 1826: Uggeri (1826), Sommario 1, Letter B ("Vota della Accademia..."), pp. 3–5. See also Uggeri and della Somaglia (1827), pp. 13–14. Fea had also advocated removing the Muro Divisorio (Fea [1826a], pp. 5–6; Fea [1826b], p. 22). Groblewski (2001) discusses this episode pp. 126–129.
7   Vincenzo Camuccini to Giulio Maria della Somaglia, 21 January 1826 (ASR: CSRBSP Segreteria b.276, f.2); printed in Uggeri (1826), Sommario 1, Letter B ("Vota della Accademia ..."), pp. 3–5.
8   Uggeri (1826), Sommario 1, Letter C ("Approvazione ..."), p. 5.
9   Beste (1826), v. 1, p. 56. On the 1825 work on the mosaics, see Uggeri's letters to Cristaldi from Summer 1825 (ASR: Camerale III b. 1910, #132; Camerale III b. 1909, #132; and Camerale III b. 1909, #137).
10   Uggeri (1826), Sommario 2, Letter A ("Stato attuale ..."), pp. 6–7.
11   Uggeri (1826), Sommario 2, Letter B ("Voto della Accademia ..."), pp. 9–10. Groblewski (2001), pp. 130–134, analyzes this debate.
12   Uggeri (1826), Sommario 2, Letter D ("Approvazione ..."), pp. 12–13; Giacomo Raffaelli, "Articoli co' quali si conviene di distaccare e rimettere in opera il Musaico dell'Arco detto di Placidia nella Basilica di San Paolo," 30 November 1826 (BNR: ARC 15 II.B.2.29; and BCALP: LP12 C79 2). On the mosaic restoration, see Biancini (2013). Raffaelli later published an article on the damage the mosaic suffered (Raffaelli [1828]). The daybook for Raffaelli's work on the mosaic is at the Biblioteca Nazionale in Rome (ARC 15 II B.2.34). Raffaelli's son Vincenzo later recounted this whole history, with detailed

descriptions of his father's innovative techniques (Vincnezo Raffaelli to Giacomo Antonelli, 3 November 1850 [ASR: CSRBSP Segreteria b. 283]).

13 Strozzieri (2021), p. 154.

14 Beste (1826), v. 1, p. 56. See Beste's amusing account (p. 57) of the English "Milordino" who was thwarted by a custodian when he tried to remove part of a marble balustrade.

15 Angelo Uggeri to Belisario Cristaldi, 23 June 1827 (ASR: Camerale III b. 1911, #259).

16 Uggeri (1827b).

17 See also Groblewski's extensive account of these debates (Groblewski [2001], pp. 102–134).

18 Guglielmo Closse to Belisario Cristaldi, 14 August 1823 (ASR: Camerale III b. 1909, #19). Closse had first contacted Cristaldi on 20 July 1823 (ASR: Camerale III b. 1909, #19).

19 Closse, "Offerta," as in Chapter 5, n. 69, and "Offerta," 20 July 1825 (ASR: Camerale III b. 1909, #19). This caused considerable excitement in the Simplon region (Luigi Alberghetti to Belisario Cristaldi, 27 December 1825 [ASR: Camerale III b. 1910, #154]).

20 *Osservazioni sul marmo* di Cottanello in Sabina (1825).

21 Fea (1826a). The text bears the date 10 December 1825 but it could not have been published before the end of January 1826, for it discusses Morel de Bauvine's offer.

22 Fea (1826a), p. 7.

23 Uggeri (1826), Sommario 4, Letter C ("Offerta de' marmi …"), pp. 20–21; tiG pp. 332–333.

24 Uggeri (1826), Sommario 4, Letter B ("Trasmissione della offerta de' marmi …"), pp. 19–20; tiG p. 332.

25 Uggeri (1826), Sommario 4, Letter D ("Voto dell'Accademia …"), pp. 21–22; tiG pp. 333–334.

26 Uggeri (1826), Sommario 4, Letter A ("Proggetto del Sig. Closse …"), pp. 18.

27 L. S. (1826).

28 Fea (1826b).

29 Vincenzo Camuccini to Giulio Maria della Somaglia, 5 June 1826; tiG pp. 340–344 and published in Uggeri (1826), Sommario 4, Letter F ["Voto della Accademia …"], pp. 32–37.

30 It is not clear from the documents whether at this point Closse was still proposing a red granite or one of a different color.

31 Camuccini (5 June 1826), as in Chapter 8, n. 29.

32 Groblewski (2001), p. 110.

33 Uggeri (1832a), Plate VIII bis.

34 Uggeri (1826), Sommario 6, Letter A ("Progetto …"), p. 49. Some of the columns he proposed to reuse came from the Basilica Ulpia – a remarkable notion given Uggeri's beliefs about the relationship of that structure to San Paolo!

35 Uggeri (1826), Sommario 6, Letter B ("Biglietto …"), pp. 49–50.

36 Giovanni Filippini to Nicola Maria Nicolai, 28 July 1826 (ASR: Camerale III b. 1910, #220); Uggeri (1826), Sommario 5, Letter A ("Progetto …"), pp. 39–40, and Letter C (*Incipit*: "La Pontificia Accademia …"), pp. 43–44.

37 Carlo Fea, "Per le colonne da farsi nella basilica di S. Paolo," 18 September 1826 (ASR: Camerale III b. 1911, #225; Camerlengato, P. II, Tit. IV, b. 155, f. 204); tiG pp. 356–357. The copy in the Camerlengato archive is signed by Fea. He had advocated Carrara columns in his "Parere" (1824) and in Fea (1825).

38 Uggeri (1827a), Part I ("SCELTA DE' MARMI") p. 4; Sommario 1, Letter D ("ARTICOLI…"), pp. 11–12; and Sommario 5, Letter C ("Notificazione …"), pp.35–7.

39 Berthel Thorwaldsen to Giulio Maria della Somaglia, 21 January 1827 (ASR: Camerale III b. 1911, #244). The contract was signed on 14 March 1827 (Uggeri [1827a], Sommario 1, Letter C ["ARTICOLI…"], pp. 6–8). The price was to be 6,000 scudi apiece, including transport to the building site by the end of September 1827.

40 Angelo Uggeri to Giovanni Francesco Zelli, May 1827 (ASP: 30/c, libro rosso 2).

41 Uggeri (1827a), Part I ("SCELTA DE' MARMI"), pp. 7–9, and Sommario 5, Letter [F] ("Lettera del Cavalier Presidente …"), pp. 40–47; Uggeri's refusal to sign is recorded on p. 47.

42 BAV: Vat.Lat. 13444, f. 1–8. See the extensive discussion in Groblewski (2001), pp. 135–145.

43 Uggeri (1831a), p. 25 (Preface). See also Groblewski (2001), p. 136 n. 4.

44 *Gazzetta di Milano*, 28 December 1827, p. 1436; *Gazzetta Piemontese* (Turin), 8 January 1828, p. 26.

45 The journey of these immense monoliths from Simplon to Rome had been tracked in the press with much fanfare: *DdR*, 4 August 1827, p. 2; *DdR: NdG*, 4 October 1827, p. 1; *DdR: NdG*, 11 October 1827, p. 1; *Gazzetta di Milano*, 11 October 1827, p. 1125; *DdR*, 20 October 1827, p. 1; *L'ami de la Religion* (Paris), 24 October 1827, p. 333; *Giornale del Regno delle Due Sicilie* (Naples), 5 November 1827, p. 1028; *DdR: NdG*, 8 November 1827, p. 1; *Giornale del Regno delle Due Sicilie*, 16 November 1827, p. 1068; etc. The second column (*DdR*, 5 January 1828, p. 1; *Gazzetta Piemontese* [Turin], 12 January 1828, p. 48; etc.) eventually was the subject of a published pamphlet: Visconti (1828). On Fea and the Sempione granite, see Fea (1826a), p. 4.

46 Luigi Poletti to Geminiano Poletti, 10 January 1828 (BCALP: LP23b C16).

47 The document in which Belli expressed his intention seems to have vanished, but Uggeri's urgent letter of protest is dated 10 January 1828 (Uggeri [1828] ("Lettera…"), pp. 3–4).

48 Seroux d'Agincourt (1823), Book 4, plates VI and VII; Pallottino (1995), p. 40.

49 Betti (1833), p. 359; Moreschi (1837), p. 3.

50 Uggeri (1828), Letter C, 25 January 1828 ("Dispaccio …"), pp. 6–7.

51 Uggeri (1828), Letter D, 27 January 1828 ("Proposizione …"), pp. 7–9.

52 Uggeri (1828), Letter E, 30-31 January 1828 ("Lettera …" and "Primo Processo Verbale"), pp. 9–12.

53 Uggeri (1828), Letter F, 13 March 1828 ("Lettera …"), pp. 12–13.

54 Uggeri (1828), Letter G, 16-17 March 1828 ("Lettera …" and "Secondo Processo Verbale"), pp. 13–15 and 16–17.

55 Uggeri (1828), Letter H, 18 April 1828 ("Dispaccio …"), p. 16.

56 Uggeri (1828), Letter K, 18 April 1828 ("Lettera …" and "Protesta …"), pp. 21–24

57 Uggeri (1828), Letter I, April 1828 ("Lettera …"), pp. 16–21.

58 "Umilissimi riflessi … nel dì 10 Luglio 1828" (ASR: Camerale III b. 1911, #289); Seroux d'Agincourt (1823), v. 1, p. 13.

59 This anticipates the Romantic Christian critique of classical art that developped just a few years later; see Chapter 16.

60 Uggeri (1831a), Sommario 2, Letter F and G ("Offerta …" and "Offerta …"), pp. 16–18

61 Uggeri (1828), Letter L ("Dispaccio …"), p. 25.

62 Uggeri (1828), 6 July 1828 ("Processo verbale…"), pp. 26–27.

63 Uggeri (1831a), Introduction ("ISTRUZIONI"), pp. 6–7.

64 Uggeri (1831a), Sommario, 1–2; II, pp. 1–3.

65 Carpi (1828).

66 Dagnet (1828), p. 88.

67 Uggeri (1831a), Sommario II, Letter H, 4 August 1828 ("Lettera …"), pp. 19–22.

68 Ceccarini (1828).

69 Uggeri (1831a), Introduction, pp. 8–10. On p. 10, it says that this final decision was taken at a meeting on 29 September 1829, but this is surely a typographical error for 29 September 1828.

70 Uggeri (1831a), Introduction, p. 10 and Sommario III, Letter A ("Contratto …"), pp. 23–26; Galloni (1988).

71 Uggeri (1831a), pp. 40–41.

72 *DdR*, 11 February 1829, pp. 1–2.

73 Belli contrived to tilt these columns slightly forward on the original bases toward the nave so that they aligned with the flat western face of the rebuilt arch (Strozzieri [2021], pp. 137–138, fig. 23). Notices were published in the *Diario di Roma* after the erection of each of the two columns, on 2 July and 6 August (*DdR*, 4 July 1829, p. 1; *DdR*, 8 August 1829, p. 1).

74 *DdR*, 4 July 1829, p. 1; *Gazzetta Piemontese* (Turin), 14 July 1829, p. 522.

75 *Cronaca* II, 6 August 1829.

76 Uggeri (1831a), p. 40.

77 Uggeri (1831a), p. 49. See also Groblewski's discussion of Belli's project (Groblewski [2001], pp. 151–154).

78 Pasquale Belli, "Disegni per la riedificazione di S. Paolo sulla via Ostiense," 16 November 1830 (BNR: Vitt.Em.638; tiG pp. 381–386 with illustrations pp. 553–555, and transcribed in Uggeri [1831a], pp. 42–48).

79 Uggeri (1831a), pp. 42–44; tiG pp. 381–383.

80 Vote of the Academy of Saint Luke, Architecture Section, 21 January 1831 (AASL: *Miscellanea Congregazioni* II, no. 101; v. 80,5; tiG pp. 386–388).

81 *Gaceta de Madrid*, 27 January 1831, p. 48.

82 Belli (1889), v. 1, p. 222: "La Fin der Monno" (25 November 1831). See Bovet (1898), p. 236.

83 *Neue Augsburger Zeitung*, 23 January 1831, pp. 90–91.

NINE

THE END OF A GENERATION

As the bureaucratic wheels began to turn in response to Belli's long-awaited master plan, Church leaders were preoccupied with electing Pius VIII's successor and, more despairingly, with the revolutionary mood then ripening across Europe. In Rome itself, two young nephews of Napoleon I (one was the future Emperor Napoleon III) attempted in December 1830 to instigate an uprising and failed only when they were betrayed to the police. A month later bombs went off on consecutive Sundays, one outside a window where the conclave was meeting.[1] But these proved to be mere comic-opera preludes to the real storm, which broke instead to the north, on 4 February, when full-scale insurrections routed the authorities in the Duchy of Modena and in Papal Bologna, and began spreading to the other Papal Legations (Forli, Ravenna, Imola, Ferrara, Pesaro, Urbino). A group of Bolognese insurgents even marched on Rome.[2] These rebellions began just two days after the archconservative Cardinal Bartolomeo Alberto (Mauro) Cappellari was finally elected Pope Gregory XVI, following the longest conclave in 175 years[3] (**Figure 51**). Relieved that the military support for the rebels promised by the French crown never materialized, the new Pope Gregory urgently invited Austrian troops to come restore order in the pontifical territories. The Austrians obliged in March 1831 and began liquidating the disillusioned insurgents with brutal efficiency.

As a Camaldolese Benedictine monk, Gregory was among the rare 10 percent of popes to emerge from the regular clergy.[4] He took his regnal name

51. Paul Delaroche, *Portrait of Pope Gregory XVI*, 1844.
Source: © RMN-Grand Palais / Art Resource, New York.

from the first such pope, St. Gregory the Great (590–604), the most celebrated pope of Christian antiquity, who had asserted papal authority both within and beyond the Church and helped lay the foundations for medieval theology and especially scholasticism. Gregory XVI at the time of his election had been cardinal-priest of San Callisto in Trastevere, the summer house of the San Paolo Benedictines, which meant that he knew their community intimately and had a special connection to the reconstruction of the basilica. On 16 March 1831, as the Austrians mopped up rebels in the north, Gregory made his first visit as pope to the San Paolo construction site.[5] The *Diario di Roma* ventured that the new pontiff's warmly expressed satisfaction might offer a fresh impetus to the work, which, with Belli's master plan now complete, seemed poised to move ahead at full steam. It was not to be, however, or at least not during the two and a half remaining years of Belli's life. These were instead filled with a suite of new challenges, new debates, and new reversals at the worksite, all unfolding against the backdrop of the architect's deteriorating health.

Despite these frustrations, a turning point in the reconstruction was reached during these years with the emergence of Belli's eventual successor, a young Modenese engineer-architect named Luigi Poletti. Poletti officially acceded to the post of architect director just a few days after Belli's death in October 1833, but by that time he had already been effectively supervising the work for more than a year. The passage from Belli to Poletti marked the start of a generational shift, as older *in pristinum* militants like Fea and Uggeri began withdrawing on account of age, infirmity, and eventually death – Fea in 1836 at the age of eighty-two and Uggeri in 1837 at eighty-three. Free of such opponents and determined to avoid the paralysis that had undermined Belli, Poletti was to take a very different approach to his work at San Paolo.

After the Architects' Section's favorable report on Belli's master plan in January 1831, it took three more months before the full Academy voted to endorse its recommendation. In the apologetic cover letter addressed to Secretary of State Bernetti, this delay was blamed on the "great public unease that the rebellion in the provinces has so lamentably provoked," but the real reason was that consensus had been surprisingly elusive.[6] A first General Assembly had been convened back on 20 February to review the architects' report, but the majority of academicians present voted to postpone debate until they could visit the basilica to evaluate elements of Belli's project that "many members have serious doubts about." That visit occurred a month later and led to a "long and frank discussion," after which the whole Academy voted to approve only four of the eight approved articles of the project: those concerning the overall plan and elevation, the retention of arches atop the nave columns, the coffered ceiling proposed for the nave, and the placement of a similar coffered ceiling over the side aisles. But on raising the pavement they ruled that they could not overlook the "grave defect" it would provoke in the proportions and overall dignity of the building. Plus it violated the Chirograph. As for the architectonic ordonnance Belli had proposed for the upper walls, the academicians were unresolved and requested still more time to reflect in anticipation of a subsequent General Assembly.[7] That assembly did not occur until 17 April 1831, and there, following more "long discussions," a new written statement was distributed by Belli's camp.[8] This, however, did not come from Belli himself, but from his new assistant Poletti, a thirty-eight year-old recently minted academician who back in January had been part of the Architects' Section that had recommended Belli's proposals.

Before discussing Poletti's statement, there is the question of how this hitherto obscure figure came to occupy such a vital position at Belli's side in

THE END OF A GENERATION   189

the first place. Neither the voluminous archive of the reconstruction workshop nor Poletti's own personal archive provide a definitive answer. Poletti had been in Rome since 1818, first as a student and then as a provincial outsider struggling to break into the clannish Roman architectural scene.[9] His controversial election to the Academy in September 1829 had provoked opposition from a cardinal and the resignation of an academician.[10] The closest we can come at this point to an explanation for Poletti's sudden appearance at San Paolo is a hypothesis based on two ambiguous archival documents.

The first is a note of just a few lines preserved in Poletti's personal archive. It was sent from a procuror called Clemente De Donatis on 21 January 1830. In it, De Donatis informs Poletti that "monsignor Nicolai" had yesterday presented "the request" to "the whole Congregation," suggests that "the thing looks like it will work out," and then asks to see Poletti the following evening.[11] "Monsignor Nicolai" was Nicola Maria Nicolai, author of the 1815 monograph on San Paolo and someone we know Poletti had been acquainted with from at least 1827. By "Congregation" De Donatis was likely referring to the Special Commission for the Reconstruction of San Paolo, of which Nicolai was a permanent member, and which contemporaries referred to interchangeably as both a Congregation and Commission. It is harder to identify the "thing" ("la cosa") he was referring to, although one possible answer can be hypothesized based on the second document. This is a supplication Poletti sent to Pope Gregory XVI two years later, in September 1832, in which he listed among his professional achievements the "important repairs he had just executed at the Monastery of S. Callisto."[12] San Callisto was of course the city house of the San Paolo Benedictines, where Gregory himself had been cardinal-priest prior to his election in 1831. None of Poletti's biographers mention that he had a commission at S. Callisto, but in his archive in Modena there are eight undated autograph drawings of the chapel there.[13] Also in the archive are two other clues. The first is a cover letter from Uggeri to Poletti, dated 6 April 1830, accompanying Uggeri's (now missing) counter-project for a roof over the nave to replace one recently approved by the Academy. In the letter, Uggeri addresses Poletti familarly and asks him to come visit him "at any hour, throughout the day" to talk over the proposal, so that they might overturn the plainly defective plan recently approved by the Academy.[14] The second clue, then, is a note to Poletti from Belli, dated 1 June 1831, asking if Poletti would be so kind as to sign the annexed sheet (now missing) and apologizing for the inconvenience.[15] The possible substance of that missing annexed sheet is suggested by an official confirmation Poletti received three weeks later, on 21 June 1831, of his new post as architetto supernumero of the *monastery* (not the basilica) of San Paolo, which explicitly stated that he would henceforth have duties "at both San Paolo and San Callisto."[16]

Now to put all this together. The "request" that De Donatis passed to Nicolai in January 1830 might have concerned an application from Poletti to carry out repairs on the San Callisto buildings; this would not have been an official responsibility of the Special Commission, but it is easy to imagine that Abbot Zelli, who also sat on the Commission, would have consulted on such matters with its other members, including his old friends Uggeri and Nicolai. Uggeri's letter concerning the roof proposal three months later seems to indicate that Poletti by then was in a position to have at least some influence on events. All this would then provide a possible path via which Poletti had come to be acting as Belli's advocate on 17 April 1831 – a path that, if it began with successful lobbying to perform repairs at San Callisto, led from there to becoming known not just to the leaders of the monastic community but also to their cardinal-priest, the future Gregory XVI, and from there brought him to the attention of the aging Belli, who at San Paolo found himself increasingly in need of just the sort of practical and intellectual support Poletti could provide.

Let us return now to the statement Poletti presented in advance of the 17 April 1831 meeting at the Academy. Based on a longer draft in Poletti's archive, it is clear that he was not just the messenger that day, but rather the author of the statement's quite original argument.[17] The text was principally concerned to confront the objection that the order of pilasters with which Belli wished to decorate the upper wall was not justified by the old elevation. Poletti's argument was simple: pilasters were more in keeping with the basilican building *type*, which Constantine had deliberately chosen as the basis for the Christian church, and Belli was therefore fully justified in emphasizing them.[18] Poletti reminded the company that a host of Early Christian basilicas had had superposed orders, from old St. Peter's and S. Agnese fuori le mura to Santa Maria Maggiore (which he did not admit was Belli's model, but which he did say "presents the true type of the middle nave"). He observed that the original nave at San Paolo had "clearly" had a coffered ceiling, and that it therefore followed logically that there had been a pilaster order. It did not matter if no one had ever seen it; it had to have been present originally, and it therefore was no violation of the Chirograph to reconstruct it.

In an impressive success for the young Modenese, the assembly voted on the spot to approve all three of the contested articles.[19] More impressive still was the fact that Poletti had almost surreptitiously introduced an entirely new rationale for the reconstruction. No longer was the goal to recreate the old basilica of San Paolo in its original form. The goal now was to create an ideal Early Christian basilica.

THE END OF A GENERATION   191

This new rationale was again implicit in a second memorandum addressed to the Special Commission on 13 May, which aimed to relitigate Belli's proposal to raise the floor. Presented as though from Belli, this too was largely by Poletti, for it is also anticipated by the draft in Poletti's archive.[20] It pointed out that the San Paolo community had been forced long ago to protect the basilica against floods by rebuilding the original nave floor with a slope and by raising the original transept pavement; indeed, the bases of the colossal columns supporting the Arch of Placidia had been completely immured in the pavement by the time of the fire. Some contemporaries had complained that raising the floor would entail reducing the columns, wrote Poletti, but in reality the antique aisle columns were but a motley grab bag of shafts with different diameters, different marbles, and decadent mismatched capitals: "What really would be the loss if such columns were cut back by three palmi?" Plus their bases were all at least partly swallowed up at one end of the nave by the sloping floor. The Academy had expressed the commendable wish that "the plan of the ancient pavement shall be preserved," but a sloping floor was hardly worthy of the dignity of a basilica, especially as it did little to protect from flooding. The choice, then, was between a successful reconstruction and an irrationally slavish adherence to the letter of the Chirograph.[21] A more enlightened approach, he concluded, would be to raise not only the pavement but the entire reconstructed basilica, thereby preserving the original proportions in their entirety.

Belli and Poletti presented this memorandum to Uggeri, who packaged it along with various annexed documents in a printed booklet for the Commission to study in advance of a meeting scheduled for 7 July 1831.[22] This meeting had been convened by Pope Gregory himself, who was said to have grown so interested in the matter of raising the floor that he had begun personally studying the relevant documents.[23] Uggeri indicated four questions for the commissioners to decide. The first two were: Should Belli's general plan for the building, as approved by the Academy, be approved by the Commission? And should the Commission accept the Academy's negative verdict about raising the nave pavement?[24] On the first, the Commission temporized: Belli's plan should be followed for the altars and ceiling, but otherwise work must remain in conformity with the Chirograph. On the second, they voted to accept the Academy's negative verdict on the pavement. Of the other two questions, which Uggeri added just before the meeting, the most important was clearly a last-ditch effort to buy time: it asked whether work on the nave ought to be set aside altogether until the transept was complete. In the days or weeks prior to the meeting, Uggeri had printed up a four-page *Proposizione* with which to lobby the commissioners on this point.[25] It stressed "our responsibility towards all those who have contributed so generously to the reconstruction of the basilica":

> ... it is proper, and I would actually say prudent, to provide a tangible
> proof that the Basilica is rising again; that so many sacrifices by the most
> humble functionaries, so many voluntary offerings from foreign persons,
> have not been used up in mere preparations, without any part of the
> building being completed to its perfection. For it seems to me that those
> who made those offerings and those sacrifices have a right to see some
> definitive results.

The Simplon granite columns for the nave were finally arriving, he acknowledged, but would benefit from being left exposed to the air for a time. He added philosophically that "desire, when it goes unsatisfied for too long, transforms itself into a true moral evil," and urged the Commission members to focus the reconstruction effort on "a single, unique goal":

> It is necessary, in choosing that goal, that it be achievable within a short
> span of time. It is necessary also to avoid those parts that might be subject
> to contingencies, and that will necessarily be subject to long and indeter-
> minate delays on account of the materials being employed.

Only by focusing everything on the transept, in sum, could they fulfill "the promises made by Leo XII to all those who contributed, or would contribute." Uggeri offered a religious rationale too: if the purpose of the whole reconstruction was to honor and conserve the sepulcher of St. Paul, then the first area to be rebuilt should be where he was buried, so that masses could resume. If the ancients were rebuilding a temple, would they not rebuild the cella before the pronaos? It was a choice between completing the essential or diverting resources to the accessory.

The Commission offered Uggeri only the maddeningly noncommittal reply that, yes, the transept should be done first, but working on the nave should also not be ruled out. Belli was thus soon reluctantly supervising the installation of the bases for the nave columns at the original floor level. But as he did so, he – or perhaps it was mainly Poletti – became so afflicted by the thought that the reconstructed basilica would thereby be marred with a permanent, objective flaw that he returned to urge the Commission to reconsider the matter yet again.[26]

Carlo Fea erupted when he learned of this, and published a pamphlet claiming that Belli was wildly exaggerating the threat: "Seriously!? After six years of work it enters the architect's head to raise the pavement by 3 palmi ... on the argument that every so often, if the Tiber rises enough, a little bit of water comes into the church?"[27] Fea marveled that the idea could even still be in play. It had been soundly voted down by all the competent authorities. There were no instances in living memory of the river having caused any catastrophic damage at the basilica. And anyway, could a letter directed by Leo XII to the whole Catholic world really be swept aside on the whim of an architect? Fea quoted canon law to suggest that only a second papal letter could effect such a change. And what about the rights of the innumerable pious faithful donors, lovers of the arts, lovers of antiquity, who had contributed from all across the Catholic world – "even from America"? How could one contemplate betraying the trust they had placed in the promise that they were contributing to an exact reconstruction? A raised nave floor would make the new San Paolo the only basilica in its class where the choir was not elevated above the nave. With the surviving doors of the old perimeter walls shortened at their bases, he quipped, one would be obliged to enter the new basilica with head bowed, as though visiting a grotto. Fea ended on a rant about how the basilica would be practically done by now if his original solution of using two-part columns of Carrara marble had been adopted. Instead, everything imaginable had been done to prolong the work, with columns dragged all the way from the Alps, and of an unattractive and inappropriate color to boot. The ludicrous idea of raising the floor would only delay things further and surely extinguish whatever generosity might yet linger in the hearts of the faithful.[28]

On 28 October, Gregory XVI returned to the construction site. A brief report in the *Diario di Roma* described only his perfect satisfaction with everything he saw and made no mention of these controversies.[29] Belli and Poletti, meanwhile, worked furiously behind the scenes. In November, they invited three key members of the Special Commission – Treasurer General Mattei, Cardinal Secretary of State Bernetti, and Cardinal De Gregorio – to meet them at the basilica, where they provided a detailed explanation of the virtues of their proposal and demonstrated why it would not in any way alter the proportions or form of the building.[30] By mid-December, all three had agreed to reverse their 7 July vote against raising the floor.[31] When Mattei reported this to Gregory XVI, the pope ordered him to poll the other four cardinals on the Commission, and by the end of April 1832 they too had all decided to reverse their votes.[32] Gregory duly authorized Belli to start raising the level of the pavement.[33] Forty travertine blocks were ordered to boost the columns of the aisles, and by October eight were in place and work was proceeding on the rest.[34]

Angelo Uggeri and Carlo Fea now mounted desperate eleventh-hour campaigns to halt this work, which each regarded as a blatant violation of Leo XII's Chirograph. In December, Fea published a short series of articles arguing that a far simpler flood prevention system could be used, not just at San Paolo but in Rome as a whole: namely, the network of overflow channels proposed in Giovanni Battista Barattieri's *Architettura d'acque* in 1656.[35] Fea's essay appeared in the *Giornale di commercio*, a new weekly paper focusing on manufacturing, technology, and commerce, probably because he hoped to expand the debate to a more practically oriented readership.[36] The editor of the *Giornale* prefaced Fea's essay by juxtaposing the worldwide outpouring of contributions to San Paolo with the academic controversies that had paralyzed progress. He described the raising of the floor as "one of the fatal innovations" of the reconstruction, and echoed Fea's claim that the risk of flood was exaggerated. He warned that raising the floor would destroy the building's "entire architectonic system," and invited all lovers of the fine arts to suggest other remedies.

A few weeks later, the indefatigable Fea spun out these complaints in the didactically titled pamphlet *La basilica ostiense liberata dalle inondazioni del Tevere senza bisogno di innalzarne il pavimento*.[37] Little here was new aside from Fea's intimation that dark forces had been at work when the original resolution against raising the floor had been overturned. Also, everyone had overlooked the old drain in the center of the nave floor: it might still function and offer the simplest solution to the whole problem.[38] It was to be Fea's final contribution to the debates on San Paolo.

Uggeri, for his part, distributed a printed sheet to the Special Commission pointing out that its reversal on this matter would have dire consequences.[39] By placing the sanctuary and nave on the same level, the majesty of the building would be diminished and Leo XII's promise to preserve the original form of the basilica would be broken. The change would also add ten years onto the reconstruction, Uggeri estimated, even as it would deprive posterity of a key surviving element of the old basilica. It would also do little to preserve the interior from floods. Uggeri urged the commissioners to examine their consciences. Instead of ruining "this entire edifice from top to bottom," might it not be better to build a flood wall outside? Such a wall would take six or seven months and cost about 3,000 scudi, whereas raising the floor would take eight to ten years and cost about 20,000 or 30,000 scudi. The Arts Council could examine the economics of the matter, and the Academy of Archaeology (not the Academy of St. Luke) might consider the aesthetics.

The passion with which the venerable Fea and Uggeri protested got Pope Gregory's attention and led him to pause the work and reopen the whole question yet again.[40] Belli was told to respond in detail to the sheet Uggeri had circulated, and this he did – surely assisted by Poletti – on 22 January 1833. He also published an engraving that showed that the nave would not be raised to the same level as the choir but was to remain slightly lower, and that the level of the 1805 flood – the major one in living memory – would now only reach to the top of the raised column bases.[41] It also illustrated Belli's solution for the aisles, which had already proven controversial: that of leaving the aisle columns on their existing footings, immuring their original bases and lower parts within the raised pavement and clipping new stucco bases around them at floor level, like anklets[42] (**Figure 52**).

THE END OF A GENERATION

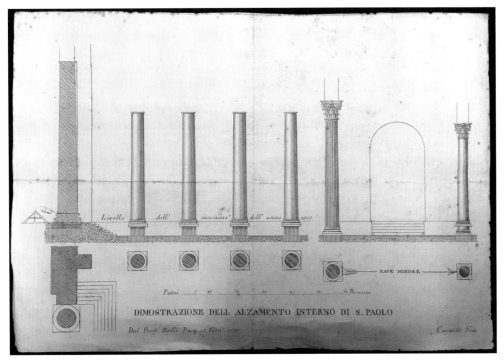

52. Pasquale Belli (and Luigi Poletti?), demonstration of how the nave floor at San Paolo was to be raised, 22 January 1833.
Source: Archivio di Stato, Rome. Su concessione del Ministero della Cultura; reproduction prohibited.

While Belli was preparing this, Gregory quietly commissioned a confidential report on Uggeri's proposed flood wall from Giuseppe Venturoli, the inspector from the Arts Council who nine years earlier had been among the experts who evaluated the projects of Valadier and Salvi. While Venturoli had expertise in hydraulics and was therefore a logical choice, he also happened to be an early protector of Luigi Poletti, and this may or may not have compromised his objectivity.[43] Whatever the case, Venturoli's report came down unambiguously on Belli's side: a flood wall would only aggravate the problem by slowing the remission of the floodwaters. Raising the floor was the only solution.[44]

Still Gregory XVI hesitated. He returned to the basilica in person on 18 February 1833 to observe for himself the effect that raising the floor would make. Probably hosted there by Poletti, Gregory was satisfied and brought debate to a definitive end the following day by ordering the resumption of the floor raising originally approved in May of the previous year.[45]

Well before this latest defeat, Uggeri's health had begun to worsen. From as far back as 1830 he had been almost completely deaf, which had often prevented him from discharging the public functions of his office as secretary to the Special Commission. Many of these were taken over by his young assistant, Luigi Moreschi, to the point that in June 1832 the treasurer general had written to Pope Gregory to say that Moreschi was effectively doing Uggeri's job, and ought to receive the title and salary that went with it.[46] Uggeri's defeat on raising the floor seems to have been the last straw for him; henceforth he retreated almost entirely from the scene, resurfacing mainly as a signature at the base of documents that had in fact been prepared by Moreschi. (We shall have much more to say about Moreschi in what follows.)

But if Uggeri's personal participation more or less ended after February 1833, his ideas lived to fight another day. During the very months when he was campaigning against raising the floor, Uggeri was also supervising the publication of *Della basilica Ulpia* (1833), his definitive statement on the Ulpian basilica, which summed up three decades of research around his cherished and by now familiar thesis that the Ulpia had been the model for San Paolo.[47] Fully one-fifth of its plates depicted San Paolo, either in isolation or in parallel with the Ulpia. The book still had no immediate impact on the San Paolo reconstruction, but it planted important seeds for the future.

The first plates comparing the two basilicas established the similarity in their overall proportions. One showed almost identically proportioned columns from the two basilicas as a suggestion that Constantine's architect had intended to borrow not just the proportions but even the actual columns of the Ulpian basilica. Another illustrated a nave column from San Paolo alongside two other columns: on the right is one of the new Simplon columns, which Uggeri tersely suggested be shifted to the exterior for use in a new Ionic quadriporticus, while the one in the center is one of the Elba granite columns donated by Morel de Bauvine, "chosen by the Academy of Saint Luke in their seance of 4 June 1826" (**Figure 53**). Even after six years, Uggeri had not made his peace with the loss of these columns.

Plate VIII ter offered a larger version of the famous "In Pristinum" plate from his *Della basilica di S. Paolo* of 1823, with little concession to the many changes that had been approved in the interim (**Figure 54**). It showed fluted columns – presumably pale Elba ones – with capitals based on those of the old basilica, supporting not arches but a flat entablature ornamented with roundels depicting Pius VII, Leo XII, Pius VIII, and Gregory XVI. The two levels of frescos up above closely mirrored those of the old basilica, only framed now by painted laurel-leaf torus moldings rather than the former assortment of painted pilasters.[48] A last trio of comparative plates aimed to demonstrate that the Basilica Ulpia had dictated the basic proportions of all the Early Christian basilicae (**Figure 55**). Two other plates, finally, gave updated versions of Uggeri's plan of the original San Paolo from his 1823 book and of his 1827 master project for the restoration (**Figure 56**). The changes to the latter were minor: a flood barrier to the north, obviously related to the debates about

THE END OF A GENERATION

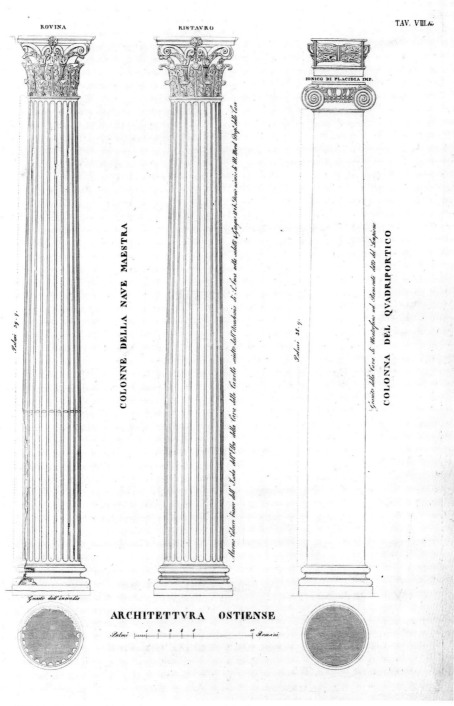

53. Plate VIII bis from Uggeri (1832a), comparing an original nave column from San Paolo (L), a proposed new column cut from Morel de Bauvine's donated granite (C), and one of the Simplon granite columns (R), which Uggeri here proposes shifting to the exterior quadriporticus.
Source: http://arachne.dainst.org/entity/16029.

54. Plate VIII ter from Uggeri (1832a), showing the original elevation (L) and Uggeri's proposed reconstruction (R) of the nave of San Paolo. Compare Figure 30.
Source: http://arachne.dainst.org/entity/16029.

raising the floor, and a new quadriporticus to the west to absorb the forty Simplon granite columns (at the cost of demolishing the eighteenth-century narthex). In the upper left of this plan, Uggeri rather pointedly placed the "no innovations" passage from Leo XII's Chirograph.

Uggeri's long campaign to link San Paolo with the Imperial precedent of the Basilica Ulpia lay at the heart of his larger project to ennoble Early Christian building as a whole. By arguing that the aesthetic intentions of the Early Christian builders were much more respectable than the results their troubled age permitted them to achieve, and that it was by their intentions that they should be judged, Uggeri expected to convince the Special Commission that it would not violate the Chirograph to rebuild the basilica with the entablature he advocated. It can only have been maddening to him, having failed in this, to see how readily other changes were approved without anything like the elaborate historical rationales he provided, and sometimes purely on their supposed aesthetic merits.[49] One suspects that Uggeri went to his grave feeling that he had failed to protect the true image of the pristine basilica – true, at least, according to his lights.

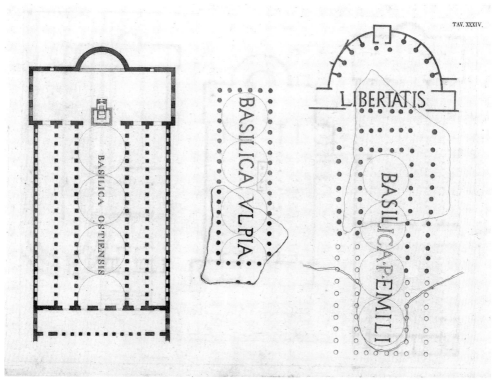

55. Plate XXXIV from Uggeri (1832a), comparing the plans of Roman civic basilica to that of old San Paolo.
Source: http://arachne.dainst.org/entity/16029.

Uggeri's historical imagination was nonetheless to resonate powerfully for the generation of Roman architects that came to the fore in the 1830s and 1840s. Men born for the most part in the 1790s, who came of age in a period when the traditional continuities binding the present to history were widely felt to be disintegrating, they were to expand upon the embryonic historicism of Uggeri's approach. We are more accustomed to find such efforts in contemporary Paris, Berlin, or London, whose architects cast their eyes back across Gothic and Greek histories in hopes of conjuring just the architectural lineage they felt their modern nations required. But as we have seen, Italians and especially Romans had endured their own violent sense of rupture, even if from a very different position, and faced their own challenges in rethinking how history might orient the modern present, and how the architectural needs of the present might draw upon the achievements of the past.

Della basilica Ulpia was dedicated to (and published on presses operated by) Uggeri's young "amico carissimo," Luigi Canina (1795–1856), an architect and archaeologist from Turin who since arriving in Rome in 1818 – the same year as his contemporary Poletti – had swiftly established himself as a leading authority on Roman architectural history.[50] A decade later, Canina was to publish his own

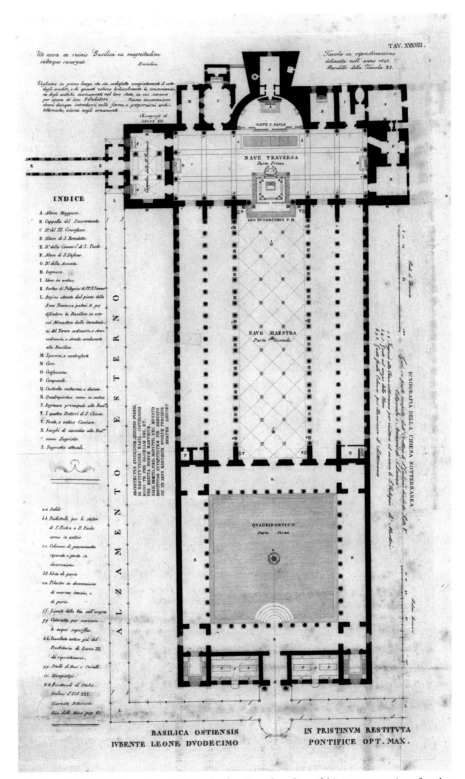

56. Plate XXXVIII from Uggeri (1832a), showing the plan of his counterproject for the reconstruction. Compare Plate 6.
Source: http://arachne.dainst.org/entity/16029.

THE END OF A GENERATION

highly influential *Ricerche sull'architettura più propria dei tempj cristiani*, which with explicit acknowledgment extended Uggeri's theses on Roman civic and Early Christian basilicae in the hopes of sparking a full-blown neo-Paleochristian revival in Roman ecclesiastical architecture.[51] Uggeri's approach offered a theorist like Canina a very attractive route toward a new and more authentic model for contemporary design: one that referred to the quintessentially Roman and Catholic idiom of Paleochristian architecture but with the solecisms typical of real Early Christian works ironed out. Such a solution bears a superficial resemblance to the efforts of Belli and his academic allies at San Paolo, but intellectually it was worlds apart. Belli and company were still in thrall to the idea of a normative classicism and would never have dreamed of putting forward a reformed Paleochristian idiom as a model for future design, whereas that was exactly what Uggeri's disciple Canina envisioned.

Canina was not the only Roman architect of the period to harbor such ambitions. So too did Luigi Poletti, albeit from a very different standpoint. The typological argument about basilican elevations that Poletti used in defending Belli's proposals was of the same general type used by Uggeri in his reflections on the Basilica Ulpia, only rather than particularizing it as the story of two buildings, Poletti generalized it as a story about the development of a building type. In so doing, he wrestled in his own way with the great questions of the day concerning the claims of tradition and the universality of aesthetic truth. As we shall see next, however, Poletti's paradoxical angle on the debate was that of a strident classicist who was also an incognizant historicist – one who saw the Christian classicism of the Renaissance masters more than that of pagan Rome as the quintessentially Roman and Catholic architecture. It was an architecture still in his view tied to absolute aesthetic values, but whose genius for modern Rome derived from its religious and geographical specificity.

After taking over the San Paolo workshop in October 1833, Poletti was to extend this line of thinking, sweeping aside Belli's vision altogether and implementing in its place a new rationale for the reconstruction: the creation of an idealized model of the Christian basilica to serve as a new basis for modern ecclesiastical architecture. This program shared much in common with Canina's *Ricerche*, including common roots in the arguments formulated by Uggeri. For like all of these projects, it was driven by that implacable contemporary compulsion to stabilize a destabilized historical moment by making new the old, and old the new.

NOTES

1   Berkeley and Berkeley (1932–1940), v. 1, pp. 99–102; Korten (2012), p. 22.
2   Frost (1876), v. 2, pp. 30–39.
3   Korten (2012).

4 On Gregory, see Bartoli et al. (1948) and Longo et al. (2008). Christopher Korten's forthcoming study of Gregory is eagerly awaited.

5 *DdR*, 26 March 1831, p. 1.

6 Uggeri (1831a), Sommario IV, Letter E ("Dispaccio Accademico …," 20 April 1831), p. 50; AASL: *Miscellanea Congregazioni* II, no. 113, v. 80, 83; tiG pp. 391–392.

7 Uggeri (1831a), Sommario IV, Letter E ("RAPPORTO"), pp. 51–58; AASL: *Miscellanea Congregazioni* II, no. 113, v. 80, 83; tiG pp. 391–392.

8 Uggeri (1831a).

9 On Poletti, see Strozzieri (2021).

10 Strozzieri (2021), p. 75.

11 Clemente De Donatis to Luigi Poletti, 21 January 1830 (BCALP: LP48 C1).

12 Luigi Poletti, Memo for Pope Gregory XVI, 25 September 1832 (ASP: 30/c, libro rosso 3).

13 BCALP: C10 1348 to 1355. Documents in the AAV indicate that unspecified work started at San Callisto in the spring of 1829, funded at 500 scudi per month through June 1832 (Mario Mattei, "Copia di escritto per i restauri dei due Monasteri di S. Paolo e S. Callisto dell'Ordine Benedettino," 23 May 1829 [AAV: Archivio Particolare di Gregorio XVI, b. 3, f. 172]).

14 Angelo Uggeri to Luigi Poletti, 6 April 1830 (BCALP: LP48 C1).

15 Pasquale Belli to Luigi Poletti, 1 June 1831 (BCALP: LP48 C2).

16 Vincenzo Bini to Luigi Poletti, 21 June 1831 (BCALP: LP48 C2).

17 Uggeri (1831a), Sommario IV, Letter E ("RAPPORTO"), pp. 56–57. Cf. also Luigi Poletti, "Alcune osservazioni di Luigi Poletti accademico a maggior chiarezza del rapporto della classe architettonica intorno ai disegni della riedificazione di S. Paolo," [April 1831] (BCALP: LP37 C132 3; tiSAD doc. 111, pp. 44–46).

18 Poletti cited Giovanni Marangoni's eighteenth-century treatise to support his claim that Constantine had deliberately chosen the basilica rather than the pagan temple as the type for the Christian church (Marangoni [1744]).

19 Uggeri (1831a), Sommario IV, Letter E ("RAPPORTO"), pp. 57–58; tiG pp. 391–392; also in AASL: *Miscellanea Congregazioni* II, no. 113, v. 80, 83.

20 Uggeri (1831a), Sommario IV, Letter G ("Rilievi …"), pp. 59–65.

21 Uggeri (1831a), Sommario IV, Letter G ("Rilievi …"), pp. 61–62.

22 Uggeri (1831a).

23 See *DdR*, 26 March 1831, p. 1. Gregory's interest is described in a note in *CAPDR*, pp. 51–64.

24 Uggeri (1831a), pp. 32–33 and unpaginated preface ("Dubbj che si propongono …"). The 7 July 1831 congress also established protocols for the collection and disbursment of funds (Uggeri (1831a), p. 33 and Sommario V, pp. 66–70).

25 Uggeri (1831b).

26 *CAPDR*, p. 52.

27 Republished as Fea (1832), dated 16 September 1831, quote on p. 39. On Fea's previous writings on the Tiber and its floods, see Guarna (1871), pp. 37–43.

28 Fea (1832), pp. 41–44.

29 *DdR*, 2 November 1831, p. 1; *Cronaca* II, 28 October 1831. This *Diario di Roma* account is reproduced in *CAPDR*, with a long note (pp. 51–64) on the struggle over raising the floor.

30 "Rapporto sul progetto d'innalzare il piano della nave grande dalla Basilica di San Paolo …," 5 May 1832 [ASP: 30/c, libro rosso 3]. See also *CAPDR*, p. 55. Belli followed this up with a memo addressed to the trio: "Osservazioni e riflessioni dell'Architetto Direttore della Basilica di S. Paolo …," 25 November 1831 (ASR: Camerlengato, P. II, Tit. IV, b. 155; tiG pp. 401–404).

31 Tommaso Bernetti to Mario Mattei, 5 December 1831 (ASR: Camerlengato, P. II, Tit. IV, b. 155; tiG p. 404); "Rapporto …," as in Chapter 9 n. 31; Emmanuele de Gregorio to Mario Mattei, 15 December 1831 (ASR: Camerlengato, P. II, Tit. IV, b. 155; tiG pp. 404–406).

32   *CAPDR*, pp. 55–57; "Rapporto . . .," as in Chapter 9 n. 31.

33   "Rapporto . . .," as in Chapter 9 n. 31.

34   *CAPDR*, pp. 58–59; *DdR*, 31 October 1832, p. 1.

35   Fea (1832); cf. Barattieri (1656), pt. I, bk. 8, pp. 265–271.

36   On the *Giornale di commercio*: Majolo Molinari (1963), v. 1, pp. 452–453; Luseroni (2012), p. 401.

37   Fea (1833). The text is dated 4 January.

38   Fea (1833), pp. 4–8.

39   Uggeri (1832), discussed in *CAPDR*, p. 60, from which the approximate date is deduced.

40   *CAPDR*, p. 59.

41   Pasquale Belli, "Dimostrazione dell alzamento interno di S. Paolo" (13 January 1833) (ASP: 30/c, libro rosso 3; BNR: ARC 15 II B 2.11 [Carte Raffaelli, Raccolta Ceccarius]).

42   On the controversy generated by this idea – ultimately not approved – see Strozzieri (2021), p. 137.

43   Strozzieri (2021), p. 23.

44   *CAPDR*, p. 61. The report is transcribed pp. 62–63.

45   *CAPDR*, p. 64. When the Tiber flooded in 1843, the monastery chronicle pointedly noted that barely any water entered the basilica (*Cronaca* II, 7 February 1843).

46   See *CAPDR*, pp. 103–104, n. 2.

47   Uggeri (1833), dated on the basis of the second supplementary plate, which gives the year as the second in the pontificate of Gregory XVI.

48   Uggeri's idea of replacing the nave arches with entablatures died hard: in an unrelated engraving depicting a *capella pontificia* of Gregory XVI, Uggeri showed the nave rebuilt in the background with entablatures and a coffered ceiling (BiASA, Roma. XI. 47. inv. 31928; tiG p. 547, fig. 74).

49   Cf. the book's dedication to Canina.

50   *DdR: NdG*, 4 April 1833, p. 4. On Canina, see Raggi (1857); Bendinelli (1953); Pasquali (1993).

51   Canina (1843), pp. 69–70. A significantly expanded second edition (Canina [1846]) appeared in the wake of a London trip during which Canina developed a friendship with C. R. Cockerell (Bendinelli [1953], pp. 147–149 and 251–254).

PLATE 1. Luigi Rossini, *View of the Ruin of the Basilica of San Paolo*, 1824.
Source: Architekturmuseum der TUM.

PLATE 2. Carlo Marchionni, New Vatican Sacristy, Vatican City, 1776–1784.
Source: Author.

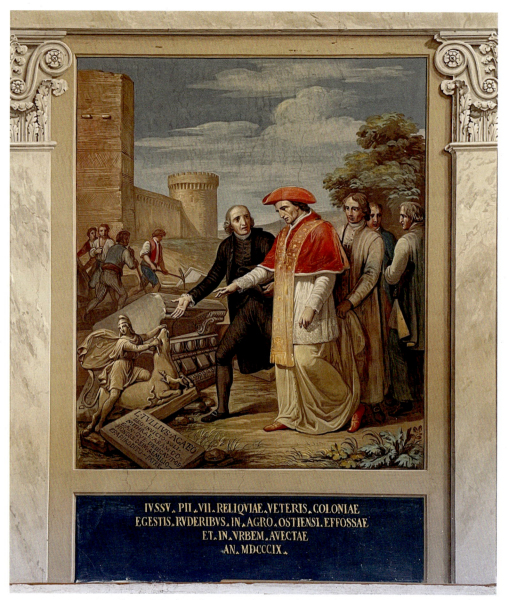

PLATE 3. Commissioner of Antiquities Carlo Fea showing Pope Pius VII the new archaeological discoveries at Ostia, from the cycle of frescos depicting episodes from the life of Pius VII Chiaramonti by Domenico De Angelis and Domenico Del Frate, c. 1818, in the Clementine Gallery in the Vatican Library.
Source: Author.

PLATE 4. Giovanni Paolo Panini, *Interior of San Paolo fuori le mura*, oil on canvas, c. 1750.
Source: Private Collection / Photo © Christie's Images / Bridgeman Images.

PLATE 5. Milvian Bridge, Rome, as reconstructed by Giuseppe Valadier, 1805–1806.
Source: Author.

PLATE 6. Elevation of the basilica of San Paolo fuori le mura, showing its prefire state (left) and Angelo Uggeri's vision for its repair and reconstruction (right) (from Uggeri [1823]).
Source: Collection of the author.

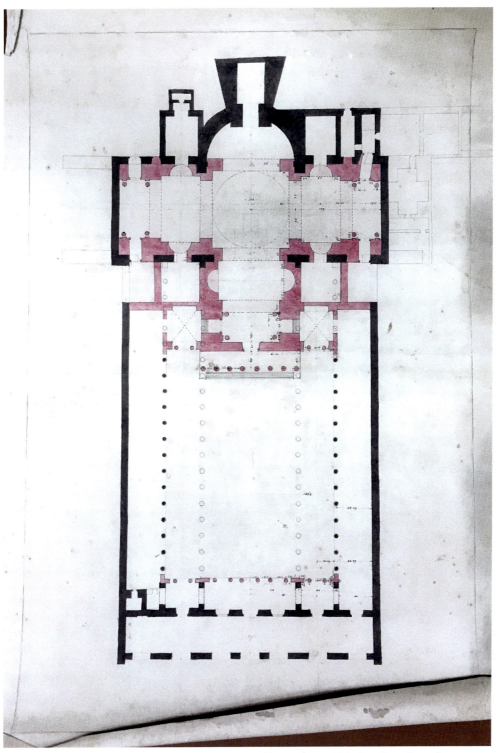

PLATE 7. Unidentified plan project for San Paolo, possibly Gianbattista Martinetti's project of April 1824.
Source: © 2022 Archivio Storico dell'Abbazia di San Paolo f.l.m.

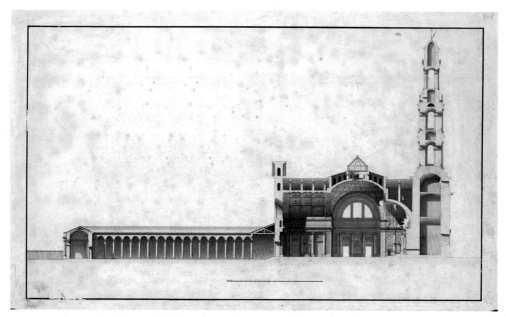

PLATE 8. Giuseppe Valadier (assisted by Gaspare Salvi), longitudinal section, revised project for San Paolo, June 1824.
Source: © Accademia Nazionale di San Luca, Roma.

PLATE 9. Jean-Victor-Louis Faure, *San Paolo fuori le mura after the Fire of July 1823*, 1823. The arch of Galla Placidia with its mosaics is visible in the distance.
Source: Private collection.

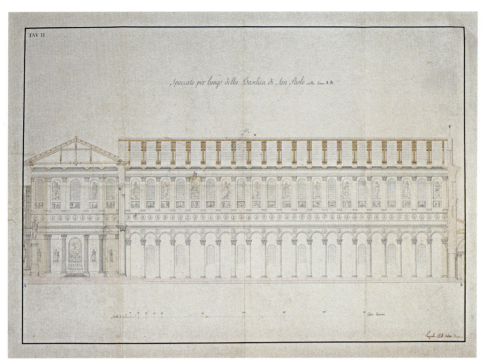

PLATE 10. Pasquale Belli, proposed longitudinal section for the reconstruction of the basilica of San Paolo, 16 November 1830.
Source: Biblioteca Nazionale Centrale 'Vittorio Emanuele II' di Roma, Vitt.Em. 638.

PLATE 11. View of the north porch of the rebuilt basilica of San Paolo. The Siricio column is in the second row, behind the third column from the right.
Source: Author.

PLATE 12. The apse at San Paolo as reconstructed between 1833 and 1840. Peter (L) and Paul (R) stand to either side of the enthroned Christ.
Source: Author.

PLATE 13. Inner side of the Arch of Placidia facing the apse, with fourteenth-century mosaic depictions of Peter (R) and Paul (L) redeployed from the exterior of the old west façade.
Source: Author.

PLATE 14. West face of the superstructure of Arnolfo di Cambio's ciborium over the confessio at San Paolo, as restored 1836–1840. Paul stands in the corner niche on the left and Peter in the corner niche on the right.
Source: Author.

PLATE 15. View from the nave of San Paolo looking east. Peter and Paul figure in the mosaic of the Arch of Placidia in the spandrals, with Peter on the left and Paul on the right. The colossal statues of Peter (L) and Paul (R) stand below them, in front of the arch.
Source: Author.

PLATE 16. The pontifical throne designed by Luigi Poletti, in the apse of San Paolo fuori le mura.
Source: Author.

PLATE 17. The St. Benedict chapel at San Paolo fuori le mura, designed by Luigi Poletti. *Source*: Author.

PLATE 18. A variant of Poletti's second façade option for the basilica of San Paolo, roughly corresponding to Gregory XVI's order in 1844 to reconstruct the original façade and portico. Gregory had ordered the quadriporticus eliminated from the project, and Poletti's memorandum described the project as not having one, but the variant shown in this drawing has one.
Source: Biblioteca civica d'arte e architettura Luigi Poletti, Modena. Archivio Poletti, disegni inv. 316.

PLATE 19. George Wigley, Sant'Alfonso de' Liguori, Rome, 1855–1859.
Source: Author.

PLATE 20. Area beneath the choir at San Lorenzo fuori le mura at the floor level of the fourth-century basilica, created by Virginio Vespignani following excavations in the 1850s.
Source: Author.

PART III

REIMAGINED SACRED HISTORIES

TEN

LUIGI POLETTI AND THE CHALLENGE OF REBUILDING SAN PAOLO

ON 1 NOVEMBER 1833, ONE DAY AFTER THE DEATH OF PASQUALE Belli, Luigi Poletti was officially named architect director for the reconstruction of San Paolo (**Figure 57**). The paralysis that had marked Belli's tenure was at once replaced by a brisk executive approach, as Poletti made a point of cultivating a good working relationship with Pope Gregory XVI that frequently enabled him to bypass the bureaucratic apparatus that had drained so much of Belli's energy; for Gregory too had been exasperated by the endless battles and was content to act as Poletti's accomplice in expediency. By decade's end, their joint subversion of the protocols set out in Leo XII's Chirograph had led to the completion of essential work on the transept, its consecration along with that of the high altar, and the triumphant public reopening of half the basilica.

Poletti and Gregory XVI did not form a naturally sympathetic partnership. Poletti was a complex and rather contradictory figure: a reader of several languages who was also a nationalistic xenophobe; a disciplined engineer and ruthless organizer with a sideline in sprawling historiographical theses on the essence of Italic culture; a science enthusiast and liberal sympathizer who served obscurantist popes. Gregory, as one of those popes, was a political reactionary whose worldview had been formed in the ecclesiastical cloister. The policy orientation of Gregory's pontificate amounted to an extension of Leo XII's revanchist ambitions for the Catholic Church, albeit in the face of even greater challenges. In the political sphere, Gregory's early response to the

57. Raffaele Fidanza, *Portrait of Luigi Poletti*, 1838.
Source: Biblioteca civica d'arte e architettura Luigi Poletti, Modena, Fondo Stampe inv. 1809.

uprisings of 1830–1831 had been so repressive as to turn the illiberal administration of the Papal States into a matter of international concern, prompting the Great Powers of England, France, Austria, Russia, and Prussia to issue an infamous memorandum demanding that the pontiff make urgent political reforms. Gregory's response was mostly diversionary, and fresh rebellions erupted the instant Austrian troops departed in 1831, to be quelled only the following summer with a second Austrian intervention.[1] Gregory surrounded himself thereafter with the most intransigent sort of reactionary, like his secretary of state, Cardinal Tommaso Bernetti, who organized armed bands of rural toughs, the loathed *centuroni*, to terrorize the countryside into submission.[2] It was not until 1838 that the last foreign troops finally departed the pontifical territories. But whereas the rebels of 1830–1832 had been genuine Mazzinian radicals whose politics were not widely popular, the cumulative effect of Gregory's despotism was to push many of his loyalest subjects into the liberal reformist camp: educated noblemen, bourgeois professionals, even some clerics. In the cultural sphere, meanwhile, Gregory consummated Leo XII's disavowal of Lamennaisian populism with explicit condemnations, most notably in his August 1832 encyclical *Mirari Vos* and then again two years later in *Singulari Nos*.[3] These categorically denied that the Church was in need of reform, reaffirmed the supernatural character of the Church's constitution, and doubled down on condemnations of everything from freedom of opinion to the separation of Church and state. Gregory also favored the policy of ultramontanism – that is, the direct and unmediated exercise of authority from Rome over the Catholic faithful – as a way to fill the void left by the post-Revolutionary decline or demise of the old national Churches. Gregory had been honing his vision of an imperial papacy since the 1790s, and it was to leave its mark on Poletti's basilica as well.

The rebuilding San Paolo took shape in the late 1830s as an unacknowledged compromise between Gregory's institutional ambitions and Poletti's architectural ones. As it did so, ambiguities that had characterized Belli's tenure persisted. Leo XII's Chirograph lost what little remaining authority it had to steer the reconstruction, as Poletti proved even more ambivalent than Belli about the Early Christian architectural style, and far more effective at ensuring for himself the freedom to build according to his own standards. But it was not only Poletti. Pope Gregory also proved eager to reshape the building in ways that moved beyond Leo's vision. And even as these new ambitions recast the architectural program, efforts to informationalize the basilica through publicity were also expanding: dispatches in the *Diario di Roma* became richer and more frequent, with news of the reconstruction appearing in newspapers as far afield as Calcutta, Rio di Janiero, even Tasmania. This dematerialized San Paolo was the fruit of the relentless labor of Luigi Moreschi, assistant since 1825 to Secretary of the Special Commission Angelo Uggeri, and from 1830 or so his de facto successor. For all that Uggeri had been focused inwardly on the history of Rome and its buildings, Moreschi had the outward-facing spirit of a born publicist. For nearly four decades, until Poletti's death in 1869, Poletti and Moreschi were to work as a team, with Moreschi translating Poletti's vision for the physical building into flights of words that nourished a global reputation unlike anything enjoyed by any building ever before.

Luigi Poletti arrived in Rome in 1818 as a provincial twenty-six-year-old from Modena with a small scholarship to study mathematics at the school of the Pontifical Engineers. Years later he told a friend that his very first stops were the Pantheon and Colosseum, where he had been so overcome that he resolved on the spot to devote his life to architecture, not mathematics.[4] Poletti dutifully enrolled with the Pontifical Engineers to study mechanics and hydraulics (where he was taken under the wing of Giuseppe Venturoli), but he was soon also attending architecture courses at the Academy of St. Luke.

Despite this education, Poletti habitually described himself as a self-made architect: the product, he liked to say, not of academies but of himself. Young Poletti's hunger for knowledge was not easy to satisfy in the Rome of the 1810s, as he explained in a letter to his beloved brother Geminiano in 1818:

> ... the book dealers and all the public and private bookstores here are stocked with sacred works and literature. The libraries are thirty to forty years behind the times, and the monastic libraries only grudgingly bring down from their shelves what few books they possess.[5]

Poletti responded by assembling a private library that eventually grew into one of the richest private architecture libraries in Europe, with works in Italian, French, Latin, English, and German – the first three of which he read fluently – and encompassing technical works, historical studies, biographies, topical pamphlets, and most of the major theoretical works from the Renaissance onward.[6] Poletti also cultivated ties with foreign institutions in areas of interest to him, including the Institut Historique in Paris and the Royal Institute of British Architects in London. Poletti cut an unusually cosmopolitan figure in the often-insular world of contemporary Roman architecture.

But knowledge and erudition could only carry a young provincial so far. One also needed the right protectors, and so Poletti contrived early on to ingratiate himself with Raffaelle Stern, one of the two professors whose architecture courses he attended at the Academy. Stern gave Poletti some early architectural work, mainly on temporary festival decors, but then died unexpectedly. Poletti shifted his attentions to Giuseppe Camporese, his other professor at the Academy, who also gave him minor design tasks; he also insinuated himself into the studio of no less a figure than Antonio Canova, whom he assisted with the architectural aspects of a few tomb designs.[7]

By the early 1820s, Poletti was trying his hand at short theoretical essays with such titles as "Observations on the Architectural Styles" and "New Hypotheses on the Origins of the Orders and their Meanings."[8] These reveal an author conversant with the early Romantic questioning of Vitruvian dogma and cognizant that stylistic choices could no longer be justified purely in terms of truth or beauty but rather had to refer to contingent factors like climate, materials, and cultural mores. Yet at the same time, the young Poletti was also making connections with the classically minded anti-Romantic intellectuals at the *Giornale arcadico* in Rome, where beginning in 1823 he published a series of articles on a wide range of topics. His first described excavations at the ancient Roman town of Bovillae, in which he had participated, while his second, from 1824, related to his projects for what would have been Rome's first iron cable suspension bridges, at the Porta di Ripetta and on the remains of the Ponte Rotto.[9]

With these first two publications, we catch an early glimpse of two sides of Poletti's nature: the historical scholar and the questing engineer. Both sides were on display again in the letter Poletti addressed to Geminiano on 16 July 1823, describing the catastrophe that had unfolded the previous day:

> The great temple of San Paolo fuori le mura, a primary monument of the Christian era, founded by Constantine and enlarged by Theodosius and Honorius, has burned and in a matter of a few hours been destroyed. The value and extent of the loss for the arts is incalculable, because in addition to its beauty it contained 100 columns of rarest Asian and African marbles, while the roof, burned by the negligence of a workman, was of wood from Lebanon covered with copper tiles. This short letter will not permit me to go into detail, but I say to you that it was an artistic marvel. This event recalls the famous fires of the Temple of Diana at Ephesus, which Vitruvius tells us was set by Erostratus in an effort to immortalize his name, and that of Jerusalem too.[10]

Having shown his erudition, the rationalist then deduced lessons from the blaze:

> The remarkable thing is that it took just 4 or 5 hours for everything to be reduced to dust, with the columns calcinated, the walls in ruins, and the bronze doors partly liquified. This helps explain those passages in the ancient writers which, when they tell of unexpected fires that reduced immense buildings to nothing and caused rivers of metal to flow, leave modern readers who are unable to conceive of such disasters full of skepticism.[11]

He concluded with characteristic impatience toward those who discerned occult meanings in the event:

> Such a loss is felt so strongly here that everyone behaves as though he has lost something personal, and you see melancholy sages in the streets, while idiots deduce from it sad consequences, prophesying misfortune and calamity.[12]

Poletti later informed Geminiano that he was seriously considering entering the 1824 Concorso Clementino with a design for a new San Paolo, though he ultimately thought better of it, fearing that he would not have enough time to devise a sufficiently mature project.[13] It was an ironic decision given how the last thirty-five years of Poletti's life were to turn out.

In 1826, Poletti decided he was ready to apply for admission to the Academy of St. Luke. His very modest design portfolio was composed by then of one minor Roman palazzo (the Palazzo Ceccopieri), a series of unexecuted projects, a few essays in the *Giornale arcadico*, and a publishing project, officially approved but never realized, to illustrate Roman buildings from the fourteenth through seventeenth centuries.[14] Poletti's application to the Academy proved controversial – Cardinal Camerlengo Galleffi favored another candidate, against the wishes of the academicians – and the case did not advance initially.[15] Poletti's response was to see that a triumphant anonymous review of his Ceccopieri palace appeared in one of the leading Roman arts journals.[16] Eager self-promotion of this sort, by then common in Paris and London, was not yet the norm in Rome, and it was even noted in the next issue that "some people took offense," protesting that Poletti's palace was "too small and, hidden away in an obscure corner of Monte Catino, required laborious searching out."[17]

In 1827, Poletti obtained a post at the Ospizio di S. Michele a Ripa Grande, a vast orphanage, hospice, and art-and-trade school, where he directed the renowned paper-making and typographic sections and held the chair in architecture, geometry, and perspective.[18] This provided him with stability, but Poletti felt he was spinning his wheels, continually putting himself forward for commissions that always seemed to go to better connected competitors. In one letter of 1828, his brother tried to encourage him, writing uncannily that he looked forward to the day when he would pick up a newspaper to read of how "the church of San Paolo outside Rome will be restored with one of your designs, and that it will be you who directs the worksite."[19] Poletti could only reply with weary resignation: "God knows how much that would please me, but you know how difficult it is to get access to those high personages."[20]

Later that year, Poletti accepted a request from the pontifical government to go on an official mission to London with instructions to study the paper industry there.[21] On the way back, he stretched his meager stipend to pass several weeks in Paris, where he met the architect and engraver Paul Letarouilly. Letarouilly introduced Poletti to his circle, including Charles Percier, and was to become a lifelong friend and supplier of French books for Poletti's library.[22] Not many other details of the sojourn have survived, but Poletti wrote and spoke French fluently, and one feels sure that he would have visited the new Parisian churches then being built on basilican plans, including Notre-Dame-de-Lorette (1823–1836) (**Figure 58**), Notre-Dame-de-Bercy (1823–1826), or Saint-Denis-du-Saint-Sacrement (1826–1835).[23]

58. Louis-Hippolyte Lebas, Notre-Dame-de-Lorette, Paris, 1823–1836.
Source: Author.

Only in 1829, after Poletti's return to Rome (in company with Letarouilly), did his admission to the Academy of St. Luke become official.[24] He was thirty-seven years old, and as though a switch had been thrown, his Roman career took off. He published a treatise on the application of geometry to the fine and mechanical arts that won considerable acclaim.[25] In 1831 he was named to an ongoing position as assistant engineer in the Congregazione di Acque e Strade, and in May 1832 was sent to inspect public buildings damaged by the recent earthquakes in Umbria. This led a few years later to one of the other major commissions of his career, the reconstruction of the basilica of Santa Maria degli Angeli in Assisi.[26] As we have seen, Poletti's association with the San Paolo workshop also began around this time.

Between his appointment as architetto supernumero of the monastery of San Paolo in June 1831 and Belli's death in October 1833, Poletti steadily expanded his role at San Paolo. When Gregory XVI visited the worksite in October 1832, the *Diario di Roma* for the first time made no mention of Belli even being present.[27] One also finds little trace of Belli in the archive after this point, beyond his increasingly ruined signature on the weekly salary authorizations for the workers.[28] When Poletti was officially appointed Belli's successor-in-waiting in March 1833, it reflected the fact that he had already assumed many of Belli's responsibilities.[29] Decades later, Poletti's friend and biographer Cesare Campori recalled how Poletti, without asking anyone's permission, had accelerated the work at San Paolo in order to get the transept walls erected and their roof built in just "a few short months."[30] This occurred before Poletti became architect director, for when Pope Gregory visited again in October 1833, three days *before* Belli's death, the *Diario di Roma* reported that he was stunned to see the transept walls complete and the roof over them two-thirds finished, with the remaining third in pieces on the ground and ready to mount. Gregory lavished praise on Poletti for the "unexpected speed" with which the basilica now progressed.[31] Poletti had actually worked himself to exhaustion in anticipation of Gregory's visit, to the point that friends for a time feared for his life.[32] Campori recalled that the new energy Poletti brought to the construction site did not pass unnoticed in Rome:

> A remarkable buzz went up in the city concerning the daring of the architect, who with such beautiful grace had cast aside the leaden cape thrown over him by those metaphysical discussions [at the Academy of St. Luke] which, if he had done otherwise, would have left the fallen basilica to its ruin, whereas instead we see it today [1865] rebuilt.[33]

Worksite accounts of these weeks tell of workers earning extra pay by laboring through their midday breaks.[34] Poletti himself boasted to the Special Commission two years later that whereas Belli had chipped away "with extreme slowness" at the construction of the roof, so that "in five months barely a third was executed," he himself had been able to execute "two thirds . . . in a month and a half."[35]

After this tour de force helped Poletti secure his position as architect director, one of his first tasks after Belli's death was to convince Pope Gregory that Belli's approved designs, which Poletti himself had once so effectively defended, were unusable – unusable because they neglected to specify basic information about many of the changes they envisaged, and moreover were limited to just the transept and nave, neglecting everything else from the east chapels and apse to the campanile and façade.[36] A year and a half after his appointment, Poletti roundly criticized the deficiencies of Belli's project to the Special Commission, "whether with respect to the chapels, the apse, the ceiling, the marbles for the altars and for the terminal walls; all things on which no foresight whatsoever had been brought to bear in the manner required for the regular conduct of work."[37] Poletti knew because he had had to deal with these deficiencies already in the months before Belli's death, when for instance he had improvised reinforcement

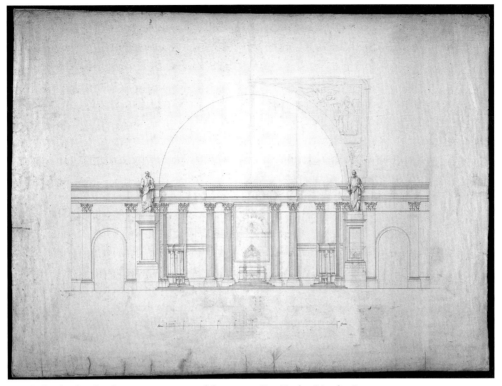

59. Poletti's plan for the rearrangement of the apse at San Paolo, March 1834.
Source: Biblioteca civica d'arte e architettura Luigi Poletti, Modena, Archivio Poletti, disegni inv. 325.

for the collapsing west façade with a brick wall bound by chains (proudly displayed to Pope Gregory during his visit).[38]

In drawing attention to the deficiencies of Belli's plan, Poletti was laying the groundwork to put forward a new master plan of his own.[39] On 3 March 1834, he presented the Special Commission with his initial requests as head architect. In the first, he asked permission to replace the early seventeenth-century altar in the apse and to construct two new chapels off the transept.[40] The altar, he wrote, was unattractive and damaged, it obscured parts of the apse mosaic, and was not worthy by the terms of the Chirograph to be reconstructed. In its place he proposed a lower altar flanked by four large fluted columns identical to the ones then being prepared for the altars in the transept terminal walls (**Figure 59**).[41] These eight, following Belli's project, were being fabricated from fragments of the *pavonazzetto* columns of the old nave, applied as a veneer around travertine cores and carefully blended together so as to appear monolithic.[42] As for the two proposed chapels, Poletti echoed what Valadier had proposed in 1823–1824 (and, perhaps not coincidentally, had recently published): a tidy perimeter wall enclosing the whole east end and concealing the apse and two flanking chapels.[43] Poletti concluded his request on what was to be a characteristically time-is-money note, asking for a speedy verdict so that his masons might take full advantage of the warm spring and summer months.[44]

Poletti's second request sought to cancel the reuse of the original columns in the nave aisles. Most of these columns had more or less survived the fire, but Poletti claimed to have subjected several of the best-preserved ones to stress tests that showed them susceptible to cracking if loaded with weight. He proposed to replace them all with granite monoliths from Simplon to match those of the main arcade and to switch to Carrara marble for their bases and capitals as well as for the arch voussoirs of the nave and for all cornices throughout the basilica.[45]

With these two requests we get a first glimpse of one of Poletti's guiding convictions: namely, that visibly historic remains of the old basilica should not be reused or retained in their original form. When it was a question of a post-Paleochristian element, Poletti usually referred to the Chirograph to justify demolition, as in the case of the Baroque altar. When it was a Paleochristian element like the aisle columns, he tended to manufacture a structural or technical argument. But behind these arguments was the fact that Poletti, rather like the academic adjudicators during Belli's tenure, hated the idea of incorporating elements of visibly different vintage into his new building. He wanted his building to be coherent and uniform, in form as in texture, and the reuse of patinaed or irregular historic elements could only rupture that. When he rejected a counterproposal to keep at least eight or ten of the more solid aisle columns and only replace the others, he said that this would destroy the "uniformity" of the interior by mixing two sets of columns in two different colors and materials, "some old, some new."[46] He was later to describe Belli's plan to retain the old columns as a "monstrous expedient."[47] Poletti's was emphatically not a Romantic vision in this respect.

Poletti should have addressed these two requests to the Academy via the Special Commission, but instead he addressed them directly to Pope Gregory. No one seems to have objected, and Gregory returned a relatively quick response on the first request, granting permission to demolish the apse altar and to fabricate four more veneered columns for its replacement.[48] He hesitated, however, on the second.[49] Poletti decided at this point, in October 1834, to reach for the grand prize: he went in person to the pontiff's country residence at Castel Gandolfo on a mission to convince Gregory to abandon Belli's project in favor of an entirely new master plan. They ended up having a two-hour meeting there.[50]

Economy was surely part of Poletti's pitch, for it was becoming apparent that funding for the reconstruction had entered a critical phase. The year 1833 had marked the end of Leo XII's fundraising campaign, while new hardships related to the 1830–1831 rebellions were forcing the Special Commission to provide poor relief for much of the San Paolo workforce.[51] Even worse, at the end of 1833 the Congregazione di Revisione – a body of clerics instituted by Leo XII to review the myriad endeavors bankrolled by the papal Treasury – had ordered that Leo's annual pledge of 50,000 scudi for the reconstruction be reduced to 24,000 scudi, with the difference "deferred until the Treasury finds itself in better circumstances."[52] But as dire as that sounded, the reality was worse, for in the massive official registry where all pledges promised and received were meticulously recorded, we see that this subsidy had barely been paid at all since Leo's death:

1826: 50,000 (Leo XII)
1827: 50,000 (Leo XII)
1828: 16,000 (Leo XII)
1829: 82,000 (Leo XII / Pius VIII)
1830: 26,000 (Pius VIII)
1831: 2,000 (Gregory XVI)
1832: 0 (Gregory XVI)
1833: 0 (Gregory XVI)
1834: 0 (Gregory XVI)[53]

This astounding default reflects the economic chaos that had enveloped the pontifical government following Leo's death, when a combination of incompetence and northern rebellions exploded the state deficit from 219,000 scudi in 1830, to 1,925,000 in 1831, to 4,520,000 in 1832. The fiscally hapless Gregory resorted to funding day-to-day government with loans from the Rothschilds, and things only deteriorated from there.[54] Between 1835 and 1845, the state did not even publish its budgets, while Gregory's profligacy became more and more the subject of whispers and laments.[55] Here is a disapproving American after a visit in 1834:

> The present pope, it is believed, in executing plans for the advancement of his own views, is gradually undermining one of the strong holds of his power. The re-erection of St Paul's church, in the environs of Rome, in a costly style, and the creation of five new cardinals – both measures in every respect unnecessary, are among the extravagant plans with which he is charged. The means of carrying on these is obtained from extensive loans, for the payment of which his most valuable revenues are pledged, and year after year, these are sacrificed to his inability to meet the annual demand. I have heard it confidently estimated that, adopting the past as a criterion, in the space of thirteen years, the resources of the government will be absorbed; and if the ability of the governed to support taxation, at that juncture, is not better than at present, there is no conceivable means of furnishing an adequate supply to sustain the papal credit.[56]

And so Poletti apparently offered a bargain to Gregory at Castel Gandolfo, one not attested to in any document but whose broad outlines may be deduced from subsequent events. Poletti likely explained to Gregory that the pressure on the depleted papal Treasury could be mitigated by a second fundraising drive, but that this would only succeed if the enthusiasm of the faithful were first rekindled with some demonstrable and well-publicized progress on the reconstruction.[57] Poletti might then have promised that he could deliver such progress if only Gregory would liberate him from the oversight of the Academy and permit him to continue seeking approval for his designs directly. It would not have been an unreasonable request: with the nave floor raised and carrying dark unfluted granite columns with capitals copied from the Pantheon, the Chirograph's imperative that continual oversight was required to preserve the basilica's original appearance had lost its logic.

In the end, Poletti again proved persuasive. Less than a month after his meeting with the pope, a breathless memo arrived from Luigi Moreschi informing him that Gregory had ordered funds released for everything Poletti had requested back in March; "Would you like anything else?" Moreschi concluded giddily.[58] Shortly thereafter, Gregory made San Paolo the beneficiary for five years (1836–1840) of about 21,000 scudi annually, to be redirected from a tax levied for the canalization of the Aniene River near Tivoli.[59] The Academy, meanwhile, was to play almost no role at San Paolo over the next decade. A provincial noble visiting Rome a few weeks later toured San Paolo and was told there that Gregory "is extremely anxious to see this work reach its completion soon, perhaps as a means of eternalizing his memory."[60]

From Poletti's perspective, liberation from the Academy simplified matters tremendously. Gregory was innocent in technical matters of architecture and, preoccupied with countless other responsibilities, had little option but to trust Poletti when they arose. Poletti did not hesitate to take advantage. When he asked Gregory for permission to substitute Carrara marble for travertine in the arch voussoirs of the nave, he suggested that the worrying profusion of air pockets in travertine made it a less than ideal material for a load-bearing role. The argument was patently ridiculous: any member of the Academy would have pointed out that they were surrounded in Rome by buildings – the Colosseum, the great aqueducts, even St. Peter's itself – with heavily loaded travertine arches. Yet Gregory saw the apparent logic of Poletti's argument and agreed to the switch.[61] There was likewise never any technical scrutiny of the experiments by which Poletti claimed to have proven that the old columns of the aisles all had to be replaced. Poletti encouraged trust by always urging quick decisions, pointing out that administrative expenses accrued whether the building site was buzzing or idle, and reminding the aging pope that their common goal was to have the transept and high altar

60. The 1:50 wooden model for the reconstruction of San Paolo created on Poletti's orders in 1834 stands today (2021) in the south aisle of the nave.
Source: Author.

consecrated during the present pontificate. Poletti's relations with Gregory amounted, in effect, to exactly the freedom Belli had longed for but never dared to request: that of approaching San Paolo not as a reconstruction but as a new design conceived loosely in homage to the old basilica.

The exact details of Poletti's new master plan for San Paolo have, however, proven difficult to pin down. In a memorandum more than a decade later, the architect noted that "for greater clarity and ease I had [my design] represented in 1834 in a model, which I then deposited in the workshop," and that work had followed this model since then.[62] A magnificent 1:50 wooden model of the basilica stands today in the nave aisle and depicts the entire basilica with both executed elements as well as elements that we know Poletti intended but never executed (**Figure 60**). Is this the model in question? Michael Groblewski has argued that it is, but Italian scholars reached the opposite conclusion based on a plaque on the base of the model that reads, "*Serafino Colagiacomi / Ascolano fecit 1844*" ["Serafino Colagiacomi / from Ascoli, made this, 1844"].[63] For the Italian scholars this offered definitive dating of the model and indicated that the 1834 model must have been either lost or destroyed.

New documentation all but proves that in fact Groblewski was right, and that the model currently on display is indeed the original of 1834. A document written in 1872 by Luigi Moreschi, who had been working at San Paolo for almost half a century by then, recalled that when Poletti took over the directorship of the reconstruction, he had been asked to provide "general and complete designs" and to "execute that wooden model *which remains in one of the workshops of the building site*, and which shows the entire architectonic plan of the basilica."[64] A similar recollection is found in an 1852 document, in which the archaeologist Giuseppe Marchi explained that "from the moment when the current head architect [Poletti] was made the successor of the deceased Pasquale Belli ... a scale model was made which is still visible to everyone."[65] Both authors, in short, explicitly state that the model before their eyes was the one Poletti had executed in 1834 and make no mention of a second model. What, then, do we make of the 1844 plaque? It almost certainly refers to a modification rather than to the model's initial fabrication.[66] In support of this argument is a second plaque on the base of the model, which reads G. S. *f*[ecit] *giugnio 17, 1861* ["G. S. made this, 17 June 1861"]. The similar wording suggests a similar intervention.[67] Several apparent modifications are visible on the model still today, as we will see in a moment. What this controversy reveals is that Poletti's model was not a static document, but rather a constantly evolving image of his working plans, as Groblewski first suggested.

Bearing all this in mind, and assisted by a few other drawings, we may essay a tentative inventory of Poletti's 1834 vision.[68] The most ambitious new features were farthest from where work was under way, and they bear vivid witness to Poletti's remorseless attitude toward what survived of the old building. He proposed to demolish the eighteenth-century entrance narthex and the adjacent medieval campanile and to erect in their place a classical pronaos façade with colossal columns.[69] This was one of the elements Poletti was later forced to change, which is why the façade on the model today – which conforms to the one actually built – is divided from the model's nave by a visible open seam: the original pronaos façade was presumably cut off (**Figure 61**). Poletti also envisaged a broad colonnaded quadriporticus to evoke the open Paleochristian atrium that documents indicated had once existed there[70] (**Figure 62**), Punctuated with triumphal arch-like entries on its two side flanks, this vast enclosure was to be almost three-quarters as long as the nave and dramatically extended the building's horizontal profile. At the center of the model quadriporticus is a classicizing votive column, but this may have been added later. Along the western range of the quadriporticus, Poletti placed a new baptistry, an homage in Renaissance garb to the fourth-century

61. Detail of Poletti's wooden model of San Paolo showing the join where the nave (left) and the west façade (right) meet. This join indicates where the pronaos façade originally built onto the model was removed sometime after 1852 and replaced with the current one, following the decision to build the façade in the Paleochristian style.
Source: Author.

baptistry at the Lateran.[71] Poletti hoped to move Arnolfo's Gothic ciborium from the crossing to stand astride the baptismal font here, where, as a kind of erudite joke, it might have been intended to inspire meditations on rebirth and regeneration; for Arnolfo's ciborium was inevitably said to mark the "rebirth" of the arts from medieval darkness.[72] This is further evidence of Poletti's desire to remove visibly historic elements as far as possible from the key interior spaces of his basilica, though in this case the widespread belief that the ciborium's survival had been a miracle caused Pope Gregory to overrule him. But one can still see the holes in the wooden floor of the model baptistry where the ciborium briefly stood before it was returned to the confessio.

The other end of the model depicts Poletti's two new chapels and east perimeter wall, while at the eastern tip of the building stands a tall classical

62. Older photographs of Poletti's wooden model before it was placed in its plexiglass case. The proposed quadriporticus and baptistry are on the center and right of the upper photo and the center and left of the lower one.
Source: Unknown provenance.

campanile where the main axis meets the via Ostiense. The cynicism of Poletti's use of the Chirograph is perhaps nowhere so evident as here, for while the Chirograph possibly authorized the demolition of the old campanile (though one of the very earliest examples in Rome, it was unquestionably post-Paleochristian), it manifestly did not authorize the construction of a new one, since the earliest Roman campanili dated to the eleventh century.[73] Poletti's campanile again reflected Renaissance aesthetics, with Doric, Ionic, and Corinthian levels canonically stacked; it also functioned like a sistine obelisk, visible down the entire length of the via Ostiense from Rome and bringing the basilica into a closer visual relationship with the city. (Valadier had offered a similar idea in his 1823–1824 projects.)[74] And finally Poletti proposed to add a classical entrance porch along the north face of the transept facing Rome, orchestrating a more dramatic arrival experience for the visiting pilgrim. This too had been suggested by Valadier, as well as by Uggeri, and also recalled sistine precedents, for instance Domenico Fontana's entrance porch on the north transept of San Giovanni. In Poletti's iteration, a classical entablature with a low attic would be supported by twelve columns in two rows.

On the interior, Poletti proposed several changes to Belli's program. Over the confessio, he proposed to replace Arnolfo's ciborium with a classical one of his own composition (**Figure 63**). He also modified Belli's wall elevations throughout the basilica, and although the exact evolution of his thinking here remains unclear, the key change was to eliminate the frescoed panels envisaged by Belli in favor of a purely architectonic arrangement of marble panels, pilasters, and stringcourses. One sees this design as it was executed in illustrations from the 1840s (see **Figures 81, 83, and 92**), even if Poletti was forced after 1850 to dismantle it in order to accommodate the fresco cycle we see today (see Chapter 15).[75] His original scheme, however, aimed to make the interior more luminous, the architectonic ordonnance more assertive, and the whole less obviously dependent on Fuga's restored Santa Maria Maggiore.

What emerges from this inventory is that Poletti was hoping to use the freedom he had won from Pope Gregory to imagine an idealized basilican type that filtered old San Paolo through the aesthetic codes of Renaissance classicism. One might object that such a vision was not, after all, so very different from what Belli had been trying to do or even what Valadier had been forced by the parameters of the commission to attempt. But unlike those predecessors, Poletti was not just trying to make Vitruvian lemonade from Early Christian lemons. His vision was instead more indebted to that of Uggeri, for it was genuinely historicist: it viewed the reconstruction as an opportunity to reorient the future by reaching back and correcting a crucial missed cue in architectural history.

In this, Poletti was part of a new generation in Rome whose reflection on Renaissance architecture was far more engaged with the anxieties orienting architectural thought in the rest of Europe than is credited. The eighteenth-century collapse of classicist universalism was understood in Rome as well as anywhere else. The revolutionary critique of traditional classical theory formulated by the mid-eighteenth-century Venetian theorist Carlo Lodoli was widely available through the publications of Francesco Algarotti and Andrea Memmo (the latter published in Rome itself) and had been debated in Roman learned circles.[76] Historical and theoretical works by local figures including Winckelmann, Seroux d'Agincourt, the provocative synthesist Francesco Milizia, and of course the cantankerous Piranesi had brought virtually every aspect of the classical tradition into question.[77] Poletti's library contained the essential texts of all of these authors. The continual stream of foreign artists and scholars who traveled to Rome further guaranteed that Roman artistic discourse after 1815 was anything but provincial.[78] Architects like Poletti were well aware that growing knowledge of Greek, Roman, and Etruscan architectures had undermined old verities about the classical ideal; that architectural traditions were increasingly related to climate, cultural mores, institutions, and technologies; that

63. Luigi Poletti, initial project for a ciborio over Paul's tomb to replace Arnolfo di Cambio's ciborium. Signed by the architect: "L Poletti inv. e dis. 1833."
Source: © 2022 Archivio Storico dell'Abbazia di San Paolo f.l.m.

hardly anyone seriously believed anymore that architecture had its origin in a wooden hut; that other peoples in other parts of the world had sophisticated architectural traditions totally unrelated to those of Mediterranean classicism; and that the idea of architecture as an imitation of nature was increasingly questioned.

The anxieties that fueled the great nineteenth-century retheorization of architecture centered on the past, in Rome as elsewhere. How could the past continue to live and bear meaning in a present that recent social and political upheavals seemed to have severed from its historical moorings? How could venerable traditions continue to orient building practice? As products of long-ago vanished cultures, what was their contemporary relevance? These anxieties hinged on mounting doubts about the possibility of ideal forms and universal aesthetic truths and resulted in a quest for other ways of thinking about what a truthful architecture might look like. Notwithstanding the Church's claim that Catholic Rome stood apart from modern incertitudes, these questions had been driven to the forefront of cultural reflection in Rome by the barrage of traumas the city and Church had experienced in the decades after 1800. But whereas reflections on history had authorized northern architects and theorists either to discard old universalisms in favor of indigenous traditions like the Gothic, or to reframe classical traditions in local terms (as Germans like Klenze or Schinkel had done), in Rome the situation had a unique complexity. Roman architects had to reckon with the fact that the classical tradition, whatever claims of universality had burdened it in the past, was their local indigenous way of building. Their challenge therefore was not so much to switch styles as to learn to think about the same style in new ways: more locally, more historically, more relativistically.

The achievement of Renaissance architecture took on a new significance in this context. Already back in 1785, a declaration of principles published in the new journal *Memorie per le belle arti* had admitted that "our customs and needs are rather different to those of the Greeks and the Romans," and that therefore the best solution was to follow "the modern classicists, from the fifteenth century especially," who had adopted ancient architecture to modern uses.[79] Roman thinkers were not the only ones who saw the Renaissance as a solution to contemporary historical-theoretical dilemmas. French architects led by Percier and Fontaine also responded to the discovery of antique contradictions and complexities by developing a more flexible mode of imitation – one that embraced the picturesque diversity of the classical past, and especially of the Renaissance, and eschewed the systematicity that their contemporary Jean-Nicolas Durand tried to impose on it.[80] After 1814, reflection on the Renaissance heritage resurfaced with urgency in Rome as well. In 1820, the young Poletti read some "Observations on the Architectural Styles" to the Accademia Tibertina, in which he proposed to determine via systematic rational analysis which style was most appropriate for present-day needs in

Italy: Egyptian, Greek, Roman, or Renaissance. (He considered including Chinese too but disqualified it on the grounds that it lacked apparent solidity and ornamental variety.) Anticipating Heinrich Hubsch's investigation of nine years later, *In welchem Style sollen wir bauen?*, Poletti conducted his analysis with reference to Italian landscape forms, building materials, culture, history, and climate. His verdict in favor of the Renaissance partly hinged on its relevance to contemporary building problems for which the antique heritage offered little of use. Examples included domestic architecture, where Renaissance architects had first formulated the normative models, and ecclesiastical architecture, where Renaissance architects revolutionized the underdeveloped models inherited from the Early Christian era and Middle Ages. This was decidedly not a universalizing discourse. Poletti even noted at one point that the steep roofs required in wet northern climates mitigated against the use of Greco-Roman styles there.[81]

Perhaps the most important advantage of Renaissance architecture, in a nineteenth-century context of Roman Catholic trauma and disillusionment, was that it offered a specifically *Christian* iteration of a local style whose pagan origins had become more troubling in the aftermath of the French Revolution and Napoleon. After the fire at San Paolo, these intimations continued to develop alongside, and increasingly in dialogue with, the nascent reflection on Early Christian architecture we surveyed in Chapter 1, which was also nourished by an identitarian longing for a Christian classicism. What took shape over the second quarter of the century in Rome was a sophisticated synthetic meditation on what the Early Christian and Renaissance traditions could offer as a basis for a new Roman Catholic classical architecture. The central site for this meditation was to be Poletti's reconstruction of San Paolo.

Poletti was reputed one of the more intellectual Roman architects of his era. His friend Gaspare Servi called him an "architect-philosopher," while a former student memorialized him as "an artist and at the same time a scholar."[82] As we saw, he was an avid reader in several languages who made it "my custom always to be up to date on the works being published" in the fields of interest to him.[83] The rationale for his ambitious reimagining of San Paolo was not lightly nor provincially conceived but rather reflected a sophisticated understanding of Italian architectural history and its significance in the present.[84]

At the core of Poletti's historical and political worldview was a fierce Italian patriotism that held the cultural genius of the Italian nation in almost mystical esteem. Already in his twenties, Poletti had acquired and admired the classics of Italian irredentism, like Carlo Botta's stridently patriotic *Storia d'Italia dal 1789 al 1814*, which blamed France for thwarting the natural course of Italian political unity.[85] In the more open atmosphere that briefly followed the election of Pope Pius IX in 1846, Poletti was to reveal his hopes of liberal reform and economic modernization – until 1848, that is, when his bourgeois mistrust of "the mob" led him back into chastened incrementalism. He was, in other words, a typical example of the patriotic liberal intellectual who was to assume so much of the political initiative in Italy after 1830.

Poletti's thought was deeply informed by recent developments in national historiography and in particular by new understandings of the ancient Etruscans.[86] Antiquarian speculation on the Etruscans has a long history in Italy, but in the eighteenth century it had taken on significant political resonances, as private excavations at the Etruscan tombs around Volterra, Siena, Cortona, and Arezzo fortified local patriotic sentiments and fueled grievances about foreign domination. The scholar Mario Guarnacci in 1757 founded an Etruscan Museum in his hometown of Volterra and a decade later began publishing his influential *Origini italiche* (of which Poletti owned a copy), which made the radical claim that the arts and sciences had not been introduced into Italy from Greece but rather vice versa, and that the mysterious Pelasgians, who the Greeks cited as their forefathers, were in fact an Italic people.[87] Patriotic Etruscomania further expanded in the decades after 1792, in works like Vincenzo Cuoco's three-volume novel *Platone in Italia* (1804–1806; two copies in Poletti's library), which offered a purported translation of an ancient manuscript describing the astonished travels of Plato amid the superior civilizations of ancient Italy. Its conclusion reiterated Guarnacci's thesis that the Etruscans were the storied Pelasgians and effectively anointed them the founders of Western civilization.[88] Similar claims underlay *L'Italia avanti il dominio dei Romani*, an explosive 1810 study published by the Tuscan scholar Giuseppe Micali (four copies in Poletti's library).[89] These works are widely recognized as foundational attempts to articulate a common historical Italian identity and as starting points for the Italian aspiration to national unity.[90] (The advocate of patriotic Etruscomania best known to art historians is undoubtedly Piranesi, whose famous polemic with Pierre-Jean Mariette helped popularize the idea that Roman architecture owed little or no debt to the Greeks, but rather derived its essential qualities from the indigenous contributions of the Etruscans.)[91]

Poletti was not just an enthusiastic consumer of this literature; he aspired to translate it into the domain of the arts. In 1835, shortly after presenting his master plan for San Paolo, he read a paper at the Istituto di Correspondenza Archaeologica concerning the recently excavated Etruscan tombs at Cerveteri.[92] His opening lines repeated Guarnacci's argument that the Etruscans were in fact the Pelasgians and presented the excavations as contributing to a seismic reconfiguration of the historiography of ancient art. A year later, Poletti went much further, reading a long lecture entitled "Delle genti e delle arti primitive d'Italia" to a joint session of the Pontifical Academy of

Archaeology and the Academy of St. Luke. Subsequently published, this quaveringly patriotic discourse echoed Micali in its very title and aimed to fill out Micali's thesis using architectural evidence[93] (**Figure 64**). Its vehemently footnoted demonstration lent material proof to the claim that the arts had originated in Italy and were brought to the barbarous Greeks by the Etruscans, and that the Etruscans had then civilized the Romans. The research drew on ancient and Renaissance texts in Latin and Greek as well as on recent scholarship in Italian, French (Lenoir, Caylus, and Petit-Radel) and English (Leake and Dodwell).[94]

The change of venue between Poletti's first and second papers, from the German-dominated Istituto di Correspondenza Archaeologica to the pontifical academies, was significant. Poletti's biographer Campori quoted Poletti on this decades later:

> "The scope of my dissertations was to oppose a German school founded here in Rome under the title of Istituto Archeologico, as well as its pedantic followers in Italy, who together propagate the verdict that nothing is made by the Italians that is not actually Greek. After the great discoveries of Etruria, Magna Grecia, and Sicily, it seemed to me that one could no longer entertain doubts as to the Italic primacy, which I was among the first to proclaim, starting in 1835. What I think I did that was new was not so much to argue that the ancient civilization of the Italians was antecedent to that of the Greeks, as this was already being said by many people, and I only amplified it with better proofs and the help of the latest discoveries; but that the Italic emigration to Greece occurred before the Hellenes ever arrived on our shores, which, as far as I know, had never been said before."[95]

The antagonistic nationalism of the quote is notable, for what Poletti's work added up to was a defiantly identitarian classicism. Over the previous half century or so, scholars and theorists had become much better informed about the complex historical reality of Etruscan, Greek, and even provincial Roman architecture and as a result were increasingly inclined to view the classical or Vitruvian tradition as little more than a latter-day historiographical fiction. The Romans in this perspective were unmasked as the mere copyists of a distinct Greek system that Rome had then superimposed upon a conceptually unrelated arcuated architecture inherited from the Etruscans.[96] Such theories were useful in northern contexts in helping to transform European architectural history from a hierarchy of geographical traditions, with the Mediterranean at the forefront and northern traditions on a secondary plane, into a series of abstract problems centered on the aesthetic ordering of architectural systems defined by local contingencies (available building materials, climate, social organization) and whichever building technologies these tended to favor. Poletti's argument also reflected aspects of this way of thinking, but only to

64. Title page from Poletti (1838a).
Source: Getty Research Institute, Los Angeles (87-B11696).

reframe the whole historical development of the classical system as intrinsically and indigenously Italian: for he reduced its Greek chapter to a brief sojourn sandwiched between an Etruscan origin and a subsequent Italic return and consummation with the Romans, later to be reconsummated and amplified in the *cinquecento*.

Poletti thus envisaged a much subtler and more palatable solution to the questions facing Roman architects after 1815 than that offered by Leo XII's Chirograph on San Paolo. The Chirograph implied a sense that the Church's originary style of the fourth through sixth centuries was really the only Roman architecture that belonged exclusively to Catholicism. Poletti saw it very differently. Poletti understood style – and especially the long Italic classical style, as he conceived it – as the manifestation of an enduring cultural unity; one marked by development certainly, but with a core essence that transcended even the passage from one religious system to another.[97] Early Christian architecture thus reflected more than just the decadent contingencies of its late antique execution, for it too belonged to the stable Italic core of development, even if only as an impoverished lull. Poletti's ambition was to reclaim that tradition in its entirety, aided by new historical insights which had revealed it to be even more aboriginally Italian than previously thought. This is what made him confortable, for example, erecting a new campanile that rejected the traditional Roman medieval models, with their blocky brick simplicity, and offered instead an ideal classical iteration of the form.[98]

One could say that in Poletti's thought the classical tradition played the role for Rome that the Gothic played for northerners – that of the organic, authentic, local tradition. And yet his system was pervaded by obvious tensions between relative and essential. Thus the Italic classical tradition, historicized and understood developmentally, still retained in Poletti's mind a powerful whiff of its old universality. Only it was no longer an absolute aesthetic universality reflecting timeless truths, but rather a historical universality that emblematized the Italic foundation of European civilization.

The challenge of rebuilding one of the great Early Christian basilicas took on a peculiar significance when one saw things this way. It became less about wrestling anachronistically with the architectural contingencies of the fourth and fifth centuries and more about reelaborating the essential *idea* of that moment in the brighter light of a longer historical understanding. The challenge became a much more self-consciously theorized version of what Fuga had essayed at Santa Maria Maggiore a century earlier and similar to what Uggeri had attempted in his proposals. Only Poletti's aim was not to rescue the original intentions of the Early Christians, but to bring forward the transcendant Italic genius that, for whatever reasons, the Early Christians had too often failed to heed when they were developing the first Christian basilicae. The goal was nothing less than the refoundation and redemption of this quintessential building type. Here is what Poletti himself later had to say about it, twenty years into his work at San Paolo, speaking to his students at the Academy of St. Luke:

> The Christian basilicae had the misfortune to rise up in a moment when the arts had declined. Thus we see a medley of ancient fragments, columns of varying diameter and height, and mismatched capitals and bases; we see entablatures with obvious variations in their dimensions, moldings, and details; while those parts that they were forced to produce anew in those times were of a raw and unformed art, with a jumbled decoration that degrades all the good rules of symmetry, unity, and elegance. Yet in the midst of such impoverished times, the general arrangement of these buildings largely conformed to the precepts of Vitruvius and the norms established by the basilicas erected in the centuries before Constantine. If only the arts had been flowering with grace and magnificence, as they had been in the time of Augustus and Trajan, we would have had Christian basilicae that surpassed the ancient ones in size and in beauty. Thus in rebuilding the basilica of San Paolo I took as my norm the precepts of Vitruvius and the most famous ancient basilicae; and I added into the general arrangement whatever a Christian temple required, and into the decoration whatever was best and most elegant in the modern arts.[99]

In his aspiration to rescue the Early Christians from the misfortunes of their historical moment, Poletti anticipates the historicist analyses of arcuated architecture proposed in the early 1840s by northern theorists like Hippolyte Fortoul, Léon Vaudoyer, and Alexandre Lenoir.[100] In their schema, Providence had handed the ancient Romans the historic task of creating an ordering system for arcuation that was equivalent to the orders the Greeks had developed for trabeation. The Romans, however, had lazily settled for superimposing the Greek system atop their arches, as on the exterior of the Colosseum, thus leaving a void at the heart of arcuated architecture that no subsequent civilization had ever been able to fill. "The problem that Rome dealt with via this lie," wrote Fortoul in 1842, "has from that time on never ceased to haunt the modern world."[101] In Poletti's analogous account, the Early Christians are handed by Providence the great architectural task of bringing forth the new building type of the Christian church; and while the general layout of what they produced reflected good Italic design, the unfortunate circumstances of the by-then collapsing empire left them bereft of competent craftspeople and forced them to fall back on the miserable expedient of reusing elements scavenged from older Roman buildings. And so they failed in their task. The subsequent history of an essential building type had been fatally compromised. It therefore fell to the architect of the nineteenth century, possessing better knowledge and better material resources, to go back and right the wrong.

Of these two advantages – better knowledge and better material resources – the crucial one in Poletti's view was certainly the former. The Early Christians had been much closer in time to the apex of Roman architecture under Augustus, but nineteenth-century architects possessed a more sophisticated understanding of the longer development of classicism, including the previously obscure roles of the Greeks and Etruscans. They also had before their eyes the magisterial *Christian* elaboration of classicism represented by the Renaissance.[102] In revisiting the flawed invention of the Christian basilica in the light of these 1,400 years' worth of accumulated knowledge, Poletti aimed at San Paolo to bring an essential building type to its long-postponed perfection, and thereby to define a new model for the future. His approach was not essentially about the past, as Leo's Chirograph had been, nor was it principally about the present, as in the idealism of Belli or Valadier. Rather it ranged in true historicist fashion across the whole arc of history, seeking to use present knowledge to remedy the deficiencies of the past for the benefit of the future.

The potential of the Early Christian basilica as an alternative to the vaulted arch-and-pilasters formula exemplified by St. Peter's has a long history.[103] It was being explored already even as new St. Peter's was being built (and as old St. Peter's was being demolished) in Giulio Romano's reconstruction of Mantua Cathedral, starting in the 1540s (**Figure 65**). What always held it back as a model was the problem of vaulting: unlike the more heavily built St. Peter's type, the Early Christian basilica was based on isolated columns that carried a wooden ceiling, as they were generally not strong enough to carry a stone vault.[104] The Early Christian model nonetheless exerted an enduring attraction, whether for aesthetic or historical reasons, and not just in Italy. In both England and France, a fascination with the Paleochristian basilica type emerged as far back as the seventeenth century, as in the proposals debated within the Commission for Building Fifty New Churches in London after the fire of 1666, or in the Perrault brothers' contemporaneous proposed reconstruction of the church of Sainte-Geneviève in Paris.[105] The ambition of this latter project exerted a deep influence in eighteenth-century France, satisfying a taste for structural lightness that was also associated with Gothic architecture, and eventually influencing the construction of a series of basilican churches starting in the 1760s, including Saint-Symphorien at Montreuil and Saint-Philippe du Roule in Paris.[106] And then in the 1820s and 1830s there was a second wave of basilican churches in and around Paris, including Notre-Dame-de-Lorette (**see Figure 58**), Notre-Dame-de-Bercy, and others that Poletti himself likely saw on his trip in 1828.[107] Interest in the basilican form was lively also in the German-speaking

65. Giulio Romano, Mantova Cathedral, nave, 1545–1546.
Source: Wikimedia Commons: Creative Commons Attribution-Share Alike 4.0 International license.

lands. The Bavarian Crown Prince Ludwig, who was in Rome at the time of the fire at San Paolo, subsequently directed his architect Friedrich Ziebland to study Early Christian basilicae in Rome before then commissioning him to build the basilica of St. Bonifaz in Munich (1836–1847), which Ziebland packed full of references to old San Paolo[108] (**Figure 66**). Even in Protestant Berlin, Karl Friedrich Schinkel – who had attended the 1824 Concorso Clementino exhibition in Rome – drew up plans for a new Berlin cathedral in the form of a five-aisled basilica that Groblewski aptly characterizes as a "synthesis of San Paolo and Santa Maria Maggiore."[109]

The fifth-century Santa Maria Maggiore was a key stimulus for such reflections for Roman architects too, largely on account of Fuga's pioneering restoration of the 1740s. Rather than hide the Early Christian building beneath a more up-to-date modern skin, as Borromini had done at the Lateran, Fuga's method had been to discern the underlying ideals of the Early Christian design and to reconstitute them independently of their decadent late antique realization.[110] We have already seen that Fuga's work formally influenced Belli's design for San Paolo in 1830, and that his conceptual approach informed the work of Belli's antagonist Uggeri. Another important Roman starting point for such reflections – one that also influenced Uggeri – was the work of Francesco Milizia,

66. Friedrich Ziebland, St. Bonifaz, Munich, 1836–1847. Photograph taken before the damage inflicted during the Second World War.
Source: Postcard – public domain.

who in 1787 had suggested that the Christian basilicae were in some ways truer to the architecture of the Greeks than many of the greatest Roman works, because, like their civic predecessors, they used columns as primary supports rather than as mere decorative accents.[111] And of course the Roman scene was also shaped by Seroux d'Agincourt, who from the 1770s to his death in 1814 had assembled in his *Histoire* a visual documentation for Milizia's insights.

All these local rethinkings of the Early Christian heritage were known to Poletti, as were at least some of the French and German ones as well.[112] By the time Poletti finally came to the task of devising a master plan for San Paolo in 1834–1835, the idea of a purified and rejuvenated Early Christian idiom was very much in the air.[113] We have seen that Uggeri's 1832 *summa* on the subject was dedicated to Luigi Canina, who was soon to publish his *Ricerche sull'architettura piu propria dei tempj cristiani*, a systematic argument in favor of the Early Christian basilica as a modern model. Canina's fellow Turinese Carlo Promis was also in Rome between 1828 and 1836 to study the Early Christian basilicae, after which he returned to Turin and produced texts arguing for a modern ecclesiastical architecture derived from Paleochristian norms.[114] Promis later developed this idea at length when King Carlo Alberto of Piedmont charged him in 1845 with designing a modern Christian basilica.

And in 1837 the Prussian diplomat Bunsen, who we have also already encountered, published *Les forum de Rome restaurés et expliqués* (also dedicated to Canina), which he had read previously at the Istituto di Correspondenza Archaeologica.[115] In it, Bunsen stressed the importance of deepening archaeological research on the forums of Rome as a means of rejuvenating contemporary architecture. The main focus, in his view, should be on the ancient civic basilicae, because an accurate reconstruction of these – one destined to be more accurate than those essayed by the Early Christians, he felt – would "help our architects revive a new system for our churches, one that would among other advantages have that of being the expression of the oldest form of this building type."[116] Bunsen would continue to push this line in the years to come.[117]

The thread linking these various explorations, whether it was explicit or implicit, was a desire to develop a purified Early Christian style, moderated with a powerful dose of Renaissance order and sweetness. It is worth stressing again what a new aspiration this was. Instead of the quest to determine the most beautiful possible iteration of the most perfect architectural system, this was predicated on the evolution and thus the historicity of classicism. It was not a quest interested in an ostensibly universal beauty – in the *bello ideale* – but rather sought an exclusive, specific, and local expression appropriate to the history, culture, values, and needs of Catholic Rome in the early nineteenth century.

Leo XII's Chirograph of 1825 helps us to see this trend in sharper relief. With hindsight, we can recognize the Chirograph as a first, if rather one-dimensional, Catholic response to the loss of faith in the idea of a Vitruvian architecture with universal pretentions. That Leo's decree was inspired by clerics and scholars rather than by architects only highlights that it was more than just the solution to an architectural debate, but rather emblematized a deeper cultural turn. Timeless universality was under threat across the board in Rome by 1825, in a traumatized and weakened Church as much as among architects.[118] Yet at a time when the logic of recuperating the local, the historical, and the exclusive was everywhere ascendant, Romans and Roman Catholics found themselves with a heritage that had been increasingly promoted as a universal possession of humanity. The significance of the Chirograph lay in reclaiming the one part of the classical heritage that nobody else wanted, and which – partly as a result – could plausibly be identified exclusively with Rome and its Church. Thereby it had been able, at least for a time, to perform powerful identitarian service in both cultural and clerical contexts. This however required an unspoken yet radical break with tradition.

But as the debates over San Paolo during the Belli years showed, an Early Christian revival in architecture was never going to be a viable program for a culture that was simply not ready to sever its ties with classical aesthetic codes.

The required Romantic view of history was there, even if largely unacknowledged, but Romantic aesthetics were still too much associated with benighted foreign forms and influences. As we will see, Poletti in particular was prone to rage in his private papers against the "nordic frenzy" of aesthetic Romanticism.[119] To acquiesce in that foreign aesthetic would have been to repudiate all the great historical buildings, from the Forum to St. Peter's, that had earned Rome its proud identity as the Home of the Arts. Such an epic repudiation was not on the cards, which is why the *in pristinum* project at San Paolo ended up with capitals copied from the Pantheon.

What had to happen instead – and this is exactly what *was* happening by the 1830s – was a patient and systematic rethinking of the Roman classical tradition, which aimed, like contemporaneous rethinkings in France and Germany, at synthesizing a new and meaningful ideal from the fullness of a specifically local architectural history. Or to put it differently: it was a reassessment of local architectural history rooted in Romantic historicism, but that remained true to a classical, which is to say an anti-Romantic, sense of aesthetics – only it was now classical in the local, not the universal, sense. In this delicate endeavor, the architecture of the Renaissance was to play the pivotal role.

The intellect and energy that Poletti brought to the San Paolo reconstruction were obviously no guarantee on their own that the public image of the project would improve, or that the flow of donations supporting it would start again. For that, Poletti needed help – help that was providentially close at hand, it turns out, in the person of Luigi Moreschi (1802–1886), who, as we saw, had been discharging most of Uggeri's responsibilities from about 1830 onward and who officially succeeded him as secretary of the Special Commission in 1837.[120] Moreschi's rise thus paralleled that of Poletti, and for thirty years the two men proved to be allies as much as Uggeri and Belli had been antagonists.[121] A neglected figure in the scholarship on San Paolo, Moreschi was the essential force in translating Poletti's efforts at the building site into public perceptions in Rome and beyond. Moreschi's big innovation was the incessant use of publication to herald and explain Poletti's work. He ultimately published dozens of accounts in the *Diario di Roma*, as well as a handful of books and pamphlets, all explaining the intentions behind Poletti's work and putting its progress in the best possible light.

Little is known about Moreschi outside of his labors at San Paolo.[122] His appointment in 1825 as Uggeri's assistant seems to have been his first government appointment, to which he subsequently added posts as a copyist or minuter in different ministries of the pontifical government until his retirement in 1870. As a result of his labors for the Special Commission, he became associated with several academies as a fellow or associate member: the

Academy of St. Luke, the Pontifical Academy of Archaeology, the Accademia dell'Arcadia, the Congregazione de' Virtuosi al Pantheon, and the Academy of Santa Cecilia. But in the mid-1830s, all that still lay in the future.

Moreschi inaugurated the practice of placing a detailed account in the *Diario di Roma* after each papal visit to the construction site. As time went on, these grew longer and were eventually published as separate supplements. Printing costs for these supplements were paid directly by Moreschi with funds from the Special Commission's budget.[123] It was, in other words, a self-consciously propagandistic effort. The first of these accounts described Pius VIII's final visit in October 1830, two weeks before his death. Unsigned by Moreschi but certainly by him, it established several features that were to become standard in his accounts: an opening that announced the precise hour of the pope's arrival; a description of the religious observances that preceded the pope's tour; an inventory of which parts of the building he then visited and their current state; and finally an account of the words of satisfaction and congratulations with which he concluded the visit.[124] Moreschi's second report described Gregory XVI's first visit to the worksite in March 1831 and depicted the basilica as a hive of activity, which would surely have surprised readers who at that date still imagined a silent worksite mired in bureaucratic paralysis. In October 1832 Gregory visited again, and Moreschi's article went to lengths to explain that the controversial decision to raise the nave floor had been fully approved at every level, from the Academy of St. Luke to the pope himself, and would have no ill effects on the appearance of the building.[125] Moreschi occasionally introduced vivid details or tableaux into these essays. In October 1835, for example, he described how Poletti had enchanted the visiting pope with a bit of theater: after inviting him to take a seat in one of the nave side aisles, Poletti gave a sign, total silence fell, and a team of some 180 workers began raising a stone pilaster before the Holy Father's eyes. Twelve minutes later, the pilaster was in place. Recalling Domenico Fontana's famously orchestrated obelisk raisings in the sixteenth century, such anecdotes fortified perceptions of Poletti's supreme competence and total control over the worksite. Moreschi's text brought it to thousands of readers, many far beyond Rome, who thereby became eavesdroppers on the pope's personal tour.[126]

These reports were to help Poletti in innumerable ways. Moreschi rarely missed an opportunity to vouch for the supposed necessity of Poletti's many elective demolitions. In 1838, when Poletti was gearing up to demolish the old campanile, Moreschi informed readers that it was "battered" on account of its poor construction and could not be expected to last much longer.[127] Or in describing the new granite columns for the side aisles, he reminded the reader that they were being substituted for old ones that, "calcinated by the fire, would not have been capable for long of doing their jobs; and they were anyway imperfect in their workmanship and proportions, and would have seemed quite unpleasant in comparison with the magnificence and grandeur of the new ones."

But mostly Moreschi helped Poletti by simply getting out the word that work was now progressing swiftly and surely. His article on Gregory XVI's site visit in September 1834 emphasized the pontiff's eagerness to see San Paolo achieved and his happiness at what Poletti was showing him: thirty-four of forty of the main nave columns erected; the main façade newly secured with buttressing; scaffolds for the construction of the nave walls erected; materials for the nave roof amassed; and work on the terminal wall altars and coffered ceiling of the transept under way. Even when Moreschi announced something as minor as a new commission for some interior statues, he drove home the point that "the works of the basilica are progressing with supreme alacrity and with indescribable exactness; and how could it be otherwise, considering that the great Poletti is its architect director?"[128] The message was hammered home at every opportunity. After the pope's visit of October 1839, with the apse and transept nearly complete, Moreschi wrote that Gregory thanked Poletti for pursuing the work with "such speed," and declared that his long day inspecting the works had been "one of the most beautiful of my life."[129]

Moreschi also helped publicize significant features of the reconstruction that would otherwise have gone unnoticed. In his account of Gregory's visit of July 1838, he wrote that the pope had paused in the midst of his perambulations with Poletti to examine the fire-damaged columns of the north aisle, some of which were on the ground, all shortly to be replaced with new granite ones. One column in particular caught Gregory's attention: it had originally stood right inside the main entry in the north aisle, and carried an inscription at its top:

SIRICIVS EPISCOPVS TOTA MENTE DEVOTVS

and another at the bottom:

VALENTIN .. NI . AVG . IIII . ET . NE . OTERI . VC

Moreschi described how Gregory, reading this, ordered on the spot that the column be preserved in the new building, and explained to everyone why: the Siricio mentioned in the upper inscription was a fourth-century bishop, while the lower inscription referenced a consulship that corresponded to the year 390; together they supported the claim that the basilica had been consecrated by Bishop Siricio in 390 during Valentinian's consulship. The column was, in other words, a witness to the earliest days of the old basilica. Moreschi's account of this papal intervention was obviously a fiction, as Poletti was by then just days from beginning construction on the north porch where the column in question was to be installed, and the decision to foreground it had certainly been made weeks if not months earlier. When Poletti shaved the

67. Reused column from the north aisle of San Paolo fuori le mura, reemployed by Poletti among the other old aisle columns supporting the north porch of the rebuilt basilica. Like all the reused columns, the shaft has been shaved down to render it uniform; however, this one has retained a ring at the top at its original thickness, displaying an inscription that dates to the fourth-century bishopric of Siricio.
Source: Author.

column down for uniformity with all the others, the upper inscription was preserved (though the lower one was not), so that it now rings the pristine shaft like a clerical collar (**Figure 67**). It is the only element in the whole porch visibly suggestive of memorial reuse, but the unforewarned visitor is apt to walk right past it. Hence the utility of Moreschi's anecdote. Distant readers who might never visit Rome could rest easier knowing that the new basilica offered worthy recollections of the old, while readers who did visit were now equipped to notice that they were welcomed into the rebuilt San Paolo by a ghostly cohort of cleaned-up veterans from the old basilica (**Plate 11**).

The message of Moreschi's articles spread far beyond Rome, for they were continually picked up and summarized in other papers. Before long, news of how work was accelerating had found its way to the Parisian *Ami de la Religion* (20 November 1833) and the Belgian *Journal historique et littéraire* (1 December 1835); soon one could read all over Europe of how work now "goes extremely fast" (*Echo. Zeitschrift für Literatur, Kunst und Mode in Italien*, 19 August 1834) or "moves forward briskly" (*Morgenblatt für gebildete Leser*, 25 January 1839).[130] The same message soon crossed the seas, appearing in the *U.S. Catholic Miscellany* of Charleston, South Carolina (11 October 1834) and the Brazilian *Jornal do Commercio* of Rio de Janeiro (11 July 1837), among others.[131] The text in virtually all of these notices may be traced back, whether directly or via intermediaries, to Moreschi's notices in the *Diario di Roma*, which provided the only regular source of news from the Catholic metropole.

Moreschi's publicitary efforts can be hard to square with the fact that the idea of public opinion in any political or doctrinal sense was still officially regarded in Rome as a Trojan horse for the Church's enemies.[132] Moreschi's efforts to disseminate positive information about San Paolo, however, reveal the less Manichean attitude already evinced in the fundraising drive. For Church leaders were under no illusion but that their Church was increasingly dependent on Catholics beyond Rome, and they understood that the material support of those believers could no longer be guaranteed in the nineteenth century simply through habit and coercion. The active support of the Catholic laity now increasingly depended upon persuasion.

NOTES

1 Reinerman (1983). For a positive appraisal of Gregory XVI's reform efforts, see Dalla Torre (1948).

2 Farini (1851–1854), v. 1, pp. 71–73; Berkeley and Berkeley (1932–1940), v. 1, pp. 131–135; Reinerman (1991).

3 *TEPD*, v. 3, pp. 169–178, 209–212.

4 Campori (1881), p. 8. On Poletti's biography, see also Campori (1865); Stefanucci Ala (1869) (a student of Poletti); Giucci (1871); Campori (1905). Among modern studies, Vaccari and Dezzi Bardeschi eds. (1992) has now been superceded by Strozzieri (2021).

5 Luigi Poletti to Geminiano Poletti, 4 April 1818 (BCALP: LP 23 C2; tiSAD doc. 2, pp. 3–4).

6 Poletti's library today forms the patrimonial core of the Biblioteca Civica d'Arte Luigi Poletti. There is no dedicated study of Poletti's collection.

7 Strozzieri attributes to Poletti a tomb project that later became the basis for Canova's own tomb at Possagno (Strozzieri [2021], p. 39).

8 Luigi Poletti, "Osservazioni sugli stili architettonici," 5 June 1820, and "Nuove ipotesi sulle origini degli ordini e loro significato," 1821 (BCALP: LP17 C12 and LP16 C10).

9 Strozzieri (2021), pp.114–116.

10 Luigi Poletti to Geminiano Poletti, 16 July 1823 [erroneously dated 15 July] (BCALP: LP23 C5; tiSAD doc. 32, p. 12).

POLETTI AND THE CHALLENGE OF REBUILDING SAN PAOLO 241

11 Luigi Poletti to Geminiano Poletti, 16 July 1823 [erroneously dated 15 July] (BCALP: LP23 C5; tiSAD doc. 32, p. 12).

12 Luigi Poletti to Geminiano Poletti, 16 July 1823 [erroneously dated 15 July] (BCALP: LP23 C5; tiSAD doc. 32, p. 12).

13 Luigi Poletti to Geminiano Poletti, 16 May 1824 and 18 June 1824 (BCALP: LP23 C8; tiSAD doc. 40, p. 14).

14 Strozzieri (2021), pp. 63–68; Luigi Poletti, "Le fabbriche più insigni di Roma moderna dopo il risorgimento delle arti ossia dei secoli XIV, XV, XVI e XVII," 7 December 1829 (ASR: Computisteria Camerale, b. 363). On the Palazzo Ceccopieri, see Ceccopieri Maruffi (1986).

15 Strozzieri (2021), p. 75.

16 "Della fabbrica Ceccopieri a Monte Catino. Architettura di Luigi Poletti," *MRABA* 3 (1826): 313–316.

17 "Architetture del Cavaliere Gaspare Salvi professore nell'accademia pontificia di belle arti in Roma," *MRABA* 4 (1827): 219.

18 Strozzieri (2021), pp. 75, 116–118. From 1825 to 1827, the president of the Ospizio was the young Giovanni Maria Mastai Ferretti, twenty years later to become Pope Pius IX, but it is unclear whether the end of his presidency overlapped with Poletti's appointment (Monti [1928], pp. 29–31).

19 Geminiano Poletti to Luigi Poletti, 4 January 1828 (BCALP: LP23b C16).

20 Luigi Poletti to Geminiano Poletti (10 January 1828) as in Chapter 8 n. 46.

21 Campori (1881), pp. 52–53; Luigi Poletti to Geminiano Poletti, 11 April 1828 (BCALP: LP23b C16).

22 Luigi Poletti, "Prospetto dei Conti fra Poletti e Letarouilly," 17 January 1832 (BCALP: LP48 C3). On their friendship, see Strozzieri (2021), pp. 51–62.

23 Pinon (1995).

24 Campori (1881), p. 18; Strozzieri (2021), p. 75.

25 Poletti (1829). On the book's renown, see [Gasparoni] (1833).

26 Perilli (1842), p. 7; Salimbeni (2008).

27 *DdR*, 31 October 1832, pp. 1–2.

28 Cf. "Riassunti dei pagamenti e spese fatte pei lavori" of September and October 1833 (ASR: Camerlengato, P. II, Tit. IV, b. 155).

29 Tommaso Bernetti to Luigi Poletti, 6 March 1833 (BCALP: LP19 C20).

30 Campori dates Poletti's appointment as Belli's successor in waiting to 1832 rather than 1833, an error that may reflect the date at which Poletti actually began supervising the worksite (Campori [1865], p. 106).

31 *DdR* (supplement), 2 November 1833, pp. 1–4.

32 *Il Tiberino*, 28 September 1833, p. 148.

33 Campori (1865), p. 106.

34 "Riassunto dei pagamenti e spese settimanali dal. 23 al 28 Decembre 1833," 28 December 1833 (ASR: CSRBSP Computisteria b. 137). The press also noted the accelerated pace: *Il Tiberino*, 22 February 1834, p. 24; *Echo. Zeitschrift für Literatur, Kunst und Mode in Italien* (Milan), 19 August 1834, pp. 395–396; *DdR: NdG*, 13 March 1834, 1 (also see *CAPDR*, p. 73).

35 Luigi Poletti, Untitled ms., March 1835 (ASR: CSRBSP Segreteria b. 275); "Specifica delle regalie accordate a titolo dei maccaroni ai lavoranti, che hanno portata a compimento la copertura della Nave traversa," 30 December 1833 (ASR: CSRBSP Computisteria b. 137).

36 Luigi Poletti, "Relazione dell'Architetto Direttore intorno alle quattro proposizioni da sottaporsi alla Congregazione Speciale," 20 May 1846 (ASR: CSRBSP Segreteria b. 276, f. 11; BCALP: LP37 C132 4).

37 Poletti (March 1835) as in Chapter 10 n. 35.

38 Poletti, "Relazione . . ." as in Chapter 10 n. 36; *DdR* (supplement), 2 November 1833, p. 3.

39 Poletti, "Relazione . . ." as in Chapter 10 n. 36.

40 Luigi Poletti, "Rapporto per S[ua] S[antità] sull'altare nell'abside, e sulle due capelle nella nave traversa della Basilica Ostiense," 3 March 1834 (ASR: CSRBSP Segreteria b. 276, f. 6; ASP: 32/c, b.1828-50, f. 3; tiG pp. 412–413).

41 BCALP: CM3 325. The two edicules flanking the high altar and the two statues of Peter and Paul would later be eliminated from the design (Luigi Poletti, Untitled ms., [1835] [BCALP: LP12 c87 11; tiSAD doc. 112, p. 46]).

42 Gregory XVI was fascinated by the process by which these columns were fabricated (*DdR*, 31 October 1832, p. 1).

43 See Valadier's designs: Valadier (1833); tiG pp. 513–514. These chapels will be discussed further in Chapter 12.

44 Poletti, "Rapporto ..." as in Chapter 10 n. 40.

45 Poletti, "Rapporto ..." as in Chapter 10 n. 40. This request is discussed in *CAPDR*, pp. 85–88, n. 1, which however dates it to "3 marzo 1833," which is clearly a typo for 3 March 1834, the date when Poletti submitted his other requests. The notes in *CAPDR* describe all these requests being made on the same day, and documents available in the archive leave no doubt that the other request was made on 3 March 1834. See Strozzieri (2021), pp. 146–147, n. 80.

46 Poletti, "Rapporto ..." as in Chapter 10 n. 40.

47 Luigi Poletti, Untitled ms., [c. 1846] (BCALP: LP37 C132 1).

48 On this altar, see Docci (2006).

49 Antonio Domenico Gamberini to Antonio Tosti, 25 June 1834 (ASR: CSRBSP Segreteria b. 276, f. 6; tiG pp. 413–414).

50 The story of this meeting appears in two places: Campori (1881) describes it on pp. 29–30, and Poletti refers to it in his "Relazione ..." (as in Chapter 10 n. 36). In cases of disagreement, I have followed Poletti's account. Campori is the source for the meeting having taken place at Castel Gandolfo, where every October Gregory habitually retired for his annual *villeggiatura. Diario di Roma* confirms that Gregory was at Castel Gandolfo from 9 October until 22 October 1834 and does not indicate any other papal stays there in 1833 and 1834.

51 Luigi Poletti, Untitled ms., [after 1 January 1849] (ASR: CSRBSP Fabbrica b. 4, f. 11).

52 "Rapporto della Computisteria della Commissione Speciale deputata alla riedificazione della Basilica di S. Paolo sullo Stato Economico dell'Azienda," 30 September 1842 (ASR: CSRBSP Computisteria b. 69, f. 14).

53 "Registro ..." as in Chapter 7 n. 30.

54 Crocella (1982), p. 28; Felisini (1990).

55 Crocella (1982), pp. 24–25.

56 Tuckerman (1835), pp. 53–54.

57 Shortly after Gregory endorsed Poletti's vision, he was quoted as declaring that it was essential to complete the transept first (*DdR* supplement, 7 March 1835, pp. 1–4; see also Poletti (March 1835) as in Chapter 10 n. 35).

58 Luigi Moreschi to Luigi Poletti, 10 November 1834 (ASR: CSRBSP Fabbrica b. 4, f. 4). For the official notice, see Antonio Domenico Gamberini to Antonio Tosti, 10 November 1834 (ASR: CSRBSP Segreteria b. 282).

59 Gamberini to Tosti as in Chapter 10 n. 58.

60 Pasolini (1887), p. 33. Pasolini's visit took place on 4 December 1834.

61 *CAPDR*, p. 86.

62 Poletti, "Relazione ..." as in Chapter 10 n. 36. The presence of a "Modello in legno della Basilica" in the "quarto magazzino" at the worksite is also documented (ASP: 6/c, b. 1834-5, n. 43).

63 Cerioni (1988); Groblewski (2001), pp. 164–165; Filippi and Pallottino, Catalog entry for X.3.12 in Susinno et al. (2003), pp. 496–498. Payment records from 1844 list Colagiacomo among the forty-five or so carpenters working at the site. See the "Riassunto dei pagamenti e delle spese settimanali dal 8 al 13 Genno 1844," 13 January 1844 (ASP: 5/c, b. 1844, f. 3).

64 Luigi Moreschi, "Relazione generica su i disegni delle architetture interne ed esterne della nuova fabbrica della Basilica di San Paolo," 6 March 1872 (ASR: CSRBSP Segreteria b. 276, f. 10). Emphasis is my own.

65 Reproduced in Ferrua (1968), pp. 266–269.

66 It is curious that no documentation of the model's construction has come to light, as it must have represented a major expense. A passage in the monastery chronacle from 1843 states that it was made "by foreman Matteo Bravi" (*Cronaca* II, 25 October 1843), but while the archive of the worksite attests to various Bravis among the skilled carpenters working at San Paolo during these years, none appears to have been named Matteo.

67 It is not immediately clear what specific modifications Coligiacomi and "G. S." might have been making in 1844 and 1861.

68 Groblewski discusses an engraved plan by Giovanni della Longa, which he dates to 1834, as a guide to Poletti's original project (Groblewski [2001], pp. 163–164; fig. 89, p. 558). But della Longa (1823–1888) was only eleven years old in 1834. The legend of one other version of this print references the 1854 consecration, which supports Pallottino's suggestion that it might have been part of a never completed series from the 1850s commemorating Poletti's work (Pallottino [2003], p. 497).

69 Cf. Chapter 15.

70 See Docci (2006), pp. 94–102.

71 These parts of the building were all built in different form after Poletti's death, but the corresponding parts of Poletti's model were never reconfigured.

72 *DdR* supplement, 29 October 1836, 1; *DdR* supplement, 28 July 1838, p. 1; Giacoletti (1840), p. 146.

73 Priester (1990).

74 Valadier (1833).

75 On the appearance of Poletti's original elevation, in addition to the figures cited, see the description in Hemans (1847a), p. 131.

76 Algarotti (1757), v. 2, pp. 183–224; Memmo (1786).

77 Piranesi (1761); Milizia (1781); Seroux d'Agincourt (1823).

78 Salmon (1995); Palazzolo (2003); Meyer (2006) and (2010); Rolfi Ožvald (2012).

79 "Architettura," *Memorie per le belle arti* 1:2 (January 1785): xi–xviii. For a thorough treatment of the question, see Pasquali (2011).

80 Garric (2004).

81 Poletti, "Osservazioni . . ." as in Chapter 10 n. 8.

82 *Il Tiberino*, 15 March 1834, pp. 34–35; Stefanucci Ala (1869), p. 215.

83 Luigi Poletti, [Dialogo con Vitruvio], n.d. (BCALP: LP17 C1).

84 See also Groblewski (2001), pp. 247–249.

85 Botta (1824); Luigi Poletti to Geminiano Poletti, 6 November 1824 (BCALP: LP23a C8).

86 Amid a vast literature, see Momigliano (1950); Banti (2000); De Francesco (2013).

87 Guarnacci (1785–1787); BCALP: POL C 1317 and 1318.

88 Cuoco (1804–1806); Mascioli (1942), pp. 366–368; Ceserani (2010); De Francesco (2013), pp. 29–50.

89 Micali (1810), v. 1, p. 28; v. 4, pp. 242–243; De Francesco (2013), pp. 51–83.

90 De Francesco (2013).

91 Piranesi (1764).

92 Poletti (1835a).

93 Poletti (1838a) and (1838b). In July 1840, Poletti read a second installment, published only in 1864 (Poletti [1864]).

94 Luigi Poletti, Bibliographic notes relating to his *Dissertazioni intorno alle genti e alle arti primitive d'Italia*, 1836 (BCALP: LP14 C2). Poletti's work on the Etruscans received at least one extremely positive review: Gasparoni (1839).

95 Campori (1881), p. 48.

96 By Poletti's day, versions of this theory were becoming commonplace, underlying major works such as Hübsch (1828) or Hope (1835), though an earlier iteration may be found already in the thought of Carlo Lodoli.

97 See Strozzieri (2021), pp. 85–87.

98 See Poletti (1835b).

99 Luigi Poletti, "Architettura Teorica" (ASL course), 1853 (BCALP: LP51 C4 1853; tiSAD pp. 67–74 [quote on p. 74]).

100 The historicist schema of arcuated architecture was expressed in various places: Fortoul (1841), v. 2, pp. 313–333; Vaudoyer and Lenoir (1842); Vaudoyer (1847), pp. 2140–2152. This system has been thoroughly analyzed in Middleton (1986); Van Zanten (1987); and Bergdoll (1994), pp. 109–134.

101 Fortoul (1841), v. 2, p. 332.

102 Strozzieri (2021), pp. 88–91.

103 This paragraph is based on Pasquali (1995); Pinon (1995); Pallottino (1997); and Groblewski (2001), pp. 165–191. On the reception of Early Christian art generally, see Reiss (2008).

104 This problem resurfaced in the early eighteenth century after the Abbé de Cordemoy tried to rehabilitate the Early Christian model (Nyberg [1967]).

105 Petzet (1957); Ruffiniere du Prey (1989).

106 In Spain too, the Early Christian basilica enjoyed renewed attention (Macsotay [2018]).

107 Pinon (1995). Pinon argues that the nineteenth-century French basilican churches were based more on Roman civic basilicae than on Early Christian prototypes.

108 Groblewski (2001), pp. 173–178; Reiss (2008), pp. 100–112.

109 Groblewski (2001), pp.178–182, 572. Cf. also Reiss (2008), pp. 127–135.

110 Minor (2010), pp. 59–90.

111 Milizia (1787), pp. 119–125; Pasquali (1995), pp. 19–20.

112 Poletti owned the Italian edition of Seroux, the complete works of Milizia, and Schinkel's *Sammlung architektonischer Entwurfe*.

113 Uggeri [1833].

114 Pallottino (1997), pp. 340–341; Groblewski (2001), pp. 188–191.

115 Bunsen (1836), pp. 207–281.

116 Bunsen (1836), p. 215.

117 Gutensohn, Knapp, and Bunsen [1842].

118 Cf. Chadwick (1957).

119 Luigi Poletti, "L'Italia moderna," c. 1848 (BCALP: LP27 C1).

120 *CAPDR*, pp. 103–104, n. 2.

121 By 1840, Poletti was addressing Moreschi in their memos as "Luigino," an affectionate diminutive of Luigi (Luigi Poletti to Luigi Moreschi, 24 March 1840 [ASP: 6/b, b. 1840–1841, f. 4]).

122 On Moreschi: *L'Osservatore Romano*, 15 August 1886, p. 3; Tiberia (2015), p. 651. Giorgio Filippi claims to have discovered Moreschi's family archive (Filippi [2004]). Moreschi should not be confused with his contemporary namesake, whose son Alessandro was the last of the Sistine castrati singers (Feldman and Piperno [2011]).

123 "Riassunto dei pagamenti e spese fatte pei lavori delle Basilica di S. Paolo Dal. 11 al 16 9mbre 1833," 16 November 1833 (ASR: CSRBSP Computisteria b. 136); Giuseppe Senatis to Luigi Moreschi, 1 October 1835 (ASP: 6/c, b. 1834–1835, f. 41).

124 *DdR*, 16 October 1830, p. 1.

125 *DdR*, 31 October 1832, p. 1.

126 The site visits of numerous European princes were also described in *DdR*.

127 *DdR* supplement, 28 July 1838, p. 2.

128 *DdR: NdG*, 13 March 1834, p. 1.

129 *DdR* supplement, 22 October 1839, pp. 1–2.

130 *L'ami de la Religion* (Paris), 20 November 1833, p. 134; *Journal historique et littéraire* (Liége), 1 December 1835, p. 433; *GASLA* 60 (July, August, September 1833): 119–130 (quote on p. 129); see also *DdR: NdG*, 7 August 1834, p. 1; *Echo. Zeitschrift für Literatur, Kunst und Mode in Italien* (Milan), 19 August 1834, pp. 395–396; *Morgenblatt für gebildete Leser* (Stuttgart and Tübingen), 25 January 1839, p. 88.

131 *United States Catholic Miscellany* (Charleston), 11 October 1834, p. 118; *Jornal do Commercio* (Rio de Janeiro), 11 July 1837, p. 4.

132 Cf. Ventura (1825d).

ELEVEN

PAUL AND PETER

Poletti's success in loosening the screws on the idea of an exact reconstruction encouraged Pope Gregory and his consiglieri to essay their own changes to the rebuilding basilica. The essence of their adjustments concerned the representation of Paul in his relationship to Peter. In the old basilica, Peter and Paul had been represented as a pair in five main locations from the apse to the west façade, whether in medieval mosaic or baroque statuary. By the consecration of October 1840, all of these representations were (or were projected to be) clustered together in the transept and crossing, whether through relocation, reconstitution from a ruined state, or simply by being rendered more visible:

(1) In the thirteenth-century apse mosaic, Peter and Paul stood to either side of the enthroned Christ. Nearly obliterated by the fire and its aftermath (**Figure 68**), by 1840 they were not only reconstituted but rendered more visible from the nave and crossing by Uggeri's demolition of the transverse wall (**Plate 12**).

(2) The upper part of the old west façade bore fourteenth-century mosaic images of Peter and Paul standing before their respective thrones. These had been taken down when Poletti reinforced the listing façade in 1833 and by 1840 were remounted on the spandrels of the inner face of the triumphal arch facing east into the transept[1] (**Plate 13**).

68. Elevation of the apse of San Paolo fuori le mura in its ruined state, by Angelo Uggeri, 1833. Badly damaged figures of Peter (L) and Paul (R) figured in the apse mosaic to either side of the enthroned Christ. Stucco statues of Peter and Paul stand atop high plinths at the left and right. The baroque altar destroyed by Poletti dominates the middle of the apse.
Source: © Istituto Nazionale di Archeologia e Storia dell'Arte, Rome.

(3) Peter and Paul had also featured in the corner niches on the upper part of Arnolfo's ciborium facing the apse. But when the restored ciborium was unveiled in 1840, it was rotated so that the two apostles now faced prominently into the nave[2] (**Plate 14**).

(4) The fifth-century triumphal arch mosaic had been taken down in 1825, preliminary to the reconstruction of the arch itself; when it was eventually reinstalled, well after 1840, Peter and Paul again appeared in the lower spandrels facing the nave, restored but essentially as they had been before the fire[3] (**Plate 15**).

(5) And finally there had been colossal stucco statues of Peter and Paul to either side of the apse in the old basilica, dating from around 1600 (**see Figure 68**). New versions of these statues were commissioned in 1834, and around 1838 it was decided that they would instead be installed in front of the two colossal columns that carried the triumphal arch, facing the nave. This work also would be completed only after 1840[4] (**see Plate 15**).

A second component of Gregory's altered program involved changes down at the confessio itself. This was one of the few areas where Pope Gregory rejected Poletti's proposals, and in particular his idea of transferring Arnolfo di Cambio's ciborium to a new baptistry. The "miraculous" survival of the ciborium had been widely offered as proof that the fire carried a message from God – Leo XII had even likened it to the deliverance of Shadrach, Meshach, and Abednego – so it is scarcely surprising that Poletti's suggestion was refused.[5] Nonetheless, God had not extended complete protection, for in 1836 it was deemed necessary to take the ciborium down for restoration. Moreschi described it in a published account of October 1836 as being in pieces in a room off the monastery cloister, where despite it having "for the most part remained prodigiously untouched by the devouring flames of 1823," it was being completely restored with "new works strictly imitating the old."[6] This work entailed digging up at least a part of the floor around the foundations of the ciborium, and while no record exists as to what this turned up, a new sense that deeper digging might expose precious relics seems to have provided the spark for what very soon became a major rethinking of this part of the basilica.

Not long afterward, Moreschi started work on the first of two historical publications, the *Osservazioni sulla sedia pontificale*, which over seventeen pages offered a more or less official presentation of this rethinking.[7] He opened with the by-now familiar story of how the earliest Christian basilicae had taken their form from the civic basilicae of the Romans, and how the Christians had modified the eastern parts of this building type so as to make it better suited to liturgical functions. With reference to various Roman examples, he described how the Early Christians typically added a presbytery enclosing the altar over the confessio, and beyond that, in the apse, the throne of the lead celebrant, flanked by exedras for assisting ministers – just as civic basilicae had had a judge's throne flanked by magistrates' benches. His point was that it had never been the practice in Early Christianity to place an altar in the apse; that practice had originated only in the seventeenth and eighteenth centuries. Moreschi turned then to San Paolo, where the historical sources left little doubt that there too the apse had once contained a pontifical throne rather than an altar. This throne probably dated to Early Christian times, though sources indicated it had been rebuilt by Pope Leo III (795–816). Moreschi then used the sources to reconstruct the old choir, presbytery, and papal throne as they had been before their demolition at the end of the sixteenth century.[8]

None of the facts here were new; it was all already in Nicolai's 1815 monograph, as Moreschi admitted. The aim in rehashing them was to advocate for rebuilding the papal throne and for reconstituting a version of the old arrangements in conformity with the command of Leo XII's Chirograph to remove elements that had been introduced into the basilica "through the whim of a subsequent era." Thus Moreschi proposed that (a) work on the replacement altar Poletti was installing in the apse be halted; (b) a pontifical throne be erected instead in its place; and (c) the altar at the confessio be reoriented so that it faced *versus populum* rather than *ad orientem*, that is, toward the congregation rather than toward the east.[9]

Moreschi presented this study to the Special Commission in late 1837.[10] It was immediately approved and forwarded to the pope, who also approved it and ordered it published. On the very first day of works, a cold morning in February 1838, what was to become an additional feature of the new program came to light. Moreschi had brought several workers to the old confessio along with Poletti's new assistant, Virginio Vespignani, and a contingent of monks from the San Paolo community to begin demolishing the old papal altar and the altar down in the old confessio.[11] The ostensible purpose was so that new foundations for the reerection of Arnolfo's restored ciborium could be laid and the altars reoriented. But Moreschi and the others – perhaps keeping a date they had promised themselves two years earlier when those foundations were first dug up – were also very interested to see what else might be down there. Sure enough, once the workers had broken up the altar down in the confessio, the delegation thrilled to discover several caskets beneath it. Sketches by Vespignani record the scene.[12] These caskets were determined to contain the remains of St. Timothy and various lesser saints. But what emerged next thrilled them even more: a great white marble sarcophagus resting on what was believed to be the floor of the original Constantinian basilica. Its inscription took everyone's breath away (**Figure 69**):

PAULO . APOSTOLO . MART.

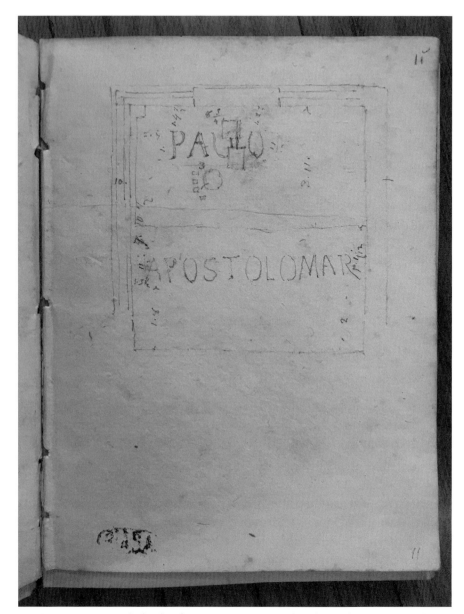

69. Virginio Vespignani's sketches from 18 January 1838, when the confessio at San Paolo was excavated. This sketch depicts the slab bearing the inscription "PAULO APOSTOLO MART." *Source*: © Istituto Nazionale di Archeologia e Storia dell'Arte, Rome.

The sarcophagus was not disturbed. But it was immediately clear that it would now have to be exposed to view as the vital center of the new arrangements in this part of the basilica.[13]

Church tradition holds that Christ chose Peter to hold supreme authority in the Church as the "keeper of the keys" and as the "rock upon which I will build my Church." This, along with Peter's subsequent efforts to build up the early Church, formed the basis of the tradition of the Petrine primacy, which hailed Peter as preeminent among the apostles and styled him Prince of the Apostles. The Petrine primacy formed the basis for the so-called Roman primacy or papal primacy, whereby each Roman pontiff, in a direct "apostolic succession" from Peter, exercised authority over the Church Universal. These traditions had a long and by no means uncontroversial history within the Church, but in the consolidated version of Catholic tradition that emerged from the Counter-Reformation, the doctrines of Petrine primacy and the apostolic succession became the crux of Catholicism's claim to represent the true Church. The sixteenth-century rebuilding of St. Peter's basilica was a spectacular affirmation of this claim.

But at the same time, Catholics in Rome had a long tradition of depicting Peter and Paul as equals.[14] The tradition of the *concordia apostolorum* first established itself in the late fourth century, in the context of the Roman Church's efforts to provide a rationale for Roman primacy at a time when, following the death of the Emperor Constantine, it was under threat from the removal of the imperial capital from Rome to Constantinople, among other factors.[15] The result in Rome at both the official and the popular levels was a reframing of the story of Peter and Paul that depicted them as the emblems of Roman primacy. The argument went like this: Peter and Paul, the greatest of Christ's earliest followers, had been pulled by divine providence from faraway lands to converge at Rome; their presence there at the exact same time (according to tradition) was no coincidence but rather proof of God's plan that the capital of the world should now become the capital of Christianity; this was then confirmed when Peter and Paul were both martyred in Rome on the same day (again according to Roman tradition).[16] God had thereby anointed Rome as his capital with the blood of two supreme martyrs, whom he then planted in the Roman soil as permanent emblems of this. In so doing, the divinely guided actions of Peter and Paul had appropriated for the Church the all-conquering prestige and power of Rome and its historic empire – something no other city could offer. The Empire had united the world, but the simultaneous martyrdoms of Paul and Peter revealed God's plan that civic unity should now give way to religious unity. Leo the Great had even spoken of them as the Romulus and Remus of Christian Rome, preaching to a Roman congregation that Peter and Paul "are your holy Fathers and true shepherds, who [...] built you under much better and happier auspices than they, by whose zeal the first foundations of your walls were laid."[17] It was no coincidence that 29 June, the supposed date of their double martyrdom and thus their shared feast day, was the date when pagans had celebrated Romulus and Remus's foundation of Rome.[18] The martyrdoms of Peter and Paul constituted a Christian refoundation of the city.

A significant early literature was devoted to this tradition.[19] Its common thread was an insistence on the unity, equality, mutual necessity, and *concordia* of the two apostles. In a sermon composed for the joint feast day of Peter and Paul, St. Augustine declared of them, *Illi duo unum erant* ("These two were as one").[20] Leo the Great had preached that

> God's Grace has raised [Peter and Paul] to so high a place among the members of the Church, that He has set them like the twin light of the eyes in the body, whose Head is Christ. About their merits and virtues, which pass all power of speech, we must not make distinctions, because they were equal in their election, alike in their toils, undivided in their death.[21]

St. Ambrose wrote a hymn about it:

> Peter is the first Apostle,
> and Paul is no less in grace;
> the vessel of holy election
> rivals the faith of Peter. [...]
>
> One would think the whole world comes forth,
> that the people of heaven converge:
> chosen city, the head of the nations!
> the seat of the teacher of the nations![22]

Ambrose's reference to Peter as head and Paul as teacher is echoed in countless contemporary reflections on the complementary gifts of the two apostles, with Peter often associated with power and Paul with doctrine, or with Peter identified as the Shepherd and Paul as the Guide.[23]

The providential Roman martyrdoms of Peter and Paul elevated them into the city's *protettori principali*, that is, its coprotectors and patron saints, a status that was constantly represented in Roman art but also deeply embedded in Roman popular culture. The two apostles appear together in sculpted form at several prominent points around the city: Clement VII had installed statues of Peter and Paul to guard one end of the Ponte Sant'Angelo; Sixtus V placed statues of Peter and Paul atop Trajan's Column and the Column of Marcus Aurelius in the urban center; Alexander VII had installed statues of Peter and Paul to guard the northern entrance to the city on the exterior face of the Porta del Popolo. When Valadier rebuilt the Milvian Bridge in 1805, there were plans to place Peter and Paul statues at the northern entrance to the bridge, although they were never executed.[24] And there were countless other reminders of their indissoluble bond. For instance, the two columns on which according to tradition Peter and Paul had been flagellated on the day of their martyrdom were preserved to the left and right of the altar in the chapel of Saints Peter and Paul in the church of Santa Maria in Traspontina.

The ever-present reality of their protection of Rome, and thus of Rome's primacy, was above all manifested in the permanent presence of their sacred remains beneath the pavements of their respective basilicae; basilicae that, in their original incarnations, had borne a close resemblance to one another. Prudentius described how together they hallowed "the Tiber marshland":

> Tiber separates the bones of the two and both its banks are consecrated as it flows between the hallowed tombs. The quarter on the right bank took Peter into its charge and keeps him in a golden dwelling ... Elsewhere the Ostian Road keeps the memorial church of Paul, where the river grazes the land on its left bank ... There you have the two dowers of the faith, the gift of the Father supreme, which He has given to the city of the toga [i.e., pagan Rome] to reverence.[25]

The fourth-century St. John Chrysostom spoke in similar terms in one of his homilies on Paul's letter to the Romans:

> Not so bright is the heaven, when the sun sends forth his rays, as is the city of Rome, sending out these two lights into all parts of the world. From thence will Paul be caught up, from thence Peter. Just bethink you, and shudder at the thought of what a sight Rome will see, when Paul arises suddenly from that deposit, together with Peter, and is lifted up to meet the Lord. What a rose will Rome send up to Christ! What two crowns will the city have about it! What golden chains will she be girded with! What fountains possess! Therefore I admire the city, not for the gold, not for the columns, not for the other display there, but for these pillars of the Church.[26]

Tradition held that Pope Sylvester I had urged Constantine to build the Vatican and Ostian basilicas at the same time and then endured the liturgical marathon of consecrating them both, one after the other, on the same day – 18 November 325 – on which date their consecrations were thereafter commemorated.[27] A common belief since the Middle Ages even held that the remains of the two apostles had been mingled at their two Roman basilicae – the *limina apostolorum* – and this claim was kept alive in the literature on San Paolo at least into the 1860s.[28]

Moreschi's publications confirm that the new concentration of prominent pairings of Peter and Paul in the rebuilt transept at San Paolo aimed to direct the knowledgeable viewer's mind toward these kinds of venerable traditions.[29] His monograph on Arnolfo's ciborium opened with a citation from the early Christian priest Caius, who had written that in Rome one could "point out the trophies of the Apostles; for if you go to the Vatican or walk along the Ostian way, you will encounter the tombs of those who founded this Church."[30] Pope Gregory repeated the passage in 1840 in his allocution at the consecration of the transept and high altar at San Paolo. The sense of Peter and Paul's equality would have been most palpable in the most visible of these representations: the two great statues that fronted the colossal columns of the Arch of Placidia, which presented the apostles as Chrysostom's two indispensable pillars of the Church upon which the stability of the whole ecclesiastical edifice must depend.

Every year after 1840, the biggest day of the year at the reopened San Paolo was the feast day of the Commemoration of St. Paul, which fell on 30 June, one day after the annual feast day of Peter and Paul was celebrated at St. Peter's. When in 1841 the two festivals were finally celebrated on consecutive days at the two basilicas for the first time since 1823, Moreschi published a commemorative book, the centerpiece of which was a twelve-page reflection on the significance of the event. This hymned the "conjunction of the souls and works of these two supreme champions of the Christian religion" and their "union in labor, hardship, and in death," and recalled the resonant formulation of St. Augustine (*Illi duo unum erant*).[31] It reminded readers of how these near-simultaneous martyrdoms had cemented the legitimacy of the papacy and permanently fused the Catholic Church to the Eternal City. In the long reports on the reconstruction that Moreschi was to publish in the *Diario di Roma* every year, always a day or two after the festival of the Commemoration of Paul, his dominant theme again and again was the unity of Peter and Paul and their role as protectors of the city and Church:

> The entire Christian Orb is, and will always be, penetrated with most pious sentiments of obsequious gratitude towards the great Apostles Peter and Paul, who interceded before our Great God, that he might liberate this eternal city from the horror and the obstinate anarchy by which it was brutally mishandled and oppressed . . . [from 1850, after the defeat of the Roman Republic of 1849].[32]

> . . . this Realm that is protected and defended by those two impregnable towers that are the two august basilicae on the banks of the Tiber, where their mortal remains are jealously guarded, and with the complete respect of the entire universe venerated [1853].[33]

> [N]ow that they are both in heaven, universally regarded as keeping vigilant watch over the Catholic Church, all glory and honor that is offered and consecrated here on earth to one of them must be given also to the other with the same equality and respect, especially in this metropolis of Christianity [1854].[34]

An essential function of the highlighted presence of Peter and Paul at San Paolo was thus to reaffirm the providential status of Rome as the world capital of Christianity and the special protection it enjoyed as a result. Setbacks there may be, it proclaimed, but Rome as the divinely chosen metropolis of Christianity could never really be threatened, thanks to their vigilant protection.

But this was not the only significance of the changes. The heightened presence of Peter and Paul was also linked to ideas about the nature of papal authority then in the ascendant in Pope Gregory's orbit.[35] The pontiff's views on this question had been expressed with remarkable consistency across his career, with two related themes predominating. One was nostalgia to reinstate the old regime, a longing typically referenced in the post-Napoleonic context as the alliance of "throne and altar." For example, in *Mirari Vos* (1832) Gregory had enjoined European princes to "understand that they receive their authority not only for the government of the world, but especially for the defense of the Church," and urged them to "persuade themselves that they owe more to the cause of the faith than to their kingdom."[36] The historical pope most identified with this kind of complementarity – between a hegemonic Church and sanctified civil institutions – was Leo III, celebrated in Church history for having completed the work of Constantine by crowning Charlemagne Holy Roman Emperor and inviting him to be the protector of the Church. It was thus significant when Moreschi repeatedly reminded his readers that Leo had been responsible for the final iteration of the original pontifical throne at San Paolo, for this linked the new arrangement to the recuperation of Leo's legacy.

Michael Groblewski has suggested that this throne and altar theme was also evoked by Poletti's design of the throne itself, in which the seat recalls a table and the backrest an altarpiece[37] (**Plate 16**). Groblewski notes that the ceremonies by which popes were enthroned deliberately blurred the lines between thrones and altars and points out that Poletti's removal of the old baroque altarpiece had exposed a hitherto hidden and, in this context, significant element of the medieval apse mosaic: a depiction of the *Hetoimasia*, or empty throne of the Second Coming, decorated with the instruments of the passion (**Figure 70**). Reexposed to view, this mediated between the enthroned Christ in the main part of the mosaic and the enthroned pope directly below, even as the altar-like architecture of the pope's throne implied that the pope was the proxy of God. All of this would have been fully in accord with Gregory XVI's writings on the subject of papal authority.

The second major theme characterizing Gregory XVI's political worldview was ultramontanism. If the throne and altar alliance represented the past, ultramontanism represented the future and would soon replace the vision of a Church-state partnership with that of an independent Church capable of defending itself against the encroachments of national governments it no longer trusted. Nineteenth-century ultramontanism held that the authority of the Roman Catholic Church should be centralized administratively in the

70. Detail of the apse mosaic at San Paolo, showing the *Hetoimasia* in the lower register at the center of the mosaic.
Source: Author.

Curia and theocratically in the pope, free of interference from civil governments and with local clerical authority minimized. The roots of ultramontanism lay in seventeenth- and eighteenth-century efforts to favor the authority of Rome in adjudicating national ecclesiastical controversies; its opponents had been any group aiming to check the reach of papal power, and above all the powerful national Catholic Churches of France and later Austria, which under the banners of Gallicanism and Josephinism insisted on autonomy and self-government. But with the decline of the national churches after the French Revolution and Napoleon, ultramontanism became the new organizational model for the international Church.[38]

In the closing decades of the eighteenth century, the future Gregory XVI, then still a thirty-something monk named Mauro Cappellari, composed a polemic entitled *Il Trionfo della Santa Sede*, which offered a learned theological demonstration that Christ had instituted the papacy as an absolute authority and that the pope was infallible.[39] The continuity between the worldviews expressed in *Il Trionfo* and in Gregory's encyclicals like *Mirari vos* and *Singulari nos* is clear. By Gregory's pontificate, ultramontanist ideas had been taken up as one of the pillars of the Romantic Catholicism associated with figures like de Maistre, Bonald, Ventura, and the early Lamennais. *Il Trionfo* made little impact when first published, but it was reissued in a much larger printing after Gregory became pope. ("After I became pope, everyone agreed that it was a magnificent work," Gregory quipped.)[40] It soon became a kind of vision statement for a Roman hierarchy actively working to refound the Church as independent and capable of protecting its interests in the post-Napoleonic political order. Here is *Mirari Vos* again:

> Remember that ... the government and administration of the whole Church rests with the Roman Pontiff *to whom the full power of nourishing, ruling, and governing the universal Church was given by Jesus Christ*, as the Fathers of the Council of Florence solemnly declared.[41]

The emblematic figure here was a different Leo: Leo I (440–461), also known as St. Leo the Great, so prominently named on the mosaic inscription of the triumphal arch that stood over the confessio at San Paolo. Gregory quoted him as saying that "*the discipline of the Canons is given to the Roman Pontiff alone, and it is for him alone, and not for any private person, to define anything about the rules of the Church fathers.*"[42] Gregory made the ultramontanist case for this kind of papal absolutism even more explicitly in 1835, in *Commissum Divinitus*: "It is a dogma of faith that the pope, the successor of Saint Peter, Prince of the Apostles, possesses the primacy not only of honor but also of authority and jurisdiction in the universal Church." Again he quoted Leo I: "to one alone is entrusted the power to preside over all."[43]

In light of pronouncements like these, the revamped core of the basilica invites interpretation as an imperial setting for an imperial pontiff or even as an imperial throne room.[44] (In his teaching, Poletti often employed a truncated etymology to remind his students that the word "basilica" meant "house of the king.")[45] The enthroned pontiff was to bask at San Paolo in a setting saturated with evidence of the papal primacy. First, he was surrounded by images of Peter and Paul, whose presence in Rome guaranteed the city's primacy within the Church and the world. The certainty that his absolute power was firmly rooted in tradition was vouched for by the ancient inscriptions and venerable objects in the basilica, which related to the same sainted popes that contemporary ultramontanism looked to for support. The (restored) papal portrait medallions populating the interior perimeter offered an emphatic demonstration of the unbroken Petrine succession from Peter to the present. And finally, Peter and Paul were present in a more tangible sense as well: Paul was there in person, in the form of his sacred body beneath the pavement, while Peter was there in the guise of the living pope sitting on his throne. Each reinforced the other, their joint protection of Rome forming the precondition for their status as pillars of the Church, referenced by the colossal statues standing before the triumphal arch. It was a setting that deployed history not to recreate the past superficially as envisaged by Leo XII's Chirograph but to demonstrate that the past authorized and authenticated contemporary ambitions.

In all the carefully footnoted documentation provided by Moreschi to prove that these transformations at San Paolo actually returned things to the way they had originally been, it is easy to detect a certain anxiety. Moreschi's other

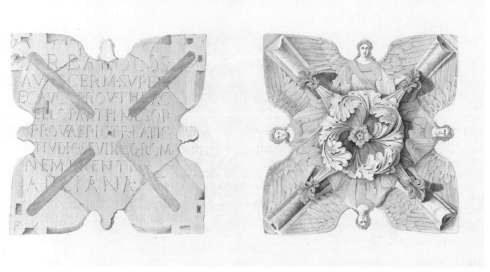

71. Engraving showing the Early Christian inscriptions discovered on the underside of one of the keystones of Arnolfo di Cambio's ciborium at San Paolo fuori le mura when it was restored in 1836–1840 – one of several such examples (from Moreschi [1838b]).
Source: Getty Research Institute, Los Angeles (85-B17567).

publication during these years was an illustrated monograph on Arnolfo's ciborium, and even this he managed to draw into his theme of the return to origins. The book disclosed that when the ciborium had been disassembled for restoration, many of its stones turned out to be spolia with Early Christian inscriptions on their versos[46] (**Figure 71**). Thereby even Arnolfo's medieval canopy became a witness to Early Christian origins. Moreschi further bound the ciborium into this history when he reported that the two figures on the spandrels facing the apse had been identified as the emperors Constantine and Theodosius, the founders of the first and second basilicas. Anita Moskowitz has pointed out that pre-1823 engravings do not appear to show these figures anywhere and registers her suspicion that they (along with some others) are nineteenth-century fabrications.[47] If this is correct, they would offer further testimony to the obsession here with affixing contemporary ideals to ancient proofs. The visitor to this rebuilt transept entered a setting that somehow claimed to be *even older* than the basilica it replaced. This willful anachronism echoed the conceptual model laid out by Leo XII's Chirograph of 1825 but transcended it with an obsessive documentary indexicality.

*
* *

The changes at San Paolo in the 1830s also implied a shift in the traditional view of Peter and Paul's respective importance for the Church Universal. During the Reformation, when authority within Christianity had been the central topic of concern facing the Roman Church, Peter provided the essential guarantee of Catholic and especially papal authority in the face of Protestant assaults. This lent impregnable prestige to the doctrine of the Petrine Primacy. The fire at San Paolo, however, and especially the manner in which it spared Paul's tomb, had been read from the start as a divine exhortation to reflect upon *Paul's* legacy, and upon what it might offer the Church in its battles against the new challenges of the nineteenth century. That legacy revolved around two poles: Paul's elaboration of a rigorous theology capable of persuading nonbelievers to enter the Church; and his peripatetic efforts as Apostle to the Nations to spread the gospel, grow the Church, and correspond with fledgling Christian communities around the Mediterranean. In both aspects, he offered an obvious model – and a far more topical one than Peter – for a nineteenth-century Church that hoped to reverse its decline, combat seductive new doctrines, and revive its global missionary presence.

It is worth considering, then, whether the sense of parity between Peter and Paul projected by the new work at San Paolo might also have affirmed a new status for Paul vis-à-vis Peter with respect to the Church's battle with its modern enemies.[48] The key to this reading lies in how this work extended Augustine's *Illi duo unum erant* from the tombs of the two apostles to the two basilicae that contained them, by first giving visibility to the confessio containing Paul's body, and by then installing a papal throne beyond that. In advocating for the recreation of the throne, Moreschi pointed out that the new St. Peter's, even though built in the Renaissance, retained its old arrangement of confessio and cathedra through Bernini's addition of the Cathedra Petri, which was believed to contain the original wooden throne of Peter.[49] Moreschi's point was that the construction of a new papal throne at San Paolo would highlight the fraternal bond that joined the two basilicas, both of which would now be centered on both a throne and a body. What Moreschi was advocating was not novel; it represented instead a return to the very old special relationship of the *limina apostolorum*. Already in the fourth and fifth centuries, the area comprising the confessio, transept, and apse at San Paolo had been configured in imitation of St. Peter's, and when this area was altered at St. Peter's during the Middle Ages, San Paolo was altered in response.[50] The sense of a long historical affinity between the two basilicae was axiomatic by the nineteenth century, and it was repeatedly invoked at the consecration ceremony for San Paolo in 1840; indeed, a liturgy was revived for it that had not been used since Clement VIII consecrated the papal altar at St. Peter's in 1594.[51]

The Counter-Reformation logic at new St. Peter's conceived that the most essential story about the Catholic Church was one that revolved around Peter. The new work at San Paolo in the 1830s implies a shift toward understanding the story of the Catholic Church as necessarily a very

Roman story that involved both Peter *and* Paul: a story of both head and teacher, of Petrine legitimacy supported by Pauline theology and evangelism, together constituting a Roman papacy absolute in its authority and infallible in its doctrine. The seed of such an image had already been implicit in old San Paolo, in the pairing of Paul's entombed body with the papal portrait medallions that lined the basilica's walls. But now it became explicit in the juxtaposition of Paul's body with the living body of Peter's current successor seated on the new papal throne, orbited by representations from across the centuries that showed the two apostles as an equal pair.[52] Such imagery invited the viewer to meditate on the distinct gifts each apostle offered the Church. Early Christian writers had recorded how Peter opened the doors of paradise to those whom Paul had instructed, or how Peter had founded the *ecclesia ex circumcisione* and Paul the *ecclesia ex gentibus*.[53] Such reflections by the 1830s might have had a more historical inflection, hinging for instance on how each apostle defended the Church at different historical moments and in the face of different challenges. Peter the rock offered an image of tradition, place, situatedness, stability, and above all authority, which had made him the natural lodestar for the Church during the Counter-Reformation. Paul instead represented doctrine, conversion, and the dissemination of infor-mation across space and populations; he was the Glory of the Whole World, the Doctor to the Gentiles, the Apostle to the Nations, who might halt the world's slide into factionalism, indifferentism, even atheism. In what was shaping up to be a century of ideologies, Paul curated the Church's armory of persuasion.

Such meditations likely had personal resonance for Pope Gregory. From 1826 until his election to the papacy in 1831, Gregory had been Prefect of the Congregation of the Propaganda Fide and thus oversaw the Church's missionary presence in the world. In that position, he had reversed seventy-five years of declining Catholic missionary activity, during which Catholic missions had been increasingly challenged by better-funded Protestant counterparts.[54] This was partly why he chose Gregory for his regnal name: Gregory the Great was famous for having reenergized mis-sionary efforts on the European periphery.[55] As part of his work, Gregory XVI had nominated numerous bishops to fill long-vacant sees outside Europe, while issuing instructions on matters as diverse as the validity of marriages in Tonkin, the celebration of masses in Bosnian Muslim house-holds, or whether local civic ceremonies in Siam were pagan. These efforts self-consciously evoked Paul's pastorality toward early Christian commu-nities in places like Corinth and Thessalonica, where he consulted on the appointment of elders and matters of doctrinal dispute. Gregory continued this work as pope, and by his death was credited with a global reinvigor-ation of Catholic missionary activity.[56] The central bas-relief of Gregory's tomb in St. Peter's depicts him resting one hand on a globe and gesturing

72. Detail of Gregory XVI's tomb in St. Peter's basilica. The bas-relief depicts Gregory resting one hand on a globe and gesturing with the other to a cross, surrounded by kneeling Middle Eastern and Asian neophites. The door below is framed in Egyptian alabaster.
Source: Author.

with the other to a cross, surrounded by kneeling Middle Eastern and Asian neophytes[57] (**Figure 72**).

From his own history, then, Gregory would have been susceptible to interpreting the divine message of the San Paolo fire as one centering on Paul's special legacy for the modern Church. The reorganized transept at Paul's basilica offers a first, but by no means the last, statement of the idea that Peter and Paul *together*, according to their different gifts, not only protected the Holy City but guaranteed the greater glory of an emphatically *Roman* Church.

262 REIMAGINED SACRED HISTORIES

NOTES

1 *DdR* supplement, 22 October 1839, pp. 1–2.
2 Moskowitz (1998).
3 The reinstallation occurred in 1852; see Moreschi (1852).
4 Giacoletti (1840). As late as 1836, the plan was still to install the statues where their prefire counterparts had been (Melchiorri [1836]). For a highly detailed analysis, though in some details still inconclusive, see Bagnarini (2015).
5 *TEPD*, v. 3, p. 30.
6 *DdR* supplement, 29 October 1836, pp. 1–4.
7 Moreschi (1838a). In parallel with the account that follows, see Groblewski's interesting analysis (Groblewski [2001], pp. 198–211).
8 Moreschi (1838a), pp. 3–16. These elements were demolished when Pontifical Masses were reintroduced at San Paolo, requiring this part of the church to accommodate more people. Moreschi's historical analysis was based on Crescimbeni (1715), Cicognara (1823), Seroux d'Agincourt (1823), and Nibby (1825).
9 Moreschi (1838a), pp. 14–20. Note that Uggeri had also considered reviving the earlier arrangement; see Groblewski (2001), pp. 138–148; fig. 87.
10 *CAPDR*, p. 78.
11 *Cronaca* II, 9 February 1838. For Moreschi's *verbale* of this incident, see Filippi (2006).
12 Virginio Vespignani, "Confessione di S. Paolo" [notebook], 9 February 1838 (BiASA: MS Lanciani 2); Lanciani (1919); Filippi and de Blaauw (2000); Filippi (2004) and (2006); Barucci (2006), pp. 162–164; Camerlenghi (2018), pp. 274–280.
13 The monastery chronacle reports that the Tiber flooded two weeks after this discovery. Belli's success may well have saved Paul's tomb from an inundation that would surely have led to further fevered prophesies (*Cronaca* II, 27 February 1838).
14 For a nineteenth-century reflection on this, see De Maumigny (1863), pp. 288–303.
15 Huskinson (1982), p. 1.
16 Pietri (1961), pp. 296–301.
17 Leo the Great, Sermon 82 (www.newadvent.org/fathers/360382.htm).
18 Erbes (1899), p. 37; Cullmann (1952), p. 116.
19 My examples of this literature are drawn from Pietri (1961).
20 Augustine of Hippo (1994), p. 201 (sermon 295); see also sermon 297 (p. 218).
21 Leo the Great, Sermon 82 (www.newadvent.org/fathers/360382.htm).
22 Ambrose of Milan, "Apostolorum passio [aka De SS. Petro et Paulo Apostolis]," in Dunkle (2016), p. 229.
23 For other examples, see Prudentius (1953), v. 2, pp. 135–137 ("Peristephanon Liber [Crowns of Martyrdom] ch. 12: Passio Apostolorum Petri et Pauli [The Passion of the Apostles Peter and Paul]"; Pietri (1961), pp. 293–295; Weidmann (2018), p. 354.
24 For details, see Guattani (1806), p. 7; Nibby (1837), v. 2, pp. 582–583.
25 Prudentius (1953), v. 2, pp. 323–325, 327.
26 Saint John Chrysostom, "Homily XXXII on the Epistle to the Romans," in Schaff (1889), v.11, p. 562.
27 This tradition is cited in *Cronaca* III, p. 32.
28 Cacchiatelli and Cleter (1865), v. 1, unpag. (text accompanying the plate, "Confessione di San Paolo"). For a nineteenth-century believer in this tradition, see Dalmières (1846), p. 491. More generally, see *DESE* v. 38, "Limina Apostolorum," pp. 221–233.
29 Indeed, Leo XII had already invoked Paul as the "companion in the merits and glories of Peter" when he launched the reconstruction in *Ad plurimas* (1825).
30 The passage occurs in Caius's "Disputation against Proclus." Moreschi's monograph was published in two volumes: Moreschi (1838b) [plates] and (1840a) [text].
31 Moreschi (1841).
32 Moreschi (1850), p. 603.

PAUL AND PETER

33 Moreschi (1850), pp. 585–586.
34 Moreschi (1854), p. 615. Many other examples could be adduced.
35 Groblewski offers a developed interpretation of this theme (Groblewski [2001], pp. 211–218).
36 *TEPD*, v. 3, p. 178.
37 Groblewski (2001), pp. 205–206. The reciprocity between altar and throne had also been a theme of the dedicatory epistle that Lelio Guidiccioni affixed to his poem, "Ara Maxima," on Bernini's baldacchino at St. Peter's (Guidiccioni [1992]).
38 This was helped by the 1814 restoration of the Jesuit order, one of the doctrine's strongholds.
39 Cappellari (1799). On the history of this text, see Korten (2016).
40 Korten (2016), p. 21.
41 *TEPD*, v. 3, p. 172. Emphasis in the original text.
42 *TEPD*, v. 3, pp. 172–173. Emphasis in the original text.
43 *TEPD*, v. 3, p. 227.
44 Groblewski (2001), pp. 197–209.
45 Poletti, 1853 ASL course, as in Chapter 10 n. 99; Campori (1881), p. 41.
46 Moreschi (1838b) and (1840a).
47 Moskowitz (1998), pp. 91–95; Moreschi (1840a), p. 68. Not everyone was fooled. The correspondant for *The Catholic Magazine* of London dryly described the restored ciborium as "similar" to the old one (cited in *Bengal Catholic Herald* [Calcutta], 13 March 1841, pp. 11–13).
48 The doctrine of the Petrine Primacy was continually in the crosshairs of Protestant critics. A long-running polemic about whether Peter had ever even been to Rome was to flare up again in the early 1840s.
49 Moreschi (1838a), p. 10.
50 For this history, see Camerlenghi (2013).
51 Moreschi (1840b), p. 6.
52 See Rolland (1866), p. 88.
53 Pietri (1961), p. 295.
54 Costantini (1948), p. 4. The suppression of the Jesuit Order in 1773 had triggered the decline.
55 Dudden (1905), v. 2, pp. 99–159.
56 *DESE*, v. 45, "Missioni Pontificie," pp. 245–250; Costantini (1948).
57 Moreschi (1857).

TWELVE

MATERIAL HISTORIES

WHEN POLETTI INHERITED THE SAN PAOLO WORKSHOP, HE ALSO inherited the ambiguity between the basilica as a space to be experienced in person and as part of a narrative that circulated informationally. Poletti's appointment seems to represent a resolution in favor of the former, since his new master plan effectively laid to rest the defiant *in pristinum* vision. But it was not quite that simple. For Poletti recognized that the loss of an exact visual congruence between the old and new basilicas left his new building at risk of appearing to have no authentic connection to the original or at best a tenuous one. This concern was indeed already in the air. Here is what a Milanese periodical had to say in 1836:

> A proverb is making the rounds in Rome: that one could construct a new Saint Peter's, but not another San Paolo. Saint Peter's has everything great that human artifice can create, but San Paolo had things that it is not in man's power to repair ... The new Saint Paul's already rises atop the old; it will be majestic and vast, but it is not in man's power to reconstitute it as antiquity left it to him; only Rome the conqueror can provide columns of *salino*, *cipolino*, and porphyry ... Saint Paul's will indeed rise up, just as perhaps one could renovate Saint Peter's; but the most ancient Christian basilica exists no more.[1]

Lamentations like this risked undermining public approval of the reconstruction. Poletti's shrewd response was to compensate the loss of the *iconic* connection with an *indexical* connection. This he did, as we will now see, through a meaningful reuse of marble remains salvaged from the original building. For these refounded the connection between the old and new basilicas as one of physical substance, and proclaimed to visitors that the new basilica still embodied the old.

Poletti's strategy here resonated with the effort to reestablish the authenticity of earlier spatial and liturgical arrangements surveyed in the previous chapter. For in both cases the effect was to elide the novelty of certain contemporary ambitions – perhaps even to the authors of these ambitions – by enveloping them in very old forms and substances. The expressive potential of such strategies depends on the spectator *knowing* that the sign has an indexical relationship to what it represents; otherwise, it would be difficult to distinguish, say, historic marbles from freshly quarried ones, or to know exactly where the historic ones had come from. But when the spectator is informed, a powerful expressivity can emerge from reflection on the links binding sign to object: binding these reused marbles to the events and personages to which they had been witness, down to the fire itself. The rebuilt building thereby took on an historical authenticity that was at once ancient and new.

The first part of this chapter will first explore the advantages, drawbacks, and consequences of Poletti's decision to redeploy the marbles of the old basilica in this way. The middle parts will then consider two other features of the reconstruction where meaning also derived from the provenance of the stones that composed them. Remaining attentive to how indexicality inspires an experience that feels objective but which depends on knowledge and interpretation, we will explore why public response to these features proved harder to control than was likely anticipated. The chapter concludes with the 1840 consecration of the transept and high altar, as a capstone to these stories about how meaning can inhere in physical matter.

Poletti was not the first to feel that material indexicality rather than an iconic replica reconstruction would be the most effective way to conjure the old basilica in the new. Valadier's proposed designs of 1823–1824 bore no physical resemblance to the old basilica but instead foregrounded architectural elements that survived from it. These elements, like the old footprint or the centrality of the confessio, would have been iconic in effect in a replica of the old basilica, but in a neoclassical project like Valadier's they read as indexical. His project really offered only one major iconic sign, and it was gestural rather than precise: the arches atop columns that framed the open court on the site of the old nave (**see Plate 8**). The new basilica envisaged by the Chirograph was thoroughly different. Not completely free of reused elements from the old basilica, it nonetheless did not highlight these as Valadier had proposed to do, nor display them as sensibly out-of-place memorial elements. If the spectator were aware, these surviving walls or columns constituted an indexical connection to the old basilica, but mainly their function would have been to reinforce an iconic relationship. The distinction between replica and reused elements, in other words, would have been read as contingent. Poletti explicitly informed the Special Commission that Belli had not intended to foreground marbles salvaged from the fire in the extensive interior wall revetments he planned: "before I took possession of my current post, no thought whatsoever had been given to the marbles that were to decorate [the interior of the transept], aside from the eight veneered columns."[2] Indeed, those eight columns were really the only significant indexical signs on offer in Belli's design. The other elements of the old basilica that survived in the new – from the mosaics and ciborium to the footprint and foundations – were retained because they reinforced a resemblance, or for reasons of economy.

By the time Poletti took the reins, the basilica – with its Pantheon capitals, unfluted granite columns, and raised floor – was well on its way to being neither iconic nor indexical. Hence the impetus to highlight the reuse of materials as a way to rebind the reconstruction to the old basilica. We have already seen that Poletti deplored the practice of redeploying visibly historic artifacts, preferring to cut up old stones for use as wall revetments. This memorial anointment of the basilica's interior surfaces permitted Poletti to avoid jarring Romantic juxtapositions of new and timeworn artifacts. An exception came on the north porch, which he supported on the old aisle columns; but this exception only proves the rule, for Poletti had those columns uniformly shaved down so that they did not disrupt the modern texture of their new setting.[3] Like the marble revetments on the interior, only the informed visitor realizes they are historic.

And the visitor got this information from reading Moreschi's reports, which repeatedly evoked the pope's excitement at encountering construction teams busily sawing up the basilica's old columns to create revetments and new veneered columns.[4] Poletti and Moreschi thus worked together to assuage any mounting concerns that the new San Paolo had sacrificed its connection to the old.

There was however one problem: the old basilica did not offer nearly enough reusable marble to revet the transept interior.[5] Poletti realized this even before he became architect director, and it was partly why he petitioned to substitute new granite columns in the side aisles: he needed the marble of the old ones to revet the upper walls. Of course, the obvious solution was to quarry more stone, but this was more complicated than it sounds because the quarries for many of the most prestigious old marbles were far away or had been exhausted in antiquity; for instance, porphyry, *pavonazzetto*, *granito rosso*, and *cipollino verde*. Their latter-day extinction was precisely what made them so evocative of Roman antiquity, as the Milanese journalist had pointed out.

Poletti tried at first to find similarly hued varieties from active quarries, but the Special Commission soon offered him an extraordinary assist: it began sending agents out to scour Roman archaeological sites for potentially usable ancient blocks of the no-longer-quarried marbles. Of the numerous fragments they located between 1835 and 1840, often using Faustino Corsi's recent inventory of the city's antique columns, several were ultimately sacrificed to the new basilica.[6] This marked a surprising return to practices of spoliation that had once been common in Rome — much of the marble for St. Peter's had been harvested in this manner — but which had been largely halted in the modern age of archaeology via a succession of pontifical proclamations and edicts between 1800 and 1820.[7] The Special Commission was fortunate here that it did not have to worry about the irascible Carlo Fea, the principal author of those proclamations, who by then was in his final ailing months.

Even without Fea, opposition arose within the pontifical government. In May 1835, Treasurer General Tosti, writing on behalf of the Special Commission, explained to Camerlengo Galleffi that the San Paolo workshop had run short of *pavonazzetto* marble and felt it had no choice but to request the use of eleven fragments of that stone from Trajan's Forum. Tosti let it be known that the request reflected the express wishes of Pope Gregory and assured Galleffi that every effort would be made to limit additional requests.[8] Galleffi consented with "the greatest displeasure" to hand over "those precious remains of ancient Roman munificence," but added that he was "extremely bitter" at having been asked and would not have permitted it if it had been up to him. He "urgently recommended" that "better diligence" be used in future.[9]

Instead, the opposite happened. The Special Commission began bypassing the reluctant Galleffi and, like Poletti, addressed its petitions directly to Pope Gregory, who always approved them.[10] This went on right up to the consecration of the transept and high altar in 1840. On at least one occasion, Galleffi's men caught the Special Commission's contractor red-handed in the Forum sawing up an antique column that had *not* been authorized.[11] (Asked to explain, Poletti professed total ignorance.) Yet after a discrete interval of six weeks, the Special Commission sheepishly requested permission to finish sawing up the column, promising to leave behind whatever they did not need.[12] Galleffi refused: it was virtually the last surviving *cipollino* column fragment at the site, all the others having been consigned to San Paolo, and he was furious about the damage that had already been inflicted on it.[13] Galleffi however died soon after, at which point the president of the Special Commission, Cardinal Gamberini, secretary of state for internal affairs and a member of Pope Gregory's inner circle, made a studied effort to cultivate his successor, Cardinal Giacomo Giustiniani. Gamberini told Giustiniani what a wonderful friend his predecessor had been to the San Paolo project and expressed the hope that he too would prove committed to Pope Gregory's vision. Giustiniani instead continued Galleffi's reluctant approach, at least at first, and at times relations between the two became chilly.[14] But by 1840, with work proceeding hammer and tongs in anticipation of the consecration of the high altar, Giustiniani offered to transfer an entire collection of ancient fragments to San Paolo, including pieces of *Porta Santa, Africano, bigio Africano, cipollino,* and *bigio brecciato*.[15] The offer was gratefully accepted, hurriedly sawn up into revetment panels, and mounted on the transept wall just in time for the ceremony in October.

These events fit into a pattern during Gregory XVI's pontificate of ambiguous official attitudes toward pagan antiquities. Gregory had continued Leo XII's excavations in the Roman Forum, but by 1837 these were winding down. Classical archaeology during Gregory's pontificate was thereafter to be increasingly private, with excavation permits becoming an important source of income for the Fine Arts Commission.[16] Like his successor Pius IX, Gregory seems to have cared less for pagan than for Early Christian Rome – as for instance when *Diario di Roma* described how he went to visit the newly discovered Baker's Tomb at Porta Maggiore in 1838 and then hastened quickly afterward to spend time in the nearby Christian catacombs.[17]

Decades earlier, Pius VII had responded to the traumas of the Repubblica Romana by redoubling archaeological efforts in the city and opening the Museo Chiaramonte to proclaim Rome's universality and providential immunity to change.[18] By Gregory's pontificate, amid continuing unrest in the Papal States and elsewhere in Italy, it was getting harder to believe in such airy conceits. What replaced them, at least for a time, is contained in the story of the marbles spoliated for San Paolo: a willfully anachronistic effort to recapture the muscular confidence of another era. One of the most rapacious epochs for the spoliation of Roman antiquities had been the Renaissance, especially during the reconstruction of St. Peter's.[19] During the fundraising campaign for San Paolo, the earlier campaigns for St. Peter's had offered a dispiriting reminder of just how diminished the Church had become since then. The return now to old practices of spoliation repudiated that sense of modern diminishment, along with the cosmopolitan fetishization of a historicized antiquity. Poletti himself probably felt a bit queasy about these acts of spoliation, but men like Gamberini likely savored them. Clerical conservatives had not forgotten that the Basilica Ulpia (which they repeatedly plundered) had been excavated by the Napoleonic authorities in a campaign that destroyed two churches.[20] The spoliation of marbles unearthed by those excavations for use at San Paolo was surely a satisfying quid pro quo in their eyes.

But practices transplanted from the sixteenth or seventeenth century to the 1830s inescapably saw their meaning transformed. The spoliations for St. Peter's had reflected the principle that Roman ruins spoke of God's providential plan for the Church Universal. Such claims were plausible then because universality was basic to the self-image of the Counter-Reformation Church. The much more limited spoliations of the 1830s occurred instead when the European consensus no longer regarded the Church as universal, and where acts of spoliation flouted the historicist sense that the scientific preservation of old artifacts saved the past from oblivion. Clerics in Rome were under no illusions that they could resuscitate the worldview that had once melted the Pantheon porch vault to make Bernini's baldachin: even the Special Commission confined its requests mostly to broken columns, and even then encountered resistance. It is also significant that none of these spoliations was ever publicized nor incorporated into the public meanings of the rebuilt basilica; all were kept secret.[21] For they were a defiant, if private, assertion by the circles around Gregory that, whatever the world may think, the Church reserved for itself, now as ever, the right to put Roman ruins in God's service however it deemed appropriate. The simultaneous awareness that broader publics saw things differently offers a revealing acknowledgment that the Church's providential history was no longer widely credited. It would have been a bitter acknowledgment, but it tasted of others to come.

We turn now to two other aspects of new work at San Paolo where the provenance of the materials used was significant: the new chapel dedicated to St. Benedict installed by Poletti in the southeast corner of the transept, and the new ciborium he built to stand over the confessio. Both works engaged with long-running debates about ancient history that had entered public consciousness on account of their political implications. The old assumption that ancient history was adequately reflected by the Bible had largely collapsed during the eighteenth and early nineteenth centuries under the twin pressures of universal histories that incorporated China, India, or the Americas and of geological and astronomical discoveries that repositioned human history as a local moment amidst the totality of space and time. These new discourses posed all kinds of problems to Catholic orthodoxy, whose guardians had often anathemized recent discoveries as dangerous invitations to unbelief. These fears were not unfounded: opponents of the Church had often been quick to celebrate their discoveries as fatal blows to Catholic sacred history, from Voltaire in his *Essai*

sur les moeurs et l'esprit des nations of 1756 to Volney in his *Recherches nouvelles sur l'Histoire ancienne* of 1814.[22]

In the 1830s, however, Church intellectuals began a pivot from dismissal to active confrontation. This confrontation eventually yielded several notable acts of artistic patronage, including Gregory XVI's foundation of the first two non-Greco-Roman museums in Rome: the Gregorian Etruscan Museum (1837) and the Gregorian Egyptian Museum (1839), each dedicated to the art and history of an ancient people that had recently come to pose a vexing challenge to traditional Catholic historiography. The two features at San Paolo to be analyzed now also both participated in this cultural shift. If Leo XII's Chirograph represented a negationist concession of the modern to the enemies of the Church, these new endeavors of the 1830s attempted a much more complex renegotiation of past and present.

We saw earlier that one of Poletti's first requests upon becoming architect director concerned the construction of two new chapels to flank those that survived to either side of the apse, and that Gregory XVI approved this request in November 1834.[23] On 4 August 1835, the Special Commission sent a memorandum to the pope asking whether Poletti could make use in one of these chapels of a set of ancient columns stored in one of the Vatican warehouses, noting that it would be "almost impossible" to obtain other ancient columns of the required dimensions from the antiquities dealers of Rome.[24] The columns in question were well known to Roman antiquarians as the smaller of two sets excavated from the ancient city of Veii, near Isola Farnese in the Papal States. The larger set comprised twelve fluted Ionic columns, while the smaller set requested by the Special Commission comprised twelve unfinished Corinthian ones.[25] Luigi Canina was later to assess them all as having been prepared for a small basilica with superposed orders that, for some reason, was never built.[26]

The columns had been sitting in Vatican warehouses since the 1820s and had already been the subject of proposals for reuse. In 1824, none other than Pasquale Belli had made plans to incorporate them into a special exhibition room in the Vatican Museum.[27] In 1833, the Commune of Albano had petitioned Cardinal Camerlengo Galleffi to employ them in its new cemetery. In a memorandum to Gregory XVI explaining his refusal of this request, Galleffi alluded to yet another petition he had previously received, which involved using the columns to decorate the Palazzo delle Poste Pontificie on Piazza Colonna in Rome. In all cases, he wrote, he refused because he thought it important not to break up the set. He urged Gregory instead to hold onto them for eventual display in the Pontifical Museums.[28]

Galleffi's advice notwithstanding, Gregory agreed less than a year later to grant the Special Commission permission to use the smaller set at San Paolo.[29]

Not long afterward, he also released the larger set for use in the same Palazzo delle Poste project that Galleffi had previously refused.[30] What had changed to convince Gregory to reject his Chamberlain's advice?

Veii had been one of the wealthiest cities of ancient Etruria from the eighth to the fourth centuries BCE, and by the nineteenth century its renown was legendary.[31] Nonetheless, the precise location of Etruscan Veii remained shrouded in uncertainty. All that was known was the location of the nearby Roman colony – the *Municipium Augustum Veiens* – which had been built after the Roman conquest. Of the Etruscan city, only isolated artifacts had ever been unearthed. The race to locate it became a cause célèbre in the 1820s, culminating in the success of Antonio Nibby and the Englishman William Gell, who published their discovery in 1832.[32] Etruscan Veii was thus much on people's minds in Rome in the mid-1830s.

The columns that had been requested for San Paolo were not, however, from Etruscan Veii. They had been excavated instead in the 1810s from the Roman colony adjacent to "the Etruscan city of Veii, previously a rival of the Eternal City," as Moreschi put it in the *Diario di Roma*.[33] Giuseppe Melchiorri described them in 1838 as representatives of "the most beautiful period of Roman architecture."[34] Once they were delivered to Poletti, he deployed them in a new chapel dedicated to St. Benedict that took the form of a Roman temple cella of the Imperial era (**Plate 17 and Figure 73**). So what was the provenance of these columns meant to signify?

Etruscan art and objects had come to play an important role in the papal collections over the first decades of the nineteenth century. After the adoption in 1802 of regulations blocking the unauthorized export of antiquities, Etruscan objects had accumulated so rapidly in government warehouses that in 1815 Pius VII opened an Etruscan collection in the Vatican Library.[35] The Pacca Edict of 1820 erected further export prohibitions and was immediately followed by spectacular discoveries in the necropoli of Tarquinia and Vulci, both inside the Papal States.[36] As a result, all through the 1820s and 1830s an ever-growing collection of Etruscan bronzes and terracottas was on display on the first floor of the Vatican Museum.[37] There was a certain awkwardness in celebrating these objects in that setting, given that so much contemporary and recent patriotic scholarship on the Etruscans presented the Roman domination of the Etruscans as an allegory of the Roman Church's subsequent domination of Italy and the foreign occupations it had fostered.[38] The presentation of Etruscan objects at the Vatican was studiously apolitical, but Church leaders were still anxious that they fed a worrisome public fascination. Already minor Etruscan objects had become sought after on the antiquities market by bourgeois buyers attracted by their patriotic associations.[39]

73. The Veii Columns along the south wall of the St. Benedict chapel.
Source: Author.

By the 1830s, however, clerical intellectuals were beginning to recognize that it was hopeless to continue dismissing modern historical scholarship, and that it made more sense to try to absorb it, when possible, into the Church's historiographical teleology. This ambition mirrored a contemporary impulse in clerical intellectual circles to confront recent discoveries in the physical and human sciences. No single factor explains this shift other than perhaps a presentment that to do otherwise was to concede too great an advantage. One of the most eloquent statements of this new outlook came in the public lectures delivered in 1835 in Rome by Cardinal Wiseman and published shortly thereafter, first in English, as *Twelve Lectures on the Connexion Between Science and Revealed Religion* (1836), and then serially in Italian in the *Annali delle scienze religiose* (1837–1838), and then later in French (1843).[40] Wiseman, who at this date was curator of Arabic manuscripts at the Vatican, professor of oriental languages at La Sapienza, and rector of the English College in Rome, led his listeners on an encyclopedic tour of recent developments in comparative linguistics, the natural history of humanity, the natural sciences, ancient history, archaeology, and oriental languages.[41] His goal was to demonstrate

> how the early stage of each [science] furnished objections to religion, to the joy of the infidel and the dismay of the believer; how many [Catholics] discouraged these studies as dangerous; and then how, in their advance, they first removed the difficulties drawn from their

imperfect state, and then even replaced them by solid arguments in favor of religion. And hence we shall feel warranted in concluding that it is essentially the interest of religion to encourage the pursuit of science and literature, in their various departments.[42]

Gregory XVI's museological practice in this period reflected this perspective. After the Camerlengato acquired the spectacular contents of the Regolini-Galassi Etruscan tomb in Cerveteri in 1836 – excavations Poletti had presented to the Istituto di Correspondenza Archaeologica – the idea of a new pontifical museum specifically dedicated to Etruscan objects began to pick up steam. Toward the end of that year, a decision was made to go ahead, and on 2 February 1837 the Gregorian Etruscan Museum was inaugurated[43] (**Figure 74**). This haste is in itself evidence of an appetite for confrontation, for it was driven by the knowledge that a blockbuster Etruscan exhibition was being prepared in London during these same months.[44] The London show was the brainchild of Vincenzo Campanari, a Tuscan archaeologist who had been vainly urging the Vatican to open an Etruscan Museum since at least 1824.[45] Campanari's wildly inventive museography in London included recreated Etruscan tombs, atmospherically darkened and toured by candlelight.[46] His show caused such a sensation that the Trustees of the British

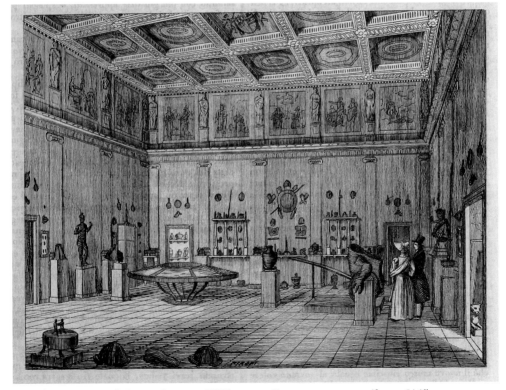

74. The interior of Pope Gregory XVI's new Etruscan museum (from *L'Album*, 24 March 1838).
Source: Getty Research Institute, Los Angeles (85-S84).

Museum ended up purchasing most of the exhibited works, while at least two popular books on ancient Etruria published in the following years credited Campanari's exhibition as their inspiration.[47] The political undertones of the exhibit also played into Italian irredentist hopes, which were well represented in London by a group of exiles headed by Giuseppe Mazzini, who had arrived in London that same year.[48] A show such as this was exactly the sort of appropriation of Italian history that Rome had resolved it could no longer leave unanswered. Gregory's new museum in Rome managed to open just days after Campanari's London exhibition.

In the encomial texts produced by curial intellectuals prior to the inauguration of Gregory's museum, the focus was on one theme: the conquest of Etruria by the Romans. This, it emerged, was how official Catholic historiography was to absorb Etruscan civilization. Like the Roman conquest of the ancient Greeks, the conquest of the Etruscans was presented as a divinely ordained and historically necessary step along the way to the triumph of the Church in the Eternal City. These courtly poems and academic orations presented the new museum as redeeming Etruscan artifacts from their pagan origins and revealing their true significance in sacred history.[49]

The contemporaneous reuse of the Veii columns at San Paolo – columns that were Roman, not Etruscan – makes sense when read against this historiographical framework: they and the chapel they were a part of were meant to evoke *Roman* Veii. They effectively restaged Rome's providential conquest and absorption of Etruscan Veii and, by inference, of Etruscan civilization. And by embedding this historical tableau within Paul's basilica, the chapel pointed ahead to the larger meaning of that conquest in preparing the way for the ultimate triumph of the Church in Rome. This is why Gregory XVI had suddenly become willing to authorize the use of these columns: their use at San Paolo was to participate in a contemporary program enfolding Etruscan history into a larger providential narrative about how Rome's conquests foretold the triumph of the Church.

The use shortly thereafter of the second set of columns at the Palazzo delle Poste confirms this reading. The Palazzo was Gregory XVI's major contemporary urban intervention, occupying a very prominent site in the urban core facing one of Rome's two great ancient victory columns, the Column of Marcus Aurelius (**Figure 75**). The juxtaposition of columns – the Veii set associated with the conquest of the Etruscans, and the historiated one memorializing a Roman triumph – spoke powerfully of the providential plan through which the supremacy of the Church in Rome was prepared. But this was not all. In 1839, shortly after the work at the Palazzo delle Poste was completed, an illustrated article about it appeared in *L'Album* that not only informed the Roman readership that the columns of the new colonnade were from Veii but also dropped the bombshell that the four *central* columns of the façade – the ones

75. Piazza Colonna, Rome, showing the Column of Marcus Aurelius (second century; with a statue of St. Paul at its summit, added by Pope Sixtus V in 1589) and the Palazzo della Posta e Gran Guardia (known today as the Palazzo Wedekind) by Pietro Camporese the Younger with input from Giuseppe Valadier, 1830–1837.
Source: Author.

that flank the projecting central archway – were from the side aisles of old San Paolo.[50] These columns (which remain in place today) were recut with flutes and given Ionic capitals and bases so as to match the Veii columns to either side (**Figure 76**). Clearly, then, the St. Benedict chapel at San Paolo and the Palazzo delle Poste façade were meant to be linked; especially as the sixteenth-century statue atop the Column of Marcus Aurelius represented none other than St. Paul, an emblem of the Church's providential triumph in Rome.[51]

These projects again bear witness to that defiant new willingness in Rome to use antique spolia, although this time the spoliation was openly acknowledged. This was likely because the columns in question were not taken from an archaeological site but had been sitting in a warehouse, already severed for decades from their original context; and because the work that the columns

76. Detail of the Palazzo della Posta e Gran Guardia. The four columns to either side of the central arch were originally in the side aisles at San Paolo. The other columns of the façade portico were excavated from the ancient Roman colony at Veii.
Source: Author.

were to perform – that of bending perceptions of the Etruscans toward orthodox Catholic optics – required publicity.

It is hard to imagine that Poletti could have been behind the decision to use these columns and still less the program of the chapel itself. In the earliest plans attributable to Poletti for this part of the building, the chapel in question is depicted as a generic rectangular space with just two columns flanking the high altar; there is no suggestion of lining the side walls with additional columns (**Figure 77**). We have already seen that Poletti was reluctant to integrate historical artifacts into his designs, and it is telling that at the St. Benedict chapel he gave extraordinarily detailed instructions to his stonecutters for how they should recut the Veii shafts so as to render them precisely identical to one another.[52] As usual, Poletti's primary concern was to preserve the uniformly contemporary texture of the chapel – an attitude that hardly seems compatible with a program that depended for its legibility on a contrast between the historic elements and their contemporary setting.

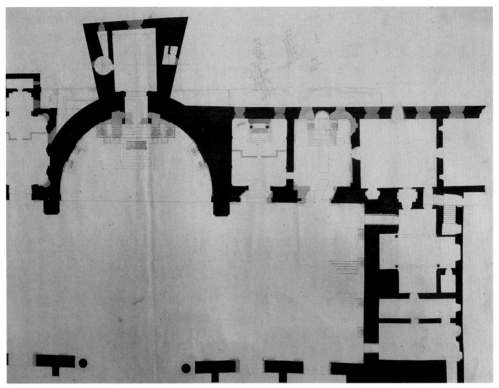

77. Detail of one of Luigi Poletti's first designs for the apse and eastern chapels of the basilica of San Paolo fuori le mura. The chapel that would eventually become the St. Benedict Chapel is the second to the right from the apse.
Source: © 2022 Archivio Storico dell'Abbazia di San Paolo f.l.m.

Moreover, Poletti harbored a powerful enthusiasm for the ancient Etruscans that can only have left him ambivalent about a *concetto* that celebrated their subjugation. Indeed, it was precisely in November 1836, just as the Veii columns were being installed in the chapel, and just as work was rushing forward on the soon-to-be-opened Etruscan Museum, that Poletti stepped to the lectern at the Pontifical Academy of Archaeology to deliver his "Delle genti e delle arti primitive d'Italia." This lecture, as we saw, stridently celebrated the foundational role of the Etruscans in Western art and civilization.[53] The timing cannot have been coincidental. If the chapel's program had been given to Poletti from on high, as part of a larger public program that encompassed the Etruscan Museum and the Palazzo delle Poste, he could hardly have voiced his displeasure openly; the lecture might have been an attempt to express his reservations by other means. When Moreschi wrote in the *Diario di Roma* about Pope Gregory's first visit to the completed chapel, he quoted him as reflecting on the "hard restrictions to which [Poletti] had been forced to conform." The reference was ostensibly to the difficulty of bringing the design into conformity with the fixed dimensions of the Veii columns, but Moreschi may have been subtly acknowledging his friend's distress at the unpalatable program he had been given.[54]

A review of the San Benedetto chapel was published in 1838 by Poletti's friend Giuseppe Melchiorri in his new Roman journal, *L'ape italiana delle belle arti*.[55] Poletti was the only Roman architect to have published previously in *L'ape*, and Melchiorri thanked him here for his "courtesy" in providing his drawings of the chapel to be engraved for this review.[56] Melchiorri may therefore have been privy to whatever ambiguous feelings Poletti harbored regarding the chapel program, and this might in turn explain why the review, extremely complimentary on the whole, adopts a typically Roman kind of linguistic indirection when it comes to speak of the Veii columns. The passage begins diplomatically, as Melchiorri compliments Gregory XVI for "having provided that [the Veii columns] should bring honor to a Christian basilica, as they once did to a pagan one." But then he employs a classic trick of the censored writer: before offering his praise, he makes a show of crocodile tears that *so many people disapproved of such acts*:

> There will always be those who blame this practice; to convert, that is, profane monuments to the ornamentation of Christian temples. But if we leaf through our histories for a moment, and visit our churches, we will only convince ourselves that the greatest number of ancient edifices ... would not have come down to us, especially through the middle ages of barbarism, if they hadn't been protected by the sanctity of religion, veneration for churches, and respect for Christian basilicas.[57]

No one by 1837 could take seriously the claim that the best way to preserve ancient architectural elements was by appropriating them as spolia – especially when the appropriation included a thorough working over by Poletti's stonecutters. By publicly reminding readers that triumphalist spoliation was widely considered inappropriate, and by offering such a weak defense of its revival, Melchiorri slyly registered scruples that may well have echoed those of Poletti himself.

In any event, it would be difficult to qualify the program of the new chapel as much of a success. The referential aspect of the columns was publicized by Melchiorri and Moreschi, but there was no public discussion whatsoever of the chapel's larger intended meaning, its relationship to the Palazzo delle Poste or to Gregory's new museum, nor even to the Catholic rethinking of the Etruscans and providential history. This is probably because public discourse on the Etruscans at this date was so dominated by the patriotic vision of Micali.[58] Poletti's "Delle genti" was in this respect more typical than exceptional. It would have seemed a thankless and perhaps counterproductive task for Church leaders to insist too much on their intended reading in such a climate. The St. Benedict chapel as a consequence ends up seeming inconsequential: an esoteric gesture meaningful to just a small crowd of clerical *cognoscenti*.

We turn now to Poletti's ciborium.[59] When Poletti proposed in 1834 to remove Arnolfo di Cambio's Gothic ciborium to the proposed baptistry, he planned to put in its place a new ciborium of his own design. The aim was to accentuate the old parallel between San Paolo and St. Peter's, where Bernini's baldachin dominates the crossing. But rather than seek to match Bernini in artistry, Poletti prudently opted to challenge him instead with extraordinary materials, and at some point in 1834 or 1835 settled on Egyptian alabaster: a rare and luminescent stone, technically a travertine, characterized by swirling tonalities of butterscotch and milk.[60] This choice emerged from conversations with Silvestro Guidi, an Egyptologist and antiquities dealer who had informed Poletti that the Ottoman Viceroy of Egypt, Mehmet Ali Pasha, had recently reopened the ancient alabaster quarries of Upper Egypt in connection with the building of his new great mosque in Cairo.[61] They agreed that Guidi would enquire with the Viceroy on his next trip about purchasing some of this precious stone. That trip occurred in 1835–1836, but while Guidi was away Pope Gregory vetoed Poletti's ciborium and ordered that Arnolfo's ciborium be kept in its original location.[62] Guidi, in any event, had no luck with the Pasha, who told him that the alabaster was uniquely for his new mosque. At this point, Poletti likely concluded that his idea for an alabaster ciborium was dead.

In fact, the story was just beginning. In October 1838, Pope Gregory sent some gifts to Mehmet Ali in thanks for the protections he had accorded to Catholics in Egypt and Syria.[63] A year later, Guidi's old friend Annibale de Rossetti, the Tuscan consul in Alexandria, took it upon himself to have another crack at getting the Pasha to sell the alabaster Poletti sought, unaware that Gregory had rejected Poletti's ciborium and that the stone was no longer needed. But as luck would have it, Mehmet Ali now changed his mind and decided to offer six alabaster columns as a personal gift to the pope, in recognition of the kind gifts conveyed to him by Gregory the year before.[64] Mehmet Ali's change of heart was almost certainly informed also by geopolitical motives. After years of attempts to gain greater autonomy vis-à-vis his Ottoman overlords, the Pasha in 1839 had launched a breakaway military campaign that conquered most of Syria, Palestine, and the Lebanon.[65] By mid-1839, the Ottoman fleet had defected to Mehmet Ali, and his troops, commanded by his son Ibrahim, stood at the southern edge of Anatolia, begging for permission to push on to Constantinople. Fearing that this would unleash a wider European war, Great Britain bullied together an international coalition that insisted Mehmet Ali relinquish his gains; the Pasha himself was vilified in the European press as a destabilizing barbarian. The offer of the alabaster columns to the pope at this very moment was undoubtedly calculated to drive a wedge into this coalition by winning sympathy from European Catholics. Mehmet Ali was canny enough to remember the global publicity that had attended the fundraising drive for San Paolo in 1825–1832 and to know that a gift as exotic as the one he was offering would receive a lot of press.[66]

Mehmet Ali was lucky in his timing, because during this same period Pope Gregory was falling into the grip of a religious Egyptomania. Scholarship on ancient Egypt had for centuries revolved around the idea that the indecipherable hieroglyphs harbored precious mystical knowledge of long-lost metaphysical truths. In Rome itself, the obelisks imported by the ancient Romans had sustained endless speculative activity in this vein, most famously by Athanasius Kircher in the seventeenth century.[67] During the eighteenth century, however, Egyptian artifacts and culture had been appropriated by one of the Church's most feared enemies, the Freemasons, who located their own origins in the Jewish exile in Egypt and counted ancient Egyptian symbology as an essential point of reference. Their conceits about Egypt came to vibrant political life during the French Revolution, informing aspects of the Revolutionary calendar, the Festival of the Supreme Being, and more.[68] This was why when Champollion deciphered the Egyptian hieroglyphs some thirty years later, clerical intellectuals in Rome leapt at what they saw as an opportunity to finally disentangle the "true" Egyptian history – which they felt sure would conform to the Bible – from Masonic fantasies. Champollion was invited to examine the Vatican collection of papyri and raved in a letter to his brother that Leo XII had told him "three times that I had rendered a beautiful, great, and good service to Religion through my discoveries."[69] But despite Leo's optimism, some in the Church still worried about what an unlocked Egyptian antiquity might add to the mounting evidence that the past exceeded the bounds of Biblical history.[70] Thus Michelangelo Lanci, chair in Arabic at La Sapienza, published a book in 1825 attacking Champollion's system and insinuating that, if correct, it would completely undermine sacred history.[71] And so by the 1830s, the main impact of Champollion's success lay outside of Rome, where Egypt had been integrated into secular narratives of civilizational development.[72] It was this secular appropriation of the Egyptians, more than the Masonic one, that finally prompted Rome to respond. Just as Etruria was to be neutralized via its integration into providential history, so too was Egypt, which henceforth was to be regarded in official Rome as an old and familiar chapter in sacred history for which new tools of understanding had now appeared. The point of departure came when Champollion's Italian disciple, Ippolito Rosellini, convinced Gregory XVI in 1833 to support the publication of the multivolume *Monumenti dell'Egitto e della Nubia* (1832–1844), which recorded the 1829 Franco-Tuscan expedition to Egypt.[73] Rossellini succeeded by assuring Gregory that the new Egyptology would offer empirical proofs of sacred history.[74] Gregory was eagerly persuaded: not only did he agree to support the *Monumenti*, but he also issued instructions to his Camerlengo to suspend all purchases for the pontifical art collections *aside from* Egyptian ones. For years the Egyptologist Guidi had been vainly trying to interest the Camerlengato in the treasures he periodically shipped to his warehouses in Rome; government buyers now abruptly cleaned him out. Gregory even authorized the use of his own personal funds.[75] By 1835, Wiseman's lectures were celebrating the confirmations of sacred history Rossellini's scholarship had yielded. One now read periodically in the *Diario di Roma* about academic papers that used the new Egyptology to pinpoint things like the exact location where the Israelites had been dwelling when Moses led them out of Egypt.[76] For "many remote facts of Egyptian history correlate to those of Hebrew history, and add new proofs of credibility to the Holy Scriptures," as Moroni wrote in his *Dizionario*.[77] The new Roman Egyptomania climaxed on 2 February 1839 with the opening of the Gregorian Egyptian Museum, one floor below the Etruscan Museum, leading Rosellini's associate, Luigi Ungarelli, to observe that the pope was "full of fervor for matters Egyptian"[78] (**Figure 78**). In opening the museum, Gregory proclaimed that "the cause of religion is not extraneous to Egyptian archaeology,"

78. The entry of Pope Gregory XVI's new Egyptian museum (from *L'Album*, 16 February 1839).
Source: Getty Research Institute, Los Angeles (85-S84).

and that "in the inscriptions, sacred philology will gain a better understanding of oriental Biblical texts." "Egyptology," in sum, "is the indivisible companion of Catholic truth."[79]

Nine months later came Mehmet Ali's canny gift of the alabaster columns.

Despite there being no use in mind at San Paolo for the columns, Gregory having by then vetoed Poletti's plans for a ciborium, the pope was nonetheless enchanted by the Pasha's offer and decided to dispatch an expedition to Egypt anyway, not just for the columns but also to explore Egypt and the Holy Land. The expedition was to study antiquities and historic sites and record data about geology, geography, flora, and fauna, in a kind of Catholic remake of the famous Napoleonic expedition of 1798–1801. This was to mark yet another step in the Catholic reappropriation of Egypt, hopefully providing fresh confirmations of sacred history and of what Wiseman had called the "utility of science to revealed religion."

On 21 September 1840, less than a year later, three ships from the Pontifical Navy – the *Fedeltà*, the *San Paolo*, and the *San Pietro* – left Civitavecchia on what came to be known as the Pontifical Expedition to Egypt.[80] The political situation in and around Egypt had by then deteriorated, with fighting throughout Syria, Palestine, and Lebanon.[81] The Holy Land component of the expedition had to be scrapped, and when they reached Egypt they found Alexandria blockaded by the British. Eventually permitted to enter the harbor, the leaders of the expedition were brought ashore and introduced to the Pasha that very evening. He laughingly told them that he had very nearly ordered them fired upon because he thought they were British ships in disguise. Also, the alabaster was not ready yet. The Romans were ultimately forced to wait several months, which they spent sailing up and then back down the Nile, exploring along the way. They paid visits to quarters of Cairo and Alexandria, to ancient monuments down to the First Cataract at Aswan and back, and to the remote sites in the Upper Egyptian desert where the alabaster was being quarried. All along the way they kept a careful written record. At the end of eleven months, 10 percent of the Roman crew had succumbed to cholera and the enterprise had cost the papal treasury the staggering sum of 17,039 scudi. But in April 1841, finally, the surviving members of the expedition collected the alabaster columns and blocks, muscled them aboard their ships, and returned to Rome[82] (**Figure 79**).

The question of what was actually to be done with these alabaster columns was not taken up until the mid-1840s and was not definitively settled even then. Even so, it is worthwhile considering the disconnect that emerged – as it had with respect to the Veii columns – between their officially intended significance and what actually emerged in public discourse. For Gregory XVI, what justified the immense investment of the expedition was the

79. The Pontifical Expedition to Egypt loading the alabaster columns donated by Mehmet Ali aboard their ships for the return to Rome (from *L'Album*, 21 August 1841).
Source: Getty Research Institute, Los Angeles (85-S84).

opportunity to place within one of Rome's two most important basilicae a tangible piece of the Holy Land, in the form of several vivid, unusual columns, unlike any others in the city. Publicity again guaranteed that everyone would know they came from Egypt. Gregory probably hoped that, as such, they would recall not only Egypt's role in sheltering the Holy Family but also its prominence in Old Testament Jewish history, to which the Church claimed to be the providential successor. Gregory and his clerical friends might also have thought of that traditional prototype for all Christian altars, the tabernacle Moses had built in the desert, formed of precious materials that God had instructed him to bring out of Egypt (Numbers 4). And even though Paul never set foot in Egypt, it would have been tempting for Roman clerics, as they remembered the well-publicized, circuitous voyage across the Mediterranean those columns had made, to contemplate Paul's evangelical voyages around the Mediterranean. It was not just that Paul's voyages and that of the columns all led ultimately to the basilica; the expedition had very deliberately paused on its way back to Rome with the columns at tiny St. Paul's Island, off Malta, traditionally regarded as the site of the shipwreck that delayed Paul on his voyage to Rome for his trial and martyrdom (Acts 28).[83]

Clerical intellectuals would have discerned still other meanings in the columns. They might have recalled the long history of Christianity in Egypt, from its status as the cradle of Christian monasticism to its contemporary position as one of the Church's main growth areas beyond Europe.[84] Thus a pious French visitor in 1849 wrote that the columns called to his mind "the providential mission that God has confided to us for the propagation of the Faith in the world."[85] Such recollections would have held special significance for Gregory, who ever since his time at the Propaganda Fide had harbored a particular concern for the Egyptian Catholic faithful.[86] Gregory also took an interest in the country's substantial Eastern Rite Catholics (Copts, Marionites, Chaldeans) and had personally appointed a Vicar Apostolic for the Copts in 1832.[87] Egypt ultimately came to be so close to his heart that it was memorialized on his tomb in St. Peter's, where the portal takes the flaring shape of an Egyptian pylon and is framed in Egyptian alabaster – not left over from the expedition, as it happens, but additional pieces donated by Mehmet Ali upon Gregory's death.[88] The Egyptian columns might have evoked all this as a reaffirmation of the old historical parallel between the Roman Empire and the Church. Like the remotely sourced marbles of the Pantheon or the city's Egyptian obelisks, both of which indexically evoked the Roman Empire's geographical reach, the new columns would have indicated the geographical reach of a Catholic Church at once ancient and modern.[89]

But once again, these high-minded intentions seem to have been rather undermined by the discourses that actually emerged in the contemporary Roman press. The expedition received substantial press coverage in the Papal States, which was then magnified by papers around the world (as Mehmet Ali had foreseen).[90] *L'Album* in particular presented a lively four-part illustrated travelogue by Camillo Ravioli, the official historian traveling with the expedition, which began appearing while they were all still in Egypt.[91] Each dispatch from Ravioli was published on the journal's front page beneath a large illustration (**Figure 80**). We might expect the Christian resonances of the expedition to be the major theme in Ravioli's text, but they are not. Instead, it is the ardent sense of Roman patriotism that dominates. Ravioli constantly insists on the audacity of the voyage, the proud flag they carried, their hopes that their "fellow citizens" would be proud of them, and their excitement at being engaged in a project that would be "appreciated by our fatherland."[92] None of this rhetoric aligned with the self-image of the absolutist, cosmopolitan papal government, whose inhabitants were subjects, not citizens, and which directed loyalties not to a fatherland but to God and to the individuals and institutions invested with his authority. Ravioli also stressed the parallel with the ancient Romans who had colonized Egypt, but not in a manner that extended it to the Church: the significance of the expedition in Ravioli's telling was rather that it proved that the Roman flair for heroic endeavor was still alive and well. At one point, having described their group, he asked rhetorically, "Was this a detachment from those cohorts which Octavius Augustus had sent to the frontiers of the Empire under the protective wings of that eagle, queen of the universe?" He also recalled the French expedition of 1832 that transported the Luxor Obelisk now in the Place de la Concorde, and coolly noted

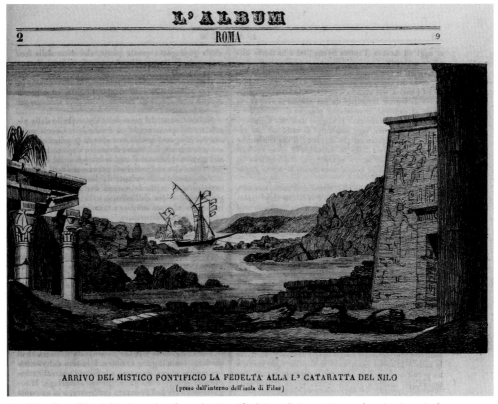

80. The first of Ravioli's dispatches from the Pontifical Expedition to Egypt, showing its arrival at the First Cataract of the Nile facing Philae (from *L'Album*, 13 March 1841).
Source: Getty Research Institute, Los Angeles (85-S84).

that while the French had traveled only two-thirds as far, they had complained twice as much.[93] The passage moves with a nationalist swagger one does not normally associate with the Papal States. Even Ravioli's decision to begin his first article in midjourney, at the First Cataract facing Philae, makes sense after one recalls that the first volume of the *Description de l'Egypte* had started at this location.

By the start of 1840, following Poletti's half-decade of feverish labor, the transept and high altar at San Paolo were nearly complete. The initial hope was to schedule the consecration on 30 June, the Commemoration of St. Paul, but in the end it was moved ahead to 5 October, the anniversary of Leo XII's election.[94] In July, a front-page article in *L'Album* announced the event beneath a dramatic half-page engraving that would have given many Romans their first glimpse of the new interior[95] (**Figure 81**). The text reassured the reader that the new basilica preserved "nearly everything that survived the rapacity of the flames, whether in whole or in part," along with "the memory of the pristine temple, and of the fire it suffered." Arnolfo's

81. The rebuilt transept of the basilica of San Paolo fuori le mura in 1840. The exedra on the right is the original eastern apse, but the exedra on the left (whence comes the ray of light) is the temporary counterwall that sealed off the transept from the ongoing construction in the nave (from *L'Album*, 11 July 1840).
Source: Getty Research Institute, Los Angeles (85-S84).

ciborium remained *votivamente* in its old position, the old façade mosaic had been reinstalled on the inner face of the triumphal arch, the apse mosaic was restored, and veneers made from the broken columns of the old church covered the walls. It added, however, that one could not help but be even more impressed "by the new work": the new pavement, the papal altar, the balustrade around the confessio, the Sedia Pontificia, the two altars in the transept end walls, and Poletti's two chapels.[96] In other words, it perfectly echoed the narratives that Poletti and Moreschi had been so patiently laying out over the previous half decade. With obeisance rendered to the old basilica via its indexical incorporation into the new, Poletti's innovations could now be freely evoked as simply "the new work."

The consecration of the transept occurred on 4 October, one day before that of the high altar. It was not a public event and began before dawn.[97] Poletti then prepared the interior for the following day, dressing the altars with borrowed cloths, laying out carpets, and installing furnishings borrowed from the Sistine Chapel in the apse.[98] In the afternoon, a crowd began arriving, but the doors were locked so that the workers would not be disturbed.[99] Work went on through the night.

Early on the morning of 5 October, elite clerical and aristocratic invitees began taking their places in the transept alongside contingents from the Roman academies and the reconstruction workshop. Admission was officially limited to invitees, though the uninvited journalist Ignazio Cantù later wrote that he had no trouble simply walking in.[100] In reviewing the ceremony, it is the tactile materiality of the rituals that most impresses: salt and ashes are mixed and spread on the altar in the shape of a cross; wine is mixed with holy water and used to trace crosses at the center and corners of the altar; the altar is circumambulated seven times and sprinkled with holy water as the choir chants the Miserere. Pope Gregory then took over "with an effusion of tears" and anointed the altar with holy oil and chrism, while at his side a priest vigorously oscillated a thurible[101] (**Figure 82**). Psalms and prayers followed, then the marking of more crosses on the altar, first with grains of incense and then wax. Finally, the blotted altar top was cleaned, and the process was repeated on the front and sides.[102]

Gregory's Latin homily foregrounded the presence in Rome of the holy bodies of Peter and Paul. It opened with the same quote Moreschi had used from the early Christian priest Caius: "if you go to the Vatican or walk along the Ostian way, you will encounter the tombs of those who founded this church."[103] Gregory juxtaposed those human remains with those of the old basilica itself, "valued not only for its antiquity and by the dignity of those who built, ornamented, and repaired it over the centuries, but also and above all by the materials that served in its construction and its architecture." The implication was that, just as Rome's special status was linked to the presence there of Peter's and Paul's remains, so too the value of the new basilica was guaranteed by the presence of the old basilica in its very substance. Like the article in *L'Album*, Gregory also finessed the point of how much of the new basilica was of novel design. In evoking Leo XII's order to reconstruct the basilica, he repeated none of the familiar but by now almost incriminating quotes from the Chirograph of 1825. He instead briskly explained that Leo's aim had been "to reproduce, following the advice of masters in art, the forms of the ancient temple, but at the same time to take advantage of the progress of modern industry and to add still more to its beauty." Poletti's new approach to the reconstruction was thereby officially consecrated as well.

82. Pope Gregory XVI consecrating the papal altar at the basilica of San Paolo fuori le mura (from *Collezione di costumi sacri Romani*, 1841–1843).
Source: Roma, Istituto centrale per la grafica, per gentile concessione del Ministero della Cultura.

This chapter has considered different aspects of the reconstruction in which meanings were understood to inhere in materials. In every case, the public reception of those meanings depended on translating those materials into a form capable of reaching the large international public that the reconstruction sought to target. In other words, the physical had to be represented as information and then disseminated, mostly via printed words and more rarely images. This was achieved relatively successfully in the two cases where the meanings in question were directly related to the building itself. The significance of Poletti's reuse of salvaged marbles was simply to establish that the new basilica had an essential relationship to the old one, and Moreschi's didactic publicity seems to have been effective in communicating this, for it was commonly echoed by commentators elsewhere. The consecration ceremony of 1840 reiterated this narrative of indexical connection, while Moreschi's published account of the ceremony then extended it even to the time and place of the ceremony itself, drilling down on the physical and spatial details of the rituals, from the seating arrangements and liturgical instruments to the variety of vestments worn. It even included a foldout illustration of the transept and assembled crowd with Pope Gregory standing before the new Sedia Pontificia, his hand raised in benediction[104] (**Figure 83**). The Catholic press abroad took it from there. Accounts of the ceremony derived from Moreschi's account appeared not only in Western Europe but by virtue of their appearance in *The Catholic Magazine* of London, even as far afield as India, where the *Bengal Catholic Herald* of Calcutta reproduced a detailed description of the day.[105] Through these means, the irreducible corporeity of the consecration ceremony was disseminated throughout the *universo mundo*.

The other two cases considered here, the Benedict chapel and the alabaster ciborium, turned out differently, with their intended messages of Catholic appropriation largely unremarked in public discourse. Here the messages were more complex, relating to the rather cerebral ambition of reclaiming ancient history from the Church's rivals. It would have required a sophisticated publicitary operation to inform a broad public what was at stake in that particular project. The expansion of the Roman press during the 1830s and 1840s coincided with the growing cultural and political engagement of parts of the Roman bourgeois public, which, as we have seen, had been shaken by the 1830–1831 rebellions and dismayed by the brutal repressions that ensued. Journals like *L'Album* were mainly aimed at this public rather than at the narrow clerical or specialized publics targeted by an earlier generation of Roman periodicals, and they were run by men from the professional classes – men who might still request and receive government subsidies but whose journals were businesses in a way that the earlier journals had not been. These periodicals had little choice therefore

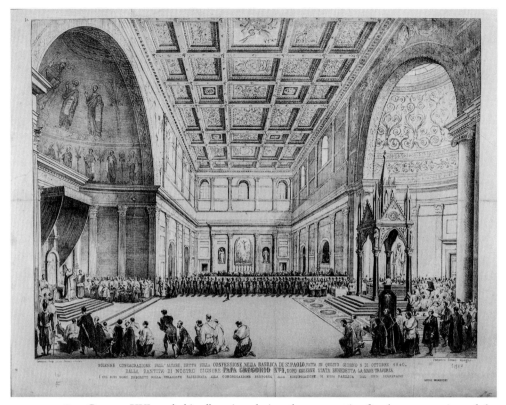

83. Gregory XVI reads his allocution during the ceremonies for the consecration of the transept at San Paolo fuori le mura in October 1840 (from Moreschi [1840b]).
Source: © Istituto Nazionale di Archeologia e Storia dell'Arte, Rome.

but to be solicitous of the tastes and enthusiasms of their readers, and thus on matters Egyptian and Etruscan they supplied patriotic narratives rather than the esoteric sacred ones that prevailed in curial encomia.[106]

In December 1840, just as the news of the newly departed Pontifical Expedition to Egypt was about to break across newspapers around the world, Gregory XVI took advantage to issue *Augustissimam Beatissimi*, an encyclical letter announcing a new fundraising drive for San Paolo.[107] A mere five months later, a complete translation was available in the *Bengal Catholic Herald* in British Calcutta, along with a preface that, like de Plessis's pastoral letter from Quebec, tackled the old question of how Catholics so far from Rome were to justify their contributions to a sacred building few of them had ever seen:

> Let it not be said that there are Churches more than enough at Rome and not enough here; that we ought to provide for our own wants in Calcutta, before we seek to embellish and adorn religion elsewhere ... Though we cannot all visit the sepulcher of the Apostle, we can at least each send our mite to restore and decorate the Church that covered it ...[108]

MATERIAL HISTORIES

Subsequent issues publicized donations collected from even the humblest members of the local Catholic community there: "Serjt. Peter Ryan ... 16 rupees," "Constable Savage ... 5 rupees."[109] These small personal gestures, coming from individuals whose connection to the Catholic metropole was as remote and as imagined as could be, surely did not spring from an intellectual reassessment of the modern world, à la Wiseman, and the same was true for most of the thousands of others across the Catholic world who were also moved to contribute. More likely, they reflected an awakening solidarity on the part of Catholics whose modern lives connected them informationally to, and left them feeling invested personally in, their Church's longing to contest a hostile secular (or Protestant) world. In the second half of the nineteenth century, names like Ryan and Savage, in their motivated multitudes, were to form the basis of a great Catholic revival. In surveying here the fortunes of these different aspects of the material San Paolo during the 1830s, we glimpse how Church leaders were already experimenting with new ways to bridge the gap between embodied sacrality and an expanded geographical horizon and hoping to inspire ecclesial renewal through new conjugations of society, discourse, and publicness.

NOTES

1   Sacchi (1836), p. 317.
2   Poletti (March 1835) as in Chapter 10 n. 35.
3   Luigi Poletti, "Contratto con Raffaele Alicata per la lavorazione di otto colonne," 19 February 1839 (BCALP: LP12 C91).
4   *DdR* supplement, 24 October 1835, pp. 1–4.
5   According to Uggeri (1823), the old basilica had sixty-two columns of *marmo salino*, twenty-eight smaller columns of porphyry, twenty-four columns of pavonazzetto, six columns of gray granite (*granito bigio*), five columns of *granito rosso*, and three columns of *cipollino*.
6   Corsi (1828). See Groblewski (2001), pp. 193–194.
7   Nineteenth-century legistation in this regard built upon earlier efforts that extended back to the Renaissance (Karmon [2011]).
8   Antonio Tosti to Pietro Francesco Galleffi, 4 May 1835 (ASR: Camerlengato, P. II, Tit. IV, b. 155, f. 204, Nr. 107; tiG pp. 414–415).
9   Pietro Francesco Galleffi to Luigi Grifi and Antonio Tosti, [10 May 1835?] (ASR: Camerlengato, P. II, Tit. IV, b. 155, f. 204; tiG pp. 415–416).
10 "Memoria per la Santita' di N[ostro] S[ignore]," 4 August 1835 (ASP: 6/c, b. "Basilica 1834–1835"); Costantino Patrizi to the Special Commission, 18 August 1835 (ASP: 6/c, b. "Basilica 1834–1835"; reproduced in *CAPDR*, p. 88); Special Commission to Antonio d'Este, 25 August 1835 (ASP: 6/c, b. "Basilica 1834–1835"); Antonio Domenico Gamberini to Pietro Francesco Galleffi, 1 July 1836 (ASR: Camerlengato, P. II, Tit. IV, b. 155, f. 204, Nr. 633; tiG pp. 417–418).
11 Luigi Grifi to Pietro Francesco Galleffi, 28 March 1837 (ASR: Camerlengato, P. II, Tit. IV, b. 155, f. 204, #102786; tiG pp. 424–425).
12 Antonio Domenico Gamberini to Pietro Francesco Galleffi, 15 May 1837 (ASR: Camerlengato, P. II, Tit. IV, b. 155, f. 204, #1093 and 103603; tiG pp. 425–427).
13 Pietro Francesco Galleffi to Antonio Domenico Gamberini, 8 June 1837 (ASR: Camerlengato, P. II, Tit. IV, b. 155, f. 204, #1093 and 103603; tiG pp. 425–427).

14 Giustiniani once accused Gamberini – wrongly – of illegally appropriating San Paolo antique marbles that had been found during roadworks near his titular church of Santa Prassade (ASR: Camerlengato, P. II, Tit. IV, b. 155, f. 204).

15 Antonio Domenico Gamberini to Giacomo Giustiniani, 20 February 1840; Giacomo Giustiniani to Antonio Domenico Gamberini, 4 March 1840; Antonio Domenico Gamberini, "Relazione alla santita di Nostro Signore Gregorio Papa XVI …," 18 March 1840 (all in ASR: Camerlengato, P. II, Tit. IV, b. 155, f. 204). On the rescheduling of the consecration: *Cronaca* II, 13 October 1839; *Australasian Chronicle* (Sydney), 26 November 1840, p. 2.

16 Brega (2008), pp. 99–100.

17 *DdR*, 8 July 1838, p. 1. Cited in Brega (2008), p. 103.

18 Springer (1987), pp. 40–43, 74–91, 95.

19 See Ridley (1992b), p. 118.

20 Ridley (1992a), pp. 154–156, 164.

21 In Moreschi's account of Gregory's visit in October 1836, the marbles are discussed at length, but their source is passed over in silence (*DdR* supplement, 29 October 1836, pp. 1–4).

22 Voltaire (1756); Volney (1814).

23 This section and the next are adapted from Wittman (2018a).

24 "Memoria …," as in Chapter 12 n. 10.

25 Delpino (1985); Liverani (1987).

26 Canina (1847), pp. 47, 87–88.

27 Liverani (1987), pp.18–19.

28 Pietro Francesco Galleffi, "Relazione della Santità di Nostro Signore Papa Gregorio XVI sulla preziosa collezione delle colonne di Vejo," 3 September 1833 (AAV: Archivio Particolare di Gregorio XVI, b. 23, f. 191–192).

29 Patrizi (18 August 1835), as in Chapter 12 n. 10.

30 Benveduti (2008), pp. 355–365; Strozzieri (2014), p. 356.

31 In 1815, the Jacobin writer Carlo Botta used it as a synecdoche for Etruria in his widely read epic poem of the Roman conquest, *Il Camillo, o Vejo conquistata* (Botta [1815]).

32 Gell (1832); Delpino (1999), pp. 73–74.

33 *DdR* supplement, 29 October 1836, pp. 1–4.

34 Melchiorri (1838).

35 Colonna (1992), p. 322; Sannibale (2009).

36 Delpino (2017).

37 Magi (1963).

38 Denina (1769); Cuoco (1804); Micali (1810), v. 1, p. 28; v. 4, pp. 242–243; Mascioli (1942), pp. 366–373; Cristofani (1992), p. 288; Ceserani (2010); De Francesco (2013), pp. 29–83.

39 Cherici (2008); Colonna (1992). Young architecture *pensionnaires* at the French Academy in Rome, most famously Henri Labrouste, also developed a keen interest in the Etruscans during these years (Van Zanten [1987]).

40 Wiseman (1836). The first Italian translation appeared serially in the *Annali delle scienze religiose* over the course of 1837–1838 (v. 4–7). Standalone translations followed in 1841–1842 and 1856.

41 *DdR*, 4 July 1835, p. 4.

42 Wiseman (1836), p. 13.

43 *DdR*, 12 February 1837, pp. 1–2; *DESE*, v. 47, "Musei di Roma," pp. 110–112.

44 Cherici (2011).

45 *DESE*, v. 47, "Musei di Roma," p. 114.

46 Barbanera (2008), p. 168.

47 Gray (1840); Dennis (1848); Haack (2013), p. 1140.

48 Cherici (2008), pp. 160–161.

49 Springer (1987), pp. 49–50, 58–63; Cherici (2011).

50 *L'Album*, 14 November 1840, pp. 293–294.

51 For a different interpretation, see Groblewski (2001), pp. 195–196.

52 Luigi Poletti, "Articoli convenuti per ristaurare le dodici colonne di marmo bigio …," 12 October 1835 (BCALP: LP12 C88 1).

53 Poletti (1838) and (1864).

54 *DdR* supplement, 22 October 1839, pp. 1–2.

55 Melchiorri (1838). Another review appeared four years later (Gasparoni [1841a]).

56 Melchiorri (1838), p. 7.

57 Melchiorri (1838), pp. 7–9.

58 See Wittman (2018a), pp. 103–105.

59 For a brief account, see Wittman (2018b).

60 Professor James Harrell via email (28 June 2015); Akaad and Naggar (1965).

61 *DESE*, v. 21, "Egitto," p. 108.

62 *DdR* supplement, 28 July 1838, pp. 1–2.

63 Driault (1830–1833), v. 1, p. 346.

64 Annibale de Rossetti to Luigi Lambruschini, 16 November 1839 (BCALP: LP37 C117 1).

65 Ufford (2007).

66 See Lacroix (1850), v. 1, p. 117. After the alabaster columns arrived in Rome, Gregory ordered the Vatican mosaic workshop to create two mosaic tables depicting views of ancient and modern Rome with Arabic captions, which were sent to Cairo in 1842 (Orazio Bruni to Luigi Lambruschini, 26 January 1842 [ASR: CSRBSP Segreteria b. 284]).

67 Iversen (1993); Curran (2007).

68 Edelstein (2010), pp. 227–239.

69 Champollion (1909), v. 1, pp. 226–227.

70 Gossman (1986), p. 33.

71 Champollion (1909), v. 1, p. 227; Lanci (1825). On Lanci, see de Minicis (1840); Marcolini (1874); Mei del Testa (2002).

72 Colla (2007), pp. 72–96.

73 Rosellini (1832–1844).

74 Ippolito Rosellini to Pope Gregory XVI, 8 November 1833; cited in Mercati (1948), pp. 293–294.

75 Lefevre (1948), p. 238; Longo (2008), p. 137 n. 9.

76 *DdR*, 3 March 1838, p. 1.

77 *DESE*, v. 21, "Egitto," p. 126; *DdR*, 3 March 1838, p. 1.

78 Lefevre (1948), pp. 248–249

79 Ungarelli (1839a), pp. 394, 397; Ungarelli (1839b), pp. 22, 55.

80 The expedition's official history is Ravioli (1870). See also *DESE*, v. 21, "Egitto," pp. 108–114; Lefevre (1947); Notarangelo (1952); Koenig (1975); Longo (2008). I am currently preparing a new study of the expedition.

81 Ufford (2007), pp. 123 ff.

82 Ravioli (1870).

83 Ravioli (1870), p. 217; Notarangelo (1952), p. 6. The course charted by the expedition especially recalled Paul's fourth voyage, landing at Crete, Malta, and Sicily.

84 It is estimated that there were 20,000 Latin Rite Catholics in Egypt by 1843 (*DESE*, v. 21, pp. 136–139; Ersilio [1958], pp. 1–21; Aubert et al. [1952], p. 161).

85 Luquet (1849), v. 2, p. 211.

86 During Gregory's pontificate, the Jesuits had returned to Syria and Beirut, joined by Catholic lay organizations like the Sisters of Charity and the Christian Brothers (Aubert et al. [1981], pp. 161–162; Gadille and Mayeur [1995], p. 140); indeed, Caliò stresses both the diplomatic and missionary value of the expedition (Caliò [2008], p. 304).

87 *DESE*, v. 21, "Egitto," p. 136.

88 Moreschi (1857). On Mehmet Ali's gift, see *DESE*, v. 64, "Sepolcro de'Romani Pontefici," pp. 94–116.

89   The *Bengal Catholic Expositor* explained to the small British Catholic community in Calcutta that with the arrival of the columns from Egypt "that country which furnished marbles and obelisks for the city of the Caesars, will again, in our days, under a milder and far different influence, contribute to the triumphs of the city of the apostles" (*Bengal Catholic Expositor*, 11 July 1840, p. 27).

90   News of the expedition's arrival in Alexandria was reported in Hobart, Tasmania, just five and a half months after the fact (*The Courier* [Hobart], 20 April 1841, p. 3).

91   Ravioli's travelogue (Ravioli [1841–42]) appeared in *L'Album* in five installments between 13 March 1841 and 19 March 1842. These articles form the basis of Ravioli (1870), where they are joined by annotations, scientific tables, and a supplemental narrative.

92   Ravioli (1870), pp. 135–137, 141.

93   Ravioli (1870), pp. 160–161.

94   *Cronaca* II, 13 October 1839. The *Australasian Chronicle* of Sydney claimed that Gregory XVI's doctors forced the change in date to save the aged pontiff from the midsummer heat (*Australasian Chronicle*, 26 November 1840, p. 2).

95   Giacoletti (1840).

96   Giacoletti (1840), p. 146.

97   This account is based on *Cronaca* II, 4 October 1839, and Moreschi (1840b).

98   On the *Cappella Papale*, see Tuker and Malleson (1900), v. 3, pt. 4, p. 378 ff.

99   *Cronaca* II, 4 October 1839.

100   Cantù (1841), p. 391.

101   *Cronaca* II, 5 October 1840, p. 235.

102   Cf. *DdR* supplement, 17 October 1840, pp. 1–4 (republished as Moreschi [1840b]); *L'Ami de la religion* (Paris), 29 October 1840, pp. 198–199; and *The Catholic Magazine* (London), December 1840, reprinted in *Bengal Catholic Herald* (Calcutta), 13 March 1841, pp. 11–13. See also *Cronaca* II, 5 October 1840.

103   The passage occurs in Caius's "Disputation against Proclus" (198 AD).

104   *DdR* supplement, 17 October 1840, pp. 1–4; Moreschi (1840b).

105   *L'Ami de la religion* (Paris) 29 October 1840, pp. 198–199; *Bengal Catholic Herald* (Calcutta), 13 March 1841, pp. 11–13; *Bengal Catholic Herald*, 1 May 1841, pp. 99–102.

106   Wittman (2020b), p. 822.

107   *TEPD*, v. 3, pp. 285–288.

108   *Bengal Catholic Herald* (Calcutta), 1 May 1841, pp. 99–102.

109   *Bengal Catholic Expositor* (Calcutta), 11 July 1840, p. 27; *Bengal Catholic Herald* (Calcutta), 13 March 1841, pp. 11–13; *Bengal Catholic Herald*, 1 May 1841, pp. 99–102; *Bengal Catholic Herald*, 8 May 1841, p. 115 [also p. 353 (4 September 1841); p. 424 (9 October 1841); p. 454 (23 October 1841); p. 495 (13 November 1841); p. 536 (4 December 1841)]; *Bengal Catholic Herald*, 19 March 1842, p. 167; *Bengal Catholic Herald*, 8 April 1843, p. 188. The enthusiasm of the Calcutta community reflected gratitude toward Gregory, who in 1834 had reestablished the vicariate apostolic of Bengal in Calcutta (Costantini [1948], p. 11; Aubert et al. [1981], pp. 198–199).

THIRTEEN

PRELUDE TO A REVOLUTION

POLETTI ENTERED THE DECADE FOLLOWING THE 1840 CONSECRATION optimistic, expecting that the next phases of work would more or less follow the master plan represented in his great wooden model. Gregory had just launched the new fundraising drive, and everything was on track for a final consecration in the presence of thousands of expected Jubilee pilgrims in the Holy Year of 1850. In every respect, Poletti was to be disappointed. Serious financial problems soon prompted Gregory to order a substantial curtailment of Poletti's master plan, and even the Holy Year was ultimately canceled. What Poletti had hoped would be the decisive final push turned instead into some of the most frustrating years of his three and half decades directing the reconstruction.

Poletti began the decade by amassing wood and stone for the reconstruction of the nave, as Moreschi's accounts of Pope Gregory's visits in 1841 and 1842 excitedly testify.[1] Yet little actual building occurred, because money was becoming a serious problem. To everyone's surprise, Pope Gregory's fundraising call of December 1840 had been a complete failure. Donations once again sailed in from distant outposts of the Catholic world, but the totals were anemic: through the end of 1841, a mere 8,836 scudi had been collected – less than half the cost of the Pontifical Expedition to Egypt.[2] By comparison, the first year of the first fundraising drive had raised over 200,000 scudi, and annual receipts had not fallen below 10,000 until three years in.[3] Things improved very slightly in 1842, so that by September the total was up to 37,549, but this was still a colossal disappointment, and donations essentially dried up after that. If Pope Gregory was counting on a windfall as his compensation for allowing Poletti to complete the transept without interference, he can only have been disheartened.

The workforce at San Paolo was soon reduced in favor of *forzati*, which is to say, forced prison laborers, of which there were between 100 and 200 at any given time, comprising over half the total personnel by the early 1840s. Sir George Head visited the worksite in 1842:

> The requisite building operations [at San Paolo] were being performed almost wholly by criminals or *forçati*, clad in their prison dresses and working continually in their clanking chains, though in all other respects they were under very trifling surveillance as regards any attempt they might think proper to make to regain their liberty. Indeed there seemed to exist hardly any impediment towards their putting such a purpose in execution, for the military guard on the spot consisted only of two sentries, both apparently careless and absorbed in their own reflections, and the civil superintendent was evidently so worn out by continual attendance, that he seemed even hardly conscious of his own existence. Meanwhile the *forçati* entered freely into conversation with the visitor, and by converting fragments of marble belonging to the ancient basilica to paper weights and other such ornamental trifles, derived a small profit.[4]

Observing a general "tone of ease and hilarity," Head described the workers as "exceedingly deliberate and slothful." Other visitors had a similar impression. Henry Noel Humphreys wrote in 1840 of seeing "the convicts of Gregorio XVI . . . lazily wandering with their half-filled wheelbarrows over the wreck," and guessed that they "will apparently be many years, at their present rate of work, in clearing the ruins."[5]

Hoping to revive the stagnant worksite, Poletti submitted a detailed petition to the Special Commission during the summer of 1842. Aware by then that Gregory XVI's fundraising drive had failed, Poletti requested a six-year increase in the annual subsidy, up to almost 112,000 scudi, and offered detailed suggestions about where the money might come from.[6] This was an immense increase – a sum considerably larger than the entire receipts of Leo XII's initial fundraising drive. As he had done at Castel Gandolfo, the architect provided an ambitious timetable: whereas at current funding levels the basilica would take about twenty-three years to complete, the requested augmentation would have the basilica ready for consecration in 1850. In addition to saving sixteen or seventeen years of administrative costs, this pace would also increase the quality and coherence of the work. Poletti doggedly reprised his promise of

PRELUDE TO A REVOLUTION

1833, that accelerated work would stimulate the generosity of the faithful, especially as 1850 was a Holy Year when thousands of pilgrims would be visiting Rome.

The Special Commission referred Poletti's request to its accountants, who responded with an overview of the finances of the entire reconstruction from 1825 to the present.[7]

Source	Amount (in scudi)	Percentage
Apostolic Chamber (as per Leo XII's Chirograph)	724,000.00	69
Leo XII's fundraising campaign (1825–1831)	286,074.40	27.2
Gregory XVI's fundraising campaign (1840–1842)	37,549.64	3.6
Sale of salvaged materials	1,846.01	0.2
Total	1,049,470.05	100

The problem was that outlays totaled 1,049,014.49 scudi, which meant that the workshop had at present less than 500 scudi on hand. There were also outstanding bills totaling 37,846.94 scudi to pay in September 1842, and they were contractually on the hook for future payments totaling 86,348.76 scudi. As for income that could be counted on in 1843, the report listed just 47,000 scudi, nearly all of which represented the annual subsidy from the Apostolic Chamber, and from which over 4,000 scudi in administrative expenses had to be deducted. The report certainly confirmed Poletti's sense that the situation was dire.

As noted, the 50,000 scudi annual subsidy decreed by Leo XII had been reduced at the end of 1833 to just 24,000 scudi per year, prompting Gregory XVI in compensation to redirect 21,000 scudi annually for five years from other budgets. The accountants who authored this 1842 report now argued that these redirected funds should not be counted against the original pledge of 50,000, because they had been used exclusively to fund work separate from the original conception approved by Leo XII, namely, Poletti's new chapels, his Carrara marble arches in the main arcade, and his decision to replace all the columns, bases, and capitals in the nave aisles. The Special Commission was therefore justified in requesting the 26,000 scudi that the Apostolic Chamber had withheld in each of the last nine years: 234,000 scudi in total, a huge sum in its own right, equivalent to 30 percent of the total paid toward the reconstruction by the Apostolic Chamber since work started. But the sum was still well short of the roughly 370,000 Poletti was seeking.

It is not clear exactly how much the Special Commission ended up asking the pope for, but on 1 March 1843 Gregory took up one of Poletti's suggestions and agreed to raid the government's sinking fund (the *Cassa di Ammortizzazione*) in order to provide the reconstruction with a boost that worked out to a bit more than 40,000 scudi per year. This, however, was made available only as a loan.[8] Gregory was perhaps persuaded by Poletti's claims about the advantages of finishing the basilica in time for the 1850 Jubilee.

The immensity of the sums in play seems nonetheless to have troubled the aging pontiff. The monastery chronicle notes that during Gregory's next tour of the worksite, in October 1843, he spent a long time in solitude looking at Poletti's model.[9] We cannot know what went through his head as he surveyed all that remained to be done: the chronicler writes that he studied the model with "true pleasure," but that seems optimistic based on Gregory's actions over the months that followed. More likely, he was beginning to ask himself whether it was wise to devote so many resources to a luxurious building in a time when the pontifical finances were increasingly in hock to the House of Rothschild.[10] With his eightieth birthday approaching, thoughts of mortality may also have entered his mind. Would Poletti's ambitious vision keep him from ever seeing the church completed? He might also have been troubled to reflect how far the project had evolved from Leo XII's vision. Gregory had already overruled Poletti's plan to move Arnolfo di Cambio's ciborium; he may now have come to feel similarly about the extension of the lacunar ceiling into the nave and the wholesale transformation of the area in front of the basilica. Certainly some of the monks at San Paolo were angry at Poletti's recent demolition of the old campanile: the monastery chronicler raged that the old campanile had been "respected by the flames!! and by lightning!!" and hissed that the new one would yield its architect "a tidy profit!!!"[11] Gregory too may have been developing misgivings about the transformations that lay ahead.

A year and a month later, in November 1844, Gregory ordered his secretary of state for internal affairs, Mario Mattei, to address a memo to Cardinal Antonio Tosti of the Special Commission indicating that the approvals given previously for a coffered ceiling over the nave and for the demolition of the eighteenth-century narthex were hereby revoked.[12] Poletti was ordered instead to reconstruct the nave timberwork as it had been before the fire, that is, open to view, and to retain the old narthex as part of a repaired façade. Any other new additions were also hereby canceled – no new quadroporticus or baptistry – other than those necessary to harmonize the old and new parts of the basilica. The bureaucratic protocols decreed by the Chirograph were also abruptly reinstituted, as Poletti was instructed to present his new plans for these elements to the Academy of St. Luke as soon as possible.

Tosti passed the news on to Poletti, who we may surmise was blindsided, for his workforce had already spent months preparing the coffered ceiling for the nave, and nearly all the materials for it were ready on site. But he had little choice but to obey and halt the work.[13] The Special Commission also asked Poletti to provide a complete accounting of the state of work on the campanile, and then in January or February 1845 decided to suspend work there as well. All available resources were now to be devoted to the completion of the walls and roof of the nave and aisles.[14]

This sudden reversal by Pope Gregory was almost certainly responsible for one of the abiding mysteries that every student of the reconstruction of San Paolo has at some point wondered about: the 1845 text known as the *Collezione degli articoli pubblicati nel Diario di Roma e nelle Notizie del giorno relativi alla nuova fabbrica della Basilica di S. Paolo*. This indispensable booklet gathers together and reprints nearly every article about San Paolo that appeared in the *Diario di Roma*, year by year, starting with the announcement of the fire on 16 July 1823, accompanied by precious commentary by Luigi Moreschi. It is basically the official history of the reconstruction, and scholars have used it as such. What makes it a mystery is that, while many pages of it were printed, it was never actually published. The title page indicates that it was published in 1845 by the Tipografia della Reverenda Camera Apostolica, but all known copies of it are unbound, and they all end on page 120 in midhyphenated word, in the midst of an article from October 1839. Most of the known copies remain unbound in bundles tied with twine in the archive of the Special Commission and at the archive of the monastery. No Roman library lists the book in its catalog aside from that of the Department of History, Design, and Restoration at La Sapienza. Their copy also ends on page 120.

It appears that Moreschi had been preparing this book in the early 1840s and had the first fifteen blanksheet proofs printed around 1845. (Fifteen standard blanksheets printed with eight pages each, four on each side, yields 120 in-quarto pages.) But then he must have abandoned the project. The book had probably been conceived as a means of stimulating interest in the reconstruction following the disappointing fundraising drive of 1840–1842 or perhaps in anticipation of the consecration during the Holy Year of 1850, but Gregory's decision to scale down Poletti's project in 1844 is almost certainly what led to its abandonment. For the *Diario di Roma* articles it republished from the late 1830s through the early 1840s had repeatedly expressed exuberant enthusiasm for the features that Gregory had now canceled. It was one thing to reproduce articles that bore witness to the long debates over which marble to use; this could be read as proof of due diligence. But it would not have reflected very well on Gregory's superintendence of the project to have republished several articles reporting on his excitement at seeing the luxurious lacunar ceiling of the nave take shape, only for that feature then to abruptly disappear without explanation. Even Moreschi would have had trouble putting a positive gloss on that.

Poletti had previously enjoyed a good relationship with Cardinal Tosti. Tosti was the patron behind a renovation of the immense Ospizio di S. Michele in which Poletti had played a leading role between 1827 and 1835, even designing a small chapel for him within the complex.[15] Tosti subsequently published a book detailing the project that spoke glowingly of Poletti's work.[16] Thus when sometime in early January 1845, a few months after delivering Gregory's bad news to Poletti, Tosti abruptly resigned as treasurer and by extension from the Special Commission as well, it was unsurprising that rumors soon arose suggesting that he had been conspiring with Poletti to circumvent the pope's order.[17] One version of the rumor is recounted in an edition of Giuseppe Gioachino Belli's poems, in the notes accompanying the sonnet "Er volo de Simommàgo" ("The Flight of Simon Magus").[18] The sonnet is dated 13 January 1845, days after Tosti's resignation and almost exactly two months after Gregory's orders; its title refers to the first-century Christian for whom the sin of simony was named. The poem depicts an imaginary conversation between Gregory XVI and Tosti in which Tosti recounts various projects that are going according to plan, prompting a satisfied Gregory to then inform Tosti that, in that case, he has no further use for his services. The editor of the edition then explains in a footnote that this referred to the circumstances of Tosti's departure as treasurer:

> ... the truth is that he was fired. I can add, because I know this from an authoritative source, that the cause, if not the only cause, of his firing, is that he disobeyed the pope, who wanted the ceiling of the basilica of San Paolo redone roughly (open), as it had been previously, whereas Tosti, without the pope's knowledge, and perhaps in order to favor artists under his protection [i.e., Poletti], initiated its reconstruction [as a lacunar ceiling]. "A thing begun, is as good as done," they said among themselves; and it proved true, but the pope made him pay.[19]

It is worth noting that the weekly accounts from the worksite at this date do indicate that some workers continued carving decorative rosettes and other details for the ceiling well after the pope's cancellation order had been received. On some of the December accounts, the description of these works is even canceled out and altered from "In progress" to "Completed," perhaps to make it appear that work done after the pope's order had actually been completed before.[20] What Poletti's intention was here one can only guess, but this may be where the rumor began. Certainly it appears that Tosti's departure did involve a whiff of scandal. An anecdote in the San Paolo monastery chronicle describes an awkward moment at the ceremonies for the Feast of the Commemoration of St. Paul in June 1845, when Tosti – no longer occupying his former powerful office – first encountered his peers:

> Amongst so many festive spirits, the spirit of Cardinal Tosti must have been full of bitterness, since in past years he would dominate more than

the pope in such circumstances, whereas today he was little more than the writer of these lines, and certainly he did not go speak to any of this very red and purple assembly [i.e., containing many cardinals and bishops]. The Pope asked Tosti how he was doing, and Tosti replied: *Very well* ["Benissimo"]. O antiphrastic word! What a thing is the world of courtiers ...[21]

Tosti never again held a powerful position in the Curia, and at the time of his death twenty years later was languishing as director of the Vatican Archives. His disgrace might also have been a factor in the abandonment of the *Collezione degli Articoli* publication, since the tireless Tosti was depicted at Pope Gregory's side in many of the reprinted *Diario di Roma* articles from the 1830s and 1840s.

What is certain is that Poletti felt cruelly betrayed by Tosti. In a letter sent from Paris in October 1845 by his old friend Letarouilly, the Frenchman responds to what Poletti, in a penciled marginal note, refers to as "the outbursts that I made to him when Letarouilly was [recently] in Rome, regarding the arrogance of Cardinal Tosti, then treasurer and deputy, who passed over and persecuted my ideas."[22] In the letter, Letarouilly counsels Poletti to resist feeling discouraged:

> Never forget that those who are hostile towards you are most often that way because of obstinacy, or vanity, and rarely because of conviction. [...] Do not permit these nuisances to get more than a secondary hold on your spirit; let the artist remain complete and ever at the high level of the great enterprise that has been confided to him. [...] I have spoken with you extensively concerning San Paolo, my dear friend, and that is natural, because San Paolo is one of your dearest children, and I too must love it, since it touches you so deeply.[23]

Poletti's strategy in the months that followed was one that had been used before on the San Paolo worksite, although not yet by Poletti: namely, to stall. To stall until Gregory's death, and then hope to persuade his successor to reinstate the original project.[24]

On 13 June 1845, Cardinal Mattei and Pope Gregory's new treasurer and deputy to the Special Commission, Cardinal Giacomo Antonelli (later to be Pius IX's long-serving secretary of state), paid a visit to the basilica with Poletti to take stock.[25] A week later, the Special Commission sent an official request to the Academy of St. Luke asking them, "in accordance with the Chirograph of Leo XII," to solicit and then adjudicate proposals from Poletti concerning four questions.[26] The first concerned the west façade, which was to be restored in accordance with Pope Gregory's new wishes. The second concerned the

deployment of the alabaster columns from Egypt. The third involved the placement of the two colossal statues of St. Peter and St. Paul that had been commissioned back in 1834.[27] These had been delivered in 1840 and 1842 respectively, and were tentatively slated for installation before the colossal columns supporting the Arch of Placidia.[28] The fourth question concerned particulars of the reconstituted sequence of painted papal medallion portraits.

Poletti was capable of working at speed when it suited him, but now he took his time. Not until 20 May 1846, nearly a year later, did he submit his plans.[29] The tone of his memorandum was defensive, reminding the Academy that he had already demonstrated back in 1834 that the plans Belli had left behind were unusable, that this was why he had elaborated the general plan represented in his 1834 wooden model, and that it was with explicit papal approval that many aspects of the basilica had been rebuilt in conformity with the model. But now that Pope Gregory ("in his profound wisdom and penetration") had taken exception to aspects of the model that had not yet been executed, Poletti hereby submitted his new proposals for those features.[30] The Special Commission read Poletti's proposals – we will consider them in a moment – and sent them on to the Academy of St. Luke for their judgment.[31]

Ten days after that, Pope Gregory XVI died, at which point all bets were off. Poletti's strategy had absorbed nineteen precious months, but in the end it had worked. As he waited to see who the new pope would be, he began quietly strategizing how to get the canceled aspects of his project reinstated.

> His name as Prince will be execrated for long years, so many were the iniquities, the revelations, the arrogance, the damages ... A weak and cowardly spirit left him little better than the servant of the powers of his century ... Distrusted by his people as a tyrant, they hated rather than loved him ... And while all was weeping, desolation, misery, and oppression, in the Papal Palace they were laughing, and jewelers were being made Cardinals ... The groans of thousands of political prisoners, the gasps of countless exiles, for fifteen years they have been awaiting this day.[32]

Such was the verdict rendered on Gregory XVI upon his death, not by an anticlerical journalist in Paris or London, but by the pious monk who kept the daily chronicle of the monastery of San Paolo. It is an extraordinary quote, one that speaks volumes about the appetite for change that gripped Rome at this date. The Anglo-German painter Rudolf Lehmann recalled that "the young Romans in the cafes received the news of the Pope's demise with ill-concealed satisfaction."[33] The San Paolo chronicler even reported that when Gregory's body was moved from the Sistine Chapel to the Vatican, some of the attending cardinals were seen to be laughing.

The political repressions of the 1830s had only worsened in the 1840s following further revolts in Savigno and Rimini. For most observers, it was self-evident that mounting deprivations fueled the political unrest, but Gregory and his advisors insisted on seeing the situation in terms of the incompatibility of theocracy with the new liberal ideas. Political liberalism placed limits on the power of sovereign heads of state, and in Gregory's view this was fundamentally incompatible with the absolute independence a pope required to fulfill his responsibilities as head of the Catholic Church. To allow others to exercise institutional authority over the Vicar of Christ on Earth was to submit God to man. Therefore, Gregory felt he had little choice but to stake out the extreme position that political liberalism was satanic. As a consequence, not only did the Papal States become almost a pariah state in Europe in the 1830s, but Gregory and his government were tarnished in the eyes even of his most respectable and quietist subjects. It seemed to some moderates as though Italy was being fractured into Mazzinian revolutionaries on one side and intransigent reactionaries on the other. The moderate bourgeoisie had never really flexed its political muscle before, but it was now drawn into sympathy with liberal reform for fear that a cataclysmic confrontation on the order of 1793 awaited otherwise.[34]

This fear eventually crystalized into the neo-Guelph movement. Heavy on symbolism and light on specifics, the neo-Guelph vision combined disparate ingredients: the promise of economic liberalization, the exaltation of Roman Catholicism as a civilizing force, the premise that the pope was the logical man to head any new Italian state, and finally a generous serving of Italic exceptionalism. The result was a grab-bag program for an independent Italian confederation that proved immensely attractive to those who feared radical solutions to Italy's problems, including even the educated clergy, who appreciated its emphasis on Catholicism.[35] The neo-Guelph vision had been defined mainly in a series of books published in the mid-1840s by a trio of intellectuals: two nobles, Cesare Balbo and Massimo D'Azeglio (who were cousins); and a priest-philosopher, Vincenzo Gioberti.[36] All were from Piedmont, the wealthiest and most powerful Italian state, whose King Carlo Alberto projected himself as the leader of the movement to liberate the Italian peninsula of its foreign occupiers; all were to serve at some point as Carlo Alberto's prime minister.

Balbo's *Delle speranze d'Italia* (1844) argued in favor of a liberal Italian confederation led by Piedmont, with the Holy See lending international prestige. D'Azeglio's *Degli ultimi casi di Romagna* (1846) envisaged an Italian state centered on a reformed and modernized Catholic Church.[37] But it was Gioberti's work, the earliest of the three, that had the deepest influence. His *Del primato morale e civile degli Italiani* (1843) argued for a politically reformed Italian confederation in which the Roman pontiff would function as the fatherly guardian of the spirit of the nation, while Piedmont would guarantee its military security and point the way toward its national internal reforms.[38] Gioberti's insight was to recognize that the national movement could only succeed with the support of the Italian princes, and that the best way to achieve that was to keep talk of sociopolitical transformation as vague as possible. Thus in Gioberti's confederation, the Italian states would be free to retain their old forms of government under their existing ruling houses. He justified making the Roman pontiff the head of the confederation on the basis that the papacy was the essential Italian national institution, with an all-determining historical influence on Italian life and culture. Gioberti's suggestion was not an endorsement of the present pontifical state, whose failings he acknowledged, but rather a vision for a liberalizing pope who might return to the historic ideal of the papacy as Europe's spiritual father. Gioberti regarded religion as the source of civilization and saw Italy as the "religious nation par excellence" providing "the seeds of civilization to the cultured nations of the modern world."[39] Gioberti's vision was, in short, a Catholic intellectual's idea of how to preempt insurrectionary energy by reinstalling the traditional authorities on a mildly reformed footing.[40] (Luigi Poletti soon revealed himself an avid partisan, with copies of both Balbo and Gioberti in his library.)[41]

In this fevered atmosphere, Gregory XVI's death in 1846 was immediately recognized as a pivotal moment. If he were to have a likeminded successor, like his unpopular secretary of state Lambruschini, violence seemed inevitable.[42] But if his successor were to be a liberal reformer, moderates believed the crisis could be avoided. The conclave to elect that successor assembled for the first time on 14 June 1846, with Lambruschini as the odds-on favorite but with the liberal faction in the College of Cardinals hoping it could force a change of direction.[43] D'Azeglio's *Degli ultimi casi di Romagna* had celebrated the liberal Cardinal Gizzi, and he was seen at first as Lambruschini's strongest challenger, but from the first round of voting on 16 June it was clear the situation was fluid. No cardinal secured enough votes for election, and while Lambruschini led, a surprise candidate nipped at his heels: Cardinal Mastai-Ferretti, the bishop of Imola, who, at fifty-four years of age, was the candidate of youth. Mastai-Ferretti was known for his forthright criticisms of government excess and of the *centuroni* in particular, and in Imola, an area with significant insurrectionary unrest, he had enjoyed regular discussions of the latest liberal political works with local noble intellectuals.[44] One of these nobles, Count Giuseppe Pasolini, later recounted that when Mastai left to attend the conclave, he packed copies of Gioberti's *Primato*, Balbo's *Speranze*, and D'Azeglio's *Casi di Romagna*, promising that he would make whoever was elected pope read them.[45] Historians are skeptical about the veracity of the anecdote, but the point is clear enough. When Mastai himself was then elected pope, and on just the fourth ballot, it was a shocking result that would likely have been

PRELUDE TO A REVOLUTION

84. José Galofre y Coma, *Portrait of Pope Pius IX*, 1847.
Source: Château de Versailles, France / Bridgeman Images.

preempted by late-arriving Austrian cardinals had voting dragged on just a little longer.[46] Mastai took the name Pius IX in honor of Pius VII, who had preceded him at Imola and whom he admired for his measured responses to the upheavals that engulfed his pontificate (**Figure 84**).

And just like that, the chain of reaction inaugurated with the election of Leo XII in 1823 seemed to have been broken. The election was greeted in Rome by surprise that soon gave way to euphoria. Here is the chronicler at San Paolo:

> It is agreed by everyone that a better choice could not have been made. Great are the needs of Rome and of the State, and everyone places their hopes in him: a miracle, this, in a people who for fifteen years have grown accustomed to not love their Prince, and to hope only in a final revolution.[47]

Pius quickly won over the Roman masses with a series of unprecedented liberal reforms. Just a month after his election, and over the strenuous objections of the conservative holdovers from the pontificate of Gregory XVI – the so-called *Gregoriani* – he issued a general amnesty liberating political prisoners in the Papal States and political exiles outside of it.[48] Romans saw this as proof of a dramatic about-face in official attitudes toward the national cause, and it led to spontaneous public celebrations. As the painter Lehmann recalled,

> No words can give an adequate idea of the popular enthusiasm which the new pope's first liberal actions aroused in Rome ... Night after night crowds would assemble with torches and music in front of the Quirinal Palace, and not rest until, in response to their vociferous clamoring, the Pope had come out and given them his blessing from the balcony.[49]

A stream of other reforms followed.[50] After Gregory XVI's refusal to build railroads, Pius appointed a commission which in just two months produced a blueprint for the creation of a rail network in the pontifical territories.[51] (Letarouilly urged Poletti from Paris to seek the commission for one of the new stations: "It is a very beautiful building type and very important ... .")[52] Pius issued orders instructing local administrators throughout the Papal States to find or create work for the masses of unemployed; he also reformed the procedural norms of the law courts; he took steps to address the high cost of grain; he initiated the foundation of the first political periodical in the Papal States, *Il Contemporaneo*.[53] All this occurred before the end of 1846, and more followed in the new year: an agricultural institute, a gas works to provide streetlighting throughout the city, and contracts with an engineering company to construct four new suspension bridges across the Tiber.[54] Additional periodicals were also authorized – *L'Italico*, *Il Popolare*, *Il Viminale* – until finally in March Pius issued a new law on press freedoms that transformed Rome overnight from having the least to the most liberal public sphere in Italy.[55] Pius now had everyone's attention. Even Protestant organizations in the United States and England voiced their admiration.[56] Within Italy too, skeptics were hard to find; Giuseppe Mazzini, no less, expressed "immense hopefulness."[57] It was as though Gioberti's world-historical pope had suddenly materialized in reality.

The artistic community meanwhile swooned in anticipation of a transformative wave of pontifical commissions. The new *Giornale degli architetti* published a giddy article with the title, "Works of Architecture and Industry Attributable to [previous] Roman Pontiffs Who Bore the Name *Pius*."[58] By the end of August 1846, a Commission of Roman nobles was raising funds by public subscription for a Roman monument in Pius's honor. They specified that the winning project, "far from limiting itself to a purely decorative, sterile, and exterior pomp," would please His Holiness more if it aspired instead to the "more noble and beautiful scope which is that of public utility."[59]

In reality, the situation was more complicated than it looked. The reforms Pius was implementing were indeed advanced by European standards, and all but revolutionary in the context of the Papal States, but the many contemporaries who assumed that they were just a foretaste of still greater liberties to come, such as popular sovereignty were not paying attention to the other things Pius was saying.[60] Pius had entrusted the composition of his first encyclical, *Qui Pluribus* (9 November 1846), to Cardinal Lambruschini, in part to reassure the *Gregoriani* that he planned no revolutionary departures in essential matters. The text praised "our superior predecessor Gregory XVI," railed against "the doctrine of human progress," condemned freedom of religion, loosed a broadside against the "unspeakable doctrine of Communism," and finally decried the "filthy medley of errors" that resulted from "the unbridled license to think, speak, and write."[61] This document was at least as representative of Pius's worldview as his reforms, for Pius believed as profoundly as Gregory ever had that the authority of the Holy See was sacred and absolute. Where he differed was only in his estimate of how much governmental reform could be accommodated without impinging on that authority. Pius claimed to represent continuity, not revolution, even if he was perhaps too intoxicated by the affection of the crowds to risk declaring more clearly the limits of his reformism.[62]

Poletti immediately identified himself as an enthusiastic supporter of Pius's program. Within weeks he was corresponding with Pius's advisors about the new street-lighting system, and a year later published an ambitious proposal for the construction of a new Roman district – Borgo Pio – to be named for the new pope.[63] A few weeks after that, he published a breathlessly patriotic essay in the *Giornale arcadico* endorsing Pius's program and calling for Italian unity as the necessary prelude to restoring the Italian peninsula's economic prosperity and political influence.[64] Poletti was an exact contemporary of the pontiff (both were born in 1792), and he seems to have found him easier to relate to than he had the octogenarian Gregory. In every way, then, the pontificate got off to an excellent start from Poletti's perspective, and for the moment it appeared that work at San Paolo would soon regain its former momentum.

The first order of business for Poletti and Moreschi at San Paolo was to preempt the role of the Academy of St. Luke in adjudicating the four proposals Poletti had submitted on Gregory's orders. Pius's first visit to San Paolo came on 30 June, less than two weeks after his election. After a mass, he briefly toured the reconstruction site, where he especially admired the lacunar ceiling of the transept and the alabaster columns donated by Mehmet Ali.[65] That must have been music to Poletti's ears. By then, Moreschi had printed up a series of documents and historical testimonies relating to the four questions for circulation within the Special Commission.[66] The plan was to have the Commission vote on these independently of the Academy, in hopes that they would agree to send a request for full reinstatement of Poletti's original project directly to the pope.

Pius made another visit on 12 November.[67] When it was pointed out to him that several of the great wooden crossbeams were already in place atop the high nave walls, Pius spontaneously expressed a desire to mount the scaffolds to see up close how they were installed. Poletti obliged and climbed up with him, explaining that the roof could be completed by the end of the year. Moreschi writes of how Pius "passed excitedly amongst the thirty-two beams already in place, [and] marveled at their astonishing effect." Back at ground level, Poletti patiently maneuvered the pontiff over to his wooden model – something he was to do more than once in the months to come.[68] In so doing, he likely recalled Letarouilly's encouragement a year earlier to use the same tricks that Bernini and Antonio da Sangallo had used to persuade their popes: the "elegant model" of San Paolo, wrote the Frenchman, might be "presented at a favorable moment ... [and] could lead to a favorable solution."[69] Once Poletti had Pius before the model, he set to work explaining the virtues of his original project for the nave ceiling, the main façade, and quadriporticus. Letarouilly's advice was again apposite:

> ... for the sacred enclosure that must stand before your façade, go to the pope himself and speak to him as an artist of profound conviction and you will be eloquent. You are reproducing the system of the old churches, so everything should be complete, so that religious enclosure will stamp the monument with its true character. Nowadays, since religious ceremonies are modified, your church would be nonsensical if, after having adopted an ancient building type, one stopped before completing it, in violation of all the laws of unity and harmony. Use every means of persuasion with the pope ... his glory ... it is the monument that will honor his reign ... bring a whole range of considerations to his attention and you will triumph, I predict.[70]

Sheets of talking points for these occasions survive in Poletti's archive. One outlines the formal evolution of the Christian basilica with special emphasis on the "small forum or anti-temple or quadriporticus" that under Constantine became the key feature that distinguished the major basilicae from lesser ones that had only a narthex.[71] Moreschi did his part by writing in the *Diario di Roma* of how much Pius appreciated "those aspects of the architecture that, in addition to making the new fabric more magnificent, gave a full idea of the primitive basilicas of Christianity, among which the Ostian temple preserved to a large extent the architectonic forms and proportions that are now maintained in its reconstruction."[72]

Just one month later, Pius's new secretary of state, the liberal Cardinal Gizzi, wrote to the Academy of St. Luke officially canceling Cardinal Mattei's request from May 1846. Instead of reviewing all four of the proposals Poletti had prepared, Pius wanted the Academy instead to study only the matter of the west façade and quadriporticus; Pius would decide for himself about the rest – the alabaster columns, the papal chronology, and the statues of Peter and Paul.[73] With respect to the alabaster columns, Poletti had been at work mere days after Pius's election on a large presentation drawing of a new variant of his ciborium project, in which the alabaster columns now carried their superstructure directly *over* Arnolfo's ciborium[74] (**Figure 85**). Pius now agreed to this design, with the remaining two columns to be affixed to the interior wall of the west façade flanking the central door. Pius also decided that the chronology of papal portraits should be executed in mosaic throughout the church.[75] (Shortly thereafter Pius formed a committee to select painters to execute the oil sketches from which the mosaic versions would be derived, which immediately became the object of lobbying efforts by powerful patrons hoping to obtain posts for their pet artists.)[76] And finally, Pius decided that the nave at San Paolo should be covered with a lacunar ceiling after all. Gregory XVI's change of heart was thus swept entirely aside.

As for the two colossal statues of the apostles, Pius announced his decision about these at his weekly Monday audience on 1 February 1847.[77] Poletti had proposed installing them in front of the Arch of Placidia, effectively turning these two Pillars of the Church into *paragone* of the two great columns that supported the arch.[78] Pius's very different idea instead took everyone by surprise. He ordered that the statues be removed to St. Peter's Square and set up at the outer corners of the stairway that leads up to Maderno's vast façade.[79] The understanding seems to have been that new statues of Peter and Paul would eventually be commissioned for San Paolo to go in the places Poletti had recommended.[80] A diary entry in late March by Principe Don Agostino Chigi described Paul's journey by oxcart from San Paolo to his installation at St. Peter's; Peter followed within days[81] (**Figure 86**). Moreschi then published an account on the front page of the *Diario di Roma*.[82]

85. Luigi Poletti's project to reinstate his ciborium proposal by erecting it over that of Arnolfo di Cambio. Signed by Poletti and dated "June 1846," that is, just weeks after the election of Pius IX. *Source*: © 2022 Archivio Storico dell'Abbazia di San Paolo f.l.m.

This newly installed Peter and Paul joined the other prominent Peter and Paul pairings in Rome discussed in Chapter 11. This new pair affirmed yet again the *concordia fratrum* linking the two basilicae, even as it also affirmed that the protection of the two apostles over the city and over the Church were all one, because city and Church were inextricably bound. As a powerful public

86. Façade of St. Peter's basilica. The statues of Peter and Paul stand on plinths to the far left and right (partially obscured by video screens).
Source: Author.

gesture that offered meanings for both ordinary and erudite Romans, Pius here announces his rare instinct for employing the arts as a means of political communication. But for the very same reason, the move also risked the same danger that was to overshadow some of his other deeds in the coming months: namely, that a public yearning for political deliverance might misread it as evidence of intentions Pius did not harbor. That Pius should have chosen as his very first act of public art patronage in Rome to transfer these two protecting statues to St. Peter's, and thereby to affirm the unique religious status of the Eternal City, at a time when Gioberti's description of Italy as "the religious nation par excellence" was ringing in everyone's ears, and his vision of Italian national self-determination seemed more within reach than it ever had – this can only have encouraged the multitudes already determined to see Pius as the agent of Italy's coming national awakening.

As for the façade and quadriporticus, Poletti re-presented his drawings and accompanying memorandum to the Academy early in January 1847.[83] The memorandum opened with a stout defense of his original plan to demolish the old façade, which was so out of plumb that even Nicolai in 1815 had feared its imminent collapse.[84] In working to stabilize it in 1833, Poletti had become convinced that both it and the eighteenth-century narthex were beyond repair.

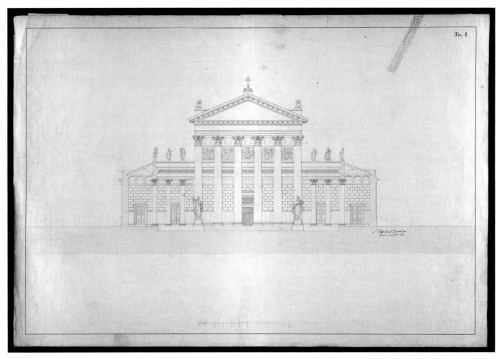

87. Elevation drawing of Poletti's pronaos façade option for the west front of the basilica of San Paolo fuori le mura, with the quadriporticus extending to either side. Signed by Poletti and dated November 1845.
Source: Biblioteca civica d'arte e architettura Luigi Poletti, Modena, Archivio Poletti, disegni inv. 315.

Moreover, the raising of the nave floor had disrupted the alignment between the façade and the nave behind it, while the removal of the façade mosaic for use in the transept had robbed it of its only notable feature. As for the narthex, Poletti anathemized it as a work in the "barbaric style of the last century" with "niches in the Chinese manner" [sic] that were wholly out of keeping with the rest of the edifice. The Chirograph, he affirmed, required its demolition.

The first of Poletti's three new façade proposals showed a colossal pronaos with six columns supporting a pediment (**Figure 87**). Beneath it sheltered a large mosaic of Christ with the apostles that more or less replicated the lowest register of the medieval mosaic in the apse of the basilica.[85] This was Poletti's original and preferred design, and it can be found illustrated in various other sketches in Poletti's archive (**Figure 88**). Poletti also remarked that this was the arrangement that one could "currently see on the model deposited in the basilica," which is not the case today because, as discussed earlier, the model was later altered to reflect the design that was ultimately approved.

Poletti also offered a second project that, with a notable lack of enthusiasm, he said responded to Gregory XVI's command to preserve the eighteenth-century narthex and eliminate the planned quadriporticus. The surviving drawing closest

PRELUDE TO A REVOLUTION

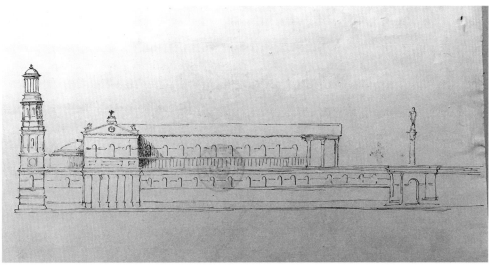

88. Undated sketch by Poletti showing the north flank of his vision for the reconstructed San Paolo fuori le mura. The pronaos façade is visible just to the left of the triumphal column shown rising up out of the quadriporticus.
Source: Biblioteca civica d'arte e architettura Luigi Poletti, Modena, Archivio Poletti, disegni inv. 554C.

in conception to this façade option is in the architect's archive in Modena, though it does in fact depict a quadriporticus[86] (**Plate 18**). Its execution, Poletti deadpanned, would pose major challenges. The whole wall would have to be essentially demolished and rebuilt to eliminate its being out of plumb and to align it with the new horizontal lines of the rest of the church. New columns would also have to be introduced since the old spolia ones would not have enough diameter for the new arrangement, while the old mosaic would have to be reconstituted, since the original had been removed to the crossing. In his drawing of these massive interventions, Poletti could not stop himself from also eliminating nearly everything of the old façade that he found unsightly (**Figure 89**). The upper part was the least changed, but in the middle zone he removed the original arrangement of squat arched windows framed by pilasters and bounded by curved volutes. In its place he depicted an austere colorless expanse containing just a pair of small inscriptions and a stemma. And then at the level of the narthex he changed everything. Gone is the "Chinese" arcading, along with the projections and recessions in the entablature. The only remaining echo of the original design sounds in the rhythm of the columns. The old design had presented single Ionic columns flanking the central archway and paired Corinthian ones flanking the others. Poletti gritted his teeth and reproduced this irregular rhythm but punished it by translating it into the humorless form of identical Corinthian columns fronting an arcade beneath an unbroken entablature.

Because this second project lacked a quadriporticus, Poletti offered a third option that included one, and which, he explained, better reflected the norms

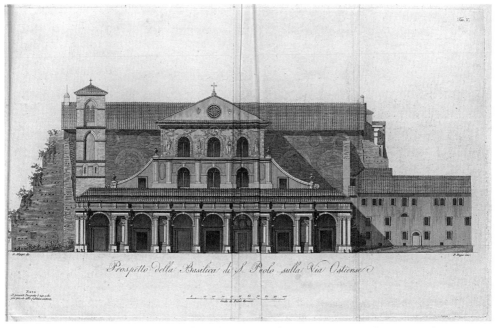

89. Engraving by Andrea Alippi showing the façade and portico of San Paolo fuori le mura before the fire of 1823 (from Nicolai [1815]).
Source: Bibliotheca Hertziana – Max Planck Institute for Art History.

of a traditional Early Christian basilica[87] (**Figure 90**). This mirrored the previous project in its upper and middle portions, but offered a more regular solution at narthex level: a long and even file of freestanding columns supporting the same uninterrupted entablature from project #2. Echoing Letarouilly, Poletti wrote that since the Early Christian basilicas all had had quadriportici, this project would permit San Paolo to present "the complete type of the old Christian basilicae." To save expense, he suggested that the façade be erected now and the quadriporticus left for later.

The subcommittee presented its report on 18 January 1847.[88] They announced at the start that they did not think one could in good conscience support Gregory XVI's orders, for all the reasons Poletti had listed. That eliminated option #2. The choice instead came down to the first and third projects, not least because each had a quadriporticus, which "revives in us the memory of the first times of the apostolic era," and recalled ancient religious practices that were fading from memory. The entirety of the Academy of St. Luke was convoked on 1 February to hear this report and vote on a final recommendation.

Poletti's personal correspondence indicates that his own preference was for his original project; around this same time, he was busily adding similar pedimented pronaos façades to the medieval church of San Venanzio in Camerino and to the seventeenth-century church of S. Maria dell'Orto in

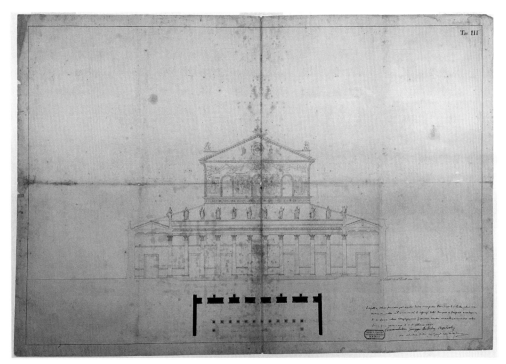

90. Poletti's third façade option for the basilica of San Paolo, representing a rationalized Paleochristian-style façade and quadriporticus.
Source: © 2022 Archivio Storico dell'Abbazia di San Paolo f.l.m.

Chiavari, while just a couple of years earlier he had lobbied unsuccessfully to introduce one at Santa Maria degli Angeli in Assisi.[89] As for San Paolo, Poletti wrote in a letter to Giovanni Domenico Navone the day before the Academy was to vote, "I confess that I have more affection for the first [option], because it was the first creature of my mind and my studies, it was born in unity with all the rest that I have done here, and because, being of our Roman style, it is founded on the classics."[90] But this project had apparently encountered serious resistance from a group that Poletti in his letter calls "the German school" – a group that, "with its handful of followers," wanted the façade to possess elements that Poletti could only regard as "essential defects ... inherent to the architecture of that period of decadence."[91]

Poletti was referring here to the painter Tommaso Minardi and his allies. Minardi was the longtime professor of drawing at the Academy of St. Luke, and though he was not German, he was one of the foremost representatives in papal Rome of artistic Romanticism, which Poletti unfailingly disparaged as "foreign," "nordic," or "German." Minardi was also associated with the German Nazarene painters in Rome, led by Friedrich Overbeck.[92] We will have much more to say about this milieu in Chapter 15, but for now suffice it to say that Minardi was a rare species in papal Rome: a Romantic academician who was critical of the pagan origins and worldly aesthetics of artistic classicism. For years, and with limited results, Minardi had been advocating a religious art that would draw on what he regarded as the spiritually authentic painting of the fourteenth and fifteenth centuries, from Giotto to the early Raphael.[93] Minardi had been on the subcommittee that issued the initial report recommending Poletti's first and third projects for the façade, but clearly had been unhappy with that verdict, for he read out a minority report to the general congress a month later. This strongly criticized Poletti's first project, pointing out that there were no examples of pronaos façades in early Christian architecture. Such a thing might look well on the Pantheon, he wrote, but would be completely disharmonious here; it would also appear out of scale and would reduce the columns of the nave to a disappointing anticlimax. And in case anyone was still keeping track, it also violated the Chirograph.[94]

Minardi's opposition to Poletti's pronaos was not of recent vintage. Already in October 1845, in his correspondence with Letarouilly, Poletti had written bitterly about "the painter" who was opposing him. Letarouilly had replied:

> As for the façade, try to bring the painter himself into your interests. Have him understand that on the exterior his work will be short-lived and a poor fit; start today working on him, to compensate him with a choice spot on the interior, on the great arch of the apse, or on a frieze above the papal portraits, where he'll be able to operate his paintbrush for a nice long time. Despite how badly painting understands its true interests, it will soon be in agreement with the architect.[95]

Unfortunately for Poletti, it had not worked out that way, and he had been compelled to include option #3 in hopes of mollifying "the painter."

In the end, Poletti faced the vote of 1 February with equanimity, claiming in his letter to Navone that "I don't mind either result, because whether they choose the first or the third project, my interests will be equally well served."[96] On the big day, two other members also weighed in with minority reports: the architect Antonio Sarti, who had been on the original subcommittee with Minardi, and the painter Ferdinando Cavalleri.[97] In their brief statements, both argued that the task at hand was not to judge the beauty but rather the appropriateness of the designs to the style of the existing building. Cavalleri did not explicitly signal a preference but clearly regarded Project #1 as the beautiful one ("the style of Pericles and Augustus") and Project #3 as the more appropriate one (the style "of Constantine and his successors").[98] Sarti made the same point but came down unambiguously in favor of Project #3, pointing out that Project #1 was a clear-cut violation of the Chirograph.

After hearing all this, the Academy voted unanimously for Project #3. In their final statement, they noted that they did not regard it to be the most magnificent option, and had selected it only because it accorded best with the

PRELUDE TO A REVOLUTION

Chirograph and with the style of the rest of the building.[99] The decision marked a significant change from the attitudes that had prevailed in the Academy during the 1820s and 1830s and suggests that a new generation of academicians hoped to mark its distance from the less preservationist instincts that only recently had dominated the company. We will return to this theme in the pages ahead.

NOTES

1   *DdR*, 16 October 1841, pp. 1–2; *DdR*, 13 September 1842, pp. 1–2.
2   The global reach of the effort is illustrated vividly by a donation pledge forwarded to Cardinal Secretary of State Luigi Lambruschini in December 1841 in a battered envelope bearing the postal stamps "India," "Colombo," "Malta," "Antibes," "Paquebots de la Mediterranée," "Genova," and "Roma" (ASP: 6/a, b. 1841, f. 3).
3   "Nota delle Oblazioni avutesi in favore della riedificazione della Basilica Ostiense da Gennaro 1841, a tutto Febraro 1842," 28 February 1842 (ASP: 6/a, b. 1841, f. 6).
4   Head (1849), pp. 80–81.
5   Humphreys (1840), p. 60.
6   Luigi Poletti, "Rapporto sulla riedificazione della Basilica di S. Paolo," 1842 (ASR: CSRBSP Computisteria b. 69, f. 14; a draft appears in BCALP: LP37 C129 20).
7   "Rapporto . . ." as in Chapter 10 n. 52.
8   Special Commission to Pope Pius IX, October 1864 (ASR: CSRBSP Segreteria b.282); Luigi Poletti, "Relazione con Allegato riguardante tanto lo stato attuale de lavori nella nuova fabbrica della Basilica di San Paolo," 25 November 1867 (ASR: CSRBSP Segreteria b. 283).
9   *Cronaca* II, 25 October 1843.
10 Crocella (1982), pp. 21–30; Felisini (1990).
11 *Cronaca* II, 22 December 1839.
12 Mario Mattei to Antonio Tosti, 25 November 1844 (ASR: CSRBSP Segreteria b. 276, f. 12). Groblewski suggests that Gregory might also have hoped to signal a hierarchy between the transept, with its altars, and the nave, which had none (Groblewski [2001], pp. 235–236).
13 Luigi Poletti to Antonio Tosti, 29 November 1844 (BCALP: LP37 C121; ASR: CSRBSP Segreteria b. 276, f. 10); Luigi Poletti to Antonio Tosti, 30 December 1844 (BCALP: LP37 C121; ASP: 32/c, b. 1828-50, f. 4).
14 Luigi Poletti to Antonio Tosti, 30 December 1844 (BCALP: LP37 C121; ASP: 32/c, b. 1828-50, f. 4); Luigi Moreschi, Notes for a General Congress of the Special Commission, 1845 (ASR: CSRBSP Segreteria b. 276, f. 10).
15 Strozzieri (2021), p. 117.
16 Tosti (1835).
17 *DdR*, 18 January 1845, p. 1.
18 Belli (1889), v. 5, p. 272.
19 Belli (1889), v. 5, pp. 272–273.
20 Riassunto dei pagamenti e delle spese settimanali dal 16 al 21 Xbre 1844, 12 December 1844 (ASP: 5/c, b. 1844, f. 1).
21 *Cronaca* II, 30 June 1845.
22 Paul Marie Letarouilly to Luigi Poletti, 8 October 1845 (BCALP: LP48 C16; tiSAD doc. 79, pp. 25–26).
23 Letarouilly to Poletti, as in Chapter 13 n. 22.

24 Poletti all but admitted his strategy of delay to his assistant Vespignani (Luigi Poletti to Virginio Vespignani, 19 February 1845 [BCALP: LP37 C122]).

25 Luigi Poletti, Memo for Pope Pius IX, 12 August 1845 (ASR: CSRBSP Segreteria b. 276, f. 6; tiG pp. 437–438). Mattei and Antonelli also spoke with Poletti about the altars for the terminal walls of the transept. Following a visit to San Paolo in 1839 by Russian crown prince and future Tsar Alexander II, the reigning Tsar Nicolas of Russia had sent Pope Gregory a gift of green malachite for the basilica. The gift came at a moment of rupture in relations with the tsar following Russia's suppression of the Rutherian Church in 1839 and was probably intended as a diplomatic offering. Poletti planned to employ the malachite on the transept altar fronts, but by the time Mattei and Antonelli visited this still had not been executed. They told Poletti that Tsar Nicolas was expected toward the end of the year, and that Gregory wanted the malachite in place by then. Poletti obeyed, and on 16 December Tsar Nicolas made an incognito visit and was shown the newly installed panels. (In addition to Poletti's memo, cited earlier, see *Cronaca* II, 3 January 1839 and 16 December 1845; Antonio Tosti to Luigi Poletti, 31 August 1842 [ASR: CSRBSP Segreteria b. 276]; *DdR*, 28 October 1845, pp. 1–2; Chigi (1906), v. 1, pp. 173–174.) On Gregory's relations with the tsar, see Korten (2015). For a different interpretation of the tsar's gifts, see Groblewski (2001), pp. 224–227.

26 Mario Mattei and Luigi Moreschi to the ASL, 21 June 1845 (AASL: v. 105, no. 81; tiG pp. 436–437).

27 *DdR: NdG*, 13 March 1834, p. 1.

28 Moreschi (1846), Sommario Num. IV, first section on statues of Peter and Paul, Letter N ("Dichiarazione del ricevimento …"), p. 14, and Letter O ("Avviso del Prof. Tadolini …"), p. 15. On Tadolini's San Paolo, see Melchiorri (1836). On these statues generally, see Bagnarini (2015).

29 Among the plans he submitted that day, I have been able to track down the following:
(1) Tav. I. [Watercolor showing option 1 for the west façade], November 1845 (BCALP: C3 315).
(2) Tav. II. [Watercolor showing option 2 for the west façade], November 1845 (BCALP: C3 316).
(3) Tav. III [Drawing of façade option 3], November 1845 (ASP: uncatalogued).
(4) [Color version of façade option 3] (ASP: uncatalogued; *Maestà* [2003], p. 499).
(5) Tav IV [Drawing depicting one of the projects for the inner face of the main façade], [April 1846] (BCALP: C3 319).
(6) Tav. V. [Watercolor showing one of the alternatives for the inside of the west façade], November 1845 (BCALP: C3 317).
(7) Tav. VI [Drawing depicting one of the projects for the inner face of the main façade], [April 1846] (BCALP: C3 318).

30 Poletti, "Relazione …" as in Chapter 10 n. 36.

31 Mario Mattei to Giovanni Silvagni, 22 May 1846 (AASL: v. 105, no. 81; tiG pp. 445–446). The ASL meeting on 29 May 1846 is discussed in the "Rapporto della Commissione speciale della I[nsigne] e P[ontificia] Accademia di S Luca sui desegni della facciata principale della Basilica di S. Paolo," 18 January 1847 (AASL: v. 106, no. 33; tiG pp. 451–453).

32 *Cronaca* II, 1 June 1846.

33 Lehmann (1894), p. 92.

34 Haddock (1998), pp. 705–707.

35 Haddock (1998), p. 720.

36 Berkeley and Berkeley (1932–1940), v. 1, pp. 135–193.

37 Balbo (1844); D'Azeglio (1846).

38 Gioberti (1843).

39 Gioberti (1843); Berkeley and Berkeley (1932–1940), v.1, pp. 154–173; Lo Curto and Themelly (1976), pp. 124–130; Haddock (1998), pp. 714–715.

40 De Rosa (1970), pp. 285–297.

41 Poletti later published a neo-Guelph proposal for an Italian free-trade agreement and railroad network (Poletti [1848a] and [1848b]).

42 This was the same Lambruschini who, while still archibishop of Genova, had authored the 1825 pastoral letter soliciting donations for San Paolo. See Chapter 5.

43 Berkeley and Berkeley (1932–1940), v. 1, pp. 267–276; Martina (1974–1990), v. 1, pp. 81–96.

44 Pasolini (1887), pp. 57–58.

45 Pasolini (1887), p. 61. Martina casts doubt on the accuracy of the claim (Martina [1974–1990], v. 1, p. 91).

46 Berkeley and Berkeley (1932–1940), v. 1, p. 273; Martina and Gramatowski (1996).

47 *Cronaca* II, 17 June 1846.

48 Berkeley and Berkeley (1932–1940), v. 2, pp. 35–54; Martina (1974–1990), v. 1, pp. 97–121.

49 Lehmann (1894), pp. 95–96.

50 Berkeley and Berkeley ([1932–1940], v. 2, pp. 55–71) provide a handy summary.

51 The famous quote of Gregory XVI ("chemin de fer, chemin d'enfer") comes from Pasolini ([1887], p. 220); it is now recognized as apochryphal. For a more even-handed study of Gregory XVI's attitude toward railways, see Negri (1968).

52 Paul Marie Letarouilly to Luigi Poletti, 6 September 1846 (BCALP: LP48 C17).

53 Majolo Molinari (1963), v. 1, pp. 239–241

54 D'Onofrio (1970), p. 174.

55 Majolo Molinari (1963), v. 1, pp. xxiii–xxv.

56 Aubert (1952), pp. 20–21.

57 Mazzini (1847), unpag.

58 Gasparoni (1846) and (1847).

59 *Programma* (1846). Proposals soon began appearing in the press, for instance in *Il Viminale* and the *Giornale degli architetti*.

60 Hearder (1975), p. 170.

61 Aubert (1952), pp. 19–20; *TEPD*, v. 4, pp. 13–23.

62 Aubert (1952), pp. 27–31; Hearder (1975), p. 170. On these questions, see Veca (2018a).

63 Alessandro Cisterni to Luigi Poletti, 26 September 1846 (BCALP: LP48 C17 A); [Luigi Poletti], "Progetto per un Rione XV in Roma col nome di PIO," *Il Viminale*, 30 December 1847, 156–157; reprinted in "I progetti fioccano," *Il girovago farfalla*, 15 February 1848, pp. 33–34.

64 Poletti (1848a).

65 *DdR*, 7 July 1846, p. 1; *Cronaca* II, 30 June 1846; *L'Amico cattolico* (Milan) 6:18 (September 1846): p. 234.

66 Moreschi (1846).

67 *DdR*, 17 November 1846, p. 1.

68 For example: *DdR*, 23 October 1847, p. 1.

69 Letarouilly to Poletti, as in Chapter 13 n. 22.

70 Letarouilly to Poletti, as in Chapter 13 n. 22.

71 Luigi Poletti, Untitled notes, [1846?] (BCALP: LP37 C132 5).

72 *DdR*, 17 November 1846, p. 1.

73 Tommaso Pasquale Gizzi to the ASL, 12 December 1846 (AASL: v. 106, no. 46); Borgnana (1847).

74 The drawing is uncataloged in the ASP. It is signed by Poletti and dated June 1846 in the bottom-right corner.

75 Borgnana (1847); *DESE*, v. 53, "Pio IX, Papa CCLV regnante," p. 191; Capitelli (2011), p. 26.

76 Capitelli (2011), p. 39.

77 Lorenzo Lucidi to Giacomo Antonelli, 3 February 1847 (ASR: CSRBSP Fabbrica b. 4, f. 9); *DESE*, v. 53, "Pio IX, Papa CCLV regnante," p. 191 incorrectly claims the decision was taken in March 1847.

78 Poletti, "Relazione . . ." as in Chapter 10 n. 36.

79 Lucidi to Antonelli, as in Chapter 13 n. 77.

80 This did not happen until 1856, after the nave was largely completed. Bagnarini (2013).

81 Chigi (1906), p. 186.

82 *DdR*, 27 March 1847, p. 1.

83 Poletti, "Relazione . . ." as in Chapter 10 n. 36.

84 Nicolai (1815), p. 311.

85 BCALP: LP C3 315 (illustrated in Susinno et al. [2003], p. 499). Poletti depicted the colossal statues of Peter and Paul standing before the façade, as they were not yet slated for reassignment to St. Peter's.

86 BCALP: LP C3 316 (illustrated in Susinno et al. [2003], p. 499).

87 ASP: Drawer 1 in large cabinet (illustrated in Susinno et al. [2003], p. 499).

88 "Rapporto . . ." as in Chapter 13 n. 31.

89 Salimbeni (2008), p. 317.

90 Luigi Poletti to Giovanni Domenico Navone, 31 January 1847 (BEM: Autografoteca Campori, "Poletti, Luigi" [cc. 92], c. 82; tiSAD doc. 55, p. 18).

91 Poletti to Navone, as in Chapter 13 n. 90.

92 Ricci (2006).

93 Susinno (1982), pp. i–xxxi; Ricci (2011).

94 Tommaso Minardi, "Parere," 1 February 1847 (AASL: v. 106, no. 45; tiG pp. 449–450). These critiques mirrored Minardi's theories about the restoration of paintings. See Ventra (2013).

95 Letarouilly to Poletti, as in Chapter 13 n. 22.

96 Poletti to Navone, as in Chapter 13 n. 90.

97 Ferdinando Cavalleri, "Alcune brevi osservazioni che il Segretario del Consiglio prega di rassegnare ai Sig. Professori prima che di venga all'Esame dei progetti per la facciata della Basilica Ostiense," 1 February 1847 (AASL: v. 106, no. 43; tiG pp. 447–448); Antonio Sarti, "Parere," 1 February 1847 (AASL: v. 106, no. 44; tiG pp. 448–449); Minardi, "Parere," as in Chapter 13 n. 94. All of these are present in copy as well in ASR: CSRBSP Segreteria b. 276, f. 11.

98 Cavalleri, "Alcune brevi osservazioni. . ." as in Chapter 13 n. 97.

99 Giuseppe De Fabris and Salvatore Betti, "Congregazione generale Straodinaria tenuta nella Patriarchale Basilica di S. Paolo," 1 February 1847 (AASL: v. 106, no. 46; ASR: CSRBSP Segreteria b. 276, f. 11).

FOURTEEN

EIGHTEEN FORTY-EIGHT

B Y THE LATE SPRING OF 1847, POPE PIUS'S REFORMIST ASPIRATIONS were increasingly undermined by political realities. Radicals had adopted the menacing strategy of reminding Pius in raucous public assemblies of just how bitterly disappointed they would be if he were ever to let them down; Pius's efforts to correct their misunderstanding naturally made little impression.[1] On Pius's other flank, the *Gregoriani* who remained as what might almost be called the "deep state" of the papal government – especially in the police – were widely suspected to be plotting provocations that would justify a crackdown. The table was thus set for the genuine crisis that unfolded after 5 July when, after months of pressure and hesitation, Pius signed off on the formation of an armed Civic Guard. The aim was to create a force capable of keeping order in uncertain times, but the risk was that it placed arms in the hands of civilians whose reliability was far from guaranteed. Secretary of State Gizzi at once resigned, leaving the most important office in the papal government empty at a crucial moment. The Austrians, meanwhile, were incensed that Pius intended to hand out arms to the citizenry, especially after the Guard swelled with anti-Austrian dissidents enticed by the promise of a weapon.[2] A series of unofficial celebrations scheduled for the first anniversary of Pius's amnesty of political prisoners in mid-July left Rome teetering on the brink of insurrection. By August, skirmishes between armed liberals and the Austrians garrisoned at Ferrara had badly damaged relations between Austria and the papacy.

As a direct consequence, relations between Piedmont and the papacy improved. Pius had been working hard to organize an Italian customs union, which he viewed as a forerunner to a Giobertian confederation spanning the whole peninsula (this was the union that Poletti endorsed in his pamphlet about Italian unity), and in November 1847 a series of very productive meetings on this proposal took place between representatives of Pius, King Carlo Alberto of Piedmont, and the Grand Duke of Tuscany. Pius regarded the union as the best alternative to a national war of liberation against the Austrians, which, because the Austrians were Catholic, he knew he could never approve. Carlo Alberto, on the other hand, viewed such a war as desirable and inevitable, and was keen to lead a united Italian force into it with the Vicar of Rome by his side. Divergent agendas notwithstanding, Pius IX was very popular in Turin by October–November 1847.[3]

These were the circumstances that produced the publication in November of a remarkable article about San Paolo in Turin's leading illustrated magazine, *Il mondo illustrato*.[4] This magazine was a liberal journal whose politics were announced by a masthead that showed a reclining figure of Piedmont sending out a winged herald bearing *Il mondo illustrato* toward a crowded landscape of famous monuments from across Italy but mainly from Rome. The article was signed by a certain Girolamo Amati, who later served as a polemicist-for-hire for Pius's government.[5] The article was therefore Roman in origin, with the ostensible purpose of shaping opinion in Piedmont. (The paper's publishers, however, revealed their distance from Roman ecclesiastical culture when they used two rather famous engravings of old St. Peter's to illustrate the article, cluelessly captioned as views of "the basilica of San Paolo.")

Amati's article opened with a history that said not one word about St. Paul or religion, but instead connected the basilica to the history of Italy: to the invasions by the Lombards and Saracens, the donation of Charlemagne during his visit to Rome in 800, and so on. It then offered a rapid description of the old basilica, heavy on the quantities and varieties of marble employed, before abruptly declaring that "this edifice, which spoke to us in the imposing language of fifteen centuries, and which married the majesty of its site to the most honored memories of our religious and civil history," was destroyed by fire in 1823.

Amati then turned to the reconstruction, quoting at length from the Gioacchino Ventura essay published in *Diario di Roma* in 1825, which we discussed in Chapter 5.[6] Ventura had reflected upon Rome's eternal resilience, its providential status as the seat of the Catholic religion, its universality as the city in which "no one, Catholics in particular, is a stranger; which is the fatherland of everyone," and whose sacred monuments, finally, were also universal. At the time, Ventura had been a disciple of Lamennais, and his essay had sought to situate the reconstruction of San Paolo in a providentialist reading of a resacralized Eternal City.[7] Amati, however, provided a very different contextualization, writing that the essay had constituted "the first germs of those theories which, developed and disseminated by Gioberti, have after 20 years returned Rome to the dignity of its ancient primacy." Amati's appropriation of Ventura's text for the neo-Guelph cause might have been plausible to readers because Ventura, after withdrawing from public life in 1832 after Gregory XVI's condemnation of Lamennasian ideas, had just recently returned to fame across Catholic Europe with a text that was to become an instant classic of liberal Catholicism: his funeral oration for Daniel O'Connell, an Irish statesman who had devoted his life to the struggle against British anti-Catholicism in Ireland.[8] Ventura's thinking had thus evolved; he now embraced the view that all men bore within their souls an essentially Christian yearning for freedom, and that the Church therefore needed to embrace revolution, though always bending it in a Christian direction. The alternative was to end up standing always with the oppressor.[9] Ventura had quickly gained a place in Pius IX's circle of advisors, and it was Pius who had selected Ventura to deliver O'Connell's funeral elegy when the Irishman died in Genoa on 15 May. Ventura mesmerized a standing-room-only crowd at the Roman church of Sant'Andrea della Valle over two nights with a stirring depiction of this exemplary Catholic revolutionary who had liberated his people without ever resorting to violence, and who had advanced the causes of both religion and political freedom. Ventura's words were soon published in several languages. Amati thus invoked a European celebrity when he quoted Ventura as "the illustrious lauder of O'Connell," and this was all it took to cast Ventura's words from two decades earlier in an entirely new light. And this allowed Amati to expand his presentation of San Paolo as a key monument of Italian history and national culture into something even broader: a neo-Guelph statement about the specifically religious quality of Italian culture. The result is an essay on San Paolo unlike any that had been written before. Rather than describe a Roman San Paolo chiefly of interest to Catholics, the article depicted its reconstruction as a national event, in Italy's most storied city, and therefore of natural interest to a patriotic readership in Piedmont.

The remainder of the essay manifested this shift by discussing the basilica in a frank and objective manner entirely different to the mandarin *Diario di Roma*. The budget, for instance, is discussed openly and in detail, as is the regrettable fact that some aspects of the design were less successful than others. To read these paragraphs is to witness San Paolo's abortive audition for the role, not of religious icon, but of an emblematic national monument: a Cologne Cathedral for the new Italian nation.

By January 1848, the political situation was unraveling all over Italy. Political pressures and local uprisings had prompted the Kingdom of the Two Sicilies, the Kingdom of Piedmont, and the Grand Duchy of Tuscany all to grant constitutions within days of one another. Meanwhile, the appetite for a war of national liberation to expel the Austrians had reached a fever pitch, intensifying pressure on Pope Pius to signal his support. His refusal to sanction a war against another Catholic state also prevented him granting his subjects a constitution, for he knew that if even a modicum of political power were placed in their hands, they would demand exactly such a war. In despair, he redoubled his efforts in favor of a Giobertian league of Italian nations, but events overtook him: uprisings in Paris (24 February) and Vienna (13 March) narrowed his options, and on 15 March, against his better judgment, he too gave his subjects a constitution. This provided for an elected Council of Deputies and an appointed High Council (to which, among other luminaries, Pius named Luigi Poletti).[10]

As Piedmont girded itself to launch the long-awaited war against Austria, Pius sent Papal troops north to assume a defensive posture at the frontier. But once fighting erupted and Piedmont won its first successes against the Austrians, Pius's troops broke ranks and flocked over the border to join the fighting. Pius responded with his fateful Allocution of 29 April, which stated unequivocally that the papal government could never be a party to a war against a fellow Catholic country. This was a crushing blow to patriots across Italy who still hoped that national liberation might be sanctified by papal participation.[11] Pius's entire cabinet of ministers resigned. Pius himself was genuinely puzzled that people failed to understand his position, for personally he remained sympathetic toward the Italian cause. As he put it to a representative of the Piedmontese government in March, "If I could still sign *Mastai*, I'd grab the pen immediately and it would be done, because I'm Italian too. But I have to sign *Pius IX*, and this name obligates me to kneel down before God and entreat the infinite wisdom of God to illuminate me."[12]

The precarity of the moment was certainly palpable at the San Paolo worksite. In the first days of 1848, Pius transferred to San Paolo the poor relief work crews that previously had been laboring at Verano Cemetery.[13] Poletti protested that he had no need of three hundred unskilled workers, but he was ignored and incidents of rebellion, insolence, and theft were soon reported at the worksite.[14] Yet the work ground slowly on. When the Frenchman Théodore Belamy visited in March or April 1848, he found "the five naves still entirely obstructed by the immense scaffolds of the masons, stone cutters, sculptors, and plasterers, and I could barely make my way through all the debris, as though I were in the middle of a working stone quarry."[15] That spring Pius ordered the erection of a full-scale painted cardboard model of Poletti's ciborium, while the Special Commission met to hash out details for the gilding of the nave ceiling, the papal chronology portraits, and the provisionment of materials.[16] In summer, Pius agreed to a request from the Special Commission to redirect a variety of rents, tributes, and taxes to the San Paolo workshop for one year so that the work could be completed in time for the Jubilee of 1850.[17] Funds were released for the nave ceiling, and the temporary counterapse from 1840 that divided transept and nave was torn down. Pius also had a large red granite column transferred from the Pontifical Armory to San Paolo and ordered Poletti to draw up a project to erect it in front of the north porch as a triumphal column. Capped by a bronze statue of St. Paul, it was to announce the basilica to pilgrims coming down the via Ostiense from the city.[18] A model of the column with four plaster figures was soon erected so that the effect could be judged. But despite these small developments, the atmosphere at the basilica was anxious. In October, Moreschi's annual progress report for the renamed *Gazzetta di Roma* ran to half its usual length.[19]

On 26 October Pius somehow found time to visit the basilica. There, in the company of his newest prime minister, the formidable Pellegrino Rossi, he studied the cardboard model of the ciborium. The monastery chronicler said Pius felt it was "not bad" but ordered that it stay in place longer so that more opinions could be collected. After recording this, the chronicler allowed himself an editorial aside:

> What is extraordinary in all this is to see everybody thinking so calmly about the San Paolo workshop, as though the Papal States were rolling in wealth and basking in the warmth of an agreeable peace. Instead, gold and silver have vanished, some paper money is circulating, and government affairs have been brought to such a state of affairs by the rampant revolution that fear has invaded every soul. One's hopes are placed entirely in the consumate expertise of Minister Rossi. But when hopes are reduced to a single man, the smallest breath can blow them away.[20]

Written immediately after this somber reflection, in different ink, is an even somberer coda: "*And so it was.*" For just twenty days after these words were written, on 15 November 1848, Rossi was assassinated as he arrived at the Cancelleria for a meeting of the Consulta. With this act, the revolution began. A mob descended upon Pius's residence at the Quirinal throwing rocks and firing shots, and a bishop peering through a window was killed by a stray bullet.[21] A panicked Pius offered new concessions, then about a week later surprised even his closest associates by disguising himself behind a pair of enormous spectacles and fleeing the city.[22] He made for the Kingdom of Naples, unsure of where he would end up and for how long.[23] The monastery chronicler at San Paolo wrote now of payback for the "intemperate joy of the past few years" and bitterly repented his harsh assessment of Gregory XVI's pontificate two years previously. Now calling Gregory "immortal," he showered the late pontiff with praise for having recognized what everyone else was now learning the hard way: that there "could be no accommodation between light and dark."[24]

The government that Pius left behind in Rome was implicated in the unrest. The assassination of Rossi was probably planned by Pietro Sterbini, who was a member of the Council of Deputies as well as a medical doctor and journalist. When Pius hurled anathemas from his refuge at Gaeta, the Deputies regretted that no one knew for certain whether he was speaking of his own free will. On 29 November, the government created a new State Council to organize elections for a full Constituent Assembly.

One might assume that the San Paolo worksite would close in such times, but that did not happen. The Special Commission even submitted a budget request for 1849 to the government, doggedly noting that the pope had not rescinded his intention to unveil the completed basilica at the 1850 Jubilee.[25] But long before this could be considered, San Paolo received funding through other means. On 4–7 December, Sterbini, newly appointed as minister of public works, requested funds from the Council of Deputies to create employment for the legions of newly idle laborers and artisans, two hundred of whom he planned to send to San Paolo as the papal administration had done the previous year.[26] Radical deputies initially complained that public monies could not legally be spent on San Paolo as it was technically not a state project, but they withdrew their objections when the plan was reframed as an emergency measure. In December, Sterbini ordered Poletti to prepare for the arrival of the workers.[27] In January 1849, Sterbini decided it was most efficient to deploy the new men on the papal chronology and so ordered Poletti to restart work on it.[28] (No one in the circumstances seems to have noticed the irony of the order.)[29] A week later, Sterbini suspended all the existing painters' contracts pertaining to the portraits for the chronology and created a commission to review each one.[30] He was aware that clientism and lobbying had attended the distribution of these contracts in 1847, and probably hoped to assemble a more politically reliable or even more artistically meritorious team.[31]

Elections for the new Constituent Assembly were meanwhile scheduled for 21–22 January. Revolutionary orators including the famous Ciceruacchio made repeated campaign appearances at the now-swarming San Paolo worksite, urging the workers to repudiate clerical government and to elect republican candidates. On election day, a group reported to contain some eight hundred laborers worked themselves up into such a frenzy that the monks of the monastery felt compelled to hide. Amid chants of "Death to the priests," a tricolor republican flag was flown over the basilica – a profanation so grave that two spry monks clambered up and tore it down. The workers then assembled in the piazza before the basilica to declare the day an official holiday in honor of "Love of Country." Speeches were given and then they marched off to the Capitoline to vote, though not before walking once more around the monastery chanting revolutionary slogans beneath the monks' windows.[32]

On 6 February, the newly elected Constituent Assembly declared the pope's temporal power at an end. Rome was henceforth a republic. The new government continued supporting the work at San Paolo in the context of Sterbini's public-works scheme, but the tone changed. Less than a week after the election, a *bando* from Sterbini's office went up around the basilica announcing new regulations that forbade smoking, drunkenness, theft of tools or material, the carrying of open flames or weapons, and insubordination. All supervisors were ordered to assess the skills of the men working for them and to report those lacking the requisite competences. (The notice also affirmed that the government was not in a position to satisfy recent demands for pay raises.)[33] Two weeks after that, Sterbini informed Poletti that all workers, the architect director included, would have to sign a declaration of loyalty to the Republic. Some of Poletti's assistants – Pietro Bosio, for instance – signed immediately, but Poletti put Sterbini off by replying that technically he was not an employee: his post, he wrote, was "an honor, and in no sense a civil employment," and therefore he considered himself exempt.[34] On 23 March, the Constituent Assembly opened a new credit of 18,000 scudi for the workshop at the Ministry of Commerce, specifically earmarked to pay workers' salaries.[35] According to Sterbini's own testimony after the fall of the Republic, his efforts ultimately increased the number of workers at the basilica to as many as 1,000.[36]

The larger political situation remained fluid. Sixteen days after Pius IX arrived in Gaeta, Louis-Napoleon Bonaparte, a nephew of Napoleon I, was elected president of the French Republic. It was an exciting result for Roman republicans, who recalled that in 1831 Louis-Napoleon with his brother had tried to foment a revolt in Rome against Gregory XVI.[37] In March 1849, Pius IX and his wily new secretary of state, Giacomo Antonelli, convoked a Conference of Catholic Powers at Gaeta.[38] By this point, Pius had unsuccessfully begged the Austrians to intervene militarily in Rome and was growing desperate.[39] Louis-Napoleon's envoys to the conference proposed that France would recapture Rome for the papacy if Pius would agree to rule thereafter according to the Constitution of 1848. This suited both Louis-Napoleon's convictions and his domestic political requirements, but Pius and Antonelli flatly refused. Louis-Napoleon brushed this aside and on 24 April, with no agreement in place, landed a French military force at Civitavecchia, led by General Charles Nicolas Victor Oudinot.[40] Within days, a team from Rome's municipal government arrived at San Paolo to construct a barricade. According to the monastery chronicle, the workers inside the basilica took this as a signal to begin brazenly stealing whatever took their fancy.[41] But on 29 April, the Republic's plan changed: the barricade was abandoned and the troops were withdrawn to create a defensive perimeter closer in, at the Aurelian wall. San Paolo, lying 2 kilometers outside of the wall, was now in no-man's land.[42]

The first French assault came on 30 April to the northwest and was badly mismanaged. Expecting to be welcomed as liberators, the French were instead savagely ambushed by Garibaldi's irregulars. The rumor that a number of priests had been murdered at their city house of San Callisto reached the monks of San Paolo that day, prompting some to flee and others to volunteer as scouts for the French.[43] In Paris, the French government was dismayed by the ferocity of the Roman resistance and sent an envoy, Ferdinand de Lesseps, to negotiate a fraternal resolution with their fellow republicans in Rome.[44] But after the failure of de Lesseps's brief mission, the humiliated General Oudinot unilaterally declared war on the Roman Republic. On the eve of his assault, he sent a force to secure the monastery and basilica at San Paolo against damage.[45] (Within the delighted monastery, this move was explained with a characteristically paranoid rumor: a spy from the city had supposedly gotten word to Oudinot that Mazzini was planning to destroy all religious buildings and slaughter all clerics the following day.)[46] Oudinot's men built fortifications from Poletti's stockpiled building materials, and the general himself made several appearances, even holding a series of meetings there with the archaeologist Giovanni Battista de Rossi concerning a most improbable plan to penetrate the city militarily via the ancient catacombs.[47] Finally, at the end of June, the French mounted a second and this time overwhelming assault on the city. The Romans fought bravely but quickly surrendered. The leaders of the Republic melted away, Mazzini to Switzerland, Garibaldi to New York, vowing to fight another day. The basilica emerged from the conflict essentially intact aside from the cardboard model of the honorary column Pius hoped to dedicate to St. Paul, which had mysteriously vanished.[48]

Pius and Antonelli had never agreed to Louis-Napoleon's terms for how the "liberated" city was to be governed, and they now quickly dispatched a trio of Cardinal Commissioners from Gaeta to take possession of the city on the pope's behalf. A wary Pius remained for now in Gaeta. The cardinals at once imposed repressive punitive measures that caused a scandal back in Paris and prompted Louis-Napoleon to protest, even threatening at one point to withdraw his forces. Ultimately the French accepted that Pius would pursue a limited path of reform, more or less consistent with the Memorandum of 1831, but when this news was published in Rome late in 1849 it pleased no one: the population was disappointed by its timidity and clerical conservatives by its liberality.[49] Pius finally returned to Rome on 12 April 1850, more than nine months after the French victory.

EIGHTEEN FORTY-EIGHT

His government from this point on bore little resemblance to that of those heady first months in 1846–1847. Instead, Pius and Antonelli spent the coming decades laying what most modern historians agree were the foundations of an historically unprecedented institution: the modern papacy. And in this dramatically transformed context, the meaning of the San Paolo reconstruction was to shift yet again.

NOTES

1   Farini (1851–1854), v. 1, pp. 226–227; Berkeley and Berkeley (1932–1940), v. 2, pp. 197–198; Hearder (1975), pp. 170–175.

2   In the midst of this chaos, Pius went to inspect the works at San Paolo on 6 July (*DdR*, 6 July 1847, pp. 1–2).

3   Berkeley and Berkeley (1932–1940), v. 2, p. 262.

4   Amati (1847).

5   See "Rapporto sulla nuova Direzione del Giornale Romano," October 1849 (ASR: Ministero Interno 1946, tit. 162, 1849).

6   Ventura (1825).

7   Boutry (1997), p. 344.

8   Ventura (1847).

9   See the essays in Guccione (1991).

10   Terenzio Mamiani to Luigi Poletti, 13 May 1848 (BCALP: LP20 C18).

11   *GdR*, 29 April 1848, pp. 1–2.

12   Cited in De Rosa (1970), p. 286.

13   Luigi Moreschi, Memo for Pope Pius IX, 8 June 1850 (ASR: CSRBSP Segreteria b. 282).

14   Girolamo Bravi to Luigi Poletti, 28 January 1848 (ASR: CSRBSP Fabbrica b. 4, f. 11).

15   Belamy (1849), v. 1, pp. 218–219.

16   "Proposizioni pel Congresso di S. Paolo," 17 May 1848 (ASR: CSRBSP Fabbrica b. 4, f. 11); *Cronaca* II, 30 June 1848.

17   Luigi Moreschi, Memo for Pope Pius IX, 24 July 1848 (ASR: CSRBSP Computisteria b. 69, f. 13; tiG pp. 457–458).

18   Angelo Vannini, Memo for Pope Pius IX, 30 August 1848 (ASR: CSRBSP Segreteria b. 276, f. 7); Pallottino (2003), pp. 500–501 (reproducing Poletti's autograph drawing for the column from the Modena archive, dated October 1848 [BCALP: C3 321]). The column in question was ultimately erected in front of San Lorenzo fuori le mura.

19   *GdR*, 30 October 1848, p. 1.

20   *Cronaca* II, 26 October 1848.

21   Hearder (1975), p. 169.

22   Coppa (1990), p. 64.

23   Martina (1974–1990), v. 1, pp. 295–302.

24   *Cronaca* II, 15 and 16 November 1848.

25   "Rapporto A Sua Eccellenza Il Sig. Ministro delle Finanze," November 1848 (ASR: CSRBSP Computisteria b. 69, f. 13).

26   *Le Assemblee del risorgimento* (1911), v. 7 [Rome, v. 2], pp. 160–178; *La Pallade*, 18 December 1848, [p. 3: "Restauri delle Chiese di Roma"].

27   See the documents concerning the San Paolo workforce during the Repubblica Romana in ASR: CSRBSP Fabbrica b. 4, f. 11.

28   Pietro Sterbini to Luigi Poletti, 20 December 1848 (ASP: 6/b, b. 1840–1841, f. 5); Hearder (1975), p. 180.

29   The chronology had come up more than once in discussions of contemporary European politics. In 1844, the French clergyman Olympe-Philippe Gerbet had written of it that "In a century in which so many governments totter and fall, this image of fixity and religious perpetuity seems only to grow in majesty" (Gerbet [1844], p. 255). One year earlier, however, the Irish Catholic priest Jeremiah Donovan had set the chronology in parallel with the so-called "Prophesy of the Popes" associated with the twelfth-century St. Malachy, according to which the Catholic Church was rapidly nearing its end (Donovan [1842], pp. 427–434).

30   Pietro Sterbini, *Ordinanza* [Bando], 29 January 1849.

31   See Gasparoni (1847). The review commission met on three occasions in February (Ministry of Commerce to Luigi Poletti, 12 February 1849 [ASR: CSRBSP Fabbrica b. 4, f. 12]). The original twenty-nine painters were a mix of future talents and relative nobodies (listed in Capitelli [2011], p. 133 n. 51).

32   *SPF*, v. 1, bk. 1, ch.1, pp. 7-10; *Cronaca* II, 23 January 1849; Bravi to Poletti, as in Chapter 14 n. 14.

33   Pietro Sterbini, *Ordinanza Ministeriale per la rinascente Basilica Ostiense* [Bando], 12 February 1849 (BSMC: BANDI a. 193/65).

34   Pietro Sterbini to Luigi Poletti, 1 March 1849; Luigi Poletti to Pietro Sterbini, 2 March 1849; Pietro Bosio to Luigi Poletti, 3 March 1849 (ASR, CSRBSP Fabbrica b. 4, f. 12).

35   *Repubblica romana. In nome di Dio e del popolo* [Bando], 23 March 1849 (BSMC: BANDI a. 196/35); Lancellotti (1862), p. 104.

36   Valeriani (1850), v. 2, p. 107.

37   Berkeley and Berkeley (1932–1940), v. 1, pp. 99–102.

38   Coppa (1990), p. 69.

39   Engel-Janosi (1950), pp. 145–146.

40   *Cronaca* II, 25 April 1849.

41   *Cronaca* II, 26 April 1849.

42   *Cronaca* II, 29 April 1849.

43   *Cronaca* II, 2–3 May 1849; Lancellotti (1862), p. 134.

44   Lesseps later played a central role in developing both the Suez and Panama canals (Courau [1932]).

45   *SPF*, v. 1, bk. 2, chs. 9–11, pp. 87–92; Farini (1851–1854), pp. 69–73; Lancellotti (1862), p. 151 (with incorrect date).

46   *SPF*, v. 1, bk. 2, ch. 10, pp. 91–95.

47   *SPF*, v. 1, bk. 4, chs. 2–3, pp. 149–152.

48   *Rapport de la Commission Mixte* (1850), p. 55.

49   Engel-Janosi (1950), pp. 155–160.

PART IV

FROM PAUL TO MARY

FIFTEEN

PIUS IX AND ROMANTIC AESTHETICS

Having dodged Sterbini's demand that he sign a loyalty oath to the Republic, Poletti fled to a friend's cottage in bucolic Grottaferrata, where in "tranquil and serene" company he awaited the liberation.[1] After the Republic fell, he returned to Rome and got the San Paolo worksite up and running again.[2] When Pius IX reentered the city in April 1850 – the Jubilee having obviously been canceled – he conferred knighthoods upon Poletti and a handful of other artists for their loyalty during the Republic.[3]

The French victory over the Republic had occurred on 30 June 1849, on the feast day of the Commemoration of Paul, and this inspired Pius to make a public gesture of gratitude for the apostle's intercession.[4] So when he went to San Paolo to celebrate Paul's feast one year later, he informed the Special Commission that "in his sovereign munificence" he wished to establish certain "arrangements": a special donation of 30,000 scudi from his personal *peculio* for the construction of the façade design that Poletti had had approved back in 1847.[5] Poletti responded to this happy news by making one last play to reinstate his original pronaos project, which was still at that point depicted on the wooden model. Why did he do this? The short answer would be that he still held stubbornly to his original ambition to perfect the basilican building type. As he told his students during these very months, the Christian churches of the best architects (he listed Palladio, Sanmicheli, Sansovino, Calderari, and Quarenghi) were "typically adorned with porticos and pronaoi. And truly, these contribute significantly to imprint character and nobility upon the buildings."[6] And as we have seen, Poletti had no interest in reproducing what he saw as the immature and imperfect forms of Early Christian design just to maintain stylistic unity. He had previously enjoyed success with Pius IX reinstating other aspects of his original project. What was there to stop him now, newly knighted for his loyalty, from trying again?

Yet the question went deeper than that. While Poletti had been thrilled by Pius's election four years earlier, important areas of concern had subsequently emerged with respect to the arts.[7] These could be summed up in the large influence Pius had accorded the painter Tommaso Minardi, who had become his most trusted artistic advisor.[8] Minardi had been placed in charge of coordinating new decorative campaigns at the Vatican and Quirinal palaces and entrusted with key paintings at the latter; he was also the only painter, and one of just two nonarchitects or nonarchaeologists, appointed to the commission charged with organizing a large-scale campaign of Roman church restorations for the Jubilee of 1850.[9] These new duties represented a dramatic shift in Minardi's fortunes. Minardi's record of artistic accomplishment was modest enough that in 1840 the *Neues allgemeines Künstler-Lexicon* reported that he "no longer paints," and, what is more, had "done little [painting] in the past."[10] Minardi was famously insecure about his skills with the brush and much preferred to exercise his greater talent as a draftsman. Minardi's reputation by 1846 instead rested on his influence as a theorist and in the generations of loyal students he had taught over twenty years as professor of drawing at the Academy.[11]

Minardi had of course emerged during the 1840s as an opponent of Poletti's vision for the reconstruction of San Paolo, first giving him trouble about the lack of figurative painting on the interior and then orchestrating the opposition to the pronaos façade. But these were only symptoms of a larger conflict from Poletti's perspective, for Minardi, in his view, was Rome's most prominent advocate of Romanticism in the arts. Minardi would more properly be described as an exponent of Purism, a maturation of the Romantic primitivism of a few decades earlier, but Poletti used the term "Romantic" in a generic sense to cover the whole range of contemporary doctrines critical of classical hegemony – all of which he opposed implacably. To make matters worse, Poletti had good reason to believe that Minardi's "Romanticism" was precisely what Pius IX liked about the painter. It was no secret that Minardi had known the pontiff prior to his election, having worked for him when he was still archbishop of Spoleto, and they had subsequently cultivated a friendship marked by Catholic patriotism and, initially, Giobertian enthusiasms.[12] Pius's patronage prior to 1848 had also favored not just Minardi personally, but also his allies, including his friend Friedrich Overbeck, to whom Pius had entrusted key elements of the redecoration at the Quirinal. Overbeck, a German convert to Catholicism who earlier in the century had led the group of Rome-based German-speaking religious painters known as the Nazarenes, had been in Rome for thirty-six years at the time of Pius's election without ever receiving a single pontifical commission. With his long hair and ostentatious spirituality, Overbeck was regarded as an oddball by the Roman artistic establishment, and the antipathy was mutual: the classically oriented approach of most Roman artists was for Overbeck intellectually and spiritually bankrupt.[13] Poletti had first seen Overbeck's work in 1820, when he wrote that the German's decision to emulate "a century in which art was still childish" (i.e., the Middle Ages) could only be "censured by intelligent people."[14] Yet Pius IX had changed everything, inserting Overbeck even into the world of the San Paolo reconstruction, where he was appointed to the four-person committee overseeing the papal chronology portraits.[15] Pius also favored Minardi's students. He granted Minardi's closest disciple, the painter Luigi Cochetti, his first independent commissions in Rome in 1846–1847, mostly at the Quirinal Palace, while he commissioned an entire cycle of frescos for the nave walls at San Girolamo degli Schiavoni from another, Pietro Gagliardi, who had never before had a commission on remotely such a scale.[16] Pius also favored Minardi's vocal ally on artistic reform, the accomplished sculptor Pietro Tenerani.[17]

Poletti was personal friends with some of these men, Tenerani in particular, and in some cases respected their work. But his opposition to what he viewed as their Romantic theory of the arts was fierce, as reflected in his longstanding association with the conservative classicists at the Roman *Giornale arcadico*. The anti-Romanticism of this periodical was political as much as aesthetic. As proud Italian patriots and, one might say, Roman chauvinists, the men of the *Giornale* circle, Poletti included, were bitterly indignant at foreign claims that modern Italy was backward and formed a pathetic contrast with the heroic memories that clung to its ancient ruins.[18] But doubly traitorous in their eyes were the Italian partisans of Romanticism, for not only did they favor a foreign aesthetic doctrine, but one that specifically condemned classicism, Italy's essential cultural achievement. Poletti and his *arcadici* friends saw Romanticism in the arts and in literature as little better than a jealous plot to drag Italian culture down to the pitiful level of France, England, or Germany – countries that had never created anything anyone had ever been tempted to imitate, and which, indeed, had spent most of their histories aping Rome.[19]

So as Poletti got back to work in 1850, he cannot have helped feeling a certain anxiety. Like all Roman artists, he was eager for the resumption of pontifical arts patronage. But he also had to be wondering whether Roman institutional classicism was at risk. Had 1848 interrupted the early stages of a Romantic revolution in the arts in Rome? One that was now poised to resume? His plan to try again with his pronaos façade was at least in part a way to find out.

Already in his early twenties, in the first decade of the nineteenth century, Minardi had been captivated by the work of the so-called "primitives" or, as he called them, "antichi maestri," by which he meant the Florentine and Tuscan painters of the late fourteenth and fifteenth centuries.[20] In his first decades in Rome, Minardi educated himself relentlessly, building up a deep personal network of international artists bound by Romantic ideals, pursuing study trips to Umbria, Tuscany, and Emilia and forming what was to be a lifelong interest in art pedagogy.[21] When Overbeck and the Nazarenes arrived in Rome, as pious medievalizing outsiders determined to undo the dominance of Greco-Roman classicism, Minardi was drawn to them as well, and a long relationship of reciprocal influence was born.[22] A specifically Italian vision of Romantic artistic reform soon took shape in Minardi's mind, one that was pietistically Christian and deeply nationalist though in a less rigidly ideological manner than some of his northern European peers; above all, it was a vision that revolved around Italian painting of the two centuries up to the middle of Raphael's career. In 1821, the position of professor of drawing at the Academy of St. Luke in Rome fell vacant, and before the position could be filled the academy students took the unprecedented step of petitioning Pope Pius VII to give the post to Minardi, who had left Rome two years earlier to direct the academy in Perugia. This "declaration of war by the youth" in favor of the new Romantic ideals (in the words of one scholar) was actually looked upon with favor by Pope Pius, though furious opposition from the neoclassical painters Vincenzo Camuccini and Jean-Baptiste Wicar delayed Minardi's appointment for a full year.[23]

Minardi spent the next twenty-five years quietly working from within to loosen the Academy's engrained classicist orientation. He had some successes here and there, and built a reputation as a dedicated and inspiring teacher.[24] His reformist vision for the arts also matured, and by the 1830s he and his allies elsewhere in Italy were identifying their ideals under the umbrella name of *Purismo*.[25] In 1831, Minardi contrived to have Overbeck accepted into the Academy of St. Luke as an *accademico di merito*, but only after another struggle with Camuccini. Minardi's own artistic production meanwhile waned, while resistance to his ideas in the Academy remained strong.[26] Minardi's criticisms of Poletti's façade design the 1840s exemplify one form of influence he sought to wield there: that of the principal critic of classical claims to innate superiority.

Minardi was known beyond Rome as perhaps the leading Italian advocate of Romantic Christian arts reform. His fame was consummated by a paper he read in September 1834 entitled, "On the Essential Qualities of Italian Painting from Its Rebirth until the Period of Its Perfection," which neatly superimposed a moral history over the formal history of Italian painting.[27] This manifesto of Minardi's Purism located the origin of painting in a spiritual impulse that every artist gradually learned to reconcile with materiality: the spiritual power of the work decreased as its material quality increased, until perfection arrived at the moment of equilibrium. This dynamic marked individual works and careers as well as national art histories. Decadence, when it inevitably arrived, was essentially a moral failure: that of *copying* perfection rather than actually striving after it, and of being satisfied with its appearance rather than its reality. Medieval painting, Minardi felt, had erred on the spiritual side, Quattrocento painting had then achieved equilibrium, while the Renaissance had fallen prey to decadence with its barren fetish of material perfection. In Minardi's view, the revival of painting in Italy would have to mirror the path of Christian redemption. Just as one aspiring to sainthood must have a saintly heart and not just a saintly appearance, so also to be a new Raphael one would have to learn to see the dynamic of nature and spirit as Raphael had done, rather than just make paintings that resembled his.

After about 1835, Minardi found his views increasingly seconded in a flood of Romantic Christian publications by French authors like Antoine-Frederic Ozanam, Charles Forbes de Montalembert, and Alexis-François Rio. These works sanctified a narrative of Italian art history as a long and virtuous path leading from the Christian catacombs to the heights of the Quattrocento, followed by the long, corrupted decline formerly known as the Renaissance. The common refrain of this discourse was that classicism was irreducibly the product of paganism and that Christian stories should never be told in such a language. Overbeck, in their view, was the great hope for the future.

If Poletti nourished hopes that Pius IX's recourse to Minardi and Overbeck reflected something other than enthusiasm for this broadly Romantic program, the publication in Rome in 1848 of Camillo Laderchi's hagiographic biography of Overbeck would have given him pause.[28] For Laderchi made it clear that Pius knew exactly what he was doing:

> One day, the Superior Commission for Opera Pia for the Propagation of the Faith was presented to [Pius IX]. When he had examined the names of the people that composed it, he read aloud that of Overbeck, exhibiting great joy, and called [the artist] to him. Pius told him that he deserved a special benediction for his virtue, and for the good that he was doing for the young [painters]. And so he had him kneel, and extending his hands over the humble artist's head, Pius blessed him with such visible emotion that all the bystanders were moved by it.[29]

Laderchi explained that Overbeck had received his commissions at the Quirinal Palace when, in response to an inquiry from Pius for a suitable subject for certain frescos, he had devised erudite Biblical allegories that deeply impressed the pope. Over the years, Overbeck was to prove a faithful ally of Pius, who thanked him with periodic studio visits and acquisitions of his work for the Vatican Museums.[30]

It is scarcely surprising that Pius should have been attracted to the moralizing artistic program sketched out by the Nazarenes and Purists. It certainly conformed to Pius's worldview far better than the tendentious official classicism of the Academy, with its lingering Napoleonic associations. Platitudes about universal aesthetic truth would likely also have rung hollow to a pope who presided over a Church surrounded by enemies, and who was himself inclined to use art propagandistically. In place of academic rhetoricalism, Overbeck and Minardi had concrete ambitions: they aspired to reach ordinary people in service to Christianity's mission of redemption.[31] And Pius had had fifteen years to take Minardi's measure; he knew and trusted the depths of the painter's faith. What is surprising, really, is that artistic Romanticism had to wait so long for a pope who finally embraced it.

The idea common to Romantic theories that most enraged Poletti was that of "Christian art": the belief that the religious faith of an artist inescapably inhered in his work and authorized an absolute distinction between Christian and pagan art. Poletti told his students that he hesitated as to whether this idea was "more stupid or more ridiculous." He was sure, however, that "it comes to us, to our shame, from the gelid peoples of the north, along with the no less absurd matter of Romanticism." Poletti held instead to an austerely classical understanding of artistic creation, in which the character of the artwork resulted from an autonomous operation of aesthetic reflection. Whether pagan or Christian, the best artists had always been "imitating nature in keeping with the aim of the work."[32] Poletti saw red when confronted with the deterministic claim that classicism was irreducibly pagan and therefore unsuitable for Christian buildings, and that Gothic was the only true Christian style: "Was the Temple of Jerusalem, sanctified by God's very word, unworthy of the Most High because it was not *ogival architecture*? Because it didn't *point upwards*?" He ranted to his students that "perhaps the underground forms of the earliest churches in the catacombs were Gothic, or perhaps when the Christians got out from under the yoke of the pagans they got the type for their first sumptuous temples from Germany, France, or England!"[33]

The "Christian art" thesis with respect to architecture was popularized in Italy in the 1840s by the critic, historian, and occasional architect Pietro Estense Selvatico (about whom more in a moment). But Poletti knew that Minardi had been making this same argument to his students at the Academy in Rome already in the late 1830s. In one lecture of 1837, Minardi had argued that the men of the Middle Ages were the best models for contemporary architecture because they never thought of pagan or mythological things but always of Christian matters when they designed their buildings.[34] The result, Minardi claimed, was a rebirth of the arts infused with Christian spirit, majestic like the majesty of God, but purged of "the proud and strutting majesty of earthly power" signified by classical art:

> And so vast temples rose up as had never before been seen, composed and ornamented in every part with imagery expressing all the beings of nature – plants, flowers, fruits, animals of every species – woven together in a thousand different ways, as though all of nature were competing to celebrate and give glory to its God.[35]

These Gothic buildings were like hymns unto the Divinity, he marveled, rising up and surpassing even the clouds. They offered a symbol of "the elevation, the spiritual sublimnity, to which the human mind was raised up by the God-made-man, by the Redeemer." They also formed a telling contrast with the materialism of pagan works: "temples to the gentile gods surprise and enchant by the majestic robustness of their construction," which he conceded did provide a powerful experience of beauty, but only "terrestrial beauty, expressive only of power, the haughty power of the human animal." Gothic churches instead "transcend every earthly argument, and, almost spiritualized in their very material, proceed by a completely different means, and are beautiful for an opposite reason." Rather than "robust Doric columns" that seem like proud Hercules carrying the world heroically on his shoulders, Minardi saw in Gothic churches a plethora of elements joining together to carry the load:

> ... every element, every part refining itself and thinning itself out, rises up to the sky, like a delicate plant that loves the sun, and is attracted to it; and one balancing atop the other, and closely gripping one another, all of a single will, rise up, and hurling themselves on high, form an ardent ray of fire that flies to its sphere and carries with it the mind of whoever sees it.[36]

If classical buildings gave the spectator the satisfaction of a manly triumph over matter, in the Gothic building instead "you will find no support, as it is held up almost by miracle ... so that it seems to you that human force had no part in it. This is what it is to spiritualize inert matter!"[37]

Minardi's lecture was soon excerpted in the *Annali delle scienze religiose*, a theological journal from Rome aimed mainly at a clerical readership.[38] The *Annali* rarely carried articles on the arts, and the appearance there of Minardi's lecture testifies to the high religious value its clerical editors saw in it. Lady Chiara Colonna was a noble whose domestic gatherings regularly brought Minardi together with Archbishop Mastai-Feretti of Imola (the future Pius IX), and in October 1837 she wrote to Minardi from Bologna to apologize for not yet having read his no doubt "bellissimo" new article in the *Annali*. The reason? She planned to read the essay in the copy of their mutual friend Mastai, who was a subscriber, but he was still awaiting its delivery by post.[39] Pius's acquaintance with Minardi's ideas on the arts thus dated to well before he became pope.

Poletti's animus toward Romanticism was intensified by the attacks that his own work at San Paolo increasingly faced from Romantic critics in the 1840s. He must have been startled, for instance, as he read Lederchi's biography of Overbeck, to encounter a footnote, seemingly apropos of nothing, that implored Pius IX to rescind his permission to Poletti to erect a new ciborium at San Paolo:

> [It is to be hoped that] the elegant tabernacle of Arnolfo might be left on its own to decorate the sepulcher of the Apostle to the Gentiles; that the artists will respect what God forced the devouring flames to respect; that the eye of the devout, who enters to pray in the basilica, will be able to penetrate immediately to the apse, that is, to the most noble and sacred part; and that its sublime character will be preserved as it was before, in accordance with the intent of the Bull with which the rebuilding was ordered.[40]

This was nothing, however, compared to what Poletti could have read in 1841 in the Milanese *Rivista europea*, where the arts rubric was edited by the aforementioned Pietro Selvatico. Selvatico was an ardent partisan of neo-Catholic aesthetic theories, and he made a point of bringing French, English, and German Romantic art theory to Italian readers via reviews, translations, or simply via absorption into his own essays.[41] In 1841, he used his perch at the *Rivista europea* to publish his own translation of an essay that had appeared in France the previous year, by the painter, critic, and travel writer Frédéric Mercey.[42] Mercey's text was precisely the type of condescending foreign commentary on Italian art that enraged Poletti and his *arcadici* brethren. After multiple expressions of incredulity at the continued influence at Rome of such "démodé" painters as Camuccini and Agricola, Mercey turned to architecture, and in particular to "the capital work of the present moment," Poletti's reconstruction of San Paolo. After the fire of 1823, wrote Mercey, there had been an option to leave a grandiose "Christian ruin" that would have held its own beside the ruins of antiquity. Instead, it was decided to attempt a "useless" reconstruction that, in mixing the old and the new, caused even the old parts to acquire a "modern sheen" that "destroys the old harmony of the edifice, and strips it of that austere and Christian appearance that formerly distinguished it."[43] Poletti's ambition to create a timeless aesthetic ideal from the historic reserves of the Italic tradition here runs up against the Romantic sense of a linear historical time in which the value of ancient artifacts is expressed in their visible antiquity: Poletti had tried to smooth over the uneven historical texture of his hybrid monument, whereas Mercey wanted to see the meaning of the building expressed through juxtapositions of old and new. But even the new elements were, for Mercey, lacking. The new granite columns, for instance, lacked the elegance and lightness of the beautiful old marble ones; they replaced the originals, "but not suitably." The new capitals were "enormously expensive" and "of a rather dry workmanship." But what most disturbed Mercey were the great coffered ceilings that Poletti was installing, for these gave the church that "gay and worldly aspect" associated with Jesuit churches and Santa Maria Maggiore – "a serious defect that an architect of genius would not have committed." He then inserted the dagger: "But on the other hand, an architect of genius would not have wanted to copy a monument. He would have built another building following his own designs."[44] The remark is of course unfair and untrue: one could hardly describe what Poletti was doing as a "copy" of the old basilica, and he would surely have preferred still more aesthetic liberty. Nonetheless, in Mercey's view San Paolo was "half ruin, half new," and, in a decidedly noncomplimentary way, "one of the most curious monuments in Italy today."[45]

It was then Selvatico's turn. Lurking in the endnotes, he delivered a nasty gloss on Mercey's text that likened Poletti's work to the Ælia Lælia Crispis, a sixteenth-century tomb slab famous for its enigmatic Latin inscription:

> It is most correct and entirely true what [Mercey] has to say about the reconstruction of S. Paolo in Rome, a most expensive pile lacking any character, that could be called the Ælia Lælia Crispis of architecture, that is, *nec vir, nec mulier, nec androgynus, nec puella, nec juvenis, nec anus, sed omnia* ["neither man, nor woman, nor hermaphrodite, nor girl, nor boy, nor old woman, but all at once"].[46]

It should be clear by now why someone of Poletti's convictions might have been apprehensive as he awaited Pius IX's return in 1850, and why he might have wanted to see where he stood by pushing for the reinstatement of his pronaos façade.

When Poletti first launched his gambit we do not know. In January 1851, when Moreschi published an article announcing the news of Pius's gift for the façade, he explicitly stated that the money would function to build the "third project" Poletti had presented to the Academy in 1846, which "reflected the architectonic character of the ancient Christian basilicae."[47] The first suggestion that Poletti had other plans came a month later when he erected a temporary brick reinforcement of the old façade.[48] This would be a puzzling decision unless either (a) the old façade had coincidentally chosen that moment to become dangerously unstable, or, more plausibly, (b) Poletti wanted to make sure that no one could invoke the urgent instability of the old façade as a way to cut short a renegotiation of its replacement. Poletti may have begun laying the groundwork for this renegotiation when he showed off this reinforcement to Pius during his visit to the construction site in June; he certainly lobbied Pius on other matters during this visit, immediately after which the pope reaffirmed his approval for the ciborium and made new donations for the gilding of the nave ceilings.[49] All of this can only have encouraged the architect since, as we saw, both features had recently been criticized by Romantic writers.

The first document that explicitly discusses the reinstatement of the pronaos dates from April 1852. It comes not from Poletti but rather from the minutes of the new Pontifical Commission for Sacred Archaeology, inaugurated by Pius less than a year earlier.[50] The Commission was the brainchild of Padre Giuseppe Marchi, conservator of the Roman catacombs and author of the pathbreaking *Monumenti delle arti cristiane primitive nella metropoli del cristianesimo* (1844).[51] Marchi had been petitioning Gregory XVI and then Pius IX for the better part of a decade for permission to secure the Early Christian catacombs from devotional plunder and other unauthorized uses and to reorganize them as an officially protected category of sacred monument.[52] Upon Pius's return from Gaeta, the value of Marchi's vision was finally recognized and the new Commission was formed. Of the two nonclerical members, one was Marchi's brilliant protégé, collaborator, and eventual successor, the archaeologist Giovanni Battista de Rossi. The other was the suddenly omnipresent Tommaso Minardi, who happened also to be one of Marchi's close friends.[53]

The minutes of the meeting in question record that Padre Marchi informed his fellow commissioners that the idea of building the new façade of San Paolo as "a pronaos or anti-temple of the same form as the ancient pronaos of the Pantheon" was apparently back in play. Marchi reminded them that this had been rejected once already by the Academy of St. Luke, and so he proposed that the Commission register its opposition. They had never before intervened with respect to a noncatacomb monument, but Marchi harbored ambitions of expanding the Commission's purview, and San Paolo was to represent something of a trial balloon for this. Marchi's colleagues invited him to write up a statement of protest for the pope.[54] When the Commission met again a month later, Marchi arrived with his statement in hand, but to ensure that they did not disturb Pius needlessly, it was decided to hold off until it was confirmed that the pronaos really was being contemplated.[55] Remarks from the minutes of a subsequent meeting a few months later indicate that such confirmation was obtained and that Marchi's protest was indeed submitted.

It is unclear exactly when this protest was submitted, but most likely this occurred in June 1852.[56]

Marchi's memo announced that Poletti's pronaos project was well known to everyone, since it was depicted on the wooden model that Poletti had built after inheriting his post from Belli.[57] But, it continued, Gregory XVI had been "advised by many people of the inappropriateness of this design" and had decided to submit it to the Academy for judgment. Gregory then died, Pius was elected, and the Academy subsequently met and voted unanimously to rule out "not just the construction, but even *the idea* of this anti-temple." The wording here is noteworthy, for it implies that the vote repudiated not just a design but the whole underlying ambition to create an idealized Christian basilica. Marchi wrote that two members of his Commission wished to elaborate on why this anti-temple was inimical to a Christian basilica. One, he added, was an academician of St. Luke, which could only mean Minardi, and in fact much of this part of the document closely follows the memorandum Minardi presented in 1846.[58]

Minardi's argument was predicated on the Romantic distinction between pagan and Christian artforms. An "anti-temple," he announced, was something affixed to the front of a pagan temple that acted as a portico or vestibule to protect worshippers from the elements. This excluded a priori any idea of connecting such a thing to a basilica, which was a different sort of building entirely: "if an anti-temple is not an anti-basilica, then it should not and cannot be." Minardi also noted that the quadriportici of Early Christian basilicae had sheltered the unbaptized during certain portions of the Mass, and that if part of the quadriporticus were to be taken over by a pronaos, it would interfere with that function. This would in turn defeat the intent of rebuilding San Paolo, which was "to preserve the true form that the Roman Church of the fourth century had given to its grand basilicae." This was a dig at Poletti, who of course sought to move beyond that original intention. The next argument was then aesthetic: a colossal order on the façade would create a monstrous discordance with the columns of the nave, which would be left looking disappointingly small. The final arguments were then that a pronaos would conceal the façade's mosaic imagery and thereby diminish its fidelity to the original; that it would be impossible to harmonize with the quadriporticus, since it would be nearly three times as tall; and that it would deprive the façade of its windows, which constitute "the principal spirit of the basilica" and provide essential interior illumination.

All these complaints had been publicly stated in 1846. But now Minardi also went back to a complaint that, to judge by Letarouilly's correspondance with Poletti, he had made informally in the early 1840s.[59] He asserted first that any honest reading of Leo XII's Chirograph could only conclude that the copious paintings that formerly decorated the upper nave wall ought to be reconstituted in the reconstruction, for "by representing stories and holy images," these frescos were what "rendered the place fully sacred." But instead, "the new architects" had appropriated this whole area "with pilasters and completely meaningless frameworks that extend all the way to the ceiling." This purely architectonic decoration gives "the whole thing an appearance that no one could call either Christian or holy":

> As a result one hears the very justified lament that the transept presents itself to the eye more like a pagan chamber, or like a Protestant church, with a kind of magnificence that aims at a stupid form of marvel, rather than as a Catholic basilica that preaches the virtues of the saints, the omnipotence and grace of the eternal God, and of Christ the Redeemer.[60]

The Romantic critique of the un-Christian nature of classical forms is front-and-center here. Minardi continued:

> This very grave transgression of Pope Leo's decree is all but irreparable. Simple painting and mosaic painting are forever banned from the basilica. Only the great windows now might give rise to some painting – painting on glass, an art that today flourishes anew in so many parts of Europe, above all in northern Italy, Germany, France, England, and that could be introduced in Rome too. If it is desired that the windows of San Paolo should be painted with colored glass, painting will be able to provide its worthy effects all along the entire perimeter of the basilica – except for at the extremity of the main nave. Because here the pronaos will impede the passage of light, especially in the afternoon hours when Romans and pilgrims come in their largest numbers to visit the sepulcher of the Apostle to the Gentiles. It will rob from those three essential windows the effects of painting, which, if the windows existed, could render them both holy and apt to inspire holy thoughts.[61]

The revival of stained glass in northern Europe had been a function of the revival of the Gothic style and the restoration of Gothic buildings.[62] That Minardi should have been keen to see this movement introduced in Rome is wholly consistent with his allegiances, as is his assertion that Poletti's preferred aesthetic would render the basilica worthless as an instrument for the production of holy thoughts.

We still do not know how close Poletti really came to success in reinstating his pronaos façade. Nor do we know exactly when or why the Commission for Sacred Archaeology decided that the threat was real enough to submit Padre Marchi's memorandum to the pope. But we do know that in July 1852, when Moreschi published a write-up of the pope's latest visit to the basilica in the *Giornale di Roma*, he once again stated that the façade was to be "designed with the character of the old Christian basilicae, following the approved design and project of Head Architect Professor Luigi Poletti."[63] This public declaration, just two months after Marchi first composed his memo, suggests that the memo had been submitted in the interim and had had its desired effect. Confirmation then comes when Moreschi adds the momentous news that Pius had also announced his wish to see "the entire sacred edifice rendered more magnificent and dignified by means of painting in the second architectonic order." That is, he wanted to have the panels between the high windows of both nave and transept – the architectonic revetments Minardi had dismissed as "meaningless frameworks" – replaced with the very frescos whose absence Minardi had lamented.[64] Minardi's memorandum had apparently had quite an effect. Over the decade following the 1854 consecration of the basilica, Poletti was compelled to remove the white marble revetments and clear windows he had initially installed and to redesign the upper wall completely in both transept and nave, transforming it into a richly colored frame for a great fresco cycle depicting Paul's life.[65]

The apprehensions about Romantic influence that Poletti had suffered in the months leading up to Pius's return to Rome in 1850 would have been resoundingly confirmed by this experience. He could not now doubt that Romantic ideas had breached his classical citadel, and that the result risked spoiling his whole vision for the reconstructed San Paolo.

Poletti often designed ephemeral structures for the so-called *girandola* celebrations: big public fireworks shows at the Castello Sant'Angelo that marked important festival days. These always centered on a large ephemeral structure that usually represented an imaginary building but on certain occasions depicted a real monument. In June 1854, for a *girandola* celebrating the Festival of the Commemoration of St. Paul, Poletti designed one that replicated the neo-Paleochristian façade he had just built at San Paolo, in commemoration of the fact that Pius IX had funded its construction[66] (**Figure 91**). The sight of this façade engulfed in a gargantuan pyrotechnical spectacle must have been unsettling for those who could still remember 1823, but Poletti may have had private reasons for savoring it. For he was known in his other *girandola* entertainments to design structures in the Gothic and even Egyptian styles – styles he would never have used in a proper building – and he may have secretly delighted to see the Paleochristian façade forced on him by Minardi and company consumed as a similarly inconsequential example of architectural exoticism.

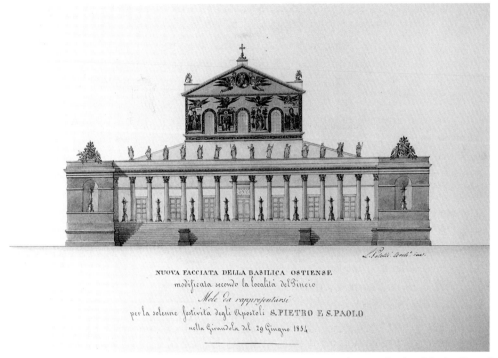

91. Luigi Poletti's design for a *girandola* structure representing the new façade of the basilica of San Paolo fuori le mura, created for the public celebrations of the festival of Peter and Paul, 29 June 1854.
Source: Biblioteca civica d'arte e architettura Luigi Poletti, Modena, Archivio Poletti, disegni inv. 979.

NOTES

1. Luigi Poletti to Ferdinando Ranalli, 21 July 1849 (BCALP: LP48 C19). Poletti lamented that a Republic that "promised a pure democratic republic" had ended up "a socialist government representing the collapse of society."
2. Luigi Poletti to Ferdinando Ranalli, 21 July 1849 (BCALP: LP48 C19); Luigi Moreschi to Camillo Jacopini, 29 August 1849 (ASR: Camerlengato, P. II, Tit. IV, b. 155, fasc. 204, #9142).
3. *GdR*, 20 May 1850, p. 459.
4. Giacomo Antonelli to Angelo Vannini, 23 December 1850 (ASR: CSRBSP Computisteria b. 69, f. 16).
5. *GdR*, 2 July 1850, p. 603. Not until December, however, was this donation announced publicly, ostensibly because of the need first to undertake urgent repairs around the city (*DESE*, v. 53, "Pio IX, Papa CCLV regnante," p. 226).
6. Luigi Poletti, "Architettura Teorica" (ASL course), 1851-2 (BCALP: LP51 C3).
7. On Pius's art patronage, cf. Capitelli (2003) and (2011).
8. On Minardi, see Susinno (1982); Ricci (2011) and (2012); Ventra (2013); and Racioppi (2018).
9. *La Pallade*, 18 December 1848, n.p.[3]; Capitelli (2011), pp. 28–30; Mulder (1994), p. 100; Dall'Olio (1864).
10. Nagler (1840), v. 9, pp. 301–302 (cited in Faldi [1950]).

PIUS IX AND ROMANTIC AESTHETICS   347

11 Ovidi (1902); Ricci (2011), pp. 77–133; Ricci (2012).
12 De Sanctis (1899), pp. 133–135; Ricci (2011), p. 84 n. 165.
13 Andrews (1964).
14 Poletti, "Osservazioni" as in Ch. 10 n. 8.
15 Capitelli (2011), p. 26.
16 Ovidi (1902), p. 114; Caperna (1992).
17 Grandesso (2003).
18 Cf. O'Connor (2005).
19 In addition to Poletti's manuscripts, see *L'illustre Italia* by his *arcadico* friend Salvatore Betti (Betti [1841]).
20 Ricci (2012), p. 243.
21 Susinno (1982), i–xxxi; Ricci (2011), pp. 29–48, and (2012), pp. 240–253.
22 Ricci (2006); (2011), pp. 49–76 .
23 Falconieri (1875), pp. 296–308; Corbo (1969); Ricci (2011), p. 101.
24 Jervis (1997), pp. 743–758.
25 Cardelli (2005), pp. 15–16, 111–124; Ricci (2011), pp. 78–115.
26 Racioppi (2018), p. 18.
27 Minardi (1835); Ricci (2011), pp. 135–190.
28 Laderchi (1848) (written in June 1847).
29 Laderchi (1848), p. 41.
30 Negro (1943), p. 194; Capitelli (2011), p. 30.
31 Cardelli (2005), p. 33.
32 Luigi Poletti, "Architettura Teorica" (ASL course), n.d. (BCALP: LP51 C8).
33 Luigi Poletti, "Architettura Teorica" (ASL course), 1860 (BCALP: LP51 C5). Emphasis is my own.
34 Minardi (1837).
35 Minardi (1837), p. 292.
36 Minardi (1837), p. 293.
37 Minardi (1837), p. 294.
38 Majolo Molinari (1963), v. 1, p. 30.
39 Ovidi (1902), pp. 271–272. Donna Colonna was rumored by anticlericals to have been Mastai-Feretti's lover (cf. Bianchi-Giovini [1863], p. 204). Poletti once dedicated a work of literary criticism to her (Poletti [1827]).
40 Laderchi (1848), pp. 22–23.
41 Bernabei (1974); Auf der Heyde (2013). Selvatico and Minardi were unsurprisingly on good terms (Ovidi [1902], pp. 258–259).
42 Mercey (1841). Original French version: Mercey (1840).
43 Mercey (1841), p.7.
44 Mercey (1841), p.8.
45 Mercey (1841), p.8.
46 Mercey (1841), p. 24 n. 3 (note by Selvatico). Selvatico continued criticizing the reconstruction even after Poletti's death (cf. Selvatico [1879], v. 2, p. 23).
47 *GdR*, 27 January 1851, p. 81.
48 "Rapporto per la Santità di Nostro Signore su la Porta Santa della Basilica di San Paolo," 10 February 1851 (ASP: 30/c, libro rosso 3).
49 *GdR*, 2 July 1851, pp. 593–594; *DESE*, v. 53, "Pio IX, Papa CCLV regnante," p. 230; *GdR*, 27 January 1851, p. 81.
50 Ferrua (1968), pp. 251–278.
51 Marchi (1844).
52 Tizzani (1886); Ferrua (1968), pp. 251–278.
53 De Sanctis (1899), p. 138.
54 PCAS: Sessione 5.a tenuta Venerdì 30. Aprile 1852. all'ore 10 ½. a.m., 30 April 1852.

55 PCAS: Sessione 6.a. tenuta Venerdì 4. Giugno 1852. all'ore 10 ½. a.m., 4 June 1852.

56 PCAS: Session 1.a. tenuta Mercoledi 10. Novembre 1852. all'ore 10 1/2 a.m., 10 November 1852.

57 Reproduced in Ferrua (1968), pp. 266–269. Emphasis is my own.

58 Marchi also referred to the Commission as the "Commission of ancient Christian monuments," hinting at his larger ambitions for it.

59 Letarouilly to Poletti, as in Chapter 13 n. 22.

60 Reproduced in Ferrua (1968), p. 269.

61 Reproduced in Ferrua (1968), p. 269.

62 On Italian stained glass of this period, see Silvestri (2006).

63 *GdR*, 5 July 1852, pp. 597–598.

64 The decision was confirmed on 4 March 1853 (Luigi Moreschi, "Rapporto su le pitture a fresco ne trentasei interpilastri del secondo ordine architettonico nelle navi traversa e media della Basilica Ostiense," 4 January 1856 [ASR: CSRBSP Segreteria b. 283]).

65 On the frescos, see Moreschi, "Rapporto" (as in Chapter 16 n. 64) and Moreschi (1867).

66 Luigi Poletti, "Nuova facciata della Basilica Ostiense modificata secondo la località del Pincio. Mole da rappresentarsi per la solenne festività degli Apostoli S. Pietro e S. Paolo nella Girandola del 29 Giugno 1854," June 1854 (BCALP: C8 979).

SIXTEEN

TWO DAYS IN DECEMBER

WHILE PIUS IX WAS GRATEFUL FOR PAUL'S INTERCESSION IN liberating Rome in 1850, it was the intercession of the Virgin Mary that he most deeply credited with the victory. This resolved him to move ahead forcefully with an old idea to which he had already been committed for many years: the proclamation of the dogma of the Immaculate Conception of Mary. The Immaculate Conception refers to that divine dispensation by which the Virgin, alone among humans, was preserved from original sin at the moment of her conception. This proclamation finally came in 1854 and effectively opened a new chapter in the collective life of the Roman Catholic Church, one that was to be far more alert to the institutional benefits of accommodating popular religious energies and traditions. Church historians often refer to the period 1850–1950 as the Church's Marian Age, but it was also the age of a great popular Catholic revival in the Western world, of the development of potent Catholic political movements and eventually parties in many countries, and of an unprecedented Catholic expansion in the world beyond Europe.[1] Not all of that can be attributed to Pius's proclamation of the dogma of the Immaculate Conception, but the rampant energies and ambitions that reinvigorated the Church during this period were to a significant extent first unleashed when Pius IX placed his official seal of approval on this popular, yet also theologically controversial, aspect of Marian devotion.

Two days after the long and elaborate ceremony at St. Peter's at which the dogma was proclaimed and celebrated, in December 1854, a second ceremony almost as long and almost as elaborate was held at San Paolo to celebrate the final consecration of the basilica. This had been scheduled not because of any particular milestone in the construction but rather to capitalize on the legions of bishops, archbishops, Catholic nobles, and ordinary pilgrims who had assembled in Rome to attend the other ceremony two days earlier. What was at stake in these two momentous days of Catholic proclamation and consecration is the subject of this final chapter.

The contested term "Tridentine Catholicism" refers in part to the rebarbative vision of Catholic devotion formulated around the time of the Council of Trent in the sixteenth century and propagated, with greater or lesser effectiveness in different contexts and locales, over the three centuries that followed.[2] This was at bottom a Catholicism obsessed with sin and guilt, suspicious of joy, and steeped in fear; one that mandated a strict separation of sacred and profane. As a religious practice, it demanded extraordinary levels of discipline and aesceticism, of the kind exemplified by heroes like François de Sales in the seventeenth century. By the eighteenth century, this vision of Catholicism was increasingly thought to have been as responsible for alienating many of the ordinary faithful and for a long decline in popular involvement in the life of the official Church. The crisis was then dramatically amplified by the Revolution and its aftermath, which punctured the Church's aura of permanence and inevitability and devastated the clergy in many regions. In great swaths of Europe, a whole generation grew up that not only lacked a religious education but had received an actively anticlerical one. Gone was the old sense that Catholicism was as natural as the air one breathed.

Of the many convictions that 1848–49 reinforced in the heart of Pius IX, one of the strongest was that the Church needed to accelerate its heretofore tentative efforts to move in favor of more humane and affective paradigms of devotion.[3] Socially progressive Romantic reformers like Lamennais had desperately hammered this point decades earlier but ended up condemned by Gregory XVI in his timorous commitment to a top-down model of authority.[4] Yet what clerical leaders had been mostly unwilling to hear in the 1830s, they began more and more to heed in the 1840s and 1850s. The middle years of the nineteenth century thus witnessed the emergence of an institutional Catholic "theology of love," centered on social inclusiveness, divine succor, and intercession.[5] The rediscovery of the eighteenth-century writer Alphonsus of Liguori (1696–1787) in particular helped to reorient diocesan and parochial-level outreach to the masses.[6] Liguori had argued that the poor tended toward immorality because the succors of religion were too often withheld from them by overeducated clerics who, with their dim Augustinian view of human moral rectitude, restricted sacraments only to the pure. Liguori instead urged much more intense and supportive moral engagement between clergy and faithful, with frequent communion as an affective means for good Catholics to internalize their loving God. Church leaders also followed Liguori after 1850 in his innovative approach to pastorage, including his radical embrace of popular religiosity. This represented a major institutional reversal for a hierarchy that for over two centuries had censured popular religious traditions that lacked Rome's imprimatur as superstition or idolatry.

A culminating moment in this epochal turn came with the proclamation of the Dogma of the Immaculate Conception in 1854.[7] Catholic Mariology was nothing new. It had a deep history stretching back at least to the Middle Ages, with origins in the rural European base of the Church, whose practices of tending local or regional Marian shrines, many of them deemed miraculous, likely reflected the vestigial survival of prehistoric mother cults. From the period of the Counter-Reformation onward, the institutional Church as a rule had mistrusted and thwarted such practices (even if in practice it sometimes accommodated them), and this had contributed to the gap in sensibility separating it from the mass of ordinary Catholics.[8] Still, devotion to the Immaculate Conception only developed institutional support during the seventeenth and eighteenth centuries, when the idea of an official dogma was first mooted.[9] This did not occur, however, because Catholic theologians were unable to explain in their habitual rational manner exactly how the Immaculate Conception worked. It was not, after all, a belief that had come about through rational deduction, nor was there a word of scriptural evidence for it. Protestant intellectuals delighted in mocking it as Catholic obscuritanism, and so the Catholic hierarchy preferred to trust to the negative verdict rendered by Thomas Aquinas in the thirteenth century. Yet Mary's immaculacy remained a popular if unorthodox belief, especially among rural Catholics, as well as among the kind of Catholic intellectuals who positively savored its resistance to rational analysis.

Marian devotion enjoyed new prominence amid the traumas of the Revolutionary and Napoleonic eras. Starting in 1802, at least one new religious order dedicated to Mary was founded somewhere in Europe every year for the remainder of the century.[10] By the time Gregory XVI became pope, Marian experiences were multiplying. In 1830, the first of the great nineteenth-century apparitions occurred in Paris, when the Virgin appeared to Sister Catherine Labouré, standing on a globe in an oval frame inscribed, "O Mary, conceived without sin, pray for us who have recourse to thee."[11] Mary reappeared to Labouré shortly thereafter to recommend that her image be mass produced on medals and distributed to the faithful. The tens of thousands of medals subsequently put into circulation played an important role in building popular support in Europe for the concept of the Immaculate Conception.[12] These new devotional practices were soon avidly promoted in Rome, for instance during the cholera epidemic of the late 1830s when Gregory XVI named Mary the protector of the city and twice ordered the venerated Salus Populi Romani icon taken out of Santa Maria Maggiore for extended processions across the city.[13] Gregory also promoted the Immaculate Conception, broadly extending the privilege to attach the word "Immaculate" to the feast of Mary's conception, and showing himself open to the idea of proclaiming a dogma of Mary's immaculacy.[14] In 1839, a treatise by the Dominican Mariano Spada argued persuasively that Aquinas's critique of the doctrine had been misinterpreted, and this removed a key obstacle for many orthodox Catholics.[15] The recent French enthusiasm sparked by the visions of Sister Labouré arrived powerfully in Rome shortly thereafter when a well-to-do French Jew, Alphonse Ratisbonne, who had been given a Labouré medal by an acquaintance, had a vision of the Virgin that mirrored the Labouré imagery while he was sightseeing in S. Andrea delle Fratte. His subsequent conversion and Catholic baptism in January 1842 were heavily publicized, and the chapel where the vision occurred was redecorated, rededicated and became a major site of devotion.[16] But Gregory's policy was still to promote a strictly official version of Marian devotion while discouraging whenever possible any genuinely popular manifestations that exceeded the Church's oversight.[17]

Pius IX, for his part, had a long history of attachment to Mary's immaculacy, and is known to have preached on the subject twice, and with great erudition, as a young cleric in Rome in the 1820s.[18] In 1846, the Catholic bishops of the United States petitioned Pius to make Mary the patroness of the United States under the title of the Immaculate Conception.[19] Also in 1846, in the remote mountains of southern France, the second of the nineteenth-century's great apparitions occurred when Mary appeared before two girls, ages fifteen and eleven, to impart a stern message about contemporary impiety and irreligion. La Salette swiftly became a major pilgrimage center.[20]

Early in 1848, Pius IX convoked a council of theologians to evaluate the idea of a new dogma. The Council's work was interrupted by the uprising later that year, but discussions continued during Pius's exile. On 2 February 1849, from Naples, Pius issued the Encyclical *Ubi primum*, in which he asked the whole Catholic episcopate to interrogate their consciences on the matter and to inquire what their clergy and faithful felt about it. Over six hundred responses arrived back, 90 percent in favor.[21] After his return to Rome, Pius relaunched his theological council, and from that point it was just a matter of defining the dogma. By September 1854, this work was nearly complete, and Pius was able to send a circular letter to his apostolic nuncios instructing them to select two bishops from each kingdom and have them in Rome in time for a ceremony proclaiming the new dogma that was being planned for the upcoming 8 December, the annual feast day dedicated to the Immaculate Conception.[22]

TWO DAYS IN DECEMBER 353

Over the following weeks, the international Catholic hierarchy descended on Rome in their hundreds. It was esteemed a good omen when 8 December dawned sunny and clear following days of hard rain. Already by 8 a.m., the streets around St. Peter's were jammed with people and vehicles, as more than 30,000 people were estimated to have attended the day-long ceremonies. Afterward there were processions, and the dome of St. Peter's was illuminated, while street orchestras played into the night.[23] News of the ceremony soon found its way into newspapers worldwide, with some Catholic papers devoting pages and pages to it over the weeks to come. It was one of the first times in the half-expired nineteenth century that Roman Catholics truly felt again that their metropole stood as the *ombelico del mondo*.

*
**

On "the first or second day of November" 1854, according to the monastery chronicle at San Paolo, an official letter reached the Special Commission indicating that Pius IX wished to take advantage of the coming presence of the Roman Catholic hierarchy in Rome to schedule the consecration of San Paolo two days after the proclamation of the new dogma, on 10 December, the feast day celebrating the miraculous translation of the Holy House of Loreto.[24] Excitement quickly gave way to horror, however, as everyone realized that they too were now going to have to perform a kind of miracle: for with less than a month's warning, Poletti and the monastery community had to transform a busy construction site into the setting for a long, mobile ceremony involving virtually the entire hierarchy of the Catholic Church. This necessarily involved completing or at least tidying up a host of unfinished aspects of the basilica itself. The nave, for example, was still unpaved. There were also scaffolds everywhere; it was estimated that in normal times it would have taken several months to dismount and remove them all. All around the basilica were staging areas for different kinds of carving and cutting and polishing and soldering, as well for materials storage; these would all have to be cleared away. A mass of liturgical furnishings had to be located and borrowed, as well as damasks, wall hangings, and decorations to conceal the unfinished areas. To make matters worse, Poletti, who was to coordinate all this, had already been tapped for the massive responsibility of organizing the décor of St. Peter's basilica for the Immaculate Conception ceremony two days earlier.[25]

A frenzy of activity began at once. The abbot of San Paolo spent much of the following month bouncing between the Vatican, the Lateran, and the other churches of Rome rounding up aspergilla, censors, and vessels for holy oil. Poletti, meanwhile, prepared the basilica. The nave was paved with slabs of unpolished marble as a temporary measure. (Because these slabs would be sprinkled with Holy Water during the ceremonies, they all had to be reused in the permanent floor.)[26] The façade was to be one of the focal points of the ceremony, owing to Pius's gift, but the quadriporticus that was to extend from it had not yet been built. So it was decided to erect a wooden portico against the façade, much larger than the one eventually built in stone, to be hung with damasks borrowed from the Vatican and Lateran. Within this temporary portico, Poletti created an elevated reliquary chapel hung with silks, while right in front of the basilica's main door he built a throne for Pius IX, framed by a triple crown of benches for the attendant cardinals. New doors were cut in the existing walls and structures all around the basilica to create a circulation corridor along the building's perimeter. Inside the basilica, another crown of benches was built around the Sedia Pontificale in the apse (these were not finished until the wee hours of the morning of the ceremony). Poletti even found time to design new liturgical furnishings, including several candlesticks which, in the circumstances, had to be made from wood and painted gold.[27]

The rain had returned on 9 December, and when day broke on 10 December the sky was gray and threatening. As on 8 December, a massive movement of carriages and people began at the crack of dawn, surging this time toward San Paolo: "men, women, monks, children, soldiers (above all French soldiers), were all there, pell-mell, trying to get through the lines of carriages containing cardinals, prelates, or simple foreigners like us," one visitor recalled.[28] Far more people showed up than could be admitted: "The number of faithful who arrived was in such disproportion to the dimensions of the church, gigantic though they are, that it became necessary to shut the doors before half of those present had been able to enter."[29] A substantial contingent of French troops had deployed to the basilica to prevent disruptions, and the interior soon echoed with drums, bugles, and orders barked in French.[30] At 8:15 a.m., Pius emerged from the main door of the façade into the wooden portico. He went first to the reliquary chapel Poletti had created, then to his throne in front of the main door, where he was surrounded by forty-nine cardinals on their benches along with some 140 bishops and archbishops.

The ceremony then started. Six bishops from six different countries (Cardinal Wiseman of Westminster among them) assisted the pope in sprinkling the exterior walls with holy water. The benediction of the façade was reserved to Pius. The ceremony then moved to the interior, where after more prayers and antiphons Pius and the six bishops fanned out to sprinkle the walls and pavement with more holy water (**Figure 92**). From there everyone went back out to the reliquary chapel under the wooden portico to get the urn containing the holy relics that were to be implanted in the altar of the Conversion of Paul on the north terminal wall of the transept (since the main altar at the confessio had already been consecrated in 1840). Before reentering, they sang Psalm 94, a plea from the Israelites to God to crush their enemies; its relevance to the recent travails of the Roman Church was obvious to everyone present. Pius then read out a more upbeat homily, which, after touching on

92. The consecration ceremony at the basilica of San Paolo fuori le mura on 10 December 1854 (from *L'Album*, 16 December 1854).
Source: Getty Research Institute, Los Angeles (85-S84).

the hardships the basilica had endured, announced his delight at being able to bring this third iteration of the building to conclusion and exhorted everyone to place themselves under Paul's protection. The relics were then brought to the Altar of the Conversion of Paul, and Psalms 149 and 150 were sung. These too did not lack for passages that savored a coming "vengeance upon the heathens," and the binding "of their kings with chains, and their nobles with fetters of iron." The relics were then introduced into the altar, which was sealed with blessed cement and ritually rubbed with chrism and ashes.

Contemporary politics surfaced once again when passages from the Council of Trent were read out affirming the excommunication of those who trespassed against the rights and properties of the Church. All eyes were said to have turned to Archbishop Fransoni of Turin, at that date exiled from Piedmont on account of his intransigent opposition to that kingdom's anticlerical Siccardi laws.[31]

The consecration was over by about 2 in the afternoon, by which time the rain had started again. Pius left first to return home to the Vatican, leaving hundreds of clerics and dignitaries to follow in what quickly became a muddy traffic jam snaking for a mile up the via Ostiense. After several hours, the basilica was finally opened to the waiting crowd that was said by one witness to extend "as far as the eye could see."[32] French soldiers kept close watch. By all accounts, the affusion of people was terrific, and the basilica was thronged until evening.

In his monograph on the reconstruction, Michael Groblewski offers an ingenious interpretation of how the consecration of San Paolo related to the Proclamation of the Dogma of the Immaculate Conception two days earlier, and why the two events were paired.[33] In Groblewski's view, the dogma was a means of rejecting the new secularist world order and of reasserting the Catholic vision of a divinely ordered world; Pauline theology, meanwhile, was where that vision was set forth and explained. The consecration of Paul's basilica, in the company of the entire Church hierarchy, offered a reminder of Paul's teaching to the whole world, and of the Church's subsequent assumption of that teaching authority. Mary and Paul, belief and theology, vessel of salvation and *Vas electionis* – mutually reinforced one another in a resounding proclamation of the Catholic vision for the world.

One feels sure that a Catholic clergyman of 1854 would have endorsed this reading. But it is useful to reflect not only on what bound the events together, but also on what made them different. One thing that certainly made them different was their weight for the international Catholic community and the amount of public attention they received. The proclamation of the dogma on 8 December was covered by newspapers all over the world, from the Catholic to the secular to the anti-Catholic. The consecration of San Paolo two days later, on the other hand, was barely covered by anybody. Even the most ardent Catholic papers in Europe, like *L'Univers* or the *Dublin Review*, made no mention of it. Secondary and tertiary events held in distant provinces weeks later in connection with the new Marian dogma received more attention than the consecration of San Paolo.

This is not surprising. The consecration of San Paolo was the culminating act of a three-decade, internationally publicized campaign of Roman Catholic

TWO DAYS IN DECEMBER

rebuilding, both metaphorical and literal – one centered, as we have seen, on the figure of Paul the theologian, the evangelist, and that projected Paul as a catalyst for Catholic popular mobilization, renewal, rededication, and resistance. As we have also seen, this communal renaissance under the Pauline sign had failed to materialize during the decades that separated the 1825 Chirograph from the 1854 consecration. Paul may have been the elite male cleric's ideal image of where a Catholic revival might start, but his limitations as the fulcrum for a mass movement are in retrospect obvious. Paul's stern letters to the early churches were the very emblem of the aescetic Tridentine Catholicism that had been in part to blame for the popular decline of the Church during the eighteenth century. Historically, both Protestant and Catholic thinkers have turned to Paul most eagerly when it has been a question of forming theological arguments – during the Protestant Reformation, for instance, or the Council of Trent – and 1825 felt to Church leaders like another such occasion. What took them some time to recognize was that they were wrong: theological arguments were not what the Church needed in its great confrontation with the changed world of the nineteenth century. The words of that great prophet of Catholic modernization, Ernest Renan, in his 1869 book on St. Paul, are apposite here:

> Scarcely any one before the sixteenth century is called by [Paul's] name. He hardly appears in the emblematical monuments. He has no devotees; they build him but few churches … There was too little sympathy between Paul and the popular conscience … [But] the Reformation opens for St. Paul a new era of glory and authority. Catholicism itself, through more extended studies than those of the middle ages, is led back to quite just views concerning the apostle of the Gentiles. Dating from the sixteenth century, the name of Paul is omnipresent. But the Reformation, which rendered so much service to science and reason, was not able to create a legend. Rome, throwing a pleasing veil over the rudeness of the Epistle to the Galatians, elevates Paul upon a pedestal almost equal to that of Peter. Paul does not therefore become to any great extent the saint of the people.[34]

In retrospect, this was a real problem, and by 1850 it had become apparent. A genuinely popular Catholic revival required a catalytic figure who offered better gifts than Paul could: maternal love and patience, compassion for suffering and failure, and intimate proximity to the supreme power of divinity.

The expansion of Marian devotion that occurred so organically during the first half of the nineteenth century responded to the social, historical, and political challenges that ordinary and especially poor and rural Catholics increasingly faced. The un-Catholic or sometimes anti-Catholic values of an ostensibly secular capitalist society did not hesitate to mock Catholic belief as a pathetic holdover from less enlightened eras. At the same time, Catholics from the humbler classes found themselves progressively victimized by processes of capitalist development, which uprooted, impoverished, disempowered, isolated, and alienated them. In such contexts, ordinary Catholics were not crying out for another authoritative patriarch dictating commandments about how to live a purer life. The longing, rather, was for a loving intercessor who might help the vulnerable believer to lay hold to God's mercy and power. This was Mary, the ultimate Catholic intercessor, who, it went without saying, had the ear of her divine Son. Ordinary rural Catholics had known this all along. Through her prayers and intercession, the oppressed, the lonely, the poor, and the alienated discerned the promise of mercy and could count on divine protection and justice. This combination of the cosmic and the intimate proved irresistible to millions of people. It was not something Paul could compete with.

This contrast between Paul and Mary is worth drawing out a little further still. Paul was a stern, authoritative philosopher-cleric whose teachings had been synthesized by learned theologians into the basis of a rational system. Mary was a mother whose love, mercy, compassion, and intercession needed no explanation and who often chose to deliver her messages to humanity via small children in the rural provinces. Paul was emblematically a material being with all the limitations that implied, whether in his vital form as the tireless traveler forever dragging himself from city to city across land and sea, or as the immobile body now entombed beneath a monumental building on the via Ostiense. Mary instead had no need of Paul's laborious mobility. She simply *appeared*, miraculously, wherever and whenever she wished, and not infrequently in remote, neglected locales. There was no tomb of Mary, for her body had already been assumed to heaven on the third day after her death. Paul was a sinner whose whole career turned on an epic act of repentance for his prior persecution of Christians. Mary was free of sin, immaculate, and occupied a unique point of intermediacy between humanity and the Godhead.

An essential attraction of Marian devotion was that, in a secular age of reason, it hinged on affect. Such devotion could be relished as a way of living a principled refusal of modern reason's self-sufficiency; of what Pius IX referred to as "naturalism" and "absolute rationalism."[35] Certainly for Pius this formed one of the attractions of the doctrine of the Immaculate Conception: it was a "truth" that could not be proved by science, history, or analysis. If in the past it had not been proclaimed a dogma because Church theologians could not explain it satisfactorily, under Pius IX this became a point in its favor. As an act of defiance – not unlike Leo XII's decision to choose the most lavish option in rebuilding San Paolo – the proclamation of a rationally indefensible dogma asserted before the whole world that the Catholic Church believed in the superiority of revelation to reason. That it was theologically controversial, even ridiculous to the Church's enemies, only made the provocation more potent; it was yet another example of the "wisdom of God which seems as foolishness in men's eyes." On 9 December 1854, Pius told a gathering that the new dogma would confound those "who exaggerate the forces of reason in order to deny or lessen the benefit of Revelation," and expressed the hope that the Blessed Virgin would "uproot and destroy this dangerous error of Rationalism, which in our unhappy times not only afflicts and torments civil society, but more deeply afflicts the Church."[36] Just four years later, Pius seemed to be triumphantly vindicated by the sensational visions at Lourdes, in rural southern France, where for the first time a Marian apparition, appearing, as usual, to a child, explicitly identified herself as the Immaculate Conception. The age of the Marian pilgrimage industry soon dawned.[37]

Increasingly encouraged in more emotional and affective forms of spiritual practice, ordinary Catholics did not delay in asserting themselves as a source of energy and power within the institutional Church. Over the second half of a century famous to historians above all for its secular liberalism, the numbers of self-identifying Catholics rebounded, Catholic lay associations came to exercise major political influence, and a deep, broad, popular Catholic revival took root.[38] Protestants predictably excoriated the new "Marian idolatry," but unlike their Tridentine forefathers, late nineteenth-century Catholic leaders were too busy to care, savoring an international revival they had been dreaming of since at least the time of Leo XII. The basilica of San Paolo, meanwhile, began what was to be a long retreat from public consciousness – replaced there by the Marian pilgrimage churches now going up in places like Lourdes and La Salette.[39]

On 7 December 1854, the day before the Dogma of the Immaculate Conception was to be proclaimed, Pius IX was presented with a project for a monument commemorating the occasion: a giant statue of the Immaculate Conception in her traditional Labouré configuration, standing atop a globe and crushing representations of heresy[40] (**Figure 93**). A few days later, a visiting Frenchman claimed that the newspapers were abuzz about a project to build a whole church in Rome dedicated to the Immaculate Conception, entirely with funds raised by subscription.[41] On 12 December, Italian papers first reported that Pius IX had indeed decided to erect such a commemorative monument: a column surmounted by a statue of Mary in Piazza di Spagna in front of the Palazzo di Propaganda Fide.[42] In a by-now familiar pattern, donations began pouring in from organs of the Pontifical State, ecclesiastical entities, clerics, and later from individuals all over the world.[43] The column that was to be used was an ancient colossal column excavated in 1778 – the year of Voltaire's death, as a noted Immaculate Conception enthusiast pointed out in a celebratory article in *L'Album*.[44] In January 1855, it was brought to

93. Giuseppe De Fabris's project for a monument in Rome dedicated to the Immaculate Conception of Mary, December 1854 (from Orioli [1855]).
Source: Courtesy of BSR Library, L.306.71.DEF(2).1.

94. Luigi Poletti, Colonna dell'Immacolata, Rome, 1855–1857.
Source: Author.

Piazza di Spagna and deposited there.[45] The architect selected to design the new monument was none other than Luigi Poletti. Ground was broken in May, and the now-iconic Colonna dell'Immacolata was inaugurated with great pomp two years later, on 9 September 1857[46] (**Figure 94**).

95. Poletti's 1846 project for a Pauline column to be erected outside the north porch of San Paolo fuori le mura.
Source: Biblioteca civica d'arte e architettura Luigi Poletti, Modena, Archivio Poletti, disegni inv. 320.

Poletti later told his friend and biographer Campori of the remarkable circumstances that led to its design. The night after he received the commission, Poletti had been lying awake in bed, suffering from his gout and trying to think of a worthy design for such a momentous memorial. Suddenly, the Virgin Mary appeared before him – one more Marian apparition in an age full of them. She did not speak to Poletti of the state of the world or his soul, but just gestured to a drawing on his drafting table: one he had made in 1846 for the Pauline column Pius IX had wanted to erect outside the north porch at San Paolo (**Figure 95**). Poletti understood her gesture to mean that she wanted him to reuse that design, swapping out Paul for her and recomposing all the auxiliary bas reliefs.[47]

Poletti leapt from bed and began erasing Paul and sketching in Mary. The symbolism of Poletti's vision is sublime, for it transforms the Colonna dell'Immacolata into a monument of Mary's displacement of Paul as the new fulcrum of Catholic revival. As it was in Catholic culture, so it was also with Mary's monument.

NOTES

1   Mazzonis (1981), pp. 265–266.
2   The literature on the Council of Trent and its impact on early modern Catholicism has expanded enormously in recent decades. Some good starting points are Ditchfield (2013) and Pollmann (2013), both in Bamji et al. (2013); and Firpo (2016).
3   Aubert (1952), pp. 451–478; Bouritius (1979), pp. 125–139, 147–154; Lagrée (1979); Mazzonis (1981), pp. 271–275; Rusconi (2005).
4   Stearns (1967); Oldfield (1969).
5   Cf. Gibson (1989), pp. 15–29, 138–145.
6   Gibson (1989), pp. 260–265; Printy (2005).
7   Hocedez (1947), v. 2, pp. 372–375; O'Connor (1958); Warner (1976), pp. 236–254; Mazzonis (1981), pp. 273–275; Pope (1985).
8   Doctrinal policing was generally weaker the further one got from Rome. See Delbeke (2017).
9   Merluzzi et al. (2022).
10 Bouritius (1979), pp. 122–123.
11 Martina (1974–1990), v. 2, p. 262.
12 Gibson (1989), p. 145.
13 On the promotion of Marian devotion under Gregory XVI, see Caliò (2008).
14 *TEPD*, v. 3, pp. 338–339.
15 Cecchin (2010), p. 61.
16 Caliò (2012).
17 Caliò (2008), p. 288.
18 Cecchin (2010), p. 61.
19 Martina (1974–1990), v. 2, p. 262
20 Gibson (1989), pp. 146–147.
21 Martina (1974–1990), v. 2, pp. 264–265.
22 Sardi (1905), v. 2, p. 123.
23 Le Mire (1855); *Cronaca* III, pp. 676–684; *L'ami de la Religion* (Paris), 16 December 1854, pp. 657–661, and 26 December 1854, pp. 741–746.

24 *Cronaca* III, pp. 659–660.

25 De Maumigny (1863), pp. 78–79.

26 *Cronaca* III, p. 660.

27 *Cronaca* III, p. 664.

28 Le Mire (1855), p. 47.

29 Le Mire (1855), p. 48.

30 Le Mire (1855), p. 49.

31 *Cronaca* III, p.725; Mellano (1964).

32 *Cronaca* III, p. 723.

33 Groblewski (2001), pp. 250–252.

34 Renan (1869), p. 328.

35 *TEPD*, v. 4, p. 272 (*Sillabo dei principali errori . . .*, no. I).

36 Quoted in Pope (1985), p. 182. Full text in *TEPD*, v. 4, pp. 143–149.

37 Agostino (2020).

38 Sperber (1984); Gibson (1989); Blackbourn (1991); Anderson (1995) and (2000).

39 Basciano (2012).

40 De Fabris (1854); Orioli (1855).

41 Le Mire (1855), pp. 49–50.

42 The news was reported as far away as Paris by December before finally being confirmed in the *Giornale di Roma* on 2 January (*L'ami de la Religion*, 21 December 1854, p. 703; *GdR*, 2 January 1855, p. 1).

43 *DESE*, v. 73, "Teatine della SS. Immacolata Concezione," p. 76.

44 Anivitti (1855), quoted in Caliò (2008), p. 305.

45 Gregorovius (1907), p. 17; *DESE*, v. 73, "Teatine della SS. Immacolata Concezione," p. 77.

46 *GdR*, 8 May 1855, p. 427; *GdR*, 9 September 1857, p. 815; Martini (1987); Tolomeo (1990).

47 Poletti's final design also resembled a project to re-erect the same antique column that was published in *L'Album* in November 1846 by the architect Paolo Belloni. In 1863, Gasparoni wrote that Belloni "claimed, and still resolutely claims" that Poletti had plagiarized his design, and in protest had had a large engraving of his project mounted in a prominent shop on the Corso and in an exhibition space in Piazza del Popolo. One hesitates to interpret Poletti's Marian vision as a fabrication to insulate himself from Belloni's charges – or as a way to safeguard his project from criticism or forced revisions – but if that is what it was, it was a cynical ploy indeed (Borgnana [1846]; Gasparoni [1863], p.2; Verzili [1874]).

CONCLUSION

THE OLD CLASSICAL UNITY OF ROMAN ARCHITECTURE SO PRIZED BY Poletti gradually disappeared after 1850. The Gothic revival had arrived in the city even earlier, first with the small Cappella del Sacro Cuore erected in 1841–1843 in the monastery of the sisters of the Order of the Sacred Heart on the fringes of Trastevere, and then more visibly with the restoration of Santa Maria sopra Minerva (1848–1855), a medieval building whose Dominican restorers, influenced by French Romantic art theory, stripped away its seventeenth-century veneers and redecorated it in a rubicund neo-Gothic manner[1] (**Figure 96**). In 1855, a Scottish neo-Catholic architect named George Wigley began a new neo-Gothic church dedicated to Sant'Alfonso de' Liguori (1855–1859) on the Esquiline Hill near Santa Maria Maggiore[2] (**Plate 19**). Classicism still maintained a strong presence in Rome, for instance in the High Renaissance style of the new church of San Giovanni della Malva in Trastevere (1851) or in Vespignani's chapel of Santa Maria della Misericordia in Verano Cemetery (1855–1859), with its neo-Paleochristian exterior and Renaissance interior[3] (**Figure 97**). A sober classicism also prevailed in non-ecclesiastical architecture, in city gates and government buildings, for instance at the Porta San Pancrazio (1854), at Poletti's own Piazza Pia (1856–1861), at the new barracks of Castro Pretorio (1862), or at the Tobacco Manufactory in Trastevere (1860–1863).[4] All told, Roman architecture of 1850–1870 would probably have pleased Poletti more than Selvatico. But it was also undeniable that the old premise of a unified Italic cultural continuity was losing its magic.

96. Santa Maria sopra Minerva, Rome, fourteenth century; restored between 1848 and 1855 by the Dominican fathers of the adjacent monastery following designs by Fra'Girolamo Bianchedi. *Source*: Author.

The way architectural *history* was deployed in the city, however, changed more profoundly after 1850, in ways that help us to understand the stakes of the long struggles over history we have witnessed around the reconstruction of San Paolo.[5] Over a twenty-eight-year campaign of urban transformation conducted by Pius IX after his return to Rome, the city's patrimony of historic sacred buildings was thoroughly reimagined, in parallel with the reimagined modern papacy that he and Secretary of State Antonelli were forging. After 1849, and as the drumbeat for Italian unification intensified in the mid-1850s, Pius and his advisors increasingly separated the temporal and spiritual components of the pope's office: the everyday government of the pontifical territories was now overseen principally by Antonelli, while Pius's public image was instead associated with the spiritual leadership of the supranational Catholic Church.[6] In keeping with Ultramontanist ideals, Church authority was concentrated in Pius's hands and an international personality cult was built up around his personage.[7] The public image of Rome was adjusted accordingly. The old Sistine ambition of trumpeting temporal glory and power with triumphalist piazzas, boulevards, and monuments was, after two and a half centuries, laid mostly to rest.[8] The urban image of Rome was more and more

97. Virginio Vespignani, Santa Maria della Misericordia, Verano Cemetery, Rome, 1855–1859. *Source*: Author.

to be before the eyes of Catholics as an emblem of the benevolent spiritual father's ancient and supranational dominion of light and love, and with the continuity of Catholic past and Catholic present under strain during this period of unprecedented institutional change, it was essential that Rome's historic fabric conjure that continuity in fresh and plausible ways. This was accomplished through Pius's unprecedented push to foreground the historical remains of Rome's Christian past at the expense of the antique monuments that anchored the old providentialist narratives of Catholic sacred history.[9] A whole lost world of ancient Christian catacombs, cemeteries, and places of worship were excavated by Marchi's Commission for Sacred Archaeology, then studied, stabilized, sheltered, publicized, and opened to the public[10] (**Figure 98**). Pius also commissioned a new Christian Museum in the Lateran Palace to house objects extracted from these excavations.[11] Entirely new circuits of sacred attractions confronted visitors to the city.

This historical turn was of a fundamentally different type from that which followed Pius VII's return to Rome following the Napoleonic occupations. The watchword then had been "restoration," and it referred to the resumption

98. The excavations under the southeast side of the Palatine Hill (from Cacchiatelli and Cleter [1865]).
Source: Bibliotheca Hertziana – Max Planck Institute for Art History.

of a providential continuity following an aberrant disruption. The continuity that Rome spoke of after 1850 was instead historical in a modern sense. An excavated catacomb was still seen to betoken divine protection and to reflect God's will, but it did not require faith to understand, in the way that one needed faith to see the Arch of Septimius Severus as evidence of God's providential plan for the Church. The demonstration now aspired to objectivity: the Church had been in Rome worshipping the one true God for a millennium and a half, and these excavated catacombs proved it. This shift spoke to the new anxieties of the period after 1850, when not only was the Church entering a period of unprecedented doctrinal, political, and territorial change, but was also finally embarking on its long-postponed adjustment to the new realities of mass-cultural modernity. The urge to celebrate the fragile emblems of an authenticating past was not a "return to normal" following a shock. Rather, it aimed to offer objective historical reassurance that the Church was durable and would endure these latest challenges as well.

99. Annibale Angelini, *Il Ponte del Soldino*, 1869. Depicts the new iron suspension bridge over the Tiber at S. Giovanni de' Fiornetini.
Source: Courtesy Berardi Galleria d'Arte.

To put it another way: past and present were not presented in the Roman cityscape prior to 1850 principally in terms of their radical distinctness, whereas that was increasingly the implication after 1850. In the earlier period, even after the traumas of revolution and occupation, Roman architects and planners were still conditioned to think of themselves as working within a long tradition in which Renaissance and Baroque precedents remained vitally and unproblematically relevant. (When in 1824 Poletti proposed what would have been the first iron suspension bridge in Rome, he dwelled at length on why it was better than the bridge proposed by Carlo Fontana for the site in 1692.)[12] We have of course also seen that this belief in continuity was by then at risk, undermined by multiplying proofs of historical rupture, the most spectacular response to these being the decision to reconstruct San Paolo *in pristinum*, a gesture that yearned to reverse a slipping sense of intimacy with a beloved past. After 1850, however, the extent of the rupture was undeniable.

It is significant, for example, that the other essential component of Pius IX's work in Rome was an infrastructural modernization that transformed the Eternal City far more than the Napoleonic reforms of a half-century earlier. Pius installed gas lighting throughout the city; he commissioned a series of iron suspension bridges over the Tiber, two of which were built (**Figure 99**); he

100. Electric-telegraph wires extending out of Rome to the southeast (from Cacchiatelli and Cleter [1865]).
Source: Bibliotheca Hertziana – Max Planck Institute for Art History.

ordered the construction of broad new streets and piazzas in connection with new public housing for the poor; he sponsored new enterprises aimed at improving the local economy, like the aforementioned Tobacco Manufactory, with its streets of adjacent workers' housing; he commissioned new buildings to house orphans, deaf-mutes, and other disadvantaged populations; he expanded the Campo Verano cemetery beyond the city walls; he connected Rome to the surrounding regions with a new railway network and telegraph service (**Figure 100**); and he founded new public museums that initiated the Roman public into scientific matters such as human anatomy, physics, and mineralogy, which previous pontifical governments had regarded with suspicion. All of these endeavors were then celebrated in official publications.[13]

The archaeological and modernizing components of Pius's transformations worked together to ensure that past and present began speaking to one another in a new way. The jarring modernity of gaslights and iron bridges now served paradoxically to throw the venerable churches and newly exposed ancient

CONCLUSION

101. The Ponte Senatorio, a new iron suspension bridge over the Tiber built atop the second-century BCE remains of the Pons Aemilius (from Cacchiatelli and Cleter [1865]).
Source: Bibliotheca Hertziana – Max Planck Institute for Art History.

Christian ruins into an even deeper historical focus, making them seem definitively old in a new and peculiarly modern way. One of Pius's two iron bridges was even attached directly to the second century BCE remains of the Pons Aemilius (Ponte Rotto) – not a Christian relic, to be sure, but the gesture exemplified the new historicist logic[14] (**Figure 101**).

This logic also underlay Pius's extensive campaign of church restorations, in which no less than seventy-two historic churches were restored and/or redecorated.[15] These churches were testimonies of the past – sometimes the remote past – which meant that they were vulnerable and in need of protection. Yet they were also in continual use as a vital part of the city's daily life. The architect who most often took the lead in this work was Virginio Vespignani, Poletti's former student as well as his assistant and eventual successor at San Paolo. Vespignani undertook major restorations at San Marcello al Corso, Santa Maria Maggiore, Santa Maria in Trastevere, San Pietro in Vincoli, and San Carlo ai Catinari, among others, but his emblematic work came at San Lorenzo

102. The basilica of San Lorenzo fuori le mura, mainly from the sixth and thirteenth centuries; restored by Virginio Vespignani, 1855–1864. As the photograph was taken before the bombing of 1943, it shows the now-lost fresco paintings along the nave walls.
Source: Hungarian National Digital Archive/Kuny Domokos Múzeum. CC BY 4.0.

fuori le mura (1855–1864)[16] (**Figure 102**). At San Lorenzo, Vespignani aimed to render a tortuous construction history explicitly and objectively legible – a strategy outside the traditional spectrum of approaches, which ran from simply renewing old buildings with new elements to placing a building's historical development in thoughtful tension with its presumed perenniality.[17] Vespignani instead foregrounded the basilica's uneven historical texture, with exactly the sort of unashamed juxtapositions of ancient and modern that Poletti had always recoiled from at San Paolo. Poletti's San Paolo insisted on a quasi-anachronic historicity, but Vespignani's restorations situate the spectator in an identifiable present from which the remote antiquity of historical elements is thrown into sharp relief. Historic elements are accented as such, especially those representing the faraway early Christian and medieval periods, whereas the new elements that Vespignani contributed were self-evidently modern, even if in broadly historical styles. The best example is the new space Vespignani created when he cleared the infilled area below the thirteenth-century floor that subdivided the old sixth-century sanctuary. If this work had been done in the 1820s or 1830s, this space would likely have been rendered in a historicizing idiom that offered an immersive experience of an exemplary past. Vespignani instead rendered it as fully modern. One descends to it directly from the thirteenth-century aisles of the nave, only to find a grid of crisply uniform Doric columns in an austere neoclassical ordonnance (**Plate 20**). The new is thereby unapologetically present, underscoring the antiquity of everything else. One encountered a similar effect on the upper part of the medieval nave walls where, before their destruction in the Second World War, there was a cycle of frescoes in the latest pictorial language of circa 1865. This implication of historical distancing was also present more generally in the alien sense of didactic order Vespignani imposed on the old building's chaotically layered fabric.

Like the iron suspension bridge that takes you to an Early Christian catacomb, the apposition of these brightly modern elements with the venerable framing fabric all around frankly admits that the old hope of timeless intimacy with the historical past is illusory. The past actually is remote, fragile, and mysterious, and it is only through comparison with the pristine present that the true depth of the historical field emerges. The contemporary constitutes the past *as past* in the viewer's experience, by revealing objectively the temporal weight that anchors the present and prevents it drifting away.

The way Christian archaeological sites were handled further illustrates the unacknowledged historicism of Pius IX's new manner of marshaling the past. Proponents of the new school of Christian archaeology at the start of the century had been motivated partly by an identitarian refusal to accept that Christian remains were less worthy than pagan ones. Before long, excavated Christian antiquities were held up as models for contemporary architecture, as we saw in the work of Canina, Promis, Bunsen, and, in his own fashion, Poletti. Pius IX's Christian archaeology after 1850 took its distance from such ambitions. In subterranean excavations such as those beneath San Clemente or the columbarium near the Porta San Sebastiano, the priority was once again to underscore the remoteness of the antiquity being revealed. When reinforcing arches were introduced to stabilize these excavated areas, or when public access was provided via new stairwells, they were executed in an abstract brick and arch style that made no effort to present itself as anything but modern, and so formed a sharp contrast with the patinaed tufa of the ancient work[18] (**Figure 103**). The era that had conducted the excavation was thereby made present in ways that made the old site available, not for immersive time travel, nor for suggestive reflections on temporality and providence, but as something inexorably remote seen across a temporal chasm.[19]

The same impulse was in evidence at newly excavated sites. When in the 1850s two lost early Christian basilicas were unearthed on the outskirts of the

SCAVI A S. CLEMENTE
Parte superiore della Navata di mezzo dell'antichissima Basilica

103. Excavations beneath the church of San Clemente, Rome, showing the brick supporting arches and vaults created in order to render the excavated area visitable by the public (from Cacchiatelli and Cleter [1865]).
Source: Bibliotheca Hertziana – Max Planck Institute for Art History.

city – Sant'Alessandro on the via Nomentana and Santo Stefano on the via Latina – contemporaries made no reference to their relevance for the design of new churches, nor were they garnished with historicizing frames. Rather, they were spoken of purely as testimonies of a distant past that proved the long continuity of Catholic worship. The low excavated walls of S. Stefano were simply left exposed in all their broken mystery (**Figure 104**). At S. Alessandro, a more elaborate presentation was envisaged. Its discovery had occurred in December 1854, at the very moment when Rome was packed with clerics for the proclamation of the Dogma of the Immaculate Conception. Clerical scholars had identified it as the burial place of the second-century pope St. Alexander I. Such a discovery, coming promptly at a moment of doctrinal mutation and significant political anxiety, was at once read as a divine reassurance – as a reminder that, as a book published on the occasion stated, "the present worship of the Catholic Church is the same

CONCLUSION 375

104. The basilica of Santo Stefano in the via Latina on the southern edge of Rome, excavated starting in 1859 (from Cacchiatelli and Cleter [1865]).
Source: Bibliotheca Hertziana – Max Planck Institute for Art History.

as in the times of Alexander."[20] When Pius IX visited the site the following spring (on what was to prove an eventful day[21]), he had an emotional response to the ruin and at once approved plans by the architect-engineer Luigi Boldrini to erect a modern, three-aisled church that was to shelter and display it down in its crypt.[22] Pius laid the cornerstone for this church in 1857, in an act that a fundraising appeal subsequently described as "reuniting the present to the past, and assuring the future to the present."[23] But construction lasted just a few years before being suspended and then abandoned shortly after 1860, partly because of the wars associated with the Risorgimento, and partly because concerns had emerged that the Alexander referenced in the inscriptions at the site might be a different Alexander. An engraving from 1865 shows that Boldrini's half-built church had by then received a simple roof that served as a basic shelter for the ruins (**Figure 105**). To judge by this image, the church was to have been in the same modern brick-and-arch style that Pius's architects had used when

105. The basilica of S. Alesandro on the via Nomentana, discovered in 1854, surmounted by the half-built church begun by the architect Luigi Boldrini in 1857 but abandoned in the early 1860s (from Cacchiatelli and Cleter [1865]).
Source: Bibliotheca Hertziana – Max Planck Institute for Art History.

reinforcing contemporary excavations.[24] Here too, then, it was through contrast with an openly modern frame that the grave and awful antiquity of the ruin was to shine forth.

Minardi's opposition to Poletti's pronaos façade can also be related to these changing ideas about the life of the past in the present. Minardi's claim was that the only authentic rationale for reconstructing San Paolo as a replica was to make its essential forms available for the edification of future generations. In Minardi's theory of painting restoration, the cardinal sin of the restorer was to add new elements to a work, since the very purpose of restoration in his view was to ensure that future generations would have access to an objective and authentic history of previous art.[25] San Paolo was a reconstruction, not a restoration, but a similar logic applied. Whereas the present had been made visible at the restored San Lorenzo in order to emphasize the authentic antiquity of all the other parts of the building, at the rebuilt San Paolo historical value instead inhered in the early Christian stylistic *form*, while its uniform modern texture vouched for the modernity of the enterprise. For Minardi, this ruled out a pronaos solution but not nave frescoes in a modern pictorial style, because modern frescos both underscored the building's status as a simulacrum and served the spiritual edification of the modern worshipers who were to use San Paolo.[26]

In all these examples, whether in archaeological sites or church restorations, or in Minardi's vision for San Paolo, the sincere manner in which the present was acknowledged invited forms of distancing. It is fascinating then to observe how during these same decades the literature on early Christian buildings began to divide into two opposed modes. On one side, scholarly publications on the catacombs and early basilicas increasingly took on a progressive scientific tone, relinquishing general concerns like the contribution of the Early Christian basilica to the future of Christian architecture, and accepting instead the specificity and acknowledged provisionality of modern historical research. Examples include Paolo Belloni's 1853 reassessment of the original form of Constantinian San Paolo and Joseph Anton Messmer's 1854 attempt to demonstrate that the Christian basilica derived not from the civic basilica but from the private court rooms typical in a larger Roman domus.[27] The corollary to this scientific turn was an exactly simultaneous burst of popular historical fiction on the life of early Christianity and the spaces it had inhabited. The most famous examples were Cardinal Wiseman's *Fabiola; or, the Church of the Catacombs* (1855) and John Henry Newman's *Callista: A Sketch of the Third Century* (1856), both bestsellers destined to be translated into several languages and remain in print for decades.[28] These elaborate Romantic fictions offered a vivid and personal sense of intimacy with the past, almost as if in acknowledgment that the objective lens of modern historiography – predicated on a sense of the past as remote, mysterious, incomplete, uncertain – had drained the past of its affective power. Such fictions became necessary with the loss of the traditional anachronic, providentialist historical consciousness, a loss whose first bitter cessions were announced in the movement for an *in pristinum* rebuilding of San Paolo.

This coming to terms with historicist consciousness was but one component of the Church's broader determination to rebound from the traumas it had endured in the period around 1800. San Paolo was thrust into its role as a catalyst for this recovery by the fire of 1823, an act of God that was read as a divine incitement to reconnect with the Pauline legacy: to embrace Paul as the Church's greatest resource in combating the assaults of modern philosophy, reuniting an alienated Catholic faithful and rechristianizing a godless world.

This reconnection was first actualized in the fundraising campaigns, which sought with unprecedented reach to reanimate the faithful as a supranational community united in pious personal sacrifice. The vital contemporary relevance for Catholics of Paul's tireless evangelizing, his stern theological rigor, his self-sacrifice, and ultimately his martyrdom were all highlighted anew in hopes of sparking the yearned-for revival.

What the latter chapters of this book have shown is that this endeavor was a failure: there had been no discernable Pauline revival in Catholic thought after 1825, and the fundraising drives, while unprecedented, could never be confused with a genuine mass movement. This failure had little to do with the reconstruction itself but rather occurred because Church leaders underestimated the depth of institutional transformation that such a revival required. In fact, a host of other reforms and recalibrations had to occur first. One of the most important had been gradually unfolding since 1815: the reconstitution of the European clergy so that it could relate more sympathetically to laypeople, so that its origins would no longer skew so much toward masculinity and social privilege and its efforts might be directed more toward socially useful forms of service, like education or medical care.[29] Another recalibration involved encouraging ordinary Catholics to develop a stronger affective connection to the quotidian life of the Church, for instance through more frequent participation in the sacraments.[30] Such efforts had already pushed church attendance in many parts of Europe to start trending upward again in the 1830s and 1840s. These shifts formed an essential precondition for any kind of large-scale Catholic revival, and they had simply not yet come to fruition when the effort on behalf of San Paolo was launched. As a result, Church leaders were unable to leverage the crusade to rebuild San Paolo into a larger movement.

In the course of this failure, however, Church leaders learned several key lessons that were to prove essential for the Catholic revival that did occur after 1850. The failure of Paul to ignite popular enthusiasms partly reflected his status as an icon of the rigid Tridentine Catholicism that many Church leaders had already identified as an obstacle to popular religious engagement. One doubts whether Church leaders would have been so ready by midcentury to open up to popular religiosity – to the pastoral solicitude of Alfonso de' Liguori and the popular mysticism of Marian devotion – if they had not first experienced not just the burgeoning popular devotions to Mary but equally Paul's failure to incite comparable enthusiasm; whether they would have been capable of embracing an intercessor rather than a figure of doctrinal authority; a mother rather than an elder; or one who spoke simple messages to peasant children rather than one whose philosophical dictums kept an army of theologians busy. Underlying these shifts was a recognition that the Church's greatest earthly resource in meeting modern challenges was no longer the ruling houses of Europe – indeed, this was becoming less and less the case – but rather the

CONCLUSION

ordinary faithful.[31] The immense fundraising drive for San Paolo had by then already shown that other paths to influence and independence were conceivable. It had hinted at the reserves of energy that might be unlocked if the Church loosened its traditional commitment to top-down control and instead cultivated a sense of identitarian belonging in ordinary Catholics. Learning that lesson enabled the Catholic Church, against all odds, to finish a secular, liberal, capitalist nineteenth century in a far healthier position than it had occupied at the century's start.

The lesson was reinforced in 1847 when French Catholics began organizing grassroots fundraising drives to mark their support for Pius IX's increasingly threatened campaign of liberal reform.[32] They referred to these as an "Obolo," a term that evoked the old medieval collections known in English as Peter's Pence. The choice of words was significant, for it conjured the old period of Christian unity in Europe and positioned the Obolo as an instrument for reestablishing it. As Ignazio Vega has observed, the Obolo was a popular political movement to which adhesion carried an identitarian component; it was at once transversal and mass, for it united people from across the Catholic world from different social classes and ideological perspectives.[33] The growing Catholic press in France supported these efforts by publishing lists of subscribers that testified eloquently to the breadth of engaged support for Pius's government. As a result, French Catholic leaders were able to exert pressure on the national government on behalf of their community, pushing it for example to end its support for Austrian efforts to intimidate the pope. Catholics beyond France were also able to see the power of the Obolo, and within months had extended it to Piedmont, Belgium, Holland, Ireland, Scotland, England, Mexico, and the USA.[34] That first revival of the Obolo was to prove temporary, but it offered Pius IX and Antonelli another thrilling glimpse, after the fundraising drives for San Paolo, of the slumbering energies that the Church could awaken in the international faithful in the context of an emerging mass politics.

It was Antonelli who seems to have first grasped the significance of this.[35] The bold idea in his mind already at Gaeta was that the best way forward was to prepare for and even to embrace the previously unthinkable, namely, the eventual loss of the pope's temporal powers.[36] The idea that this might actually benefit the Holy See was certainly not original to him; the chronicler at San Paolo wrote on the very day of Pius IX's return to Rome in 1850 that "it is publicly disputed whether the temporal power is beneficial to the pope," adding that "one hears even ecclesiastics declare themselves against it."[37] But it was apparently Antonelli who convinced Pius that such a future was inevitable, and that it could bring advantages. Liberation from the burden of ruling a territory might permit the Church to reacquire the supranational dimension it had enjoyed in its greatest periods of power and influence, and which the recent success of the Obolo had reawakened. It would also free the Church from the pernicious interference of Catholic monarchs – monarchs who, to take but one famous example, had been in a position in 1773 to force Clement XIV to dissolve the Jesuits, very much against his will.[38] Pius IX would never have willingly surrendered a temporal power that he felt was a divinely conferred responsibility, and in principle he remained an implacable defender of it.[39] But much of what he began doing already in the 1850s suggests that he too saw a deterritorialized future as inevitable and recognized that it need not be an entirely bad thing.

The challenge was to ensure that when that loss finally occurred, the Church would be capable of reconstituting the independence that the temporal power had been intended to guarantee.[40] Antonelli and Pius were reminded once again in Gaeta what an ally the Catholic faithful could be as they negotiated the handover of Rome with Louis-Napoleon following the defeat of the Republic. For Pius had only been able to refuse the French president's demand that he return to the liberal constitution of 1848 because he and Antonelli knew that Louis-Napoleon was under significant pressure from Catholics at home – the same ones who had started and publicized the Obolo a year earlier. They formed an essential part of Louis-Napoleon's political support, and they wanted to see the pope returned to Rome much more than they wanted to see him forced to govern with a liberal constitution.[41] Louis-Napoleon's surrender on this point indicated how popular support from ordinary Catholics abroad could translate into greater pontifical independence at home.

Over the coming decades, Church leaders exploited every means to repeat this kind of success. They fostered new kinds of Catholic associations and pressure groups, nurtured a European Catholic press, and generally encouraged the formation of a specifically Catholic public, all of which expanded Catholic influence in the political sphere.[42] The Protestant and Orthodox churches of Europe had responded to the triumph of quasi-religious nationalisms in Europe by associating themselves with the cause of the nations sympathetic to them. But the Catholic Church still held to the idea of a divinely ordained authority that superseded that of kings and nations, and what remained of this Catholic universalism militated against too deep an association with particular nationalisms. So instead the Church embarked after 1850 on a far-reaching process of bureaucratization; of homogenizing international Catholic cultures, practices, and beliefs; and of mass popular mobilizations centered on a pervasive Ultramontanist ideology.[43] In short, and as Peter Raedts has argued, the Church began reimagining itself as a kind of supranational nation.[44] The cumulative effect was to position the Church as the ultimate nation, one that "because of its divine origin and its universal destination" surpassed all others. And just as in the secular nation-states, the Church's new nation was justified

CONCLUSION   381

with an appeal to history; in a strategy that we have glimpsed also at San Paolo, these new arrangements were presented not as innovations but as a salutary return to the supranational Church of yore.[45]

With the Italian Risorgimento in 1858–1861, the Holy See lost 71 percent of its national territory and 76 percent of its population while remaining responsible for the lion's share of its debts and expenses. Almost at once, a second and far more comprehensive revival of the Obolo blossomed, again from below, to vindicate the wisdom of the Church's strategy.[46] The Obolo of 1847–1848 had laid the conceptual and administrative groundwork, but what began in 1859 was on another scale altogether. What it produced was no longer a helping hand but rather an essential lifeline; without it, the survival of the Church in its traditional form would have been doubtful.[47] Reprising the script developed during the fundraising campaigns for San Paolo, Antonelli organized the papal nuncios actively to foster the revived Obolo by churning out, promoting, and coordinating propaganda and by streamlining the transfer of funds to Rome.[48] Ordinary Catholics responded robustly, glad of an opportunity to take concrete political action in support of a cause and a pope to which their affective ties had been cultivated for nearly a decade. Long lists of subscribers were again published, revealing donors from every social stratum. By February 1860, well before the economic losses inflicted by the Risorgimento were fully felt, a special account had been created in the Apostolic Chamber to absorb the sums pouring in from England, Austria, France, Italy, Germany, Belgium, Poland, Switzerland, Canada, the United States, Cuba, Martinique, Brazil, Peru, Jerusalem, Turkey, and the East Indies.[49] And that was just the first year. Over time, contributions from the United States and Latin America would increase, and donations would eventually arrive from China and India as well.[50] The Obolo was ultimately what permitted the Church to pay for the pope's civil list, the academies, university, schools, beneficent institutions, and general government of Rome; the maintenance of the papal palaces, museums, and libraries; and the Roman congregations, pensions, and diplomatic corps abroad.[51] In the words of the Obolo's first great scholar, Carlo Crocella, this "mass phenomenon" succeeded in "prolonging the life" of an organism that was "no longer alive."[52]

Crocella pinpoints the Obolo as the key moment in the Church's great modern pivot from linking its fortunes to aristocracies and governments to instead drawing its sustenance from the faithful at large; or, to use Raedts's expression, to reconceiving of the Church as a supranational nation.[53] Exclusivity is a defining characteristic of the modern nation, and the Obolo helped the Roman hierarchy to retire the anachronistic identification of the Church with society as a whole and instead to recognize the faithful for what they now were: one sharply defined part of society with agency, capable of functioning as a pressure group among others, or even in some places eventually as a political party, within the framework of nation-states.[54] By the late nineteenth century, this reconception extended even to efforts to make common cause with the subaltern classes, where the Church highlighted its critique of capitalism and stressed its identification with the common victims of the new liberal bourgeois order.[55] This sanctified alternative to the godless doctrines of socialism was disseminated through the Catholic press, intensified preaching missions, and a popular printed imagery heavy on types like the Sacred Heart of Jesus or the suffering Christ, in which the poor were encouraged to see a reflection of their own misery.[56] Even in Rome itself, already by the 1860s the tone had changed profoundly from the days of Leo XII or Gregory XVI. New semiofficial journals from the bourgeois *Civiltà Cattolica* to the proletarian *Il Veridico* now continuously celebrated the loyalty, goodness, intuitiveness, and resiliance of the Roman *popolani* in an effort to build as well as to publicize warmer relations between the people and their Holy Father.[57] A more sympathetic and tolerant attitude also prevailed with respect to popular festivals and amusements, whose palliative social function was increasingly respected.[58]

The San Paolo reconstruction played an essential part in the prehistory of this epochal turning point. Premonitions of these future developments in the San Paolo saga are not difficult to discern, from the leveraging of individual affect to prompt voluntary financial contributions, to the role of the press in naming even the humblest participants; from the ways this could stimulate further donations and effect contemporary political debates, to the uneasy balance of opportunism and humility required of the institutional Church to accept this dependency. The Obolo and the deeper changes of which it is emblematic thus help us perceive an essential yet largely overlooked aspect of the legacy of the massive San Paolo reconstruction: its key part in the trial-and-error process of institutional reinvention by which Church leaders moved past their old anathemas to begin engaging productively with the challenges and possibilities of a changed world.

This book has invited the reader to consider three intertwined early nineteenth-century histories: that of Roman architecture, that of Roman Catholic understandings of time and history, and that of the institutional Church in its relationship to the changing cultural, social, political, and religious possibilities of contemporary modernity. With respect to architecture, the book has argued that international scholarship, still too much oriented by an outdated hegemonic understanding of modernity, has underestimated the conceptual sophistication of early nineteenth-century Roman architecture and theory, too often dismissing it as a backward-looking and ultimately irrelevant foil to experimental northern Romanticisms. The analysis here suggests that

CONCLUSION

we gain much more – including an adequate understanding of the San Paolo reconstruction as an early landmark of European architectural historicism – if we approach the Roman experience instead as a sophisticated if also contradictory local iteration of the new currents of thought; one born of related traumas and anxieties but based on a very differently positioned experience of them. With respect to understandings of time and history, I have tried to demonstrate how a modern historicist temporality ostensibly incompatible with the Church's traditional conception of a providential, teleological history was gradually absorbed into even the most propagandistically antimodern cultural projects of the Holy See. The implication here, again, is that contemporary Catholic claims about the Church's principled rejection of the modern cannot be taken at face value – even if apologists and critics alike have often conspired in doing so. And finally, I have attempted to build out from this analysis a larger argument about how the Church as an institution became modern even as it claimed it never would, as everyone from architects to popes learned to avail themselves of new conceptual, technological, epistemological, and communicative possibilities – possibilities that we must certainly regard as "modern" – all in the name of, and in defense of, a declaredly antimodern worldview; and how these acquisitions, many of which came about in the course of the San Paolo reconstruction, form an essential part of the prehistory of the Catholic revivial of the Church's Marian age.

By insisting on framing all three of these histories as *modern* transformations, this book aspires also to encourage the reader to question a stubbornly durable view of early nineteenth-century European modernity as predominantly northern and secular in character.[59] In reality, early nineteenth-century Rome could be described much as everywhere else in Europe at this date: as a paradox. A paradox born of ancient expiring dreams and barely grasped new possibilities, of sanctified routines and intrepid experiments, of willful blind spots and breakthrough insights. This paradox, in Rome specifically, was shaped by the necessity of reimaging how a very ancient Church – not just the institution but its people and its culture – might respond to, act upon, and thrive within an emerging new world of mass politics, socioeconomic liberalism, and informationalized popular culture.

NOTES

1   Palmerio and Villetti (1989); Mulder (1989–1990); Rivetti (1990). For a contemporary account, see Leoni (1855).

2   Caiola (1990).

3   The ten interior and exterior columns of Vespignani's Verano Chapel were taken from the aisles of old San Paolo (Barucci [2006], p. 115). Appropriately, Angelo Uggeri is buried there amid them.

4   All of these may be seen in Cacchiatelli and Cleter (1865).

5 See Wittman (2021b), on which portions of this conclusion draw.

6 Mazzonis (1981), p. 259; Coppa (1990), pp. 80–81.

7 Veca (2018a), pp. 57–94.

8 Spagnesi (2003), pp. 167–168.

9 Spagnesi (2003), pp. 167–168; Caliò (2008).

10 Caperna (2007); Capitelli (2012) and (2013). Many of these projects are described and illustrated in Cacchiatelli and Cleter (1865).

11 Marucchi (1929).

12 Strozzieri (2021), pp. 114–115. Many similar examples could be adduced.

13 Atti (1864); Cacchiatelli and Cleter (1865).

14 Poletti had proposed the same thing in 1824 (Poletti [1824]).

15 Mulder (1992); Pastorino and Pastorino (1995); Caperna (1999–2002); Capitelli (2011);.

16 Cacchiatelli and Cleter (1865); Barucci (2006); on San Lorenzo specifically, see also Mulder (1992).

17 See for instance the discussion of Alberti's Tempio Malatestiano in Rimini (1450s) in Nagel and Wood (2010), pp. 175–178.

18 Caperna (2007), pp. 452–453.

19 Cacchiatelli and Cleber (1865) contains numerous examples.

20 Atti del martirio di S. Alessandro Primo, pontefice e martire e memorie del suo sepolcro al settimo miglio della via Nomentana (1858), p. 54.

21 Pius's visit occurred on 12 April 1855, just hours before he "miraculously" escaped injury when a floor in the nearby convent of Sant'Agnese, overloaded by dozens of students waiting to kiss his foot, collapsed – an event that contributed handsomely to the cult forming around Pius during these years (Martina [1974–90], v. 2, p. 25; Caliò [2008], p. 323).

22 Atti del martirio di S. Alessandro Primo, pontefice e martire e memorie del suo sepolcro al settimo miglio della via Nomentana (1858), pp. 65–68. On Boldrini, see Scarfone (1980).

23 Atti del martirio di S. Alessandro Primo, pontefice e martire e memorie del suo sepolcro al settimo miglio della via Nomentana (1858), p. 75; GdR, 18 April 1857, p. 349.

24 These remains were demolished in the 1930s and replaced with a new structure: Fumasoni Biondi (1943), pp. 282–283.

25 Ventra (2013), esp. pp. 89–93.

26 Baronio's Paleochristianizing restoration of SS. Nereo ed Achilleo in 1596–1597, where past and present relate to one another very differently than at San Paolo, also incorporates a fresco program in a thoroughly contemporary stylistic idiom. See Herz (1988), pp. 606–610.

27 Belloni (1853); Messmer (1854). See also Hübsch (1862; earliest sections published 1858).

28 Wiseman (1855); Newman (1856).

29 Gibson (1989), pp. 256–260; Doyle (2017), pp. 113–115.

30 Gibson (1989), pp. 63–78.

31 For example, the Siccardi laws of 1850 in deeply Catholic Piedmont (Mazzonis [1981], p. 256; Coppa [1990], pp. 77–78).

32 (2018b), p. 1034.

33 (2018b), p. 1042.

34 (2018b), p. 1047.

35 Coppa (1990).

36 Aubert (1952), p. 86 n. 8; Mazzonis (1981), pp. 256–263; Coppa (1990), p. 82.

37 Cronaca II, 12 April 1850. As far back as 1848, Terenzio Mamiani, who briefly served as Pius IX's Minister of the Interior, had also urged such a separation (Martina [1974–1990], v. 1, p. 266; Coppa [1990], pp. 58–59).

38 Raedts (2004), p. 479.

39 In 1866, for instance, he appointed Catherine of Siena a co-patron of the city, in a clear reference to her role in ending the Babylonian Captivity of the Papacy in 1376 (Caliò [2008], pp. 310–311).

40 Crocella (1982), p. 16.

CONCLUSION

41 Coppa (1990), pp. 73–77.
42 Mazzonis (1980).
43 Mazzonis (1980).
44 Raedts (2004).
45 Raedts (2004), p. 484.
46 Crocella (1982), pp. 95–153; Campobello (2017).
47 Crocella (1982).
48 Crocella (1982), p. 99.
49 Crocella (1982), pp. 98–101, 108.
50 Crocella (1982), pp. 128, 135
51 Crocella (1982), pp. 40–41.
52 Crocella (1982), p. 109, 40–41.
53 Raedts (2004).
54 Gellner (1997), pp. 6–9.
55 Crocella (1982), p. 23.
56 Bouritius (1979), pp. 147–154.
57 Caliò (2008), pp. 334–337.
58 Caliò (2008), p. 338.
59 Cazzato (2017a).

BIBLIOGRAPHY

ARCHIVES

Archives Nationals, Paris (ANF)

Archivio dell'Accademia di San Luca, Rome (AASL)

Archivio Apostolico Vaticano, Vatican City (AAV)

Archivio del Monastero di San Paolo fuori le mura, Rome (ASP)

Archivio di Stato, Rome (ASR)

Archivio Storico Capitolino, Rome (ASC)

Biblioteca Apostolica Vaticana, Vatican City (BAV)

Biblioteca Civica d'Arte Luigi Poletti: Archivio Luigi Poletti, Modena (BCALP)

Biblioteca di Archaeologia e Storia dell'Arte, Rome (BiASA)

Biblioteca di Storia Moderna e Contemporanea, Rome (BSMC)

Biblioteca Estense, Modena (BEM)

Biblioteca Nazionale Vittorio Emanuele, Rome (BNR)

Fondazione Achille Marazza, Borgomanero (FM)

Pontificia Commissione di Archaeologia Sacra, Vatican City (PCAS)

PUBLISHED SOURCES

Only the most significant periodical articles cited in the text are cited in the bibliography.

Unless otherwise indicated, all the pre-1870 periodicals were published in Rome.

For papal encyclicals and allocutions, consult Bellocchi (1993–), abbreviated TEPD in the footnotes.

BEFORE 1823

Algarotti, Francesco, "Saggio sopra l'architettura," in *Opere varie del Conte Francesco Algarotti*, Venice: Pasquali, 1757, v. 2, pp. 183–224.

Allegranza, Giuseppe, *Sepulcris Christianis*, Rome: Galeatium, 1773.

Andrés, Giovanni, *Dell'origine, progressi e stato attuale di ogni letteratura*, Parma: Stamperia Reale, 1787.

Andrews, William Eusebius, "Entrance of the Sovereign Pontiff into Rome," *The Orthodox Journal and Catholic Monthly Intelligencer* 2:13 (June 1814): 244.

Barattieri, Giovanni Battista, *Architettura d'acque*, Piacenza: Bazachi, 1656.

Boldetti, Marc'Antonio, *Osservazioni sopra i cimiteri de' santi martiri ed antichi christiani di Roma*, 2 v., Rome: Salvioni, 1720.

Botta, Carlo Giuseppe Guglielmo, *Il Camillo, o Vejo conquistata*, Paris: Chez l'auteur, 1815.

Cancellieri, Francesco, *Storia de' solenni possessi de' Sommi Pontefici*, Rome: Lazzarini, 1802.

Cancellieri, Francesco, *Lettera del Rmo Padre Abate D. Giuseppe Giustino di Costanzo sopra le sue memorie inedite della basilica di S. Paolo*, Rome: 1816.

Cappellari, Mauro, *Il trionfo della Santa Sede*, Rome: Zempel, 1799.

Ciampini, Giovanni, *De sacris aedificiis a Constantino Magno constructis*, Rome: Apud Joannem Jacobum Komarek Bohemum Typographum, 1693.

Crescimbeni, Giovanni Mario, *L'istoria della basilica diaconale collegiata e parrocchiale di S. Maria in Cosmedin di Roma*, Rome: De Rossi, 1715.

Cuoco, Vincenzo, *Platone in Italia*, 3 v., Milan: Nobile, 1804.

Denina, Carlo, *Delle rivoluzioni d'Italia*, Turin: Fratelli Reycends, 1769.

Eaton, Charlotte Anne, *Rome in the Nineteenth Century*, 3 v., Edinburgh: Archibald Constable and Co., 1820.

Eustace, John Chetwode, *A Classical Tour Through Italy*, 4 v., London: Mawman, 1815.

Fea, Carlo, *Notizie degli scavi nell' anfiteatro Flavio e nel Foro Traiano*, Rome: Lino Contedini, 1813.

Fea, Carlo, *Nuova descrizione di Roma antica e moderna*, 3 v., Rome: Puccinelli, 1820.

Fea, Carlo, "Lezione sopra quattro basiliche Romane dette Costantiniane," *DPARA* 3 (1829): 74–99.

Fontana, Carlo, *Templum Vaticanum*, Rome: Bagni, 1694.

Guarnacci, Mario, *Origini italiche*, 3 v., Rome: Giunchi, 1785–1787.

Guattani, Giuseppe Antonio, "Roma. Ristaurazioni," *Memorie enciclopediche romane sulle belle arti, antichità* 1 (1806): 5–10.

Gutensohn, Johann Gottfried, and Johann Michael Knapp, *Monumenti della religione christiana*, Rome: de Romanis, 1822–1826.

Gutensohn, Johann Gottfried, and Johann Michael Knapp, *Denkmale der christlichen Religion*, Rome: de Romanis, 1822–1827.

Kotzebue, August von, *Souvenirs d'un voyage en Livonie, à Rome et à Naples*, 3 v., Paris: Barba, 1806.

Marangoni, Giovanni, *Delle cose gentilesche, e profane trasportate ad uso e adornamento delle chiese*, Rome: Niccolo e Pagliarini, 1744.

Memmo, Andrea, *Elementi dell'architettura Lodoliana*, Rome: Pagliarini, 1786.

Micali, Giuseppe, *L'Italia avanti il dominio dei Romani*, 4 v., Florence: Piatti, 1810.

Milizia, Francesco, *Principj di architettura civile*, 3 v., Finale: de'Rossi, 1781.

Milizia, Francesco, *Roma delle belle arti del disegno*, Bassano: Remondini, 1787.

Nicolai, Nicola Maria, *Della basilica di S. Paolo*, Rome: de Romanis, 1815.

Orsi, Giuseppe Agostino, ed., *Della istoria ecclesiastica*, 21 v., Roma: Pagliarini, 1747–1762.

Piranesi, Giambattista, *Della magnificenza ed architettura de' Romani*, Rome: 1761.

Piranesi, Giambattista, *Osservazioni di Gio. Battista Piranesi sopra la Lettre de M. Mariette*, Rome: Salomoni, 1764.

Pouillard, "Review of *Della basilica di San Paolo* by Nicola Maria Nicolai," *Revue encyclopédique* (Paris) 5 (September 1817): 154–176.

Reinolds, Jean Baptiste, *Tableau de Rome vers la fin de 1814*, Brussels: Weissenbruch, 1816.

Rondelet, Jean Baptiste, *Traité théorique et pratique de l'art de batir*, 5 v., Paris: Chez l'auteur, 1812.

Roscoe, William, *Vita e pontificato di Leone X*, Milan: Sonzogno, 1816.

Severano, Giovanni, *Memorie sacre delle sette chiese di Roma*, Rome: Mascardi, 1630.

Tambroni, Adamo, "Review of *Monumenti della religione cristiana* by Johann Gottfried Gutensohn and Johann Michael Knapp," *GASLA* 16 (1822): 402–404.

Uggeri, Angelo, *Edifices de la décadence*, Rome: 1809.

Uggeri, Angelo, *Edifices de Rome antique déblayés par S.S. le pape Pie VII depuis l'an 1804 jusqu'au 1816*, Rome: Bourliè, 1817.

Vasi, Mariano, *Itinérario istruttivo di Roma antica e moderna*, 2 v., Rome: L'autore, 1816.

Vermiglioli, Giovanni Battista, "Review of *Della basilica di S. Paolo* by Nicola Maria Nicolai," *Biblioteca italiana* (Milan) 1:2 (April 1816a): 22–30; and 1:2 (May 1816b): 161–167.

Vermiglioli, Giovanni Battista, *Lezioni elementari di archeologia*, 2 v., Perugia: Baduel, 1822.

Volney [Constantin-François Chassebœuf de La Giraudais, comte de Volney], *Recherches nouvelles sur l'histoire ancienne*, 3 v., Paris: Courcier, 1814.

Voltaire, *Essai sur les moeurs et l'esprit des nations*, Paris: Cramer, 1756.

Waldie, Jane, *Sketches Descriptive of Italy in the Years 1816 and 1817*, 4 v., London: John Murray, 1820.

1823 TO 1854

"Architetture del Cavaliere Gaspare Salvi professore nell'accademia pontificia di belle arti in Roma," *MRABA* 4 (1827): 219–222.

"Della fabbrica Ceccopieri a Monte Catino. Architettura di Luigi Poletti," *MRABA* 3 (1826): 313–16.

Osservazioni sul marmo di Cottanello in Sabina, Rome: 1825.

Rapport de la Commission Mixte instituée à Rome pour constater les dégats occasionnes aux monuments ou établissements artistiques, par les armées belligérantes, pendant le siége de cette ville, Paris: Imprimerie Nationale, 1850.

Roma compiutamente descritta in sette giornate per comodo de' forastieri, Rome: Poggioli, 1830.

Amati, Girolamo, "La Basilica Ostiense," *Mondo illustrato* (Turin), 27 November 1847, pp. 761–762.

Balbo, Cesare, *Delle speranze d'Italia*, Paris: Tip. Elvetica, 1844.

Belamy, Théodore, *Rome: impression et souvenirs*, 2 v., Paris: Vermot, 1849.

Belloni, Paolo, *Sulla grandezza e disposizione della primitiva Basilica Ostiense*, Rome: Tipografia Forense, 1853.

Beste, John Richard Digby, *Transalpine Memoirs*, 2 v., London and Bath: Longman, Rees, Orme, Brown, and Green, 1826.

Betti, Salvatore, *L'illustre Italia: dialoghi*, 2 v., Rome: Tip. delle Belle arti, 1841.

Betti, Salvatore, "Elogio di Giambatista Martinetti, ingegnere ed architetto," *GASLA* 48:4 (October 1830): 105–110.

Betti, Salvatore, "Notizie intorno alla vita e alle opere di Pasquale Belli architetto romano," *GASLA* 58:3 (March 1833): 357–366.

Bisson, E., *Du séjour, de l'épiscopat et du martyre de Saint Pierre à Rome*, Paris: le Clere et Cie., 1845.

Boni, Filippo de, *Biografia degli artisti*, Venice: Gondoliere, 1840.

Borgnana, Carlo, "La colonna di marmo caristio ora giacente presso la Curia Innocenziana," *L'Album*, 14 November 1846, pp. 317–318.

Borgnana, Carlo, "Il nuovo campanile della Basilica Ostiense, Opera del Cav. Luigi Poletti," *Il Viminale*, 30 March 1847, pp. 10–13 [also published as a pamphlet with the same title].

Botta, Carlo Giuseppe Guglielmo, *Storia d'Italia dal 1789 al 1814*, 4 v., Paris: Didot, 1824.

Brancadoro, Cesare, *Intimazione di collette per la riedificazione della sacrosanta basilica di San Paolo*, 2nd ed., Rome: Bartolini, 1825.

Bunsen, Christian Carl Josias, "Les forum de Rome / restaurés et expliqués par Ch. Bunsen ... ddres ddressee à M. le chev. Canina," *Annali dell'Instituto di Corrispondenza Archeologica* 8:2 (1836): 207–281.

Bunsen, Christian Carl Josias, Johann Gottfried Gutensohn, and Johann Michael Knapp, *Die basiliken des christlichen Roms*, 2 v., Munich: Cotta, [1842].

Burgess, Thomas, *The Great Jubilee of the Year 1825*, Dublin: Napper and White, 1825.

Cancellieri, Francesco, "Prospetto delle memorie istoriche della basilica Ostiense di S. Paolo, disposte da Francesco Cancellieri secondo il piano indicatogli in una lettera dal p. Abate don Giuseppe Giustino di Costanzo benedittino," *Effemeridi Letterarie di Roma* 11 (June 1823): 363–365.

Canina, Luigi, *Ricerche sull'architettura più propria dei tempj cristiani*, Rome: Tipi delle stesso Canina, 1843 [2nd ed. 1846].

Canina, Luigi, *L'antica città de Veii*, Rome: Tipi dello stesso Canina, 1847.

Cantù, Ignazio, "Roma. Articolo secondo," *L'Album*, 6 (February 1841): 390–392.

Cardinali, Luigi, "Di un teatro architettato a Codogno nel Cremonese di Angiolo Uggeri," *MRABA* 3 (1826): 321–324.

Carpi, Pietro, *Relazione dell'accesso fatto all'isola del Giglio dalla Commissione deputata per osservare i graniti di detta isola proposti per le quaranta colonne della nave grande della basilica di S. Paolo*, Rome: 1828.

Ceccarini, Giovanni, *Lettera di G. Ceccarini, scultore, al Signor C. Vanelli di Carrara, relativa al granito dell'Isola del Giglio*, Rome: Salviucci, 1828.

Chateaubriand, François-René de, *Mémoires d'Outre-Tombe*, Paris: Penaud Frères, 1850.

Cicognara, Leopoldo, *Storia della scultura dal suo risorgimento in Italia*, 2nd ed., Prato: Giachetti, 1823.

Corsi, Faustino, *Delle pietre antiche libri quattro*, Rome: Salviucci, 1828.

Costanzi, Guglielmo, "Patriarcale Basilica di S. Paolo," in *L'Osservatore di Roma*, v. 2 [supplement], Rome: Puccinelli, [1831], pp. 35–45.

Dagnet, P.-N., *Journal, ou Notes descriptives du voyage en Italie fait par P.-N. Dagnet*, Paris: Didot, 1828.

Dalmières, *Itinéraire du voyageur catholique a Rome*, 2 v., Avignon and Paris: Seguin, 1846.

D'Azeglio, Massimo, *Degli ultimi casi di Romagna*, Lugano: Tip. della Svizzera italiana, 1846.

De Fabris, Giuseppe, *Descrizione del progetto o bozzetto di un monumento alla gran madre Maria, immacolatamente concetta, in memoria del giorno 8 Decembre 1854, presentato alla Santita di Papa Pio IX*, Rome: Bertinelli, 1854.

De Minicis, Gaetano, *Biografia del Cavaliere D. Michelangelo Lanci*, Macerata: Viarchi, 1840.

De Romanis, Filippo, Review of *Della Basilica di S. Paolo sulla via Ostiense* by Angelo Uggeri, *Effemeridi letterarie di Roma* 13 (October 1823): 35–42.

Dennis, George, *The Cities and Cemeteries of Etruria*, 2 v., London: John Murray, 1848.

Donovan, Jeremiah, *Rome, Ancient and Modern: And Its Environs*, Rome: Puccinelli, 1842.

Fabi Montani, Francesco, "Uggeri," *L'Album* 2 (December 1837): 309–312.

Fabi Montani, Francesco, *Elogio storico di Angelo Uggeri*, Rome: 1838.

Farini, Luigi Carlo, *The Roman State: From 1815 to 1850*, 4 v., London: John Murray, 1851–1854.

Fea, Carlo, "Belle Arti," *Giornale di commercio*, 5 December 1832, p. 4; 12 December 1832, p. 4; and 19 December 1832, pp. 3–4.

Fea, Carlo, *Aneddoti sulla basilica ostiense di S. Paolo*, Rome: Poggioli, 1825.

Fea, Carlo, *Continuazione degli aneddoti sulla basilica ostiense di S. Paolo*, Rome: Poggioli, 1826a.

Fea, Carlo, *La basilica ostiense liberata dalle innondazioni del Tevere senza bisogno di innalzarne il pavimento*, Rome: Nella stamperia della R. C. A., 1833.

Fea, Carlo, "Riflessioni sopra l'innalzamento che si è progettato del pavimento della Basilica di S. Paolo," in *Opuscoli tre idraulici e architettonici*, Rome: Nella stamperia della R. C. A., 1832, pp. 38–44.

Fea, Carlo, *Rivista di varie opinioni riprodotte in stampa da un sedicente scarpellino sulle colonne da farsi nella basilica ostiense di S. Paolo*, Rome: 1826b.

Folchi, Clemente, "Relazione," in *La distribuzione dei premj solennizzata sul Campidoglio li 5 ottobre 1824 dall'insigne Accademia delle Belle Arti Pittura, Scultura, ed Architettura in S. Luca*, ed. Angelo Mai, Rome: de Romanis, 1824, pp. 1–11.

Fortoul, Hippolyte, *De l'Art en Allemagne*, 2 v., Paris: Labitte, 1841.

Gandolfi, Stefano, *Notificazione per la riedificazione della Basilica Ostiense ossia del Tempio di S. Paolo di Roma*, Viterbo: Stamperia Camerale del Patrimonio, 1825.

[Gasparoni, Francesco] ("F. G."), "Delle simmetrie degli ordini di Architettura estratte dalla Geometria applicata alle Arti belle e alle Arti meccaniche del Professor Luigi Poletti," *Il Tiberino*, 16 (March 1833): 34–36.

Gasparoni, Francesco, "Frammento di lettera intorno una dissertazione del ch. prof. Luigi Poletti, *sulle genti e sulle arti primitive d'Italia*," *La Pallade*, 23 (March 1839): 47–48.

Gasparoni, Francesco, "La nuova cappella di S. Benedetto nella basilica di S. Paolo sulla via Ostiense," *L'architetto girovago* 1 (1841a): 26–29.

Gasparoni, Francesco, "Opere d'architettura e d'industria appartenute a que' Romani pontefici che hanno portato il nome di Pio (articolo primo)," *Giornale degli architetti*, 15 (October 1846): 17–21.

Gasparoni, Francesco, "Opere d'arte dei pontefici di nome PIO," *Giornale degli architetti*, 30 (January 1847): 73–75.

Gasparoni, Francesco, "Si fa un poco di anatomia a sette moderne fabrichette romulee in sette separati articolucci," *L'architetto girovago* 1 (1841b): 160–161.

Gell, William, "Gli avanzi di Veji," *Memorie dell'Instituto di Corrispondenza Archeologica* 1 (1832): 1–23.

Gerbet, Philippe, *Esquisse de Rome chrétienne*, 2 v., Louvain: Fonteyn, 1844.

Giacoletti, Giuseppe, "La rinnovata basilica di San Paolo sulla via Ostiense," *L'Album*, 11 (July 1840), pp. 145–148.

Gioberti, Vincenzo, *Del primato morale e civile degli italiani*, 2 v., Brussels: Meline, Cans e Compagnia, 1843.

Gray, Elizabeth Caroline, *Tour to the Sepulchres of Etruria*, London: Hatchard and Son, 1840.

Grimaldi, Giuseppe Maria, *Lettera di Giuseppe Maria Grimaldi vescovo di Vercelli al clero e al popolo per la raccolta dei fondi promossa da Leone XII per la riedificazione della basilica di San Paolo*, n.p.: 1825.

Head, George, *Rome: A Tour of Many Days*, London: Longman, Brown, Green, and Longmans, 1849.

[Hemans, Charles Isidore], "The Restoration of the Basilica of St. Paul," *The Roman Advertiser*, 13 February 1847, pp. 130–131 [Hemans 1847a] and 27 February 1847, pp. 147–148 [Hemans 1847b].

Hope, Thomas, *An Historical Essay on Architecture*, London: John Murray, 1835.

Hübsch, Heinrich, *In welchem Style sollen wir bauen?* Karlsruhe: C. F. Müller, 1828.

Humphreys, Henry Noel, *Rome, and Its Surrounding Scenery*, London: Charles Tilt, 1840.

Lacroix, Louis, "École Française d'Athènes: Sur les écoles fondées par les lazaristes à Alexandrie," in *Archives des missions scientifiques et littéraires, choix de rapports et instructions publie sous les auspices du ministere de l'instruction publique et des cultes*, Paris: Imprimerie nationale, 1850, v. 1, pp. 113–118.

Laderchi, Camillo, *Sulla vita e sulle opere di Federico Overbeck*, Rome: Menicanti, 1848.

Lambruschini, Luigi, "Lettera pastorale di Monsignor Luigi Lambruschini Arcivescovo di Genova per far concorrere i suoi diocesani con generose offerte alla riedificazione del tempio di S. Paolo," *Giornale ecclesiastico di Roma* 4:21 (November 1825): 131–139.

Lambruschini, Luigi, "Rom. Die Beitage zur Allgem. Zeitung vom 20 April d. J. theilt folgendes Rundschreiben Sr Heil des Papste Gregor XVI mit, in welchem alle Christgläubigen zu mit den Beiträgen für den Unbau der St Paulskirche aufgeferdert werden," *Allgemeine Kirchenzeitung* (Darmstadt), 22 May 1841b, pp. 653–656.

Lambruschini, Luigi, "Rome: Basilic of St. Paul," *The Catholic Telegraph* (Cincinnati), 24 April 1841a, p. 130.

Lancellotti, Luigi, *Diario della rivoluzione di Roma dal 1 Novembre 1848 al 31 luglio 1849*, Naples: Guerrera, 1862.

Lanci, Michelangelo, *Osservazioni sul bassorilievo fenico-egizio che si conserva in Carpentrasso*, Rome: Bourrliè, 1825.

Leo XII (Pope), *Chirografo della Santità di Nostro Signore Papa Leone XII in data dei 18 settembre 1825 sulla riedificazione della Basilica di S. Paolo nella via Ostiense*, Rome: Poggioli, 1825.

Lovery, Enrico, "Esposizione pel concorso Clementino nella gran sala del palazzo Senatorio in Campidoglio," *MRABA* 1:2 (1824): 33–37.

L. S. ["Lo Scarpellino"], *Riflessioni sulla continuazione degli aneddoti della Basilica di S. Paolo del Sig. Avvocato Carlo Fea*, Rome: Bourrliè, 1826.

Luquet, Jean-Felix-Onesime, *Souvenirs de l'expédition française a Rome*, 2 v., Rome: Paterno, 1849.

Marchi, Giuseppe, *Monumenti delle arti cristiane primitive nella metropoli del cristianesimo*, Rome: Puccinelli, 1844.

Marocchi, Giuseppe, *Dettaglio del terribile incendio accaduto il di 15 luglio 1823 della famosa basilica di S. Paolo di Rome*, Rome: Ajani, 1823.

Mazzini, Giuseppe, *A Pio IX. Pontefice Massimo*, Paris: de Bailly, 1847.

Melchiorri, Giuseppe, "Lettera d'un socio ordinario dell'accademia archeologica di Roma ad altro socio della medesima in Firenze. Lettera I," *Antologia* (Florence) 17:50 (February 1825a): 131–134; and 17:51 (March 1825b): 153–157.

Melchiorri, Giuseppe, "La nuova cappella a cornu Epistolae nella Basilica di S. Paolo di Poletti," *L'Ape italiana delle belle arti* 4 (1838): 7–9.

Melchiorri, Giuseppe, "San Paolo del Professore Adamo Tadolini, Statua Colossale alta Metri 5:57, per la nuova Basilica di San Paolo sulla via Ostiense," *L'Ape italiana delle belle arti* 2 (1836): 48.

Mercey, Frédéric Bourgeois de, "La Peinture et la Sculpture en Italie," *Revue des Deux Mondes* (Paris) 23 (1840): 256–278.

Mercey, Frédéric Bourgeois and Pietro Selvatico (trans.), "La Pittura e la Scultura in Italia (part 2)," *Rivista europea* (Milan) 4:3 (July 1841): 5–28.

Messmer, Joseph Anton, *Ueber den ursprung: die entwickelung und bedeutung der basilika in der christlichen baukunst*, Leipzig: Weigel, 1854.

Minardi, Tommaso, *Ragionamento detto alle Pontificie Accademie Romane di Archeologia e di San Luca in solenne adunanza*, Rome: Tipografia Camerale, 1835.

Minardi, Tommaso, "Estratto di un ragionamento del Prof. Minardi Presidente dell'Accademia di S. Luca," *Annali delle scienze religiose* 5:14 (September–October 1837): 291–294.

Moreschi, Luigi, Obituary for Angelo Uggeri, *DdR*, 17 October 1837, pp. 3–4.

Moreschi, Luigi, *Descrizione del tabernacolo che orna la confessione della basilica di san Paolo sulla via Ostiense*, Rome: Tipografia dell'Ospizio apostolico, 1840a.

Moreschi, Luigi, *Intorno la Festività della Commemorazione di San Paolo solennizzata il di' 30 di Giugno 1841 nella sua basilica fuori della Porta Ostiense dalla Santità di nostro Signore Gregorio XVI felicemente regnante*, Rome: Tipografia della R.C.A., 1841.

Moreschi, Luigi, *Osservazioni sulla sedia pontificale ch'era nell'abside della basilica di san Paolo sulla Via Ostiense*, Rome: Dalla tipografica della R.C.A., 1838a.

Moreschi, Luigi, *Prospetto spaccato e dettagli della confessione nella Basilica di S. Paolo*, Rome: Nella Calcografia della R.C.A., 1838b.

Moreschi, Luigi, *Relazione della consecrazione fatta da papa Gregorio XVI della nave traversa della basilica di S. Paolo*, Rome: 1840b.

Moreschi, Luigi, (ed.), *Collezione degli articoli pubblicati nel Diario di Roma e nelle Notizie del giorno relativi alla nuova fabbrica della Basilica di S. Paolo*, Rome: Tipografia della R.C.A., 1845 (abbreviated *CAPDR* in the text).

Moreschi, Luigi, *Commissione speciale deputata alla riedificazione della basilica di San Paolo nella via Ostiense*, Rome: 1846.

Moreschi, Luigi, "Congregazione Speciale deputata alla riedificazione della Basilica di S. Paolo," *Giornale di Roma*, 2 July 1850, p. 603.

Moreschi, Luigi, "Congregazione Speciale deputata alla riedificazione della Basilica di S. Paolo," *Giornale di Roma*, 5 July 1852, pp. 597–598.

Moreschi, Luigi, "Congregazione Speciale deputata alla riedificazione della Basilica di

S. Paolo," *Giornale di Roma*, 3 July 1854, pp. 615–616.

Moreschi, Luigi, *Indicazione dei dipinti a buon fresco rappresentanti le principali geste dell'apostolo San Paolo ed eseguiti nella sua basilica sulla Via Ostiense*, Rome: Tipografia della R.C.A., 1867.

Moroni, Gaetano, *Dizionario di erudizione storico-ecclesiastica*, 103 v., Venice: Tipografia Emiliana, 1840–1861 (abbreviated *DESE* in the text).

Nagler, Georg Kaspar, "Minardi, Tommaso," in *Neues allgemeines Künstler-Lexicon*, Munich: Fleischmann, 1840, v. 9, pp. 301–302.

Napione, Gian Francesco Galeani, "Notizia del libro intitoloato: *Della Basilica di S. Paolo*; opera di Nicola Maria Nicolai," *L'amico d'Italia* (Turin) 3:5 (1824): 150–158.

Nibby, Antonio, *Analisi storico-topografico-antiquaria della carta de' dintorni di Roma*, Rome: Tip. delle Belle arti, 1837.

Nibby, Antonio, "Della forma e della parti degli antichi templi cristiani," *DPARA* 2 (1825a): 401–434.

Nibby, Antonio, *Della forma e delle parti degli antichi templi cristiani: dissertazione*, Rome: de Romanis, 1825b.

Odescalchi, Pietro, "Elogio di Monsignore Niccola Maria Nicolai," *DPARA* 6 (1835): 381–412.

Perilli, Scipione, *Relazione storica sul risorgimento della Basilica degli Angeli presso Asisi* [sic], 2nd ed., Rome: Tipografia dell'Ospizio Apostolico, 1842.

Piale, Stefano, *Esame di un qualche aneddoto sulla venerabile basilica di S. Paolo*, Rome: Puccinelli, 1833.

Poletti, Luigi, "Delle genti e delle arti primitive d'Italia," *DPARA* 8 (1838b): 145209.

Poletti, Luigi, *Delle genti e delle arti primitive d'Italia: Dissertazione I*, Rome: Stamperia della R.C.A., 1838a.

Poletti, Luigi, *Geometria applicata alle Arti Belle e alle Arti Meccaniche*, Rome: Stamperia dell'Ospizio Apostolico, 1829.

Poletti, Luigi, "Il campanile di Urgnano nel Bergamasco, dell'Architetto Marchese Luigi Cagnola," *L'Ape italiana delle belle arti* 1 (1835b): 52–54 and plate 33.

Poletti, Luigi, "Intorno alla lega commerciale e alla rete delle strade ferrate d'Italia," *GASLA* 114 (January 1848a): 33–51.

Poletti, Luigi, *Intorno alla lega commerciale e alla rete delle strade ferrate d'Italia*, Rome: Bertinelli, 1848b.

Poletti, Luigi, "Intorno alla costruzione dei ponti sospesi sulle fila di ferro," *GASLA* 22 (1824): 195–222.

Poletti, Luigi, *Intorno alla Silvia di Cincinnato Baruzzi. Lettera*, Rome: Boulzaler, 1827.

Poletti, Luigi, "Osservazioni intorno alle tombe etrusche di Cere," *Annali dell'istituto di corrispondenza archeologica* 7:2 (1835a): 177–186.

Raffaelli, Vincenzo, "Fine dell'articolo concernente le Belle Arti*," DdR: Notizie del Giorno*, 24 December 1828, pp. 3–4.

Ravioli, Camillo, "Al Sig. Cav. Gio. de Angelis Direttore dell'Album," *L'Album*, 13 March 1841, pp. 9–12.

Ravioli, Camillo, "Rapporto del Viaggio della Spedizione Romana in Egitto," *L'Album*, 3 July 1841, pp. 137–144.

Ravioli, Camillo, "Quarto ed Ultimo Rapporto della Spedizione Romana in Egitto," *L'Album*, 12 March 1842, pp. 9–16.

Ravioli, Camillo, "Quarto Rapporto della Spedizione Romana in Egitto (Continuazione e fine V. pag. 9)," *L'Album*, 19 March 1842, pp. 22–23.

Ravioli, Camillo, "Terzo Rapporto del Viaggio della Spedizione Romana in Egitto," *L'Album*, 21 August 1841, pp. 193–199.

Rosellini, Ippolito, *I monumenti dell'Egitto e della Nubia: disegnati dalla spedizione scientifico-letteraria toscana in Egitto*, 9 v., Pisa: Capurro, 1832–1844.

Sacchi, Defendente, "San Paolo a Roma," *Cosmorama Pittorico* (Milan) 2:40 (1836): 316–317.

Seroux d'Agincourt, Jean-Baptiste-Louis-Georges, *Histoire de l'Art par les Monumens depuis sa décadence au IVe siècle jusqu'a son renouvellement au XVI*, 6 v., Paris: Treuttel et Wurtz, 1823 (Italian edition 1826).

Servi, Gaspare, *Notizie intorno alla vita del cav. Giuseppe Valadier, architetto romano*, Bologna: Tipi delle muse alla Capra, 1840.

Settele, Giuseppe, "Memoria sull'importanza dei monumenti che si trovano nei cemeteri degli antichi cristiani del contorno di Roma letta nell'accademia Romana di archeologia nell'adunanza del 3 giugno 1824," *DPARA* 2 (1825): 43–104.

Sherer, Moyle, *Scenes and Impressions in Egypt and in Italy*, 3rd ed., London: Longman, Hurst, Rees, Orme, Brown, and Green, 1825.

Simond, Louis, *Voyage en Italie et en Sicile*, Paris: Sautelet et Compagnie, 1828.

Stefanelli, Giovanni Domenico, *Lettera pastorale sui pericoli della propaganda anticattolica ai Bagni di Lucca e richiesta di oblazioni per la Basilica di San Paolo a Roma*, Lucca: Benedini, 1841.

Stendhal [Beyle, Marie Henry], *Promenades dans Rome*, 2 v., Paris: Delaunay, 1829.

Taillefer, Louis, *Saint Pierre a-t-il jamais été à Rome: Réponse à un défi de M. l'abbé Bisson,* Paris and Geneva: Pagny, 1845.

[Tambroni, Giuseppe], "Relazione esatta e veridica delle circostanze che precedettero il fatale incendio della Basilica di S. Paolo fuori le mura, con alcune notizie intorno alla sua fondazione e ai danni che ora ha sofferti," *DdR*, 26 July 1823, pp. 1–3.

Teloni, Francesco Ansaldo, *Lettera enciclica di Sua Santità Papa Leone XII a tutti i patriarchi, primati, arcivescovi e vescovi pubblicata al clero e popolo delle due diocesi da Monsignor Vescovo di Macerata e Tolentino*, Macerata: Fratelli Rossi, 1825.

Tosti, Antonio, *Intorno la origine e i progressi dell'Ospizio apostolico di S. Michele*, Rome: Stamperia della R.C.A., 1835.

Tuckerman, Henry Theodore, *The Italian Sketch Book*, Philadelphia: Key & Biddle, 1835.

Udalric de St. Gall [pseudonimo di Auguste Scheler], *Étude historique sur le séjour de l'Apôtre St. Pierre à Rome,* Brussels: Chez tous les principaux libraires, 1845.

Uggeri, Angelo, *Della Basilica di S. Paolo sulla via Ostiense*, Rome: 1823 [2nd ed. 1825].

Uggeri, Angelo, *Sommarj*, Rome: 1826.

Uggeri, Angelo, *Commissione speciale deputata dalla Santità di Nostro Signore Leone Papa XII alla riedificazione della Basilica di San Paolo nella via Ostiense*, 4 luglio 1827, Rome: 1827a.

Uggeri, Angelo, "Dell'arco trionfale detto di Placidia. Lezione prima," *MRABA* 4 (1827b): 113-24.

Uggeri, Angelo, *Commissione speciale deputata dalla Santità di Nostro Signore Leone Papa XII alla riedificazione della Basilica di San Paolo nella via Ostiense, il di 10 Luglio 1828*, Rome: 1828.

Uggeri, Angelo, *Commissione speciale deputata alla riedificazione della Basilica di San Paolo nella via Ostiense, Quinta congregazione generale del dì 7 Luglio 1831*, Rome: 1831a.

Uggeri, Angelo, *Proposizione del Segretario della Commissione Speciale*, Rome: 1831b.

Uggeri, Angelo, *Riedificazione della Basilica Ostiense*, n.p., n.d. [1832].

Uggeri, Angelo, *Della Basilica Ulpia nel Foro Trajano; istoria e ristaurazione agli amanti delle antichita romane*, Rome: [1833].

Uggeri, Angelo and Giulio della Somaglia, *Relazione de' principali acquisti, e lavorazioni eseguite per la riedificazione della Basilica di S. Paolo nella Via Ostiense*, Rome: 1827.

Ungarelli, Luigi Maria, *Descrizione dei nuovi Musei Gregoriani, etrusco ed egizio aggiunti al Vaticano,* 2nd ed., Rome: Tip. dell'Belle Arti, 1839b.

Ungarelli, Luigi Maria, "Nuovo Museo Gregoriano-Egizio nel Vaticano," *L'Album*, 16 February 1839a, pp. 393–397.

Valadier, Giuseppe, *Opere di architettura e di ornamento*, Rome: 1833.

Valeriani, Gaetano, *Storia della Repubblica Romana*, 2 v., Rome: Ajani, 1850.

Vaudoyer, Léon, "Histoire de l'architecture en France," in *Patria: la France ancienne et moderne, morale et matérielle,* ed. Jean Aicard, Félix Bourquelot, and Auguste Bravais, Paris: Dubochet, Lechevalier, 1847, pp. 2113–2200.

Vaudoyer, Léon, and Albert Lenoir, "Études d'architecture en France," *Magasin pittoresque* (Paris) 10 (April 1842): pp. 121–128.

Ventura, Gioacchino, "Della disposizione attuale degli Spiriti in Europa rispetto alla Religione; e delle necessita' di propagare i buoni principj per mezzo della stampa," *Memorie di religione, di morale e di letteratura* (Modena) 7 (1825e): 385–421.

Ventura, Gioacchino, *Elogio funebre di Daniello O'Connel,* Rome: Filippo Cairo, 1847.

"Lettera enciclica del regnante Sommo Pontefice LEONE XII, relativamente alla riedificazione della basilica di S. Paolo apostolo," *Giornale ecclesiastico di Roma* 1 (March 1825b): 161–169.

Ventura, Gioacchino, "Spirito Pubblico Religioso. Della disposizione attuale degli Spiriti in Europa rispetto alla Religione; e delle necessita' di propagare i buoni principj per mezzo della stampa," *Giornale ecclesiastico di Roma* 3 (July 1825c): 17–70.

Ventura, Gioacchino, "Spirito Pubblico Religioso: La Francia nel suo rapporto col cristianesimo," *Giornale ecclesiastico di Roma* 3 (September 1825d): 194–247.

Ventura, Gioacchino, "[Untitled]," *DdR*, 12 March 1825a, pp. 1–2.

Vermiglioli, Giovanni Battista, *Opuscoli di Gio. Battista Vermiglioli,* 4 v., Perugia: Bartelli e Costantini, 1825.

Visconti, Pietro Ercole, *Notizie intorno la colonna sbarcata il giorno 4 di Gennaro del corrente anno 1828, per servire alla riedificazione della basilica di S. Paolo sulla via Ostiense, etc,* Rome: Da' Torchj del Salviucci, 1828.

Visconti, Pietro Ercole, *Orazione funebre in lode del Commendatore Gaspare Salvi Architetto,* Rome: Pallotta, 1850.

Wiseman, Nicholas, *Twelve Lectures on the Connexion Between Science and Revealed Religion,* London: Joseph Booker, 1836.

Woods, Joseph, *Letters of an Architect, from France, Italy, and Greece,* 2 v., London: John & Arthur Arch, 1828.

1854 TO 1899

Atti del martirio di S. Alessandro Primo, pontefice e martire e memorie del suo sepolcro al settimo miglio della via Nomentana, Rome: Morini, 1858.

Anivitti, Vincenzo, "La Colonna della Concezione," *L'Album,* 26 May 1855, pp. 108–109.

Atti, Alessandro, *Della munificenza di sua santità Papa Pio IX,* Rome: Pallotta, 1864.

Baldassari, Pietro, *Relazione delle avversità e patimenti del glorioso papa Pio VI negli ultimi tre anni del suo pontificato,* 4 v., Rome: Tipografia Poliglotta, 1889.

BIBLIOGRAPHY

Belli, Gioachino, *I sonetti romaneschi di G.G. Belli*, ed. Luigi Morandi, 6 v., Città di Castello: Lapi, 1889.

Bianchi-Giovini, Aurelio, *Le prediche domenicali*, Milan: Sanvito, 1863.

Bovet, Ernest, *Le peuple de Rome vers 1840 d'après les sonnets en dialecte transtévérin de Giuseppe-Gioachino Belli*, Neuchâtel and Rome: Attinger Freres, 1898.

Bunsen, Christian Carl Josias Freiherr von, and Friedrich Nippold, *Christian Carl Josias Freiherr von Bunsen: Aus seinen Briefen u. nach eigener Erinnerung geschildert von seiner Wittwe*, Leipzig: Brockhaus, 1868.

Cacchiatelli, Paolo, and Gregorio Cleter, *Le Scienze e le Arti sotto il Pontificato di Pio IX*, 2nd ed., 2 v., Rome: Aurelj, 1865.

Campori, Cesare, *Biografia di Luigi Poletti, architetto*, 3rd ed., Modena: Viscenzi e Nipoti, 1881.

Campori, Cesare, "Notizie biografiche del Comm. Prof. Luigi Poletti Modenese, architetto di S. Paolo di Roma," *Memorie della Reale Accademia di Scienze, Lettere ed Arti in Modena* 6 (1865): 95–122.

Carcani, Michele, "Il Ponte Milvio e le sue Memorie," *L'Album*, 29 May 1858, pp. 116–117.

Ciampi, Ignazio, *Vita di Giuseppe Valadier architetto romano*, Rome: Tip. delle belle arti, 1870.

Dall'Olio, Luigi, *Descrizione della pittura rappresentante la propagazione del cristianesimo operata dal Professore Tommaso Minardi nel Palazzo Apostolico del Quirinale l'anno 1864*, [Rome]: 1864.

de Maumigny, Victor, *Les Voix de Rome. Impressions et Souvenirs de 1862*, Paris: Victor Palmé, 1863.

De Sanctis, Guglielmo, *Tommaso Minardi e il suo tempo*, Rome: Forzani, 1899.

Erbes, Carl, *Die Todestage der Apostel Paulus und Petrus und ihre römischen Denkmäler*, ed. Adolf von Harnack and K. G. Goetz, Leipzig: Hinrichs, 1899.

Falconieri, Carlo, *Vita di Vincenzo Camuccini, e pochi studi sulla pittura contemporanea*, Rome: Stabilmento tipografico italiano, 1875.

Frost, Thomas, *The Secret Societies of the European Revolution, 1776–1876*, 2 v., London: Tinsley Bros., 1876.

Gasparoni, Francesco, "Il monumento di piazza di Spagna," in Arti e lettere. *Scritti raccolti da Francesco Gasparoni*, Rome: Menicanti, 1863, v. 1, pp. 1–2.

Giucci, Gaetano, "Biografia di Luigi Poletti architetto (segue l'elenco compilato da Gaspare Servi e relativo alle opere realizzate dall'architetto)," *Roma artistica* 1:4 (1871): 25–28.

Guarna, Baldassarre Capogrossi, *Il Tevere e le sue inondazioni*, Rome: Tipografia delle scienze matematiche e fisiche, 1871.

Hübsch, Heinrich, *Die altchristlichen Kirchen nach den Baudenkmalen und älteren Beschreibungen und der Einfluss des altchristlichen Baustyls auf den Kirchenbau aller späteren Perioden*, Karlsruhe: Grosh. Bad. Ministerium des Innern, 1862.

Le Mire, Noel, *Lettres sur l'Italie*, Lyon: Bauchu, 1855.

Lehmann, Rudolf, *An Artist's Reminiscences*, London: Smith, Elder & Company, 1894.

Leoni, Quirino, "Santa Maria sopra Minerva ristaurata per cura dei pp. Domenicani," *L'Album*, 1 September 1855, pp. 217–220; 29 September 1855, pp. 249–251; and 13 October 1855, pp. 265–268.

Lesueur, Jean-Baptiste-Ciceron, *La basilique Ulpienne (Rome) Restauration exécutée en 1823 par M. Lesueur*, Paris: Firmin-Didot, 1877.

Madden, Richard Robert, *The literary life and correspondence of the Countess of Blessington,* 3 v., London: T. C. Newby, 1855.

Marcolini, Camillo, *Su la vita e le opere di Michelangelo Lanci: Discorso di Camillo Marcolini*, Fano: Lana, 1874.

Moreschi, Luigi, *Relazione sul monumento sepolcrale eretto alla santa memoria di Gregorio XVI sommo pontefice nella Basilica vaticana*, Rome: Cairo, 1857.

Newman, John Henry, *Callista: A Sketch of the Third Century*, London: Burns and Lambert, 1856.

Orioli, Francesco, *Di un monumento ideato, ed eseguito in modello, dall'insigne scultore signor commendatore Giuseppe De-Fabris ... per eternare la memoria della solenne dichiarazione del domma dell'immacolato concepimento di Maria ...*, Rome: Bertinelli, 1855.

Pasolini, Pietro Desiderio, *Giuseppe Pasolini. 1815–1876. Memorie raccolte da suo figlio,* 3rd ed., Turin: Bocca, 1887.

Poletti, Luigi, "Delle genti e delle arti primitive d'Italia. Dissertazione II," *DPARA* 15 (1864): 449–545.

Raggi, Oreste, *Della vita e delle opere di Luigi Canina Architetto ed Archeologo da Casal Monferrato,* Casal Monferrato: Nani, 1857.

Ravioli, Camillo, *Viaggio della spedizione romana in Egitto fatto nel 1840 e 1841 dalla Marina dello Stato sotto gli ordini del commendatore Alessandro Cialdi compendiato sui documenti ufficiali,* Rome: Tipografia delle Belle Arti, 1870.

Renan, Ernest, *Saint Paul,* trans. Ingersoll Lockwood, New York: G. W. Carleton, 1869 [French edition 1869].

Rolland, L'Abbé, *Rome: ses églises, ses monuments, ses institutions: lettres à un ami,* Paris and Brussels: Régis Ruffet, 1866.

Sala, Giuseppe Antonio, *Scritti di Giuseppe Antonio Sala: Diario romano degli anni 1798–99,* 2 v., Rome: Presso la Società, 1882.

Schaff, Philip, ed., "Chrysostom, Saint John: Homily XXXII on the Epistle to the Romans," in *A Select Library of the Nicene and Post-Nicene Fathers of the Christian Church. First Series,* ed. George B. Stevens, New York: Christian Literature Company, 1889, v. 11, pp. 559–564.

Selvatico, Pietro, *Le arti del disegno in Italia,* 3 v., Milan: Vallardi, 1879.

Stefanucci Ala, Alessandro, "Il morte del Prof Luigi Poletti, ricordo del suo discepolo Alessandro Stefanucci Ala," *Il Buonarroti* 4:9 (September 1869): 213–224.

Têtu, Henri, and Charles-Octave Gagnon, eds., *Mandements, lettres pastorales et circulaires des évêques de Québec,* 4 v., Québec: Imprimerie Générale A. Coté, 1888.

Tizzani, Vincenzo, *Della commissione di archeologia sagra del museo Cristiano-Pio e dell'antica basilica di S. Clemente,* Rome: Accademia dei Lincei, 1886.

Trollope, T. Adolphus, "Francesco Cancellieri," *British Quarterly Review* 82:166 (April 1886): 280–304.

Verzili, Giuseppe, "I Tre Capi d'Opera del Commendatore Luigi Poletti," *Il Buonarroti* 9:6 (June 1874): 196–200.

Viollet-le-Duc, Eugène-Emmanuel, *L'art russe: ses origines, ses éléments constitutifs, son apogée, son avenir,* Paris: Vve A. Morel, 1877.

Wiseman, Nicholas Patrick, *Fabiola; or, the Church of the Catacombs,* London: Burns and Lambert, 1855.

Wiseman, Nicholas Patrick, *Recollections of the Last Four Popes and of Rome in their Times,* London: Hurst and Blackett, 1858.

1900 TO THE PRESENT

Le Assemblee del risorgimento. Atti raccolti e pubblicati per deliberazione della Camera dei Deputati, 15 v., Rome: Tip. della Camera dei deputati, 1911.

Agostino, Marc "The Golden Age of Pilgrimages in France in the Nineteenth Century," in *Nineteenth-Century European Pilgrimages: A New Golden Age,* ed. Antón M. Pazos, New York and London: Routledge, 2020, pp. 121–237.

Akaad, M. K., and Naggar M. H., "Geology of the Wadi Sannur alabaster and the general geological history of the Egyptian alabaster deposits," *Bulletin de l'Institut du Desert d'Égypte du Caire* 13:2 (1965): 35–63.

Anderson, Margaret Lavinia, "The Divisions of the Pope: The Catholic Revival and Europe's Transition to Democracy," in *The Politics of Religion in an Age of Revival,* ed. Austen Ivereigh, London: 2000, pp. 22–42.

Anderson, Margaret Lavinia, "The Limits of Secularization: On the Problem of the Catholic Revival in Nineteenth-Century Germany," *The Historical Journal* 38:3 (1995): 647–670.

Andrews, Keith, *The Nazarenes, a Brotherhood of German Painters in Rome,* Oxford: Clarendon Press, 1964.

Aubert, Roger, *Le Pontificat de Pie IX, 1846–1878,* Paris: Bloud & Gay, 1952.

Aubert, Roger, Johannes Beckmann, Partick H. Corish, and Rudolf Lill, *The Church between Revolution and Restoration,* trans. Peter Becker, ed. Hubert Jedin and John Dolan, New York: Crossroad, 1981.

Auf der Heyde, Alexander, *Per l'« avvenire dell'arte in Italia » : Pietro Selvatico e l'estetica applicata alle arti del disegno nel secolo XIX*, Pisa: Pacini, 2013.

Augustine of Hippo, *The Works of Saint Augustine. A Translation for the 21st Century. Sermons III/8 (273-305A) on the Saints*, trans. Edmond Hill, ed. John E. Rostelle, Hyde Park: New City Press, 1994.

Bagnarini, Nadia, "Fonti inedite per l'attività romana di Salvatore Revelli dal fondo 'Commissione Speciale per la riedificazione della Basilica di San Paolo fuori le mura'," in *Salvatore Revelli (1816–1859): l'ambiente, i percorsi, le committenze*, ed. Franco Boggero and Francesca De Cupis, Pisa: ETS, 2013, pp. 37–59.

Bagnarini, Nadia, "La Basilica di San Paolo fuori le mura: storia di una committenza pontificia. Le sculture degli altari della 'Nave traversa' e i Ss. Pietro e Paolo dell'arco di Placidia," *Annali della Pontificia Accademia di Belle Arti e Lettere dei Virtuosi al Pantheon* 15 (2015): 241–263.

Bamji, Alexandra, Geert H. Janssen, and Mary Laven, eds., *The Ashgate Research Companion to the Counter-Reformation*, Aldershot: Ashgate, 2013.

Banti, Alberto Mario, *La nazione del Risorgimento: parentela, santità e onore alle origini dell'Italia unita*, Turin: Einaudi, 2000.

Barbanera, Marcello "The Impossible Museum. Exhibitions of Archaeology as Reflections of Contemporary Ideologies," in *Archives, Ancestors, Practices. Archaeology in the Light of its History*, ed. Nathan Schlanger and Jarl Nordbladh, New York and Oxford: Berghahn Books, 2008, pp. 165–175.

Barry, Fabio, "Building History: The Baroque Remodellings of S. Anastasia al Palatino," *Storia dell'arte* 95 (1999): 45–102.

Bartoli, Alfonso, Pio Ciprotti, and Giuseppe Bozzetti, eds., *Gregorio XVI: Miscellanea Commemorativa*, 2 v., Rome: Camaldolesi di S. Gregorio al Celio, 1948.

Barucci, Clementina, *Virginio Vespignani: architetto tra Stato Pontificio e Regno d'Italia*, Rome: Argos, 2006.

Basciano, Jessica Ruth, "Architecture and Popular Religion: French Pilgrimage Churches of the Nineteenth Century," Ph. D. Columbia University, 2012.

Becchetti, Nino, "Ponte Milvio e i restauri di Giuseppe Valadier," *Strenna dei Romanisti* 50 (1989): 61–72.

Bellini, Federico, "L'interno della basilica liberiana nel rifacimento di Ferdinando Fuga," *Palladio* 15 (1995): 49–62.

Bellocchi, Ugo, ed., *Tutte le encicliche e i principali documenti pontifici emanati dal 1740: 250 anni di storia visti dalla Santa Sede*, 12 v., Vatican City: Libreria editrice vaticana, 1993– (abbreviated *TEPD* in the main text).

Bendinelli, Goffredo, *Luigi Canina (1795–1856). Le opere, i tempi, con documenti inediti*, Alessandria: Società di storia arte e archeologia, Accademia degli immobili, 1953.

Bénichou, Paul, *Le temps des prophètes: doctrines de l'âge romantique*, Paris: Gallimard, 1977.

Benveduti, Carlo, "La cultura architettonica al tempo di Gregorio XVI: la figura di Pietro Camporese il Giovane," in Francesca Longo, Claudia Zaccagnini, and Fabrizio Fabbrini, ed., *Gregorio XVI promotore delle arti e della cultura*, Pisa: Pacini, 2008, pp. 353–384.

Bercé, Yves-Marie, "Rome, 1796–1814," in *Camille de Tournon: le préfet de la Rome napoléonienne, 1809–1814*, ed. Bruno Foucart, Rome and Boulogne-Billancourt: Palombi and Bibliothèque Marmottan, 2001, pp. 25–32.

Bergdoll, Barry, *Léon Vaudoyer: Historicism in the Age of Industry*, New York; Cambridge: MIT Press, 1994.

Berkeley, George Fitz-Hardinge, and Joan Berkeley, *Italy in the Making*, 3 v., Cambridge: Cambridge University Press, 1932–1940.

Bernabei, Franco, *Pietro Selvatico nella critica e nella storia delle arti figurative dell'Ottocento*, Vicenza: Pozza, 1974.

Biancini, Laura, "'Quest'opera religiosissima'. Giacomo Raffaelli e la ricostruzione della basilica di San Paolo," in *1823. L'incendio della basilica di San Paolo. Leone XII e l'avvio della ricostruzione*, ed. Ilaria Fiumi Sermattei,

Genga: Consiglio Regionale; Assemblea Legislativa delle Marche, 2013, pp. 99–114.

Blackbourn, David, "The Catholic Church in Europe since the French Revolution: A Review Article," *Comparative Studies in Society and History* 33:4 (1991): 778–790.

Blix, Göran, *From Paris to Pompeii: French Romanticism and the Cultural Politics of Archaeology*, Philadelphia: University of Pennsylvania Press, 2009.

Boiteux, Martine, "La Croce luminosa, un rito della Settimana Santa nella basilica di San Pietro," in *La religione dei nuovi tempi. Il riformismo spirituale nell'età di Leone XII*, ed. Ilaria Fiumi Sermattei and Roberto Regoli, Ancona: Consiglio Regionale Assemblea legislativa delle Marche, 2020, pp. 281–316.

Bonella, Anna Lia, Augusto Pompeo, and Manola Ida Venzo, eds., *Roma fra la Restaurazione e l'elezione di Pio IX. Amministrazione, Economia. Società e Cultura*, Rome, Frieburg, and Vienna: Herder, 1997.

Bouritius, Gerben J. F., "Popular and Official Religion in Christianity: Three cases in 19th-century Europe," in *Official and Popular Religion: Analysis of a Theme for Religious Studies*, ed. P. H. Vrijhof and Jean Jacques Waardenburg, The Hague: Mouton, 1979, pp. 117–165.

Bouritius, Gerben J. F., Boutry, Philippe, "La restaurazione (1814–1848)," in *Roma moderna*, ed. Philippe Boutry and Giorgio Ciucci, Rome: Laterza, 2002a, pp. 371–413.

Bouritius, Gerben J. F., Boutry, Philippe, *Souverain et Pontife: Recherches prosopographiques sur la Curie Romaine à l'âge de la restaura–tion (1814–1846)*, Rome: EFR, 2002b.

Bouritius, Gerben J. F., Boutry, Philippe, "Une théologie de la visibilité: Le projet zelante de resacralisation de Rome et son échec (1823–1829)," in *Cérémonial et rituel à Rome (XVIe–XIXe siècle)*, ed. Maria Antonietta Visceglia and Catherine Brice, Rome and Paris: EFR, 1997, pp. 317–367.

Branchetti, Maria Grazia, "Leone XII e il restauro dell'Arco di Placidia della basilica ostiense: la vicenda iniziale alla luce di due progetti non attuati," in *1823. L'incendio della basilica di San Paolo. Leone XII e l'avvio della ricostruzione*, ed. Ilaria Fiumi Sermattei, Genga: Consiglio Regionale; Assemblea Legislativa delle Marche, 2013, pp. 79–98.

Brega, Giuliana, "L'archeologia classica a Roma durante il pontificato di Gregorio XVI," in *Gregorio XVI promotore delle arti e della cultura*, ed. Francesca Longo, Claudia Zaccagnini, and Fabrizio Fabbrini, Pisa: Pacini, 2008, pp. 81–120.

Bressani, Martin, and Christina Contandriopoulos, eds., *Nineteenth-Century Architecture. The Companions to the History of Architecture*, v. 3, Hoboken: Wiley & Sons, 2017.

Brigante Colonna, Gustavo, "La basilica di San Paolo completata col monumentale quadriportico," *Capitolium* 5:8 (August 1929): 385–392.

Bujanda, Jesús Martínez de, and Marcella Richter (eds.), *Index Librorum Prohibitorum, 1600–1966*, Geneva and Montreal: Librairie Droz and Médiaspaul, 2002.

Caiola, Antonio Federico, "Il neogotico a Roma: la chiesa di Sant'Alfonso de' Liguori e le sue trasformazioni," in *Neogotico nel XIX e XX secolo*, ed. Rossana Bossaglia and Valerio Terraroli, Milan: Mazzotta, 1990, v. 2, pp. 357–366.

Caliò, Tommaso, "Corpi santi e santuari a Roma nella seconda Restaurazione," in *Monaci, ebrei, santi. Studi per Sofia Boesch Gajano, Atti delle Giornate di studio (Roma, 17–19 febbraio 2005)*, ed. Antonio Volpato, Rome: Viella, 2008, pp. 305–373.

Caliò, Tommaso, "I santuari di Gregorio XVI," in *Lo spazio del santuario. Un osservatorio per la storia di Roma e del Lazio*, ed. Sofia Boesch Gajano and Francesco Scorza Barcelona, Rome: Viella, 2008, pp. 279–312.

Caliò, Tommaso, "Sant'Andrea delle Fratte," in *Santuari d'Italia. Roma*, ed. Sofia Boesch Gajano, Tommaso Caliò, Francesco Scorza Barcellona, and Lucrezia Spera, Rome: De Luca, 2012, pp. 158–161.

Calzolari, Monica, "Leone XII e la ricostruzione della basilica di San Paolo fuori le mura," in *Il pontificato di Leone XII: restaurazione e riforme nel governo della Chiesa e dello Stato*, ed.

Gilberto Piccinini, Ancona: Consiglio regionale delle Marche, 2012, pp. 87–106.

Camerlenghi, Nicola, "Splitting the Core: The Transverse Wall at the Basilica of San Paolo in Rome," *Memoirs of the American Academy in Rome* 58 (2013): 115–142.

Camerlenghi, Nicola, *St. Paul's outside the Walls: a Roman Basilica, from Antiquity to the Modern Era*, Cambridge and New York: Cambridge University Press, 2018.

Camerlenghi, Nicola, "The Life of the Basilica of San Paolo fuori le mura in Rome; Architectural Renovations from the Ninth to the Nineteenth Centuries," Ph.D. Princeton University, 2007.

Cameron, Rondo E., "Papal Finance and the Temporal Power, 1815–1871," *Church History* 26:2 (1 June 1957): 132–142.

Campobello, Francesco, *La Chiesa a processo: il contenzioso sugli enti ecclesiastici nell'Italia liberale*, Naples: Edizioni scientifiche italiane, 2017.

Campori, Matteo, *Luigi Poletti, discorso inaugurale della statua, dell'atrio e della galeria Poletti, Modena, IV dicembre MDCCCCIV*, Modena: Rossi e Cie, 1905.

Caniglia, Emma, "Il concorso clementino del 1824. Storia e cronaca di una celebrazione accademica," in *Le scuole mute e le scuole parlanti: studi e documenti sull'Accademia di San Luca nell'Ottocento*, ed. Paola Picardi and Pier Paolo Racioppi, Rome: De Luca, 2002, pp. 357–394.

Caperna, Maurizio, "Archeologia cristiana e restauro nella Roma di Gregorio XVI e Pio IX," *Quaderni dell'Istituto di Storia dell'Architettura* 50 (2007): 447–460.

Caperna, Maurizio, "Il restauro delle chiese romane durante il pontificato di Pio IX: preesistenze e rinnovamento figurativo," *Quaderni dell'Istituto di Storia dell'Architettura* 34/39 (1999–2002): 505–516.

Caperna, Maurizio, *La Basilica di Santa Prassede. Il significato della vicenda architettonica*, 2nd ed., Rome: Quasar, 2014.

Caperna, Maurizio, "La Chiesa di San Girolamo dei Croati (già 'degli Schiavoni' o 'degli Illirici')," *Storia architettura* 1 (1992): 255–285.

Capitelli, Giovanna, "Icone del culto in difesa dell'identità anti-moderna," in Stefano Susinno, Sandra Pinto, Liliana Barroero, and Fernando Mazzocca, eds, *Maestà di Roma: Da Napoleone All'unità d'Italia: Universale ed Eterna, Capitale delle Arti*, Milan: Electa, 2003, pp. 248–253.

Capitelli, Giovanna, "L'archeologia cristiana al servizio di Pio IX: 'la catacomba in fac-simile' di Giovanni Battista De Rossi all'Esposizione Universale di Parigi del 1867," in *Martiri, santi, patroni: per una archeologia della devozione*, ed. Adele Coscarella, Paola De Santis, Rende: Università della Calabria, 2012, pp. 555–566.

Capitelli, Giovanna, *Mecenatismo pontificio e borbonico alla vigilia dell'Unità*, Rome: Viviani, 2011.

"Redescendons aux catacombes. Note sulla fortuna dei monumenti cristiani primitivi nella cultura figurativa dell'Ottocento," *RSdA* 110–111 (2013): 45–58.

Cardelli, Mascia, *I due purismi: la polemica sulla pittura religiosa in Italia, 1836–1844*, Florence: Capponi, 2005.

Carpi, Umberto, *Letteratura e società nella Toscana del Risorgimento. Gli intellettuali dell'«Antologia»*, Bari: De Donato, 1974.

Cazzato, Luigi, "Fractured Mediterranean and Imperial Difference: Mediterraneanism, Meridionism, and John Ruskin," *Journal of Mediterranean Studies* 26:1 (2017b): 69–78.

Cazzato, Luigi, *Sguardo inglese e Mediterraneo Italiano. Alle radici del meridionismo*, Milan: Mimesis, 2017a.

Cecalupo, Chiara, "Sulla nascita dell'archeologia cristiana: il cantiere della Basilica Vaticana nova," *Papers of the British School at Rome* 89 (2021): 211–231.

Ceccarelli, Francesco, *L'intelligenza della città. Architettura a Bologna in età napoleonica*, Bologna: Bononia University Press, 2020.

Cecchin, Stefano Maria, "La proclamazione del dogma dell'Immacolata Concezione: una vicenda storica e teologica," in *La Sala dell'Immacolata di Francesco Podesti: storia di una committenza e di un restauro*, ed. Micol Forti, Vatican City: Edizioni Musei Vaticani, 2010, pp. 53–67.

Ceccopieri Maruffi, Franco, "Luigi Poletti, architetto modenese a Roma," *Strenna dei Romanisti* 47 (1986): 111–122.

Cerioni, Anna Maria, "L'incendio de 1823. Problemi, polemiche per la ricostruzione e la sua realizzazione," in *San Paolo fuori le Mura a Roma,* ed. Carlo Pietrangeli, Rome: Nardini, 1988, pp. 67–83.

Cerutti Fusco, Annarosa, "Salvi, Gaspare," in *Architetti e ingegneri a confronto: l'immagine di Roma fra Clemente XIII e Pio VII*, ed. Elisa Debenedetti, Rome: Bonsignori, 2008, v. 3, pp. 205–210.

Cerutti Fusco, Annarosa, "Gaspare Salvi (1786–1849), architetto e professore di architettura teorica nell'Accademia di San Luca e il dibattito architettonico del tempo," in *La cultura architettonica nell'età della Restaurazione*, ed. Giuliana Ricci, Giovanna D'Amia, and Francesco Cherubini, Milan: Mimesis, 2002, pp. 279–290.

Cerutti Fusco, Annarosa, "Gaspare Salvi (1786–1849), architetto, restauratore e archeologo romano," in *Saggi in onore di Gaetano Miarelli Mariani*, ed. Maria Piera Sette and Gaetano Miarelli Mariani, Rome: Bonsignori, 2007, pp. 243–260.

Ceserani, Giovanna, "Classical Culture for a Classical Country: Scholarship and the Past in Vincenzo Cuoco's Plato in Italy," in *Classics and National Cultures*, ed. Susan Stephen and Phiroze Vasunia, Oxford: Oxford University Press, 2010, pp. 59–77.

Chadwick, Owen, *From Bossuet to Newman: the Idea of Doctrinal Development*, Cambridge: Cambridge University Press, 1957.

Chakrabarty, Dipesh, *Provincializing Europe: Postcolonial Thought and Historical Difference*, Princeton: Princeton University Press, 2000.

Champollion, Jean-Francois, *Lettres de Champollion le jeune, recueilliés et annotées par H. Hartleben; tome premier: Lettres écrites d'Italie*, ed. G. Maspero, Paris: Ernest Leroux, 1909.

Cherici, Armando, "Gregorio XVI e gli studi sull'antico, tra contingenza politica e strategia culturale. Una riflessione," in *Gregorio XVI promotore delle arti e della cultura*, ed. Francesca Longo, Claudia Zaccagnini, and Fabrizio Fabbrini, Pisa: Pacini, 2008, pp. 149–168.

Cherici, Armando, ""Mirari Vos": La politica museale di Gregorio XVI tra storia e antistoria," in *La Fortuna degli Etruschi nella Costruzione dell'Italia Unita*, ed. Giuseppe M. Della Fina, Orvieto: Quasar, 2011, pp. 51–67.

Chigi, Augustino, *Diario del Principe D. Agostino Chigi dall'Anno 1830 al 1855*, 2 v., Tolento: Filelfo, 1906.

Cochrane, Eric, "Giovanni Lami e la storia ecclesiastica ai tempi di Benedetto XIV," Archivio Storico Italiano 123: 1 (445) (1965b): 48–73.

Cochrane, Eric, "Muratori: The Vocation of a Historian," *CHR* 51:2 (1965a): 153–172.

Coen, Paolo, ed., *The Art Market in Rome in the Eighteenth Century: A Study in the Social History of Art*, Leiden: Brill, 2019.

Colapietra, Raffaele, "Il Diario Brunelli del Conclave del 1823," *Archivio storico Italiano* 120:1 (1962): 76–146.

Colapietra, Raffaele, *La chiesa tra Lamennais e Metternich. Il Pontificato di Leone XII*, Brescia: Morcelliana, 1963.

Colapietra, Raffaele, "Una riflessione sul Giubileo di Leone XII," in *'Si dirà quel che si dirà: si ha da fare il Giubileo'. Leone XII, la città di Roma, e il giubileo del 1825*, ed. Ilaria Fiumi Sermattei and Raffaele Colapietra, Genga: Consiglio Regionale; Assemblea Legislativa delle Marche, 2014, pp. 15–35.

Colini, Antonio Maria, "L'abate Angelo Uggeri Architetto, antiquario e vedutista milanese a Roma," in *Studi offerti a Giovanni Incisa della Rocchetta*, Rome: Biblioteca Vallicelliana, 1973, pp. 139–161.

Colla, Elliott, *Conflicted Antiquities: Egyptology, Egyptomania, Egyptian Modernity*, Durham: Duke University Press, 2007.

Collins, Jeffrey, *Papacy and Politics in Eighteenth-Century Rome: Pius VI and the Arts*, Cambridge and New York: Cambridge University Press, 2004.

Colonna, Giovanni, *"L'avventura romantica,"* in *Gli etruschi e l'Europa*, ed. Massimo Pallottino, Paris: Fabbri, 1992, pp. 322–339.

Connors, Joseph, and Louise Rice, eds., *Specchio di Roma Barocca. Una guida inedita del XVII secolo*, 2nd ed., Rome: Elefante, 1991.

Coppa, Frank J., *Cardinal Giacomo Antonelli and Papal Politics in European Affairs*, Albany: State University of New York Press, 1990.

Corbo, Anna Maria, "Tommaso Minardi e la scuola romana di San Luca," *Commentari. Rivista di critica e storia dell'arte* 20:1–2 (January–June 1969): 131–141.

Costantini, Celso, "Gregorio XVI e la missioni," in *Gregorio XVI: Miscellanea Commemorativa*, ed. Alfonso Bartoli, Pio Ciprotti, and Giuseppe Bozzetti, 2 v., Rome: Camaldolesi di S. Gregorio al Celio, (1948), v. 2, pp. 1–28.

Courau, Robert, *Ferdinand de Lesseps. De l'apothéose de Suez au scandale de Panama*, Paris: Grasset, 1932.

Cremona, Alessandro, "Consalvi e i progetti del 1805 per l'area Flaminia," in *Cardinale Ercole Conslavi: 250 Anni dalla Nascita*, ed. Roberto Regoli, Trieste: Biblioteca Civica "A. Hortis", 2008, pp. 124–145.

Cristofani, Mauro, "Le mythe etrusque en Europe entre le XVie et le XVIIIe siecle," in *Gli etruschi e l'Europa*, ed. Massimo Pallottino, Paris: Fabbri, 1992, pp. 276–291.

Crocella, Carlo, *Augusta miseria: aspetti delle finanze pontificie nell'età del capitalismo*, Milan: Nuovo istituto editoriale italiano, 1982.

Cullmann, Oscar, *Saint Pierre: disciple, apôtre, martyr: histoire et théologie*, Neuchâtel, Paris: Delachaux & Niestlé, 1952.

Curran, Brian A, *The Egyptian Renaissance: The Afterlife of Ancient Egypt in Early Modern Italy*, Chicago: University of Chicago Press, 2007.

Curzi, Valter, "Per la tutela e la conservazione delle Belle Arti: L'amministrazione del Cardinale Bartolomeo Pacca," in *Bartolomeo Pacca (1756–1844). Ruolo pubblico e privato di un Cardinale di Santa Romana Chiesa*, ed. Claudia Zaccagnini, Velletri: Blitri, 2000, pp. 49–79.

Dalla Torre, Paolo, "L'opera riformatrice ed amministrativa di Gregorio XVI," in *Gregorio XVI: Miscellanea Commemorativa*, ed. Alfonso Bartoli, Pio Ciprotti, and Giuseppe Bozzetti, 2 v., Rome: Camaldolesi di S. Gregorio al Celio, 1948, v. 2, pp. 29–121.

De Francesco, Antonino, *The Antiquity of the Italian Nation: The Cultural Origins of a Political Myth in Modern Italy, 796–1943*, Oxford: Oxford University Press, 2013.

De Rosa, Gabriele, "La crisi del neoguelfismo e la questione romana," *Studi Romani* 18:3 (1970): 285–297.

Debenedetti, Elisa, "Valadier e Napoleone: diario architettonico," in *Villes et territoire pendant la période napoléonienne (France et Italie)*, Rome: EFR, 1987, pp. 519–556.

Debenedetti, Elisa, "Vita di Giuseppe Valadier attraverso nuovi documenti," in *Architetti e ingegneri a confronto: l'immagine di Roma fra Clemente XIII e Pio VII*, ed. Elisa Debenedetti, Rome: Bonsignori, 2008, v. 3, pp. 7–30.

Del Signore, Roberto, "La Basilica ricostruita," in *San Paolo fuori le Mura a Roma*, ed. Carlo Pietrangeli, Rome: Nardini, 1988, pp. 85–150.

Delbeke, Maarten, "Religious Architecture and the Image in the Southern Netherlands after the Beeldenstorm. Shrines for Miracle-Working Statues of the Virgin Mary," in *Renaissance and Baroque Architecture. The Companions to the History of Architecture*, v. 1, ed. Alina Payne, Hoboken: Wiley-Blackwell, 2017, pp. 434–466.

Delpino, Filippo, *Cronache veientane: storia delle ricerche archeologiche a Veio*, Rome: Consiglio nazionale delle ricerche, 1985.

Delpino, Filippo, "La "riscoperta" degli Etruschi e dei loro monumenti in eta' leonina," in *Antico, conservazione e restauro a Roma nell'età di Leone XII*, ed. Ilaria Fiumi Sermattei, Roberto Regoli, and Maria Piera Sette, Ancona: Consiglio Regionale, 2017, pp. 175–192.

Delpino, Filippo, "La "scoperta" di Veio etrusca," in *Ricerche archeologiche in Etruria meridionale nel xix secolo*, ed. Alessandro Mandolesi and Alessandro Naso, Florence: All'Insegna del Giglio, 1999, pp. 73–85.

Demarco, Domenico, *Il tramonto dello stato pontificio. Il papato di Gregorio XVI*, Turin: Einaudi, 1949.

Di Marco, Fabrizio, "Belli, Pasquale," *Studi sul settecento Romano* 22 (2006): 146–151.

Di Nola, Annalisa, "Dal pellegrinaggio alla gita turistica: un'analisi quantitativa dette guide di

Roma," *Dimensioni e problemi della ricerca storica* 1 (1989): 181–262.

Di Nola, Annalisa, "Mutamenti della coscienza storica e dei moduli cronologici nelle Guide di Roma dell'età moderna," *Archivio della Società romana di storia patria* 111 (1988): 311–345.

Di Nola, Annalisa, *"Percorsi reali e percorsi simbolici nelle guide di Roma tra XVI e XIX secolo,"* in *Luoghi sacri e spazi della santità*, ed. Sofia Boesch Gajano and Lucetta Scaraffia, Turin: Rosenberg & Sellier, 1990, pp. 483–506.

Di Sante, Assunta, and Simona Turriziani (eds), *Quando la fabbrica costrui San Pietro: un cantiere di lavoro, di pietà cristiana e di umanità: XVI–XIX secolo,* Foligno: Il Formichiere, 2016.

Ditchfield, Simon, ""Historia Magistra Sanctitatis"? The Relationship between Historiography and Hagiography in Italy after the Council of Trent (1564–1742 ca.)," in *Nunc alia tempora, alii mores: storici e storia in età postridentina*, ed. Massimo Firpo, Florence: Olschki, 2005, pp. 3–23.

Ditchfield, Simon, "Tridentine Catholicism," in *The Ashgate Research Companion to the Counter-Reformation*, ed. Alexandra Bamji, Geert H. Janssen, and Mary Laven, Aldershot: Ashgate, 2013, pp. 15–31.

Docci, Marina, "L'altare di Onorio Longhi: Prime indagini su un'architettura perduta," *BMMGP* 25 (2006): 159–162.

Docci, Marina, *San Paolo fuori le mura: dalle origini alla basilica delle "origini"*, Rome: Gangemi, 2006.

Donato, Maria Pia, "Lo specchio di un progetto politico: l'antichita nella Repubblica giacobina romana," *Dimensioni e problemi della ricerca storica* 1 (1994): 82–119.

D'Onofrio, Cesare, *Il tevere e Roma*, Rome: Bozzi, 1970.

Doyle, Ann Margaret, "Catholic Church and State Relations in French Education in the Nineteenth Century: The Struggle between *Laïcité* and Religion," *International Studies in Catholic Education* 9:1 (2017): 108–122.

Driault, Edouard, *L'Egypte et l'Europe, la crise de 1839–1841: correspondance des consuls de France et instructions du gouvernement*, 5 v., Cairo: Société royale de géographie d'Égypte, 1930–1933.

Dudden, Frederick Homes, *Gregory the Great: His Place in History and Thought*, 2 v., London: Longmans, Green, and Company, 1905.

Dunkle, Brian, *Enchantment and Creed in the Hymns of Ambrose of Milan*, Oxford: Oxford University Press, 2016.

Edelstein, Dan, "The Egyptian French Revolution: Antiquarianism, Freemasonry and the Mythology of Nature " in *The Super-Enlightenment: Daring to Know Too Much,* ed. Dan Edelstein, Oxford: Voltaire Foundation, 2010, pp. 215–241.

Eisenstadt, Schmuel Noah, "Multiple Modernities," *Daedalus* 129:1 (2000): 1–29.

Engel-Janosi, Friedrich, "The Return of Pius IX in 1850," *CHR* 36:2 (July 1950): 129–162.

Ersilio, Michel, *Esuli italiani in Egitto, 1815–1861*, Pisa: Domus Mazziniana, 1958.

Faldi, Italo, "Il purismo e Tommaso Minardi," *Commentari* 1:4 (1950): 238–246.

Falsetti, Francesca, "La Visita Apostolica per il giubileo del 1825. Uno strumento per verificare lo stato di conservazione e pianificare gli interventi di restauro della Roma sacra," in *'Si dirà quel che si dirà: si ha da fare il Giubileo'. Leone XII, la città di Roma, e il giubileo del 1825*, ed. Ilaria Fiumi Sermattei and Raffaele Colapietra, Genga: Consiglio Regionale; Assemblea Legislativa delle Marche, 2014, pp. 93–115.

Fancelli, Paolo, "Gregorio XVI e il restauro dei monumenti," in *Gregorio XVI promotore delle arti e della cultura*, ed. Claudia Zaccagnini and Fabrizio Fabbrini, Pisa: Pacini, 2008, pp. 265–313.

Federici, Daniele, "L'influenza di Lamennais in Italia e la sconfitta degli intransigenti nel 1826 alla luce del carteggio Baraldi-Ventura," in *La religione dei nuovi tempi. Il riformismo spirituale nell'età di Leone XII*, ed. Ilaria Fiumi Sermattei and Roberto Regoli, Ancona: Consiglio Regionale Assemblea legislativa delle Marche, 2020, pp. 63–80.

Feldman, Martha, and Martina Piperno, "Moreschi and Fellini: Delineating the Vernacular Castrato in Post-Unification Italy," *voiceXchange* 5:1 (Fall 2011): 1–34.

Felisini, Daniela, *Le finanze pontificie e i Rothschild, 1830–1870*, Naples: Edizioni scientifiche italiane, 1990.

Ferraris, Angiola, *Letteratura e impegno civile nell'«Antologia»*, Padua: Liviana, 1978.

Ferrua, Antonio, "I primordi della Commissione di Archeologia Sacra 1851–1852," *Archivio della Societa romana di storia patria* 91 (1968): 251–278.

Filippi, Giorgio, "La tomba di San Paolo e le fasi della Basilica tra il IV e VII secolo. Primi risultati di indagini archeologiche e ricerche d'archivio," *BMMGP* 24 (2004): 187–224.

Filippi, Giorgio, "Nuovi documenti sul lavori del 1838 nella Vecchia Confessione," *BMMGP* 25 (2006): 87–95.

Filippi, Giorgio, and Sible de Blaauw, "San Paolo fuori le mura: la disposizione liturgica fino a Gregorio Magno," *Mededelingen van het Nederlands Instituut te Rome* 59 (2000): 5–25.

Filippi, Giorgio, and Sible de Blaauw, Marina Docci, and Claudio Noviello, "Le iscrizioni pavimentali della basilica tra il 1600 e il 1823," *BMMGP* 25 (2006): 97–121.

Firpo, Massimo, "Rethinking 'Catholic Reform' and 'Counter-Reformation': What Happened in Early Modern Catholicism – a View from Italy," *Journal of Early Modern History* 20 (2016): 293–312.

Fiumi Sermattei, Ilaria, ed., *1823. L'incendio della basilica di San Paolo. Leone XII e l'avvio della ricostruzione*, Genga: Consiglio Regionale; Assemblea Legislativa delle Marche, 2013.

Fiumi Sermattei, Ilaria, "'Ut nova ex ruinis Basilica ea magnitudine, cultuque resurgat.' Leone XII e l'avvio della ricostruzione della basilica di San Paolo," in *1823. L'incendio della basilica di San Paolo. Leone XII e l'avvio della ricostruzione*, ed. Ilaria Fiumi Sermattei, Genga: Consiglio Regionale; Assemblea Legislativa delle Marche, 2013, pp. 15–26.

Fiumi Sermattei, Ilaria, and Raffaele Colapietra, eds., "Il reimpiego degli antichi marmi superstiti dall'incendio della basilica di San Paolo fuori le mura," in *Antico, conservazione e restauro a Roma nell'età di Leone XII*, ed. Ilaria Fiumi Sermattei, Roberto Regoli, and Maria Piera Sette, Ancona: Consiglio Regionale, 2017, pp. 147–173.

Fiumi Sermattei, Ilaria, and Raffaele Colapietra, *'Si dirà quel che si dirà: si ha da fare il Giubileo'. Leone XII, la città di Roma, e il giubileo del 1825*, Genga: Consiglio Regionale; Assemblea Legislativa delle Marche, 2014.

Fiumi Sermattei, Ilaria, and Raffaele Colapietra, "What Origins for the Restoration of the Church? Remote Past and Recent History in Leo XII's Cultural Policy," in *Re-thinking, Re-making, Re-living Christian Origins*, ed. Ivan Foletti, Manuela Gianandrea, Serena Romano, and Elisabetta Scirocco, Rome: Viella, 2018, pp. 235–252.

Fiumi Sermattei, Ilaria, and Raffaele Colapietra, and Roberto Regoli, eds., *La religione dei nuovi tempi. Il riformismo spirituale nell'età di Leone XII*, Ancona: Consiglio Regionale Assemblea legislativa delle Marche, 2020.

Fraschetti, Cesare, "Lo Stato Romano all'alba del secolo XIX," in *Diario del Principe D. Agostino Chigi dall'Anno 1830 al 1855*, Tolento: Filelfo, 1906, v. 1, pp. 9–68.

Fumasoni Biondi, Pietro, "Ficulea e la Basilica Cimiteriale di Sant'Alessandro," *Roma: rivista di studi e di vita romana* 21:8 (August 1943): 279–285.

Gadille, Jacques, and Jean-Marie Mayeur. eds., *Libéralisme, industrialisation, expansion européenne des origines à nos jours 1830–1914 (Histoire du christianisme, v.11)*, Paris: Desclée, 1995.

Galloni, Egisto, *Le colonne di granito di Montorfano della Basilica di San Paolo fuori le mura*, Mergozzo: Antiquarium Mergozzo, 1988.

Gardner, Julian, "Gian Paolo Panini, San Paolo fuori le Mura and Pietro Cavallini. Some Notes on Colour and Setting," in *Mosaics of Friendship: Studies in Art and History for Eve Borsook*, ed. Ornella Osti Francisi, Florence: Centro Di, 1999, pp. 245–254.

Garric, Jean-Philippe, *Recueils d'Italie: les modèles italiens dans les livres d'architecture français*, Sprimont: Mardaga, 2004.

Gellner, Ernest, *Nationalism*, New York: New York University Press, 1997.

Geoffroy de Grandmaison, Charles-Alexandre, *Le jubilé de 1825: la première année sainte du XIXe siècle; étude historique*, Paris: Bloud, 1902.

Gibson, Ralph, *A Social History of French Catholicism 1789–1914*, London: Routledge, 1989.

Gossman, Lionel, "History as Decipherment: Romantic Historiography and the Discovery of the Other," *New Literary History* 18:1 (Autumn 1986): 23–57.

Grandesso, Stefano, *Pietro Tenerani: (1789–1869)*, Cinisello Balsamo: Silvana, 2003.

Gregoire, Réginald, "Une visite apostoliquc à Rome en 1824–25," *Rivista di storia della chiesa in Italia* 21 (1967): 482–489.

Gregorovius, Ferdinand, *The Roman Journals of Ferdinand Gregorovius, 1852–1874*, trans. Annie Hamilton, ed. Friedrich Althaus, London: George Bell & Sons, 1907.

Groblewski, Michael, *Thron und Altar: Der Wiederaufbau der Basilika St. Paul vor den Mauern (1823–1854)*, Freiburg, Basel, Vienna: Herder, 2001.

Guccione, Eugenio, ed., *Gioacchino Ventura e il pensiero politico d'ispirazione cristiana dell'Ottocento*, Florence: Olschki, 1991.

Guidiccioni, Lelio, *Latin Poems: Rome 1633 and 1639*, ed. John Kevin Newman and Frances Stickney Newman, Hildesheim: Weidmann, 1992.

Haack, Marie-Laurence, "Modern Approaches to Etruscan Culture," in *The Etruscan World*, ed. Jean MacIntosh Turfa, New York and London: Routledge, 2013, pp. 1136–1146.

Haddock, Bruce, "Political Union without Social Revolution: Vincenzo Gioberti's Primato," *The Historical Journal* 41:3 (1998): 705–723.

Hearder, Harry, "The Making of the Roman Republic, 1848–1849," *History* 60:199 (1975): 169–184.

Herz, Alexandra, "Cardinal Cesare Baronio's Restoration of SS. Nereo ed Achilleo and S. Cesareo de'Appia," *Art Bulletin* 70:4 (1988): 590–620.

Hjort, Oystein, "L'incendie de San Paolo fuori le mura," *Meddelelser fra Thorvaldsens Museum* (1970): 157–162.

Hocedez, Edgar, *Histoire de la théologie au XIXe siècle, 3v.*, Brussels: Édition universelle, 1947.

Huskinson, J. M., *Concordia Apostolorum: Christian Propaganda at Rome in the Fourth and Fifth Centuries: A Study in Early Christian Iconography and Iconology*, Oxford: B.A.R., 1982.

Ilari, Annibale, "Le visite pastorali a Roma sotto Leone XII e Leone XIII," *Rivista diocesana di Roma* 3–4, 5–6, 7–8: (1967–1969): 350–359, 601–611, 844–850.

Iversen, Erik, *The Myth of Egypt and its Hieroglyphs in European Tradition*, Princeton: Princeton University Press, 1993.

Izzi, Giuseppe, "Giuseppe Melchiorri: dall'antiquaria alla storia," in *Fictions of Isolation: Artistic and Intellectual Exchange in Rome during the First Half of the Nineteenth Century*, ed. Lorenz Enderlein and Nino Zchomelidse, Rome: L'Erma di Bretschneider, 2006, pp. 49–57.

Jervis, Anna Valeria, "Per "il giusto sviluppo del genio della gioventù". Note e documenti sulla polemica tra Camuccini e Minardi circa l'insegnamento accademico della tecnica dell'affresco," in *Roma fra la Restaurazione e l'elezione di Pio IX. Amministrazione, Economia. Società e Cultura*, ed. Anna Lia Bonella, Augusto Pompeo, and Manola Ida Venzo, Rome, Frieburg, and Vienna: Herder, 1997, pp. 743–758.

Johns, Christopher M. S., "Clement XI and Santa Maria Maggiore in the Early 18th Century," *JSAH* 45:3 (1986): 286–293.

Johns, Christopher M. S., *Papal Art and Cultural Politics: Rome in the Age of Clement XI*, Cambridge and New York: Cambridge University Press, 1993.

Johns, Christopher M. S., "The Entrepot of Europe: Rome in the Eighteenth Century," in *Art in Rome in the Eighteenth Century*, ed. Edgar Peters Bowron and Joseph J. Rishel, Philadelphia and New York: Philadelphia Museum of Art, 2000, pp. 17–45.

Jonsson, Marita, *La cura dei monumenti alle origini: restauro e scavo di monumenti antichi a Roma 1800–1830*, Stockholm and Göteborg: Svenska instututet i Rom, 1986.

Karmon, David E., *The Ruin of the Eternal City: Antiquity and Preservation in Renaissance Rome*, New York: Oxford University Press, 2011.

Kertzer, David I, *The Popes against the Jews: The Vatican's Role in the Rise of Modern Anti-Semitism*, New York: Knopf, 2001.

Koenig, Duane, "The Last Cruise of the Pope's Navy, 1840–1841," *The Social Studies* 66:6 (1975): 270–273.

Korten, Christopher, "Against the Grain: Pope Gregory XVI's Optimism toward Russia in His Censure of Polish Clerics in 1831," *CHR* 101:2 (Spring 2015): 292–316.

Korten, Christopher, "Against the Grain: Pope Gregory XVI's Optimism toward Russia in His Censure of Polish Clerics in 1831," *CHR* 101:2 (Spring 2015): 292–316.

Korten, Christopher, "Financial Policies in the Papal States, 1790s–1848. A Comparative Study of Napoleonic Europe," *Journal of Modern Italian Studies* 23:3 (2018): 234–255.

Korten, Christopher, "Il Trionfo? The Untold Story of Its Development and Pope Gregory XVI's Struggle to Attain Orthodoxy," *Harvard Theological Review* 109:2 (2016): 1–24.

Korten, Christopher, "The Conclave of 1830/1: how Mauro Cappellari was elected and other reflections," in *Gregorio XVI tra oscurantismo e innovazione: stato degli studi e percorsi di ricerca*, ed. Romano Ugolini, Pisa: Serra, 2012, pp. 9–31.

Koselleck, Reinhard, *Futures Past: On the Semantics of Historical Time*, trans. Keith Tribe, New York: Columbia University Press, 2004 (original German edition 1979).

Lagrée, Michel, "Religion populaire et populisme religieux au XIXe siècle," in *Histoire vécue du peuple chrétien, tome 2: Vers quel christianisme?*, ed. Jean Delumeau, Toulouse: Privat, 1979, v. 2, pp. 157–78.

Lambert, James H., "Plessis, Joseph-Octave," in *Dictionary of Canadian Biography*, v. 6, Toronto: University of Toronto/Université Laval, 2003–. www.biographi.ca/en/bio/plessis_joseph_octave_6E.html

Lanciani, Rodolfo Amedeo, "Delle scoperte fatte nel 1838 e 1850 presso il sepolcro Paolo Apostolo," *Bullettino di archeologia cristiana* 23 (1919): 727.

Le Guillou, Louis, "Lamennais fut-il créé cardinal par Léon XII ?," *Société des Amis de Lamennais* 9 (1978): 1–9.

Lefevre, Renato, "Il colera in Egitto e la spedizione del 1841," *L'Osservatore Romano*, 5 October 1947, p. 3.

Lefevre, Renato, "La fondazione del Museo Gregoriano Egizio al Vaticano," in *Gregorio XVI: Miscellanea Commemorativa*, ed. Alfonso Bartoli, Pio Ciprotti, and Giuseppe Bozzetti, 2 v., Rome: Camaldolesi di S. Gregorio al Celio, 1948, v. 1, pp. 223–287.

Leflon, Jean, *Histoire de l'Église. 20. La crise révolutionnaire 1789–1846*, ed. Augustin Fliche and Victor Martin, Paris: Bloud et Gay, 1951.

Leniaud, Jean-Michel, "Les travaux de François Debret (1777–1854) à Saint-Denis," *Bulletin de la Société de l'histoire de Paris et de l'Ile-de-France* 122–124 (1995–1997): 221–268.

Liverani, Paolo, *Municipium Augustum Veiens*, Rome: L'Erma di Bretschneider, 1987.

Lo Curto, Vito, and Mario Themelly, *Gli scrittori cattolici dalla Restaurazione all'Unità*, Rome: Laterza, 1976.

Longo, Francesca, "Gregorio XVI e l'Egittologia: la spedizione romana in Egitto (1840–1841)," in *Gregorio XVI promotore delle arti e della cultura*, ed. Francesca Longo, Claudia Zaccagnini, and Fabrizio Fabbrini, Pisa: Pacini, 2008, pp. 133–148.

Longo, Francesca, Claudia Zaccagnini, and Fabrizio Fabbrini, eds., *Gregorio XVI promotore delle arti e della cultura*, Pisa: Pacini, 2008.

Low, Setha M., "Embodied Space(s): Anthropological Theories of Body, Space, and Culture," *Space and Culture* 6:1 (2003): 9–18.

Löwy, Michael, and Robert Sayre, *Romanticism against the Tide of Modernity,* trans. Catherine Porter, Durham: Duke University Press, 2001.

Luseroni, Giovanni, "La stampa periodica ed il pontificato di Gregorio XVI: prime ricerche," in *Gregorio XVI tra oscurantismo e innovazione: stato degli studi e percorsi di ricerca*, ed. Romano Ugolini, Pisa: Serra, 2012, pp. 389–405.

Macsotay, Tomas, "The Distracted Believer and the Return to the First Basilica: Marqués de Ureña's Reflexiones sobre la Arquitectura, Ornato, y Música del Templo of 1785," *Architectural Histories* 6:1 (2018): 1–15.

Magi, Filippo, "Il Museo Gregoriano Etrusco nella storia degli scavi e degli studi etruschi," in *Etudes étrusco-italiques, mélanges pour le 25e anniversaire de la chaire d'étruscologie à l'Université de Louvain,*

Louvain: Publications universitaires, 1963, pp. 119–130.

Majolo Molinari, Olga, *La stampa periodica romana dell'Ottocento*, 2 v., Rome: Istituto di studi romani, 1963.

Marconi, Paolo, *Giuseppe Valadier*, Rome: Officini Edizioni, 1964.

Mariani, Gaetano Miarelli, "Il 'Cristianesimo Primitivo' nella riforma Cattolica e alcune incidenze sui monumenti del passato," in *L'architettura a Roma e in Italia (1580–1621)*, ed. Gianfranco Spagnesi, Rome: Centro di studi per la storia dell'architettura, 1989, v. 1, pp. 133–166.

Martina, Giacomo, *Pio IX*, 3 v., Rome: Pontificia università gregoriana, 1974–1990.

Martina, Giacomo, and Wiktor Gramatowski, "La relazione ufficiale sua conclave del 1846: Nel 150° anniversario dell'elezione di Pio IX," *Archivum Historiae Pontificiae* 34 (1996): 159–212.

Martini, Antonio, "Il monumento all'Immacolata in piazza di Spagna," *Bollettino del Circolo S. Pietro* 119:1 (1987): 41–53.

Martone, Sonia, "1797–1814. L'alternanza dei Governi francese e pontificio a Roma. Note sui criteri adottati per la conservazione dell'architettura ecclesiastica," in *Restauro Architettonico a Roma nell'Ottocento*, ed. Maria Piera Sette, Rome: Bonsignori, 2007, pp. 87–106.

Marucchi, Orazio, "Il Museo Cristiano Lateranense fondato da Pio IX e completato da Pio XI con il Museo Missionario," *Angelicum* 6:1/2 (1929): 67–76.

Mascioli, Frederick, "Anti-roman and pro-Italic sentiment in italian historiography," *Romanic Review* 33:4 (1942): 366–384.

Matthiae, Guglielmo, *Piazza del popolo: attraverso i documenti del primo ottocento*, Rome: Palombi, 1946.

Mazzonis, Filippo, "Pio IX, il tramonto del potere temporale e la riorganizzazione della chiesa," in *Storia della Società Italiana (vol. XVIII): Lo stato unitario e il suo difficile debutto*, ed. Bartolo Anglani, Milan: Teti, 1981, v. 18, pp. 251–285.

Mazzonis, Filippo, "Storia della Chiesa e origini del partito cattolico," *Studi Storici* 21:2 (1980): 363–400.

Meeks, Carroll L. V., *Italian Architecture 1750–1914*, New Haven and London: Yale University Press, 1966.

Mei del Testa, Alberto, *Michelangelo Lanci e l'interpretazione dei geroglifici*, Fano: Biblioteca Federiciana, 2002.

Mellano, Maria Franca, *Il Caso Fransoni e la politica ecclesiastica piemontese (1848–1850)*, Rome: Pontificia Università Gregoriana, 1964.

Mercati, Angelo, "Ippolito Rosellini e Gregorio XVI," in *Gregorio XVI: Miscellanea Commemorativa*, ed. Alfonso Bartoli, Pio Ciprotti, and Giuseppe Bozzetti, 2 v., Rome: Camaldolesi di S. Gregorio al Celio, 1948, v. 1, pp. 289–303.

Merluzzi, Manfredi, Gaetano Sabatini, and Flavia Tudini, eds., *La Vergine contesa: Roma, l'Immacolata Concezione e l'universalismo della Monarchia Cattolica (secc. XVII–XIX)*, Rome: Viella, 2022.

Meyer, Susanne Adina, "La "pierre de touche": riflessioni sul pubblico romano tra Sette e Ottocento," *RSdA* 90 (2006): 15–22.

Meyer, Susanne Adina, "Il giudizio del pubblico e il ruolo dei critici. Il panorama europeo e il caso romano," in *Il Settecento negli studi italiani: Problemi e prospettive*, ed. Anna Maria Rao and Alberto Postigliola, Rome: Edizioni di Storia e Letteratura, 2010, pp. 323–337.

Middleton, Robin, "The Rationalist Interpretations of Léonce Reynaud and Viollet-le-Duc," *AA Files* 11 (1986): 29–48.

Milbach, Sylvain, "«Jusqu'à présent l'Église a toléré, négocié, dissimulé». Les conseils de Lamennais à Léon XII (1827)," in *La religione dei nuovi tempi. Il riformismo spirituale nell'età di Leone XII*, ed. Ilaria Fiumi Sermattei and Roberto Regoli, Ancona: Consiglio Regionale Assemblea legislativa delle Marche, 2020, pp. 51–62.

Minor, Heather Hyde, *The Culture of Architecture in Enlightenment Rome*, University Park: Pennsylvania State University Press, 2010.

Momigliano, Arnaldo, "Ancient History and the Antiquarian," *Journal of the Warburg and Courtauld Institutes* 13:3/4 (1950): 285–315.

Momigliano, Arnaldo, "Mabillon's Italian Disciples," in *Essays in Ancient and Modern*

Historiography, Chicago: University of Chicago Press, 2012, pp. 277–293.

Monti, Antonio, *Pio IX nel Risorgimento italiano*, Bari: Laterza, 1928.

Moskowitz, Anita F., "Arnolfo, non-Arnolfo: new (and some old) observations on the ciborium in San Paolo fuori le mura," *Gesta* 37:1 (1998): 88–102.

Mulder, Suzanne, "Il risorgimento del tempio Minervitano: il restauro ottocentesco di S. Maria sopra Minerva," *Rassegna di architettura e urbanistica* 23: 69–70 (September 1989–April 1990): 96–104.

Mulder, Suzanne, "Image Building by Means of Church Restorations, Conservations of Ancient Monuments, Evangelic Diligence and Church Policy under the Pontificate of Pius IX during the Years 1850–1870," in *The Power of Imagery: Essays on Rome, Italy & Imagination*, ed. Peter van Kessel, Rome: Apeiron, 1992, pp. 83–97.

Mulder, Suzanne, "La tutela del patrimonio culturale a Roma tra il 1800 e il 1870," *Mededelingen van het Nederlandse Institut te Rome* 53 (1994): 81–133.

Nagel, Alexander, and Christopher S. Wood, *Anachronic Renaissance*, New York: Zone Books, 2010.

Nardi, Carla, *Napoleone e Roma: dalla consulta romana al ritorno di Pio VII (1811–1814)*, Rome: Gangemi, 2005.

Nardi, Carla, *Napoleone e Roma: La politica della Consulta romana*, Rome: EFR, 1989.

Negri, Pietro, "Gregorio XVI e le ferrovie in alcuni documenti degli Archivi di Stato di Roma e di Bologna," *Rassegna degli Archivi di Stato* 28:1 (1968): 103–126.

Negro, Silvio, *Seconda Roma 1850–1870*, Milan: Hoepli, 1943.

Notarangelo, R., "Gli Alabastri Egiziani della Basilica di S. Paolo," *Rivista di cultura marinara* (1952): 3–7.

Nyberg, Dorothea, "La Sainte Antiquité: Focus of an Eighteenth-Century Architectural Debate," in *Essays in the History of Architecture Presented to Rudolf Wittkower,* ed. Douglas Fraser, Howard Hibbard, and Milton Lewine, London: Phaidon, 1967, pp. 159–169.

O'Connor, Anne, "L'Italia: La Terra dei Morti?," *Italian Culture* 23 (2005): 31–50.

O'Connor, Edward D., *The Dogma of the Immaculate Conception: History and Significance*, Notre Dame: University of Notre Dame Press, 1958.

Oldfield, John J., "The Evolution of Lamennais' Catholic-Liberal Synthesis," *Journal for the Scientific Study of Religion* 8:2 (1969): 269–288.

O'Meara, Thomas F., *Romantic Idealism and Roman Catholicism: Schelling and the Theologians*, Notre Dame: University of Notre Dame Press, 1982.

Ovidi, Ernesto, *Tommaso Minardi e la sua scuola*, Rome: Rebecca, 1902.

Palazzolo, Maria Iolanda, "Tra antico e moderno. La cultura romana nel primo Ottocento," in Stefano Susinno, Sandra Pinto, Liliana Barroero, and Fernando Mazzocca, eds, *Maestà di Roma: Da Napoleone All'unità d'Italia: Universale ed Eterna, Capitale delle Arti*, Milan: Electa, 2003, pp. 53–60.

Pallottino, Elisabetta, "Architettura e archeologia intorno alle basiliche di Roma e alla ricostruzione di S. Paolo f.l.m.," in *Roma fra la Restaurazione e l'elezione di Pio IX. Amministrazione, Economia. Società e Cultura*, ed. Anna Lia Bonella, Augusto Pompeo, and Manola Ida Venzo, Rome, Frieburg, and Vienna: Herder, 1997, pp. 329–347.

Pallottino, Elisabetta, "La nuova architettura paleocristiana nella ricostruzione della basilica di S. Paolo fuori le mura a Roma (1823–1847)," *RSdA* 56 (1995): 30–59.

Pallottino, Elisabetta, "La ricostruzione della basilica di San Paolo fuori le Mura," *Roma moderna e contemporanea* 20:2 (2012): 677–697.

Pallottino, Elisabetta, "La ricostruzione della basilica di San Paolo fuori le mura (1823–1829)," in *1823. L'incendio della basilica di San Paolo. Leone XII e l'avvio della ricostruzione*, ed. Ilaria Fiumi Sermattei, Genga: Consiglio Regionale; Assemblea Legislativa delle Marche, 2013, pp. 27–40.

Pallottino, Elisabetta, "La ricostruzione della basilica di San Paolo fuori le mura (1823–1854)," in *Capitale delle Arti*, ed. Stefano Susinno, Sandra Pinto, Liliana

Barroero, and Fernando Mazzocca, Milan: Electa, 2003, pp. 484–489.

Palmerio, Giancarlo, and Gabriella Villetti, *Storia edilizia di S. Maria sopra Minerva in Roma, 1275–1870*, Rome: Viella, 1989.

Pasquali, Susanna, "Basiliche civili e cristiane nell'editoria romana d'architettura tra Sette e Ottocento," *RSdA* 56 (1995): 18–29.

Pasquali, Susanna, "Eredità del Cinquecento romano osservate e reinterpretate tra il 1760 e il 1790," *RSdA* 105 (2011): 55–62.

Pasquali, Susanna, "Luigi Canina, Architect and Archaeologist," *Rassegna* 55:3 (1993): 44–51.

Pastorino, Armanda, and Laura Pastorino, "I restauri delle chiese a impianto basilicale a Roma durante il pontificato di Pio IX," *RSdA* 56 (1995): 60–72.

Petruccioli, Attilio, and Antonio Terranova, "L'asse nord-sud di Roma napoleonica, principio ordinatore per una architettura della citta imperiale," *Controspazio* 13 (1981): 178–189.

Petzet, Michael, "Un projet des Perrault pour l'église Sainte-Geneviève à Paris," *Bulletin Monumental* 115:2 (1957): 81–96.

Pietrangeli, Carlo, *Scavi e scoperte di antichità sotto il pontificato di Pio VI*, Rome: Istituto di studi romani, 1958.

Pietri, Charles, "Concordia apostolorum et renovatio urbis (Culte des martyrs et propagande pontificale)," *Mélanges de l'école française de Rome* (1961): 275–322.

Pinon, Pierre, "La pianta basilicale nell'architettura religiosa francese: dalla basilica civile alla basilica paleocristiana," *RSdA* 56 (1995): 6–17.

Pirri, Pietro, "Il Movimento Lamennesiano in Italia. Nel Centenario dell'Enciclica "Mirari Vos"," *Civiltà cattolica*, 12 August 1932a, pp. 313–327 and 9 September 1932b, pp. 567–583.

Plessis, Joseph Octave, *Journal d'un voyage en Europe, 1819–1820,* ed. Henri Têtu, Québec: Pruneau & Kirouac, 1903.

Pollard, John F., *Money and the Rise of the Modern Papacy: Financing the Vatican, 1850–1950*, Cambridge and New York: Cambridge University Press, 2005.

Pollmann, Judith, "Being a Catholic in Early Modern Europe," in *The Ashgate Research Companion to the Counter-Reformation*, ed. Alexandra Bamji, Geert H. Janssen, and Mary Laven, Aldershot: Ashgate, 2013, pp. 165–182.

Pommier, Édouard, "La Révolution et le destin des oeuvres d'art," in *Lettres à Miranda sur le déplacement des monuments de l'art,* ed. Édouard Pommier, Paris: Macula, 1989, pp. 7–67.

Pope, Barbara Corrado, "Immaculate and Powerful: The Marian Revival in the Nineteenth Century," in *Immaculate & Powerful: The Female in Sacred Image and Social Reality*, ed. Clarissa W. Atkinson, Constance H. Buchanan and Margaret Ruth Miles, Boston: Beacon Press, 1985, pp. 173–200.

Priester, Ann, "The Belltowers of Medieval Rome and the Architecture of Renovatio," Ph.D dissertation, Princeton University, 1990.

Printy, Michael, "The Intellectual Origins of Popular Catholicism: Catholic Moral Theology in the Age of Enlightenment," *CHR* 91:3 (2005): 438–461.

Prudentius, "Peristephanon Liber [Crowns of Martyrdom] ch. 12: Passio Apostolorum Petri et Pauli [The Passion of the Apostles Peter and Paul]," in *Prudentius*, trans. H. J. Thomson, v. 2, London and Cambridge: William Heinemann and Harvard University Press, 1953, pp. 322–337.

Racioppi, Pier Paolo, "The Men of Letters and the Teaching Artists: Guattani, Minardi, and the Discourse on Art at the Accademia di San Luca in Rome in the Nineteenth Century," *Journal of Art Historiography* 19 (2018): 1–19.

Raedts, Peter, "The Church as Nation State: A New Look at Ultramontaine Catholicism (1850–1900)," *Nederlands archief voor kerkgeschiedenis / Dutch Review of Church History* 84 (2004): 476–496.

Reardon, Bernard M. G., *Religion in the Age of Romanticism: Studies in Early Nineteenth-Century Thought*, Cambridge: Cambridge University Press, 1985.

Regoli, Roberto, "Storiografia intorno al conclave di Leone XII (1823)," in *Il Conclave del 1823 e l'Elezione di Leone XII*, ed. Ilaria Fiumi Sermattei and Roberto Regoli, Genga: Consiglio Regionale; Assemblea Legislativa delle Marche, 2016, pp. 23–41.

Regoli, Roberto, "Un pontificato religioso. Gli anni di Leone XII," in *La religione dei nuovi tempi. Il riformismo spirituale nell'età di Leone XII*, ed. Ilaria Fiumi Sermattei and Roberto Regoli, Ancona: Consiglio Regionale Assemblea legislativa delle Marche, 2020, pp. 17–50.

Reinerman, Alan J., "Papacy and Papal State in the Restoration (1814–1846): Studies since 1939," *CHR* 64:1 (1978): 36–46.

Reinerman, Alan J., "The Concert Baffled: The Roman Conference of 1831 and the Reforms of the Papal State," *International History Review* 5:1 (1983): 20–38.

Reinerman, Alan J., "The Failure of Popular Counter-Revolution in Risorgimento Italy: The Case of the Centurions, 1831–1847," *The Historical Journal* 34:1 (1991): 21–41.

Reiss, Anke, *Rezeption frühchristlicher Kunst im 19. und frühen 20. Jahrhundert: ein Beitrag zur Geschichte der christlichen Archäologie und zum Historismus*, Dettelbach: Verlag J. H. Röll, 2008.

Ricci, Saverio, "Agli albori del Purismo. Il riflesso degli antichi maestri nell'opera del giovane Tommaso Minardi," in *La ricerca giovane in cammino per l'arte*, Rome: Gangemi, 2012, pp. 238–261.

Ricci, Saverio, "Da Roma a Perugia, da Perugia all'Europa. Tommaso Minardi, gli artisti tedeschi e i puristi italiani alla scoperta dell'"Umbria Santa'," in *Arte in Umbria nell'Ottocento*, ed. Francesco Federico Mancini and Caterina Zappia, Cinisello Balsamo: Silvana, 2006, pp. 88–99.

Ricci, Saverio, "Il magistero purista di Tommaso Minardi, 1800–1850. Il contributo dell'artista e della sua scuola al dibattito teorico sul primitivismo romantico, nella riforma della didattica accademica, per la diffusione in Europa dei fenomeni di Revival," Università degli studi della Tuscia – Viterbo, Viterbo, 2011.

Ricci, Saverio, Richardson, Carol M., and Joanna Story, "Appendix: Letter of the Canons of Saint Peter's to Paul V Concerning the Demolition of the Old Basilica, 1605," in *Old Saint Peter's, Rome*, ed. Rosamond McKitterick, Cambridge and New York: Cambridge University Press, 2013, pp. 404–415.

Ridley, Ronald T., "In Defence of the Cultural Patrimony: Carlo Fea Goes to Court," *Xenia Antiqua* 5 (1996): 143–158.

Ridley, Ronald T., *The Eagle and the Spade: Archaeology in Rome during the Napoleonic Era*, Cambridge and New York: Cambridge University Press, 1992a.

Ridley, Ronald T., *The Pope's Archaeologist: the Life and Times of Carlo Fea*, Rome: Quasar, 2000.

Ridley, Ronald T., "To Protect the Monuments: The Papal Antiquarian (1534–1870)," *Xenia Antiqua* 1 (1992b): 117–154.

Riemann, Gottfried, ed, *Karl Friedrich Schinkel: Reisen nach Italien. Tagebücher, Briefe, Zeichnungen, Aquarelle*, Berlin: Rütten & Loening, 1979.

Rivetti, Guglielmo, "La cappella del Sacro Cuore a Villa Lante," in *Neogotico nel XIX e XX secolo*, ed. Rossana Bossaglia and Valerio Terraroli, Milan: Mazzotta, 1990, v. 2, pp. 376–380.

Roberts, Daniela, "Angelo Uggeri – Von den Veduten Roms zu den malerischen Ruinen des antiken Latium," in *Souvenir de Rome: Ansichten aus Rom und Umgebung von Angelo Uggeri (1754–1837)*, ed. Julia M. Nauhaus, Daniela Roberts, Gerd Bartoschek, and Sarah Kinzel, Altenburg: Lindenau-Museum, 2015, pp. 9–26.

Robinson, John Martin, *Cardinal Consalvi, 1757–1824*, New York: St. Martin's Press, 1987.

Rolfi Ožvald, Serenella, *"Agli Amatori delle belle arti Gli Autori". Il laboratorio dei periodici a Roma tra Settecento e Ottocento*, Rome: Campisano, 2012.

Ruffinière du Prey, Pierre de la, "Hawksmoor's "Basilica after the Primitive Christians": Architecture and Theology," *JSAH* 48:1 (March 1989): 38–52.

Rusconi, Roberto, "Devozione per il pontefice e culto per il papato al tempo di Pio IX e di Leone XIII nelle Pagine di «La Civiltà Cattolica»," *Rivista di storia del cristianesimo* 2:1 (2005): 9–37.

Sabene, Renata, "Fede, accoglienza e indulgenze nella Fabbrica di San Pietro in Vaticano," in ed., Assunta Di Sante and Simona Turriziani, *Quando la fabbrica costrui San Pietro: un cantiere di lavoro, di pietà cristiana e di umanità: XVI–XIX secolo*, Foligno: Il Formichiere, 2016, pp. 43–62.

Sabene, Renata, *La Fabbrica di San Pietro in Vaticano: Dinamiche internazionali e dimensione locale*, Rome: Gangemi, 2015.

Salimbeni, Lorenzo Bartolini, "La Basilica di San Pio V," in *San Francesco e la Porziuncola: dalla "chiesa piccola e povera" alla Basilica di Santa Maria degli Angeli*, ed. Pietro Messa, S. Maria degli Angeli (Perugia): Porziuncola, 2008, pp. 301–324.

Salmon, Frank, "'Storming the Campo Vaccino': British Architects and the Antique Buildings of Rome after Waterloo," *Architectural History* 38 (1995): 146–175.

Sannibale, Maurizio, "Il Museo Gregoriano Etrusco: le sue trasformazioni e il suo ruolo nella storia dell'Etruscologia," in *I Musei Vaticani nell'80 anniversario della firma dei Patti Lateranensi*, ed. Antonio Paolucci and Cristina Pantanella, Rome: Edizioni Musei Vaticani, 2009, pp. 57–79.

Santanicchia, Mirko, "Francesco 'riscoperto'. Il santo e la basilica di Assisi nel contesto romantico europeo," in *Luoghi, figure e itinerari della Restaurazione in Umbria (1815–1830)*, ed. Chiara Coletti and Stefania Petrillo, Rome: Viella, 2017, pp. 315–337.

Sardi, Vincenzo, *La solenne definizione del dogma dell'Immacolato Concepimento di Maria Santissima*, 2 v., Rome: Tipografia Vaticana, 1905.

Scarfone, Giuseppe, "Luigi Boldrini, architetto pontificio," *Strenna dei Romanisti* 41 (1980): 475–482.

Sebastianelli, Fabio, "L'Incendio della Basilica di S. Paolo fuori le mura," *Roma Moderna e Contemporanea* 12:3 (December 2004): 539–566.

Segarra Lagunes, Maria Margarita, *Il Tevere e Roma: storia di una simbiosi*, Rome: Gangemi, 2004.

Sette, Maria Piera, "Restauri Romani di Pasquale Belli," in *Saggi in onore di Guglielmo de Angelis*

d'Ossat, ed. Sandro Benedetti, Gaetano Miarelli Mariani, and Laura Marcucci, Rome: Multigrafica, 1987, pp. 491–498.

Sette, Maria Piera, (ed.), *Restauro architettonico a Roma nell'Ottocento*, Rome: Bonsignori, 2007.

Sgarbozza, Ilaria, *Le spalle al Settecento: forma, modelli e organizzazione dei musei nella Roma napoleonica (1809–1814)*, Rome: Edizioni Musei Vaticani, 2013.

Silvestri, Silvia, *Vetrate italiane dell'Ottocento: storia del gusto e relazioni artistiche fra Italia e Francia, 1820–1870*, Florence: SPES, 2006.

Spagnesi, Gianfranco, *L'architettura a Roma al tempo di Pio IX*, Rome: Multigrafica, 1978.

Spagnesi, Gianfranco, "Roma capitale dello Stato pontificio e il "programma" di Pio IX (1846–1878)," in *Roma: la Basilica di San Pietro, il borgo e la città*, Milan: Palombi, 2003, pp. 165–181.

Sperber, Jonathan, *Popular Catholicism in Nineteenth-Century Germany*, Princeton: Princeton University Press, 1984.

Springer, Carolyn, *The Marble Wilderness: Ruins and Representation in Italian Romanticism, 1775–1850*, Cambridge and New York: Cambridge University Press, 1987.

Stearns, Peter N., *Priest and Revolutionary: Lamennais and the Dilemma of French Catholicism*, New York: Harper & Row, 1967.

Stewart, Herbert L., "Theology and Romanticism," *The Harvard Theological Review* 13:4 (1920): 362–389.

Strozzieri, Yuri, *Luigi Poletti: gli orientamenti del restauro nella prima metà dell'Ottocento: stile, filologia, storia*, Rome: L'Erma di Bretschneider, 2021.

Strozzieri, Yuri, "L'ultimo Valadier: i progetti per il Palazzo della Posta e Gran Guardia a piazza Colonna e per Porta Maggiore," in *Antico, città, architettura, I. Dai disegni e manoscritti dell'Istituto Nazionale di Archeologia e Storia dell'Arte*, ed. Elisa Debenedetti, Rome: Quasar, 2014, pp. 349–375.

Susinno, Stefano, "Introduzione," in *Disegni di Tommaso Minardi (1787–1871)*, ed. Stefano Susinno, Rome: De Luca, 1982, pp. i–xxxi.

Susinno, Stefano, Sandra Pinto, Liliana Barroero, and Fernando Mazzocca, eds.,

Maestà di Roma: Da Napoleone All'unità d'Italia: Universale ed Eterna, Capitale delle Arti, Milan: Electa, 2003.

Terdiman, Richard, *Present Past: Modernity and the Memory Crisis*, Ithaca: Cornell University Press, 1993.

Tiberia, Vitaliano, *La Congregazione dei Virtuosi al Pantheon da Pio VII a Pio IX*, Rome: Congedo, 2015.

Tolomeo, Maria Grazia, "Il monumento della Immacolata Concezione di Luigi Poletti. Arte e Architettura della Restaurazione," *Bollettino dei Musei Comunali di Roma* 4 (1990): 87–101.

Tuker, Mildred Anna Rosalie, and Hope Malleson, *Handbook to Christian and Ecclesiastical Rome*, 3 v., London: A. and C. Black, 1900.

Ufford, Letitia Wheeler, *The Pasha: How Mehemet Ali Defied the West, 1839–1841*, Jefferson: McFarland & Company, 2007.

Vaccari, Monica, and Marco Dezzi Bardeschi, eds., *Luigi Poletti: architetto (1792–1869)*, Bologna: Nuova Alfa Editoriale, 1992.

Van Liere, Katherine, Simon Ditchfield, and Howard Louthan, eds., *Sacred History: Uses of the Christian Past in the Renaissance World*, Oxford: Oxford University Press, 2012.

Van Zanten, David, *Designing Paris: The Architecture of Duban, Labrouste, Duc, and Vaudoyer*, Cambridge: MIT Press, 1987.

Veca, Ignazio, *Il mito di Pio IX: storia di un papa liberale e nazionale*, Rome: Viella, 2018a.

Veca, Ignazio, "Nascita dell'obolo di san Pietro. Le origini politiche di una moderna devozione (1847–49)," *Studi Storici* 4 (2018b): 1031–1054.

Ventra, Stefania, "Tommaso Minardi e il restauro come condizione necessaria per una storia dell'arte," in *La cultura del restauro. Modelli di ricezione per la museologia e la storia dell'arte*, ed. Maria Beatrice Failla, Susanne Adina Meyer, Chiara Piva, and Stefania Ventra, Rome: Campisano, 2013, pp. 85–100.

Verdi, Orietta, "L'istituzione del Corpo degli ingegneri pontifici di acque e strade (1809–1817)," in *Roma fra la Restaurazione e l'elezione di Pio IX. Amministrazione, Economia. Società e Cultura*, ed. Anna Lia Bonella, Augusto Pompeo, and Manola Ida Venzo,

Rome, Frieburg, and Vienna: Herder, 1997, pp. 191–220.

Vessey, Mark, "Cities of the Mind: Renaissance Views of Early Christian Culture and the End of Antiquity," in *A Companion to Late Antiquity*, ed. Philip Rousseau, Hoboken: Wiley-Blackwell, 2009, pp. 43–58.

Warner, Marina, *Alone of All Her Sex: The Myth and the Cult of the Virgin Mary*, New York: Knopf, 1976.

Weidmann, Clemens, "Maximus of Turin. Two Preachers of the Fifth Century," in *Preaching in the Patristic Era. Sermons, Preachers, and Audiences in the Latin West*, ed. Anthony Dupont, Shari Boodts, Gert Partoens, and Johan Leemans, Leiden and Boston: Brill, 2018, pp. 347–372.

Wittman, Richard, "A Partly Vacated Historicism: Artifacts, Architecture, and Time in Nineteenth-Century Papal Rome," *Grey Room* 84:3 (Summer 2021b): 6–37.

Wittman, Richard, "Architecture in the Roman Periodical Press, 1770–1848," *The Journal of Architecture* 25:7 (2020b): 809–843.

Wittman, Richard, *Architecture, Print Culture, and the Public Sphere in Eighteenth-Century France*, New York and London: Routledge, 2007.

Wittman, Richard, "Churches and States," *Places Journal*, September 2019, https://doi.org/10.22269/190917.

Wittman, Richard, "Churches and States (Updated)," *Future Anterior* 17:1 (2020a): 19–45.

Wittman, Richard, "Félix Duban's Didactic Restoration of the Château de Blois: A History of France in Stone," *JSAH* 55:4 (1996): 412–434.

Wittman, Richard, "Imprinting Patriotism: Etruria and Egypt in Papal Rome (1834–41)," in *The Printed and the Built*, ed. Mari Hvattum and Anne Hultzsch, London: Bloomsbury, 2018a, pp. 97–119.

Wittman, Richard, "Space, Networks, and the Saint-Simonians," *Grey Room* 40 (2010): 22–49.

Wittman, Richard, "Sulla ricostruzione della basilica di San Paolo fuori le mura: nuovi documenti sul Concorso Clementino del 1824," in *Roma in età napoleonica. Antico, architettura e città da modello a laboratorio*, ed. Jean-Philippe Garric, Susanna Pasquali, and Marco Pupillo, Rome: Officina Libraria, 2021a, pp. 199–218.

Wittman, Richard, "The Alabaster Columns from the Pontifical Expedition to Egypt, 1840–1841," in *Images of Egypt*, ed. Mari Lending, Eirik Arff Gulseth Bøhn, and Tim Anstey, Oslo: Pax Forlag, 2018b, pp. 164–165.

Wittman, Richard, "A Partly Vacated Historicism: Artifacts, Architecture, and Time in Nineteenth-Century Papal Rome," *Grey Room* 84:3 (Summer 2021b): 6–37.

Wünsche, Raimund, "Ludwigs Skulpturenerwerbungen für die Glyptothek," in *Glyptothek München, 1830–1980*, Munich: Staatliche Antikensammlung und Glyptothek, 1980, pp. 23–84.

Yack, Bernard, *The Fetishism of Modernities: Epochal Self-Consciousness in Contemporary Social and Political Thought*, Notre Dame: University of Notre Dame Press, 1997.

Zuccari, Alessandro, "La politica culturale dell'Oratorio Romano nelle imprese artistiche promosse da Cesare Baronio," *Storia dell'arte* 42 (1981): 171–185.

INDEX

Academy of Santa Cecilia, 237
Academy of St. Luke, 2, 32, 72, 74, 79, 88, 89, 92,
        93, 94, 97, 120, 157, 161, 162, 164, 165,
        172, 173, 174, 175, 180, 182, 188, 189,
        190, 191, 196, 210, 212, 213, 216, 218,
        228, 231, 237, 298, 301, 302, 308, 309,
        311, 314, 316, 334, 336, 338, 341, 342,
        343
Accademia dell'Arcadia, 237
Accademia Tibertina, 225
Ælia Lælia Crispis, 341
Agricola, Filippo, 340
Albani, Giuseppe, 175, 176
Alexander I, pope, 374
Alexander VII, pope, 252
Alexander the Great, 50
Alexandria, 279, 282
Algarotti, Francesco, 223
Alippi, Andrea, 52, 74, 75, 79, 92, 119,
        121
Amati, Girolamo, 322
Ambrose of Milan, saint, 252
Ami de la Religion, 55, 240
Andrés, Giovanni (Juan), 29, 30, 80
Annali delle scienze religiose, 272, 339
Antologia, 106, 107, 109
Antonelli, Giacomo, 301, 327, 328, 329, 366, 379,
        380, 381
Antoniacci, Nicola, 46
Antonine Column. *See* Rome:Column of Marcus
        Aurelius (aka Antonine Column)
Aquinas, Thomas, 351, 352
Arcadius, Emperor, 1
Arnolfo di Cambio, 44, 221, 223, 248, 249, 253,
        258, 279, 285, 298, 309, 340
Assisi
    Basilica of St. Francis of Assisi
        Lower Church, 74
    Santa Maria degli Angeli, 213, 315
Aswan, 282
Athens, 17
Augustine of Hippo, St., 252, 254, 259
Augustus, Emperor, 17, 109, 174, 231, 232, 284,
        316

Austria, 34, 57, 147, 149, 186, 187, 208, 256, 305,
        321, 324, 327, 379, 381

Balbo, Cesare, 303, 304
    Delle speranze d'Italia (1844), 303, 304
Barattieri, Giovanni Battista
    Architettura d'acque (1656), 193
Baronio, Cesare, 14
Battisti, Pietro, 45
Bavaria, 116, 142, 148
Belamy, Théodore, 324
Belgium, 143, 379, 381
Belli, Giuseppe Gioachino, 23, 181, 300
    "Er volo de Simommàgo" (1845), 300
    "La Fin der Monno" (1831), 182
Belli, Pasquale, 52, 74–75, 79, 89, 90, 119, 120, 121,
        139, 158, 159, 169–176, 177, 186, 187,
        188, 189, 190, 191, 192, 193, 194, 201,
        209, 213, 214, 215, 216, 220, 223, 232,
        233, 235, 236, 266, 270, 343
    death, 188, 207
    master plan for San Paolo (1830), 169, 177–182
Belloni, Paolo, 377
Benedict XIV, pope (Prospero Lorenzo
        Lambertini), 14, 15
Benedict, St., 271
Bengal Catholic Herald, 7, 289, 290
Beretta (building contractor), 46
Berlin, 5, 6, 37, 199, 233
    Cathedral project by K. F. Schinkel, 233
Bernetti, Tommaso, 174, 175, 188, 193,
        209
Bernini, Gianlorenzo, 259, 269, 279, 308
Bertazzoli, Francesco, 121
Berthier, Louis Alexandre, 18
Beste, John Richard Digby, 161
Blix, Göran, 34
Boldrini, Luigi, 375
Bonald, Louis de, 127, 256
Borromini, Francesco, 14, 15, 233
Bosio, Antonio, 31
    Roma Sottoterranea (1630), 31
Bosio, Pietro, 121, 327
Bosnia, 260

413

Botta, Carlo, 226
  Storia d'Italia dal 1789 al 1814 (1824), 226
Bottari, Giovanni, 14, 15, 16
Boutry, Philippe, 53
Bovillae, 211
Bracci, Pietro, 89
Bramante, Donato, 108
Brancadoro, Cesare, 115
Brandolini, Luigi, 79
Bravi, Matteo, 243
Brazil, 116, 149, 381
Brizi, Giuseppe, 74
Bunsen, Christian Carl Josias, 53, 55, 61, 89, 116, 142, 235, 373
  Les forum de Rome restaurés et expliqués (1837), 235

Cairo, 279, 282
  Mehmet Ali Mosque, 279
Calcutta, 7, 209, 289, 290
Calderari, Ottone, 333
Calzolari, Monica, 53
Camerino
  San Venanzio, 314
Campanari, Vincenzo, 273, 274
Camporese, Giuseppe, 210
Camporese, Pietro (the younger), 89, 93
Campori, Cesare, 214, 228, 363
Camuccini, Vincenzo, 336, 340
Canada, 149, 153, 381
Cancellieri, Francesco, 31, 49, 71, 73
Canina, Luigi, 199–201, 234, 270, 373
  Ricerche sull'architettura più propria dei tempj cristiani (1843), 201, 234
Canova, Antonio, 19, 22, 210
Cantù, Ignazio, 287
Carlo Alberto, king of Piedmont, 234, 303, 322
Carlo Felice of Sardinia, king, 142
Castel Gandolfo, 216, 218
Catholic Magazine, 289
Cavalleri, Ferdinando, 316
Centuroni, 209, 304
Cerveteri, 227, 273
Champollion, Jean-François, 280
Charlemagne, 255, 322
Charles X of France, king, 147, 176
Charleston, South Carolina, 146, 240
Chateaubriand, François René Vicomte de, 49, 57
Chiavari
  S. Maria dell'Orto, 315
China, 7, 269, 381
Chlumčansky, Václav Léopold von, 143
cholera, 282, 352
Chrysostom, John, saint, 253, 254
Ciceruacchio (Angelo Brunetti), 326
Civiltà Cattolica, 382
Clement VII, pope (Giulio de' Medici), 252
Clement VIII, pope (Ippolito Aldobrandini), 259
Clement XI, pope (Giovanni Francesco Albani), 14

Clement XIII, pope (Carlo della Torre di Rezzonico), 16
Clement XIV, pope (Giovanni Vincenzo Antonio Ganganelli), 16, 19, 380
Closse, Guglielmo, 119, 162, 163, 164, 165, 174, 175
Cochetti, Luigi, 335
Codogno
  Theater (by Uggeri), 159
Colagiacomi, Serafino, 219
Colapietra, Raffaele, 57
Colonna, Lady Chiara, 339
Commission des Embellissements, 24
Commissione delle Chiese, 24
Commission for Building Fifty New Churches (1711), 232
concordia apostolorum tradition, 251
Concorso Clementino (1758), 2
Concorso Clementino (1775), 71
Concorso Clementino (1824), 88–97, 100, 212, 233
Congregation of Propaganda Fide, 150, 260, 284
Congregazione de' Virtuosi al Pantheon, 237
Consalvi, Ercole, 25, 35, 36, 37, 52, 53, 54, 57, 58, 73, 74, 97, 121, 140
Conservatori of Rome, 109, 145, 146
Constantine, Emperor, 1, 28, 36, 44, 62, 105, 119, 166, 190, 196, 211, 231, 251, 253, 255, 258, 308, 316
Constitutionnel, Le, 55
Corsi, Faustino, 267
  Delle pietre antiche (1845), 267
Costanzo, Giuseppe Giustino di, 31, 71
  "Memoria della Basilica di San Paolo" (1780s), 31
Counter-Reformation
  Catholicism, Tridentine, 131, 350, 357, 359, 378
  Council of Trent, 350, 356, 357
Cristaldi, Belisario, 74, 75, 77, 79, 80, 87, 96, 98, 115, 117, 118, 119, 121, 143, 145, 146, 162, 172
Crocella, Carlo, 381
Cuba, 381
Cuoco, Vincenzo, 227
  Platone in Italia (1804-06), 227

D'Argenteau, Carlo Giuseppe Benedetto Mercy, 121
D'Azeglio, Massimo, 303, 304
  Degli ultimi casi di Romagna (1846), 303, 304
De Donatis, Clemente, 189, 190
De Gregorio, Emmanuele, 121, 193
De Romanis, Filippo, 71, 73
De Rossi, Giovanni Battista, 328, 342
Della Longa, Giovanni, 243
Della Porta, Giacomo, 43
Della Somaglia, Giulia Maria, 59, 64, 79, 80, 83, 98, 110, 115, 116, 119, 121, 122, 123, 124, 141, 142, 143, 145, 146, 154, 159, 163, 165, 169, 170, 172, 173, 174, 182
Denon, Vivant, 41, 42, 43

INDEX

415

Description de l'Egypte (1809–22), 285
Diario di Roma, 31, 50, 53, 54, 58, 81, 96, 112, 120,
      121, 143, 146, 148, 175, 187, 193, 209,
      213, 214, 236, 240, 254, 268, 271, 277,
      281, 299, 301, 309, 322, 323
Donati, Carlo, 79
Dublin Review, 356
Durand, Jean-Nicolas, 225

East Indies, 381
Eaton, Charlotte, 44
*Echo. Zeitschrift für Literatur, Kunst und Mode in
    Italien*, 240
Effemeridi letterarie di Roma, 71
Egypt, 279, 280, 281, 282, 283, 284, 302
Emilia, 336
England, 129, 143, 148, 208, 232, 306, 335, 338,
      344, 379, 381
Enlightenment, 17, 114, 127, 128, 130, 132, 133
Ephesus
    Temple of Diana, 211
Erostratus, 211
Eustace, John Chetwode, 41, 42, 55

Fea, Carlo, 19, 22, 31, 32, 52, 71, 73, 97, 100, 101,
      102, 103, 104–109, 112, 116, 131, 132,
      163, 164, 165, 169, 174, 188, 192, 193,
      194, 267
    Anedotti sulla basilica ostiense (1825), 104–109
    Continuazione degli aneddoti sulla basilica ostiense
      (1826), 163
    *La basilica ostiense liberata dalle inondazioni del Tevere
      senza bisogno di innalzarne il pavimento*
      (1833), 194
    Nuova descrizione di Roma (1820), 31
Ferri, Isidoro, 45
Folchi, Clemente, 89, 96
Fontaine, Pierre-François-Léonard, 225
Fontana, Carlo, 369
Fontana, Domenico, 43, 222, 237
Fortoul, Hippolyte, 231
    De l'Art en Allemagne (1842), 231
Fossati, Gaspare, 175
France, 19, 23, 37, 49, 57, 127, 134, 148, 149, 208,
      226, 232, 236, 256, 327, 335, 338, 340,
      344, 352, 359, 379, 381
Francesco I of Naples, king, 142
Franco–Tuscan Expedition to Egypt (1829), 280
Fransoni, Giacomo Filippo, 116
Fransoni, Luigi, 356
French Revolution, 3, 4, 9, 17, 21, 23, 27, 37, 49,
      114, 130, 133, 140, 209, 226, 256, 280,
      350, 351
Friedrich Wilhelm III of Prussia, king, 116, 141, 147
Fuga, Ferdinando, 15, 17, 177, 180, 223, 230, 233

Gaceta de Madrid, 55, 146, 180
Gaeta, 326, 327, 328, 342, 379, 380

Gagliardi, Pietro, 335
Galla Placidia, 44, 166
Galleffi, Pietro Francesco, 121, 145, 212, 267, 270
Gallicanism, 256
Gamberini, Antonio Domenico, 267, 268, 292
Garibaldi, Giuseppe, 328
Gazzetta di Milano, 55
Gazzetta di Roma, 325
Gazzetta Piemontese, 55, 146, 147
Gell, William, 1, 271
Germany, 57, 236, 335, 338, 344, 381
Giacomo (tinsmith), 59
Gilly, Friedrich, 37
    Friedrichsdenkmal project, 37
Gioberti, Vincenzo, 303, 304, 306, 311, 323
    Del primato morale e civile degli Italiani (1843), 303,
      304
Giornale arcadico, 32, 211, 212, 307, 335
Giornale degli architetti, 306
Giornale di commercio, 193
Giornale di Roma, 345
Giornale ecclesiastico di Roma, 103, 112, 113, 114, 127,
      142
Giustiniani, Giacomo, 116, 268, 292
Gizzi, Tommaso Pasquale, 304, 309, 321
Gnassi, Gaetano, 89, 90, 92, 93, 94, 96, 97, 99
Gniezno, 149
Gregory I (the Great), pope, 187, 260
Gregory XVI, pope (Bartolomeo Alberto
    [Mauro] Cappellari), 126, 186, 189, 190,
      191, 193, 195, 196, 207, 213, 217, 237,
      238, 246, 248, 255, 256, 260, 268, 270,
      273, 274, 278, 280, 282, 284, 287, 289,
      290, 295, 296, 297, 298, 299, 300, 301,
      302, 303, 304, 306, 307, 309, 312, 314,
      323, 325, 327, 342, 343, 350, 351, 352,
      382
    Augustissimam Beatissimi (1840), 290
    Commissum Divinitus (1835), 257
    Il Trionfo della Santa Sede (1799), 256
    Mirari vos (1832), 209, 255, 256, 257
    Singulari nos (1834), 209, 256
Groblewski, Michael, 219, 220, 233, 255, 356
Grottaferrata, 333
Guarnacci, Mario, 227
    Origini italiche (1785–87), 227
Guatemala, 149
Guidi, Silvestro, 279, 281
Gutensohn, Johann Gottfried, and Johann Knapp,
      32
    Monumenti della religione cristiana (1822), 32

Heinrich Hübsch
    In welchem Style sollen wir bauen? (1829), 226
Hobart, 7
Honorius, Emperor, 1, 44, 211
Hübsch, Heinrich, 226
Hungary, 149

416 INDEX

Ibrahim Ali, 279
Il Contemporaneo, 306
Il Popolare, 306
Il Veridico, 382
Il Viminale, 306
Immaculate Conception, 8, 9, 349, 351, 352, 353, 356, 358, 359, 374
   Proclamation of the Dogma of, 9, 349, 351, 353, 356, 358
India, 7, 269, 289, 381
Innocent X, pope (Giovanni Battista Pamphilj), 14, 163
Ireland, 148, 149, 323, 379
Isoard, Gioacchino Giansaverio d', 121
Italy, 13, 23, 55, 106, 112, 115, 116, 149, 152, 162, 176, 226, 227, 228, 232, 268, 271, 303, 304, 306, 311, 322, 323, 324, 335, 336, 337, 338, 341, 344, 381

Jerusalem, 211, 381
Jerusalem, Temple of, 54, 61, 338
Jesuit Order, suppression of (1773), 380
Jornal do Commercio, 240
Josephinism, 256
Jourdan, Sempliciano, 89
Journal des débats, 55
Journal historique et littéraire, 240
Jubilee of 1775, 17
Jubilee of 1825, 58, 59, 81, 88, 104, 110, 113, 126, 127, 131, 133
Jubilee of 1850 (canceled), 295, 298, 325, 326, 333, 334
Julius II, pope (Giuliano della Rovere), 106, 108

Klenze, Leo von, 225
Knapp, Johann. *See* Gutensohn, Johann Gottfried

L'Album, 274, 284, 285, 287, 289, 359
L'ami de la Religion, 146
L'Italico, 306
L'Univers, 356
La Salette, 8, 352, 359
Labouré, Catherine, 351, 352, 359
Labrouste, Henri, 5
Laderchi, Camillo, 337
   Sulla vita e sulle opere di Federico Overbeck (1848), 337
Lambruschini, Luigi, 115, 142, 304, 307
Lamennais, Félicité Robert de, 57, 58, 112, 126, 127, 130, 209, 256, 322, 350
   Essai sur l'indifférence en matière de religion (1817 ff), 126
Lanci, Michelangelo, 280
   Osservazioni sul bassorilievo fenico-egizio (1825), 280
Lanciani, Pietro, 109
Le Maistre, Joseph, 127, 256
   Du Pape (1819), 114, 127
Lebanon, 211, 279, 282

Ledoux, Claude Nicolas, 37
Lenoir, Alexandre, 231
Leo I, pope (Leo the Great), 57, 160, 251, 257
Leo III, pope, 249, 255
Leo XII, pope (Annibale Francesco Clemente Melchiorre Girolamo Nicola della Genga), 2, 7, 56, 57, 61, 73, 74, 75, 78, 89, 90, 92, 97, 98, 103, 104, 109, 110, 113, 118, 121, 126, 127, 130, 131, 132, 134, 140, 141, 143, 146, 152, 159, 160, 161, 166, 175, 192, 194, 196, 207, 209, 216, 217, 248, 268, 280, 285, 287, 296, 297, 305, 358, 359, 382
   Ad plurimas easque gravissimas (1825), 110–112, 113, 115, 116, 120, 139, 142, 153
   Chirograph on the Reconstruction of the Basilica of San Paolo (1825), 120, 128, 133, 139, 140, 141, 142, 157, 158, 159, 160, 162, 164, 166, 167, 169, 172, 173, 177, 180, 188, 190, 191, 193, 198, 207, 209, 215, 216, 218, 222, 230, 232, 235, 249, 257, 258, 265, 270, 287, 297, 298, 301, 312, 316, 344, 357
   Quod Hoc Ineunte (1824), 58, 81
   Ubi Primum (1824), 58, 61, 126, 127
Leopold II, Grand Duke of Tuscany, 322
Lesseps, Ferdinand de, 328
Lesueur, Jean-Baptiste-Ciceron, 69, 180
Letarouilly, Paul, 212, 301, 306, 308, 314, 316, 343
Liguori, Alphonsus, 350, 378
limina apostolorum, tradition of the, 253, 259
Lodoli, Carlo, 13, 223
London, 5, 6, 199, 210, 212, 232, 273, 274, 289, 302
   British Museum, 274
London Times, 152
Loreto
   Holy House of Loreto, 353
Louis-Philippe d'Orléans of France, king, 176
Lourdes, 8, 359
Lovery, Enrico, 93, 94
Löwy, Michael, 127, 130
Lucina, 1
Ludwig I of Bavaria, king, 116, 143, 233

Macao, 150, 152
Macchi, Vincenzo, 141
Madrid
   Espiritu Santo, 60
Mantua
   Cathedral of Saint Peter, 232
   Sant'Andrea, 90
Marchetti, Giovanni, 126
Marchi, Giuseppe, 220, 342, 343, 344, 345, 367
   Monumenti delle arti cristiane primitive nella metropoli del cristianesimo (1844), 342
Marco y Catalan, Jean Francisco, 121
Marengo, Battle of (1800), 19
Mariette, Pierre-Jean, 227

INDEX

Marocchi, Giuseppe, 61
  Dettaglio del terribile incendio accaduto il di 15 luglio 1823 della famosa basilica di S. Paolo di Rome (1823), 61
Martinetti, Gianbattista, 79, 80, 81, 84, 89, 90, 93, 98
Martinique, 381
Mary (Virgin), 9, 349, 351–353, 356, 358, 359, 363, 378
  Marian Age of Catholic Church, 349, 383
  Marian devotion, 8, 9, 349, 351, 352, 357, 358, 359, 378
Mattei, Mario, 193, 298, 301, 309
Mazzini, Giuseppe, 274, 306, 328
Mehmet Ali, 279, 280, 282, 284, 308
Melchiorri, Giuseppe, 106, 107, 109, 271, 278
  L'Ape italiana delle belle arti, 278
Memmo, Andrea, 223
Memorandum of 21 May 1831, 208, 328
Memorie per le belle arti, 225
Memorie romane di antichità e belle arti, 93, 162
Mercey, Frédéric, 340, 341
Messmer, Joseph Anton, 377
Mexico, 149, 153, 379
Micali, Giuseppe, 227, 228, 278
  L'Italia avanti il dominio dei Romani (1810), 227
Michoacán, 149
Milan
  San Lorenzo, 84
Milizia, Francesco, 13, 69, 223, 233
Mill, John Stuart, 129
  Principles of Political Economy (1848), 129
Milner, John, 143
Minardi, Tommaso, 315, 316, 334, 335, 336–340, 342, 343, 344, 345, 376, 377
  "On the Essential Qualities of Italian Painting from Its Rebirth until the Period of Its Perfection" (1834), 336
  attitudes toward Gothic architecture, 338–340
missions, Catholic, 3, 259, 260
Molli, Giovanni, 89, 90, 93, 94
Mondo Illustrato, 322
Montalembert, Charles Forbes de, 337
Montreal, 148
Montreuil
  Saint-Symphorien, 232
Morel de Bauvine, 146, 151, 163, 165, 166, 196
Moreschi, Luigi, 196, 209, 218, 220, 236–240, 248, 249, 253, 254, 255, 266, 271, 277, 278, 286, 287, 289, 308, 309, 325, 341, 345
  Collezione degli articoli pubblicati nel Diario di Roma e nelle Notizie del giorno relativi alla nuova fabbrica della Basilica di S. Paolo (1845), 299, 301
  Indicazione dei dipinti a buon fresco (1867), 345
  Intorno la Festività della Commemorazione di San Paolo (1841), 254

Osservazioni sulla sedia pontificale (1838), 248, 249, 259
Prospetto spaccato e dettagli della confessione nella Basilica di S. Paolo (1838), 253, 258
Relazione della consecrazione fatta da papa Gregorio XVI della nave traversa della basilica di S. Paolo (1840), 289
Morgenblatt für gebildete Leser, 240
Morgenblatt für gebildete Stände, 106, 109
Moroni, Gaetano, 281
  Dizionario di erudizione storico-ecclesiastica (1840–61), 281
Moskowitz, Anita, 258
Munich
  St. Bonifaz, 233

Napoleon I, 3, 4, 9, 18, 19, 23, 35, 41, 42, 49, 121, 186, 226, 256, 327
Napoleon III, 186, 327, 328, 380
Navone, Giovanni Domenico, 89, 93, 315, 316
Nazarenes, the, 334, 336, 338
Neo-Guelph movement, 303, 323
Neo-Thomism, 126
Netherlands, 142, 148, 149, 379
Neue Augsburger Zeitung, 182
Neues allgemeines Künstler-Lexicon, 334
Newman, John Henry, 377
  Callista, A Sketch of the Third Century (1856), 377
Nicolai, Nicola Maria, 29–31, 43, 46, 74, 115, 118, 120, 121, 165, 189, 190, 249, 311
  Della Basilica di S. Paolo (1815), 30, 31, 43, 46, 74, 189, 249
Niles' Weekly Register, 147
North America, 7, 78, 150, 193, 269
Nueva Caceres, 149
Nueva Segovia, 149

Obolo (Peter's Pence), 8, 379, 380, 381, 382
O'Connell, Daniel, 323
Oesterreichischer Beobachter, 146
Olomouc, 149
Origo, Giuseppe, 47, 55
Ostia, 20
Oudinot, Charles Nicolas Victor, 327, 328
Overbeck, Friedrich, 315, 334, 336, 337, 338, 340
Ozanam, Antoine-Frederic, 337

Pacca, Bartolomeo, 32, 71, 72, 73, 90, 95
  "Pacca Edict" (1820), 25, 271
Palazzi, Giacomo, 89
Palestine, 279, 282
Palladio, Andrea, 333
Paris, 5, 6, 18, 24, 35, 55, 73, 141, 176, 199, 210, 212, 302, 324, 328, 351
  barrières de Paris, 37
  Notre-Dame-de-Bercy, 212, 232
  Notre-Dame-de-Lorette, 212, 232

INDEX

Paris (cont.)
  Place de la Concorde
    Luxor Obelisk, 284
  Saint-Denis-du-Saint-Sacrement, 212
  Sainte-Geneviève, 232
  Saint-Philippe du Roule, 232
Patane, Francesco, 89
Paul V, pope (Camillo Borghese), 14, 105
Paul, St., 1, 7, 8, 18, 43, 62, 81, 99, 107, 110,
    111–112, 113, 115, 116, 133, 139, 142,
    145, 153, 242, 246–261, 275, 283, 287,
    293, 317, 318, 319, 320, 322, 328, 349,
    355, 356, 357, 358, 363, 377, 378
  Festival of the Commemoration of, 254, 285,
    300, 333, 345
Percier, Charles, 212, 225
Pericles, 316
Perrault, Charles, 232
Perrault, Claude, 232
Peru, 381
Perugia, 146
  Academy of Fine Arts, 336
  University, 30, 33
Peter, St., 43, 105, 111, 112, 246–261, 287, 357
Petrine primacy, tradition of, 251, 259
Philae, 285
Philippines, the, 7, 153
Piale, Stefano, 106
Piazza, Tommaso Domenico, 53, 54, 61, 78
Piedmont, 234, 303, 304, 322, 323, 324, 356, 379
Piranesi, Giovanni Battista, 223, 227
Pius VI, pope (Giovanni Angelo Braschi), 17, 18,
    61, 71
Pius VII, pope (Barnaba Niccolò Maria Luigi
    Chiaramonti), 19–26, 28, 30, 31, 34, 35,
    49, 50, 56, 57, 58, 59, 110, 140, 142, 196,
    268, 271, 305, 336, 367
  Chirograph on Antiquities and Fine Arts in
    Rome (1802), 19, 22, 23
Pius VIII, pope (Francesco Saverio Maria Felice
    Castiglioni), 175, 176, 182, 186, 196, 217,
    237
Pius IX, pope (Giovanni Maria Battista Pietro
    Pellegrino Isidoro Mastai-Ferretti), 7, 9,
    129, 227, 268, 301, 305, 322, 323, 324,
    327, 333, 334, 337, 339, 341, 342, 345,
    349, 350, 352, 353, 354, 358, 359, 363,
    369, 373, 375, 379, 380
  Allocution of 29 April, 324
  Qui Pluribus (1846), 307
  Ubi primum (1849), 352
Plessis, Joseph-Octave, 153, 154, 290
Poland, 381
Poletti, Geminiano, 59, 210, 211, 212
Poletti, Luigi, 6, 59, 188–191, 192, 193, 194, 195,
    199, 201, 207–236, 237, 238, 246, 248,
    249, 255, 257, 264, 265, 266, 267, 268,

    269, 270, 271, 276, 277, 278, 285, 286,
    287, 295, 296, 297, 298, 299, 300, 301,
    302, 304, 306, 307, 308, 309, 311, 313,
    314, 316, 324, 326, 327
  early life and career, 210–213
  history and theory of art, 210–212, 223–236
    attitudes toward Romanticism, 236, 315, 335,
    338
    interest in Etruscans, 226–230, 273
    Delle genti e delle arti primitive d'Italia,
    227–230, 277, 278
  library, 6, 304
  master plan for San Paolo (1834), 219–224
Pontecorvo, 145
Pontifical Academy of Archaeology, 30, 32, 100,
    104, 106, 108, 162, 194, 228, 237, 277
Pontifical Commission for Sacred Archaeology,
    342, 344, 367
Pontifical Expedition to Egypt, 282, 283, 290, 295
Portugal, 141, 149
Poznań, 149
Promis, Carlo, 234, 373
Prudentius, 105, 253
Prussia, 141, 147, 208
Purism, 334, 336, 338

Quarenghi, Giacomo, 333
Quebec, 148, 149, 290
Quin, Frederic Forster, 1

Raedts, Peter, 380, 381
Raffaelli, Giacomo, 161
Raimondi, Quintiliano, 89, 93
Raphael (Raffaello Sanzo), 108, 118, 316, 336, 337
Ratisbonne, Alphonse, 352
Ravioli, Camillo, 284, 285
Reinolds, Jean-Baptiste, 41
Renaissance, 7, 13, 17, 26, 37, 69, 90, 114, 177, 201,
    210, 220, 222, 223, 225, 226, 228, 232,
    235, 236, 259, 268, 337, 365, 369
Renan, Ernest, 357
  Saint Paul (1869), 357
Repubblica Romana (1798), 18, 21, 22, 24, 73,
    268
Repubblica Romana (1849), 254, 327, 328, 333,
    380
Revolutions of 1830, 176
Riario Sforza, Tommaso, 121
Rio, Alexis-François, 337
Rio de Janeiro, 209, 240
Rivista Europea, 340
Romano, Giulio, 232
Romanticism, Catholic, 125–135
Rome
  Arch of Constantine, 20, 28
  Arch of Janus, 24
  Arch of Septimius Severus, 20, 269

INDEX

Arch of Titus, 65, 108, 118
Archivio Storico Capitolino, 145
Aurelian wall, 1, 328
Basilica Aemilia, 43, 172
Basilica Ulpia, 69, 104, 105, 159, 166, 180, 196, 198, 201, 268
Campo Verano cemetery, 24, 324, 365, 370
Capitoline Hill, 18, 46, 89, 96, 102, 327
Castro Pretorio barracks, 365
Collegio Romano, 15
Colosseum, 20, 24, 25, 65, 108, 118, 210, 218, 231
Column of Marcus Aurelius (aka Antonine Column), 18, 252, 274, 275
Column of the Immaculate Conception, 361, 363
Early Christian catacombs, 268, 328, 337, 338, 342, 367, 368, 377
Festival of the Federation (1798), 18
Forum, 20
Girandola (fireworks), 345
guidebooks, 17, 31, 129, 150
Horti Caesaris, 24
Istituto di Correspondenza Archaeologica, 227, 228, 235, 273
Lateran Christian Museum, 367
Mausoleum of Hadrian (Castello Sant'Angelo), 43, 172, 345
Milvian Bridge, 34–37, 71, 73, 131, 252
Ospizio di S. Michele, 212
Palazzo Caffarelli, 46, 89
Palazzo Ceccopieri, 212
Palazzo delle Poste Pontificie (Palazzo Wedekind), 270
Palazzo di Propaganda Fide, 359
Pantheon, 21, 169, 172, 173, 174, 178, 210, 218, 236, 266, 269, 316, 342
Piazza Colonna, 270
Piazza del Popolo, 24, 73, 164
Piazza di Spagna, 359, 361
Piazza Pia, 365
Pincian Hill, 24, 73
Pons Aemilius (Ponte Rotto), 211, 371
Ponte Sant'Angelo, 252
Porta del Popolo, 34, 252
Porta San Pancrazio, 365
Porta San Sebastiano, 373
Quirinal Palace, 59, 306, 325, 334, 335, 337
Roman Forum, 24, 268
S. Andrea delle Fratte, 352
Sacro Cuore di Gesù a Villa Lante, 365
San Bonaventura, convent, 73
San Callisto, 42, 47, 187, 189, 190, 328
San Carlo ai Catinari, 371
San Clemente, 15, 373
San Crisogono, 16
San Francesca Romana, monastery, 73

San Giovanni della Malva, 365
San Girolamo degli Schiavoni, 335
San Lorenzo fuori le mura, 32, 372, 373, 376
San Marcello al Corso, 371
San Paolo fuori le mura
    1840 consecration, 207, 246, 253, 259, 265, 267, 268, 285, 287, 289, 295
    1850 consecration (postponed), 295, 296, 299
    1854 consecration, 9, 350, 353–356, 357
    apse, 45, 47, 77, 84, 94, 158, 214, 215, 216, 238, 246, 248, 249, 255, 259, 270, 286, 302, 312, 316, 340, 354
    Arch of Galla Placidia, 31, 44, 52, 77, 84, 158, 160–162, 165, 169, 175, 191, 246, 248, 254, 257, 286, 309
    Belli's master plan (1830), 177–182
    ciborium (Arnolfo di Cambio), 8, 44, 158, 221, 223, 248, 249, 253, 258, 266, 279, 286, 298, 309
    ciborium (Poletti), 223, 269, 279, 282, 289, 309, 324, 340, 342
    cloister, 31
    confessio, 44, 77, 86, 94, 221, 223, 248, 249, 259, 265, 269, 286, 354
    dividing wall, 159–160
    fire of 1823, 1, 4, 8, 45–55, 59–62, 66, 77, 78, 81, 97, 102, 104, 107, 110, 111, 112, 114, 118, 131, 132, 133, 226, 248, 259, 261, 299, 322, 340, 377
    forzati (prison labor), 100, 296
    frescos, 43, 48, 177, 196, 344, 345, 377
    fundraising, 77–78
    fundraising drive, 7, 8, 54, 110, 111, 112, 114, 115, 116, 117, 119, 133, 139–154, 216, 218, 240, 268, 280, 290, 295, 296, 299, 378, 379, 381
    Hetoimasia, 255
    in pristinum option, 2, 71, 73, 98, 102, 103, 104, 106, 109, 110, 113, 118, 119, 120, 125, 128, 131, 132, 133, 139, 141, 158, 188, 196, 236, 264, 358, 369, 377
    mosaics, 16, 31, 41, 44, 45, 48, 77, 78, 84, 109, 158, 160, 162, 215, 246, 248, 255, 257, 266, 286, 309, 312, 313, 343, 344
    nave capitals, 158, 164, 165, 169, 172, 173, 174, 178, 191, 216, 218, 231, 236, 266, 297, 341
    nave columns, 27, 29, 33, 43, 44, 47, 48, 66, 69, 75, 76, 84, 102, 105, 111, 119, 120, 132, 150, 157, 159, 162–175, 177, 180, 191, 192, 193, 196, 198, 211, 215, 216, 218, 231, 237, 238, 266, 275, 286, 297, 341, 343
    north façade portico, 222, 238, 266, 325, 363
    papal portrait medallions, 43, 49, 59, 77, 90, 109, 177, 257, 260, 309, 325, 326, 335
    papal throne, 249, 255, 257, 259, 260, 286

420 INDEX

Rome (cont.)
    Poletti's master plan (1834), 219–224
    quadriporticus, 196, 198, 220, 308, 309, 311,
        312, 314, 343, 354
    raising floor, 158, 177, 180, 191, 192, 193, 194,
        195, 196, 198, 218, 237, 266, 312
    stained glass, 344
    St. Benedict chapel, 269, 270–279, 289
    Valadier's 1st project (1824), 75–77
    Valadier's 2nd project (1824), 84–87
    west façade, 41, 80, 214, 220, 238, 246, 286,
        298, 301, 308, 309, 311–317, 333, 334,
        335, 336, 341–343, 344, 345, 353, 354,
        376
    wooden model (Poletti), 219–220, 221, 295,
        298, 302, 308, 312, 333, 343
    wooden model (Valadier), 76, 100, 108
  San Pietro in Vincoli, 371
  San Sebastiano fuori le mura, 73
  Sant'Agnese fuori le mura, 32, 190
  Sant'Alessandro, 374, 375
  Santa Croce in Gerusalemme, 16
  Santa Eufemia (demolished), 73
  Santa Maria del Popolo, convent, 73
  Santa Maria della Febbre, 17
  Santa Maria della Misericordia, 365
  Santa Maria in Traspontina, 252
  Santa Maria in Trastevere, 16, 371
  Santa Maria Maggiore, 15, 17, 49, 81, 177, 180,
      190, 223, 230, 233, 341, 352, 365, 371
    Salus Populi Romani icon, 352
  Santa Maria sopra Minerva, 365
  Santa Prassede, 16
  Sant'Alfonso de' Liguori, 365
  Santo Spirito (demolished), 73
  Santo Stefano (ruin), 374
  SS. Apostoli, 15
  St. John Lateran, 14, 15, 54, 77, 81, 221, 222, 233,
      353
    Paleochristian basilica, 14, 17, 32, 69, 190, 232,
      259, 322
  St. Peter's, 1, 2, 7, 43, 49, 58, 59, 65, 76, 81, 90,
      105, 106, 108, 111, 114, 141, 163, 218,
      232, 236, 251, 253, 254, 259, 260, 264,
      267, 269, 279, 284, 311, 349, 353, 354
    Cathedra Petri, 259
    Paleochristian basilica, 69
    Sacristy, 17
    square, 18, 309
  Temple of Fortuna Virilis, 24
  Temple of Peace (Basilica of Maxentius), 24, 163
  Temple of Venus and Rome, 165
  Temple of Vesta, 24
  Tobacco Manufactory in Trastevere, 365, 370
  Trajan's Column, 24, 73, 252
  Trajan's Forum, 165
  Vatican Museums, 270, 271, 337

  Gregorian Egyptian Museum, 270, 281
  Gregorian Etruscan Museum, 270, 273, 274,
      277, 278, 281
    Museo Pio-Clementino, 16, 20
  Vatican Palace, 16, 59, 334
Rondelet, Jean-Baptiste, 33
  Traité de l'Art de Batir (1812), 33
Roscoe, William, 114
  Life and Pontificate of Leo X (1805), 114
Rosellini, Ippolito, 280, 281
  Monumenti dell'Egitto e della Nubia (1832–44),
    280
Rossetti, Annibale de, 279
Rossi, Pellegrino, 325, 326
Rothschild banking family, 217, 298
Rousseau, Jean-Jacques, 130
Royal Institute of British Architects, 210
Russia, 134, 149, 208

Sala, Domenico, 121
Salvi, Gaspare, 79, 80, 81, 87, 89, 90, 92, 121, 195
Salvigni, Pellegrino, 145
Sangallo, Antonio da, 308
Sanmicheli, Michele, 333
Sansovino, Jacopo d'Antonio, 333
Santelli, Antonio, 77, 78, 143
Santini, Francesco, 90
Sarti, Antonio, 109, 316
Sayre, Robert, 127, 130
Scaccia, Girolamo, 89, 90, 96
Schinkel, Karl Friedrich, 5, 89, 225, 233
Scotland, 379
Selvatico, Pietro Estense, 338, 340, 341, 365
Seroux d'Agincourt, Jean-Baptiste-Louis-Georges,
    26–28, 29, 31, 44, 170, 174, 223
  Histoire de l'art per les monuments (1810–23), 26,
    234
Servi, Gaspare, 226
Sherer, Moyle, 49
Siam (Thailand), 260
Siccardi laws (1850), 356
Simond, Louis, 41
Siricio, bishop, 238
South America, 7, 78, 149, 193, 269, 381
Spada, Mariano, 352
Spain, 141, 149
Special Commission for the Reedification of the
    Basilica of San Paolo, 110, 114, 115, 117,
    118, 121, 145, 158, 159, 162, 164, 165,
    166, 169, 173, 174, 175, 189, 190, 191,
    193, 194, 196, 198, 209, 214, 216, 236,
    237, 249, 266, 267, 269, 270, 296, 297,
    298, 299, 300, 301, 302, 308, 324, 325,
    326, 333, 353
Speroni, Gregorio, 59
Stendhal, 24, 49, 59, 63, 64, 393
Sterbini, Pietro, 326, 327, 333

INDEX

Stern, Raffaelle, 65, 210
St. Paul's Island, 283
St. Petersburg, 149
Strambi, Vincenzo Maria di San Paolo, 78
Switzerland, 328, 381
Sylvester I, pope, 253
Symmachus, pope, 167
Syria, 279, 282

Tambroni, Giuseppe, 55
   "Relazione esatta e veridica delle circostanze che
      precedettero il fatale incendio della
      Basilica di S. Paolo fuori le mura" (1823),
      53–56
Tasmania, 7, 209
Teloni (bishop of Macerata and Tolentino), 115
Tenerani, Pietro, 335
The Courier, 7
Theodosius, Emperor, 1, 44, 174, 211, 258
Timothy, saint, 249
Tonkin (North Vietnam), 260
Tosti, Antonio, 267, 298, 300–301
Tournon, Camille de (Camille Philippe Casimir
      Marcellin, comte de Tournon-Simiane), 24
Trajan, Emperor, 231
Turkey, 381
Tuscany, 174, 324, 336

Uggeri, Angelo, 28, 29, 33, 68, 69, 70, 71, 73, 74,
      97, 104, 115, 117, 118, 119, 121, 145, 158,
      159, 160, 162, 163, 164, 165, 166, 167,
      169, 170, 172, 173, 174, 175, 178, 180,
      188, 189, 190, 191, 192, 193, 194, 195,
      196, 198, 201, 209, 222, 223, 230, 233,
      236, 246
   Della Basilica di S. Paolo (1823, 65, 66, 69, 70, 71,
      118, 196
   Della Basilica Ulpia (1833), 196, 199
   Edifices de la décadence (1809), 28–29, 65
ultramontanism, 57, 126, 209, 256, 257, 366, 380
Umbria, 213, 336
Ungarelli, Luigi, 281
United States Catholic Miscellany, 146, 152, 240
United States of America, 78, 306, 352, 379, 381

Valadier, Giuseppe, 35, 36, 37, 65, 71–74, 75, 77,
      79–81, 84–97, 98, 100, 102, 103, 105,
      107–110, 112, 115, 117, 118, 119, 120,
      121, 125, 131, 132, 133, 135, 139, 195,
      215, 222, 223, 232, 252, 265
Valentinian II, Emperor, 1, 166, 238
Vasi, Mariano, 31
Vaudoyer, Léon, 231
Vega, Ignazio, 379
Veii, 270, 271, 274
   columns reused at San Paolo, 271, 274, 275, 276,
      277, 278, 282
Ventura, Gioacchino, 112, 113, 114, 126, 127, 130,
      256, 322, 323
Venturoli, Giuseppe, 79, 195, 210
Vermiglioli, Giovanni Battista, 30, 31, 33, 80
Vespignani, Virginio, 249, 365, 371, 372
Vienna, 324
Viollet-le-Duc, Eugène Emmanuel, 134
Volney (Constantin-François Chassebœuf de
      La Giraudais, comte de Volney)
   Recherches nouvelles sur l'Histoire ancienne (1814), 270
Voltaire (François-Marie Arouet), 17, 130, 359
   Essai sur les moeurs et l'esprit des nations (1756), 270
   Le mort de César (1731), 18
Volterra
   Etruscan Museum, 227

Waldie, Jane, 41, 44
Wicar, Jean-Baptiste, 336
Wigley, George, 365
Winckelmann, Johann Joachim, 223
Wiseman, Nicholas, 43, 45, 49, 50, 52, 58, 59, 78,
      272, 281, 282, 291, 354, 377
   Fabiola, or, the Church of the Catacombs (1855), 377
   *Twelve Lectures on the Connexion between Science and
      Revealed Religion* (1836), 272
Woods, Joseph, 43, 44
Wrocław, 149

Zante, 148
Zelli, Giovanni Francesco, 74, 75, 107, 108, 119,
      143, 165, 166, 190
Ziebland, Friedrich, 233